P9-DHG-164

FROM THE LIBRARY OF
BERNARD GOODMAN

The First New Deal

Also by

Raymond Moley

The Republican Opportunity
The American Century of John C. Lincoln
The Political Responsibility of Businessmen
What Price Federal Reclamation?
How to Keep Our Liberty
27 Masters of Politics
The Hays Office
After Seven Years
Tribunes of the People
Our Criminal Courts
Politics and Criminal Prosecution
Parties, Politics and People
Commercial Recreation
Lessons in Democracy
The State Movement for Efficiency and Economy
Lessons in American Citizenship

The author and the President-elect in the library at Hyde Park at the time work on the first inaugural address was completed

Raymond Moley

With the assistance of Elliot A. Rosen

The First New Deal

Foreword by Frank Freidel,
Harvard University

Harcourt, Brace & World, Inc., New York

First edition

Library of Congress Catalog Card Number: 66-22282

Printed in the United States of America

Foreword

by Frank Freidel

The crisis years of the early New Deal brought some of the most momentous changes in the history of the United States. In response to the acute distress of the great depression, the Federal government abandoned the policy of aloof neutrality it had pursued during earlier nineteenth-century economic debacles. Rather, President Franklin D. Roosevelt marshaled the massive energies of the government upon behalf of the economic welfare of the American people. He also tried to make a reality the dream of the progressives that the government should play a dynamic role in maintaining an impartial balance among the large, complex forces in the economy. In time he went further than the progressive ideal in assuming for the Federal government a position of dominance within the economy.

In the beginnings of the New Deal, no single other person was more essential to Roosevelt in translating ideas into action than Raymond Moley, the chief Brains-Truster. By 1936 the New Deal had swept beyond what Moley regarded as prudent limits, and in subsequent years, like many another one-time progressive, he became outspoken in his opposition. In 1939 he published the most lively and penetrating of those critical memoirs, *After Seven Years.* Appearing on the eve of a Presidential campaign in which it was already likely that Roosevelt would run for a third term, it was in part significant as a political manifesto. Moley set forth in emphatic tones his alarm at the more recent directions in which Roosevelt had taken the New Deal. President Roosevelt reacted privately in kind. On October 13, 1941, two years after the book appeared, his secretary, Grace Tully, sent a memorandum to Samuel I. Rosenman:

"Quite a long time ago, the President, in discussing Moley's book I think, said to you that he would like you to go through the book sometime for inaccuracies. He himself, just at a glance, has discovered two or three and he knows there are many more. This is a job that cannot be turned over to anyone else because they would not know the background of what really did happen. Just another job for you!"

Judge Rosenman suggested to Roosevelt that others like Harry Hopkins, William Bullitt, Jesse Jones, and Cordell Hull should be consulted on events after March 4, 1933, when Rosenman was not in Washington. Roosevelt replied on October 15:

"Will you ask these people to check, with the exception of Secretary Hull, who is doing his own checking? I really don't believe Jesse Jones could be very helpful, but you might add Berle and Tugwell and anybody else you can think of when you read the book."

Whatever the results may have been, nothing from this fact-finding enterprise ever saw light at the time, or is to be found in the Roosevelt papers. Cordell Hull vented his feelings in his *Memoirs,* but presented no specific evidence. Moley has commented, "I am rather proud of the fact that nobody ever delivered the goods on this assignment, for the simple reason that they couldn't find anything worth using."

The fact was, as historians of the New Deal began to discover, that Moley had brought to the writing of *After Seven Years* the respect for the facts and the precision in handling details that had distinguished him both as a professor of political science and as a public servant. He had depended less upon his memory than upon detailed correspondence, memoranda, notes, and diaries. His is a rich, indeed indispensable collection of manuscripts, on some points more informative on the planning of the New Deal than even the Roosevelt papers at Hyde Park. Moley has repeatedly made these papers available without the slightest restriction to several historians and biographers even though their viewpoints and his might by no means coincide. The papers corroborate at countless points the factual evidence in *After Seven Years* and in this book.

Even in the fullest of manuscript collections much is missing that can be supplied only by the memories of the participants. As the reverberations of the New Deal battles have died out, the Roosevelt era has been removed as a political issue, but has remained a vital historical phenomenon.

It is fortunate indeed that from the perspective of these calmer years Moley has written a second account to set forth dispassionately his memories and evidence on the vital events in which he was a prime participant. Those seeking a whiff of gunpowder or a far-off aroma of scandal may be disappointed. Here, rather, is a meticulously careful, clearly organized report on one of the great epochs of American history. It is magisterial in approach and monumental in perspective.

As an account of a stewardship it is perhaps most comparable to Theodore Sorensen's memoir of John F. Kennedy. Both these books, focusing upon dynamic Presidents, are also noteworthy as unconscious self-portraits of the writers.

Moley brought to Roosevelt's service a rare ability to clarify and simplify complex, sometimes dull, issues and to present them in vivid language. He marshaled for Roosevelt a brilliant array of academic talent, some that was not academic—altogether a group of considerably divergent views. In his work on speeches, Moley, as he has written, was able "to help crystallize [Roosevelt's] own ideas and inclinations, reflect them accurately, and extend them where necessary, and present them congruously—in brief, to relieve him of a good deal of personal drudgery." Altogether, Moley worked endless hours for Roosevelt as, he says far too modestly, a "packhorse in his great affairs."

The qualities that made Moley so valuable to Roosevelt are apparent in his background. He was nurtured in the great Ohio school of reform that flourished in the early twentieth century, and through his graduate training at Columbia University became a master of scientific analysis applied to politics.

Moley began his political schooling young. He was born in 1886 into a Catholic household in the predominantly Protestant Western Reserve area of Ohio. His Dublin-born father indoctrinated him in Democratic politics so early that he remembers asserting his party views vociferously in the campaign of 1892 when he was only six years old. Financial stringency, which soon turned into acute depression, created unusual bitterness in the political battles of the time. In Olmsted Falls, "where my father was struggling with his small 'gent's furnishings store,' loaded with debts," Moley has reminisced, "I heard nothing but hard times." He well remembers a division of Coxey's Army passing through town in 1894—unemployed men bound for Washington to petition Congress for relief. Bryan was Moley's first political hero:

"In 1896 I was intensely interested in the Bryan-McKinley campaign. . . . Campaign buttons in those days were sold, not given away, and I sold a lot of . . . Bryan buttons. Bryan aroused my childish imagination with his handsome demeanor, his oratory, and his professed concern for the down-trodden. . . . I was so overwhelmed when Bryan lost that I stayed out of school for three days because I was afraid to face the opposition."

Moley's enthusiasm for Bryan soon waned, permanently. Several other Democratic leaders made a lasting impression upon him. Especially there was Tom Johnson, the reform mayor of Cleveland and disciple of Henry George:

"In 1901 there was great excitement in the Cleveland newspapers, which we read and which I sold in my town, over the election of Tom L. Johnson. . . . He was an exciting figure, a successful businessman who had been converted by Henry George's books to a low-tariff position and to a belief in heavier taxes on land. As I followed Tom Johnson's long career, running until 1909, I read everything in the newspapers about him. He was essentially a Georgist, but as an immediate issue he favored a 3-cent fare on the Cleveland streetcar lines, rather than 5 cents. He was an experienced operator of streetcar lines and believed . . . 3 cents would be sufficient. In those days Cleveland was alive with Georgism, and my copy of *Progress and Poverty* is dated when I was sixteen years old."

In recent years, Moley has written of Henry George: "In my judgment George brought home, with perhaps the most easily understood illustration, the concept of social value which inspired the whole Progressive movement in the United States. . . . For anyone can see that the individual who holds a piece of land with no effort to improve it and who has small taxes to pay cannot help but be enriched by those whose industry enriches the entire community. He toils not and neither does he spin, but his land increases in value.

"But the subjects George considered in his many speeches and his writings touched almost all of the corrective influences which were the result of the Progressive movement. The restriction of monopoly, more democratic political machinery, municipal reform, the elimination of privilege in railroads, the regulation of public utilities, and the improvement of labor laws and working conditions—all were in one way or another accelerated by George." *

Woodrow Wilson early became a hero of Moley's, when Wilson was McCormick Professor of Jurisprudence and Politics at Princeton University: "I wondered then if this thing called politics could be taught, and I think that fixation remained until I actually did take graduate work. But I followed Wilson's career with great concern before and during his own entrance into politics."

As a young man, Moley not only studied politics but, in addition to earning a living as a schoolteacher, became a precocious political practitioner. At the age of twenty-one he was superintendent of schools in Olmsted Falls, with jurisdiction over three teachers. He was also elected town clerk. Four years later he was elected mayor. He had intended to go to law school, but his savings had to be spent on a sojourn in New Mexico and Colorado recuperating from tuberculosis. Therefore he decided to follow the route of Wilson into politics, by becoming a professor of political science. He did graduate work at Columbia University under

* Raymond Moley, *The American Century of John C. Lincoln* (New York: Duell, Sloan and Pearce, 1962), p. 160.

Charles A. Beard, an ardent progressive, who in 1913 set forth an iconoclastic view of the Founding Fathers, *An Economic Interpretation of the Constitution.* Beard laid stress upon scientific fact-finding as a first step toward reform.

Moley spent ten years in Cleveland, first as a high-school teacher and debating coach, then as teacher in Western Reserve University, and finally as director of the Cleveland Foundation. In the foundation he played a significant part in reforming the administration of criminal justice in that city. He brought to Cleveland Dean Roscoe Pound and Professor Felix Frankfurter to conduct a comprehensive study of the various aspects of the administration of the criminal law.

Moley's achievements in Cleveland led to a professorship in Columbia University in 1923. Then he embarked upon studies of police, prosecution, and the courts in a number of states. He met Louis Howe, Roosevelt's secretary, who enlisted him to work in Roosevelt's gubernatorial campaign in 1928. After his election Governor Roosevelt appointed Moley to a Commission on the Administration of Justice in New York State.

In the Presidential campaign of 1932, Moley served as the head of a group of policy advisers and speech writers, which came to be known as the Brains Trust. After the campaign the Brains Trust ceased to exist as a cohesive body; it never again met as a group. But Roosevelt continued to utilize the advisory services of its members in planning the New Deal.

Moley coordinated their activities, all their proposals and countless others from all over the nation. By Roosevelt's direction, these were channeled through Moley. During the months of the interregnum between Roosevelt's election and his inauguration, he was the key adviser, engaged in planning, in the enlisting of personnel and the drafting of speeches—especially the inaugural address.

He was also one of those assigned to liaison with the outgoing Administration, and accompanied Roosevelt to two of the dramatic meetings with President Hoover.

Through the hectic first months of the early New Deal, the close relationship between Roosevelt and Moley continued. Ernest K. Lindley described Moley as "the second strongest man in Washington." He was a focal point of incessant interest, curiosity, and occasional malice on the part of the newspapermen. Because of the nature of his work, Moley seemed of necessity elusive and mysterious, slipping in and out of the White House, working until all hours at his room in the Carlton Hotel, and dashing to New York City to meet his Barnard College classes. He was constantly conferring with notables, but never gave interviews to the press. As was inevitable with someone so close to the center of power, he became the target of jokes—the sort always told about a

President and his intimates. One of Roosevelt's oldest friends was supposed to have telephoned the White House: "Franklin, can you do me just one favor? Can you get me an appointment with Moley?"

George Creel, who earlier had been a notable progressive newspaperman, thus described him:

"Here is one who has been set down by the press as a 'mystery man,' but the mystery springs entirely from the fact that he is utterly lacking in the publicity instinct, and has no liking whatsoever for interviews, feature stories and personal exploitation. The one thing that interests him is the *job,* and to it he brings an absolute concentration that leaves no room for anything else.

"A rather hard-boiled person this Dr. Moley, and about as different from the timid, absent-minded professor type of fiction as could be imagined. There is a jut to his jaw, a steel-trap effect around the mouth, and behind his glasses are a pair of clear eyes that have the bore of gimlets." *

With his quick directness, his no-nonsense ways, Moley made many friends in Congress and in the new Administration. In the Senate he won the admiration of the old-line progressive Republican, Hiram Johnson, the incoming chairman of the Foreign Relations Committee, Key Pittman, and the most vigorous expediter of Roosevelt's legislative proposals, James Byrnes. His closest friends in the Cabinet were Secretary of the Treasury William Woodin and Postmaster General James A. Farley. No one would have thought of using the term "Irish Mafia," but there was no more vital trio in the drafting and furthering of New Deal bills than Moley, Farley, and Byrnes.

Not everyone was a friend. Policy differences and personal animosities developed almost immediately. While Moley was a faithful coordinator and speech drafter for Roosevelt, he did bring to his task the firm views to which he had long subscribed. In both domestic economic matters and foreign policy he was an emphatic nationalist. He and Tugwell had tried energetically and unsuccessfully to counter the influence upon Roosevelt of the outgoing Secretary of State, Henry L. Stimson. They were appalled when Roosevelt endorsed the Stimson Doctrine toward Japan, fearing it would lead ultimately to war. Moley, bent upon achieving a domestic recovery shielded by the tariff from foreign interference, was ideologically at odds with the new Secretary of State, Cordell Hull, an old-fashioned Southern free-trader. Yet it was Moley's misfortune, because Howe's jealousy made a desk in the White House impossible, to be put into the State Department as an assistant secretary. Hull and most of his lieutenants differed with Moley and resented his presence. It was particularly distasteful to Hull, who had been unhappy that

* *Colliers,* June 17, 1933, p. 36.

Roosevelt failed to consult him during the planning period, and who seldom was summoned to the White House in the spring of 1933. Moley's daily conferences with the President and his authority in war debt negotiations were repugnant to those believing in chain-of-command.

Moley had taken the position intending to hold it for a few months at the most, but even in that brief term Hull focused on Moley the same smoldering resentment he later developed toward Sumner Welles. Roosevelt had given Moley an untenable appointment. Further, he expected Moley to carry out White House assignments of the utmost importance with little or no formal authorization. The denouement came in July 1933 at the London Economic Conference. Moley, hurrying to the conference on Roosevelt's orders, for several days was the center of world attention. He acted cautiously within the letter and spirit of Roosevelt's instructions to expedite a limited monetary stabilization arrangement. Then Roosevelt suddenly changed his mind, torpedoing the arrangement and thus the conference. Hull could not attack Roosevelt without relinquishing his prestigious position as Secretary of State; he vented his wrath on the only vulnerable target, Moley.

Not long thereafter Moley put into effect his plans of several months. He resigned as assistant secretary of state to become editor of a new magazine, *Today*. In time *Today* evolved into the present *Newsweek*. Moley, disappearing from the public scene, continued his quiet services at the White House. As the New Deal evolved in new directions in 1935, he became less and less sympathetic. The last speech for which he prepared a draft was that in which Roosevelt accepted renomination in 1936. Others put in the denunciations of "economic royalists" which Moley found distasteful, but it was he who wrote the stirring call to a "rendezvous with destiny."

Moley and Roosevelt parted amicably enough; in later years whenever Moley dreamed of Roosevelt, it was of making up with him. Reconciliation never came since Moley, like many of his generation of Ohio reformers intellectually rooted in the doctrines of Tom Johnson and Henry George, moved permanently into emphatic opposition. Numerous Wilsonians also went into the opposition, and, over foreign policy more than domestic matters, some of the Republican progressives. Moley's teacher Charles Beard became one of the most bitter opponents. "Beard and I had many conversations in his later days, in the 1940's," Moley recalls, "and perhaps he and I both went through a change in which we reexamined all of our earlier preconceptions." Thus it was that Moley, who had worked so long and skillfully for reform, fearing excesses, left Roosevelt's Democratic Party. In the years since, he has employed his talents upon behalf of the Republican Party and its Presidential candidates from Wendell Willkie to Barry Goldwater.

In viewing Moley's remarkable public services, one may apply to him what have long been his own favorite words from the speeches of Franklin D. Roosevelt. On election eve in 1932, Roosevelt declared:

"A man comes to wisdom in many years of public life. He knows well that when the light of favor shines upon him, it comes not, of necessity, that he himself is important. Favor comes because for a brief moment in the great space of human change and progress some general human purpose finds in him a satisfactory embodiment.

"To be the means through which the ideals and hopes of the American people may find a greater realization calls for the best in any man; I seek to be only the humble element of this restoration."

FRANK FREIDEL

Harvard University
Cambridge, Massachusetts
March, 1966

Preface

The Genesis and Purpose of This Book

More than nine years ago I decided to write this story of the First New Deal. One of the factors that constrained me to undertake such a formidable task was the persistent urging of an old friend, René Wormser, a distinguished member of the New York Bar, with whom I had shared some of my recollections of the early New Deal period. He argued that I could, by writing such an account, provide for a generation born since 1933 a useful personal story of what happened in a decisive moment in the life of the nation and contribute something to the future histories of these times. He said that I should do it while my memory was fresh and before the primary records of that time were scattered or lost. Thus there might measurably be lessened the danger, which is already apparent, that the virulent growth of mythology be intertwined with the accounts of events so long past.

I had often considered the writing of such a book, but the pressure imposed by my professional responsibilities as a journalist made it clear that I could not spare the time and effort to write about the past. For the composition of such a book would involve much more than a mere recital of my own recollections. An enormous body of literature about that period has accumulated in the years since, and it is still growing rapidly. There are basic materials such as memoirs, articles, the papers of contemporaries, official records, and newspaper reports. Most contemporaries are gone, but those who remained would have to be interviewed.

My own papers—notes, diary, letters, and other material in my possession—while well organized and catalogued, would, I realized, need to be examined with care. Moreover, the serious histories of that period would necessarily have to be checked in search of new leads and new information. I simply could not, I told Wormser, take the time for such a diversion. If I should undertake such a story, it would have to be something more than a mere memoir. It would have to be comprehensive, thorough, documented, and also embody my own reflections over the years since.

In 1957 the opportunity offered itself to enlist the services of a young friend, Elliot A. Rosen, whose professional interest in teaching and writing lay in the period to be considered. Dr. Rosen after his graduate training had embarked on a career as a historian. He was and is a member of the faculty of Rutgers University. And so I engaged him to undertake the preliminary research. He spent as much time as he could spare from his teaching on that assignment over a period of five years. He examined not only my own papers but those of many contemporaries in various depositories. And he supplemented what he found by an examination of the literature and the newspapers of the period. The result of his labor was a manuscript of five hundred pages of his own composition. This in itself is a contribution to history, for it revealed a fine historical sense, judgment, and discrimination.

After those preliminaries were finished, I was diverted for a year, writing a book on current politics. Then I spent nearly three years on this written account. As I proceeded, I found it necessary to do a great deal of additional research myself. Living contemporaries needed to be consulted, and they supplied me with written records and recollections. During this later period Dr. Rosen has assisted not only by checking my own account but by further traveling from place to place to examine the papers of deceased contemporaries.

From time to time in the text I have referred to my account as a story. It is written in the first person singular and is largely limited to the events in which I played some part or of which I was an intimate witness. It begins with Franklin D. Roosevelt's election in November 1932 and covers in some depth the events of the year that followed. Finally, there are chapters extending the account, so far as my own activities were concerned, during the years up to the Presidential campaign of 1936.

Still, I do not claim this to be a comprehensive history. For a great deal happened in Washington and in the far-flung projections of Federal authority over the nation which I knew little about. Thus, I choose to speak of a "story" rather than a "history." But I cherish the hope that history may profit by what I have written.

The first sentences of Pollock and Maitland's classic *The History of English Law* often came to my mind when I was writing this book:

"Such is the unity of all history that any one who endeavours to tell a piece of it must feel that his first sentence tears a seamless web. . . . A statute of limitations must be set; but it must be arbitrary. The web must be rent; but, as we rend it, we may watch the whence and whither of a few of the severed and ravelling threads which have been making a pattern too large for any man's eye."

As I was writing this "piece," however small, of the history of my country, I was constantly reminded of the long threads that ran back many years before the New Deal came by its name. All of us who had a part in creating what was called "new" brought with us to the task lessons we had learned in earlier years. My earliest impressions were of the great depression of the 1890's, when leaders in politics and government were grappling with most of the same anxieties that prevailed in the early 1930's. I had learned then that, without accepting the prescriptions of Populism as expounded by William Jennings Bryan, the American economy had recovered because of the simple fact that a powerful nation regained its confidence in itself. It remained to the next decade, in the name of Progressivism, for reformers to draw the specifications for the correction of the imbalance created by a ruthless capitalism by means more refined than greenbackism and free silver. Intellectually, the New Deal was born in that newer moral and economic perspective, which emerged in the years before 1914. Thus, we learned in 1933 that, while the restoration of public confidence was imperative, certain remedial and corrective measures were long overdue. It would have been useful in composing this account to follow those threads back two or three decades. But a "statute of limitations" was imposed by time and space. That extension of my story must wait for another occasion and perhaps another author.

Moreover, limits had to be imposed on tracing the threads of policy into the era in which we are now living. Here again I have observed a "statute of limitations."

I have not attempted to draw the heavy cloak of generality over the events in the period with which I have concerned myself. There is great danger in attempting to encompass a whole period in a phrase or even in a philosophic capsule. In February of this year I participated in a symposium at Claremont Men's College, which considered the meaning of the 1930's in the American tradition. My old friend Rex Tugwell was there with me to bring to a newer generation some of the realities that we had witnessed as participants. Several papers were read by younger scholars who sought to impose philosophical generalizations upon the history of the early New Deal. I realized as never before the perils in such historical exercises.

For the New Deal was not of one piece. Nor was it the product of a single integrated plan. It was, as I shall attempt to show, a loose collection of many ideas—some new, most borrowed from the past—with plenty of improvisations and compromises. Those of us who participated were too busy for mature reflection or to create a system or an over-all pattern. Too often a philosophy is created long after the facts upon which it is based have ceased to exist. Even the philosophical—or, as they called it, "scientific"—efforts of Brooks and Henry Adams to create a "scientific" interpretation of history in the 1890's seem futile in the light of what happened after they wrote—developments that were already under way when they were observers.

As I reflect upon those exciting months of 1933, I realize that we were dealing with two pressing necessities: to keep the machinery of government in motion, to help individuals and businesses to stay alive; and at the same time to revive the confidence of the people in their capacity to recover from the depths of the depression. The people of the nation didn't understand what we were doing. But they were convinced that a lot of things were being done. And that alone gave them the spirit to carry on.

It was the confidence of the public rather than any specific reforms that led to the recovery that followed.

That is a lesson that historians should learn.

In 1939 I wrote an account of the years that followed Roosevelt's early quest for the nomination in 1932. After it appeared serially in the *Saturday Evening Post,* it was published as my book *After Seven Years.* This appeared in a climate of intense political controversy, when Roosevelt was preparing to shatter the two-term tradition and the United States was seriously divided in its attitude toward the war in Europe. Already the sinister shadow of that war was moving over the Atlantic and the Pacific and threatening to embroil us. My book invited controversy, but in writing it I had made a calculated choice. Either I must shade my conclusions and thus invite the judgment that the book was something less than the whole truth, or I must be utterly candid and invite criticism of the author. I chose the second course. In the years since, the book has stood the test of truth even though it was said that I should have chosen another time to write it.

The mood and temper of this book are suited to the climate in which it will appear. The old controversies have faded with the years. A great majority of my present contemporaries were either unborn in 1933 or were too young at that time to comprehend what was happening. My maturity and objectivity have grown with the years, although I have surrendered none of the convictions that guided me in 1939. The differences between the books are in emphasis, mood, and detail. In the present instance, my story is enlarged by a vast amount of material that was unavailable when that earlier book was written.

Considering the evolution of political parties and policies in the thirty-three years since Roosevelt's first inauguration, the injection of partisanship in such an account as this would not only mar its authenticity but be an exercise in futility. Republicans today are not running against Roosevelt, nor are Democrats running against Hoover.

A new generation must deal with a transformed nation, with a world that no one could envision in the 1930's. But, although methods and names may change, great principles abide and are deeply embedded in American character. And the extent to which they were observed in 1933 and the beneficial results that emerged, and also the extent to which they were disregarded with unhappy results, are lessons for any future generation.

Except where anecdotal items have been essential to the over-all story, I have rejected the temptation to introduce those juicy but irrelevant bits, which may excite but never inform. As Frank Freidel says in his Foreword to this book, whoever seeks "the whiff of gunpowder or a far-off aroma of scandal" in this may be disappointed. There is plenty of that sort of thing in the reporting of the doings of the living present. Taste as well as truth should be an essential component of all history.

Many acknowledgments are due to those upon whom I have called for help during the years of planning and writing this book. I have already mentioned Dr. Rosen. Marjorie Wilson, my editorial assistant, has contributed not only indefatigable labor with the manuscript but her judgment and comprehension of the text, which have been of inestimable help.

Frank Freidel, professor of history at Harvard and the distinguished biographer of Franklin D. Roosevelt, read the manuscript, made many vital suggestions, and also generously wrote the Foreword.

Rex Tugwell has been most helpful with his personal recollections, his reading and correction of the chapters on agriculture, and the loan of his unpublished diary and memoranda. Also very helpful has been Adolf Berle, another of the original members of the Brains Trust, who read a chapter in which I describe the planning for the Hundred Days legislation.

Since I have put together the first comprehensive account of the banking crisis and the rescue of the banks, I needed a great deal of assistance. Mrs. Arthur A. Ballantine permitted me to use her late husband's papers accumulated during that period. F. Gloyd Awalt, who as acting comptroller of the currency in 1933 was a major factor in the rescue of the banks, has not only read and checked my account but has generously permitted me to use freely his own unpublished history of that operation. Walter Wyatt, at that time general counsel of the Federal Reserve Board and after 1946 reporter of decisions for the Supreme Court of the United States, read two successive drafts of the banking section and contributed many essential facts and incidents. He was, as I indicate, the author of the Emergency Banking Act. Lewis Douglas, director of the budget in 1933, supplied me with the history of the Economy Act of that year.

Januarius Arthur Mullen of Detroit, my assistant in 1933, has checked and verified a part of my account of my mission to the London Economic Conference.

In the year before his death, I enjoyed a considerable correspondence with Henry Wallace and profited from his recollections of the early days of the agricultural program.

My son, Raymond, Jr., assisted me in reconstructing several chapters. Annette Pomeranz Gettinger, who was my secretary in 1933, has checked and verified my account of the writing of the inaugural address. Florence Ahrens, in typing the entire manuscript, intelligently found her way through a very complicated assignment.

Frances Sleeper Moley, whose first vote was cast against Roosevelt in 1932, and who remained a devoted admirer of Herbert Hoover, always wondered about my early attachment to "that man in the White House." Nevertheless, during the long months of labor while this book was being written she made my life at home comfortable and happy.

RAYMOND MOLEY

New York City
May 1, 1966

Contents

Part Three

The Struggle for Solvency

Part Four

The Hundred Days

Part Five

Contemporaries

Part Six

International Frustrations

Part Seven

Summing Up

Prelude

The President

IN this account of what happened in the First New Deal the central figure is necessarily Franklin D. Roosevelt. But except for inferential revelations and occasional comments, it is neither a biography nor a character portrayal of that extraordinary individual. I am seeking to portray a movement, a change in national purposes and direction, not the epic of a hero. On two occasions in the past, in 1939 and 1949, I have published books in which I incorporated brief personality sketches of Roosevelt. Neither sought to be a comprehensive study of the man. The first was mainly concentrated in revealing the change in Roosevelt after his second election—a change which was to have vast influence on our national policies and our national destiny. The second sought to reveal the singular capacity of Roosevelt in practicing the art of politics. This present sketch has an equally limited purpose. It seeks to make my text understandable by describing Roosevelt as I knew him in the momentous year 1933.

Every man reveals more than one aspect of personality, depending upon the circumstances of a particular time and the influences that shape his conduct and course of action. As we shall see, even in that short period of 1933 Roosevelt revealed two quite different sides of his character—the one covert, secretive, and unreliable; the other frank, dependable, open, and unbelievably agreeable to work with. For the most part I knew only the better side. In later years there were great changes which came as political successes accumulated. Vast self-confidence grew and, as is inevitably the case with a man possessed of great authority, the virus of power had its way. With that evolution of character, this account has nothing to do.

In describing the Roosevelt of 1933 I shall certainly not hide behind those meaningless adjectives which have so often been used to portray him. He was neither "complex" nor "subtle" as I knew him at that time. He may have given this impression to some who had casual contacts with him. But this can be explained by the fact that his mental processes were essentially political. At times, either because he was uncertain about a subject or deliberately sought to evade a commitment, he felt it best to maintain an air of mystery. He could, when he chose, be as foggy as the Oracle at Delphi. When he nodded, he did not necessarily mean agreement. He had that habit because he wanted to convey the fact that he understood what was said to him. As we shall see, this completely deceived Hoover at their first meeting and Hoover carried the impression of agreement to his grave. There were many lesser people who were deceived by that nod, including many crackpots who came to him with odd and impractical ideas for recovery. He listened politely, indicated that he understood, and sent such people away believing they had convinced him.

While my knowledge of Roosevelt's character and behavior before his illness in 1921 comes only from secondary sources, I am inclined to believe that the romantic concept of a great change because of that misfortune is an exaggeration. It has been believed that the illness changed an individual from a carefree, venturesome, and superficial young man into a serious and dedicated statesman. Most of the characteristics that distinguished Roosevelt in his early life remained to the end.

Roosevelt was not deeply philosophical or reflective. Although the Harvard he attended and the leisure afforded him by his material means provided a rich potential for the intellect, his knowledge of political and constitutional history and theory was distinctly limited. During all the time I was associated with him I never knew him to read a serious book. That is a pattern quite common among politicians. Reading is a personal experience between the reader and the author, and Roosevelt was too restless to enjoy that. Like most political figures, he learned by listening. It was said of Alfred E. Smith that he always brushed aside a book and said he preferred "to talk with the author." In this respect Roosevelt was quite unlike his cousin Theodore, who was a voracious reader and who acquired a comprehensive store of knowledge that suited his purposes and prejudices. This encyclopedic knowledge excited the wonder of his contemporaries.

Perhaps that is why Franklin D. Roosevelt never developed the easy command of language which characterized so many who preceded him in the Presidency. Roosevelt was quite aware of his limitation and sought to make up for it by the help of others. Nevertheless he had a keen sense of language, and this was shown in the magnificent manner in which he delivered a written speech.

Because of his limited store of book learning, many of his contemporaries wrote him down as quite superficial. Many who knew him well believed he was living beyond his intellectual means. In cultural and pseudo-cultural circles in New York it was the fashion in the days of his governorship and even later to write Roosevelt off, as did Walter Lippmann in one of the most unfortunate pieces he ever wrote, as "a pleasant man who, without any important qualifications for the office, would like very much to be President."

Those who shared this view failed to understand that had Roosevelt given the same prodigious attention to the law, business, or scholarship that he gave to politics, he would have attained great distinction in those professions. Politics, regardless of the low estimate in which it is held, is a major art and one of the oldest professions. The perfection of Roosevelt's equipment in this field enabled him not only to compensate for his limitations but to accomplish as President, however one may appraise the record, far more than any President in a long time.

Roosevelt's approach to the problems of society and the nation was essentially pragmatic. He considered serious questions with that carefree and tentative and experimental attitude which suggests a comparison with William James, the great pragmatic optimist. When Roosevelt outlined to me his idea of what became the Civilian Conservation Corps, I asked him whether he had ever taken a course with James at Harvard, for the idea he was expressing had a distinct likeness to what James had said in his essay "The Moral Equivalent of War." He answered that he had never studied with James, but remembered him in the Yard as the famous professor who had such abundant whiskers.

In George Santayana's essay on James there is much that might be applied with equal pertinence to Roosevelt. Santayana mentioned James's boundless optimism, his love of mankind, his desire to solve men's problems, and his constant appeal that something be done about those problems without delay. But Santayana added, "Love is very penetrating but it penetrates to possibilities rather than to facts. . . . What is good is to believe rationally, holding what seems certain for certain, what seems probable for probable, what seems desirable for desirable, what is false for false."

In the perspective of the years, this pragmatic optimism is what contributed to Roosevelt's greatest failures. But in the context of 1933, it was marvelously effective because it was so contagious. His activism was a correlative of his optimism and his love of experimentation. His belief ran in some such form as this: "To perceive a wrong is 'good.' To deplore that wrong is also 'good.' Therefore to do something about it is 'good.' Not to act is to be untrue to the insight that made the wrong apparent in the first place." *

* Raymond Moley, *After Seven Years* (New York: Harper, 1939), p. 392.

Some of Roosevelt's decisions in the early weeks of his Administration were based upon the careful thought and long preparation by the expert people who were already in the government. This was especially true of the methods used in saving the banks and of his backing of economy measures. It was true also of his agricultural program, which was the result of years of study by farm leaders; and of his effective use of the Reconstruction Financc Corporation, a Hoover creation.

But these measures succeeded because Roosevelt won for them the confidence of the American public. The capacity of Roosevelt to act experimentally and to act with incredible expedition was the indispensable factor in the recovery which moved the country out of the darkest days of the depression. He was not, however, unaware of the experimental nature of these measures.

During the months of the campaign and in the early months of the Administration, Roosevelt's abundant hospitality to novel ideas was a problem for those who were advising him. All sorts of plans for ending the depression were coming in. These plans ranged from pure crackpotism to serious communications from business and academic people. Quacks who had been active in earlier years reappeared with their long-treasured nostrums. Greenbackers, free-silverites, and socialists of every variety offered their wares. A good deal of this assortment was brought to Roosevelt through the mediation of old friends and associates. It was Louis Howe's plan that all this stuff should be relayed to me, and my well-advertised position as an adviser brought many plans to me directly. There was little time to see all these economic seers or even to read what they submitted. Often this neglect brought down on me bitter criticism which forced its way into the newspaper columns.

On the other hand, when friends have told me that I should have used my influence to prevent the adoption of this or that reform, I have answered, "You ought to see some of the ideas and plans which I was able to nip in the bud."

Roosevelt's knowledge of economics was limited. It was, like Sam Weller's knowledge of London, "extensive but peculiar." But a practical streak in him caused him to lean upon orthodoxy when grappling with the immediate problems before him. He had been an economical governor of New York. Measurably, he believed in free enterprise. And his main reliance in those early days was upon such practical people as Jesse Jones, Will Woodin, Lewis Douglas, and other people who had business experience.

One of Roosevelt's characteristics stood him in good stead and was a wholesome restorative for the country in those early months and somewhat later. This was his genuine concern for people for whom life had not offered the advantages and enjoyments he himself had possessed from birth. He truly loved all sorts and conditions of people, with some notable and distinguished exceptions. And this is why in middle life he focused his attention upon the pressing economic dislocations with which Americans were confronted. He wanted to help them.

Roosevelt's incredible capacity to project this personal concern—through face-to-face relationships, through his dauntless optimism, and through his mastery of the spoken word over the radio—not only cemented his political ascendancy but provided the public confidence that turned the tide of the depression.

I shall leave to other analysts the question of cause and effect here. Was he concerned with people because they had votes, or because of his liking for and understanding of them?

This raises the question of his sincerity. I have been asked many, many times by people who knew of my long association with Roosevelt a simple question about his sincerity. In 1949 I wrote the following reply to that question:

> . . . sincerity, as a quality known to the generality of people, is not fairly applicable to a politician. Or to put it another way, in a category of virtues appropriate to a politician, sincerity occupies a less exalted place than it does among the qualities of a novelist, a teacher or a scientist. And that is in no way damning the politician, for he may exalt virtues such as kindness, understanding and public service far beyond those who sniff at his lack of sincerity.*

Most politicians will stoutly disagree with this interpretation of the political mind. For no politician would wish his words and actions to be known as political; to deny political motives is a first principle in the political art. Frederick the Great wrote a discourse refuting the arguments in Machiavelli's *Prince*. Someone at that time, reputedly Voltaire, commented that if Machiavelli had been alive he would have heartily approved of this enterprise of Frederick. For the first rule of a prince is that he must deny that he is concerned with his own personal fortunes.

Despite this harsh judgment concerning those who dedicate their lives to politics—a necessary service, considering the failure of most people to manifest any interest in the way they are governed except when their personal concerns are touched—there were strong reasons for realizing that Roosevelt entertained an overmastering concern for other people. He was intensely loyal to the people in his official family in the period when I knew him best. In one or two instances my own blunders might have caused him great embarrassment. But he never uttered a disapproving word.

Above all, he hated to hurt people, except those who were his political critics, enemies, and opponents. And he had a genuine horror of dis-

* Raymond Moley, *27 Masters of Politics* (New York: Funk & Wagnalls, 1949), p. 42.

charging an incompetent subordinate. Generally, that unpleasantness in 1933 devolved upon Louis Howe. When a change in personnel was required, Roosevelt sought to soften the blow by creating an alluring alternative, either another position in the Administration or a special mission of some kind. During the final months of the National Recovery Administration, Roosevelt realized that General Hugh Johnson must be removed. And so he proposed to that forthright individual a mission to Europe "to study recovery methods over there." Johnson exploded: "If you want to fire me, say so. Don't beat around the bush." Subsequently, Johnson resigned.

This reluctance to make clear-cut personnel decisions was the source of some of the indescribable confusions that marred Roosevelt's administration of the Presidency. Often he would not remove a person who was not doing the work assigned to him, but would appoint another person with a new title such as "coordinator." Thus, two people would be doing the job which should have been assigned to one.

His lack of directness in personal relations, which grew from his desire to make everyone—or nearly everyone—happy, is what gave him the reputation of being devious. Some of those historians who have admired him greatly, including Arthur Schlesinger, Jr., flatly accuse him of lying. But those who were close to Roosevelt and knew this trait formulated ways of checking among themselves to determine what the facts were. On my own account, I was never during this early period seriously misled except on one notable occasion, which I shall describe later.

It may surprise some who knew Roosevelt only in later years that in the time which I am considering here, in 1932 and 1933, there was a lovable humility in Roosevelt. He well realized that in the years since he left the Wilson Administration his knowledge of national affairs was only that of the ordinary newspaper reader. As governor he had been immersed in state affairs. Campaigning for President against a regime which had been established for twelve years was a formidable task, and in his inmost self he realized that he was an amateur. This induced him to place great reliance upon those whom he gathered around him to supply what was needed concerning national issues. During his years as governor he had made a great deal of use of academic people, notably in finance, agriculture, and electric power development. But when the campaign started in early 1932 he said to me more than once that his Albany advisers "didn't know beans about national issues." The members of my small group would have been presumptuous to say we were experts. We had enjoyed no part in government, but we had, because of our teaching, a considerable familiarity with national affairs. And we were in general sympathy with Roosevelt's slowly evolving sense of direction. Our greatest value probably was that we knew where to get the information we lacked.

Our many conferences with Roosevelt in the pre-convention days during the spring of 1932 were pitched on a most informal level. It was never a relationship that suggested master and servant. Everybody could speak his mind, critically or otherwise. He was one with us in trying to shape a program which would have appeal to the American public. He was never dogmatic; he always asked in such terms as "What do you think about this approach?" At first he was cautious in dealing with long-experienced Congressional leaders, and it was I who suggested that more practical experience with Federal affairs was needed and asked that Senators Byrnes and Pittman be added to our group.

One of the most remarkable characteristics of Roosevelt in those early days was his lack of confidence in addressing large city audiences. He said to me that he did not feel comfortable in cities. He was at his best in small towns and amid rural scenes. He commented somewhat wistfully in 1932, "Al Smith knows these city people better. He can move them. I can't."

He had fought the city bosses in New York years before when he was a state senator. He disliked and distrusted Tammany. And when he sought the Presidential nomination, the bosses fought him. This he could not forget until much later in his Presidency. His attachment to Edward Flynn of the Bronx was the exception. But Flynn had been close to him since the 1928 campaign.

Roosevelt's dislike for the methods of urban politics revealed a broad streak of idealism in the man which he carried with him into the Presidency. It deserves special note that in his Administration there was maintained a climate in the government that inhibited not only the lower forms of scandal but the shadowy tone that was to characterize the Truman years later. During the year with which I am concerned in this book I knew nothing in or about the Administration that even savored of dishonesty. True, there was some unavoidable jobbery and plenty of patronage-peddling. There were even some rogues lurking about. Some may discount the idealism in Roosevelt to which I refer. Nevertheless it was clear that political advantage was not to be gained by shady deals. The real political advantages were to be gained by tremendous and spectacular efforts to relieve distress and to get the economy moving again.

It is true that the humility of which I speak here disappeared in later years when vast power and popularity had their way with Roosevelt, as they have always afflicted individuals in history. No temperament is immune to the vitrifying effect of power. Anyone who occupies the Presidency has a way of closing the windows of his mind to invigorating opinion from without. Day after day there is the subtle flattery from those who come to ask favors or to win the ingratiating smile. The endless streams of those who have appointments do not use the time to purvey unpleasant truths. And if a man is told hour after hour and day after day how right he is, he will, unless he has extraordinary defenses, come to believe that he can never be wrong.

But this change never manifested itself in the period in which I knew Roosevelt best and which is the subject of the account that follows. I could not have worked with a man more kind, more considerate, and more of a friend than Roosevelt. Without this in view, the events which follow lose all meaning and all pertinence.

Those who worked with him never thought about the infirmity which had reduced his legs to useless appendages. He never discussed it or complained about this handicap. When occasion demanded it, such as making a speech, he wore steel braces, and someone, usually in those early days his guard Gus Gennerich and sometimes his son James, walked with him and kept him upright. The braces were not comfortable, and in the daily routine he removed them and conducted his business in a sitting posture. When he had to move from place to place, as from room to room or to an automobile or train, he used his wheel chair.

Like his cousin Theodore, he had a singular freedom from physical fear. The perils that lurk about a President, which had been shown in three assassinations, never seemed to concern him. Once when I was riding with him through the streets of Washington, we discussed this grim subject. He merely said that a President could not be protected from gunfire. All that the elaborate security measures could accomplish was to make sure that an assassin or a would-be assassin should never escape.

It may be noted by some readers that there is virtually no mention of Roosevelt's wife, Eleanor, in this book. That is because this story is limited to the making and execution of public policy. I have ruled out all concern with anyone's private life. Mrs. Roosevelt seldom if ever intruded her ideas into policy-making at that time. She had limitless outlets for her remarkable energies. Subsequently, especially in the war period and after Roosevelt's death, she became a public figure in her own right.

Nor have I, except incidentally, mentioned Roosevelt's masterful and class-conscious mother, Sara.

Autobiographical Note

I offer these personal observations largely because I have been asked on innumerable occasions how I first became associated with Franklin D. Roosevelt and also because it may be useful at the outset of this story to recite the qualifications in experience and training I brought to the responsibilities that he bestowed upon me in 1932 and thereafter.

My first contact with Roosevelt was in the autumn of 1928. Louis Howe, whom I had known for approximately two years, told me that his "boss" wanted to talk with me about the campaign in which he was a candidate for the governorship of New York. Louis took me to Roosevelt's campaign office at the Democratic headquarters in New York City.

Roosevelt was at his desk sorting letters, some of which he laid aside for the drafting of replies by Howe and others. The first impression he conveyed was of his handsome figure, a most attractive face, and powerful shoulders and arms. He turned to me with the smile that was so soon to win the affection of many million Americans.

He came directly to the reason for which he had summoned me. As a candidate for governor, he intended to propose the simplification, through law and practice, of the administration of justice in the state. He cited some examples of the failure of the courts to administer justice with more dispatch and efficiency. And, he said, if elected governor, he intended to create a remedial commission. He wanted me to prepare a memorandum, which would be the basis of a speech on the subject. I prepared the material he wanted. The speech was delivered later in the campaign.

Louis's belief in my qualifications for this assignment arose from the relations I had enjoyed with him. There had been created, two or three years before, a group called the National Crime Commission. Roosevelt was a director of this organization along with a number of notable Americans, including Charles Evans Hughes. Louis, a dedicated reader of detective stories and a former newspaperman, learned of my interest in criminal justice and had enlisted my help in some of the commission's reports, notably one on payroll robberies.

My interest in the subject went back to 1920, when as director of the Cleveland Foundation I had promoted and managed a comprehensive survey of criminal justice in Cleveland. The report of this survey, which was directed by Dean Roscoe Pound and Professor Felix Frankfurter of the Harvard Law School, had attracted a good deal of attention at the time. Subsequently, I was employed as research director of similar studies in Missouri and Illinois. In 1926, I was appointed research director of the New York State Crime Commission. Governor Alfred E. Smith had secured the creation of this commission from a Republican legislature. In 1928 and 1930 I published two books that summarized the conclusions of my various researches, *Politics and Criminal Prosecution* and *Our Criminal Courts.* At the time of my first meeting with Roosevelt and later, until 1952, I was a professor of public law at Columbia.

In 1930, Judge Samuel Seabury began his investigation in New York City, first of the magistrates' courts, and then of the New York County district attorney. I served on the Seabury staff in those investigations and assisted the judge in shaping his findings.

Because of these various services, Roosevelt, as governor, appointed me a member of a committee that prepared and secured the passage of a new parole system for New York State. And in 1931 he made me his major representative on the Commission on the Administration of Justice in the State of New York.

Thus, my relationship with Roosevelt developed during his years as governor.

This relationship became especially meaningful in late 1931 and early 1932, because the Republican legislature had appointed a committee charged with the investigation of New York City's government. Seabury was the counsel for that committee, and a series of sensational exposures of incompetence and corruption was developed. The major Seabury objective was the removal of Mayor James J. Walker. I declined to serve on the Seabury staff in this investigation because of my relationship with Roosevelt. For it became evident that Seabury was determined to embarrass Roosevelt in his quest for the Presidential nomination by dumping charges against Walker on the governor's desk. The mayor's removal from office or exoneration would be the responsibility of the governor. I was aware at the time that Seabury, a Democrat who had once been a candidate for governor, entertained the idea that by eliminating Roosevelt he might himself secure the Presidential nomination.

This turn of affairs brought my services to Roosevelt into the realm of national politics. In early January 1932, Roosevelt invited me to lunch at his office in Albany. Presumably I was to contribute a section on judicial reform to his annual message. The talk, however, turned to politics, for he was already actively seeking the Presidential nomination. The man upon whom he leaned most heavily for political counsel—the astute Edward J. Flynn, his secretary of state—had assigned James A. Farley the task of gathering delegate pledges over the country.

I told him of my long interest in politics and offered to help in any way I could. He said he would be glad to call on me.

This opportunity to participate in a campaign for the Presidency was especially attractive to me. My abiding interest from the time of my boyhood, in the small town of Olmsted Falls in Ohio, had been politics. I had managed to graduate from Baldwin University (now Baldwin-Wallace College) in 1906. After my graduation I secured a teaching job in Olmsted Falls and in 1907 became "superintendent." (There were only four teachers in the "system.") But long before there was any turmoil in educational circles about academic freedom, I exercised my right to run for village clerk in 1907 and was elected. My opponent, incidentally, was president of the School Board but he observed the amenities of politics and, as one of the best friends I ever had, continued to support me in my school job. In 1909 I was re-elected clerk. I contracted tuberculosis and spent two winters in the West, one in New Mexico and the other in Denver. I recovered and in 1911 ran for mayor of Olmsted Falls and was elected.

Once when Farley said to me in 1932, "What the hell [or whatever else he used for emphasis] do you, a college professor, know about politics?" I reminded him that I had been elected to office three years before he won as a candidate for clerk of Stony Point and Roosevelt was elected to the New York State Senate. We all, incidentally, had Republican constituencies and we all were Democrats. I was two years Farley's senior and four years younger than Roosevelt.

The foregoing tells something of a political sophistication that had its beginning back in a small town and was developed later in Cleveland and New York when I participated in campaigns at the state and local level.

Meanwhile I had absorbed the ideas and spirit of the Progressive movement, although I was never an admirer of Theodore Roosevelt. I doubted his sincerity and was repelled by his ham acting. I preferred Wilson's more intelligent approach to reform. And he was a Democrat! As I shall note later, I also preferred the more concise specifications in

Charles Van Hise's *Concentration and Control* to the voluminous writings of Herbert Croly.

All in all, it was Wilson who determined my occupation, and the Progressive movement my political faith. Maturity came with the years after that, but these early influences were still alive when the exciting events of 1932 began.

When Roosevelt asked me to assist him in his quest for the nomination in January 1932, I was confident that my study, observation, and professional interest in national affairs could play a role in the formulation of campaign issues. Also, my experience in directing the various research projects had equipped me to organize the ideas and knowledge of others. My heritage had made me a Democrat, and I believed sincerely that the state of the nation at that time demanded a change of government. And finally, I believed that the nomination and election of Roosevelt would be assured if he could clearly formulate a course of action designed to end the depression, which had shortly before entered its third year.

At this point and in this context, my earlier services to Roosevelt in the field of law enforcement meshed with his problem of bringing national support for his Presidential ambitions.

In February, Seabury placed before the governor serious charges about the mysterious enrichment of Thomas M. Farley, sheriff of New York County. In his hearings before Roosevelt, Farley was unwilling or unable to explain this enrichment beyond his income from the office he held and other rather modest means. Roosevelt dismissed him from office, holding that in such a case involving a public official the governor was not bound by the judicial rule that the state must prove wrongdoing. In such an instance, the accused must establish the legitimacy of the sources of his income beyond his official compensation.

Roosevelt asked me to write the order of removal, and I complied with a strongly worded expression about integrity in public office. Those accused must be held to "a stern and uncompromising rectitude." This expression of Roosevelt's position won high praise far beyond New York, and Farley's removal firmly fixed the governor's image as a strong and forthright executive.

This stand was not at all inconsistent with Roosevelt's earlier attitude. His relations with Tammany had never been cordial, and two decades before, as a state senator, he had been the leading figure in a group of reformers who bitterly opposed Tammany's candidates for a United States Senatorship.

Samuel I. Rosenman in his book *Working with Roosevelt* * has an interesting story about the origins of the Brains Trust (an expression I never relished but which has found its way into the dictionaries).

Rosenman at that time held the office of counsel to the governor. He

* New York: Harper, 1952.

and Basil O'Connor, Roosevelt's law partner, during the preceding years had helped Roosevelt with his speeches on state affairs. But Rosenman realized that in the campaign for the Presidency which loomed ahead, talent more familiar with national affairs needed to be recruited for Roosevelt's help. He says that in March he decided that the national issues with which Roosevelt would have to deal in his quest for the Presidency were "beyond my own experience." And so he suggested that there be recruited a number of professors familiar with national problems, and he said to Roosevelt: "The first one I thought I would talk with is Ray Moley. He believes in your social philosophy and objectives, and he has a clear and forceful style of writing. Being a university professor himself, he can suggest different university people in different fields."

Roosevelt assented but suggested that "We'll have to keep this whole thing pretty quiet." That was about as futile a suggestion as Roosevelt ever made, for secrecy under the surveillance of the many newspapermen who were already following the governor was impossible.

After our group had got under way, we were, in a phrase used by Hugh Johnson on another occasion, "as easy to track as a herd of elephants in six feet of snow."

The first production, however, was my own handiwork, a ten-minute radio address on the "Lucky Strike" program. Rosenman says in his book that it was "beautifully written" and it crowded into its short space the very general outlines of the philosophy of the campaign that followed. To characterize it, I inserted the phrase "forgotten man," which I lifted from William Graham Sumner's famous essay which bore that title. This composition apparently qualified me for the task that was then assigned to me.

Rosenman at about that time was appointed by Roosevelt to a vacancy on the New York Supreme Court, and I saw very little of him in the months that followed.

The organization of my group began with an evening meeting with Rosenman and O'Connor. Then I presented to them a list of topics that seemed to me to be the major issues of the campaign. Opposite each topic I wrote the names of people who could be drawn upon for expert and detailed information suitable for speeches. (I have in my papers the original draft of this list, written on O'Connor's stationery.)

I then began the business of recruiting. This procedure I can best illustrate by what happened with Rexford G. Tugwell, who was a professor of economics at Columbia. He was primarily interested in agriculture, and I believed that this would be a major, if not the major, issue in the campaign. I brought him with me to dinner with Rosenman and O'Connor. He presented his views, and after a long discussion I took him to Albany for a dinner and an evening's discussion with Roosevelt at the governor's residence. In this instance and in the many that followed with other prospects, I carefully noted the man's ideas and considered how he would fit into the plans for the campaign. Since these recruits would, if selected, have to deal directly with Roosevelt, I watched his own reactions. In Tugwell's case Roosevelt immediately reacted favorably. And so he was the first choice.

The next was Adolf A. Berle, Jr., a junior member of the Columbia Law School faculty. He, too, elicited Roosevelt's keen interest.

Thus the nucleus of our group was formed.

I took several others to Albany for this screening process, but most seemed unsuitable and were dropped.

During the pre-convention period most of the speech material was provided by Tugwell and Berle.

After the nomination, Hugh Johnson was recruited. And a bit later, in order to provide practical advice based on long service in Congress, I asked Roosevelt to add Senators James F. Byrnes of South Carolina and Key Pittman of Nevada.

Although many others were on the periphery and helped with ideas, these six—Tugwell, Berle, Johnson, Byrnes, Pittman, and I—were the real Brains Trust.

In August, Roosevelt validated my status by writing a letter addressed to the following Democratic leaders: Newton D. Baker, Owen D. Young, Bernard M. Baruch, Melvin A. Traylor, Guy A. Thompson (president of the American Bar Association and an old friend of mine), Colonel Edward M. House, and Senators Pittman, Walsh, Robinson, Hull, and King.

The letter was this:

> Between now and the end of the campaign a good many matters for immediate decision will arise—matters relating to issues and policies of various kinds—and I am asking a small group to hold themselves in readiness for consultation. This will not be in any sense a formal advisory committee but only a few people whose judgment I value.
>
> Professor Raymond Moley, of Columbia University, an old friend who has been assisting me in many ways, is acting as a sort of clearing house for me. This part of my task has nothing to do with those who are engaged in the strictly political management of the campaign, but has in a sense a more personal relationship. It would help me in a very practical sense if you would give me your thought on matters from time to time, and if Professor Moley calls you up or writes to you on any specific point, I hope you will feel that it comes from me and that you will confer with him.

The importance of this communication was that it clearly differentiated my group from the political managers, headed by Flynn, Farley, and Howe. They had their headquarters in the Biltmore Hotel. My group had a suite at the Roosevelt Hotel. By agreement the two operations were kept strictly separate. The line of command from each led directly to Roosevelt. There was no interference about the content of speeches from the Biltmore at any time in the campaign.

Another principle of organization that I established was that in the preparation of a speech the members of my group reported directly to me. They occasionally had access to Roosevelt directly but only for discussion. When I had sorted out the material supplied by members of my group, I made the selections and wrote my own draft. Then this draft was worked over with Roosevelt. No one came between us in this procedure. Otherwise there would have been utter confusion. A speech cannot be written by a committee.

It is regrettable that in subsequent Presidential campaigns these two rules have not been followed and in many cases the result has been disastrous.

The expression Brains Trust was applied to our group by James Kieran, a reporter for the New York *Times*. I didn't like it, but it was better than the original expression applied to us by Roosevelt. He called us his "privy council."

It is essential to an understanding of this story to describe my relationship with Roosevelt which matured in the years between our first meeting in 1928 and the election in 1932. I was not, in the current use of the term, a mere "speech writer" for him. An intimacy developed during the 1932 campaign which offered him the relief and satisfaction of thinking aloud when we were together. Policies and strategy had to be debated and discussed, and my reactions provided him with at least a sympathetic and trusted friend. My academic equipment helped in these discussions. I also had seen enough, heard enough, and experienced enough to have developed a good deal of political sense and some understanding of public opinion. I had entered his service not only because I believed in him and his cause, but to enrich my own knowledge of the art of politics. I had no ambition to hold public office or to wield political authority. I was quite happy to continue to enjoy the freedom provided by a university professorship. Roosevelt knew this, and for that reason could count on my lack of any personal political ambition.

Moreover, I was free, so far as I know, of those inner-circle contentions and jealousies so common on the slippery ground that surrounds great official authority. My role was recognized and respected by those close to Roosevelt—his political experts Flynn, Farley, and Howe, his prospective secretaries Stephen Early and Marvin McIntyre, and Marguerite LeHand. In short, I had become a member of his official family.

This is what made the transition so easy after the election from chief of the Brains Trust to an unofficial assistant to the President-elect and later to the President. This relationship continued even after I resigned from the government in September 1933. It lasted until 1936.

In December, after our first conference with Hoover, Roosevelt talked with me about an official position in his Administration. Since he wanted to call on me for many assignments, it was obvious that I should be relieved of administrative responsibility in any government agency. It was also understood that I wished to remain in any official position only for the relatively few months after the inauguration in March. And so in December he suggested an appointment as one of the four assistant secretaries of state. That particular post had no specifically assigned responsibilities. It would, he said, leave me free to assist him directly. As matters developed, it would have been much better to continue an office, "administrative assistant to the President," which had existed in the Hoover Administration. But Louis Howe, in reorganizing the White House staff, had abolished that office. With certain misgivings, I agreed with his suggestion.

Part One

International Complications

Chapter One

Hoover and Roosevelt Meet in November

WHEN the polls closed on November 8, 1932, the returns showed that the Roosevelt-Garner ticket had been elected with a popular plurality of seven million votes. In both houses of Congress, Democrats had substantial majorities. This seemed to be a clear mandate for Roosevelt to deal with the depression on terms that had been presented to the electorate in the long campaign which began, so far as Roosevelt was concerned, in the very early spring.

On the morning after the election I went to Roosevelt's house on East Sixty-fifth Street and found Gus Gennerich, Roosevelt's bodyguard borrowed from the New York State Police, sorting out a big pile of congratulatory telegrams. I poked about among them, located Hoover's message of good wishes and went up to Roosevelt's bedroom, where he was finishing breakfast. I presented the Hoover message and he dictated a suitable reply, which I scribbled on the back of the Western Union envelope.

After a time, friends and party leaders began arriving, and the day was spent in reminiscences and congratulations. Toward evening, Roosevelt returned to Albany.

I went back to my apartment near Columbia University. Despite my post-campaign weariness, in the days that immediately followed I prepared for the full resumption of my class work. Although I had taken no leave of absence, it had suffered considerable neglect since September.

On Sunday morning, the thirteenth, this peaceful interlude was interrupted by a telephone call from Roosevelt. He said he had received a telegram from Hoover which needed consideration and asked me to join him in Albany to discuss an answer. The Hoover message was read to me over the telephone. It said that a critical situation had arisen concerning the European debts and suggested that Roosevelt meet Hoover for a discussion in Washington later that month. This suggested the beginning of a new phase of public policy for which there had been little or no thought during the campaign.

It must be difficult for those who have reached maturity during the past three decades to realize that there had been no discussion of foreign affairs by Roosevelt during the campaign. The Western world was at peace, and the governments of Europe were grappling with internal economic distress. The echoes of Locarno still prevailed, and Hitler was only a strident voice in the beer halls. In Italy the people were undergoing the Fascist ministrations of Mussolini. Britain had been through an election in 1931 which resulted in a national government with Ramsay MacDonald as Prime Minister and Philip Snowden in the Exchequer. Both were refugees from the Labour Party, and most of the remainder of the Cabinet were Conservatives. The government there had abandoned the gold standard in 1931.

In Roosevelt's campaign speeches the only comment on foreign affairs was some mention of tariffs. A month before the election Roosevelt had received memoranda on foreign policy from Francis Sayre and Sumner Welles, who were old friends of his family. He had discussed these with me. We felt that they were unsuitable for campaign material. I had read Hoover's defenses of his foreign policy and suggested that no real issue could be drawn from these. Roosevelt agreed, saying, "Yes, old Hoover's foreign policy has been pretty good." And so foreign affairs had vanished from our minds until that November day when the telegram came from Hoover.

If the people in Roosevelt's circle who were so lighthearted the day after the election could have known what was going on in government offices in London and Paris and could have foreseen the outcome of those activities so far away, there would have been less joy and new worry. For the decision that was made abroad immediately after our elections was destined to divert Roosevelt from domestic affairs during the greater part of two months and, what was even more serious, bring very close a perilous division in his triumphant party.

That decision, in which Britain was joined by other debtor countries, was to tear open the severely controversial issue of the foreign debts to the United States. The news, which Henry L. Stimson described in his diary as a "bombshell," was delivered to our State Department on November 10, 1932, in the form of two notes demanding not only that the debt payments due on December 15 be deferred but that we review the whole debt situation with debtor nations.

Secretary of State Stimson and Ogden Mills, Secretary of the Treasury, immediately began telephone conversations with Hoover, who was resting in Palo Alto. Hoover agreed with them that in this critical situation he should confer with Roosevelt personally, since the issue had ramifications with which the outgoing Administration could not deal effectively. Stimson and Mills drafted a message for Hoover to send to Roosevelt and dispatched it to Palo Alto. Hoover immediately terminated his holiday and boarded a train for Washington. He made substantial changes in the Stimson-Mills draft and dispatched his communication to Roosevelt on Saturday at Yuma.*

The lengthy message Roosevelt received, which we carefully examined in Albany that Sunday, recited some of the recent history of the debts so far as the Hoover Administration and Congress were concerned. Hoover cited the British request for a suspension of the December payment and for a review of the entire debt situation, and similar requests by other debtor nations. Thus, said Hoover, "our government is now confronted with a world problem of major importance to this nation."

Hoover reiterated his prior public statements that he did not favor debt revision in any form. But he was willing to bargain if, in compensation for some readjustments on our part, we should receive benefits in an expansion of markets for the products of our labor and our farms.

But he called attention to the firm resolution of Congress, at the time of the moratorium, that no new debt commission be created, and that it was clearly declared national policy that the debts be neither canceled nor reduced.

Since any such negotiations as were suggested could not be concluded by the Administration then in office, the President rather indirectly suggested that the new Administration join in some reply to these requests. Therefore, he proposed a meeting with Roosevelt to review the subject. Roosevelt, he said, might bring with him any Democratic Congressional leaders or other advisers as he might wish. He said that, since he had learned that Roosevelt was contemplating a trip South, it might be convenient for him to stop in Washington for such a conference at the White House.

In considering a response to this appeal, certain factors were reviewed that day in Albany after I arrived. It was clear that if Roosevelt acceded to such cooperation, he would be bound, perhaps for years to come. Certainly, Roosevelt could not commit himself before he was appraised

* Stimson Diary, Yale University Library, entries for Nov. 10 and Nov. 12, 1932. We could not know it at that time, but the evidence is now revealed in Secretary Stimson's diary that there had been a sharp disagreement about the content of Hoover's invitation to Roosevelt. In very considerably revising a draft of the invitation that had been prepared by Stimson and Secretary of the Treasury Ogden Mills, Hoover took a decidedly harder line against any suggestion of cancellation. This disturbed Stimson because he believed that it would stiffen the British position. He believed, too, that Hoover's recital of his troubles with Congress would make

of all the long history of the debts. Congress also was to be considered, for its approval was necessary before any debt concession could be authorized. Roosevelt felt that, although the new Congress would have in its membership most of the Democratic leaders inherited from the Congress that had approved the moratorium, it would take a hard line toward any proposal to revise the debts. And Roosevelt must count upon this Congress for its help in enacting any measures he contemplated after his inauguration. Any suggestion that he disagreed with the policies previously fixed by Congress would engender strong opposition and endanger his programs.

The clear course, therefore, would be for Roosevelt to deny any constitutional authority to commit himself to any proposal before his inauguration.

The reply that was composed at Albany that Sunday was cordial but firmly noncommittal. Roosevelt indicated his willingness to cooperate and to meet with Hoover, when "you and I can go over the whole situation." He said he would be meeting with Democratic leaders later that month in Warm Springs. But he ended his reply by saying that "the immediate question raised by the British, French, and other notes creates a responsibility which rests upon those now vested with executive and legislative authority."

Roosevelt less amenable to some sort of cooperation. Stimson was greatly concerned about Hoover's determination to fight for the vindication of his policies in a future election. After Hoover returned to Washington, a sharp disagreement arose between Hoover and Mills on one side and Stimson on the other. Stimson feared the effect of Hoover's hard line upon the European debtor countries, for a forced default might be very embarrassing in his future relations with them. Hoover and Mills were more concerned about the domestic reaction to the invitation and a conference with the President-elect. It was Stimson's opinion that Hoover and Mills were viewing the subject in political terms—both of them, Stimson seemed to believe, were looking forward to another election. As the events proved in the weeks to come, Stimson was most anxious to establish a close relationship with Roosevelt while Hoover and Mills were irreconcilable so far as Roosevelt was concerned. It is also evident that Stimson's sympathies for any relationship with the New York banking community were greater than Hoover's and Mills's. Stimson had a considerable number of contacts with those New York interests during that week and in the months that followed. These differences no doubt caused Hoover to omit Stimson from the conference with Roosevelt. He did, however, ask Stimson to stand by in the White House during the conference because someone had guessed that Roosevelt would call upon Garner and if that happened he wanted Stimson present. This idea of Garner's participation never occurred to Roosevelt, and so Stimson's vigil was unnecessary. After the conference, however, Hoover called Stimson and recited to him much of what had happened. Perhaps this stand-by presence of Stimson is what prompted Hoover in his memoirs to say that Stimson was actually present at the conference with Roosevelt. Stimson Diary, Nov. 12, Nov. 18, and Nov. 19, 1932.

The bare facts, which I gathered during the week that followed and which I transmitted to Roosevelt, were these:

After the United States entered the war, and following the armistice, our government had loaned a number of the Allied powers more than $10,000,000,000. Of this amount, approximately $7,000,000,000 was advanced during the war and $3,200,000,000 after the armistice. Most of this money was spent in the United States for foodstuffs, munitions, and cotton. Most of this lending was done under the authority of the Liberty Loan Act. And that act stipulated that these advances were loans, not gifts. Promissory notes were required. Repayments were to be used to retire Liberty Bonds. In 1922 Congress created the World War Debt Commission, which agreed to reduce the original obligations to about 51.3 per cent. This plan, named for the commission chairman, Charles G. Dawes, fixed interest rates. Britain, Finland, Hungary, Poland, and Czechoslovakia were to pay at the rate of 3.3 per cent; France, 1.6 per cent, and Italy .4 per cent.

Up to June 15, 1931, we had received $750,000,000 on principal and $1,900,000,000 in interest.

However, most of our debtors had received more than that in reparations payments from Germany, whose ability to pay had substantially been made possible by private loans from the United States. When our own economic troubles began and these private loans stopped, Germany ceased to pay reparations. And then the various European Allies considerably reduced the amount of Germany's reparations.*

In June 1932 Hoover proposed a moratorium on payments for a year. This was approved in the recess by Congressional leaders and later by Congress. But with its approval Congress resolved that "any of the indebtedness of foreign countries to the United States" should not be canceled or reduced.

Despite the opposition of a majority in Congress and Hoover's own views, there was a considerable body of opinion in the United States, largely centered in the East, which favored cancellation or major reductions of the debts. Late in 1932 a group of American economists argued for leniency, saying that it would help in the revival of business. This view was strongly held by the international bankers.

Tugwell pointed this out to me, saying in effect that while the debtor

* One of the arguments the debtors used when they asked us to reconsider—that is, reduce—what was due us was this remission of reparations which they had made for Germany. Later that year, in the summer of 1933, I met James J. Walker, former mayor of New York in England. He said that people he met over there had brought up this argument and asked me to explain the difference between what the British owed us and what Germany owed them. I explained, and he replied, "I see. The debts are debts and the reparations are fines." I have never heard a better summation of the subject.

countries were able to pay their installments, the international bankers wanted the government debts out of the way to help the revival of their business abroad.*

It was apparent that France could easily pay her December installment, for her supply of gold was very considerable. Britain, Italy, and Greece could do so with more difficulty. This was set forth by Berle in a very illuminating memorandum to me.† Berle further pointed out that the various countries' budgets showed that the amount set aside, except by Britain, for debt payments was only 5 per cent of total expenditures. The complicating factor was the transfer problem—that is, the ability of the debtors to secure dollars to meet the payments. Berle's general conclusion was this:

> In fundamental economics, any payments from abroad diminish the chance of disposing of an export surplus of farm products. But the debt payments are relatively unimportant in comparison with the interest on the private debts (foreign bonds, etc.) and payments on short-term bank paper of which eight hundred millions (about) are in New York. The significance of the debt payments is therefore appreciable but not determinative; the psychological factor outweighs the financial or economic.

With the assistance of Berle and others, I drafted a series of questions which I believed might help Roosevelt in his Washington conference. These were typed separately on three-by-five cards which could be held unobtrusively in his massive hand.‡

The purpose of these questions was to learn directly from Hoover certain facts that were not clear to us: Why did the debtor countries not avail themselves of the provision that they should bring up any wish for adjustment ninety days before the payments were due? Why was a new debt commission necessary? What were the gold holdings of the various debtor nations?

It had been rumored that when Pierre Laval, as Premier of France, had visited Hoover in 1931, there had been some sort of agreement to reopen debt negotiations. Accordingly, one of the questions was: "Has any promise been made to European governments that debts will be re-examined because of agreements in Europe to forgo reparations payments?" The concept of some sort of secret agreement was in Roosevelt's mind, because he wrote on one of the cards in longhand, "Secret agreements with Pres." Fortunately, in the conference the following week he did not propound this question. The situation was tense enough as it was.

* Tugwell's comment on this is in his book *The Democratic Roosevelt* (Garden City: Doubleday, 1957), p. 256.

† R. M. Files, Adolf A. Berle to Raymond Moley, November 15, 1932.

‡ These questions appear in the Appendix, pp. 555–56.

On Thursday, the seventeenth, I visited Albany to deliver what information I had accumulated and to talk over the conference with Roosevelt. To my astonishment, Marvin McIntyre, who had been a general manager of appointments during the campaign and who became appointments secretary in the new Administration, told me on my arrival that Roosevelt had decided that I should accompany him when he talked with Hoover and Mills. I received this news with mixed feelings. It was obvious, since Hoover had announced that Mills was to be present with him, that someone must accompany Roosevelt. My selection was logical enough. Roosevelt had not announced his prospective Secretaries of State and Treasury. Indeed, these selections were not to be made for three months. And the selection of Senator Glass or Owen Young or any other prominent person who had been talked about would indicate a commitment that lay far in the future. I was not then a prospect for any office in the new Administration. And I had enjoyed a close confidential relationship with Roosevelt for many months. But my position had been more or less anonymous, not to say anomalous, so far as the public press was concerned. This assignment would bring upon me a blaze of publicity, accompanied by an almost terrifying responsibility in the months ahead, perhaps for longer. It was a turning point in my life—whether for good or not, I could not know. But I dismissed the risks and accepted the task as a new and interesting adventure.

I accompanied Roosevelt on the train to Washington that morning and rode with him in a White House car to the meeting. Accompanying us in the car was Warren Delano Robbins, who was protocol officer in the State Department. The fact that Robbins was Roosevelt's cousin was a delicate touch of hospitality which did not escape Roosevelt. There was also, resplendent in gold braid, Captain Walter N. Vernou, the President's naval aide, another compliment to a "former naval person."

I still recall the sense I had of the atmosphere in the streets as we passed along to the White House. There was some applause for the President-elect from the people looking on. But in general I had the sensation of passing through an occupied city whose inhabitants were not quite clear as to what it was all about.

There are three versions of what happened in the meeting. Mills, so far as I know, left no record. Roosevelt wrote later * that "on the subject of foreign debts no tangible suggestion was forthcoming." That is incorrect, because Hoover's suggestions were very clear. Roosevelt also said later that "little discussion took place." There was, in fact, a great deal of discussion.

* *Public Papers and Addresses of Franklin D. Roosevelt,* Vol. I (New York: Harper, 1938), p. 867.

Hoover's version is this:

He [Roosevelt] had expressed a wish to bring some adviser, and I thought it might be one of the senators, Glass, Hull, Swanson or Walsh, who were being discussed as members of his Cabinet and were familiar with these problems. He, however, brought Raymond Moley, who had been one of his aides. Moley was an able man with a mind quick to grasp public problems. . . . Of course, neither Roosevelt nor Moley could be familiar with the background of these complicated matters; worse still, they were obviously suspicious that we were trying to draw them into some sort of trap. Moley took charge of the conversation for Roosevelt. I, therefore, directed myself to primary educational work upon him, as he would influence the action of the President-elect.*

But he adds in his *Memoirs* that he understood that we

agreed to all our proposals. On these promises, I suggested that Roosevelt join me in a meeting with Congressional leaders of both parties which I would call for the next day at the White House, where we would jointly urge the reactivation of a War Debt Commission. This would at once display our united front in the foreign field. Mr. Roosevelt stated he would rather not attend such a joint meeting but would communicate his approval to the Democratic leaders.

We suggested that after this White House meeting with the Congressmen we should draft a press statement upon the debt question to be issued in our joint names, stating our agreement as to what should be done. However, Roosevelt and Moley stated that they preferred that I alone should issue such a press statement after agreement with them as to its terms; and that Roosevelt should then issue an approving statement, the terms of which would also be jointly settled. It was agreed that Secretary Mills would meet with Roosevelt and Moley the next day to settle the texts.

When I met the Congressional leaders, I was astonished to find that Mr. Roosevelt had not communicated with the Democratic members.†

Hoover then adds that the Democratic members said they would oppose any reactivation of the Debt Commission.

The aspects of this version which were not as Roosevelt and I understood them at that time might be attributed to faulty memory, since Hoover wrote that account nearly twenty years later. But that he left the meeting with a belief that Roosevelt had agreed to his program is attested by the notation in Stimson's diary, written at the time, that Hoover told him an hour after the meeting concluded that Roosevelt had promised to come out in favor of the Hoover-Mills plan. ‡

My own version of what happened and what was said in that conference differs markedly from those of Hoover and Roosevelt. Perhaps

* *The Memoirs of Herbert Hoover,* Vol. III (New York: Macmillan, 1952), p. 179.

† *Ibid.,* pp. 180–81.

‡ Stimson Diary, Nov. 22, 1932.

this was inevitable because the meeting was informal and there was no stenographer present. Fortunately, in the light of these differences, Bernard Baruch came to my quarters in the Mayflower Hotel that evening after dinner. I told him what had happened at the conference in some detail, for on a subject like this I greatly valued his advice. When I finished, he said with the friendly sharpness which was so characteristic of his relations with his friends, "Young fellow, see that bed? Well, don't you dare get into it until you have written down what happened this afternoon. Do it while your memory is fresh, because there may be a lot of disagreement between Hoover and Roosevelt about what was agreed to."

This was one of those flashes of insight which have made Baruch's reputation legendary. Needless to say, I did what he told me to do and six years later, when I wrote my book *After Seven Years,* I had my notes with me. There were also other contemporary sources such as the memories of other people to whom I told the story, to help me with my account.*

We met somewhat past mid-afternoon in the Red Room of the White House. Hoover sat alone at my far left, pausing occasionally in his preliminary discourse to puff on a cigar. Roosevelt and I sat on a couch, with the President-elect next to Hoover. Mills sat at my far right. Roosevelt, as was his custom, was smoking cigarettes.

Behind Mills I saw the White House portraits of Jefferson and John Adams. General Grant was on the wall before me, and a table with cigars, cigarettes, and water stood in the center. From the outside, through the red hangings, came the dimming light of a typical November twilight.

There were a few pleasantries. Roosevelt twitted Mills, saying, "The only thing I objected to in the campaign was when the Republican National Committee printed a picture of your private golf course and said it was mine." Mills took this with good humor and replied, "Well, Franklin, the misinformation seems to have been pretty general." Then he added that "the course isn't any more mine than yours. The sole satisfaction I get out of it in recent years is that I pay dues to the club that owns it. I can't remember when I played it last."

Hoover opened the conversation with a long analysis and history of the debts. He spoke with scarcely any interruption for nearly an hour. Shyness, so characteristic of him, caused him to fix his eyes at the outset upon the beautiful seal of the United States which was woven into the red rug. After a while, he began to address himself to me, primarily, as he explained to Stimson that evening and also in his memoirs years later, to educate me and thus to influence the course of Roosevelt.

* My account of the conference in the next few pages is in part taken from my book *After Seven Years,* pp. 72–77.

There was never a more attentive student, for I realized as he went on that on this subject we were in the presence of the best-informed man in the world. I was amazed at the wealth of his detailed knowledge and the cogent manner in which he expressed himself without even a scrap of a note. Never once did he find it necessary to fall back on his competent Secretary of the Treasury.*

His Administration, Hoover said, had observed four principles with respect to debts. First, these were not political debts, but substantially honest business obligations. Second, each debtor should be dealt with as an individual unit; each debt was an individual transaction to be judged upon its specific merits. Third, the debts and reparations were not related, so far as the United States was concerned. The United States had taken no responsibility for the fixing of German reparations, had accepted no reparations, had suffered no devastation at home. It could therefore not accept the contention of the European debtors that since they had reduced reparations payments we should for that reason reduce the debts.† Fourth, capacity to pay should be considered. We should take account of proven inability on the part of the debtors to pay us.

Roosevelt agreed to these four principles. They were, in fact, the basis of negotiations by the new Administration in 1933.

Hoover then argued that cancellation or default would shake international credit and cause economic shivers to pass through the United States. While both cancellation and default must be avoided at all costs, he said, we could not insist upon payment without extending some hope of revision or re-examination, unless we were to invite a united front against us on all economic questions.

At this point, Roosevelt, relying upon the cards he held, interjected a number of questions. Hoover, and occasionally Mills, replied. While both Hoover and Mills expressed a bitter attitude toward France, they were sympathetic with Britain. They pointed out that the British had

* Perhaps it was because I gave Hoover such rapt attention when he was reciting the history of the debts that he was prompted to say in his memoirs that he directed himself to "primary educational work" on me. In his account to Stimson that evening after the conference he made a similar reference to my education. He said then that he and Mills spent most of their time "educating a very ignorant [but] . . . a well-meaning young man." Considering his bitterness toward Roosevelt, I am sure that Hoover would not have said that his late opponent was "well-meaning." Therefore, I accept the charge of ignorance as well as the compliment as applied to me. I am certainly not at this time offended. I was ignorant. I learned a lot that I never knew before. And I cherished the education. Stimson Diary, Nov. 22, 1932.

† At the Lausanne Conference of June and July, 1932, German reparations had been reduced from $30,000,000,000 to about $700,000,000. However, there was a "gentlemen's agreement" that the reduction of reparations should be ratified only if the United States reduced or canceled the debts.

only about $78,000,000 over here and would face difficulties in meeting the December payment. The pound would fall and, with it, employment, wages, prices, and the standard of living.

At last Hoover came to the crux of the situation. He recounted in detail the history of Congressional domination of the debt issue. If he alone were to negotiate a settlement of the debts with the debtors, Congress would refuse to approve. He would like to have the old Debt Commission revived, to be made up of three representatives of the President—to be named or at least approved by Roosevelt—three Senators, and three Representatives. In the meantime, we would insist that the December payments be made. Thus negotiations could begin under the Hoover Administration even though no commitments were made until Roosevelt assumed office.

When Hoover finished, Roosevelt nodded.* He said that obviously the European countries ought to have a better means of presenting their claims. He said, "I see no reason why the old legal maxim that a debtor ought to have access to the creditor shouldn't prevail." Then turning to me he said, "Don't you think so, Ray?" My answer was that "even a horse trader does that."

But Roosevelt continued to look at me and said, "Well then, where do we go from there?" Thus encouraged by Hoover's attention to me and by Roosevelt's question, I ventured my views.

I said that the appointment of such a commission as the President had suggested, played up dramatically by the press, would precipitate such uncertainty about the future that a stoppage rather than an acceleration of business would result. Further, that in view of the opposition in Congress to any debt revision, the idea of such a commission would surely result in its rejection by Congress. (In saying this, I had in mind that Roosevelt's joining in such a proposal would at once ignite opposition to him in a Congress that he counted upon to work with him on measures of recovery.)

I said that debt discussions could take place just as conveniently through the executive department, specifically through normal diplomatic channels. I said further that what I knew of the constitutional powers of the President led me to believe that there was no way that Congress could deprive him of the authority to carry on negotiations on any subject with any foreign government. Certainly, there was no need to ask Congress in advance for approval to negotiate with governments on the debts they owed to us.

* Roosevelt's habit of nodding may be the reason that Hoover believed he agreed. Roosevelt, those who were close to him knew, nodded to express his understanding of what had been said. It did not at all mean that he agreed with what had been said. This habit was destined to cause grave misunderstandings about many matters in the years to come.

It seemed to me, I continued, that it would be best to insist upon the debt payments in December, but to say at the same time that the channels of diplomatic intercourse were open to suggestions for later revision. I added that Governor Roosevelt ought to accept the President's four principles, with this one added: constant negotiation for revision by the Executive through diplomatic channels. This suggestion I had not discussed with Roosevelt before the conference.

Hoover and Mills were visibly annoyed—in part, because of the nature of my argument and also, no doubt, because I was so ready with advice. Roosevelt, however, immediately embraced my formula rather than the revival of the Debt Commission. After this, the discussion became strained.

Hoover seemed to decide, finally, that the time had come to make the best of things. He suggested that, since he and Roosevelt had blocked out certain opinions in which they agreed and others in which they disagreed, it might be desirable for them to issue separate statements. Perhaps the preponderance of agreement might indicate a sufficient harmony to reassure the country. For the moment, a brief, noncommittal note could be issued jointly to the press. Hoover wrote this out on a pad and read it to us:

> The President and Governor Roosevelt traversed at length the subjects mentioned in their telegraphic communications. It is felt that progress has been made. The President confers with members of Congress tomorrow, when the subject will be further pursued.

Roosevelt approved of this note, and the conference ended. There was a private talk between Hoover and Roosevelt for about ten minutes, the nature of which I was not informed about. Mills and I meanwhile agreed to meet at the Mayflower the next morning.

When Mills appeared at my room at the hotel the following morning, he announced that he had the President's statement, and I took him immediately to Roosevelt's apartment.*

Between these two men, Hudson Valley neighbors, members of the same generation of prominent families, and Harvard classmates, there existed mutually implacable political enmity and personal animosity. On this occasion Mills was grave and tense, Roosevelt gay and casual. As Mills sat down and opened a typewritten manuscript, Roosevelt commented, "Well, Ogden, you must have sat up all night writing that." Mills's face hardened as he retorted, "This is a very important document." He proceeded to read the statement.

Roosevelt declined to comment upon what he had heard and said that,

* In Hoover's memoirs he says that Roosevelt refused to see Mills. This must have been a slip of memory.

since he had spent the evening before conferring with Congressional leaders, he had not prepared his statement but would do so that afternoon and release it in the evening.

I escorted Mills to the door. When we were outside, he turned to me and said most earnestly, "I wish you would do what you can to impress him with the seriousness of this matter and the need for developing a constructive policy about it." I replied that it seemed to me that we had a formula that Roosevelt believed to be constructive.

Hoover met Congressional leaders of both parties that morning at the White House, when he carefully went over the entire subject as he had with us on the day before. It was the consensus of the group that the December installment should be demanded and that there should be no reconsideration of the existing debt agreements. Some said that no new facts had been advanced to warrant a change of policy. And there was little or no support among Republicans and no support at all among the Democrats for the revival of a debt commission.

Hoover issued his statement on the conference on the day after the meeting. It was a somewhat lengthy exposition of the subject, with his earlier proposal for mutual trade and other concessions—his *quid pro quo* policy. It was apparently designed to inform the country and thus to bring about a different attitude in Congress. The statement reiterated the principles he had stated to us which had guided him in dealing with the debts; it brought in the necessity to prepare for the World Economic Conference, and referred also to the disarmament conference then in progress; it suggested that the new agency which he was asking Congress to authorize should have a partial "identity of membership" with those who would represent or were representing us in those two conferences; it also made his point that there should be some mutual concessions on our part by a readjustment of the debts, and on the part of the debtors of some economic advantages to us; and he urged that there be cooperation from Congress to these ends.*

I had made some notes for the Roosevelt statement the night before, but on the southbound train I discussed the form Roosevelt's statement should take with Bernard Baruch and Charles Michelson, the latter at that time an employee of the Democratic National Committee. Then, with Roosevelt, we put it in final form and released it when we reached Richmond. In general, Roosevelt reiterated his view that the responsibility was with the President and Congress in office at that time. It accepted Hoover's four principles, but said that rather than the re-creation

* Major excerpts from this statement can be found in *The Hoover Administration* by William Starr Myers and Walter H. Newton (New York: Scribner's, 1936), pp. 283–87.

of a debt commission, the normal channels of diplomacy should be used for exploration of the requests of debtor nations. This point, which I had invented at the conference, was somewhat elaborated. So far as the December payments were concerned, the statement made clear that the President and Congress should make that decision.

The following is the text of the statement:

My conferences with the President and with leaders of my party have been most illuminating and useful. I wish to express my appreciation of the opportunity thus afforded me.

At this time I wish to reaffirm my position on the questions that have been the principal subjects of our discussions.

As to the debt payments due December 15th, I find no justification for modifying my statement to the President on November 14th when I pointed out that "the immediate questions raised by the British, French and other notes create a responsibility which rests upon those now vested with executive and legislative authority."

With regard to general policies respecting these debts I firmly believe in the principle that an individual debtor should at all times have access to the creditor; that he should have opportunity to lay facts and representations before the creditor and that the creditor always should give courteous, sympathetic and thoughtful consideration to such facts and representations.

This is a rule essential to the preservation of the ordinary relationships of life. It is a basic obligation of civilization. It applies to nations as well as to individuals.

The principle calls for free access by the debtor to the creditor. Each case should be considered in the light of the conditions and necessities peculiar to the case of each nation concerned.

I find myself in complete accord with four principles discussed in the conference between the President and myself yesterday and set forth in a statement which the President has issued today.

These debts were actual loans made under the distinct understanding and with the intention that they would be repaid.

In dealing with the debts each government has been and is to be considered individually, and all dealings with each government are independent of dealings with any other debtor government. In no case should we deal with the debtor governments collectively.

Debt settlements made in each case take into consideration the capacity to pay of the individual debtor nations.

The indebtedness of the various European nations to our government has no relation whatsoever to reparations payments made or owed to them.

Once these principles of the debt relationships are established and recognized, the methods by which contacts between our government and the debtor nations may be provided are matters of secondary importance. My view is that the most convenient and effective contacts can be made through the existing agencies and constituted channels of diplomatic intercourse.

No action by the Congress has limited or can limit the constitutional power of the President to carry on diplomatic contacts or conversations with foreign governments. The advantage of this method of maintaining contacts with foreign governments is that any one of the debtor nations may at any time bring to the attention of the Government of the United States new conditions and facts affecting any phase of its indebtedness.

It is equally true that existing debt agreements are unalterable save by Congressional action.*

This statement brought sharp and unhappy reactions from the international banking community in Wall Street. Some of the Eastern newspapers expressed disappointment. And from then on there was a disposition to blame Roosevelt's "advisers" for failure to cooperate with Hoover.

But there was vigorous support in Congress from the Democratic side and from the progressive Republicans.

It should be noted that this statement and the formulas it presented were to be the new Administration's policy throughout the year that followed Roosevelt's inauguration.

The position taken by Roosevelt at that time made it clear that by keeping the debts as living obligations we were serving notice that European nations were not to count upon the United States as a potential war treasury in case the old hatreds and rivalries reappeared. Moreover, this was the first public indication that Roosevelt held views on international affairs in sharp distinction not only from those of the Hoover Administration but from the large American community of advocates of joining the League of Nations, of pro-sanctionists, and of the vast private foreign lending operations, which in the 1920's had been one of the contributing causes of our economic collapse.

This was also warning that the foreign policy of the New Deal would not ally us with France and Britain as policemen of the world determined to maintain the status quo by enforcing peace through the threat of joint action in case of war.

The position of Roosevelt and of the majority in Congress earned them the characterization as isolationists by those who, in the phrase of President Nicholas Murray Butler of Columbia, were possessed of an "international mind." But our firm belief, based upon American experience, was that while European countries had been anxious to have American help when trouble erupted, they had failed to seek our counsel in making the decisions that had led to hostilities. In short, while we were summoned at the crash, we had no part of the takeoff.

That was Roosevelt's position as I understood it at that time. But as events proved within a few weeks, his convictions were not so firm as some of us conceived them to be. In fact, I was destined to entertain

* *Ibid.*, pp. 287–88.

grave doubts about his firmness at the dawn of the New Year, when new influences other than Hoover's were brought to bear upon him.

But at that moment in November, as well as later, most of the people around Roosevelt believed that the first order of business was to put the domestic economy in order.

Chapter Two

Roosevelt Wavers at the Crossroads

IN December and January there reappeared a deep cleavage in policy among Democrats that more than ten months before had nearly defeated Roosevelt for the nomination. At that time, the battle had centered not only on personalities but on the course of policy to be followed in a campaign that, considering the depressed condition of the country and the unpopularity of Hoover, would almost certainly result in the election of a Democratic President. Old Wilsonians, powerful financial interests in the East, and the internationalists of all degrees and both party affiliations had mounted a very serious drive to block the nomination of Roosevelt and, in a deadlocked convention, to nominate someone who represented the lost cause that Wilson embodied in the final years of his Administration. The most probable result of this effort, had it succeeded, would have been the nomination not of Alfred E. Smith but of Newton D. Baker, Secretary of War in Wilson years. It is certain that if Roosevelt had failed to win the nomination on the critical fourth ballot, his delegate strength would have crumbled and Baker would ultimately have been the choice of the convention. After the election of Roosevelt, these allied forces had lost their bid, but they were still vigorously influential.

In the Wilson period the issues were membership in the League of Nations, tariff reduction, and closer relations, financial and political, with Europe. In the new context, the League of Nations was hardly mentioned. The issue was economic. Because of the crisis over the debts, it now centered not only on that subject but on the need for lower tariffs, less emphasis upon purely domestic recovery, and closer financial and economic relations with Europe. It will be convenient here to describe this issue as between internationalism and intranationalism, the latter being an expression quite commonly used in those days to describe a concentration on domestic affairs.

In this phase of the conflict for the mind of Roosevelt, the outgoing Administration was to play a powerful part. Some reduction in the debts was a central issue, but many other economic matters chiefly concerned with our relations with Europe came to be part of the pattern. Baker himself, it should be emphasized, had no part in this new phase; but many others in the Democratic Party, as well as powerful financial interests, were most active.

Roosevelt's rejection of cooperation with Hoover in debt negotiations seemed to resolve the issue after the November White House conference. But as the time for the end of the moratorium and the December payments approached, Hoover renewed his appeals to Roosevelt.

A series of exchanges with the British and French governments, managed on the American side by the Secretary of State, culminated in the payment by the British of the December installment (with the reservation that it be "regarded as a capital payment on which account should be taken in any final settlement"). The French, without pleading inability, simply refused to pay. Premier Herriot tried to persuade the Chamber of Deputies to follow the course of Britain. But that body authorized payment only if the United States would join an international conference designed to adjust all international obligations. On this issue the Herriot Government fell.

After my return from Warm Springs, I had several conferences with Secretary Stimson, because it had been understood that I should be the intermediary between him and Roosevelt. These contacts were mostly routine and amicable, and all of them at that time dealt primarily with the exchange of views with the debtor nations. But in December serious complications arose because of the determination of the Hoover Administration to associate the debts with other international questions. This effort, Roosevelt believed, ran counter to the principles that had developed from the White House conference and our subsequent statement. I was determined to maintain that stated position so far as I was able.

But the most serious of the complications arose from the plan for the World Monetary and Economic Conference which had been decided upon at the Lausanne Conference of European powers in 1932. Hoover at our meetings with him and with Mills had made no suggestion that the debts be associated with such a conference, although he had mentioned the conference casually. The United States and the other principal nations of the world had appointed delegate members of a preparatory commission of experts, which convened in Geneva during the autumn of 1932.

Our representatives were Edmund E. Day, then an official of the Rockefeller Foundation, and Professor John H. Williams of Harvard. At our meeting Hoover had said that no date had been fixed for the conference. There seemed to be nothing urgent about it.

But when I saw the preliminary agenda, which had been brought back by Day and Williams, I realized that this would thrust a new and troublesome element into the debt situation. For it was proposed that the conference would seek a restoration of the international gold standard, debt reduction, monetary stabilization, and other measures of international cooperation which would lay a heavy hand upon the Roosevelt programs for domestic recovery. A troublesome paragraph in this document was this:

> One important development in the intergovernmental situation is indispensable: a definitive settlement of the war debts must be clearly in prospect, if not already attained, before the Commission comes together again. To have this question overhanging the next meetings of the Preparatory Commission would be to cloud the discussion with such suspicion and ill-feeling as to preclude any effective progress. With a satisfactory debt settlement in hand, or in the making, and with a willingness on the part of two or three of the principal powers to assume initiative in working out a program of normalization of the world's economic order, the next meeting of the Preparatory Commission may be expected to yield highly important results. . . .*

Obviously, Day and Williams, who were to return to Geneva, must be informed about the views of the incoming Administration. In dealing with this problem in the weeks that followed, I relied heavily upon Rex Tugwell, whose views as well as my own stressed domestic recovery first and strongly rejected such international entanglements as were suggested by draft of the agenda.

On December 16, Tugwell and I discussed with Roosevelt the agenda brought back by Day and Williams. He responded by asking Tugwell to confer with Day and Williams, to tell them of the policies we had laid down on the debts, and of his determination that no international entanglements should stand in the way of the domestic recovery program outlined in the campaign.

Apparently, the return of Day and Williams reminded Hoover of the planned World Monetary and Economic Conference, and on December 17 he dispatched a long telegram to Roosevelt without giving any notice of it to the press. In this he said that the debts could not be dissociated from the other problems that would come before the Economic Conference, and that the conference should be assembled as soon

* Department of State, "Report of American Delegates to the Preparatory Committee of Experts on the World Monetary and Economic Conference," p. 7.

as possible. While he repeated that the debts must be considered with each country separately and not in an international conference, he said it would be desirable if before such a conference there be some progress with the individual countries on the debts. Hoover concluded by asking Roosevelt to join with him in selecting a delegation that would give "co-ordinate consideration" to the debts, disarmament, and the questions that would come before the coming Economic Conference.

Two days later, Hoover covered much the same ground in his annual message to Congress.

Obviously, this was a commitment Roosevelt could not make. It was clearly impossible to agree to calling the conference before the new Administration was in office. It would necessarily be held sometime after March 4; and a delegation jointly selected by the outgoing and incoming Administrations would not represent the government of the United States. Moreover, such a jointly selected delegation could not possibly speak for a Congress, overwhelmingly Democratic, that would not meet until March. This would also place upon Roosevelt the responsibility for negotiations over which he would have only partial authority. And the belief, which would almost certainly arise, that Roosevelt contemplated trading the debts for concessions that were at that time indeterminate would ignite tempers in a Congress that had already made it clear that the debts were to be inviolate.

And so Roosevelt's reply on December 19, in the composition of which I took part, was a polite refusal. It made clear that all the questions raised by the Hoover message required separate or "selective" treatment. Roosevelt regarded Hoover's activities in behalf of disarmament as satisfactory. But so far as debts were concerned, the reply reaffirmed the November principle that negotiations could be conducted by the "existing machinery of diplomatic intercourse," which at that moment meant the Hoover Administration.

"As to the Economic Conference," Roosevelt said, "I am clear that a permanent economic program for the world should not be submerged in conversations about disarmament and debts." He added a point that I regarded as cardinal, and which was measurably maintained in the new Administration, that discussions about debts and about other economic matters should be strictly separate. There is a "relationship but not an identity," he added. Finally Roosevelt suggested that the selection of the delegates and "the final determination of the program of the Economic Conference be held in abeyance until after March fourth."

Hoover stubbornly refused to yield and on December 20 he replied with a further plea for "solidarity of national action." He suggested that he would be glad if Roosevelt would designate Owen D. Young, Colonel House, or "any other man of your party possessed of your views and confidence" to sit with officers of the Hoover Administration to see what steps could be taken and thus save valuable time and losses.*

Roosevelt immediately sent this new message from Hoover to me. I was at home on Claremont Avenue, ill and in bed. After I considered a suitable reply, I drafted some language, and since Owen Young had been mentioned in the Hoover message, I asked him to come and talk it over with me. Then, as always, I had great respect and affection for Young. He had been the chief in the second debt settlement, and its text bore the name "Young Plan." I believed that there was an implied obligation on Roosevelt to appoint Young as his Secretary of State.

Young was most helpful, and we agreed upon the sort of reply Roosevelt should make. I wrote a draft and sent it to Albany. On the 21st Roosevelt called me on the telephone five times to discuss the exact text of his reply, and the final and revised text was dispatched.

In it Roosevelt again refused to be committed. Doubtless, Hoover was sincere; but "for me to accept any joint responsibility in the work of exploration," Roosevelt telegraphed, "might well be construed by the debtor or other nations . . . as a commitment. . . . The designation of a man or men of such eminence as your telegram suggests would not imply mere fact finding; it would suggest the presumption that such representatives were empowered to exchange views on matters of large and binding policy." Roosevelt suggested that the President select his own representatives to conduct preliminary explorations with our debtors "and representatives to discuss the agenda of the World Economic Conference" (thus distinguishing between the two), but made it clear that "none of these representatives is authorized to bind this government as to any ultimate policy." Roosevelt would be "happy to receive their information and their expressions of opinion. . . . I also shall be happy to consult with you freely during this period."

The failure of this interchange moved Hoover to give out the entire correspondence to the press on December 22 with this terse comment:

"Governor Roosevelt considers that it is undesirable for him to accede to my suggestions for cooperative action on the foreign proposals outlined in my recent message to Congress. I will respect his wishes. . . ."

Roosevelt then said to the press that he was willing to cooperate and had proposed a method to that end which was consistent with the incoming Administration's policies. The President was free to adopt it or not, as he saw fit.

* It was obvious that Hoover hoped that Roosevelt would not choose me for such conferences. The suggestion of Colonel House was unacceptable to Roosevelt, for in his opinion, expressed to me, House, a very old man, had long outlived his usefulness. This mid-December exchange is fully described in Hoover's *Memoirs,* Vol. III, pp. 185–87.

For the moment the Hoover-Roosevelt relationship ended, and no doubt both men at that time had no intention to continue it.

It seemed to me that Roosevelt's position had been made clear in his various communications with Hoover and in his November statement: He would under no circumstances enter into a series of negotiations over the debts with representatives jointly selected by him and Hoover. The debts and the plans for the Economic Conference should be strictly separated in any contacts Hoover might have with the British. Delegates to the Economic Conference should not be selected before March 4; after that Roosevelt would assume complete responsibility. Hoover's argument for trading the debts or a modification thereof for concessions —the *quid pro quo* idea—was unsound because, while we had a definite quid, we were unable to know what the quo might be.

I believed that Roosevelt thought we were through with the whole thing until the new Administration should take office. This was an immense relief to me because I could see that otherwise we could not devote our time and energy to preparations for the domestic program for recovery that would be the order of business when Roosevelt was inaugurated.

But this respite was only ephemeral, for in the four weeks ahead I was destined to undergo the most difficult period of my whole association with Roosevelt. Roosevelt, under the potent influence of two men, was to waver at the very beginning of his consideration of how his policies would be carried out after he assumed office—"wobble" is what Stimson called it in his diary.

This vacillation was caused by the return from Europe of Norman H. Davis, an old friend of the Wilson days, and by the determination of Stimson to keep the negotiations going despite Hoover's statement that the subject of cooperation was closed. The pressure of these two men, supported by elements in the Eastern press and by the international banking community, seemed in this period of four weeks to raise doubts in Roosevelt's mind about the wisdom of his earlier commitments and—much more important—to shake his faith in the central proposition of his 1932 campaign, which was to give all priority to domestic recovery.

In the struggle for Roosevelt's mind that ensued, Tugwell and I were arrayed not only against these two individuals, Davis and Stimson, who seemed to be much more influential with Roosevelt than we had expected, but against a revival of the internationalism that had so nearly denied Roosevelt his nomination the year before.

The details that immediately follow are not so important in themselves, for in the long perspective of years since then, such issues as were involved have faded with changing conditions in the United States and Europe. They serve, however, to make clear that for a time it was very doubtful whether we were to have a New Deal or a virtual continuation of the policies that had so signally failed in the Hoover years. They also reveal most vividly a side of the Roosevelt character and personality that so often caused him to believe that he could successfully reconcile the irreconcilable.*

After the Hoover-Roosevelt negotiations in November and early December had ended in stalemate, Stimson shrewdly concluded that the failure was because of the mutual antipathy which prevailed between the two men, but that by establishing more direct contacts he himself might persuade Roosevelt to change his mind.

Stimson's orientation during most of his life when he was not engaged in public service had been that of a New York lawyer in close contact with the great international financial and cultural community that centered in that city. His friends, his intimates, and his intellectual commitments were all there. It was to be expected that these relations were profoundly important to him as Secretary of State. He had sought persistently, and often with measurable dissent from Hoover, to establish strong ties with Europe. In addition to the international economic relations with those countries, there was his concern with the imperialistic designs of Japan in Manchuria, a concern which he shared with the British government of that time. It is apparent that during this period he leaned heavily upon advice from New York, especially from the partners of the Morgan company.

He tells in his diary of the vigorous efforts of Hoover and Mills in September and October to have him take an active part in the campaign. He finally acceded to their wishes, but hesitated for some time in framing the sort of speeches he had agreed to make. He was reluctant to make a direct attack upon Roosevelt's record as governor of New York. He finally concentrated his fire not upon Roosevelt personally, but upon the advisers who had, he said, written Roosevelt's speeches. And he determined to make his speeches in the East where, he noted, people know something. His first essay was at the venerable Union League

* I have described in a much more summary fashion the events during this period in my book *After Seven Years*. But now there is available a great deal of information which was not available when that book was written in 1939. One of those sources is Stimson's diary and papers in the library of Yale University. Another is Tugwell's *Notes from a New Deal Diary,* an unpublished manuscript at the Roosevelt Library at Hyde Park, and his book, *The Democratic Roosevelt* (New York: Doubleday, 1957). Another is the collection of the papers of Norman Davis in the Library of Congress. Finally, there is the third volume of Hoover's *Memoirs,* published in 1952. And I have as a guide to day-by-day events my own diary, which was written at the time and was, of course, available when I wrote my book twenty-seven years ago. Rather than mar this text with innumerable footnotes and quotations, I shall in general, with the use of those sources, merely narrate the events and state the opinions of the participants with a minimum of specific references.

Club in Philadelphia. Another was in New York. Thus the stage was set in late December for an effort to discredit Roosevelt's advisers, while he sought at the same time to establish by personal contacts an influential relationship with the President-elect.

Like so many New Yorkers, he manifested a lack of comprehension of the currents of opinion to the West and South. He was quite unfamiliar with the economic factors in the United States that contributed to the depression. And strangely enough, he had failed to read and understand the factors that contributed to Roosevelt's election.

While Stimson's differences of opinion with President Hoover were only dimly recognized by us at the time, his diary and papers reveal them to be sharp and of long standing. Hoover had far less confidence than had Stimson in the advice coming from New York, and especially from the Morgan partners; Hoover's contacts with those ever-present advisers were officially cordial, but he entertained toward them a deep suspicion of their disinterestedness and, indeed, their competence. His experiences during the war, the peace conference, and the aftermath had implanted in Hoover an inclination to be cautious in dealing with European diplomacy, while with their vast network of contacts the great banking firms in New York more often than not conformed to the policies generated in foreign offices. This applied not only to the political field but to financial and monetary policies. In his memoirs Hoover attributed blame for the reckless stock-market inflation in large part to the domination of Federal Reserve policies by Benjamin Strong, head of the New York "Fed." Strong, he said, was in turn too close to Montagu Norman, at that time governor of the Bank of England.*

In dealings with the British, Hoover was wary and toward the French he was almost hostile. Hoover, moreover, was emotionally always a Westerner, despite his long years abroad. And when Hoover rewrote and dispatched his November invitation to Roosevelt, Stimson was distressed at its tone and its specifics. He was not happy about Hoover's determination not to cancel the debts without an adequate *quid pro quo* or about the President's refusal to link the debts with reparations.

It seems clear, in the light of these differences, why Hoover omitted Stimson from the November meeting.†

In late December Hoover was reluctant to meet Roosevelt again and very dubious about Stimson's seeking a direct contact with the President-elect. But Stimson from here on decided to take things into his own hands.

He was determined to break through the advisers, directly appeal to Roosevelt himself, resolve the doubts the President-elect had expressed

* Strong died in late 1928.

† Hoover in later years told me that he had doubts about Stimson's policy toward Japan. He said it was like "sticking a pin into a rattlesnake."

in two interchanges with Hoover, reverse the policy of nationalism to which the Democratic candidate had committed himself in the campaign, induce through this a change in Congressional opinion, and succeed in achieving on his own terms that concert of policies in which Hoover had so signally failed.

Stimson when aroused was a man of bold resolution. He had shown that by adopting a policy toward Japan in Manchuria that even the British had only measurably adopted, which ran counter to the ardent desire for peace among Americans and about which his President had grave doubts. In seeking this, he also tried with consummate skill to swing Roosevelt over to a policy of international economic relations. This he boldly attempted to do in the fading weeks before he was to leave his high office. And it is clear in what was to follow that he came very close to a stunning victory.

As a factor favoring his success, he counted on the low, almost contemptuous estimate of Roosevelt he had absorbed from his friends in New York. In the community that was Stimson's political home, Roosevelt was regarded as an ambitious politician who had bent with the winds of expediency, who had no very clear convictions, and who in complex matters of international financial relations was a superficial amateur. This estimate was strengthened by Hoover's account of the November meeting and the texts of the December correspondence.

When Norman Davis arrived from Geneva, Stimson was provided with a powerful and willing ally. Davis was a Democrat whose international predilections were shared by an important segment of his party. He had an access to Roosevelt which he had maintained over the years. And Davis, who was ambitious to become Secretary of State in the new Administration, immediately injected himself into the situation with all the skill that he had acquired in many years of diplomacy. At the moment, Davis was Hoover's designation not only as the American representative in the disarmament talks in Geneva, but also as a member of the group that had been preparing the agenda for the World Monetary and Economic Conference. Thus, he enjoyed close relations with Stimson and Hoover. In outlook, ideology, and personal associations with the international community, Stimson and Davis perfectly complemented each other.

Davis was a native of Tennessee whose early career, before he entered government service in 1917, had been in business—chiefly banking and land speculation—in Cuba. In the Wilson Administration he enjoyed the powerful patronage of Colonel E. M. House and had worked up through various official positions to that of undersecretary of state. After the Republicans came to power, Davis had been negotiating in various roles for twelve years.

But as Roosevelt's star rose in early 1932, Davis joined with many others whose views were imbued with the Wilsonian tradition in urging Newton D. Baker to seek the nomination. He said in a letter to Baker:

"I cannot abandon the conviction that our only hope is through you, and that it is not too late for you to do it. . . . As nearly as I can gather, there is no genuine enthusiasm for Roosevelt on the part of any of the more important men who have come out for him."

But with Davis, nothing was so successful as success, and three months after writing his letter to Baker he wrote to Roosevelt congratulating him and offering his services.*

I was not unfamiliar with the career of Norman Davis and his bent of mind, for during the campaign he had written long letters to Roosevelt, whom he had known well in the Wilson years. He urged Roosevelt to make the tariff a major issue, believing, as did Cordell Hull and other old-line Cleveland-Wilson Democrats, that enlarged foreign trade would cure the depression. Roosevelt ignored this advice, and as the campaign progressed the tariff faded out as an issue. In October, Davis suggested the desirability of general agreements with Europe in which the debts, disarmament, tariffs, and a monetary stabilization would all be lumped in a vast game of give-and-take. To facilitate this, Davis suggested that Roosevelt, if and when elected, should make a trip to Europe before his inauguration. He said that he had talked with Ramsay MacDonald about such a trip.

I was unaware of the continuation of this correspondence after the election, but the Davis papers now show that there were a number of exchanges. Roosevelt invited further confidential information and advice and this set the stage for the Davis approaches to Roosevelt after he arrived in the United States on December 22.

Since Rex Tugwell had talked with Day before he left in October with Williams to attend the discussions preliminary to the World Monetary and Economic Conference, and since these American representatives had returned to the United States late in November, I felt that Tugwell should establish contact with them and make sure that they were fully briefed on Roosevelt's position before they returned to Geneva. As I have already indicated, the preliminary agenda which they had helped to prepare lumped many international issues with the debts for treatment at the conference. With this, both Tugwell and I were in complete disagreement.

* Norman Davis to Newton Baker, April 7, 1932, Davis Papers, Library of Congress, Container 3.

Chapter Three

Roosevelt Reaches a Decision

IN late December Felix Frankfurter entered the scene, possibly without knowing of the difficulties Tugwell and I were having over the concentrated effort of Davis and Stimson to sway the mind and policies of Roosevelt. According to the Stimson diary, Herbert Feis, on December 23, acting in his role as economic adviser of the State Department, relayed several messages from Frankfurter to Stimson. In part, these told of a number of conversations that Frankfurter had with Roosevelt. Frankfurter said that Roosevelt had not decided whom he would appoint as Secretary of State, but that while Davis would be useful in establishing contacts between Stimson and Roosevelt, Stimson should not assume that Davis should be used as "a substitute Secretary of State."

When Davis saw Stimson in Washington on December 29, he told the Secretary that Roosevelt had suggested that he should return abroad and continue his disarmament talks. Stimson noted that "Davis turned this down apparently unless he is made Secretary of State [in the new Administration]." Then Stimson confided in his diary that Frankfurter had told him of a case against Davis that had gone to the Supreme Court and which involved a land deal (or deals) in which Davis had participated when he was in business in Cuba in the early 1900's.

In his defense, Davis told Stimson that the case concerned a land transaction when he was only twenty-five years old, that his colleagues in the business knew about his activities but had denied that they knew about the fees he had received. He said that the case had been badly handled in the courts. Stimson accepted this explanation and continued to have a high estimate of Davis.*

* This suit, which reached the Supreme Court, is reported in the Court's opinion at 227 U.S. 80. I learned about this in January from a source other than Frankfurter. Stimson Diary, Dec. 23 and Dec. 29, 1932; Jan. 19, 1933.

The supposition of Stimson that Davis was being seriously considered as a possibility for Secretary of State was wide of the mark. For in December, well before Frankfurter had appeared on the scene, I had a long talk with Roosevelt in Albany about prospects for that office. Several names were brought up—Owen Young, Cordell Hull, Key Pittman, and even Robert Bingham. Davis was not mentioned. If he had been, Roosevelt would have dismissed the idea because he had repeatedly told me of the Davis associations with the Morgan people and also of his pro-League leanings. Howe had been busy promoting Hull and no doubt Roosevelt had been convinced that the Tennessean Senator should be offered the job well before he gave me his Cabinet list in January.

According to Hull's memoirs, Roosevelt made the offer on January 19, or perhaps the next day, the twentieth.*

Frankfurter's incredible capacity to influence affairs, including appointments, which continued for years afterward, is shown in the manner in which he acted as middleman in bringing about a private meeting between Stimson and Roosevelt.†

Largely because of Frankfurter's mediation, Roosevelt wrote a letter to Stimson on December 27 saying he would be glad to have a talk with him, by telephone or in person. Then Frankfurter went to see Stimson and told him of his conversation with Roosevelt. Frankfurter told Stimson of his earlier relations with Roosevelt. He had served with Roosevelt on the War Labor Board during Wilson's Administration. And from Frankfurter's glowing description of Roosevelt, on December 29, Stimson

* In Julius W. Pratt's book on Hull, *Cordell Hull, 1933–1944,* in the series *The American Secretaries of State and Their Diplomacy,* Vol. XII (New York: Cooper Square Publishers, 1964), pp. 77ff., the author tells about Davis' activities in the State Department. His relations with Hull were intimate and very informal: " 'He would,' Hull says in his memoirs, 'come into any conference I was having.' " Also, Pratt adds, Davis "was equally informal in dropping in on Under and Assistant Secretaries. 'Norman Davis was in and out all day' was a common item in their chronicles, suggesting sometimes a shade of annoyance." I should add that he never "dropped in" at my office. I was made aware in the spring, through gossip columns whose authors were briefed by Davis, that he blamed me for frustrating his ambitions.

† The source of Frankfurter's great influence on Stimson and, through him, a very considerable influence in the Hoover Administration was a friendship that went back many years. When Frankfurter graduated from the Harvard Law School, he secured a position in the U.S. Attorney's office in New York. Stimson was then U.S. Attorney for the Southern District in New York. He served under Stimson in that capacity for four years. Stimson resigned to become the unsuccessful Republican candidate for governor in 1910, and in 1911 he was appointed Secretary of War by President Taft. While in that office he brought Frankfurter to Washington as a law officer in the War Department, where Frankfurter remained until he was appointed in 1914 a professor in the Harvard Law School. Frankfurter was, in effect, a Stimson protégé and warm friend.

received "a much more attractive" opinion of the governor than he had hitherto enjoyed. And so after various telephone calls and after a delay due to Hoover's reluctance, Stimson visited Roosevelt at Hyde Park on January 9.

There is no record of the Stimson-Roosevelt meeting that day, so far as I know, except in a memorandum in Stimson's diary. The talk ranged over several subjects—Cuba, the Far East, disarmament, debts, and the planned World Monetary and Economic Conference.

Roosevelt, according to Stimson, had a hereditary interest in the Far East. He approved of the Stimson policy there and only wished it had been adopted earlier. He had an ancestor who had a "position" there and had a grandmother who went there in a sailing vessel and was nearly captured by the Confederate ironclad *Alabama.* This strange reason for his interest was later told to Tugwell and me at the house on Sixty-fifth Street.

As for the coming Economic Conference, Roosevelt said he had talked with Day and Williams but, according to Stimson, had not thoroughly digested the report. Stimson told him of the psychological importance of the debt question as a barrier to the conference. Roosevelt told Stimson why he had not agreed with Hoover's suggestion for a new debt commission, because he believed he could get a settlement through Congress if he did the negotiating himself rather than through a commission.

Roosevelt then suggested that a high British official (Stanley Baldwin) come over and talk about debts with him. Roosevelt also suggested a similar mission from France.

After this conference Stimson reported to Hoover, who wanted to think about it.

Stimson telephoned to Davis three days later, on January 12, and told him of his conference with Roosevelt. Davis said that he was keeping in touch with Roosevelt, and Stimson noted that Davis "has been very helpful in getting the right atmosphere about it."

Stimson was most anxious to have another conference at the White House and finally brought Mills to agree that it was desirable. Hoover in a memorandum to Stimson on January 15 doubted the effectiveness of Roosevelt's suggestion that he talk with one person from the British government but preferred a delegation to confer with an American group. Such an arrangement should not be before March 1, when the new Secretaries of State and Treasury would have been selected. But "if the Governor wants an Englishman to come over and if *he* will do all the negotiating we can facilitate it."

Then on the fifteenth Stimson had a long telephone conversation with Roosevelt. Here, too, there is no record except in Stimson's diary. Stimson said that even if debt negotiations were to be separate from plans for the Economic Conference, Roosevelt would surely want to be assured of British cooperation before he agreed to a debt settlement. He said also that the British should give assurance that they would stabilize sterling as a means of raising world prices, and unless this was secured, an inflationary race would take place. Roosevelt, Stimson said, expressed the view that he wanted no such race.

Stimson said that Britain would want to send several men to discuss things with Roosevelt, rather than one man. Roosevelt replied that he wanted only a few. Obviously, Stimson said, Hoover representatives could not negotiate. Any plan should be Roosevelt's, not Hoover's. Roosevelt agreed to this.

Roosevelt told Stimson that he had been talking with Russell Leffingwell and that the Morgan partner had agreed with Stimson that the debts and plans for the Economic Conference should be interconnected.

Then Roosevelt agreed to meet Hoover on January 20 and suggested that Stimson meet him on the afternoon of the nineteenth at the Mayflower.

Stimson reported this talk to Hoover.

On January 17, Stimson called Roosevelt and made arrangements for the meetings in Washington. Stimson was to see Roosevelt on the nineteenth and in the morning of the twentieth the White House conference would be held. Mills and Stimson would be present with Hoover. Roosevelt said that he "will bring Moley."

On January 17, Tugwell observed in his *Notes from a New Deal Diary:* "I had my first real difference of opinion with FDR last night." The papers had made a great deal of Roosevelt's assurance after his conference with Stimson that he agreed with the Stimson policy on the Far East. Tugwell said that this might lead to war with Japan.

"He, however, seemed very pleased at Stimson's cooperation with him; says he has called him on the phone every day lately and says, furthermore, that he is quite prepared to see the policy through. He has a strong personal sympathy with the Chinese; and this, added to a sudden trust in Stimson carried him over."

I was present during that argument and well remember Tugwell's passionate disagreement. My fears of Stimson's influence were as great as Tugwell's. But since the fat was in the fire so far as Manchuria was concerned, I realized that Roosevelt could not contradict himself at once. Moreover, Roosevelt repeated what he had told Stimson about his forefather's trading with China. "I have always had the deepest sympathy for the Chinese. How could you expect me not to go along with Stimson on Japan?"

This was so incredible a reason for such a far-reaching commitment on a matter of foreign policy that I lacked words to express my disagreement. Tugwell held the floor and argued with intensity and, I believed, convincing logic. But it was a vain dissent.

At that moment in January I was mainly concerned with what other commitments Roosevelt had made with Stimson concerning debts and other international questions. Arguments about Japan and Manchuria might wait for calm debate in a new Administration. What I feared then was that Roosevelt, confronted by the skillful designs of Stimson, had abandoned the positions he had taken in November and December and had agreed to policies that would endanger his entire domestic program.

The stage was set, I realized, for a real battle at the White House on January 20. And my head had to be clear for the encounter.

At the last moment before leaving New York, Roosevelt invited Davis to travel on the train with him to Washington, along with Tugwell, Will Woodin, and me.

The presence of Davis prompted reporters to ask Roosevelt if Davis was to be present at the White House. Roosevelt said "No." And he made it clear to the reporters that there was no connection between his talks with Davis on the train and the planned meeting with Hoover et al.

Meanwhile, I had explored the subject with Roosevelt. He told me that after talking with Stimson he could see no reason why he should not have talks with British representatives after March 4. This was clearly in line with the position we had taken at the November "summit," which was that the debtor always should have access to the creditor. But he made it clear that he agreed with Tugwell and me that debt discussions should not be linked or conditioned upon discussions concerning matters to come up at the World Conference. The two sets of negotiations might even be concurrent, but they were to be conducted by different people and physically apart. This was wholly agreeable to me, and I was determined to present these views when we met Hoover, Stimson, and Mills.

Although discussions with Roosevelt on the afternoon of January 19 at the Mayflower, after our arrival in Washington, were not conclusive, they were amiable. Stimson and Davis and I were present. Stimson, however, left with the feeling that Roosevelt was in agreement with him on all points.

But early in the morning of the twentieth Tugwell, Davis, and I met at the hotel and had a somewhat heated discussion. We went over the same ground once again, explaining to Davis why we wanted the two separate sets of discussions with the British. The attitude of Davis was exactly that of Stimson. He could not see why we were making such an issue of the separation. But he was too intelligent not to understand what we were driving at. He knew that we were determined not to put the debts on the table as trading material for concessions from the debtors on trade, monetary stabilization, disarmament, and other matters. He wanted, I was sure, to use the debt concessions as trading pawns to lift his disarmament negotiations out of the doldrums into which they had fallen over the months he had spent at Geneva. Also, I was sure he wanted to get the debts out of the way to facilitate reviving private lending to Europe.

After this argument, Davis went directly to Roosevelt and bluntly asked to be included in the White House meeting. I was disturbed but silent, and Roosevelt agreed to take him. And so we three set out for the White House.

On our way to the White House the accumulation of four weeks of frustration over Roosevelt's indecisive course, the persistence and boldness of Davis' efforts to displace me in Roosevelt's confidence, the devious approaches of Stimson to the President-elect, and my conviction that upon the outcome of this, the second White House conference, depended the entire course of the new Administration compelled me to a decision that if I were to lose my contention I would go down fighting for it. It was clear to me that only boldness and self-assurance on my part would turn the course and so I decided to make my position clear at all costs, even if one of the costs was to break my relations with Roosevelt completely. The vigorous way in which I conducted myself at that meeting stemmed from this decision.

The status of Davis at this conference was ambiguous. He was there because Roosevelt brought him. But at the same time he had official status as an employee of the Hoover Administration. In his contributions to the discussion he was wholly on the side of Stimson, Mills, and Hoover.*

The major subject of discussion was how and when the projected discussions with British representatives should be held and what was to be discussed.

Stimson's and my accounts of the meeting agree in one respect. We did most of the talking.

The reason why I was inflexible about separating the debts from other subjects I explained at some length. Hoover clung to his idea that there should be, as he stated it, a *quid pro quo*. I believed, although I refrained from saying it to the weary President, that this formula of his made no sense. In the first place, he had made it clear in November that the debts were individual agreements with each debtor nation and were stated in promissory notes. If concessions were to be made to the British, all the other nations involved would want similar treatment. Moreover, we were asked to trade a very definite "quid" for an inchoate

* There are three first-hand accounts of the White House meeting: Stimson's diary, my diary, and a sort of *aide-mémoire* by Hoover which Stimson quotes in his diary. Hoover does not mention the meeting in his memoirs.

and perhaps illusory "quo." It seemed to me that any tariff concessions or the stabilization of British and French currencies could not have much to do with the primary need for recovery in the United States. Tariff and monetary affairs would require months of negotiation and more months before their effect could be felt. Meanwhile, the restoration of public confidence by vigorous domestic measures would produce results at home almost immediately. (That is, in fact, what happened.) I knew further that the European countries that had made the concessions about German reparations were determined to demand debt concessions from us in return. And one of Hoover's own principles in November was that the two were not to be associated in any way.

If I had known then what I know now from Stimson's diary, my case would have been still stronger. Mills had reported to Stimson that in a talk in New York with Owen D. Young the latter, whose sources of information were abundant, said that the British were really driving for an independent settlement of the debt question without any concession in return.

Stimson records in his diary that before Hoover got very far in his preliminaries, the *quid pro quo* argument, "Moley, to my surprise, jumped in." He says further that he believed at our conference the previous afternoon I had agreed with him. He was mistaken, for I had never changed my position on the subject over the two months since the November meeting at the White House. And as I had understood him, Roosevelt had held the same position.

After I explained my reasons for separate discussions with the British, Stimson says that "Roosevelt became rather wobbly again, and we all took a hand, principally myself." *

Davis at this point warmly supported Stimson's position. I believe that this expression of Davis' agreement with Stimson, Mills, and Hoover is what caused Roosevelt almost immediately after this meeting to dispense with Davis' advice permanently.

The Secretary of State, greatly agitated, rose and with his back to the fireplace in his best courtroom style addressed Roosevelt as if he were a jury. He believed that in their meeting at Hyde Park and on the telephone later Roosevelt had agreed with him. I am sure that this lack of understanding rose from Roosevelt's eternal habit of seeming to agree when he did not agree. It is also possible that Roosevelt did agree with Stimson at one of those times and now decided to disagree.

At that time, to my profound relief, Roosevelt rejected Stimson's plea and backed up my position. He said in effect that the subjects were twins but not identical twins. And that there should be a physical separation in the British conferences, with different representatives for each.

Thus the meeting ended in a disagreement. Hoover picked up note

* Stimson Diary, January 20.

paper and began the composition of a statement for the press. While he was writing and then reading what he wrote, I broke in—rather rudely, since he was President of the United States—and insisted that the point of separation should be made clear. Hoover, who had agreed to this conference only under the insistent pressure of Stimson, was no doubt sick of it all. And so he changed the statement to suit me.

As the meeting broke up, Roosevelt made it clear that Stimson should work out a reply to the British in collaboration with me, since he was leaving on the train that afternoon for Warm Springs.

Stimson, who was more than ever determined to prevail and who had been encouraged to believe that he should reach Roosevelt directly without my intervention, made a final effort. He wrote, I believe in the White House, a reply to the British to hand to the Ambassador that afternoon. Then he called Roosevelt at his hotel and read it to him. Fortunately, I was in Roosevelt's room and when I realized what was happening I made gestures indicating that I was to approve whatever was sent and that there should be no hurried approval over the telephone. Roosevelt, responding to my mute appeal, answered Stimson by saying that he would have me go over to the State Department and that I was to collaborate with Stimson in writing the note.

When I entered the old State, War, and Navy monstrosity, I met Tugwell, who had been on another errand over there, and asked him to go with me to Stimson's office. There we found the Secretary with Harvey Bundy and Herbert Feis discussing the proposed note.

Then there followed what Stimson's diary describes as a "battle royal." Stimson was angry enough because of what he considered to be Roosevelt's change of face. He was hardly fond of me. But when he saw Tugwell, he was furious. I looked at the note he had prepared and said it would not do.

Stimson said that Roosevelt had earlier agreed with him. I pointed out what Roosevelt had said that morning at the White House.

When Tugwell entered the discussion, Stimson was thoroughly aroused and said, according to Tugwell's diary and my own recollection, that we were "trying to tear down everything I have been working for in my whole term." Tugwell replied that he was certain that Roosevelt's position was identical with his own.

Tugwell's account of this dispute, written not long after the event, is complete and informative:

> I . . . found Moley, Feis, Bundy, and Stimson struggling over the formulation of the note. Stimson's proposal was wholly unsatisfactory. It completely ignored the points which had been established at the morning conference; it provided for a common meeting, it identified the questions and it clearly held out concessions on the debt as a return for currency stabilization. Before I came in Moley, who had been given power by F. D. R. to O.K. the

note, had indicated that this was wholly unsatisfactory and had insisted that only one representative be asked to confer on the debt question and he with negotiating power; and that the representatives to discuss other questions should be mentioned separately. The problem was to indicate to the British that the two were so connected that we should insist on mutual satisfaction in both matters; but to keep from any commitment.

When I came in all of them were working with pencil and paper trying to find a satisfactory formula. Stimson was irritable. He insisted that he was trying to protect F. D. R. in the coming negotiations by indicating a clear linking between the two sets of conversations. Moley was most conciliatory but very firm. I spoke up after a while saying that the Secretary did not seem to understand our reasons for separation of the two issues. I said that the matters stood quite differently than he appeared to think and that we should have been happier if there had not been such quick action or such close linkage. Stimson turned on me with indignation and denounced me as trying to tear down everything he had been working for throughout his term. The connection was not quite clear. But evidently his little outburst was an accumulation of irritation at not having his way all day and at having to deal with people who must, to him, have seemed like sheer amateurs and upstarts. I was pretty angry and got red but managed to keep my mouth shut and take it out in glaring. Later I tried to explain. Stimson said that in all his conversations with the Governor there had been clear indication of intention to deal with both at once. Moley pointed out that they had been separated in the morning conversations and said that he had not understood what F. D. R. meant by saying that the sentences mentioning the "debts" and "other matters" were "twins." But that he could now see that he meant them to be treated at the same time but separately and that this must be adhered to. I explained to Stimson that I had begun to talk with F. D. R. about the debts months ago and had first taken the position that not only debts but disarmament should be linked to other economic matters; that they should, for instance, be permitted to be discussed in the Economic Conference together. That is the approach an economist would make. But F. D. R. had immediately objected and had always maintained his objection; his arguments had seemed sufficient to him and we were only carrying out instructions. I went over F. D. R.'s arguments:

1. To lay the debts on the table would be to admit that concessions were to be made.

2. Public opinion both at home and abroad was singularly determined; on the one side not to cancel, on the other not to pay. This made temporizing necessary. The realities would have their way in the long run, but political considerations had to be taken account of.

3. Other arrangements—monetary matters, tariffs, etc.—required very different handling of public opinion and might be worked out whether or not the debts could be reduced as rapidly as everyone hoped.

4. The kind of negotiations were different. The one was now at the stage of plenary negotiation, the other a matter for preliminary expert study and exchange of opinion and the rate of progress might be very different.*

* *Notes from a New Deal Diary*, pp. 71–73.

The issue, then, was divergent interpretations of Roosevelt's views. Stimson claimed that he had written an *aide-mémoire* of his talk with Roosevelt on the telephone on January 15, 1933. This, he said, did not correspond with the position stated by Tugwell and me.

Then I said with finality that since Roosevelt had left Washington and was on a train going to Warm Springs, and since before leaving he had instructed me to represent him in writing the note, my position would have to prevail. There followed a great deal of scribbling by everyone present, seeking a satisfactory formula. When Bundy had something written and attempted to read it to us, Stimson snapped at him, saying that he had "better keep out of this."

Finally, Stimson and I agreed upon a text. He then called Hoover on a telephone in a booth in his office and got the President's approval. Then he and I initialed the copy.

He warned us that he did not agree with us about the British negotiations and would leave in the State Department files a record of his own interpretation of what Roosevelt had told him earlier and of the procedure that should have been followed.

The note, which was handed to Ambassador Lindsay later that afternoon, said in effect that the President-elect would be glad to discuss the debt with the British and that he would welcome a representative or representatives for such a discussion after his inauguration. It said further that he would also welcome a discussion in Washington at that time with representatives of the British about ways and means of improving the world situation.

While the British reply to our note was ambiguous, a beginning of the end of the debt situation for the time being was provided by Roosevelt's invitation to Ambassador Lindsay to visit him in Warm Springs. They had been friends in the Wilson days in Washington, and also Lindsay was a thoroughly amiable human being. The two men had a good visit on January 28, and shortly afterward Lindsay returned to London to report. From that time on, the British government apparently decided not to press the debt and the subject was not revived until the June payment was approaching. By general agreement, there was no reply to the British answer to our suggestion for two conferences.

Tugwell then gathered a small group to consider the issues that would arise if the British-American talks should materialize after the inauguration. Some of the members of that group were Ernest M. Patterson of the University of Pennsylvania, Walter Stewart, a business economist, and James Warburg. Later, when Tugwell told Roosevelt about this informal activity, Bernard Baruch was added as a sort of chairman. When the bank crisis crashed into the orbit of the new Administration's planning, such preparations went over into April.

I had a number of contacts with Stimson in the next two weeks. These were quite amicable and of a routine nature.

Tugwell records in his diary that he and I had a long talk on January 30 "about our future." He notes that I told him that I was going to talk with Roosevelt about what official position he was to have in the new Administration. He replied that I was not to ask for any job for him:

> I said, however, that I would always be glad to do what I could in any emergency, and that I might be most useful in that way. . . . I advised Moley not to go further in his present anomalous role. He has much work, many responsibilities, and no authority. F. D. R. is certainly not treating him—or me, for that matter—fairly in requiring so much of us without clear delegation.

I shared this feeling after the strange proceedings in January. For without fully informing me, Roosevelt had made what both Stimson and Davis believed to be commitments in the specific subjects which he had delegated to me in November and December. I had received his offer of an assistant-secretaryship in the State Department in early December and had accepted. But this had not been made public. I was not feeling sorry for myself, or jealous because he had not given me his complete confidence. I was well aware of his casual habits and I assumed that he was dealing with Stimson and Davis in order to inform himself of all sides before making his own decisions.

During those four weeks, it was a relationship quite unlike that which had prevailed during the campaign when, with his remarkable skill as a political manager, he had definitely assigned responsibilities to me, to Farley, to Howe, and others concerned.

During the campaign I had specific and generally understood authority. But as I had already perceived and was to learn the hard and often embarrassing way in months to come, Roosevelt the campaigner and Roosevelt vested with great power were, so far as administrative methods were concerned, two quite different individuals. He was unsurpassed in administering a campaign. As an executive, he was one of the most imprecise, not to say inefficient, administrators who ever held the office of President.

My reflections at that time were concerned, first, with the status of the debts as a factor in our international relations; second, with the machinations of Stimson—with some rather reluctant assists from Hoover—to turn the mind of Roosevelt away from the policies he had presented in the campaign. There was also the almost certain hostile reaction in Congress if the new President should adopt the policies of the outgoing Administration.

Two precious months had been lost since the White House conference in November. That time had been dissipated in almost continuous disagreement—time during which we should have been working on a program for submission to a newly elected Congress.

I fully realized that future payments on the debts would be small and far between. But they should remain on the books. So long as they were alive, their presence would be a warning, however slight, that the European debtors should not look upon the United States as a source of new help. I felt, moreover, that the cut in German reparations had been nothing less than an invitation to the Germans, who looked upon France and England as "paper tigers," to dedicate themselves to rearmament in anticipation of another war. Lausanne, however well-intentioned its participants, was a minor Munich. Hitler in late 1932 was rapidly gaining in power. This, of course, reduced disarmament to an exercise in futility.

My mind was far more political than was Tugwell's, and I viewed the efforts of Stimson and Davis as nothing short of an inducement to betray Roosevelt's pledges to the American people. To make what Tugwell called "the grand gesture" of reducing or cancelling the debts would seem ironical to the people of the country, who were themselves sorely burdened with private indebtedness—impoverished and mortgage-laden farmers, small businesses that could barely borrow enough from the banks to stay alive, big businesses that were depressed for lack of customers. For a Presidential candidate who had so seriously planned to attack the problem of debt on the home front to make international concessions after election would be resented. And if the country were apprised that Roosevelt had adopted policies urged by the President and Secretary of State of an Administration which had been overwhelmingly repudiated by the electorate, there would be ignited a revolt in Congress against a leader whom the members had loyally supported in the campaign. Moreover, had the country known—as many members of Congress knew—that at Roosevelt's right hand was Norman Davis, who belonged to a group that had sought to wrest the nomination from Roosevelt in 1932, it would seem incredible. I knew many Senators who were quite conversant with Davis and his past associations. Davis' known affinity for the League of Nations would have set in motion a distrust of Roosevelt that might have resulted in party division and disaster.

It seemed at that point unbelievable that Roosevelt, the master politician, seemed unaware of these political perils. All these conclusions—in part political, in part ideological, and largely because I wanted Roosevelt to succeed—crossed my mind as I viewed his associations with Stimson and Davis. His bitterness toward Hoover had saved him so far.

But the Stimson-Davis-Frankfurter approach was far more subtle and, I regretted, more comfortable.

Finally, it seemed unbelievable that a regime that had so utterly failed in grappling with the depression, when it had possessed the power of the executive department and for two of its years a majority in Congress, should now try to bend the opposition to its policies. I remember that once I commented to an intimate at that time, "Who the hell do these people believe won that election—Roosevelt or Hoover and Stimson?"

Here were the makings of a struggle to influence Roosevelt's mind and for the policies that were to be followed in the first months of his administration.*

And so in the week following the White House meeting on the twentieth I decided to try to reach a clear-cut understanding with Roosevelt, much as I had in the campaign the year before.

The necessity for this was not only to effectuate my own activities, but to clear up a public impression which had appeared in the press. Various items had appeared—no doubt because of promptings from Norman Davis, whose wiles with the press were a characteristic part of his business of diplomacy—that featured a Moley-Davis rift and also the replacement of me with Davis so far as international affairs were concerned.

As a preliminary to reaching a showdown with Roosevelt, I felt that I needed the advice of veterans, and I sought out one of the wisest and most kindly of men, Senator Claude Swanson. He was most helpful. He said I should ignore newspaper stories that were obviously either inspired or written without knowledge of the facts. And he assured me that his Democratic colleagues had full confidence in me.

And so I called Roosevelt on January 22 at Warm Springs. After telling him about our meeting with Stimson and the writing of the note to the British, I told him about the newspaper stories. These, and also Davis' projection of himself into our negotiations with the Hoover Administration, had placed me in a painfully ambiguous position. The

* The crafty series of contacts by which Stimson and Davis, with occasional assists from Hoover, sought to capture Roosevelt's mind and persuade him to abandon his campaign commitments are described in great detail in Herbert Feis's book *1933: Characters in Conflict* published in March 1966 (Boston: Little, Brown) after my foregoing account was already written. Feis had been economic adviser to the State Department since 1931. His appointment had been made by Stimson because of the recommendation of Frankfurter. Feis was not only very close to Stimson but a devoted admirer. And in several of the approaches to Roosevelt, Feis was the channel through which Frankfurter communicated with Stimson. To these operations Feis devoted eight chapters of his book. They are designated as "liaison." And as he says, they ended "rancorously." Because of the urgent recommendation of Frankfurter I persuaded Roosevelt to retain Feis in the State Department.

immediate question concerned, I explained, was who was to represent him in dealing with Stimson?

Roosevelt was in one of his gay and affectionate moods. He said that, while Davis had accompanied him on part of his train journey south from Washington, when they had parted there was no mention of any future appointments. Specifically, he said, "I am through with Norman Davis." And he added that he would hold me responsible for representing him so far as the debts were concerned and also related subjects. He also said that I should establish contact with Hull, inform him about developments, try to determine whether he would accept the office of Secretary of State, and keep him (Roosevelt) informed.

This was reassuring, but my doubts about entering his Administration as an official of the State Department remained. And so, in order to obtain full guidance concerning what I should do while he was on his projected cruise with Vincent Astor, I went to Warm Springs, arriving there on February 2. The next day I had a long and what was to me a memorable talk with Roosevelt.

There was first a discussion of the Cabinet appointments and the course I was to follow in getting either acceptances or refusals from the people he had already invited to accept those offices. Then I explained my personal doubts about serving in the State Department. I had grave misgivings about serving as a nominal subordinate of Hull while at the same time assisting the President in a wide variety of subjects wholly unrelated to foreign affairs. Anyhow, I explained, I was chiefly interested in domestic affairs and only casually concerned with foreign policy. Even as patient and understanding a man as Hull would resent my anomalous position.

Roosevelt lightly dismissed any possibility of misunderstanding. He said Hull clearly understood that I was to serve the President directly.

Largely to draw him out, I suggested that it might be better for me to be removed from Washington entirely, and I mentioned the governorship of the Philippine Islands. He immediately answered, "No. You would be eight thousand miles away. I need you here."

I then said that if I were to serve in the State Department, there were a number of areas in which I was specifically interested and that I wanted him to specify these in some formal way. He then dictated and I wrote down in my notebook the following guide to my assignments:

> The foreign debts, the World Economic Conference [meaning preparations for it], supervision of the economic adviser's office [in the State Department], and such additional duties as the President may direct in the general field of foreign and domestic government.

This was indeed quite an assignment, and I believed at the moment that such written specifications might suffice. It has been said over and over that Roosevelt's optimistic and casual moods were contagious. I confess that there, under the bright sunlight near the pool where he took his therapeutic swims, and with his smiling assurances ringing in my ears, I caught the contagion and closed the subject with what then seemed to me complete satisfaction. What happened there was that a long-time friendship and mutual trust triumphed in both our minds over reason and common sense.

Later, as I reflected more coherently, I came to the firm conclusion that while such a jerry-built specification of responsibilities might serve during the intense period that would mark the first months of the Administration, it was no permanent arrangement. Apparently I told Tugwell that I had decided to stay only a month after the inauguration. But my own calculations ran to the autumn months of 1933, when I was scheduled to resume my teaching at Columbia and for which I had already listed my courses in the catalogue.*

Anyhow, I realized that there was vastly interesting work to be done in the honeymoon of the new Administration and I wanted to learn as much as I could while doing it.

A vastly more important question was answered while I was in the South with Roosevelt. This was that first in priority in the policies of the new Administration was recovery on the domestic scene; international commitments were to wait until the home front was in order. This was the central issue for which Tugwell and I had struggled during the three months since the election.

The great decision to which Roosevelt committed himself was embodied in his historic inaugural address, on which we collaborated:

> Our international trade relations, though vastly important, are in point of time and necessity, secondary to the establishment of a sound national economy. I favor as a practical policy the putting of first things first. I shall spare no effort to restore world trade by international economic adjustment, but the emergency at home cannot wait on that accomplishment.
>
> The basic thought that guides these specific means of national recovery is not narrowly nationalistic. It is the insistence, as a first consideration, upon the interdependence of the various elements in and parts of the United States. . . .

This was the commitment that we had sought in the battle for Roosevelt's mind. It was final, and irrevocable. And it was followed in spirit and action during the First New Deal for months.

* Subsequently, I had a very sincere and earnest letter from Frankfurter telling me that I ought to continue to help Roosevelt in a purely unofficial status. That, incidentally, was to be his decision when offered the position of solicitor general. To guard myself, I wrote a number of letters to friends, saying that I expected to stay in office only a few months. One of these friends, Fred Charles, a Buffalo newspaperman, returned my letter to me for my files at a time when a large part of the press and public assumed that I had resigned because of Hull's objections.

Part Two

The Administration Takes Shape

Chapter Four

Interlude at Miami

IT was Louis Howe's excessive caution that resulted in my presence in Miami on the evening of February 15. There were a good many messages to be delivered to Roosevelt verbally, mostly the latest progress reports on my negotiations with prospective Cabinet appointments. Louis hesitated to entrust this sort of information either to the mail or to the telephone or to anyone but me, since I had been the means of contact with the people under consideration. I went to Miami rather reluctantly because I had agreed to make a speech in Cincinnati on February 17. But I appealed to Trubee Davison, an old friend who at that time was assistant secretary of war in charge of air operations, to have an Army plane pick me up in Jacksonville on the sixteenth and fly me to Cincinnati.

After arriving in Miami, I went directly to Vincent Astor's yacht, *Nourmahal*, which had arrived there in the afternoon.

Astor and his friends were just completing their farewell dinner when I arrived and a number of newspapermen were interviewing Roosevelt at the dinner table, in the center of which were the remains of a birthday cake.

I delivered my confidential messages, and after some talk about future plans and assignments Roosevelt and the members of Astor's group and some newspapermen entered some automobiles that were drawn up at the dock. A sort of reception had been planned at Bay Front Park in Miami, and Roosevelt was expected to meet the crowd and say a few words of greeting.

Roosevelt was in the leading car with the mayor of Miami and Marvin McIntyre. There was also a Secret Service man or two in the car. The car carrying Roosevelt was a touring car with the top down. Other Secret Service men were in the car immediately behind Roosevelt's. In the next car, a rather small sedan, were Kermit Roosevelt, who had been in the Astor cruise, Vincent Astor, William Rhinelander Stewart, and I. Kermit was sitting with the driver in the front seat; Astor, Stewart, and I were in the rear.

On our way to the park we passed along a highway that bordered the bay. A long row of palms was between us and the water. Very few people were abroad, and the February night was not bright. By an amazing coincidence, Astor commented on the danger to Roosevelt's life from possible assassins. "Anyone could shoot him in such a place as this," he said. I replied that during the months of the campaign there had always been that possibility, and we had passed through dense crowds in a dozen cities. Living with danger becomes commonplace with a public figure such as a President or a candidate for President. And during the period before the election Roosevelt had no protection of his own. Only the local police were charged with that, and their security measures were never very adequate. But when he had been elected, Secret Service officers from Washington were assigned to him.

When we arrived at Bay Front Park, the cavalcade halted in the roadway. Roosevelt's car stopped before a small temporary stand on which were seated several local dignitaries and also Mayor Anton Cermak of Chicago. Cermak was there measurably to make amends for the fact that at the Democratic Convention in 1932 he, with the Illinois delegation, had opposed Roosevelt. He also had in mind putting in a word for a loan to Chicago from the Reconstruction Finance Corporation.

A crowd estimated at a few thousand was assembled to see and hear the President-elect. There were some flimsy chairs, but most of the people were standing. The front tiers were close to the driveway and to Roosevelt's car. Our car was about seventy-five feet behind.

Roosevelt was hoisted up on the back seat of the car and was handed a loud speaker. He talked for about two minutes—mostly pleasantries. Then he slid down into the seat. Several of the dignitaries, including Mayor Cermak, came down from the platform to shake his hand. Cermak started to return to the platform but stood for a moment to the right of the car.

We heard five distinct shots. For a moment I believed the sound was caused by automobile backfiring. But then I saw a great rushing about in the vicinity of Roosevelt's car.

Giuseppe Zangara had posted himself in the crowd at a distance of fifteen or twenty feet from where Roosevelt's car was to stop. He stood on a chair when Roosevelt was speaking but for some reason failed to take advantage of the broad target which was offered when the President-elect was sitting up high on the back seat. But as Roosevelt had settled back into the seat, Zangara apparently took a revolver from his pocket and aimed. A woman standing by grabbed at his hand and deflected his aim. That is why the succession of five bullets missed Roosevelt and struck a number of people, including Cermak, who were close to the rear of the car. Cermak fell to his knees from the shock, but with the aid of a Secret Service man rose to his feet immediately.

It was reported that more than five people were struck by bullets. A Secret Service man suffered a glancing blow on the forearm. Two women were wounded. A man whom I could not identify had blood on his white hair. And the police brought another man, who had a flesh wound in his forehead, back to our car and Astor took him in onto his lap.

Several policemen brought Zangara back to our car and put him across the trunk rack on the rear, where two officers pinned him down. Another officer mounted the running board, and I held him by his belt.

Meanwhile, Cermak was placed beside Roosevelt in his car. Roosevelt supported him with one arm while he held his pulse with the other hand. And so the cars all started for the hospital. It was a considerable distance. When we arrived Roosevelt was emerging from the hospital door, completely uninjured and calm, on the arm of Gus Gennerich.

When the policemen raised themselves from Zangara's body on the trunk rack, one of them fell to the ground because of numbness induced by the position in which he had been riding. Zangara was then taken away to the jail.

Roosevelt and his party remained in a room at the rear of the hospital to wait and learn how Cermak was resting. We must have been there for an hour or more. Roosevelt agreed to return to Astor's yacht for the night rather than to follow his plan to take the train to New York. For some time on the *Nourmahal* we discussed the events. At about two o'clock Roosevelt went to bed.

My memory went back to the time, thirty-one years before, when as a boy of fifteen I had been at the Buffalo Pan American Exposition when President McKinley was assassinated. I was not in the Temple of Music where the shooting took place, but was in the small crowd outside when Leon Czolgosz was brought out to be taken to prison. I witnessed the frenzy of the crowd that attempted to take Czolgosz from the police at that time. And in the weeks that followed, I read in the newspapers of the witch hunt for anarchists which followed that assassination.

And so now, in Miami, I decided to determine, if I could, whether Zangara had a political motive for his crime. Frederic Kernochan, a member of Astor's party, was a judge in New York City and was quite able to evaluate oral evidence. At about midnight he and I therefore visited the jail where we could question Zangara.

The prisoner was not very communicative. He seemed to feel a great deal of pain in the vicinity of the stomach and constantly complained about his suffering. We learned from him that this distress had been of long duration and concluded that it seriously affected his behavior.

He said, in the midst of his complaining, that he had wanted to shoot "big men." I asked him why, if he wanted to kill Presidents, he had not tried to kill Hoover. His response was unintelligible. But we concluded that he had been intent on shooting Roosevelt and had probably missed his chance because of the crowd, which had been pressing in on him when Roosevelt was sitting high upon the back of the rear seat.

Repeated questions designed to determine whether he had any political or ideological connections yielded nothing. And so we concluded that his case was simply that of a man who was deranged by acute pain and had conceived a hatred of people who were eminent and powerful.

I made sure the next morning that the story of our interview reached the reporters, and it appeared in the New York *Times*, among other newspapers. My concern was to forestall any sort of Communist, or anti-Communist, or anarchist witch hunt such as had followed the assassination of McKinley. Zangara's complaint about the pain he was suffering was confirmed at the autopsy which followed his execution. There were serious stomach adhesions caused by ulcers.

The fact that Cermak had been hit, however, gave rise to a myth that Zangara was a member of a Chicago gang determined to kill the mayor. There was no substance to this, because Zangara had lived in Paterson, New Jersey, prior to his trip to Miami, and no evidence was found to connect him with anyone in Chicago.

The whole affair demonstrated a complete absence of physical fear in Roosevelt. He remained perfectly calm and self-possessed. He was, as I noted at the time, "easy, confident, poised, and unmoved except for his concern about Cermak." Mayor Cermak died in the hospital two weeks later.

Two days after the Miami shooting I came close to losing my own life. The two-seat Army plane that picked me up in Jacksonville attempted to fly me to Cincinnati after a stop at Fort Bragg, North Carolina. The pilot had no means of communication with the ground. Heading northwest over the mountains and above thick clouds, he lost his course and passed over the tip of Virginia, probably a corner of Kentucky, and southward into Tennessee. He could not risk seeking the ground, for the mountains were under us, hidden by low clouds, and the sinking sun warned of approaching darkness. Providence finally revealed a break in the clouds, and he lowered the plane through. We found farm land there, soaked by spring rains. Nothing remained but to land, and the trip ended with the plane's nose deep in the mud.

We were near Maynardville, twenty-five miles north of Knoxville. I called off the engagement in Cincinnati, and we secured transportation to Knoxville, where I took a train to Washington. The pilot, Lieutenant Coons, under Army regulations had to return to the disabled plane.

The helplessness of the pilot in such an aircraft and under such weather conditions serves to explain the death toll of Army pilots later when the job of carrying the U.S. mail was imposed upon them because of Roosevelt's cancellation of the mail contracts. In that instance, Postmaster General Farley claimed that Secretary of War Dern had assured him that the Army pilots could do the job.

Chapter Five

Recruiting a Cabinet, I

OVER the years since the Virginia Dynasty, President's Cabinets have occasionally included persons of great talent and distinction. But these exceptions have served to prove the rule of mediocrity. Most came, except for the political service that won their appointment, from obscurity. They played their part for a while on the great stage. And then they slipped from sight into private life.

Certain of the reasons for this rule of mediocrity have been endlessly repeated. Political service rather than administrative capacity has had priority. Men engaged in large private enterprises cannot quit their responsibilities for the puny glory of public attention, even for a few years. They hesitate to live in the hectic climate of Washington. They know that a large part of the time and energies of a department head means endless labor in preparing for or presenting matters before Congressional committees, seeking something that is often unattainable without giving some undeserved favors in return. It means operating in an administrative system in which the rules of civil service bar any effort to impose efficiency within a teeming bureaucracy. Often, too, there are repellent rivalries among the department heads themselves. It means exposure to the merciless hammering of the press, unless valuable time is given to the cultivation of reporters.

Men of stature realize that membership in the Cabinet is a transitory and empty honor, if prominence in the press can be called honor. The member is only nominally an adviser to the President, for he is more often told rather than asked about national policy. Presidents get the better part of their advice from a variety of sources other than their Cabinets. Cabinet meetings are routine and generally boring affairs. The

President cannot feel free to discuss his decisions, because a Cabinet is almost always a very leaky vessel. Members have no vote like the Senators' and Congressmen's in shaping national policy.

In the great departments over which they preside, they are virtually the prisoners of their own bureaucracies. The technical knowledge comes from the people below, who may or may not be loyal to the man at the top. Career officers regard their politically selected superior as a necessary but temporary nuisance. The iron rules of civil service deny the department head sufficient freedom to select even a small number of subordinates of his own choice. Also those rules make it preferable to endure the incompetence of a subordinate rather than to fire him. For removal entails long and harassing hearings. And very frequently the President himself hires the more important assistant secretaries and bureau heads.

A Cabinet member has a fine car with a chauffeur to haul him about. He has an ornate office with portraits of his predecessors staring down at him. He gets a lot of invitations to dinner where his office rather than he is honored and at which there are always some fellow guests who are there to squeeze some sort of information from him—information to which they are not entitled. He has fancy stationery for his letters but the texts of these are usually supplied by some subordinate who has the proper information. Everybody calls him "Mister Secretary" except in the Post Office and Justice Department, where he is called "General." But these are perquisites attractive only to small persons.

But a most important reason why Cabinets have been so mediocre is that so many Presidents want people around with whom they can feel comfortable. This means men who by their stature and capacity will not remind him of his own deficiencies.

There have been a few in recent years who have taken a Cabinet membership because of a genuine desire to serve. But these have generally remained only until they believe they have acquitted themselves of a duty.

The drop-out rate among Cabinet members is highest among the more competent. Others stay because they have no better place to go. This mediocrity prevails even now, when some of the departments have grown to colossal size. And grave responsibilities fall upon such members as the Secretaries of Defense and the Treasury. Perhaps the least desirable place in the Cabinet is that of Secretary of State. For while protocol and custom give him priority, he is generally a mere figurehead. The President makes foreign policy. The Secretary merely expounds the President's ideas. Also the bureaucracy in the Department of State is most especially addicted to routine, red tape, and petty intrigue. It operates with little supervision from the Secretary because that functionary is occupied during most of the year flying to or attending international conferences or in greeting representatives of foreign nations in Washington.

The foregoing traditional conditions and limitations all weighed heavily in Roosevelt's choices. But there were also a number of compulsions and limitations imposed which were personal to Roosevelt.

The greatest reservoir of practical judgment and administrative talent in the United States is the business community. But in the depression years there was so much prejudice against businessmen that Roosevelt, who shared that distrust, was reluctant to look to the world of business for Cabinet material. In addition to this he had an unreasoning antipathy toward successful people in business who had been his contemporaries in college and who had never taken the young squire of Hyde Park seriously. Moreover, most businessmen were Republicans and were measurably barred for that reason. Only Woodin in the first Roosevelt Cabinet was what might be called "business-minded," but he was exonerated because he had loyally supported Roosevelt in pre-convention days. And Woodin often commented that, had the choice been his, he would have preferred a career in music. Farley had been engaged in small business but he was better known as a politician. The remainder of the Cabinet in 1933 were substantially without business experience, and in fact were almost completely destitute of executive competence.

Roosevelt was unwilling to appoint people who had served in high office under Wilson. For, a junior in that Administration, he was generally regarded by his senior colleagues as immature and irresponsible, with a hint of the playboy in his character. Roosevelt knew of this prejudice against him and deeply resented it.

In fact—and this is no compliment to me—Roosevelt always seemed to feel uncomfortable in the presence of first-rateness. He rationalized this by regarding a man's past associations with large private affairs as a reason why that man could not be trusted to guard the public interest. Henry Morgenthau, Jr., who always reflected the President's less worthy instincts, once told me when he was Secretary of the Treasury and was looking for a suitable appointee that he could not find true "intellectual integrity" anywhere except in college professors. I don't know whether this was intended as a personal compliment but I responded by recommending a professor in the Columbia Law School who served—admirably, as it happened—as Morgenthau's undersecretary for a short period.

Another limitation, which some commentators have deplored, has been the need for geographical representation. This is not so serious as it has been represented. For certain departments this sectionalism is desirable. For Interior, it is desirable to have a man from the West, because that is where the main interests of that department are concentrated. It would be a mistake to select a New Englander as Secretary of Agriculture. And other factors being favorable, the Secretary of the Treasury should come from the East. Otherwise sectional interests might well be disregarded.

It should be noted, however, that such unseemly deals as were made in securing the nomination of Abraham Lincoln, and which loaded the Cabinet of the Great Emancipator with misfits, did not encumber Roosevelt. There were, so far as I was able to determine, no such obligations, express or implied. Only twice in our months together in the campaign in 1932 was a future Cabinet position mentioned. Once when I arrived at Hyde Park in the afternoon, I found Roosevelt in a towering rage. He said that someone who had visited him that morning had offered him a large sum for the campaign if he would promise to appoint a certain person to a specified Cabinet post. Since I had an excellent clue to the identity of the two individuals concerned, I can testify that the suggested appointee did not get the job.

Roosevelt said on another occasion that he intended to appoint a woman to the Cabinet, and mentioned Ruth Bryan Owen, daughter of the immortal William Jennings Bryan, as his first choice at that time.*

On January 11 I had a long talk with Roosevelt about tentative suggestions for his Cabinet. The following possibilities, as I noted them in my notebook of that day, were:

State—Cordell Hull
Treas.—Carter Glass
Commerce—Will Woodin or Jesse Straus
Agric.—Henry Wallace
Attorney General—Thomas Walsh (if he will take it). Hiram Johnson, Phil La Follette or Bronson Cutting
War—Dern of Utah
Navy—Gardiner of N.C.
Post. Gen.—Jim Farley

In giving me this information, Roosevelt made it clear that a great deal of confidential negotiation would be necessary and that he wanted me to carry most of that responsibility. To scatter such a task among several negotiators would lead to premature and embarrassing publicity. It would also lead, if made public, to deep resentment by people who had been considered and later dropped. Another reason for assigning this task to me was that he would be excessively busy. He was planning a vacation later on Vincent Astor's yacht.

* Mrs. Owen was an extraordinarily attractive woman. After the new Administration was installed, she entertained an ambition to be appointed an assistant secretary of state. She came to me, hoping I might help her get the appointment. Our talk turned to her father, who had been one of my boyhood heroes. She indicated that she had inherited her undoubted gift as a public speaker from her father as a major qualification. She was rewarded later with an appointment as Minister to Denmark. I believe that this was the first appointment of a woman to a major diplomatic post.

One of these appointments was not only substantially mandatory. The offer had already been made and accepted. According to Farley, Roosevelt had made the offer of appointment as Postmaster General on October 10, 1932.* This was traditional, for a Postmaster General who is also National Chairman is official keeper of the plum tree.

Frances Perkins, who was not included in my negotiations, says that she agreed with reluctance to serve as Secretary of Labor in late February only after Roosevelt's acceptance of her proposals for a broad "program of labor legislation." She says further that she was reluctant to serve because she was not "a bona fide labor person." Roosevelt countered by reminding her that she had served with him as industrial commissioner of New York and that "we could accomplish for the nation the things we had done for the state." Such a "program," the details of which apparently neither Mrs. Perkins nor Roosevelt seems to have clarified then, was only partially adopted in the National Recovery Administration and the Wagner Act two years later.†

The most glorious moment in the life of William Gibbs McAdoo was when he arose in a deadlocked convention in 1932 and made Roosevelt's nomination possible by casting California's votes for the New York governor. Although the negotiations that lay behind that switch of California's votes had been made (according to their stories afterward) by people too numerous to mention, McAdoo had the intense satisfaction of announcing it. That, according to McAdoo, had earned high priority for his demands upon Roosevelt for innumerable appointments later. He himself was not under consideration for a position in the Administration, for he had been elected Senator in California in November.

But as a gesture to McAdoo, Roosevelt offered the Commerce position to Daniel C. Roper, a close friend of McAdoo's. Roper had served in the Wilson Administration as first assistant postmaster general and later as commissioner of Internal Revenue.

It is unfortunate that in the histories of that period Roper has been regarded as a complete nonentity. This neglect, as well as the light manner in which he was treated by Roosevelt and his associates, is not at all fair to a sincere, likable, and crisp administrator. Perhaps his sin in the eyes of most New Dealers was that he sought as well as he could to fulfill the responsibility that should fall upon the Commerce Department. This was to represent business in Federal affairs. He was powerless to curb Roosevelt's occasional attacks upon the business community.

* James A. Farley, *Behind the Ballots* (New York: Harcourt, Brace, 1938), p. 183.
† Frances Perkins, *The Roosevelt I Knew* (New York: Viking Press, 1946), pp. 150–52.

Serious complications attended the Roper selection. The January 11 list of preliminary preferences had listed Woodin and Jesse Straus for the Commerce position. Woodin would have been reluctant to take the post, but Straus was definitely interested. And he had certain undeniable claims. He was at that time head of the great R. H. Macy establishment. He had served as chairman and chief financial supporter of the Roosevelt Business and Professional League. Moreover, his distinguished uncle, Oscar S. Straus, had held the new position of Secretary of Commerce and Labor. He was appointed in 1906 by Theodore Roosevelt.

The selection of Roper was a bitter disappointment to Straus. The salt was rubbed into the injury by the fact that the news that he was not to get the post came by the incredible blundering of the officious Henry Morgenthau, Sr. Morgenthau had the effrontery to ask him what other position would be agreeable to him. The news of this unauthorized action of Morgenthau's was brought to me by Straus's son, Robert, who had served in a minor capacity in the 1932 campaign under my direction. I called Roosevelt directly, and he immediately had a talk with Straus, made it clear that Morgenthau had acted without authority, and said that he wanted Straus to go to France as Ambassador. Straus accepted this alternative.

The appointment of George H. Dern as Secretary of War raised many questions in the press. This was not because of any serious bar to the appointment of this good man, but because there seemed to be no good reason for the appointment. I never knew when or where the offer was made and accepted, and I had met Dern only casually when we were campaigning in Utah in 1932. He was then governor of that state. Apparently, Roosevelt simply liked Dern because of his meetings with him at a governors' conference. Farley claims that Roosevelt mentioned Dern in October as a possible Secretary of the Interior. Perhaps the overriding reason for the selection was that Dern was a Westerner. At that time, the office of Secretary of War was unimportant. The Army was very small, and war seemed a completely remote possibility.*

The appointment of the venerable and beloved Claude A. Swanson achieved a number of objectives. He had served with distinction in the Senate since 1910 and in the new Senate would have been chairman of the Foreign Relations Committee. Roosevelt very greatly desired to recognize Senator Key Pittman, who had served most effectively in the 1932 campaign. Pittman ranked next to Swanson and would succeed to the chairmanship. Also, Swanson's resignation from the Senate would make way for Harry F. Byrd, who had been governor of Virginia.

* Before my selection as assistant secretary of state, a friend and associate suggested to me that the war post was a "sinecure" and that if appointed to it I could give my time to assist Roosevelt. Needless to say, I never seriously considered the suggestion.

Swanson was in advanced years and would, Roosevelt believed, permit the President to have a free hand in running the Navy. Finally, the great prestige of Swanson in Congress would assure liberal appropriations for the Navy. No negotiations were necessary in this instance. Roosevelt made the offer and it was accepted.

This array of the circumstances may convey the impression that Swanson's own qualities and character were incidental to his appointment. That is not true. He was a man of fine intelligence and superior judgment. I had many occasions to talk with him in the period before the inauguration, and his advice, rendered with unfailing kindness and with a wisdom enriched by many years in public life, saved me many a blunder. If I had listened to him more carefully on the subject of Cordell Hull, I would not have accepted a position nominally subordinate to the new Secretary of State and would thus have saved much embarrassment to me and to Hull.

There was never any doubt about the man Roosevelt wanted for Attorney General. The fame and party standing Thomas J. Walsh had won by his exposure of the Harding Administration's oil-lease scandals were compelling facts. Walsh had also been a strong Roosevelt supporter before and after the nomination. In September, Walsh had boarded Roosevelt's campaign train and remained during the entire trip to the West Coast and back. He and Pittman collaborated with me in preparing the tariff speech, which was delivered in Sioux City. Both Senators were strong protectionists, and the speech substantially assured the farmers that no tariff cuts in their products were anticipated. This greatly distressed Cordell Hull, who spent most of the campaign at his home in Tennessee.

At Roosevelt's suggestion, I conferred twice in late January and early February with Walsh about his designation as Roosevelt's choice for Attorney General. Roosevelt wanted the announcement to be made at his return from his cruise in mid-February. Roosevelt also asked me to "sound out" Walsh about appointing Felix Frankfurter as solicitor general. Walsh's gray mustache bristled. He said he would accept the Attorney Generalship but would not have Frankfurter as solicitor general. He gave as his reason Frankfurter's lack of practical experience at the bar. He said that he didn't want a solicitor general who would lose cases in "the grand manner." In fairness to Frankfurter, it should be added that he would not have accepted the position if it were offered. For after the death of Walsh, the offer was made and he declined.

On March 2 Walsh died on a train while returning from a Southern vacation. This presented a serious problem on the eve of the inauguration. Roosevelt could not think of an alternative and had decided to let the appointment go over until after the inauguration. Edward J. Flynn gives the following account of how Homer S. Cummings was selected:

When this news [of Walsh's death] came, "Missy" LeHand, who was Roosevelt's confidential secretary, and I were in the room. . . . "Missy" said that perhaps Homer Cummings would be a good appointment.

The President-elect hesitated, for Cummings was down for Governor General of the Philippines. The longer Roosevelt thought about it, however, the more he resolved that at least a temporary appointment of Cummings as Attorney General would be an excellent solution for his needs. Cummings was sent for, and the situation was explained. He agreed that the appointment should be temporary, and that any time after the inauguration the President wished to make a change would be agreeable to him. . . .*

I had talked with Cummings a few days before this, and he seemed to be quite excited about going to the Philippines. He said he had brought with him a number of books about the islands which he intended to read on the voyage to Manila. He showed such extraordinary capacity in the early days of the Administration in bringing order in a somewhat disorganized Department of Justice that Roosevelt never thought of shifting him, and he remained in the Cabinet until 1939.

One of the most fortunate decisions that Cummings made early in his administration of the department was to retain J. Edgar Hoover as director of the Federal Bureau of Investigation. There had been terrific pressure on Roosevelt by various city politicians to replace Hoover with this or that police chief whom they believed would be amenable to them for patronage. Such a political appointment would most certainly have been the end of the effectiveness of the splendid organization Hoover had built up since he was first appointed in 1924 by Harlan Stone, who was at that time Attorney General. Louis Howe loved the subject of criminal investigation as a result of reading detective stories. He threw his weight behind the demands of the bosses for replacing Hoover. There were also lurking around at the time several disgruntled ex-members of the F.B.I. staff who were anxious to see Hoover removed and thus open the way for their reinstatement. One of these was brought to me, and he complained about the iron discipline which Hoover maintained over his subordinates. This sort of argument to me was the best commendation Hoover could have had. For a police agency must, if effective, be strictly disciplined.

I entered the argument at this point and strongly opposed Howe in my discussions with Roosevelt. For I had a considerable experience in studying law enforcement and had served, as I have indicated earlier, in several important matters in that area when Roosevelt was governor. At least I secured a stay of execution, and the decision was passed over to Cummings. It was not long before Cummings realized that Hoover was indispensable, and Hoover was retained.†

* Edward J. Flynn, *You're the Boss* (New York: Viking Press, 1947), pp. 125–26.
† More than a month before, I was directed, after a patronage conference with

From the middle of the summer of 1932, Rex Tugwell labored to induce Roosevelt, if elected, to appoint Henry Agard Wallace as Secretary of Agriculture. Tugwell had met Wallace and had read a good deal of the Wallace writings in *Wallace's Farmer and Iowa Homestead.* I concurred with Tugwell's idea and we arranged to have Wallace come to Hyde Park and meet Roosevelt. Subsequently, Wallace was one of the several people who contributed ideas for Roosevelt's speech on agriculture.

After Roosevelt showed me his tentative list of appointees, he wrote to Wallace offering him the position. But since no reply had come from Wallace, Roosevelt delegated me to call Wallace while he was cruising in early February. I called Wallace and rather bluntly, I imagine, asked him whether he would accept. There was a long pause, and I thought for a moment that something had happened to our telephone connection. I asked him again, and he replied that he would accept. When I grew to know Wallace rather well, I realized that his delay in replying to Roosevelt and his hesitation on the telephone were owing to the essential modesty of the man. He knew well the immense administrative labor that such an office would require.

After receiving the acceptance from Wallace, I sent Roosevelt a radiogram and said, in accord with a simple code we had devised before he sailed, "CORN BELT IN THE BAG." These radio messages were jointly signed by Howe and me with the quaint expression invented by Howe, "LUHOWRAY."

The simple realization by Wallace of his own limitations at that time may seem strange to those who knew him later as exceedingly articulate and unorthodox on all sorts of public affairs. But as Tugwell told me later, after his association with him in the Department of Agriculture, Wallace was a sort of "mystic." His mind was speculative and ruminative, rather than practical. But his annual reports were evidence of a comprehensive knowledge of the agricultural economy and its relation to international trade.

These were strong reasons for his appointment other than his knowledge of agriculture. His father, Henry Cantwell Wallace, had been the Secretary in the Harding and Coolidge Cabinets. In that difficult spot,

Roosevelt that I attended with Flynn and Farley, to offer Frank Murphy, then mayor of Detroit, the chairmanship of the Federal Trade Commission. Murphy, whom I had known for several years, replied that he would like to be Attorney General. After I told him that Walsh was slated for that job, he said, "How about governor of the Philippines?" That, I said, was assigned to Homer Cummings. He concluded that he would then stay as mayor of Detroit. The fantastic outcome was that after serving a term as governor of Michigan he was appointed governor of the Philippines, and then Attorney General. He ended his career on the Supreme Court. Thus, he was not only a child of fortune, but a man who always wanted something of the best and always seemed to get it.

his views collided sharply with those of his fellow native of Iowa, Herbert Hoover, Secretary of Commerce. Henry A. had succeeded his father as editor of *Wallace's Farmer*. The Wallaces were originally Republican but had joined the Progressive Party in Theodore Roosevelt's day, and after the death of the elder Wallace, Henry had opposed Republican farm policies.

Chapter Six

Recruiting a Cabinet, II

THE offer of appointment as Secretary of the Treasury to Senator Carter Glass was virtually imposed upon Roosevelt because of Glass's proven capacity and the great respect for him which prevailed in Congress, in the Democratic Party, and in the financial community. Glass, as a member of the House during the early Wilson years, had been chairman of the Banking and Currency Committee. He had carried great responsibility in writing the legislation that created the Federal Reserve System in 1913. Since that operation involved a tangle of conflicting views, the achievement of Glass is memorable. After the resignation of Secretary McAdoo in 1918, Glass was appointed Secretary of the Treasury by Wilson. He served until 1920, when he was appointed to the Senate. In 1933 he was chairman of the Appropriations Committee, but as a member of the Banking and Currency Committee he was destined to steer through the Senate the Glass-Steagall Banking Act of 1933.

Although he was highly respected by the financial community, he was far from subservient to it and was often constructively critical. As a stalwart conservative he had vigorously supported Roosevelt's candidacy in 1932. He had severely criticized both the Coolidge and Hoover Administrations because he believed they had been lax, not to say reckless, in their fiscal and monetary policies.

Roosevelt offered the Treasury appointment to Glass on January 19 in Washington and urged him to accept. But their conversation was hurried, and Glass had strong reservations and conditions. And so before Roosevelt left for Warm Springs after his offer, he instructed me to carry on the negotiations with Glass.

I had profound respect and affection for the great Virginian and essentially agreed with his conservative views. I also realized that Roosevelt had certain unorthodox views which Glass would have to contend with if he were in the Cabinet. This was the most difficult assignment that had yet been imposed upon me, but I undertook it with the determination that I would maintain a completely neutral position.

To avoid misunderstanding, I contrived a means of communication that would save me from blame if the negotiations should fail. And so when I met with Glass on January 27 in Washington I carefully wrote down his reservations and conditions and read the text back to him. Then when I talked with Roosevelt over the telephone to Warm Springs, I read that text to him. Then I wrote down Roosevelt's replies and for verification read back to him what I had written. Next, I went to Glass and read Roosevelt's replies to him. I followed this procedure throughout the negotiations.

Glass was not in the best of health at the time and had been worn down in the debate then raging in the Senate over his banking bill. The virulent attacks upon Glass and his bill by Senator Huey Long had been especially hard to bear.

Glass told me at our first meeting that he wanted answers from Roosevelt to two major questions.* Glass said first that, if he accepted, he wanted a completely free hand to name his own subordinates in the Treasury. He especially wanted Russell Leffingwell, a Morgan partner, as undersecretary. He added that if Roosevelt objected to Leffingwell because of his Morgan connection, he would yield. But otherwise he wanted to make the appointments himself.

Next, he said that he wanted Roosevelt's views on inflation. He had some doubt about Roosevelt's capacity to resist the inflationists. If there were to be any inflationary policies, he would be a "roaring lion in the Senate."

When I read these conditions to Roosevelt the next day, he replied, "Make it perfectly clear that we simply cannot go along with Twenty-three." (Twenty-three Wall Street was the Morgan address.) He also said, "So far as inflation goes, you can say that we are not going to throw ideas out the window simply because they are labeled inflation." Then he added, "If the old boy doesn't want to go along, I wouldn't press it."

The next evening I met Glass in his apartment in the Raleigh Hotel. I showed Roosevelt's answers as I had written them (except for Roosevelt's final comment). He yielded on the Leffingwell appointment, but said that inflation was another matter. He instructed me to tell Roosevelt that he was "not against inflation *in vacuo;* but you just bring me any

* In this account I am relying on my own written copies of the questions and answers and upon my own diary.

specific measure providing for inflation and see if I can't punch it full of holes."

Then Glass brought another consideration into the negotiations. He was reluctant to enter the Cabinet because its social demands would endanger not only his own health but that of his ailing wife. On that point I suggested that he consult his own physician in Virginia and determine whether he could safely stand the rigors of official life and the social obligations involved.

At this point I realized how dangerous to all concerned his acceptance of the appointment might be. Experience had taught me the capricious nature of Roosevelt's views on fiscal and monetary affairs. He was substantially committed to raising the price level—he said to 1926 prices. This would, I was sure, lead to bitter differences and to Glass's resignation within a year or so. I pictured to myself the tragedy of this fine aging Senator and magnificent human being forced by his convictions into private life at the climax of his brilliant career. For he was sorely needed in the Senate to press through his bill for the reformation of banking. I confided my feelings to Jim Byrnes, whom Glass regarded with an affection like that of a father to a son. I could not express these reflections to Glass because I was serving Roosevelt's interests. But the perceptive Glass had already read my mind.

On January 20 Roosevelt told me on the telephone to try to have Glass make an early decision. On February 10 or 11 I received two letters from Glass, one addressed to me and the other to be delivered to Roosevelt, presumably when he returned from his cruise: *

February 8, 1933

MY DEAR MR. MOLEY:

I am sending you the letter to the President-elect, under seal and registered, and will be obliged if you will communicate my decision to Mr. Roosevelt. You have been very kind and patient to hear my story and I derive infinite satisfaction from the fact that you seem to concur in my conclusions.

Hoping for you the best of good fortunes and happiness, believe me,

Sincerely yours,
CARTER GLASS

Professor Raymond Moley
Columbia University
New York City

February 7, 1933

MY DEAR FRANKLIN:

I shall never be able to tell you the measure of my appreciation of the honor which you have done me in inviting me to take the responsible post

* The texts of these letters appear in *Carter Glass, A Biography* by Rixey Smith and Norman Beasley; Introduction by Senator Harry F. Byrd and a Preface by Douglas Southall Freeman (New York: Longmans, Green, 1939), pp. 332–33.

of Secretary of the Treasury in your cabinet. It grieves me to find that I am unable to requite your confidence and kindness by complying with your wish. I have very earnestly considered the matter in all its important aspects, prompted by a compelling desire to be of service to you and to the country. You may be sure it has caused me genuine distress to reach the decision indicated.

Aside from the fact that the reaction to the suggestion among my colleagues in the Senate has been positively averse to me leaving this body, the unanimity of protest from Virginia by press and representative men has been emphatic. Without any intimation from me as to my own concurring conviction, my associates in the Senate and public sentiment in Virginia unite in the judgment that I can better serve you and the country where I am than by a transfer to the Treasury. I trust you may, upon mature reflection, reach the same conclusion, keeping always uppermost in mind that I shall ever be ready to serve your administration to the full extent of my capabilities.

That you may clearly realize that I have tried hard to overcome various difficulties of an almost insuperable nature, I may state that, at the last, hoping to allay the fears of my immediate family as to the effect of the proposed transfer on my health, I sought the frank professional opinion of my regular physician. His letter I am sending to you in strictest confidence.

I am sure you will experience no difficulty in securing a Secretary of the Treasury upon whose vision, courage and strength you may confidently rely.

With fervent good wishes for you and your administration and a further expression of gratitude for your kindness, believe me

Faithfully yours,

CARTER GLASS

Hon. Franklin D. Roosevelt,
Miami, Florida.

This, it seemed to me, was a happy termination of the effort to enlist Glass. But a few days later there were efforts to have Glass reconsider. These were stimulated by Bernard Baruch and Admiral Cary Grayson, who had been Woodrow Wilson's personal physician and who was a warm friend of both Baruch and Glass.

After Roosevelt returned to New York, he called Glass on February 19. Glass said that at the moment he was sitting beside Cary Grayson and that he was still undecided. But he added that if he did not finally accept, he would like to see a sound-money man appointed and he suggested Swagar Sherley, who had served with him for many years in the House during the Wilson Administration. Roosevelt was noncommittal.*

* Sherley and I had had many contacts in the preceding months and in 1932. He was deeply versed in fiscal affairs and had served in Wilson's years as chairman of the Appropriations Committee. Since his retirement from the House, he had practiced law in Washington and Louisville. Roosevelt had offered him the directorship of the budget and he had declined.

Later that morning, Glass called me at the Roosevelt Sixty-fifth Street house. He urged me to persuade Roosevelt to select Sherley. I replied that there was no chance that Roosevelt would select Sherley. This was based on my knowledge and Roosevelt's of Sherley's strong ideas on monetary policy, ideas that were quite as inflexible as those of Glass. That ended the Glass negotiations, and it was assumed by Roosevelt that the Senator's refusal was final.

It happened that Sherley was at Roosevelt's house with several other friends of Roosevelt's that morning. After my conversation with Glass I talked with him. Sherley had also talked with Glass and had indicated to him that he would not accept the Treasury appointment if it was offered. I was so sure that Sherley was sincere that I reported to Roosevelt that he should not be asked. Roosevelt then finally called Glass and got a final refusal.

I first met William H. Woodin in December 1932 at Warm Springs. He had been entertained at dinner by Roosevelt in his cottage. Apparently Roosevelt suggested to him that he talk with me about the plight of the railroads, which at that time was a serious problem for Woodin, an equipment manufacturer. He came to my room at the hotel, and I was immediately struck by his friendly, cheerful, and almost childlike simplicity.

Woodin had been one of the largest and most unselfish contributors to Roosevelt's pre-convention campaign for the nomination. For that reason, and also because they had been friends for a long time, Roosevelt was very fond of Woodin. And since he knew that Woodin had no axes to grind and no favors to ask, Roosevelt gave him his confidence.

Woodin had inherited a very large interest in the American Car and Foundry Company and at that time was president of the company. He was also a director of the New York Federal Reserve Bank. He was exceedingly well acquainted with the financial circles in New York. He wanted nothing except to serve unofficially in considering some of the problems that faced the incoming Administration and to be generally useful in that capacity. He said that night that he knew something about banking and railroads, "the only things, aside from music, that I know anything about." *

* In our many visits after that I had many talks about his life and ambitions with him in his beautiful apartment in New York in which, in addition to many other items of an artistic value, he had a remarkable collection of Hogarth prints. But his other-than-business interest was centered in music. He spent hours at the piano, playing and composing. During that period he had a concert at which he had an orchestra play a symphony, the basic theme of which he had composed himself. He told me with great modesty that after he had gone just so far in its composition, he employed a professional to orchestrate the work. As a young man, he said, he had been sent by his father to Europe to negotiate for the purchase of the Wagon-Lit business, but what he remembered most was an incident in Munich, where he

But in those days, with his business in secure hands, Woodin dedicated himself to the assistance of a group of harried railroad presidents with whom we met on several occasions during those weeks. His knowledge of the financial problems of the railroads was considerable because they were large purchasers of equipment from his company. As an industrialist he saw the banking situation from that detached position much more clearly than did the bankers themselves.

I realized as early as January that there were many reasons why, in the event that Glass refused the Treasury, Woodin would be a completely satisfactory substitute. Roosevelt's confidence in him was assured. Woodin had a keen understanding of Roosevelt's mind and purposes, and his temperament made it possible for him to accommodate himself to the unorthodox manner in which the banking situation might be weathered. On January 25 I noted in my diary that Woodin would be the best alternative to Glass.

In the period before the final refusal of Glass I talked with Louis Howe a number of times about Woodin as a member of the Cabinet. Howe's biographer, A. B. Rollins, Jr., says, "Louis was deeply distressed, although he recouped rapidly when Moley bounced into his Madison Avenue office one afternoon to suggest William Woodin. Howe was delighted to find here a man who was both a loyal Roosevelt partisan and a sop to the 'big boys' of business." This is the way Louis looked at it, but the suitability of Woodin was more important than that. For Woodin was, as it proved in the months that followed, able to keep those "big boys" in their place and also to teach them some sorely needed lessons.

And so, well before the final elimination of Glass, Louis and I contrived a radio message in code to Roosevelt, who was at sea on his cruise: "PREFER A WOODEN ROOF TO A GLASS ROOF OVER SWIMMING POOL. LUHOWRAY."

It came about quite naturally that in February when the final refusal of Glass had been received, Roosevelt turned to me and said, "Now call Will Woodin and bring him here late tonight."

I called for Woodin after dinner that evening and went with him to Roosevelt's home. Woodin had a quaint and joyous way of showing surprise whenever anything pleasant was announced. But when Roosevelt told him that he wanted him to be his Secretary of the Treasury, he showed a bit more unanticipated pleasure than usual. He said he

saw a zither in the window of a music shop. He not only bought the instrument, but employed a musician to accompany him and give him lessons. No doubt only his obligation to his father induced him to take over the business he inherited and abandon his ambition to make a career as a composer of music. Woodin's quaint way, as well as his love for music, was exhibited by the special license plate on his Rolls-Royce, "2T2."

would accept but needed twenty-four hours to confer with his family and business associates. The next day he left for Washington, where he could learn what he could from the people in the Treasury about the darkening cloud over the banking community.

On his earlier visits to Washington he had occupied a suite with a piano in the Carlton Hotel. I occupied a room adjoining. We spent a great deal of time together, especially after the inauguration, either there or at his office in the Treasury. He no longer had the piano, but had brought his guitar. This he would play softly while he was wrestling with the perplexities which the Treasury faced in the months that followed.

Since foreign affairs occupied so little attention during the campaign, Roosevelt, so far as I could tell, had given no thought at all to the appointment of a Secretary of State. The first thought about that position came on the day after Roosevelt's election. I was at the Sixty-fifth Street house clearing up some loose ends with Roosevelt when Colonel Edward M. House was ushered in to offer his congratulations. House, whose close associations with Woodrow Wilson until their break at the Versailles Peace Conference were a matter of national interest, had been living in quasi retirement. During the campaign he wrote long letters to Roosevelt, replete with all sorts of advice. Roosevelt turned them over to me to read, remarking on one occasion that House was "right about 50 per cent of the time." I found his suggestions only mildly interesting. In 1933 he had reached the age of seventy-five and in his manner seemed much older. His mission that day after the election was to suggest that Roosevelt appoint as Secretary of State Robert W. Bingham, proprietor of the Louisville *Courier-Journal* and a liberal donor to the Roosevelt cause. No doubt, House saw in such an appointment an opportunity in the twilight of his life to be once more a man behind the scenes (with plenty of visibility) in a Democratic Administration. Roosevelt seemed to dismiss the suggestion and only referred to it casually a month later.*

* Apparently there were close ties between House and Bingham. Some weeks later Bingham came to Warm Springs to talk with Roosevelt. He invited me to join him in his car when he returned to Atlanta. While we were discussing a number of things during the trip, Bingham took pains to extol House as a provider of rich and wise advice. He also took occasion to warn me against the influence of Bernard Baruch. He said that Baruch had been responsible in Paris for the final break between House and Wilson. I made no comment on that information, for I knew quite well from many sources the reasons why Wilson had lost confidence in House. I knew also that there had never been friendly relations between Baruch and House. Baruch always referred to the diminutive Texan as "Colonel Mouse." Bingham, as I came to know him later, had an obsession for palace intrigue. In his book of reminiscences, *The Public Years* (New York: Holt, Rinehart and Winston, 1960), pp. 141–45, Baruch discloses his low estimate of House as well as the story of why

In the early evening of December 12, in the governor's residence in Albany, the President-elect discussed with me his tentative ideas about a Secretary of State. The following is an account of that conversation as I wrote of it in 1939 in my book *After Seven Years*. In every respect it checks with my memory now:

> He talked desultorily of the qualifications of Senators Key Pittman, Cordell Hull, and Joe Robinson; of Newton Baker, Owen Young, Bernie Baruch, and Robert W. Bingham of Louisville. It was clear he had come to no final decision. But there were indications that he had already eliminated most of these men from serious consideration. Baruch could be better used elsewhere, he felt. Joe Robinson was needed as Senate leader. Robinson's supreme desire was a Court appointment, in any case. Baker simply wouldn't do. Pittman he liked, but Pittman would emerge as chairman of the Committee on Foreign Relations in the Senate if Swanson should come into the Cabinet. As such, his power and influence could be as great as that of the Secretary of State. . . .
>
> Of Hull, he spoke in completely different terms. Hull was Louis Howe's idea, originally, I knew. As far back as 1928 Louis had told me of his boundless admiration for him in explaining why he thought Hull would be the perfect candidate for Vice President on the Democratic ticket that year. All through the spring and early summer of 1932 he'd overlooked no opportunity to speak well of Hull, who had been influential among the Southern party leaders in supporting Roosevelt for the nomination.
>
> The effect of this was cumulative. By August, when Hull's name first came up in conversation between us (this was at the time F. D. R. sent out his letter about me to the elder statesmen of the party), Roosevelt was unconsciously using Louis's very words to describe his own feelings about Hull. He spoke of Hull's dignity and his high-mindedness. This was repeated on the December night we talked of Cabinet possibilities, with the added comment that Hull's appointment would be pleasing to the old-line party leaders. There was not the slightest evidence that Roosevelt saw the fundamental conflict between his New Deal and the beliefs of the old Democrats, the basic incongruity of his own program and Hull's Adam Smith economics.*

the Wilson-House break became inevitable because of House's general meddling in the affairs of the Peace Conference.

* *After Seven Years,* pp. 111–12. One other incident can be told now, since all of the individuals concerned are dead. In discussing Pittman that evening I said that, while by intelligence and long experience on the Foreign Relations Committee he was well suited for the position, he had the misfortune occasionally to drink to excess. After I pondered my remark on the way to the railroad station that night, I bitterly regretted it. For I was very fond of Pittman and believed that even with his handicap he was better equipped to be Secretary of State than any of the others mentioned except Owen D. Young and Newton D. Baker. I realized then, as always, that such casual suggestions always took deep root in Roosevelt's mind. After reaching the station I immediately took a taxi back to the governor's house and, although Roosevelt was in bed by that time, I told him to dismiss what I had said about Pittman. I am not sure that I had corrected the damage I had done to Pittman's

Of all the men mentioned that evening, only two had the qualifications to be a great Secretary of State, Newton D. Baker and Owen D. Young. I had known Baker personally quite well since his return to Cleveland after Wilson left the White House and for many years before that as a public figure in my home city. In my estimation he was the outstanding member of the Wilson Cabinet. In his mastery of the principles of government, his singular eloquence, and his dedication to the national interest he ranked with Wilson. His dedication to Wilson's policies, especially to the cause of the League of Nations, was one consideration, however, that made him unacceptable to Roosevelt. For Roosevelt wished, above all things, to create his own policies and shape for himself a niche in history. He would have been appalled at the idea that his foreign policies were merely an extension of Wilson's. Certainly, he wanted no one in the State Department whose primary dedication was to a former President. Moreover, Baker, as well as other members of Wilson's high command, had grave doubts about Franklin D. Roosevelt, whom they knew only as a rather young man who had occupied a minor position in the war years. Baker had special reservations about Roosevelt's competence. I have no doubt that he would have declined, even if the appointment had been offered.

Young would have been a towering figure as Secretary of State. From my rather slight acquaintance with him at that time, I knew him to be not only a highly respected corporate executive, but one whose dedication to public interests and wholesome public causes had won him friends and admirers far beyond business circles. He had undertaken the delicate and complicated European negotiations involved in the second debts commission. Since the problems of Europe at that time were economic, and since the United States had a vast stake in them, this would have well served him in the State Department. Moreover, he was well known to European leaders of government and business. So far as political availability was concerned, he qualified. For he was a Democrat. He was the respected friend of Alfred E. Smith and other party leaders. And his appointment in 1924 and 1929 to the Reparations Conference by a Republican Administration indicated the respect which was accorded him by the opposition.

In the months and years which followed the inauguration, I saw and consulted with Young many times. He was a wise and kindly individual whose judgment I always found helpful in making my own personal decisions.

The affection and respect which characterized Louis Howe's attitude toward Young was marked. It is my opinion that Howe would have been happy to have Young as Secretary of State, and this is cor-

chances. However, Pittman was much happier as chairman of Foreign Relations than he would have been as Secretary of State.

roborated by Howe's biographer.* On one occasion during the period in early 1932, when the campaign to nominate Roosevelt was having difficulties, I met Howe as he was taking a taxi in front of his Madison Avenue office. He told me that he was going to see Owen Young. His mission in calling on Young was, he told me, to discuss Young's attitude toward the nomination. For Young's name had been suggested widely in the press and by party leaders. Perhaps as a historian I should not suggest what I cannot prove. But I believe that when Howe saw Young that day he told him that if Roosevelt were nominated he would press Roosevelt to name him Secretary of State. Very shortly after that, Young announced that under no circumstances would he be a candidate for the nomination. This belief of mine was confirmed in January, when Howe told me frankly that Young ought to have the opportunity to refuse or accept the office of Secretary of State. Subsequently, Young made it very clear that, because of the frail health of Mrs. Young, he could not accept a Cabinet position.†

Howe, as I noted earlier, had told me prior to 1932 that he had a very high opinion of Cordell Hull and suggested in 1928 that he would be an excellent choice for Vice-President. In Howe's choices for a Cabinet position, however, he considered Hull for the Commerce Department, not State.

Roosevelt, however, made the final decision. He did not offer the position to Young, and he did offer it to Hull. There were, I am sure from what he said at that time and later, three considerations that threw the balance to Hull. Young was a proven statesman in his own right and would no doubt insist upon measurable independence in conducting foreign affairs. Roosevelt intended to follow the Wilson pattern by being his own foreign minister. Also, he did not want to place the imprint of big business upon his Administration. He did not agree with the orthodoxy of Young's economic views. And most important of all, Young as chairman of General Electric had grave doubts about the development of Federal power projects.

And so, in the Cabinet list given me in January, Hull was slated to be Secretary of State, and when Roosevelt was in Washington on January 19 and 20 he offered the position to Hull. Hull took it under advisement and formally accepted a month later.

On January 22 Roosevelt instructed me over the telephone from Warm Springs to negotiate with "the gentleman from Tennessee" and to keep him informed on developments in foreign affairs. Pursuant to these instructions, I called at Hull's senatorial office. I had met him only

* Alfred B. Rollins, Jr., *Roosevelt and Howe* (New York: Alfred A. Knopf, 1962).

† Rollins says (p. 373), "Louis also played a dangerous game with this most important of posts by using it to pay a political debt. Owen D. Young was given to understand that *he* could be Secretary of State."

once before, at the meeting of party leaders with Roosevelt in New York on January 5. I noted at that time that he said very little. At our second meeting I was impressed by his apparent kindliness. I recorded this in my notebook after the meeting: "C. H.—Lack of frankness due to kindness of heart—humility—lack of confidence in self."

I told Hull that Roosevelt had asked me to bring him up to date on debt and other developments. His few comments indicated neither agreement nor disagreement. We did not discuss the tariff, although the subject must have been on the minds of both of us. During the campaign I had, with Roosevelt's approval, sent Charles Taussig, a friend of Adolf Berle and other members of the Brains Trust, to Tennessee to talk over with Hull what Roosevelt's position should be on the tariff. Since this was a subject in which Hull's almost fanatical dedication was well known, I realized that his views might not be accepted by Roosevelt. But Roosevelt's affectionate regard for the Senator required the gesture. Taussig came back with the draft of a statement on the subject which he brought to me in California. Since in the course of the campaign Roosevelt said little about the tariff except to condemn the Smoot-Hawley measure of 1931 and ultimately disclaimed any specific efforts to reduce rates, there is no doubt that Hull was disappointed. He isolated himself from the campaign and remained at home in Tennessee until after the election.

There are few secrets in the Senate, and the news that Hull was under consideration for Secretary of State was widely rumored. And so in the course of the next few days five Democratic Senators told me to inform Roosevelt that they considered it inadvisable to appoint Hull as Secretary of State. Two of them suggested that he might be suited to the Treasury because of his experience in the House with fiscal policy. Others said that Hull was interested only in the tariff and had a limited comprehension of foreign affairs. One of them said, "Why, it's an open secret that he has only one string to his bow. And every time he makes his speech on tariffs, he clears the floor of the Senate." All said that Hull could not handle men well. Four of these Senators were Glass, Swanson, Walsh of Montana, and Pittman. The fifth is still living and must be unnamed here.

This was ticklish business for me. I told all of them that I would merely communicate their judgment to Roosevelt with no comment of my own. But the Senators who had raised the question about Hull were distinguished members of the Democratic Party, and three of them had been on Roosevelt's tentative list for Cabinet appointments. To prevent any misunderstanding, I called Roosevelt on the telephone at Warm Springs on January 31, with one of the objecting Senators in the room with me. Roosevelt listened to the report and gave this answer, "Well, you tell the Senators that I will be glad to have some fine idealism in the State Department." *

There remained for me to conduct the negotiations with Hull and to iron out any reservations he had toward accepting the appointment. I went to Warm Springs on February 1 and returned to Washington on the sixth, after traveling to Jacksonville with Roosevelt. In Washington on February 8 I had another conference with Hull pursuant to Roosevelt's order to "get a definite answer from Hull."

It was first necessary to resolve my doubts about the position to which Roosevelt intended to appoint me in the State Department. I told Hull that Roosevelt intended me to serve as assistant secretary of state and to work directly with the President on all matters to which he might assign me. This seemed to be possible because there were no statutory duties assigned to that particular position. I felt that I should have a clear understanding with Hull on this point. In his answer he was completely agreeable to the arrangement. But in his memoirs years later he wrote that he was "not enthusiastic about this sort of appointment." If that were true, Hull might have saved himself, Roosevelt, and me a great deal of later embarrassment by frankly telling me about his doubts. For I realized the dangers myself.

He made it clear that he would accept on two conditions: he did not intend, if he accepted, to concern himself with the administrative machinery of the department but wanted to devote himself exclusively to policy; and he did not want to do a lot of entertaining and to go out except very infrequently to dinners and other quasi-social affairs. This reservation about entertaining and being entertained was, he said, because he was a man of very modest means and also because he disliked such affairs. I promised to consult both Roosevelt and Howe and get assurances from the President-elect.

After talking with Howe, I dispatched this joint message by wireless to Roosevelt: "FURTHER CONFERENCE ON TENNESSEE PROJECT INDICATES POSSIBILITY OF ADOPTION PROVIDING SOME OTHER FOOD SUPPLYING AND CONSUMING MEANS CAN BE FOUND. LUHOWRAY."

The "other food supplying and consuming means," Louis said would be his choice for undersecretary, William Phillips of Boston, an old Roosevelt friend and an experienced foreign-service officer. Apparently Phillips would also handle the administration of the department as well.

Throughout February, Hull and I conferred often, and Hull began to take part in discussions about the debts and the projected monetary and economic conference with the British and French Ambassadors.

In all these conversations and negotiations there was not the slightest

* This account is recorded in my diary as of January 31, 1933. And my comment at the end is, "Well, that apparently is that."

evidence that Roosevelt was cognizant of a fundamental conflict between his New Deal, which emphasized a domestic approach to recovery, and Hull's devotion to tariff reduction as a means for universal economic prosperity and prevention of warfare. Throughout his political career on the national level, Hull had been preoccupied with this single concept. Now, in the midst of the depression, "economic disarmament and military disarmament" seemed to Hull to be the "two most vital and outstanding factors for peace and business recovery." Thus, in a statement on December 4, 1932, he proposed a truce on further tariff increases and a horizontal reduction of 10 per cent on all permanent tariff rates.*

Ernest K. Lindley keenly analyzed the situation in his *The Roosevelt Revolution:* "If he [Hull] had been a college professor, the gentlemen of the brains trust would have shunned him as they shunned many of their professorial colleagues who had only one formula." †

Hull's approach to economic problems was completely contrary to the proposed New Deal policy of placing emphasis on domestic recovery. Even worse, it was grossly naïve, considering the relative insignificance of foreign trade. In his *Memoirs* (I, p. 159) Hull reports: "We did not discuss foreign affairs to see whether we agreed in our attitudes toward them," on the ground that neither he nor Roosevelt felt the need to do so. That need would become obvious in the spring and summer of 1933.

With Hull's acceptance and the announcement of his selectees by Roosevelt after his return from his cruise in February, the task of Cabinet-making was almost finished.

It was apparent from the beginning that the Interior Department would be most important in implementing the policies to which Roosevelt had committed himself. Roosevelt was anxious that his Administration, like that of T. R., should concern itself with the public interest in the vast Federal properties in the West and promote reclamation, conservation, and river-basin development. Moreover, since both Presidents Taft and Coolidge had been afflicted with bitter controversies over their Interior secretaries, the individual selected must be very capable in protecting the public against private exploitation. It seemed also that someone who had been connected with T. R.'s Progressive movement was most desirable for this position.

Roosevelt's first choice was Senator Hiram Johnson, who told Roosevelt that he could not accept and would prefer to remain in the Senate. A second choice was Senator Bronson Cutting of New Mexico, a Repub-

* *The Memoirs of Cordell Hull,* Vol. I (New York: Macmillan, 1948), p. 155.

† Ernest K. Lindley, *The Roosevelt Revolution: First Phase* (New York: Viking Press, 1933), p. 179.

lican who had supported Roosevelt. And Roosevelt instructed me to negotiate with Cutting while he was absent on his cruise.

Cutting at that time was one of the most unusual and interesting figures in public life. He was a member of a very wealthy Eastern family. Like Roosevelt, he was a product of Groton and Harvard. He contracted pulmonary tuberculosis in 1910 and went to Santa Fe seeking recovery. After a long illness he recovered and decided to remain in New Mexico and enter politics. His wealth and political acumen enabled him to build a powerful political machine there. He was appointed to fill an unexpired term in the Senate in 1927 and was elected in 1928.

I had two long conferences with Cutting in early February. We had something in common, for I had gone to New Mexico for my own health in 1909 and was there when he came, although we had never met before these negotiations began. He was a reticent and inarticulate man who listened to my arguments but said little in reply. One stated reason for refusing the appointment was his love of New Mexico and his apprehension that the heavy obligations of an administrative office in Washington might stir up his old lung infection. But another reason, which was left to my inference, was a basic distrust of Roosevelt—in some degree a sharing of the reservations which were so common in the Eastern social and economic circles to which Cutting had belonged in his earlier years. Later this flared into opposition to a number of Roosevelt's policies. A healthy mutual dislike grew up between them. And in 1934 Roosevelt gave quiet support to Dennis Chavez, who opposed Cutting's re-election. The returns were close and there was a contest. (In the New Mexico of those days, largely because of the strange mixture of races, corruption was widespread.) In returning to his state to direct his side of that contest, Cutting was killed in an airplane crash. Chavez was subsequently appointed and elected.*

Cutting's final refusal of Cabinet membership left the Interior appointment open until the inauguration was very close.

The selection of Harold Ickes for the Interior Department was the outcome of a series of circumstances that had nothing at all to do with Cabinet-making. After our experience during the period in which Norman Davis was prominent, Roosevelt and I decided that two people should be selected to help with the foreign debts and with preparations for the international economic conference which was scheduled for June. We did not want anyone who might be influenced by the international banking community. And we were quite aware that the bureaucracies

* Senators close to Cutting, including Robert M. La Follette and Hiram Johnson, bitterly resented Roosevelt's part in covertly supporting the candidacy of Chavez and thus making necessary the trip which ended in Cutting's death. This tragedy, coupled with other factors, contributed to the alienation of Johnson, La Follette, and other progressive Senators from Roosevelt.

of the State and Treasury departments were especially hospitable to those influences from New York. And so Roosevelt suggested that I consult three progressive Republican Senators, Hiram Johnson, La Follette, and Cutting, and ask them to suggest two competent persons to take on this assignment.

In response to my request, Cutting called me from Washington and said that he and his colleagues had decided upon former Senator John J. Blaine, a La Follette man from Wisconsin, and Harold Ickes, a Chicago lawyer who had been a strong supporter of T. R. during the Progressive days twenty years before.

I discussed this with Louis Howe, and he growled in his characteristic way, "There isn't any such name as Ickes. There must be some mistake." But there was such a man and I reached him on the telephone. I asked him to come to New York for conferences on the subjects on February 21. I met him at the Roosevelt Hotel and took him up to meet Roosevelt at the Sixty-fifth Street house. There I introduced him to Roosevelt. He had actively supported Roosevelt in Chicago during the 1932 campaign and he had wanted the job of Indian Affairs commissioner.

There was a morning conference at Roosevelt's home on the debts and the forthcoming economic conference, attended by Baruch and others. I did not attend this, but arranged with Ickes to meet him in the afternoon at his hotel to give him a briefing on the two subjects involved in his assignment.

When I returned to the Sixty-fifth Street house early that afternoon, Roosevelt in a puckish mood said, "Well, I have got a Secretary of the Interior. It is Ickes."

He explained that after he had met Ickes in the morning he had called Hiram Johnson and asked him again to accept the Cabinet post. Johnson again declined. Then, in response to Roosevelt's inquiry about Ickes, Johnson expressed approval. This satisfied Roosevelt, and he had made the offer to Ickes and received his acceptance after the morning conference and before noon.

I thereupon called Ickes and, since he was not to continue his interest in international affairs, I canceled our afternoon conference and suggested that he come to the Roosevelt home after dinner that evening.

Roosevelt made no comment about his sudden decision to have Ickes in his Cabinet other than the comment, "I liked his jib."

When I went to the Roosevelt home that evening about eight o'clock, Ickes was in the reception room. On the other side of the room Frances Perkins sat in silence. I said to them that I would like to introduce the Secretary of the Interior to the Secretary of Labor.

This, I surmise, was one of the most casual appointments to a Cabinet position in American history.

The long tenure of Ickes in the Interior Department was colorful and newsworthy. He was so ostentatiously honest that he recalled Disraeli's comment that Gladstone was "honest in the most odious sense of the word." His suspicions, however, were such a fixation that one might be inclined to suspect that he believed honesty was of his own invention and that official integrity would die with him. He was not so honest, however, in what he wrote in his diaries, which appeared after his death in three large volumes. They were to be so "secret" that he required the stenographers who took the dictation to destroy their notes in his presence. Probably in more primitive times he would have required even more assurance by executing the stenographers. What was published is a hodge-podge of gossip, much of which had no foundation in fact, rumors, personal hatreds, his own unending vendettas, and bald suspicions.

Chapter Seven

The Inaugural Address

I have always resented the characterization of my service to Roosevelt as that of a "speech writer." Even more odious is the expression "ghost writer." For there is suggested by such expressions something fictitious, phony, shabby—even dishonest—when a man in high authority and vested with great responsibility delegates to someone else the writing of the expressions he presents to the public as his own. There were only two or three occasions during our long association from 1928 to 1936 when Roosevelt delivered any comments or speeches that were exclusively of my own composition. And on those occasions the matter of the speech was not consequential and there were limitations on time and opportunity for the careful collaboration which characterized our normal relationship.

Any suggestion that I wrote the words and Roosevelt delivered them is a reflection upon both of us. Roosevelt was a man who knew what he wanted to say, who was an incomparable judge of public psychology and a master of timing. With such a person as the principal, no one could have "ghost written" the exact words to fit his purposes. Nor would I have been a party to such make-believe. I had my own reputation to consider. I was no weaver of fancy phrases to fit whoever might call for such confections. If I had not believed in Roosevelt's objectives, I could not have participated. I was concerned with winning the election and then with redeeming the promises of the campaign.

As organizer and director of our policy group in 1932 I was a participant in shaping policies. This meant putting meaning and purpose into whatever the candidate and later the President said. When it came to writing speeches, they were written with, rather than for, him. They had to represent his convictions. He had to feel at home with what he read. And the only way to achieve that was to have him participate in the composition of the text.

Roosevelt was not a good extemporaneous speaker, as were Woodrow Wilson, Newton D. Baker, and, of course, Churchill. They had been trained in the law courts, legislative bodies, or, in Wilson's case, in the classroom. Roosevelt had no such training. But he was matchless in reading a manuscript. Indeed, his virtuosity was so great that in reading he brought out meanings by inflection and emphasis that those who had helped in the writing never realized were there.

The procedure Roosevelt and I had developed in 1932 began with a preliminary discussion of subject matter, arrangement, and emphasis. Then I would prepare a draft, borrowing freely from the materials and ideas contributed by members of my group. At a favorable moment Roosevelt and I would review this text, and he would interpolate his suggestions in pencil. If a passage seemed too long, he would write "boil" in the margin. Words that came more easily to him would be substituted for some of my own. A new idea would be noted for development.

After that I would rewrite the draft, incorporating his suggestions. Then he would repeat the process of examination and correction. When time allowed I would do still another draft. By this time the product was in reality a joint composition. Finally he would read the final draft slowly and carefully to familiarize himself with the phraseology and content. By this time he could assuredly feel the speech to be his own.

I can best explain this process of collaboration by describing in some detail how the first inaugural address was conceived and written. Unlike the preparation of most of the campaign and other speeches of the years up to 1936, the development of this address extended over a considerable period of time. Otherwise its composition was our standard practice.

It originated in Roosevelt's suite in the Palace Hotel in San Francisco late at night on September 22 and in the early hours of the twenty-third. It had been a hard day beginning at the Oregon border at dawn. The weather in the valley coming down was very hot and the train was unusually crowded with local politicians, newspapermen, and others. There had been an element of strain among those close to Roosevelt because he had brushed aside the advice of his political advisers, largely based upon political superstition, to skip California. That fear of bad luck in California arose from the unfortunate experience of Charles Evans Hughes, who had lost the election in 1916 because of miscalculations in that state. Above all, we realized that Hiram Johnson, the beloved native son of the state, must be brought to the support of Roosevelt. This made it necessary that a speech be prepared during the morning for delivery at Sacramento in the afternoon. I wrote one, including in it a glowing tribute to the Senator. It was delivered in the state capital in hundred-degree temperature. Then, on our way to the bay, Pittman and I went over a proposed draft of a speech prepared by Adolf Berle, which Roosevelt planned to deliver in San Francisco. But time allowed only a few changes.

The parade up Market Street was enveloped in a suffocating crowd. During and after dinner Roosevelt's suite was crowded with politicians, well-wishers, and old friends. My concern while this was going on was to get some time alone with Roosevelt to go over and edit the speech he would deliver the next day.

But when the last of the visitors left, William Gibbs McAdoo came bustling in, in that officious manner so characteristic of the man. He always wanted something that could only be gotten in private. And when he saw me he blurted out that he wanted to speak with Roosevelt—"alone." This, so far as I can remember, was the first such eviction I had received in the many months of the campaign. I left and went to my room down the hall. No doubt to give McAdoo some of his own medicine, Roosevelt presently sent the transplanted Californian to my room with an invitation to join the "Governor."

When I entered, Roosevelt ordered the telephone cut off and, after removing the heavy braces from his legs, settled down to work with me. I read the Berle draft, which was scheduled for the Commonwealth Club on the twenty-third, and with little or no change it was laid aside for copying the next day.

Roosevelt was always best late at night, and despite the strenuous day his incredible energy buoyed him up. His Western trip had assured him that the election was substantially won. He was anxious not to discuss the campaign but to reflect upon what he might say when he was inaugurated more than five months later.

He said the situation he would face could be likened to an emergency no less serious than war. The economy, he assumed, could not recover during the winter months, with a defeated Administration still in office and a divided Congress, half Republican and half Democratic, lingering on during a lame-duck session.

He would have to contend with a badly stricken and confused population. But nothing should be said by him to lessen the public's impression of the critical realities. They had already heard too much of optimistic preachment. On the other hand, the spirit of the people must not be further weakened by discouragement and despair. All must work voluntarily with the new Administration for recovery.

At that, I introduced the word "discipline," which seemed to me appropriate to a crisis as serious as war. This word was to find its way into the final draft of the inaugural speech.

This mixture of warning and of assurance must be strongly expressed in the speech. The new Administration must provide an example of positive and expeditious action.

Roosevelt commented then that there should be concentrated authority in Washington to create the impression of firmness and that the Presidential power should be freely used just as it had been used by Lincoln and others before Roosevelt in moments of crisis. Yes, there should be a strong show of executive leadership, for Congress should not be permitted to bicker and delay.

Further, there should be something to remind people of the strong fiber of their tradition.

It is most unfortunate that there could be no record of those three hours of conversation. I hesitated to take notes, for if some of these declared purposes should reach the opposition there would be dangerous cries of dictatorship. But these comments, as I recall them here, show clearly that the attitude and policies and utterances of Roosevelt in 1933 were not merely improvised at the time.

It must have been two o'clock when I ventured to break the spell. We were both worn out and there was a hard day ahead. I suggested that Roosevelt get some sleep, and I grimly reminded him that this Presidential suite might well be the place where Warren G. Harding had passed away nine years before.

We had little discussion about the inaugural speech during the months that followed, but the general tone of what he wanted remained with me. For what he said that night was to be the theme and import of his inaugural address.

During my stay in Warm Springs from February 1 to February 3, 1933, so many other subjects had to be discussed that there was no time until the night we left to consider the inaugural address. Roosevelt was preparing for the cruise on Vincent Astor's yacht and I was being charged with negotiations with several Cabinet possibilities and other responsibilities. But when we were on the train bound for Jacksonville after dinner on February 3, we resumed the subject that had been discussed in September. Edward J. Flynn and I joined Roosevelt in his room.*

Flynn's account of that evening with Roosevelt is told in his book, *You're the Boss* (p. 124):

* Flynn intended to go to Coral Gables after leaving Jacksonville, and I was bound for Palm Beach, where Joseph Kennedy had invited me for a stay of two or three days.

I accompanied Roosevelt as far as Jacksonville, and en route Ray Moley and I sat with him in his drawing room. Here he dictated the suggestions of what he wanted in his first inaugural address. The notes were then turned over to Moley for elaboration and editing.

As we talked that night about the speech, I made notes of Roosevelt's suggestions. Each point was discussed freely among the three of us. Flynn made some suggestions, for he was not only Roosevelt's most reliable and trusted strategist but a widely read and thoughtful individual. His sense of the mood of the public was his most remarkable gift.

The next morning I elaborated in my notebook at some length the ideas I had written down when we were together the previous evening.

world scale (3
— action necessary
In getting this
action must get
orderly carrying
as govt was
intended to
function &
but if govt
especially in
legislative function
necessary to initiate
these new
undertakings
either fails or
delays — then
there is but 1
recourse & that
is to reorganize

emergency & to (4
give wide & clear
cut — even tho
temporary authority
to executive to put
changes into
effect — in other
words I shall
propose to the Congress
a program designed
to meet the necessities
of the emergency — born
of it — I shall ask
the Congress to enact
this program or a
program of their own
choosing which
shall be equally
all inclusive

& equally sound — (5
But in the event
that the congress
shall fail to take
1 of these 2 courses
& in the event
that at at that
time the national
emergency is still
critical I shall
ask Cong for the 1
remaining remedy
temporary but
broad executive
powers to
conduct a war
against the world
emergency just

as great as the (6
powers that would
be given in one
invaded by a foreign
foe —
It will be my aim
to in carrying out
all normal & all
emergency administrative
functions & executive
powers to return
the country to many
fundamentals which
in a mere age of
money making have
been conveniently
forgotten — I refer
to such things as
[illegible] —

7

1. / insistence on an admin of justice without favor to the rich—

2. / the observance of laws & in the repeal of laws—proven un workable

3. / restoration of the balance of our population—by encouraging unemployable millions in industrial centers to become self sustaining on the land

8

4. Govt assistance to prevent farm owners & home owners from being dispossessed by REFORMING their debts & readjusting their interest obligations

5. National planning & supervision of all transportation—in order to readjust its capitalization—eliminate waste & provide good service;

6. National supervision of all other utilities of an interstate

9

character esp. electric power & telephones to prevent exorbitant rates—

7. Strict supervision of all national banking & natl. credit to prevent recurrence of speculation & loss of depositors money;

8 Cutting costs of operating units of Fed & State & municipal govt & greatly

10

corp—thereby reducing taxes—

Unttanamuu here—national program of this the practice not merely patched up by only emergency—but will also place the U S under stable on a sound economic basis—regardless of what may be the immediate developments of world events

After I returned to New York, I set aside two days—Sunday, February 12 and Monday, February 13—for concentrated work on a first draft of the address. I worked, as I generally did when in New York, in my small office at Barnard College. Two assistants who had worked with me for two years, Celeste Jedel and Annette Pomeranz, worked there with me on the second day. The latter, in addition to other qualifications, was an exceedingly competent stenographer. I never dictated anything but letters, however, since my habit over the years confined me in drafting speeches and articles to longhand, usually on legal size, perforated tablets.

I have in my papers the outlines, phrases, and what I call sketches of ideas that preceded the drafting of a connected composition. After I finished the first draft, Miss Pomeranz copied it on the old office typewriter. The longhand draft was destroyed, since I was concerned that visitors and others who frequented the building and my office should not see and thus anticipate the general tenor of the address.

As is obvious, the notes written after the night on the train are random, somewhat disorderly and repetitive. They consist not only of what Roosevelt actually said, but of my own interpretations and also ideas that came to me as we proceeded.

It was my habit to begin the actual composition of a draft by making a tentative and very brief outline. In such an outline I usually indicated how much language, measured by pages, should go into each section. This first outline appears as Exhibit A, on this page and the next.

MEMORANDUM

Exhibit A

1. Sick-ness — 1 page
The sickness-strife all over
2. Failure of us: of old method ½ page
3. 10 points — 1 page
4. Inter-nat ½
5. The good neighbor action needed
6. Dictatorship
7. No failure of Dem —
8. Tribute to people of U.S.
encourage them —

MEMORANDUM

Sick world—
Forged into unity by rings of fire.
A part of this is because *we*
are sick—
The failure of method not of
substance—
The failure of incentives—
The failure of balance—
intra—

No past to ignore—This put
into
good neighbor

To meet w. dictatorial powers.

Following is the text of the outline reproduced above:

1. Sickness— 1 page
   In sickness—strife
2. Failure of us—of all due to
   method—½ page
3. 10 points— 1 page
4. Intra-nat—½
5. The good neighbor
   Action needed
6. Dictatorship
7. No failure of Dem—
8. Tribute to people of U.S.
   encourage them—

Sick world—
Forged into unity by rings of fire—
A part of this is because *we* are sick—
The failure of method not of substance—
The failure of incentives—
The failure of balance—
    intra—
No past to ignore—this put
    into
  good neighbor
To meet w. dictatorial powers—

Then, having developed some order of sequence, I turned to a legal pad and began to compose phrases and expressions of ideas. There are several pages of these sketches, one of which is shown as Exhibit B.

I

The withered leaves of
industrial enterprise
lie on every side.

(1 page)

Sick nation in midst of rich world
Stoppage of business—
Frozen exchange—
Withered enterprises—institutions—
broken—bankrupt

Befuddled leaders—
People
for end
Where there is no vision the people perish.

We

In the heavy air of

II

As the
money changers
were driven
from the
temple—so
it behooves
us to restore
moral values
by driving out
— material
standards.
[last three lines
crossed out
on original]

This failure is due to method—not
substance—no shortage—not failure
of nature—not even of human
nature—but of mechanics & method—
leadership—in the traditional modes of
relief have—the philosophy of
money changers has failed—
—overproduction—
End
Not to be ministered unto but
to minister—
Not to save banks.
—Restore values—
(Equities)

The 10 points—
[Crossed out on original]

It is out of such rough sketches, which help to make the draft to be written later, that order, proportion, and emphasis are worked out. Attractive phrases and words come to mind and are written down.

On other pages of this sort there are expressions such as "action needed," "putting people to work," "the failure—not of substance—not of nature—not even of human nature—but of mechanics—but of leadership of the traditional modes."

Others are "not to be ministered unto but to minister," "the world was made for man—not man for the world," "the larger honesty—in pub affairs—in business—in foreign affairs." "Cannot on private profit motives." The "discredited captains," "the joy of creative workmanship."

I played with another expression because it appears at least three times in these notes. "We in the U.S. are forged into a new unity amid the fire that burns throughout the world." This was discarded as the first draft was written.

The idea of the ten points, which appears in the February notes, was also discarded. It would have marred the effect of the speech.

At the end of a long day, Sunday the twelfth, I developed another outline, which is Exhibit C.

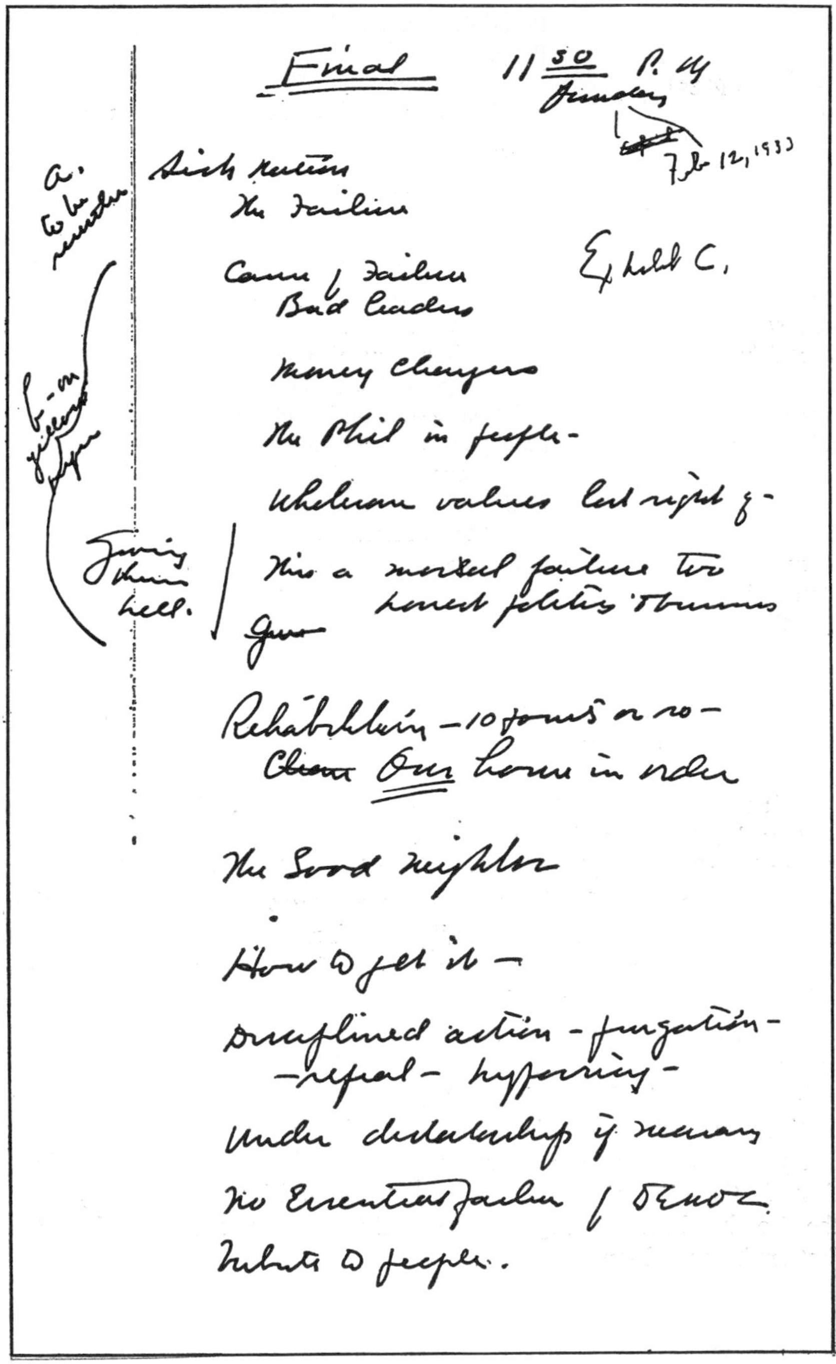

Final 11 30 P.M.
Sunday
Feb 12, 1933

Exhibit C.

a. to be rewritten

Sick nation
The failure

Cause of failure
Bad leaders

Money changers

The Phil in people–

Wholesome values lost sight of–

Giving them hell.

This a moral failure too
honest politics & business

B–on following page

Rehabilitation–10 points or so–
Clean Our house in order

The Good neighbor

How to get it–

Disciplined action–[illegible]–
–repeal– hypocrisy–

Under dictatorship if necessary

No Essential failure of Democ.

Tribute to people.

Here is the text of the final outline reproduced on the preceding page:

Final 11:30 P.M.
Sunday

a to be rewritten	Sick nations The failure
b—on yellow paper Giving them hell	Cause of Failure Bad leaders Money changers The Phil in people— Wholesome values lost sight of— This a moral failure too honest politics & business Rehabilitation—10 points or so— Clean [crossed out] *Our* house in order The Good neighbor How to get it— Disciplined action—purgation— —repeal—hypocrisy— Under dictatorship if necessary No essential failure of democ Tribute to people.

With this beginning, the drafting went on the next day. Miss Pomeranz then copied what I had written. Two of the pages from this draft are shown as Exhibits D and E (on the next two pages).*

* Miss Pomeranz, who is now Mrs. Raymond Gettinger, has verified these pages. The characteristics of the typewriting correspond with copies of my letters written in February.

about Feb 11 / Notes dictated on train by F.D.R. & notes dictated by me on Feb 3. 1933

PART I

America is a sick nation in the midst of a sick world. We are sick because of our failure to recognize economic changes in time, and to make provision against their consequences. For a quarter of a century tremendous developments have taken place. The machine age in this time has moved more rapidly in the direction of replacing men with machinery than in the one hundred years before. We have moved faster in productive capacity not only in agriculture, but to a larger extent in industry than in the entire history of our country. This is only one factor, however, in the present stagnation of enterprise. The means of exchange have become frozen all along the channels of trade. It is time to face the facts and get away from the idea that we can return to conditions that approximate those of four years ago. It is not a restoration of the old that we seek, but an evolution into a new. This evolution must be guided by informed and enlightened thought, with no disposition to reject experimental and tentative efforts merely because they are new and untried. To attempt to rebuild precisely what we had before is to invite the pain and suffering that we incurred in its failure. People registered through their vote their conviction on this question and they have the right to its fulfilment. In achieving these ends, it is necessary, moreover, to bend the entire theory of human progress away from the strivings for private money making, so characteristic of the past. It is necessary to strive to build an incentive far more permanent and humane than mere money making Behind the enterprise that ~~characterizes~~ is called life. In every one of the activities we need the incentive TC.

-5-

sound and genuinely thoughtful internationalism.

This ~~is the world policy~~ of the good neighbor. The good neighbor knows when to mind his own business.

The good neighbor respects the sanctity of his obligations in a world of neighbors. He is not moved or deceived by the unsubstantial and sometimes trivial results of broad pretentions of interrelationships. He is fundamentally concerned with the substance and not the mere form of international associations. He is not a slave to a names.

Basic in the relations of neighbors is respect for the principle that what is lent should be returned. There echos down through the essential and basic history of a contract the idea that the principal, the rem, is of fundamental consequence. The terms may be payment for use by money, by the enjoyment of advantages, by innumerable methods of exchanging value. Good neighbors can meet the emergencies occasioned by differences in methods of providing compensation for the use of principal; but the relations of a world of neighbors are disturbed profoundly when the distinction is lost between a loan and a gift.

From time to time I worked on editing the first draft. On one occasion I tried to develop an insert, which appears as Exhibit F.

Insert A

He resolutely respects himself.
He respects the rights of others. He
~~looks~~ trys to support himself ~~in~~
and in addition
He seeks ~~to not to so~~ so to
order his affairs that he
is ready for emergencies. He
makes provision against the
danger of hard times. He is
not if he can help it a public
charge when the community
falls into depression.

(Part of material prepared for Mar. 4.)

F

Washington's
Weekly
Review

(Insert A)

He resolutely respects himself.
He respects the rights of others. He
looks [crossed out] trys to support himself in [crossed out]
and in addition
He seeks to not to [three words crossed out] so to
order his affairs that he
is ready for emergencies. He
makes provision against the
danger of hard times. He is
not if he can help it a public
charge when the community
falls into depression.

Finally, some time in February another revised draft was copied, and I carried that with me to Hyde Park on February 27. There, that evening, Roosevelt first saw my draft of the speech.

There were very few people at Roosevelt's home that evening. At dinner there were only Marguerite LeHand, a stenographer named Margaret, Roosevelt, and I.

After dinner Roosevelt and I retired to the library at about nine o'clock. He sat in a chair he had used while he was governor of New York, with a folding bridge table before him. He read over my draft carefully and then said that he had better write out the text himself because if Louis Howe (who was expected the next morning) failed to see a draft in his (Roosevelt's) handwriting, he would "have a fit." I then took from my brief case a legal-size tablet for him to use and the drafting began.*

I sat on the long couch before the fireplace, in which a bright fire was burning. Then began a long process of considering every sentence and sometimes every word. We exchanged comment, and from time to time either Roosevelt or I decided upon a change. The copy in his handwriting shows some words crossed out or changed. The discussion and writing went on to the end of my draft. I told him that I had purposely omitted a peroration which, in this address, called for some sort of reference to the Deity. He then wrote: "In this dedication of a Nation we humbly ask the blessing of God. May He guide me in the days to come."

During those hours there were diversions, talk about matters wholly unrelated to the text. At eleven o'clock I took out my notebook and wrote the following:

Feb. 27 Monday evening at 11.

Before the fire in the library at Hyde Park. Alone. w. F. D. R. He is writing inaugural on a card-table. On the table letter from Lamont with direful warning re banks. Will Woodin calls. Cordell Hull calls. Silence. I am lying on couch. Glasses—whiskey for us. More writing. Talk re postal savings bank to care for the people's money. "How do you spell foreclose?"

I have been here since last night almost alone w. him. Everyone happy. Missy, Mac (dressed up) Margaret, 4 of us dined together. Margaret, Missy F. D. R. & I.

A week—yes five days—this man will be Pres. of U.S. Talk of Franklin (he was shallow) Jefferson best. T. R. range of his knowledge Wilson, F. D. R. artistic qualities, etc. Talk w. Taussig. Two

A strong man F. D. R.—

* For reasons that appear later, I have verified this from the handwritten copy now in the Roosevelt Library at Hyde Park. For some years I had been using these tablets. They were made, and still are, by Wilson Jones in Newark. I had been unable to get this kind in New York and I purchased them from time to time from Horders in Chicago. The sheets are lined and are perforated across the top.

Feb 27 — Monday Evening at 11.
Began the first in the library at Hyde Park. Alone w. F.D.R. He is writing inaugural on a card-table. On the table letter from Lamont with dreadful warning re banks. Will Woodin calls. Cordell Hull calls. Silence. [illegible] Glasses — whiskey for us. More writing. Talk of [illegible] [illegible] to [illegible] for the paper's [illegible] money. "How do you spell foreclosure?" I have been here since last night almost alone w. him. Everyone happy

Missy, Mac (dressed up) Margaret. 4 of us dined together. Margaret, Missy, F.D.R. & I.
A week — yes five days — this man will be Pres. of U.S. Talk of Franklin (he was [illegible]) Jefferson best. T.R. [illegible] [illegible] Wilson. F.D.R. artistic qualities, etc. Talk w. Tammany. [illegible]
A strong man F.D.R. —

As this note shows, I was quite aware of the historical significance of this session. And feeling a keen sense that whatever might be the authorship, he and he alone would have to carry the responsibility of what was said on the fateful day of inauguration, I rose after we had finished and, taking my copy from the table, tossed it into the still-glowing embers in the fireplace. I said as I did so, "This is your speech now."

Early the next morning, I went over Roosevelt's handwritten draft, numbering the pages, changing a few words, and making two inserts. These are in my own handwriting in the draft at the library at Hyde Park.

Then, in the morning, as had been anticipated, Howe got his hand into the composition. He proceeded to redictate the draft, adding, as had been his habit on other occasions, a first paragraph. He also measurably tightened up some passages. Apparently he preferred the use of semicolons to my habit and Roosevelt's of using short sentences. This did not mar the continuity, however. Roosevelt in his incomparable manner of reading could manage the necessary emphasis.

It will be noted that in the first paragraph, which Howe added, there appear the words "the only thing we have to fear is fear itself." This was destined to be the most famous phrase in the address. Speculation attributes it to a borrowing from Thoreau. I am sure that neither Howe at that time nor Roosevelt was familiar with Thoreau's passage. I do clearly remember that the phrase appeared in a department store's newspaper advertisement some time earlier in February. I assume that Howe, an inveterate newspaper reader, saw it, too. A somewhat cursory search of newspaper files has failed to verify my recollection of this point. To Howe's everlasting credit, he realized that the expression fully fitted the occasion. It has been pointed out that the expression must be taken figuratively, for there were actually more things to fear than the panic which prevailed at the time.

And that is how the draft stood until March 3, when there was a brief period when Roosevelt and I were alone for a final examination. Roosevelt had told me the night when we had worked on the draft that if Howe made any substantive changes he would restore the original language. We found that, except for the first paragraph and the other changes mentioned above, it stood substantially as it had been written. Roosevelt read it over very carefully in order to familiarize himself with the arrangement and the phraseology. A very few changes were made, and the text was turned over to a trusted typist to make the reading copy.

That reading copy I kept in my possession, for in the confusion that prevailed in Roosevelt's suite there was real danger that some newspaperman might have access to a preview. I well remember that I kept this copy in my jacket pocket, for it was there when I was summoned to the White House on the afternoon of the third for a final conference with Hoover, Mills, and Meyer. That night I placed it carefully under my pillow, and the next morning when Roosevelt left for the inauguration I delivered it to him.*

I have given this history of the inaugural address, which I omitted in *After Seven Years*, for two reasons:

It is the best example of the method of collaboration that Roosevelt and I had developed during the year that preceded it.

* To show the changes made by Howe and by Roosevelt and me after February 27, compare the text beginning p. 121 and the manuscript facing p. 120.

The other reason is the many distortions concerning the origins of this address that have been published in the years since it was delivered. Some of this misunderstanding comes from a note on White House stationery which is attached to Roosevelt's longhand draft now reposing in the library at Hyde Park:

THE WHITE HOUSE
WASHINGTON

March 25, 1933.

This is the original manuscript of the Inaugural Address as written at Hyde Park on Monday, February 27th, 1933. I started in about 9.00 P.M. and ended at 1.30 A.M. A number of minor changes were made in subsequent drafts but the final draft is substantially the same as this original.

Franklin D Roosevelt

****

I was not aware of the existence of this note until 1964, and so in my earlier book *After Seven Years* there is only a casual reference to the inaugural speech. It seemed unnecessary at that time to describe my participation in the preparation of the text of the address, because my function as a collaborator was well known and it was assumed by all close contemporaries that I would be involved in the preparation of this speech. Certainly everybody in the Roosevelt circle knew it and accepted it as natural and essential. I certainly did not know of Roosevelt's note at the time when its date claims it was written.

Some historians accept the note as an indication that on that night of February 27 Roosevelt sat down all alone in his library at Hyde Park and dashed off the draft. Such a concept does not square with the evidence even apart from what I have presented here. For Roosevelt was not in the habit of such extemporary composition. The very care in the organization of the text denies such an interpretation. And the seriousness of such an address precludes the idea that he would trust himself to such a method of preparing what he was to say on such an occasion. Those who accept this hypothesis are certainly not paying Roosevelt a compliment when they contend that the announcement of such portentous policies was determined on a momentary hunch.

The omission of the fact that I was present with him that night and that I had put before him a draft that I had prepared after much consideration and many conferences with him seems strange, especially if Roosevelt's note were written and attached to the draft on the date it bears. For at that moment we were on the most intimate terms, shaping and promoting the legislative measures of the Hundred Days.

The note signed by Roosevelt and dated as I have indicated is, to say the least, misleading. A notable example of those who have speculated about the writing of the address is Samuel I. Rosenman, who during Roosevelt's period in Albany was counsel to the governor and who in later years edited Roosevelt's speeches and public papers. In his book *Working with Roosevelt* Rosenman says that during Roosevelt's first term "my visits to Washington were almost exclusively social." Except for two isolated instances, he says, "I had nothing to do with any of the speeches or messages of the first term." The exceptions were the preparation of the message vetoing the soldiers' bonus in 1935 and helping "polish" the annual message of January 1, 1936. Rosenman then adds his participation in the acceptance speech of 1936. His account of the writing of the inaugural address is almost wholly speculative. He suggests that the inaugural speech "was one of those very few of which the President wrote the first draft in his own hand." As proof of this he cites the note dated March 25, 1933.

He is puzzled about the first paragraph which, as I have indicated, was added by Louis Howe on the morning of February 28 after the long session I had with Roosevelt the night before.

The supposed origin of the phrase "the only thing we have to fear is fear itself" was the subject of wide comment at the time. But since the paragraph that contains the sentence was not in Roosevelt's handwritten draft, Rosenman seems to have been unaware of Howe's addition to the speech. He then indulges in speculation. He says that after he discovered that the sentence was missing from the draft he "inquired of many people who were in a position to know." (He made no such inquiry of me or, apparently, of Howe, whose relations with Rosenman were either strained or non-existent.)

Then, since many people had suggested that Henry David Thoreau had said, "Nothing is so much to be feared as fear," Rosenman had to speculate on how Roosevelt had seen the quotation. Apparently he suggested the Thoreau idea to Mrs. Roosevelt, who claimed that someone had given a copy of some of Thoreau's writings to Roosevelt before the inauguration and that it was in Roosevelt's suite at the Mayflower. This gave Rosenman the idea that the words were inserted at the Mayflower before the inauguration. That is a colorful fancy, but it could not have been true. The "fear" paragraph was added by Howe on February 28.

But mythology grows by what it feeds upon. In a book, *Roosevelt: The Lion and the Fox,* published in 1956, four years after Rosenman's book appeared, the author, James MacGregor Burns, embellished Rosenman's theory as follows:

> The evening of February 27, 1933, at Hyde Park was cloudy and cold. A stiff northwest wind swept across the dark waters of the Hudson and tossed the branches of the gaunt old trees around the Roosevelt home. Inside the warm living room a big thick-shouldered man sat writing by the fire. From the ends of the room two of his ancestors looked down from their portraits: Isaac, who had revolted with his people against foreign rule during an earlier time of troubles, and James, merchant, squire, and gentleman of the old school.
>
> Franklin D. Roosevelt's pencil glided across the pages of yellow legal cap paper. "I am certain that my fellow Americans expect that on my induction into the Presidency I will address them with a candor and a decision which the present situation of our Nation impels." The fire hissed and crackled; the large hand with its thick fingers moved rapidly across the paper. "The people of the United States want direct, vigorous action. They have made me the instrument, the temporary humble instrument"—he scratched out "humble"; it was no time for humility—"of their wishes."
>
> Phrase after phrase followed in the President-elect's bold, pointed, slanting hand. Slowly the yellow sheets piled up. By 1:30 in the morning the inauguration speech was done.*

The Hyde Park manuscript shows that the word "humble" was not scratched out. It remains. The passage Burns has quoted does not exist as he has it. The manuscript reads as follows:

> We do not distrust the future of essential democracy. The people of the United States have not failed. In their need they have registered a mandate that they want direct vigorous action. [word crossed out] They have asked for discipline and direction under [word "vigorous" crossed out] leadership.

* New York: Harcourt, Brace, 1956, p. 161.

They have made me the instrument, the temporary humble instrument of their wishes. In the spirit of the gift I take it.

After a few paragraphs on unrelated subjects, Burns returns to the text of the address, where he seeks to place the origin of the "fear" phrase. Perhaps he noted in reading the handwritten text that this phrase is not there. So he says that on March 2, "In his hotel room Roosevelt worked over the speech. Nearby was a copy of Thoreau, with the words, 'Nothing is so much to be feared as fear.' "

The speculation of Rosenman, Burns, and Mrs. Roosevelt does not fit the facts as I have recited them. I was in Roosevelt's Mayflower suite most of the long waking hours after his arrival in Washington and until the inauguration. I saw no books there. Nor was I familiar with Thoreau. I had been with Roosevelt more than a year and never heard him mention Thoreau. I doubt whether during the many months since he first sought the nomination in the spring of 1932 he had read any book. And Howe, whose reading—which his asthma-provoked insomnia required—was confined exclusively to detective stories and newspapers, may never have heard of Thoreau. Moreover, Thoreau's ideas of civil disobedience cannot have had any appeal to Roosevelt, who proposed not to violate but to change the laws in pursuit of his objectives.* Anyhow, the "fear" expression was in the speech draft before Roosevelt went to Washington.

The great detail of the foregoing is given to provide a basic account of an address that foreshadowed the policies and mood of a new period in our government's history, which was destined greatly to influence the role of Federal authority in the future. A minor justification for its detail is to furnish a lesson in the evolution of an important public document—a story of how ideas develop into outlines and then into a completed prose composition.

History is sometimes made by sudden unpremeditated decisions and actions. But guiding and permanent innovations in public policy are more often the result of long and carefully calculated reasoning. And their announcement to an anxious and attentive nation must or should be made in terms which instruct and enlighten while they inspire and encourage. The care which characterized the composition of this address earned for it the immediate as well as the lasting recognition accorded it by the American people.

* The concept of "fear of fear" has very ancient origins. In one form or another the idea was phrased by the author of the Proverbs, by Epictetus, Cicero, Shakespeare, Bacon, Montaigne, Daniel Defoe, Burke, Lord Chesterfield, and, since Thoreau, by William James. Surely the man who wrote the advertisement where Howe found it was not the originator of the concept.

Draft of the Inaugural Address
in F. D. R.'s Hand,
February 27, 1933

The following pages are reproduced by permission of the Franklin D. Roosevelt Library, Hyde Park, New York.

I am certain that my fellow Americans expect that on my induction to the Presidency I will address them with a candor and a decision which the present situation of our nation impels. This is no occasion for soft speaking or for the raising of false hopes.

In the crisis of our War for Independence, in the poverty, the unrest and the doubts of the early days of constitutional government, in the dark days of the War between the States, a leadership of frankness and vigor has met with that understanding and support of the people themselves which is an essential to victory.

In such a spirit on my part and on yours we recognize our common difficulties. On the side of material things our values have shrunk to fantastic levels. Our taxes have risen; our ability to pay has fallen. Government of all kinds is faced by serious curtailment of income.

The means of exchange are frozen in the currents of trade; the leaves of industrial enterprise lie withered. Farmers find no market for their produce. The savings of many years in thousands of families are gone.

More important, a host of unemployed citizens face the grim problem of existence, and an equally great number toil with little return. Only a foolish optimist can deny the dark reality of the moment.

Our national distress comes from no failure of substance. We are stricken by no plague of locusts. Nature still offers her bounty, and human efforts have multiplied it; but a vast use of it languishes in the very sight of the supply. It is because the rulers of the exchange of mankind's goods have abdicated through their own stubbornness and their own incompetence.

True, they have tried; but their efforts have been lost in the pattern of an outworn tradition. Faced by a failure of credit they have offered only the lending of more money. Faced by failure of the lure of profit, they have resorted to exhortations pleading tearfully for restored confidence. When no response has come they have thrown up their hands.

Where there is no vision the people perish.

The philosophy of the money changers stands indicted in the court of public opinion, rejected by the hearts and minds of men. It is no longer the creed of the temple after many years of civilization. We can proceed
now to restore that temple to the ancient faiths. The measure of the restoration lies in a character of value more noble than mere monetary profit. The moral stimulation of work, the joy of creative effort shall no longer be submerged in the shams of evanescent profits accruing without work. We have rediscovered the truth that our true destiny is not to be ministered unto but to minister to ourselves.

Recognition of this failure of standards goes hand in hand with abandonment of the false gods of place and profit in our politics, with an end to a conduct in banking and in business which too often has given to a sacred trust the likeness of callous and selfish wrongdoing. Small wonder that confidence lags: it thrives only on honesty, on honor, on the sacredness of obligations, on faithful protection, on unselfish performance. Without them it cannot live.

Restoration calls however not for changes in standards alone. The nation asks action and action now.

Our primary task is to put people to work. That can be accomplished in part by direct recruiting by the government itself, treating the task as we would treat the emergency of a war, but at the same time through this employment accomplishing greatly needed projects to stimulate and reorganize our natural resources.

The task can be helped by frank recognition of the overbalance of population in our industrial centers and by engaging on a national scale in a redistribution to provide a better use of the land for those best fitted for the land.

It can be helped by definite efforts to raise the values of agricultural products and with this the power to purchase the output of our cities.

It can be helped by treating realistically the tragedy of the growing loss of our farms and small homes through foreclosure.

It can be helped by insistence that the federal, state and local governments act forthwith on the demand that their cost be drastically reduced.

It can be helped by the unifying of relief activities which today are often scattered, unequal and uneconomical.

So too we can accomplish much by national planning for and supervision of all forms of transportation, and of communications and other utilities which have a definitely public character.

Finally in our progress towards a resumption of work we require two safeguards against a return of the evils of the old order: a strict supervision of all banking and credits and investments; an end to speculation with other people's money; and provision for adequate but sound currency.

These are the lines of attack. I shall presently urge upon the new Congress in special session detailed measures for their fulfillment; and I shall seek the immediate assistance of the several States.

Through this program of action we address ourselves to putting our own national house in order. ~~Vastly important~~ Our international trade relations, though vastly important, are in point of time and necessity secondary to the establishment of a sound national economy. I favor as a practical policy the putting of first things first. I shall spare no effort to restore world trade by international economic readjustment, but the emergency at home cannot wait on that accomplishment.

The basic thought that guides the foregoing specific means of national recovery is not narrowly nationalistic in its purpose. It is an insistence, ~~~~ as a first consideration, upon the interdependence of the various elements in and parts of the United States — a recognition of the old and permanently important manifestation of the American spirit of the pioneer. It is the way to recovery. It is the immediate way. It is the strongest assurance that the recovery will ~~be~~ endure.

7

In the field of world policy I would dedicate this nation to the policy of the good neighbor — the neighbor who resolutely respects himself and because he does so respects the rights of others — the neighbor who respects his obligations and respects the sanctity of his agreements in and with a world of neighbors.

Our people, now inured to hardship and suffering, do not fear the rigors of discipline. They are, I know, ready and willing to submit their lives and property to a discipline which aims clearly and honestly at a larger good. This I propose to offer them, pledging to them that the larger purposes will bind upon us all as a sacred obligation, with a unity of duty hitherto evoked only in time of armed strife.

With this pledge taken, I assume unhesitatingly the sword of leadership of an army dedicated to a disciplined attack upon our common problems.

Action in this image and to this end is feasible under the form of government which we have inherited from our ancestors. Our Constitution is so simple and practical that it is possible always to meet extraordinary needs by changes in emphasis and arrangement without loss of essential form. That is why our constitutional system has proved itself the most superbly enduring political mechanism the modern world has produced. It has met every stress of vast expansion of territory, of foreign wars, of bitter internal strife, of world relations.

It is to be hoped that the normal balance of executive and legislative authority may be wholly adequate to meet the unprecedented task before us. But it may be that an unprecedented demand and need for undelayed action may ~~[illegible]~~ call for temporary departure from that normal balance of public procedure. ¶ I am prepared under my constitutional duty to indicate the measures that a stricken nation in the midst of a stricken world may require. These measures, or such other measures as the Congress may build out of their experience and wisdom, I shall, within my constitutional authority, seek to bring to speedy adoption. ¶ But in the event that the Congress should fail to take one of these two courses, and in the event that the national emergency is still critical, I shall not ~~[illegible]~~ evade. or quit. I shall ask the Congress for the one remaining instrument to meet the crisis — broad executive power to wage a war against the ~~[illegible]~~ emergency as great as the power that would be given me if we were ~~[illegible]~~ in fact invaded by a foreign foe.

For the trust reposed in me I shall return the courage and the devotion that befits the time. I can do no less.

We do not distrust the future of essential democracy. The people of the United States have not failed. In their need they have registered a mandate that they want direct vigorous action. ~~[illegible]~~ They have asked for discipline and direction under ~~[illegible]~~ leadership. They have made me the instrument, the temporary humble instrument of their wishes. In the spirit of the gift I take it.

We face the arduous days that lie before us in the warm courage of national unity; with the clear consciousness of seeking old and precious moral values; with the clean satisfaction that comes from the stern performance of duty by old and young alike. We aim at the assurance of a rounded and permanent national life.

In this dedication of a nation we humbly ask the blessing ~~and the guidance~~ of God. May he protect each and every one of us. May he guide me in the days to come.

Franklin D Roosevelt

The Inaugural Address, March 4, 1933

I am certain that my fellow Americans expect that on my induction into the Presidency I will address them with a candor and a decision which the present situation of our Nation impels. This is preeminently the time to speak the truth, the whole truth, frankly and boldly. Nor need we shrink from honestly facing conditions in our country today. This great Nation will endure as it has endured, will revive and will prosper. So, first of all, let me assert my firm belief that the only thing we have to fear is fear itself—nameless, unreasoning, unjustified terror which paralyzes needed efforts to convert retreat into advance. In every dark hour of our national life a leadership of frankness and vigor has met with that understanding and support of the people themselves which is essential to victory. I am convinced that you will again give that support to leadership in these critical days.

In such a spirit on my part and on yours we face our common difficulties. They concern, thank God, only material things. Values have shrunken to fantastic levels; taxes have risen; our ability to pay has fallen; government of all kinds is faced by serious curtailment of income; the means of exchange are frozen in the currents of trade; the withered leaves of industrial enterprise lie on every side; farmers find no markets for their produce; the savings of many years in thousands of families are gone.

More important, a host of unemployed citizens face the grim problem of existence, and an equally great number toil with little return. Only a foolish optimist can deny the dark realities of the moment.

Yet our distress comes from no failure of substance. We are stricken by no plague of locusts. Compared with the perils which our forefathers conquered because they believed and were not afraid, we have still much to be thankful for. Nature still offers her bounty and human efforts have multiplied it. Plenty is at our doorstep, but a generous use of it languishes in the very sight of the supply. Primarily this is because rulers of the exchange of mankind's goods have failed through their own stubbornness and their own incompetence, have admitted their failure, and have abdicated. Practices of the unscrupulous money changers stand indicted in the court of public opinion, rejected by the hearts and minds of men.

True they have tried, but their efforts have been cast in the pattern of an outworn tradition. Faced by failure of credit they have proposed only the lending of more money. Stripped of the lure of profit by which to induce our people to follow their false leadership, they have resorted to exhortations, pleading tearfully for restored confidence. They know only the rules of a generation of self-seekers. They have no vision, and when there is no vision the people perish.

The money changers have fled from their high seats in the temple of our civilization. We may now restore that temple to the ancient truths. The measure of the restoration lies in the extent to which we apply social values more noble than mere monetary profit.

Happiness lies not in the mere possession of money; it lies in the joy of achievement, in the thrill of creative effort. The joy and moral stimulation of work no longer must be forgotten in the mad chase of evanescent profits. These dark days will be worth all they cost us if they teach us that our true destiny is not to be ministered unto but to minister to ourselves and to our fellow men.

Recognition of the falsity of material wealth as the standard of success goes hand in hand with the abandonment of the false belief that public office and high political position are to be valued only by the standards of pride of place and personal profit; and there must be an end to a conduct in banking and in business which too often has given to a sacred trust the likeness of callous and selfish wrongdoing. Small wonder that confidence languishes, for it thrives only on honesty, on honor, on the sacredness of obligations, on faithful protection, on unselfish performance; without them it cannot live.

Restoration calls, however, not for changes in ethics alone. This Nation asks for action, and action now.

Our greatest primary task is to put people to work. This is no unsolvable problem if we face it wisely and courageously. It can be accomplished in part by direct recruiting by the Government itself, treating the task as we would treat the emergency of a war, but at the same time, through this employment, accomplishing greatly needed projects to stimulate and reorganize the use of our natural resources.

Hand in hand with this we must frankly recognize the over-balance of population in our industrial centers and, by engaging on a national scale in a redistribution, endeavor to provide a better use of the land for those best fitted for the land. The task can be helped by definite efforts to raise the values of agricultural products and with this the power to purchase the output of our cities. It can be helped by preventing realistically the tragedy of the growing loss through foreclosure of our small homes and our farms. It can be helped by insistence that the Federal, State, and local governments act forthwith on the demand that their cost be drastically reduced. It can be helped by the unifying of relief activities which today are often scattered, uneconomical, and unequal. It can be helped by national planning for and supervision of all forms of transportation and of communications and other utilities which have a definitely public character. There are many ways in which it can be helped, but it can never be helped merely by talking about it. We must act and act quickly.

Finally, in our progress toward a resumption of work we require two safeguards against a return of the evils of the old order: there must be a strict supervision of all banking and credits and investments, so that there will be an end to speculation with other people's money; and there must be provision for an adequate but sound currency.

These are the lines of attack. I shall presently urge upon a new Congress, in special session, detailed measures for their fulfillment, and I shall seek the immediate assistance of the several States.

Through this program of action we address ourselves to putting our own national house in order and making income balance outgo. Our international trade relations, though vastly important, are in point of time and necessity secondary to the establishment of a sound national economy. I favor as a practical policy the putting of first things first. I shall spare no effort to restore world trade by international economic readjustment, but the emergency at home cannot wait on that accomplishment.

The basic thought that guides these specific means of national recovery is not narrowly nationalistic. It is the insistence, as a first consideration, upon the interdependence of the various elements in and parts of the United States—a recognition of the old and permanently important manifestation of the American spirit of the pioneer. It is the way to recovery. It is the immediate way. It is the strongest assurance that the recovery will endure.

In the field of world policy I would dedicate this Nation to the policy of the good neighbor—the neighbor who resolutely respects himself and, because he does so, respects the rights of others—the neighbor who respects his obligations and respects the sanctity of his agreements in and with a world of neighbors.

If I read the temper of our people correctly, we now realize as we have never realized before our interdependence on each other; that we cannot merely take but we must give as well; that if we are to go forward, we must move as a trained and loyal army willing to sacrifice for the good of a common discipline, because without such discipline no progress is made, no leadership becomes effective. We are, I know, ready and willing to submit our lives and property to such discipline, because it makes possible a leadership which aims at a larger good. This I propose to offer, pledging that the larger purposes will bind upon us all as a sacred obligation with a unity of duty hitherto evoked only in time of armed strife.

With this pledge taken, I assume unhesitatingly the leadership of this great army of our people dedicated to a disciplined attack upon our common problems.

Action in this image and to this end is feasible under the form of government which we have inherited from our ancestors. Our Constitution is so simple and practical that it is possible always to meet extraordinary needs by changes in emphasis and arrangement without loss of essential form. That is why our constitutional system has proved itself the most superbly enduring political mechanism the modern world has produced. It has met every stress of vast expansion of territory, of foreign wars, of bitter internal strife, of world relations.

It is to be hoped that the normal balance of Executive and legislative authority may be wholly adequate to meet the unprecedented task before us. But it may be that an unprecedented demand and need for undelayed action may call for temporary departure from that normal balance of public procedure.

I am prepared under my constitutional duty to recommend the measures that a stricken Nation in the midst of a stricken world may require. These measures, or such other measures as the Congress may build out of its experience and wisdom, I shall seek, within my constitutional authority, to bring to speedy adoption.

But in the event that the Congress shall fail to take one of these two courses, and in the event that the national emergency is still critical, I shall not evade the clear course of duty that will then confront me. I shall ask the Congress for the one remaining instrument to meet the crisis—broad Executive power to wage a war against the emergency, as great as the power that would be given to me if we were in fact invaded by a foreign foe.

For the trust reposed in me I will return the courage and the devotion that befit the time. I can do no less.

We face the arduous days that lie before us in the warm courage of national unity; with the clear consciousness of seeking old and precious moral values; with the clean satisfaction that comes from the stern performance of duty by old and young alike. We aim at the assurance of a rounded and permanent national life.

We do not distrust the future of essential democracy. The people of the United States have not failed. In their need they have registered a mandate that they want direct, vigorous action. They have asked for discipline and direction under leadership. They have made me the present instrument of their wishes. In the spirit of the gift I take it.

In this dedication of a Nation we humbly ask the blessing of God. May He protect each and every one of us. May He guide me in the days to come.

Part Three

The Struggle for Solvency

Chapter Eight

The Banks on the Critical List

THE famed expression in Roosevelt's inaugural, "the only thing we have to fear is fear itself," inserted in the speech by the ubiquitous Howe, was a glittering but inspiring untruth. It was belied in the speech itself when Roosevelt told what he was going to do to banish fear. It is true that a bank's troubles are generally associated with the fear—real or imagined—of depositors; but in this instance depositors' fears had solid foundations rooted in the shaky foundations of thousands of banks. It is barely possible that had there been no depositors' panic more banks might have survived. But the reckoning would have been only postponed until another time.

Certainly a man cannot be expected to be fired with courage when his assets are frozen or when he has well-founded doubts about the institution to which he had entrusted the savings of a lifetime. Only a few hours before Roosevelt spoke those cheering sentiments, the governor of New York had reluctantly closed the doors of the banks and stock exchanges in that state, thus following a widespread suspension in other states.*

* In a letter of March 16, 1966, Walter Wyatt, general counsel to the Federal Reserve Board in 1933, wrote to the author:

"After we learned during the meeting of the Federal Reserve Board in the night of March 3–4 that the Governors of New York and Illinois had finally agreed to declare holidays simultaneously (so that neither could blame the other) on the morning of March 4, the question arose as to what should be done about the other 24 States which had not yet closed. Eugene Meyer was not willing for the Board or any of its staff to notify the governors of those States, lest it be said that the Board had asked them to declare holidays; but we knew that the banks

As in every situation of economic malaise there were remote as well as immediate causes of the banking collapse. The catastrophe of that winter had followed three years of economic dislocation. But before that, throughout the 1920's, there had been grave premonitory warnings. And years before the 1920's there had been an accumulation of unwise legislation, of bad supervision by state governments, and irresponsible risks by bankers themselves.

A major premise of Roosevelt's 1932 campaign was that roots of the Great Depression were in postwar conditions in agriculture. The accuracy of this diagnosis is shown by the widespread bank failures in predominantly rural areas after 1920. During the twelve-year period beginning in 1921, 10,484 banks with deposits of nearly five billion dollars had closed their doors. Of these, 1,571 were national banks with deposits of more than a billion dollars. The others were banks of other sorts, mostly chartered under state laws and under state supervision. These figures fail to tell the whole story. There was also the weakening of the banks that managed to stay open but suffered loss of deposits before 1929 and after that more losses because of the hoarding of depositors stricken by fear.

These failures and losses were most pronounced in the primarily rural states in the Midwest, the Northwest, and South. They reflected the deeper troubles of farmers, whose prices were declining and who were compelled to borrow to make ends meet on their land, equipment, livestock, and growing crops. They had been stricken by their own abundance, since in the First World War they had greatly expanded their acreage to provide food and fiber for a war-stricken Europe and for war conditions in the United States.

But far back beyond that war there were factors that contributed to the proliferation of small, undercapitalized banks. In 1900, under Populistic pressure Congress had enacted legislation that reduced the

in those States would be subjected to runs and great strains unless holidays were declared. It was finally decided to inform the governors of the other ten Federal Reserve Banks of the situation and leave it to their judgment as to what should be done in the States in their respective Districts where holidays had not already been declared. We divided up the job and finally succeeded in conveying the news to the Governors or other representatives of the other ten Federal Reserve Banks. Some of them had to be awakened in the middle of the night, and the news was quite a shock to them. Then some of them had great difficulty getting in touch with the Governors of some of the States in their Districts. Gov. Pinchot of Pennsylvania had come to Washington to attend the inauguration, and no one at his Washington home would answer the telephone or respond to a telegram. Finally, at the urgent request of John Sinclair, General Counsel to the Federal Reserve Bank of Philadelphia, I stopped at Governor Pinchot's house on my way home about 4:00 A.M. and succeeded in arousing someone, whom I frightened into getting the Governor to telephone his office!"

minimum capitalization of national banks from $50,000 to $25,000. Towns that barely supported a general store or a livery stable felt a thrill of civic pride when some farmer or groceryman set himself up in the banking business. Lax state laws and sloppy state administration were the rule rather than the exception from 1900 on. From 1920 to 1932, 65.7 per cent of all suspended banks had capital of less than $50,000.

These loose legal and administrative conditions had encouraged the founding of banks. From 1900 to 1920 the number of banks increased from 10,382 to 30,139, an annual increase of 988. This multiplication of banks was by no means justified by the growth of the country, either in population or economic potential. But so long as agriculture continued prosperous in the "good" years before and during the war, these puny institutions had little trouble in doing a prosperous business.*

During the supposedly boom years in the later 1920's there were some contributing causes of bank trouble other than farm distress. The relatively great prosperity of the industrial areas drew countless people from the farms to the industrial urban areas. For example, the rise of the vast automobile industry in the Detroit area made deserted villages of many towns, and high wages in the factories left many a farm to be operated by old people or by casual help. Smaller industries took flight from small cities and either moved to the big cities or were consolidated with bigger concerns. These had been the main support of the towns they left, and the withdrawal of their deposits crippled the small banks. For thirty years the nation had been moving from a predominantly agricultural economy to a gigantic industrial complex. This had been lost sight of by political regimes, which seldom looked beyond the next election. Business leaders shared the myopia. Profits this year and tomorrow absorbed their attention. They seldom looked back and only occasionally looked forward beyond the quarter- or half-year ahead. Most serious was the failure of bankers and pseudo bankers, blinded by the rising price of securities on the stock markets, who dropped from their vocabulary the prudent word "no."

One cannot expect the casual newspaper reader in Los Angeles to read much below the headlines when during the winter and spring the news appears that the snowfall and rains in the high Sierras or the Rocky Mountains have been exceptionally light. The rivers on which his very life depends seem to be running along as usual. It is only when midsummer comes and there are urgent warnings that water must be conserved that he may awaken to the fact that this shortage had its origins months before and hundreds of miles away.

Thus the stock market crash in 1929 was but the thunderclap in a

* These data are from an unpublished manuscript by F. Gloyd Awalt, acting comptroller of the currency from 1932 to May 11, 1933.

storm that had been gathering a long time before. At first the contraction on the exchanges affected banks less than other elements in the economy. But by 1931 there was a serious number of bank failures, and this time the blow was felt by larger urban institutions. The high point of bank failures came in 1931 when 2,290 banks closed their doors. Of these, 1,772 with deposits of nearly a billion dollars were not members of the Federal Reserve System. In December 1931 there were 358 failures of banks of all sorts. But in 1932, because of the creation of the Reconstruction Finance Corporation and other emergency measures, the bank failures tapered off. The number of closings fell steadily for ten months, so that in October 1932 there were only 97.

But hoarding of money was pronounced. In July 1932 it was estimated that hoarding had reached $1,500,000,000. Withdrawals of deposits for hoarding are quite unlike normal withdrawals, for in the latter case the money finds its way back into the credit stream. Hoarding, however, causes a net loss in circulating media.

In a monumental study, *A Monetary History of the United States, 1867–1960,* Milton Friedman and Anna Jacobson Schwartz call the fall in the money supply from 1929 to 1933 "The Great Contraction":

> The contraction from 1929 to 1933 was by far the most severe business-cycle contraction during the near-century of U.S. history we cover and it may well have been the most severe in the whole of U.S. history. Though sharper and more prolonged in the United States than in most other countries, it was world-wide in scope and ranks as the most severe and widely diffused international contraction of modern times. U.S. net national product in current prices fell by more than one-half from 1929 to 1933; net national product in constant prices, by more than one-third; implicit prices, by more than one-quarter; and monthly wholesale prices, by more than one-third.
>
> The antecedents of the contraction have no parallel in the more than fifty years covered by our monthly data. As noted in the preceding chapter, no other contraction before or since has been preceded by such a long period over which the money stock failed to rise. Monetary behavior during the contraction itself is even more striking. From the cyclical peak in August 1929 to the cyclical trough in March 1933, the stock of money fell by over a third. This is more than triple the largest preceding declines recorded in our series, the 9 per cent declines from 1875 to 1879 and from 1920 to 1921. More than one-fifth of the commercial banks in the United States holding nearly one-tenth of the volume of deposits at the beginning of the contraction suspended operations because of financial difficulties. Voluntary liquidations, mergers, and consolidations added to the toll, so that the number of commercial banks fell by well over one-third. The contraction was capped by banking holidays in many states in early 1933 and by a nationwide banking holiday that extended from Monday, March 6, until Monday, March 13, and closed not only all commercial banks but also the Federal Reserve Banks. There was no precedent in U.S. history of a

concerted closing of all banks for so extended a period over the entire country.*

The public, either because of fear for the solvency of banks or for other reasons, had by these withdrawals compelled many sound banks to sell investments and shorten credit. This had its impact upon security prices and other values.

In the campaign of 1932, banking, so far as Roosevelt's speeches were concerned, was not an issue. The Democratic platform made only a slight reference to it. Roosevelt and his advisers, including myself, regarded any talk about the banks as politically dangerous and against the public interest. We had heard all about the Dawes loan (which I shall presently describe) and realized that some irresponsible campaigners might be using it as an issue. But this, it seemed to us, only further disturbed public confidence, deepened the depression, and added to its miseries.

We considered bank failure as only a manifestation of a deeper illness that afflicted the whole economy, especially agriculture. And we were concerned with providing some answer to the farmer's plight.

The beginning of the crisis, which reached its acute phase in February 1933, was in early 1932. At that time, in addition to our own troubles, we were feeling the severe strains that accompanied what was happening in Europe. The failure of the Credit Anstalt in Austria marked the beginning of the breakdown of European banks. In Britain this led to the abandonment of gold in September 1931, the breakup of the socialist government there and a schism in the Labour Party itself. An election was held and a national government was created with Ramsay MacDonald, who had left the Labour Party, as Prime Minister and Philip Snowden, also a refugee from Labour, as Chancellor of the Exchequer.

The nations of the world, noting our troubles, lost faith in the American dollar, and gold in the hundreds of millions began to flow out of the United States.

As these gold shipments increased, Hoover, in December 1931, proposed and Congress, in January 1932, created the Reconstruction Finance Corporation. This was a bold and imaginative step and for its sponsorship Hoover deserves great credit. Simply described, it was designed to bring the strong credit of the United States to the support of private credit. Hoover said that when the RFC was created its major purpose was to help smaller banks and other financial institutions, the railroads, and insurance companies. But it soon appeared to Jesse Jones and Charles G. Dawes, former Vice-President, two of the original mem-

* Subtitled *A Study by the National Bureau of Economic Research, New York* (Princeton: Princeton University Press, 1963), p. 299.

bers of the board of the RFC, that the big banks and certain industries would need help too.*

The RFC secured its funds through direct withdrawals from the Treasury with specific appropriations and scrutiny by Congress. Although this was a fiscal measure essential to meet a great emergency, it set a precedent that has been most deplorable in later years and with other agencies. It came to be called "back-door" financing.

In the early months of its existence the RFC did a remarkably constructive job. Many a key banking structure was saved from ruin. As we have seen, bank failures declined in the months which followed in 1932. By the end of the year it appeared that 18,000 commercial banks with $32,000,000,000 in deposits seemed to have weathered the storm.

A flurry of criticism arose when Dawes abruptly resigned from the RFC, realizing that it was necessary for him to return to Chicago and do what he could to save the Central Republic National Bank and Trust Company, commonly known as the "Dawes" bank, which he had founded. He himself had only a small holding in the stock of the bank, but the firm of Dawes Brothers, Inc., of which he was the largest stockholder, held several hundred thousand shares as an investment. After arriving in Chicago, Dawes found the bank to be in deep trouble and that if help were not made available it would have to close. This would have shaken the Chicago banks seriously, perhaps fatally. Jesse Jones went to Chicago to survey the situation, and on his recommendation after talking to Hoover the RFC loaned the Dawes bank $90,000,000. This proved to be, according to Jones, "probably the most constructive loan the RFC ever made."

But the size of the loan, the previous membership of Dawes on the board of the RFC, and Dawes's prominence in the Republican Party drew a great deal of criticism. The loan moreover was made just as the Democrats were meeting in Chicago to nominate a President and Vice-President.

While Roosevelt refused to take political advantage of the Dawes loan, other Democrats were not so scrupulous. But an even greater

* For an account of the creation and early operation of the RFC, see Hoover, *Memoirs,* III, Chapters 9 and 10. Also *Jesse H. Jones, the Man and the Statesman* by Bascom N. Timmons (New York: Holt, 1956), Chapters 15–18; and Gerald D. Nash, "Herbert Hoover and the Origins of the Reconstruction Finance Corporation," *The Mississippi Valley Historical Review,* XLVI (December 1959). In his article Nash makes the point that the germ of the idea that resulted in the creation of the RFC was in the War Finance Corporation created in 1918 and continued until 1929. Eugene Meyer was managing director during most of the WFC's life. From this experience Meyer conceived of the RFC and urged the idea on Hoover, who was at first hesitant but later proposed it to Congress.

damage to the banking system and the usefulness of the RFC was the insistence by Speaker John N. Garner on making public the names of beneficiaries of RFC loans. I have never been clear about why Garner insisted on this. It seemed to be completely out of character. For Garner was a shrewd and prudent statesman. He had agreed with Hoover about establishing the RFC. He had secured Hoover's agreement to appoint Jesse Jones a member of its board. He himself had been in the banking business and controlled a bank in Uvalde, Texas, his home town. I have been told, while in the course of writing this account, that one motive was that certain competitors of Garner's bank had secured loans and he wanted to gain a competitive advantage. But even this motive can hardly explain such an irresponsible action.

No doubt because Garner was favorable to publicizing the loans, a measure was introduced in Congress requiring the RFC to publicize them. After bitter debate the vote in the House was a tie, which Garner broke by voting for the measure and the Senate agreed. This was shortly after the Dawes loan was made known to the press in July 1932. The RFC interpreted the legislation to apply only to monthly reports, but Garner was insistent and in early January 1933 a House resolution required all loans made prior to July 21, 1932 to be made available to the public. This was carried because Garner insisted upon it.

No one can tell how much harm this action inflicted on the banking structure. But Hoover and Arthur A. Ballantine, undersecretary of the Treasury, believed it to be one of the major reasons why there was another and much more serious sinking spell in February 1933. Certainly it had the effect of making banks that had hitherto received help from the RFC hesitate to ask for loans. This was the opinion of Jesse Jones when he wrote his book *Fifty Billion Dollars, My Thirteen Years with the RFC* in 1951.

I have two documents in my files which seem to agree with the position taken by Hoover and Ballantine. One is a letter written to George L. Harrison, governor of the New York Federal Reserve Bank, by one of his subordinates. The other is a letter that came to me from Senator Byrnes.

The letter to Harrison called attention to the situation of several large and smaller banks in the New York district. It said that the officers of those banks attributed the deepening of their troubles to the publicity. Shortly after I received this communication from Harrison (in February), I received a letter from Byrnes saying:

> Mr. Henry I. Harriman, President of the Chamber of Commerce of the United States has written me the attached letter as to the publicity of loans made by the Reconstruction Finance Corporation to banks and Insurance Companies.
>
> At the time the measure was considered in the Senate, I am satisfied that

I voted for the provision requiring publicity. Today I am convinced that it is a mistaken policy and that injury has been done to the banks and Insurance Companies. . . .

The object of a loan to a bank is to relieve its pressing needs. If the publicity results in immediate withdrawals, it defeats the very purpose of the loan.

It seems to me that the suggestion made by Mr. Harriman, that the object of publicity can be attained by having the Reconstruction Finance Corporation furnish to the appropriate committees of Congress a list of the loans made. [sic] It would enable the representatives of the people to know what is being done with the money appropriated.

Byrnes concluded on the note that he and other Senators had become convinced that publicity was a "mistaken policy," but that it would be impossible to make any change "until sentiment has developed along this line." While it was "a matter for us to handle and not one to be thrust upon Roosevelt," he did believe that an effort would be made to modify the law, and therefore hoped it would be brought "to the attention of the Governor for his consideration." *

The final verdict about the loan publicity must be that Garner's insistence upon it was an act of irresponsible demagoguery. And the strangest part of it all is that he was supported in his efforts by many of the members of Congress whom he himself, as well as Glass, regarded as "wild men." Maybe the crisis would have come anyhow. But that it was hastened and made more acute by the publicity cannot now be denied.

Another source of trouble in 1933 was the growing talk in Congress, in the press, and in semi-private talk that the gold value of the dollar would be reduced. For the first time in history, talk of a cheaper dollar was not the monopoly of populistic farmers and their representatives. This time it came from urban politicians, college professors, and even some of the more prominent businessmen. A "Committee for the Nation" was organized at about that time which included some of the ex-

* James F. Byrnes to Raymond Moley, February 13, 1933. R. M. Files. The Harriman letter to Byrnes, dated February 10, pointed up the deep concern of the U.S. Chamber of Commerce regarding the effect which RFC loan publicity was having on financial and insurance companies. "In general public expenditures should be given due publicity," wrote Harriman. "But I feel that the wide publicity given to bank and insurance loans tends to undermine confidence in the borrowing bank or company. . . . I most earnestly wish you would consider whether all the objects of publicity cannot be properly obtained by having the RFC furnish to the appropriate committee of each house a list of the loans made during the preceding month." The committee could then publicize those loans they believed the public interest required. "Already to my knowledge," concluded Harriman, "funds have been withdrawn from Washington banks because of the fear resulting from the publication of loans and what is true in Washington is, I am sure, true in many other places."

ecutives of large corporations. This was Bryanism reincarnated, a revival of Populism, although it substituted a dollar of varying gold content for the free and unlimited coinage of silver at a ratio of 16 to 1.

In the midst of all the talk of "reflation" by dollar manipulation, no one knew where the President-elect stood. The consequence was an outflow of gold and currency from the nation's banks. Arthur Ballantine wrote:

> During January, and strikingly in February, came gold withdrawals, not for normal purposes but as a means of hoarding or flight from the dollar. Earlier the trouble had been with the panic desire to turn bank deposits into cash; at this time the idea was the more disastrous one of turning cash into gold, in the belief that more gold could be obtained for the dollar then than later.
>
> Withdrawals of gold owned outside the United States had been withstood by the banking structure in 1931 and 1932. Such withdrawals of gold by domestic depositors, worried or astute about the future of the paper dollar, were a drain on the very basis of our currency and had almost no limit.*

While the RFC and other agencies of the Hoover Administration had been struggling with the banking situation throughout the months before the election in 1932, the gloom deepened as Christmas approached. There were bank runs in the Midwest in December and trouble in Pennsylvania. When January came, danger signals were flying in Cleveland, St. Louis, Little Rock, Memphis, and Mobile. Bad news came from San Francisco, New Orleans, Kansas City, and Nashville. In February the heavy doors of even some of the large banking institutions swung shut; the light went out in the lobbies, and depositors felt the cold grip of loss. Thus, we who were so close to the responsibility of taking over the government were faced with a condition more urgent than even the task of general economic recovery and the more remote problem of banking reform.

The most serious situation in those February days had arisen in Detroit. Because of the immense automobile industry, this city during the 1920's had come to be a major unit in the nation's economic structure. But with the coming of the depression the automobile industry, its employees, its managers, and its owners suffered more severely than those in most other industrial centers. Over the nation automobile owners, when they felt the pinch of necessity, could make do with their old cars. In boom years innumerable workers had been drawn to Detroit and neighboring cities and suburbs by the lure of jobs with relatively high wages. When the industry slowed down in 1931 and 1932, workers, many of whom had purchased homes on credit, left the city in droves or, jobless,

* Arthur A. Ballantine, "When All the Banks Closed," *Harvard Business Review,* XXVI (March 1948), pp. 134–35.

lost their homes in a bitter harvest of defaults. The impact of these defaults and the shrinkage of payrolls meant severe difficulties for the banks.*

The major banks in Detroit and neighboring Michigan cities were consolidated in two groups, each with its holding company: the Guardian or Ford group and the Detroit Bankers group. In July 1932 representatives of the Ford group came to the RFC and asked for a loan. They said that when the Union Guardian Trust Company, the weakest unit in the group, began to have troubles in 1930, Edsel Ford, who was a director of both the trust company and the holding company, had personally loaned them $6,000,000 in cash and securities. The next year he had given his personal credit to secure a loan for them in Chicago. Later the Ford Motor Company extended a $3,500,000 loan to the group. The RFC responded with a loan of $8,733,000 to the trust company for six months and promised that more would be forthcoming. Meanwhile, it was hoped that the Fords would themselves work out a solution.

When in the months that followed the condition of the Ford group worsened, the RFC—after making some additional loans, an aggregate of $13 million—suggested that a pool be formed to which Chrysler and General Motors would each contribute $1,000,000, Senator James Couzens $1,000,000, and the Ford interests still more. Senator Couzens, who had been an executive of the Ford Motor Company, had been mayor of Detroit before entering the Senate.

To this suggestion, made personally by President Hoover, Henry Ford agreed but Couzens flatly refused. According to Hoover, Couzens not only ranted at length against the Ford interests and the government, but said that if such a further loan were made he would denounce it publicly. And so the pool idea ended in utter failure.

Later, on February 11, 1933, Hoover sent Treasury Undersecretary Ballantine and Commerce Secretary Chapin (himself a Detroiter and

* In the account of the Michigan bank crisis which follows, I have relied mainly upon five sources already referred to: *Fifty Billion Dollars,* by Jesse H. Jones and Edward Angly (New York: Macmillan, 1951), pp. 54–69; *Jesse H. Jones,* by Bascom N. Timmons; "When All the Banks Closed," by Arthur A. Ballantine, *Harvard Business Review;* Hoover, *Memoirs,* III, pp. 206–207; and on the unpublished manuscript by F. Gloyd Awalt already referred to. A comprehensive history of the complicated episode, the distress of the banks, the recalcitrance of Henry Ford, and the long efforts of the Hoover Administration to bring about relief has never been written. In what follows I have considered only two of the critical periods in the story: the effort of Jones and Hoover to create a pool to aid the banks in 1932, and the climax in February 1933, when the governor of Michigan was compelled to close all the banks in the state. My source for the first of these is in the Jones-Angly book. For the second I have relied upon the Ballantine article and the Awalt manuscript.

industrialist) to Detroit to see if something could be worked out. These emissaries met with Henry Ford, his son Edsel, and a Mr. Liebold. This was on Monday, February 13, a legal holiday.*

Ballantine and Chapin presented a plan that they had worked out in consultation with the RFC and the President.

The trust company had already had a loan of $15,000,000 from the RFC, but by some exchanges of assets among the banks in the Ford group a further RFC loan of $8,600,000 might be possible which would be part of a larger loan of $23,000,000 from various other banks of the group. However, this would leave a gap of $11,000,000 to $13,000,000 in the assets of the trust company. To fill this gap, it would be necessary for Ford to agree to subordinate his deposit liabilities of $7,500,000 in the trust company and the Ford interests would have to supply part of the new cash needed.

Henry Ford said flatly that he would not subordinate the $7,500,000 deposit liabilities. He admitted that only a few days before he had expressed willingness to do so, but said he had changed his mind.

Ballantine countered by saying that Ford's decision would make it impossible to save the trust company and, if that went under, all the Ford group would have to close. This, Ballantine said, would throw pressure on the other group of Detroit banks and all other banks in the state. The repercussions would reach beyond the state.

Ford reiterated his decision. If this meant, he said, that the trust company was not saved (presumably by more advances from the RFC), he would immediately withdraw $25,000,000 of Ford deposits from the First National, a member of the other group.

Ballantine pointed out that such a withdrawal would make it difficult to save the First National and, if that closed, it was difficult to see how any Michigan bank could survive.

This would mean catastrophe for the deposits that were the source of support for 3,000,000 people. Thus, the epidemic would spread through the nation.

Ford then hinted that the origins of the Ballantine-Chapin plan were in a widespread plot against him. Ford had always been deeply suspicious of the New York banking community, which he believed was intent on ruining him.

The argument continued and ramified into general conditions in the automobile industry and economic and social conditions generally. Perhaps, Ford said, such a catastrophe might be useful, for it would mean that everybody would have to go to work a little sooner.

As for himself, he said this (which was reported verbatim by Ballantine and Chapin): "All right, then, let us have it that way; let the

* The facts about these negotiations were fortunately preserved for history, because Ballantine and Chapin prepared a detailed report for the President and the RFC.

crash come. Everything will go down the chute. But I feel young. I can build up again."

As a final effort, some hours later Couzens was appealed to and he talked with Ford, with Jesse Jones and Awalt listening in. This contest between the two bitter enemies ended in frustration.

Nothing remained but to prevent Ford from withdrawing his money from the two national banks, $25,000,000 from the First National and $17,500,000 from the Guardian National Bank of Commerce. Awalt states that he himself, as acting comptroller of the currency, would have closed the First National before Ford could withdraw his deposits, and he so advised the conferees. But Governor Comstock then stepped in, on the early morning of February 14, and declared a bank holiday for all Michigan. This holiday was continued by the governor up to the beginning of the national bank holiday on March 6.

As we have seen, several other states followed suit.

It is hardly necessary to add that the earlier recalcitrance of Couzens and the Ford attitude were not only cruel blows against the national interest, but were powerful factors in the general panic which followed.

The sensational collapse in Detroit and Michigan sharply brought home to all Americans the gravity of the crisis. For wherever there were Americans there were automobiles, a daily reminder of the great industry which centered in that area. No doubt this series of tragic episodes is what prompted Hoover to make his personal appeal to Roosevelt in the week following the Michigan bank holiday.*

By the afternoon of March 3, when Hoover made a face-to-face appeal to Roosevelt at the White House, the banks in twenty-four states were closed or were restricting payments of deposits. The first state had been Nevada, which declared a twelve-day holiday on October 31, 1932, which was renewed; Iowa enacted emergency legislation on January 20, 1933; Michigan declared a holiday on February 14; New Jersey restricted payments on February 21; Indiana declared a holiday on February 23; Maryland, February 25; Arkansas, February 27; Ohio, February 28; Alabama, Kentucky, Tennessee, and Nevada (again) on March 1; Arizona, California, Louisiana, Mississippi, Okla-

* There were those close to Roosevelt who failed to realize the significance of the Michigan collapse. On the Sunday following the Michigan bank closing, I was at Roosevelt's Sixty-fifth Street house most of the day. That morning Louis Howe was enjoying—as well as his frail digestion allowed—a late breakfast, with a pile of the Sunday newspapers before him. He was especially interested in an article by a feature writer describing how the people of Detroit were taking the bank closings there. Louis growled something to the effect that "All this fuss about the banks is silly. The people out in Detroit are not worried. Why should we be worried?" There was scarcely any talk about the bank crisis in Roosevelt's conversations that day. There seemed to be so many other more important things to be considered.

homa, and Oregon, March 2; Georgia, Idaho, New Mexico, Texas, Utah, Washington, and Wisconsin on March 3.*

By this time the public was in such a panic and currency was being taken out of banks and gold out of the Federal Reserve banks at such a rate that a complete suspension was inevitable. The Federal Reserve Board and the Treasury had been urging Hoover since the evening of March 2 to declare a national bank holiday, but, as we shall see, Hoover, because of the advice of his Attorney General, hesitated to use the old 1917 Trading with the Enemy Act as authority.

By March 3 the gold reserve in the New York Federal Reserve Bank was depleted, and there was talk of requiring Chicago to rediscount for New York. Then, the member banks in Chicago objected to this and started pulling gold out of the Chicago Federal.

Thus, by the night of March 3 and the early morning of March 4 the real problem was to get the governors of New York and Illinois to proclaim holidays, which would no doubt be followed by the remaining states.

This was the situation that had been gathering into more and more serious proportions and had stimulated Hoover's entreaties to Roosevelt up to his last day in office.

* Banking's Reference Supplement, American Bankers Association, 1936, p. 5.

Chapter Nine

The Rough Road to Cooperation

BECAUSE of delay occasioned by the exciting events at Miami on February 15, Roosevelt and his party did not reach the Sixty-fifth Street house until Friday, the seventeenth. During the next day the house was the center of great activity. Roosevelt was busy with callers and with many matters needing attention. My own exciting adventure on the flight into Tennessee delayed me, and I did not reach the Roosevelt house until late in the day. Roosevelt and a group of close friends were planning to attend what was known as the Inner Circle dinner, given by the New York newspapermen, the feature of which was a number of skits after the manner of the Gridiron shows in Washington. I went with the others to the dinner and sat at Roosevelt's table.

The serious matters facing the nation and Roosevelt's new Administration only two weeks later were forgotten amid the gaiety of the occasion. Dinner programs bearing the picture of Roosevelt were passed around the table for autographing, and many old New York friends at other tables came over to greet the President-elect and chat.

Close to midnight, a Secret Service agent from the White House quietly entered the dining room and handed Roosevelt a letter. Roosevelt read it hurriedly and passed it to me under the table. I was astonished to see that it was from Hoover and in his own handwriting.*

Under the circumstances I could not read it with sufficient care. I showed it to one or two of my companions and returned it to Roosevelt.

When Roosevelt, Basil O'Connor, Samuel Rosenman, Louis Howe,

* I noted that Hoover, no doubt because of the strain under which he was laboring, had in addressing the envelope actually misspelled Roosevelt's name—"Roosvelt."

and I returned later to Roosevelt's house, the letter was read by all of us with some care. The discussion that followed was short and perfunctory, for it was already past midnight.

The letter, which was lengthy, called attention to the very critical situation that faced the banks and the Administration in Washington. It recited in some detail the unsettlement of the public mind during the past months, the measures that Hoover's Administration had taken to moderate public apprehensions, and ended with a plea to Roosevelt for a statement that would help to extinguish what Hoover called the "fire" that was raging. Since Hoover would be the best judge of the important items in the letter, here is his account as recited in his *Memoirs:* *

Yet there was very little that an outgoing administration could do while handcuffed by a hostile Congress and an uncooperative President-elect. It was obvious that no encouraging statements or assurances from us, going out of office within a few days, carried any weight. Also, it was obvious that I could secure no remedies from the Congress without Roosevelt's explicit direction to the Democratic members.

As I have said, I had been trying daily for ten days to contact Roosevelt, without success. He returned on the 17th. That day, I at once sent him a longhand letter by a trusted messenger who delivered it into his hands in a few hours. It was unduly long, but I feared from the lack of understanding of such questions which he had displayed in our earlier interviews, and his two weeks' absence from the scene, that he did not fully grasp the situation.

MY DEAR MR. PRESIDENT-ELECT:

A most critical situation has arisen in the country of which I feel it is my duty to advise you confidentially. I am therefore taking this course of writing you myself and sending it to you through the Secret Service for your hand direct as obviously its misplacement would only feed the fire and increase the dangers.

The major difficulty is the state of the public mind, for there is a steadily degenerating confidence in the future which has reached the height of general alarm. I am convinced that a very early statement by you upon two or three policies of your Administration would serve greatly to restore confidence and cause a resumption of the march of recovery.

I then reviewed at length the situation which had developed.

I therefore return to my suggestion at the beginning as to the desirability of clarifying the public mind on certain essentials which will give renewed confidence. It is obvious that as you will shortly be in a position to make whatever policies you wish effective, you are the only one who can give these assurances. Both the nature of the cause of public alarm and experience give such an action the prospect of success in turning the tide. I do not refer to action on all the causes of alarm, but it would steady the

* Vol. III, pp. 203–204. The full text of the letter is in Myers and Newton, *The Hoover Administration,* pp. 338–40.

country greatly if there could be prompt assurance that there will be no tampering or inflation of the currency; that the budget will be unquestionably balanced, even if further taxation is necessary; that the Government credit will be maintained by refusal to exhaust it in the issue of securities. . . . It would be of further help if the leaders could be advised to cease publication of RFC business.

I am taking the liberty of addressing you because both in my anxiety over the situation and my confidence from four years of experience that such tides as are now running can be moderated and the processes of regeneration which are also always running can be released. . . .

HERBERT HOOVER

It should be noted here that the main import of Hoover's appeal was that, while in the final month of his Presidency his own efforts were likely to be unavailing, he believed that reassurances by Roosevelt would quiet the panic. The unsettlement of the public mind, he thought, was due to uncertainty about Roosevelt's intentions. While he did not discount other causes for the panic, he believed that the assurances he wanted Roosevelt to give offered "the prospect of success in turning the tide." These assurances were (a) that there be no tampering with or inflation of the currency, (b) that "the budget will be unquestionably balanced, even if further taxation is necessary," (c) that the government credit would be maintained by refusal to exhaust it by the issue of securities, and (d) that Roosevelt should advise the leaders in Congress to cease the publication of the RFC loans.

I am sure that Roosevelt at that time and later felt that he could not comply with Hoover's suggestions. He had communicated through me to Glass more than two weeks before that he could not be bound to reject steps that some people would deem to be inflationary. He had communicated to Glass that to foreswear "tampering" was to use an expression which could be interpreted in innumerable ways. Since the Federal government had been running a deficit in 1931 and 1932 and these deficits had been covered by issuing government securities, it would be impossible and dishonest to promise a balanced budget in that year. Later, even with the enactment of the drastic economy act in March, the budget remained unbalanced. And as for notifying the Democratic leaders in Congress to stop publication of RFC loans, that could have been accomplished, but it might further unsettle the public mind. The damage had already been done.

The Hoover conditions, upon which he said cooperation should be based, were spelled out in letters to Senator David A. Reed of Pennsylvania and Senator Simeon D. Fess of Ohio, written on February 20 and 21 respectively. These letters reasserted, in much more forcible terms, his conviction, more mildly expressed in his letter to Roosevelt, that the basic cause of panic was public fear rising from Roosevelt's plans and intentions.

He concluded the Reed letter in bald terms:

> I realize that if these declarations be made by the President-elect, he will have ratified the whole major program of the Republican Administration; that is, it means the abandonment of 90% of the so-called new deal. But unless this is done, they run a grave danger of precipitating a complete financial debacle. If it is precipitated, the responsibility lies squarely with them for they have had ample warning—unless, of course, such a debacle is part of the "new deal."

In the letter to Fess, Hoover concluded with this:

> The day will come when the Democratic party will endeavor to place the responsibility for the events of this . . . period on the Republican Party. When that day comes I hope you will invite attention of the American people to the actual truth.

There was an element here of political calculation to which I shall refer later.

Since the neglect of Roosevelt to reply promptly to the Hoover letter, which was received by Roosevelt near midnight on February 18, has mystified many who have written on this subject and has been freely used to indict Roosevelt for failing to understand the danger that confronted the banking system, it is essential that the chronology be straightened out here as far as it is possible. For there is confusion in dates even between Hoover's account in his memoirs and the Myers and Newton book.

Myers and Newton say that "President-elect Roosevelt's reply to President Hoover's appeal of February 17th arrived at the White House" on March 1 "after an elapse of twelve days."

Assuming that the Roosevelt replies are correct as published by Newton and Myers, since they had access to the Hoover papers in writing their book, the texts are these. The first is under date of March 1. The second bears the date of February 19:

> DEAR MR. PRESIDENT:
>
> I am dismayed to find that the enclosed which I wrote in New York a week ago did not go to you, through an assumption by my secretary that it was only a draft of a letter.
>
> Now I have yours of yesterday and can only tell you that I appreciate your fine spirit of co-operation and that I am in constant touch with the situation through Mr. Woodin, who is conferring with Ogden and with various people in N.Y. I am inclined to agree that a very early special session will be necessary—and by tonight or tomorrow I hope to settle on a definite time—I will let you know—you doubtless know of the proposal to give authority to the Treasury to deposit funds directly in any bank.

I get to Washington late tomorrow night and will look forward to seeing you on Friday.

Sincerely yours,
[Signed] FRANKLIN D. ROOSEVELT

The President
The White House

[Enclosure]

DEAR MR. PRESIDENT:

I am equally concerned with you in regard to the gravity of the present banking situation—but my thought is that it is so very deep-seated that the fire is bound to spread in spite of anything that is done by way of mere statements. The real trouble is that on present values very few financial institutions anywhere in the country are actually able to pay off their deposits in full, and the knowledge of this fact is widely held. Bankers with the narrower viewpoint have urged me to make a general statement, but even they seriously doubt if it would have a definite effect.

I had hoped to have Senator Glass' acceptance of the Treasury post—but he has definitely said no this afternoon—I am asking Mr. Woodin tomorrow—if he accepts I propose to announce it tomorrow together with Senator Hull for the State Department. These announcements may have some effect on the banking situation, but frankly I doubt if anything short of a fairly general withdrawal of deposits can be prevented now.

In any event, Mr. Woodin, if he accepts, will get into immediate touch with Mills and the bankers.

Very sincerely yours,
[Signed] FRANKLIN D. ROOSEVELT

The President
The White House

From the evidence in my diary, written daily at that time, and from the internal indications of dates in Roosevelt's letters, this is what happened and when:

Since I was exceedingly busy conferring with Woodin about developments, in working on the inaugural text, and in the many other odd jobs, I was not aware whether Roosevelt had replied to Hoover's letter. But my diary puts the second letter quoted above as having been written, according to Roosevelt, on February 19, the day after he received Hoover's letter at the Inner Circle dinner. Roosevelt's second letter—the first quoted above—was by internal evidence written on March 1 and delivered on the same day, by means of which I have no evidence. At the Hyde Park library the stenographic notes from which these letters were typed show that both were dictated on the same day, March 1st.

To the suggestion by Hoover in his letter of February 17 that an appointment to the Treasury should be announced soon, so that lines of communication could be established with the outgoing Administration,

Roosevelt immediately acted, on the nineteenth, by getting the final refusal of Glass and making the offer of the position to Woodin.

After Woodin had accepted the Treasury position and it was announced, a measure of cooperation immediately began. Woodin had been a director of the New York Federal Reserve Bank and had been in close touch with the banking situation for some time through that contact. On Saturday, February 18, George Harrison, governor of the New York bank, had placed in Woodin's hands a tabulation of payments in gold coin in New York which showed that such payments to individuals and banks totaled more than $3.4 million February 15 and $3.1 million on February 16, more than in the entire month of January. It seemed from this and other evidence that paralysis was setting in throughout the banking structure.

Whatever time I could spare from other obligations I spent with Woodin in New York, discussing the banking situation. While I was designated to be assistant secretary of state in the new Administration, I conceived it to be my responsibility to serve then and after we arrived in Washington as an assistant and co-worker with Woodin, since there had been no designation of a Treasury undersecretary and would not be for three months. Meanwhile, Arthur Ballantine held that official position.

When on February 28 Hoover had received no reply to his letter to Roosevelt written eleven days before, he wrote another letter asking for a declaration by the President-elect, "even now on the line I suggested." This letter when delivered must have prompted Roosevelt's reply, with enclosure, on March 1. On that day, Hoover instructed Ogden Mills, his Secretary of the Treasury, to offer "the full co-operation of the Administration to the President-elect in any line of sensible action which will meet the present banking situation."

This would indicate that Hoover had slightly receded from his position stated in his letter of February 17.

History has dwelt at length upon the failure of cooperation between Hoover and Roosevelt. This subject has been obscured by the controversy in the years since 1933. Therefore, it seems to me necessary to recite in detail what happened between the arrival of Roosevelt in Washington on March 2 and noon on March 4.*

On March 2 Roosevelt and his party, which included Woodin and me, arrived in Washington and Roosevelt and I were installed in the

* In this I am relying in large part on my account in my book *After Seven Years,* written six years after the events, when many of the participants were still living. That account was substantiated by Arthur Ballantine, who read my version in manuscript. I also have now the account of Hoover in his *Memoirs,* published in 1952. There is also the Myers and Newton book, published in 1936, to which I have already referred, and a partial account in the biography of Carter Glass by Rixey Smith and Norman Beasley, which was published in 1939.

Mayflower Hotel. Shortly after we arrived, Woodin, who had immediately got in touch with the people at the Treasury, informed us that proposals had been made that called for immediate and serious consideration.

Representatives of the Treasury and of the Federal Reserve Board were asking that Roosevelt approve the issuance of a proclamation closing all the banks. The power for this, they said, rested with the President under Section 5 of the Trading with the Enemy Act passed during World War I. The word was, further, that Hoover did not favor closing all the banks, but would consider another course that might be valid under the same powers. This would be an order to prohibit banks from paying out currency and gold except for manifest commercial needs.

This power had been considered at the time of the banking crisis in February of the year before, but Hoover had rejected the suggestion.

But the condition under which either of these steps would be taken was that Roosevelt support the proposals.

At once, the Democratic Congressional leaders were summoned to Roosevelt's apartment, and the question of Roosevelt's responsibility was discussed. The consensus was that there was no need for joint action and that Hoover was to proceed as he thought best. That was the message sent back to Hoover through his advisers by Woodin. The message was not, as is reported by Myers and Newton, that Roosevelt would not approve such action.

There were three reasons for Hoover's hesitancy to act. He had been advised by his Attorney General, William D. Mitchell, that the authority conferred by the Trading with the Enemy Act upon the President was doubtful. Hoover did not believe that the closing of the remaining banks was necessary. And he would not act alone because he believed that a Democratic Congress would not validate his action. For the latter reason, he demanded Roosevelt's assurance of support—presumably, his publicly stated assurance.*

* Letter from Walter Wyatt to Raymond Moley, March 16, 1966, states, "I found the following notation in my file:

" '*Thursday, March 2, 1933*

" 'About 8 P.M. Wyatt and Harlan sent to confer with Atty gen re powers under 5(b) Trading w. Enemy Act. A.G. opposed to action on grounds of policy. Hoover only has 36 hours to go: why not let things ride & leave it to new administration? Doubtful as to powers. After discussion, said "Tell him there is sufficient color of authority to justify issuance of executive order if he thinks emergency is great enough to require it."

" 'Later A.G. came to Mills office & assisted in preparation of first draft of Executive order.

" 'Meanwhile efforts being made to get Roosevelt to ask Hoover to issue order. Would not do so but said he would interpose no objection to declaration of bank holiday until noon March 4. I am not yet President.

" 'When he heard this, Atty Gen said Hoover should not issue executive order

Hoover's explanation of his position is this in his *Memoirs:*

Up to the day I left the White House more than 80 percent of the banks of the country, measured by deposits, were still meeting all depositors' demands. I, therefore, refused to declare a holiday but constantly proposed up to the last moment of my Presidency (11 P.M. of March 3rd) to put into effect the executive order controlling withdrawals and exchanges if Roose-

unless it was unanimously agreed by outgoing and incoming administrations that it was necessary & assurances obtained from Congressional leaders that it would be ratified promptly & that enabling legislation would be passed. I have only a "shoe string" on which to base legality of executive order.

" 'Meanwhile letter had been written by Hoover to Bd inquiring whether Bd. would recommend declaration of national holiday. Bd. voted to do so (Thursday night) & Meyer told Hoover so over the telephone.' "

The Wyatt letter continues:

"Ogden Mills asked John Harlan of the War Loan Staff of the Treasury Department and me to go to the home of the Attorney General, show him a copy of the memorandum pointing out why Section 5(b) of the Trading with the Enemy Act had not expired when the rest of the Act did, and ask him whether he agreed with my view that a proclamation closing the banks could be issued thereunder. You will observe from the above quotation that he did not give a flat negative answer. The executive order referred to above may have been the 'first draft' that Mitchell worked on; but I am pretty sure that my office had prepared a draft earlier and had had it mimeographed. I have a copy of such a mimeographed proclamation; but, unfortunately, it is not dated. I have a carbon copy of the proclamation drafted by Attorney General Mitchell and also a carbon copy of a revised draft prepared by me and Chester Morrill, Secretary of the F.R. Board. Both are dated March 2, 1933, and both applied to Federal Reserve Banks as well as other banking institutions. In fact, the definition of 'banking institution' in our revised draft of March 2, 1933, is substantially the same as that later incorporated in the proclamation issued on March 6, 1933, by President Roosevelt. 19 F.R. Bull. 113–114.

"I also have a carbon copy of a still later draft of a proclamation or executive order which was sent to President Hoover after midnight on the night of March 3–4, 1933. The 'whereas' clauses are very similar to those contained in the proclamation issued by President Roosevelt, and the definition of 'banking institutions' and the description of the transactions prohibited during the 'bank holiday' are almost word for word the same.

"I have the following pencilled memorandum about the events of March 3–4, 1933:

" 'Board in practically continuous session from 10 A.M. to 3:30 A.M. Saturday morning. N.Y. had 13 tellers windows paying out gold. Board suspended reserve requirements early in the p.m. & discussed requiring Chicago to rediscount for N.Y. When Chicago heard this, its member banks started withdrawing gold (apparently to prevent it from leaving 7th Dist). By night the situation looked desperate & by 11:30 Bd had been advised that Directors of N.Y.F.R. Bk & Executive Committee of Chicago Bk had requested Bd to urge Hoover to declare national holiday for 3 days.

" 'About 11:30 Meyer communicated these facts by telephone to Hoover and urged him as strongly as possible to issue executive order, which had already been taken to him. Hoover was very petulant & kept saying he wouldn't do it unless Roosevelt requested it. Meyer said you are President & no one else; the situation is velt would approve. This would have effectively prevented all the banks from closing and given time for the panic to subside.*

There the situation stood on the morning of March 3. During the first hours of that day Hoover apparently believed that the situation had taken a turn for the better. "Secretary Mills," according to Myers and Newton, "reported to President Hoover that the banks in the larger centers had taken various measures which he felt would prevent any general closing over the inauguration and that the President-elect's inaugural address might give the necessary assurances to stop the monetary panic" (p. 365).†

But by afternoon the situation grew worse. Hoover decided to make another appeal to Roosevelt, because the Treasury had reported devastating withdrawals of gold and currency, especially from the New York banks.

According to custom, the President-elect and Mrs. Roosevelt, with son James as his physical supporter rather than the bodyguard, Gus Gennerich, left the hotel to call upon the President and Mrs. Hoover.‡

I decided to take a short rest after the exciting twenty-four hours which had passed since we left New York. Although my nerves were

desperate, you are the only one who has power to act; and it is your duty to do it, whether Roosevelt requests it or not. Hoover quibbled and said Roosevelt ought to ask him to. Meyer said Roosevelt will not ask you and 'we are fiddling while Rome burns.' Hoover 'I can keep on fiddling. I have been fiddled at enough and I can do some fiddling myself.'

"The relations between Meyer and Hoover had become as bitter as those between Hoover and Roosevelt—or maybe more so. I understood that, even later in the night, Meyer wrote a letter along the above lines to Hoover and managed to get a Secret Service man to slip it under Hoover's bedroom door after Hoover had gone to bed. I also understood that Hoover wrote Meyer a scorching reply the next morning; but I never saw either letter."

* Vol. III, p. 213.

† Wyatt in letter of March 16, 1966, doubts this statement.

‡ In a book, *Affectionately, F.D.R.*, by James Roosevelt and Sidney Shalett (New York: Harcourt, Brace, 1959), pp. 250–52, there appears a grossly distorted account of this meeting with Hoover. James Roosevelt in his book does not follow the order of the events as they were recounted to me by Roosevelt later, nor as I saw them happen when I arrived at the White House. James reports that Hoover said, in response to Roosevelt's comment that the President need not return this call, "Mr. Roosevelt, after you have been President for a while, you will learn that the President of the United States waits for no one." That is about how Roosevelt reported the interchange when he returned to the Mayflower. It was a most unfortunate expression, it is true. But James also charges Hoover with a violation of the amenities of the occasion by having Mills waiting in another room to join Hoover and Roosevelt in a discussion of the banking situation. Mills was there, and so was Eugene Meyer, but their presence was allowable, considering the nature of the emergency. In his account, James forgets that Meyer and I joined the group after the formalities were concluded. James forgets his manners, too, by saying, twenty-six years later, that he wanted "to punch him [Hoover] in the nose."

on edge and my thoughts went to the inaugural speech, the reading copy of which I was carefully guarding in my jacket pocket, I drifted into a doze from which I was awakened by the telephone. It was Warren Robbins calling. As the protocol officer of the State Department, he was at the White House.

Robbins said that Ike Hoover, the chief usher of the White House, had whispered to Roosevelt at his arrival that Secretary Mills and Eugene Meyer, governor of the Federal Reserve Board, were waiting in a side room, presumably to be summoned for a serious talk with Roosevelt as soon as the social amenities were over. So Roosevelt whispered to Robbins to summon me so that I could be present for the discussion. I immediately went over, and when Mills and Meyer appeared, Roosevelt told Hoover that he had sent for me, and I entered the room.

The discussion which followed was fruitless. The two alternatives that seemed possible to Mills and Meyer were considered. Hoover said that under the Trading with the Enemy Act the banks might be partially or completely closed. But Hoover still contended that complete closing was unnecessary and brought up the opinion of his Attorney General that the validity of the old legislation was questionable.

Roosevelt declined to give any assurance that he would join in any action at that time. That was the province of the President. He said that he had asked an opinion from Senator Walsh, who had been his choice for Attorney General but who had died the day before, and that Walsh had believed the old legislation was still valid. He also said that Homer Cummings, who had been drafted to replace Walsh, was studying the matter at that moment. So far as he was concerned, Roosevelt said, the authority still existed. But he could not go beyond that in any assurance of sharing the President's responsibility. And so the responsibility was left with Hoover.

Roosevelt concluded the discussion by saying, "I shall be waiting at my hotel, Mr. President, to learn what you decide."

After dinner that evening and until as late as one o'clock, there was constant discussion in Roosevelt's suite. Woodin, Glass, Jesse Jones, Byrnes, and Hull were there for various periods. Others came and went. I was there for the greater part of the evening. The telephone was constantly ringing because many people were either offering advice or asking what was going to be done about the banks.

Thomas W. Lamont of the Morgan Company called to recommend that no action be taken because, he said, the leading New York bankers had told him that the banks could pull through and reopen on Monday if Roosevelt's inaugural speech were to provide sufficient stimulus to public confidence. Roosevelt was not much interested in what the bankers thought, and while he was cordial with Lamont, he was not at that time likely to be influenced by advice emanating from Morgan's.

Hoover called to say that he had word from New York and Chicago, where the bankers were still in conference. This was, according to Hoover and also Myers and Newton, at 11:30. Hoover states that in this conversation he again asked Roosevelt to give his approval of an order from the President controlling withdrawals and exchanges. Hoover concludes his account of this exchange by saying that Roosevelt "in the presence of Senator Glass, again declined." *

I believe that the Hoover version is true, for Roosevelt had not altered his earlier position, which was that Hoover should do whatever he chose to do. But it is also true that Roosevelt had by this time decided to use the Trading with the Enemy authority to close all the banks rather than to follow Hoover's secondary plan to control withdrawals of currency and gold. A confirmation of this latter decision is in the following account of a conversation between Roosevelt and Glass late that evening.† Since this was written before the death of Glass, and since it was an authorized biography, I accept it as authoritative:

"You will have no authority to do that, no authority to issue any such proclamation," protested Glass. . . .

"I will have that authority," argued Roosevelt. "Under the Enemy Trading Act, passed during the World War and never rescinded by Congress. . . ."

"It is my understanding that President Hoover explored that avenue a year or two ago—and again during the recent days," said Glass. "Likewise, it is my understanding that the Attorney General informed him that it was highly questionable if, even under this Act, though it has never been rescinded by Congress, the President has any such authority. Highly questionable because the likelihood is the Act was dead with the signing of the Peace Treaty, if not before."

"My advice is precisely the opposite."

* There are different versions of this conversation. Myers and Newton (p. 366) say, "Finally, at 11:30 that night, from a conference meeting in the White House, President Hoover telephoned to President-elect Roosevelt, who was in conference with his advisers at his hotel in Washington, and asked for their conclusions. Mr. Roosevelt stated that Senator Glass, with whom he was conferring, was opposed to national closing, that the Senator believed the country should go temporarily onto a clearing-house scrip basis. Mr. Roosevelt believed that the governors of the States would take care of the closing situation where it was necessary. He said he did not want any kind of proclamation issued. The President asked if he could repeat Mr. Roosevelt's statement to the men assembled with him at the White House, and did so."

I was, of course, not actually listening on the telephone to the conversation of the two men. But I did hear Roosevelt's end of the conversation and Roosevelt's summary of it, for the benefit of all of us there, the moment he had hung up. And neither what I remember nor what I noted down at the time jibes with the foregoing account.

† Smith and Beasley, *Carter Glass,* p. 341.

"Then you've got some expedient advice," returned Glass. . . .

"Nevertheless," declared Roosevelt, "I am going to issue such a proclamation."

Glass left the Roosevelt suite that night, dreading what this portent of the future seemed to him to mean.

While Hoover does not mention a later call, I remember it well. He called Roosevelt finally at one o'clock. He said that Mills with the Treasury and Federal Reserve people at the Treasury was considering what action should be taken. Roosevelt thanked him and suggested that both of them turn in and get some sleep.

I left Roosevelt's apartment after wishing him a good night's sleep before the ordeal of the inauguration. I was on my way to my own quarters in the Mayflower, but when I stepped out of the elevator into the lobby, there was Will Woodin. He smiled when he saw my expression of astonishment at seeing him.

"Don't say it," he said, "I really tried very hard, but I couldn't even get to the stage of undressing. This thing is bad. Will you come over to the Treasury with me? We'll see if we can give those fellows there a hand."

This decision by Woodin had incalculable consequence. It meant that with Roosevelt and Hoover hopelessly deadlocked, and with the whole banking system drifting toward catastrophe, the subordinates were to join in the sort of cooperation which they believed to be essential to the paramount interests of the nation.

Woodin believed he needed me not because I knew much about banking or of the steps needed to stem the panic, but because for many months I had enjoyed the complete confidence of Roosevelt. His contacts with Roosevelt had been close but infrequent. I could therefore learn what needed to be done and, with Woodin, get Roosevelt to agree to plans that could be worked out with the outgoing Administration and to act upon the steps he must take. The foregoing indicates that Roosevelt had already made up his mind to exercise his authority in full to close the banks and then, after a curative holiday, to reopen them. Neither Woodin nor I gave a thought to the possibility that Roosevelt would repudiate our action. But such risk as was involved we were willing to take because he had not told us to go to the Treasury. In the many years of Roosevelt's Presidency, subordinates realized that when there were no specific orders, they must move on their own responsibility, that Roosevelt would be delighted if they succeeded and believe sincerely that he had willed it so. Or, if they failed, that he would be compassionate.

We learned in time from the people in the Treasury that early morning that they were also running a great risk of repudiation. But we all realized that Hoover and Roosevelt were so fatigued and that the personal bitterness between them was so great that a meeting of minds between them was out of the question at this late and critical hour.

I had conceived a liking for Ogden Mills from the time I first met him at the November White House conference and on the morning after that, when the sparks flew when he had visited Roosevelt's room at the hotel. He was a fighter. He was able and experienced. And I trusted him. After his initial contempt for me as Roosevelt's man had faded, he seemed to generate a certain respect and liking for me. I had not known Arthur Ballantine before this moment, but out of our work together, a friendship grew which lasted to his death many years later. Woodin, of course, everybody loved and he entered upon this new adventure with characteristic enthusiasm.

From the time we entered the Treasury Secretary's office that dark morning, everyone forgot political differences. Our concern was to save the banking system, despite the confusion of some and the incompetence of many of the bankers themselves, and to save the nation from the antipathy which existed between the two men who had been elected to the Presidency.

The question of who should get the credit or take the blame for the actions that we took could not be considered. There simply was no time for such speculation.

From time to time after that, Woodin and I together reported to Roosevelt about progress in the plans or asked him to act on various subjects for which he was responsible. In the course of the next few days Ballantine had access to Roosevelt, and they got on very well indeed. For Roosevelt had no such animosity toward Ballantine as he had entertained toward Mills. Our meetings with Roosevelt were brief and to the point, for he was very busy with the multitudinous duties imposed upon a new President, official and social. We found practically no opposition from him about anything that had been done in the Treasury.

When we arrived at the Treasury, we found in the Secretary's office Mills, Undersecretary Arthur Ballantine, F. Gloyd Awalt, the acting comptroller of the currency; Eugene Meyer, and perhaps two or three others. They were haggard and red-eyed from hours of examination of bank figures. They informed us that it was their considered and unanimous conclusion that the banks would have to be protected from further runs that morning, whether the New York and Chicago bankers realized it or not. They had called the governors of states that had not already suspended or restricted banking operations, to induce them to agree to brief bank holidays. Only the big states remained to be dealt with. They had not been able to reach Governor Henry Horner of Illinois, and they had not been able to persuade Governor Herbert Lehman of New York to overrule the bankers, who were urging him to wait. While Lehman came of a banking family, he was new to the office, which he had occupied only since it had been vacated by Roosevelt's resignation three months before.

Repeated calls to Lehman were made by Mills, who stepped into another room to make them. At the same time, Meyer maintained almost continuous communication with George Harrison, who was at his office in the Federal Reserve Bank of New York. From time to time Meyer entered the Secretary's office where the rest of us were sitting. It was Harrison's contention that the New York bankers who were advising Lehman to do nothing did not comprehend that while they were indulging in vain hopes of staying open the gold withdrawals were becoming unbearable.

While this telephoning was going on, there was nothing the rest of us could do but sit and wait. It must have been about two o'clock when nearly twenty hours of activity had its way with me, and I fell asleep. Half an hour later Woodin awakened me, saying, "It's all right now. Everything is closed. Let's go now."

Lehman had yielded and had issued the order closing the New York banks. Horner had been located and had done the same thing in Illinois.

I rubbed my eyes and looked around. The scene in the Secretary's office still is vivid in my memory. Behind the desk sat Mills. Woodin occupied a chair beside the desk. Awalt, Meyer, and Ballantine were scattered around. Little was to change in that room in the long days and nights that were to follow except that Woodin and Mills changed positions.

That early morning of March 4, there was nothing further that could be done. "We stood up then, and walked through the echoing halls past the soft-footed watchmen and the deathwatch of the reporters and photographers who were to snap pictures of us, in the same rumpled clothes, bowed under the same weariness for a week of nights." *

* *After Seven Years*, p. 148.

Chapter Ten

The Unhappy Holiday

IT is probable that the best-remembered periods in this century in America, except the two wars, are the paralysis that gripped the banks in February 1933, the unhappy holiday in March, and the lifting of the clouds, which was the aftermath. I have found these to be etched in the minds of everyone now of mature years and also of those who were children at the time but who knew of the crisis from family conversation. Millions still recall the pinch of cash and the fear for savings that gripped the land.

But despite the transcendent importance of the bank crisis and its successful conclusion, most historical accounts of those times have given it only minor attention. The roots of the trouble were so widespread and so remote in time from the events in 1933, the remedies applied came from so many sources, the decisions made and actions in Washington were crowded into so few days, the individuals directly concerned were so few and so hidden from public notice at the time, and the Congressional action was so swift and so lacking in debate that the record tends to be speculative and sketchy. Moreover, the individuals concerned were so busy then and in the weeks that followed that there was little time for them to recall and recount what they did and knew.

An objective, informed, and intelligent writer, Ernest K. Lindley, in his book *The Roosevelt Revolution*, wrote this comment in late 1933:

> The press could not publish all that it knew without aggravating the panic; yet it could not ignore the situation without undermining public confidence in the press and perhaps giving wild rumor more leeway than it otherwise would have had. . . . the press experienced unusual difficulty in obtaining reliable information. The few men who had it were likewise

trying to allay rather than accelerate the panic. . . . the best informed men—in the banking centers and in Washington—were themselves meagerly informed. As in the thick of a battle on a broad front, infinite numbers of events were happening simultaneously, the lines of communication were uncertain, the reports from different points were colored by the emotional state of the men who made them. A complete picture of the rapidly changing situation could neither be assembled nor coolly judged. The more reputable newspapers adopted the sensible course of publishing the evidence of the progress of the panic as it was shown by moratoria, restrictions, and gold and currency withdrawals without frightening headlines or doleful comment which would have whipped even higher the waves of fear. It is doubtful if the story of the banking crisis and Mr. Roosevelt's first week in office ever can be put together to the satisfaction of everyone. The main participants in the drama were too numerous and they emerged from long days and nights of tension with blurred and conflicting memories.*

This challenge, that the story cannot be put together to the satisfaction of everyone, is one which this writer, who was one of the inner participants at the time, is reluctant to accept even at this distance of more than three decades. But from a variety of sources, many of them hitherto unavailable, I shall attempt to answer the implied question in Mr. Lindley's conclusion.

The public, the press, and even most of the historians have received and retained impressions only of the high and most visible over-all incidents. Roosevelt's proclaiming a bank holiday; the huddling of a small circle of officials who were formulating the steps that should be taken in reopening the banks; the rush of gold hoarders first and the currency hoarders a few days later; the moving appeal of the President on the Sunday night preceding the reopening; and the almost miraculous rise in public confidence which followed—these remain the ineradicable impressions.

Most of those who knew all or almost all of what happened in the Treasury, the Federal Reserve Board, and the White House were, for a variety of reasons, slow to tell their story. This was because they were doers rather than writers, because they were restrained by their official status, or because they were too busy. Roosevelt kept no diary, no *aide-mémoire*, and his only account is the memoranda which appear in his collected papers. The two Secretaries of the Treasury died leaving only the papers that had accumulated at the time. I wrote a somewhat abbreviated account in my book *After Seven Years*. Arthur Ballantine wrote nothing for publication until 1944 and 1948. And F. G. Awalt waited for twenty-five years before writing his unpublished manuscript to which I have already referred.

But now I have found a great deal more material that is relevant,

* Lindley, *The Roosevelt Revolution*, pp. 71–72.

which makes it possible to piece the story together in these chapters.*

The proclamation by the President declaring a bank holiday must be examined closely to show why it was so extraordinary an extension of Executive power. The proclamation was prepared at the Treasury during the period between the time when Roosevelt declared to Woodin and me that he was willing to invoke this authority and some time on Sunday, March 5.†

It was issued on Sunday, but under date of Monday, the sixth, at 1:00 A.M.

* My major sources for this account are the following, and I have refrained from marring the text with innumerable citations for each detail because I have been able, from matching and evaluating the facts, to compromise all or most of the differences among those who participated: My own memory supplemented by the notes and diary written at the time and the correspondence and memoranda in my files. Much of this material is condensed in Chapter V of *After Seven Years,* written in 1939 and checked at the time for facts by Arthur Ballantine. I am now heavily indebted to Ballantine's papers, made available to me by Mrs. Ballantine and by Ballantine's former secretary. Among these are two articles by Ballantine himself—one published in the New York *Herald Tribune* in August 1944; the other an article in the *Harvard Business Review,* XXVI (March 1948). There is a manuscript "Interview with Mr. Henry Ford," by Secretary Roy D. Chapin and A. A. Ballantine on February 13, 1933. There are also *28 Days* by C. C. Colt and N. S. Keith (New York: Greenberg, 1933); a memorandum by Woodin, Ballantine, and George W. Davison given to Roosevelt on March 7, 1933; a letter from Walter Wyatt to Ballantine, August 1, 1948; an excerpt from the diary of Charles S. Hamlin of the Federal Reserve Board. Ballantine's papers also contain copies of the many Presidential proclamations and executive orders prepared by Ballantine. There is also the *Federal Reserve Bulletin* for June 1933 (Vol. 19). Of major importance is an unpublished manuscript by F. G. Awalt, written in 1958, to which I have already referred. There are a large number of letters to Roosevelt in the Roosevelt Library at Hyde Park. There are *The Public Papers and Addresses of Franklin D. Roosevelt,* edited by Samuel I. Rosenman. Finally there are the Hoover *Memoirs,* Vol. III.

† Wyatt letter to Raymond Moley of March 16, 1966, stated:

"We had drafted and mimeographed a proposed proclamation much earlier; Attorney General Mitchell had dictated a draft on the night of March 2; Morrill and I had revised it; and a draft very similar to that finally promulgated by President Roosevelt had been sent to Hoover on the night of March 3. It may have been revised somewhat at the Treasury on March 4 and 5. When I was called to the White House on Sunday, March 5, President Roosevelt already had a draft which differed somewhat from our draft, and it was revised further in the President's study on the second floor of the White House in a conference participated in by the President himself, Attorney General Cummings, Mr. Woodin, myself and others. You must have been in the group; but my notes do not mention you. The document was ready for signature before midnight; but, at my suggestion, it was dated March 6 and actually was not signed until after midnight. I told the President that his great inaugural address had ended on a religious note, which had a great psychological effect on me and possibly on many others, and it might spoil the effect if this important document were promulgated on a Sunday. Others disagreed; but the President agreed with me on this point."

The provision of the old Trading with the Enemy Act which was cited as authority was this:

"That the President may investigate, regulate, or prohibit, under such rules and regulations as he may prescribe, by means of licenses or otherwise, any transactions in foreign exchange, and the export, hoarding, melting, or earmarking of gold or silver coin or bullion or currency." Following this were the punitive sections of the act.

It will be noted that there was not in this text any specific power to close banks. The authority to close the banks, as expressed in the proclamation, was the emergency created by withdrawals from banks and the inferences in the terms of the old act. But it was believed that in the emergency that then prevailed the terms of the act could not be exercised without closing the banks. However, in Roosevelt's proclamation he authorized the Secretary of the Treasury to make regulations, subject to the approval of the President, to permit certain prescribed activities of the banks. This was clarified by a statement by Woodin, issued later.

The expression "banking institutions" was defined in sweeping terms to include specifically names of all sorts of institutions, or persons doing a banking business.

It is important to note here that the authority cited by Roosevelt in his proclamation declaring a bank holiday to and including Thursday, the ninth of March, was not a last-minute discovery. Nor was it, as Hoover declares in his memoirs, "a weak reed for a nation to lean on in time of trouble." For nearly a year it had been quite familiar to the leading people in the Treasury and the Federal Reserve Board, and through them it was no doubt quite generally known. The existence of this authority was made known to me on January 7, 1933, by René Léon, a man who constantly had sought to transmit information to Roosevelt for many months.*

I must have communicated this to Roosevelt, or he might have heard it from many other sources with access to him.

In Awalt's unpublished manuscript, he tells the following:

In 1918, the 1917 Trading with the Enemy Act was revised by Congress. Milton Elliott, then general counsel of the Federal Reserve Board, incorporated an idea of Paul M. Warburg's that at some future time the government might find it necessary to place an embargo on the export of gold. Elliott talked with Walter Wyatt, who was then a member of his staff, and who in 1933 was general counsel of the Federal Reserve Board.† The result was that certain new language was added to

* R. M. Notebook, January 7, 1933.

† In Wyatt's letter of March 16, 1966, his account of what happened is somewhat, but not materially, at variance with Awalt's account:

"Milton C. Elliott, the first General Counsel of the Federal Reserve Board, had the 1917 Act and the amending language was enacted by Congress. Wyatt was then the connecting link between the original legislation and the situation in 1932 when the subject came up again. In June 1932 Adolph Miller, a member of the Federal Reserve Board, asked Wyatt about authority to place an embargo on the export of gold, to prohibit the hoarding of gold, or to go off the gold standard (presumably by Executive order). Wyatt advised him that there was such authority under the Trading with the Enemy Act as amended in 1918. Miller asked for a memorandum. Being too busy, Wyatt had Magruder Wingfield prepare it. Wyatt consulted his chief, Eugene Meyer, governor of the Federal Reserve Board, and Meyer advised that Wyatt's opinion should not be put in writing but given verbally.

In the fall of 1932 Secretary Mills spoke to Wyatt about the subject and was told that there was such authority and that it could be used to control the whole banking situation. A draft of an executive order was drawn up and prepared for the President's signature but was never signed.

Thus this most important tool for closing the banks was already in existence when the February crisis came.

Adolph Miller, who had believed ever since the 1932 incidents already mentioned that the Trading with the Enemy Act could be used to declare a bank holiday, urged Hoover on March 2, 1933, to exercise this authority. In response, Hoover wrote a letter to the Federal Reserve

drafted the original Trading with the Enemy Act, and in 1918 he was asked to draft certain amendments. While he was doing so, the late Paul M. Warburg, one of the original members of the Federal Reserve Board, suggested that, if the powers granted under Sec. 5(b) to prohibit the exporting or hoarding of gold, silver or currency, etc. could be made permanent, instead of expiring with the termination of the war, it might be a great help in some future emergency. However, it was feared that, if this were proposed openly to Congress, it might cause a money scare or opposition which might defeat the proposed amendments which were needed during the war. I was only a young law clerk in Milton C. Elliott's office; but he explained the problem to me and asked me to see whether I could figure out a way to make Sec. 5(b) permanent without attracting attention to it or incurring the risks mentioned above. I had had little experience, if any, in drafting legislative matters; but I went to work on the problem and, applying principles of sleight-of-hand which I had played with as a boy, I figured out how it could be done and pointed out the trick to "Judge" Elliott, who adopted it in drafting his amendments to the Act. The amendments went through in the form proposed without any difficulty. Magruder Wingfield was not on the Board's staff at that time and did not join it until 1923 or later.

"I had forgotten all about this incident when Adolph C. Miller, one of the original members of the Federal Reserve Board, called me to his office one day in 1932, reminded me of it, and asked me to look into the matter and see whether that power was still in effect and whether it might not be used to stop the exportation of gold or the hoarding of money that was then causing so much trouble to the banking system. I was then too busy to do it myself; but I called in Magruder

Board asking its advice. He also asked the board if it believed there was such authority "to limit the use of coin and currency to necessary purposes," to provide him with a draft proclamation. Hoover says in his memoirs, "The majority of the Board again declined to have any part in the proposed recommendations to Roosevelt or the Congress."

Awalt, who was present at the March 2 meeting, says that Mills and Meyer were of the opinion that a banking holiday must be declared. He says also that the board members Miller and Hamlin believed that the Trading with the Enemy powers could be used to prevent further withdrawals for hoarding and that the situation would then clear up without proclaiming a holiday. Awalt himself favored a holiday, but he was not a member of the board.

Mills said that Hoover was willing to use the authority to declare a holiday of three days, March 3 to 5 inclusive. But first he wanted an assurance that the incoming Administration would agree to such a shorter holiday and would call Congress into special session on Monday, the sixth, to validate the closing and to pass necessary legislation that might be prepared in the interim. This obviously was a very large order.

Awalt says that Mills said that Roosevelt suggested that Hoover declare a holiday until Saturday noon and that after that he would take the responsibility. Mills was unwilling to see this done. Despite his opposition to the use of the Trading with the Enemy Act, the Attorney General with the aid of Wyatt (who, as has been noted, had already

Wingfield, who had become one of my assistants, told him the above story, and asked him to study the matter thoroughly and prepare a memorandum on the subject. He did so, and his memorandum left no doubt in my mind that Sec. 5(b) was still in force and could be used to stop the exportation of gold, the hoarding of money, etc. It is my impression that someone thought the matter was "dynamite," and consequently no formal opinion on the subject was written, and the memorandum was not addressed to anyone or signed by anyone. It was kept very confidential, and at one time I was forced by Eugene Meyer to decline to give a copy to Ogden Mills, which embarrassed me greatly at the time.

"I had no doubt that the President could use this power to stop the exportation or hoarding of gold or currency; but, when it was suggested that it be used to close the banks entirely, I was a bit troubled by the fact that 90 per cent of all business transactions are settled by means of checks, and they usually result only in the transfer of bank credits from the accounts of the drawers to those of the payees—without any coin or currency changing hands. I concluded that the prohibition of this and other banking activities could be justified as necessarily incidental to the other powers in the circumstances then existing; but I knew this point was debatable. Therefore, when we started preparing drafts of a proclamation closing all the banks under a nation-wide bank holiday declared by the President under this authority, I felt that (1) such action should be ratified as soon as possible by Congress, and (2) Sec. 5(b) should be amended at the same time so as to apply also to "transfers of credits." Therefore, when we first drafted the proclamation, I also drafted legislative provisions for these purposes, and they eventually became Sections 1 and 2 of the Emergency Banking Act of March 9, 1933."

written such a proclamation months before) prepared two draft proclamations. Mills tried to reach Hoover (it was then early in the morning of the third) but the President had gone to bed. When all these efforts failed and Congress adjourned on Saturday, the day of the inauguration, nothing remained but to get all the states to declare holidays and await the actions of Roosevelt.

This is about where matters stood when Woodin and I went to the Treasury on the morning of the fourth.

On the morning of March 4, only a few hours after Woodin and I left the Treasury, we called on Roosevelt at the Mayflower. We reported to him what had happened at the Treasury. We said that the consensus there was: first, that there should be a proclamation under the powers of the old law, closing all the banks for a holiday; second, that it had been pointed out that Roosevelt should call a special session of Congress to validate his action, if necessary extend the holiday, and pass legislation providing for the reopening of banks after the holiday. We reported that it was believed at the Treasury that he should call together for consultation the important bankers of New York, Chicago, Philadelphia, Baltimore, and Richmond. These were to meet on the next day, Sunday.

Any apprehension that Woodin and I had entertained because without his explicit authority we had taken up cooperation after he and Hoover had reached a deadlock was soon disposed of. For Roosevelt was delighted that we had joined the men at the Treasury. He agreed promptly with these proposed steps.

A number of vital questions still had to be answered. When could Congress meet after the President's call? Could the Federal Reserve banks be closed by the President, or would the Federal Reserve Board be required to act? What steps should be taken to restore the confidence of the depositors when the banks were reopened after the holiday? How should the emergency legislation be drafted upon which Congress could act and when could it be ready?

The quest for these answers brought about another long session at the Treasury later that day and far into the night. The same participants were there as before. There was a brief review of some of the proposals made by various bankers and other individuals. Some of these were worth considering; most were born of desperation and were summarily rejected. There was little time for deliberation. Decisions had to be made in the prayerful hope that we were acting in the best interests of the nation and its anxious people.

After this conference, Woodin returned to the White House and brought the word that it was considered imperative that Roosevelt call Congress to meet on Thursday, the ninth. It was believed that the necessary legislation could be prepared by that time. Roosevelt agreed to issue the call and to make a public announcement of his decision.

Another question we discussed that evening of the fourth was whether the Federal Reserve banks could be closed by the President's proclamation or whether this should be done by the board itself. This was resolved by Eugene Meyer, governor of the board, who left the room for a short period and returned to say that the board had agreed to act on its own responsibility.*

A Presidential proclamation was prepared by Mills and Ballantine on the basis of Wyatt's early draft and in consultation with Awalt. It called for a general bank closing for four days beginning on Monday, the sixth. This was to carry the statement that this was in pursuance of the authority of Section 5(b) of the Act of October 6, 1917, as amended. It was issued by the President under date of March 6 at 1:00 A.M. The holiday was extended indefinitely by another Presidential proclamation on March 9.

The impact upon the country of these measures, which were immediately reported in the press over the nation, was only partially known to those of us who were working in the relative isolation of the Treasury and the White House. A letter I received from a friend whose wisdom I had learned to respect indicated what was happening even under the partial closing the week before under state authority. This letter is dated March 3 and was written by W. A. Sheaffer, president of the Sheaffer Pen Company of Fort Madison, Iowa:

> We have today our checks returned and refused from twenty-four states and it looks as though in a few days business would be at an actual standstill. Therefore, the most urgent emergency in the history of our nation is at hand. There must be adequate relief legislation immediately. It would seem that it could not wait for a week or ten days and with no money available for payrolls and salaries. It would seem to me that the country would be at a standstill.

We realized all too well the unhappy situation that prevailed in the lives of millions of people and the paramount necessity that successive bulletins and Presidential actions provide the building of confidence in the week that was to follow. We felt that the new President's inaugural speech had been effective, although it had been written before anyone

* Wyatt in his letter to Raymond Moley of March 16, 1966, explains, "There was never any doubt in my mind that, if the President declared a national bank holiday and closed all the commercial banks, he could and should at the same time close all the Federal Reserve Banks. Therefore, in drafting the proclamation, I had made it apply to 'all banking institutions' and defined that term as specifically including 'all Federal Reserve Banks.' 19 F.R. Bull. 113–114. The Federal Reserve Banks closed March 4, 1933, pursuant to holidays proclaimed by the state governors, and they remained closed the next week pursuant to the President's proclamation. The Board did not tell any of them to close."

could know what might be happening over that weekend. Fortunately, it was designed to convey to the listening public assurance that Roosevelt would invoke all possible powers to meet the general economic paralysis, which was spreading over the country. For that reason, it measurably prepared the public for the shock of the next day's proclamation of a bank holiday. But there were few people beyond the small group who were working at the center of things who knew how much needed to be done and how these needs were to be met.

The bank panic, which ended when New York and Illinois fell into line on Saturday, March 4, was succeeded by another sort of crisis. This affected people of all sorts and conditions from coast to coast. It was apparent, even before the new President issued his proclamation on Sunday, that people would have to live for an indeterminate number of days with only the cash or credit they had or could get from other hard-pressed relatives or friends.

The New York Stock Exchange was closed by its Board of Governors and the Chicago Board of Trade was shut down for the first time since 1848.

I have already made clear that until Woodin made his decision to use Federal Reserve bank notes, it was believed that scrip would become a means of exchange. Various efforts immediately got under way to provide this form of paper money. The American Bank Note Company began emergency operations. It was preparing to supply the paper for many major cities. The news came out on Monday, the first day of the Federal holiday, that Governor Lehman had received authority from the legislature to set up a corporation to issue scrip certificates. Former Governor Alfred E. Smith was named as president of this new institution.

This action in New York was erroneously interpreted to reflect the thinking in Washington, and thus only a short moneyless holiday was anticipated, with scrip being used thereafter for money. But influential voices against the use of scrip were heard. Wise people warned that the scrip, if issued generally, would drive all normal currency out of circulation and that the hoarding of scrip would supplant the hoarding of gold and cash. But by Wednesday the scrip movement died out because of the announcement that other methods would be used.

Meanwhile, from Saturday, March 4, until well into the week that began on Monday, the thirteenth, when the banks were progressively opened, millions of Americans made what efforts they could to live, move about, and, if they were in business, maintain operations. Almost every American now beyond the age of fifty has vivid personal recollections of those strange days.*

* Those of us in the center of the vortex at the Treasury and the White House could only imagine how the holiday was affecting people at the grass roots. We

Never was there so drastically shown the utter dependence of all of us upon the banks that serve us.

It is true that many frightened depositors had withdrawn their money from the banks during the February scare. These hoards were in paper money, mostly in larger denominations. But that frightened and, shall we say, foresighted few constituted a relatively small minority.

The most immediate problem was a drastic shortage of coins. A newspaper survey in a New England city showed that the average individual had pocket money amounting to only $18.23. People whose credit was good at hotels and stores nevertheless found difficulty in changing notes of ten dollars or more or in cashing their checks. Miami was in a state of dire confusion—the American Express Company declared a limit of fifty dollars in cashing checks. Across the nation, at the Huntington Hotel in Pasadena, unofficial scrip was printed for the convenience of the stranded rich. People with paper money of all denominations were unable to buy cigarettes, to pay bus fares, or to use a pay telephone. Railway clerks were unable to make change for tickets. Automats were invaded by people seeking nickels. People went to churches to exchange paper money for the change in the collection boxes. The pastors of these churches were having trouble, too, and advised the worshipers that I.O.U.'s would be acceptable when the collection plates were passed.

Stores and hotels realized early that credit was the only recourse if they were to keep in business. R. H. Macy's cash store decided to honor charge accounts of other department stores. Restaurants and similar stores soon found their cash registers crammed with I.O.U.'s from old customers. Prince Mike Romanoff, the restaurateur, said, "A good many people's checks are now as good as a great many others'." Barbershops closed for lack of business—shaves and haircuts could wait. Two race tracks closed. And movie box-office receipts dropped 45 per cent.

Weird sorts of barter developed. In his article in *Holiday,* William Manchester says, "During the first week of the new administration, stamps, phone slugs, Canadian dollars, Mexican pesos, and street-car tickets were used for currency. Mormons in Salt Lake City designed a paper money that could be used locally; the Greenwich Village Mutual Exchange issued $1,000 in tokens to member businesses; in Princeton the *Princetonian* printed twenty-five-cent scrip notes for students, to be redeemed when the banks reopened. A Wisconsin wrestler signed a con-

were all too immersed in preparing the legislation and the many orders and proclamations to see beyond Washington. There was no time even for us to read newspapers. For the colorful incidents that follow, I am indebted to the research of William Manchester, whose article, "The Great Bank Holiday," appeared in *Holiday* (February 1960), Vol. 27, No. 2. The quotations I use with the permission of the author and *Holiday.*

tract to perform for a can of tomatoes and a peck of potatoes; an Ashtabula newspaper offered free ads in exchange for produce; and a New York state senator arrived in Albany with twelve dozen eggs and a side of pork to see him through the week.

"The most spectacular experiment in barter was conducted by the New York *Daily News*, which was sponsoring the semifinals of the Golden Gloves tournament in Madison Square Garden. The price of seats was fifty cents, but any article worth that amount was accepted as admission, provided the five-cent amusement tax was paid. An appraiser was engaged, who inspected, during the evening, frankfurters, mattresses, hats, shoes, overcoats, fish, noodles, nightgowns, steaks, spark plugs, cameras, sweaters, canned goods, sacks of potatoes, gold knickers, mechanics' tools and foot balm. A boy presented his New Testament, a girl her step-ins. The items most frequently offered were jigsaw puzzles."

Regulations were issued by the Secretary of the Treasury on March 6, 7, and 8 authorizing limited banking transactions to relieve some of the distress described above. The first of many regulations authorized banks to make change, and the second allowed customers free access to their safe-deposit boxes.

While the government could provide no penalties for the hoarding of gold that began before the legislation was passed, the pressure of publicity was immediately put on to compel its return. On Wednesday, March 8, it was announced by the Federal Reserve Board that lists of persons who had withdrawn gold since February 1 and who failed to bring it back by Monday, March 13, would be published. This started a real gold rush.

On Thursday and Friday the disgorging of this gold hoard went on with frantic speed. It was mostly in New York, where millions were returned. One man brought in $700,000, and one firm $6,000,000 in gold bullion. The gold supply of the government rose rapidly, and on Friday there was a line of a thousand people with gold in their pockets and luggage of various sorts, returning the gold and receiving deposit slips. By Friday night 4,000 people had passed through the line. Altogether, by Saturday night the Federal Reserve banks had recovered $300,000,000 in gold and gold certificates—enough for the backing of $750,000,000 in additional currency.

Despite all the discomfort, there was general tolerance and good will. The President's inaugural speech, the reassuring proclamations from the Treasury and the White House, the news of prompt action by Congress, and Roosevelt's first fireside speech had been effective. One might apply a trite expression to the state of the nation when normal conditions returned, "a smiling land."

Chapter Eleven

Pre-Planned and Orthodox Rescue

THE closing of the banks was the anesthetic before the major operation. A proclamation that had been considered for weeks, assured of authority under the law, required merely the stroke of a White House pen.* The hard part lay ahead.

The attending surgeons before the patient is prepared for surgery must make complicated and minute preparations. They must have at hand the pre-operative X rays, the tools, the trained personnel, the diagnostic test records, and skilled management by the anesthetist to accompany the procedure. They must also have the foresight that looks toward the patient's restoration to consciousness and the long road through convalescence.

It was realized that prohibition of gold-holding must be enforced and hoarders must be permitted to return their metal to the Federal Reserve banks; solvent or apparently solvent banks must resume business; the shaky ones must be fortified; the casualties must be conserved and there must be currency for the people which the people would trust.†

* According to Wyatt, in a letter to Raymond Moley of March 16, 1966, "We did not begin seriously considering the possibility of a nationwide bank holiday to be proclaimed by the President under Sec. 5(b) until January or February, and it was not until then that we drafted a proposed proclamation and the legislation to ratify it and broaden the powers under Sec. 5(b). Meanwhile, it was only one of several possible alternatives being considered, including the issuance of scrip or clearing-house certificates and the guaranty of bank deposits. I find from my folder that we actually drafted a bill to authorize the issuance of clearing-house certificates, though none of us around the Federal Reserve believed in either of those remedies."

† I have used the word "solvent" in this sentence rather than "sound" because it is more correct. The solvency of a national bank is determined by the comptroller of

Despite the long vigil of the previous night, when our group in the Treasury were waiting for the governors of Illinois and New York to close the banks in their states, an after-breakfast meeting was called in Secretary Mills's office. Those present were Mills, Ballantine, James H. Douglas, Jr., assistant secretary of the Treasury; Dr. Emanuel A. Goldenweiser of the Federal Reserve Board, and Parker Gilbert, a Morgan partner and a former assistant secretary of the Treasury.*

This group not only reviewed the plan for the holiday by Presidential action but considered the form of the Presidential proclamation to be issued by Roosevelt and, of equal importance, the steps that should be followed in reopening the banks after the holiday. Plans were reviewed and with little debate were generally agreed upon.

The job remained of formulating the ideas in a written, comprehensive plan to be passed on to the new Administration. One such plan was composed by Mills in a letter to Woodin; the other by Ballantine, which was later given to Roosevelt for his approval.

That afternoon of March 4, Mills, with Goldenweiser and Awalt sitting by, dictated a letter to Woodin and enclosed a memorandum which he entitled "Tentative Outline of a Possible Line of Approach to the Solution of our Banking Problem." This memorandum by Mills was of great importance for, with some slight variations, it was the blueprint that was followed in drafting the emergency legislation for action by Congress and the steps taken by the President and Woodin in the days that ensued.

With this accomplished, Mills told Woodin that he would be at home subject to call. In fact, Mills was called and was present that night in a meeting that began at noon in Woodin's office.

Mills's plan stated at the outset that no solution could be possible except by a Presidential proclamation closing all banks and putting them "on the same basis of treatment." He then stated that the banks should be reopened on a staggered basis; and in order to classify banks in their order of possible reopening, that there would be three classes—A, B, and C.

the currency, who takes all the essential factors into consideration. State banks that are members of the Federal Reserve System are subject to examination not only by the state bank authority but by the Federal Reserve. State banks that are not members of the Federal Reserve System are within the jurisdiction of the state authorities. It is presumed that, as in the case of the national banks, the authority responsible will take into consideration all the factors, including those that are subjective as well as those that are material. In all cases it is a matter of experienced judgment rather than any arbitrary assessment of figures.

* In those days certain Morgan partners, especially Gilbert, were frequently in and around the Treasury. But now, because of the realization that the House of Morgan would not be welcomed by Roosevelt and Woodin, Gilbert was most unobtrusive and subsequently absented himself from Treasury conferences.

Awalt points out in his unpublished account that the two main questions that Mills and his associates confronted were: (1) which banks should be opened quickly in order that the country might function, and (2) how to keep them open. There was also the question of how banks that were on the doubtful list could be fortified, to open either immediately after the holiday or later on.

There was no information at the Treasury to provide positive identification of the state banks that were solvent or insolvent, especially those that were not members of the Federal Reserve System. As to the national banks, which numbered 5,938, the Treasury had reasonably accurate information. Awalt estimated that about 2,200 of these were liquid and could be reopened at once and meet all demands. These were designated as Class A banks. Class B banks were the ones that had to be bolstered in some way. Class C banks included all the rest, some of which could not be allowed to open at all, or only after they were reorganized.*

For Class B banks, according to the Mills letter, there would have to be some scaling down of deposits and additional capital which, if not available from private sources, should be supplied by issuing preferred stock to be taken by the RFC as security.

Some Class C banks could not be safely opened at all. These would, in the Mills plan, be placed in charge of "conservators" rather than "receivers." Most of those in Class C were state banks, the opening of which would have to be determined by state authority.

Inherent in these plans outlined by Mills were three important but rather novel devices:

1. Provision for the use of Federal Reserve bank notes to meet needs if withdrawals of cash continued after the holiday;

2. Provision for conservators for banks that would be kept closed, at least for the time necessary for reorganization or merger or liquidation;

3. Authority for banks to issue preferred stock to be taken by the RFC as security for loans.

All these key devices had been carefully considered by the Treasury, the Federal Reserve Board, and the White House weeks before.†

* It should be clearly understood that this classification of banks was somewhat different from the classification of banks that were opened on the three days following the holiday. An explanation of the classification of banks at that time is in a subsequent chapter.

† Wyatt in his letter of March 16, 1966, states, "At Awalt's request, I had dictated a first rough draft. I anticipated doing a lot more work on it and producing a finished draft suitable for introduction in Congress; but Awalt, to my great surprise, demanded that I give him the only two copies of the rough draft that I had, and he took them to his office and locked them in his safe. There they remained until some time after 11:00 P.M. on Tuesday night, March 7. After I was asked to draft

Putting these together was a matter of some calculation. Each was essential to the rescue operation after the holiday, and each in turn was clearly understandable by Congress when the emergency legislation would come before it for validation.

There have been considerable differences as to the origin of these devices. That is understandable, considering the number of people in government who had been present in many conferences earlier. But an examination of the evidence, along with the written accounts since then by the two present survivors of the crisis and the articles already noted written by Ballantine in 1944 and 1948, reveal these origins:

1. The plan to issue Federal Reserve bank notes, according to Awalt, was "sold" to Secretary Mills, who at first believed that it would be necessary to issue scrip. As I have indicated, Goldenweiser was present when Mills wrote his letter to Woodin. Wyatt notes that Goldenweiser later claimed credit for the idea but that he, Wyatt, did not know about it until he began the drafting of the emergency banking bill. The idea finally crystallized in the authority given the banks to borrow on anything they might have in assets from the Federal Reserve System.*

It so happened that because of the rush at reopening to redeposit cash and gold, the $200 million issue of Federal Reserve bank notes was unnecessary. They were ultimately retired.

Wyatt says that he first heard of the idea of having conservators rather than receivers "about Lincoln's birthday" in 1933, when Awalt came to him and asked him to draft legislation to authorize it. This draft was checked, revised, perfected, and mimeographed before the March crisis. It provided for the appointment by the comptroller of the currency of the conservators. It found its way into the Emergency Banking Act as Title II. There is some evidence that the idea originated with Secretary Mills. At any rate, he favored it and incorporated it in his March 4 memorandum to Woodin.

Since Jesse Jones administered the plan of taking the preferred stock of banks as security for loans, the impression has been created that it

the Emergency Banking Act, I went to Awalt's office and he got the rough draft of the preferred stock bill from his safe and gave it to me. A lot of work had to be done on it before it could be incorporated in the bill which became the Emergency Banking Act. The Bank Conservation Act, however, was in finished form and mimeographed, and a copy may have been given to Senator Glass during the latter part of February or the first few days of March."

* In my book *After Seven Years* I told of Woodin's decision to use the notes rather than scrip on the morning of the seventh. My account of Woodin's decision seems to have conveyed the impression to some readers that Woodin originated the idea of the notes. Woodin was merely affirming, as I tried to make clear at that time, a recommendation already made to him by Mills and Ballantine. It was, as Woodin said, money, unlike scrip, "that looked like real money."

was an invention of Jones's, although he never claimed this credit. Awalt says that the idea came from Franklin W. Fort, president of the Lincoln National Bank of Newark, New Jersey. Fort was earlier a Republican Congressman and a member of the Banking and Currency Committee of the House.

Fort told Hoover of this idea in March 1932 and suggested that banks could issue debentures or preferred stock as security for loans. He said that common stock with double liability would not attract investors. Hoover suggested then that Fort talk with Comptroller of the Currency J. W. Pole, who objected to the idea at the time. Later, early in January 1933, Fort brought the idea to Awalt. Secretary Mills was told about it, and Awalt asked Wyatt to draft the necessary permissive legislation, which Awalt kept in a safe in his office. This, too, including permission for the RFC to purchase such stock, went into the Emergency Banking Act.

Thus, the evidence shows conclusively that practically all the tools used in meeting the emergency were already in existence in the Hoover Administration.

Sunday, March 5, marked the beginning of four days of seemingly interminable meetings of bankers attended sporadically by members of the two Administrations. Woodin had asked that these bankers be called for three reasons: to give them a sense of participation in a solution and thus to shore up their morale; to familiarize them with the plans that had already been made or were in the making; and, if possible, to get from them constructive ideas for improving the plans.

So far as improving their morale was concerned, the meetings no doubt helped, for they were removed from the signs of disasters at home and lived for a while in the fast-moving and confident atmosphere of official Washington. Since their nerves had been badly shattered for more than a month, this experience was a blessed relief.

But their proposals were confused. Some were still unable to see any alternative to the issuance of scrip. Others were already sufficiently familiar with the idea of issuing the Federal Reserve bank notes and soon grasped its advantages. A few were so immersed in despair that they saw no way out except nationalizing the banks through some jerry-built contrivance. Some others concentrated on the argument that the banks could not be safe unless and until the state banking systems were all forced into the Federal Reserve System. And there was some talk of converting the several Federal Reserve banks into government-owned deposit banks.*

* Wyatt explains in his letter of March 16, 1966: "The meeting of bankers was held in the board room of the Federal Reserve Board on the second floor of the Treasury Building, and Chester Morrill, the board's secretary, had a large office adjoining. Mr. Meyer told Floyd Harrison, Morrill, Goldenweiser, Smead and me to stand

There was a good deal of talk about attaching the guarantee of bank deposits to the emergency legislation. But those of us who were close to the making of plans realized that this must be postponed. We knew that Roosevelt, whatever may have been the subsequent versions of his thinking, was at that time and even later opposed to it. We felt, therefore, that this should be deferred until the Glass legislation was under consideration. At that time, it was made a part of permanent banking reform, and Roosevelt at first endured and then embraced it. I am convinced that finally he made himself believe he had favored it from the beginning.

Up to Tuesday, I had attended some of these meetings as an observer and listener. It was apparent that, quite aside from the psychological task of conditioning the people of the country to the necessity of the holiday and the soundness of the plans for ending it, the bankers themselves presented a serious case of shattered nerves. Melvin A. Traylor, president of the First National Bank of Chicago, an attractive but high-strung individual, had been on the firing line for nearly a year. In the summer of 1932, before the Dawes bank had been saved by a loan from the RFC, Traylor had been compelled to mount the marble pedestal in the lobby of his bank where he attempted to assure panic-stricken depositors that their money was safe. His arguments at that time persuaded Jesse Jones that if the Dawes bank failed, all the rest of the big Chicago banks would have great difficulty in keeping open. And Jones had called Hoover from Chicago and persuaded him to approve the making of the loan. It is interesting to note that the popularity of Traylor in his home city was so great that he had been the favorite-son candidate for the Presidential nomination at the convention that nominated Roosevelt.

At the meeting of bankers on Sunday, March 5, Traylor was the most articulate member of the banking group. He argued with nervous intensity that the Treasury's refunding operation, which was scheduled for March 15, could not succeed because the Treasury certificates could not be taken by the banks. I suggested that Roosevelt in such an eventuality might by a public appeal induce the public to buy the issue. Traylor retorted that I did not know what I was talking about. This

by in that room so as to be readily available if we were needed. It was during this time that I outlined a plan entitled 'Skeleton Outline' [details and explanations omitted]. It represented our selection of what we believed to be the most practical of the many suggestions which had been considered and discussed during recent months, and it provided for the issuance of clearing-house certificates, instead of Federal Reserve bank notes. Apparently, the Federal Reserve bank note idea had not been thought of by any of us up to that time! We did not anticipate the flow of public confidence that would result from the closing and then reopening of the banks, and we feared that there would be further withdrawals of deposits, which would necessitate the issuance of emergency currency."

was probably true, because I was speaking from faith rather than knowledge of such matters. He said, "You talk like William Jennings Bryan when he said that in case of war a million Americans would take up arms and spring to the defense of the nation." *

By Monday, Woodin and I had thoroughly and finally familiarized ourselves with the plans that had largely been developed in the Treasury by Mills and Ballantine. We were also convinced that nothing much would be contributed by the bankers in the days ahead. Woodin needed to clear his mind of details, for the final decisions were clearly to be his own. Roosevelt had been so occupied with other important matters that he had, up to then, only the sketchiest notions of what remained to be done.

That Monday evening, I returned with Woodin to his room at the Carlton Hotel and, free from the day's confusion, we tried to see the situation ahead in some perspective. We had the elements of the Treasury's plan in mind and were convinced that it would work if properly and swiftly put into effect. We could, therefore, afford to skip details for the moment and consider the all-important subject of public reactions. We were assured that Roosevelt was giving and would give us his complete confidence. It was also clear that Congress would enact whatever Roosevelt might ask. Glass by this time had decided to accept the inevitability of Roosevelt's commitment to use the Trading with the Enemy Act, and on Wednesday, with a few other Congressional leaders, would be brought into the planning and would support the emergency banking legislation in Congress.

Woodin, by his earlier experience in banking, and I, by what I had learned in the preceding days and in the light of my political activity, had grasped an essential fact. We knew how much of banking depended upon make-believe or, stated more conservatively, the vital part that public confidence had in assuring solvency.

The necessity, therefore, was for swift and decisive and well-publicized action by Roosevelt and Congress. Since the great majority of people were accustomed to orthodox banking procedures, this, too, was essential to gaining their confidence. Therefore, we were determined to exclude from the group of major participants—who were known to the press, the bankers, and the public—all the reputedly radical and visionary individuals who were hovering in the background with novel, even revolutionary, ideas (which, we were to learn later, went so far as nationalizing the banking structure). There was nothing revolutionary in our plans. The only unusual feature was the boldness and swiftness of their application.

* Traylor was one of the casualties of those days. He lived only eleven months after that day, to the age of fifty-six.

It was essential to public confidence and the termination of panic that as many banks as possible be reopened at the end of the holiday. Where there was doubt about solvency, the decision should be weighted on the side of reopening, because we anticipated a flow of confidence, which would bring back a host of hitherto frightened depositors with the money they had withdrawn. The larger the number of reopened banks, the less distress and dismay among the nation's depositors. There was substantially in being the same volume of cash and credit as before the beginning of the crisis. Stability required only that it be returned to the banks.

We also took into consideration that another stimulus to confidence would be a big gesture of government economy, which Roosevelt had already promised to Lewis Douglas, his new director of the budget.

Finally, Roosevelt himself should announce the plans to the press on the Saturday following and to the people on Sunday night on the radio networks. There was magic, we knew, in that calm voice.

When I left Woodin that night, only one decision remained, and he had to make it before work on the emergency legislation was to resume the next day. This was the option between scrip which so many banks favored, and the issuance of Federal Reserve bank notes, which the Treasury favored. This issue, it appeared later, occupied Woodin's mind during most of the night that followed.

When I joined Woodin at breakfast in his room the next morning, he announced with youthful enthusiasm that he had resolved this question.

His explanation of how he had made the decision was characteristic of his nature—half artist and half businessman.

He said that music helped him to clear his mind and that he played on his guitar for a while, read a novel for an hour or so, and had snatches of sleep. But his thinking went back always to what he called "the scrip thing."

He said that he finally went back to the idea of issuing Federal Reserve bank notes.

"We don't have to issue scrip. Those bankers have hypnotized themselves. We can issue currency against the assets of the banks through the Federal Reserve. The Federal Reserve Act permits us to print all we need. It won't frighten people. It will be money that looks like money."

Now all the elements of the plan were in order, and Woodin and I went to the White House and with little discussion secured Roosevelt's approval.

Then we went to the Treasury and Woodin announced his decision and Roosevelt's approval. Then Woodin, Ballantine, and George W. Davison, the wise, capable president of the Hanover Bank in New York, went to the White House and presented Roosevelt with a written summary of the whole plan. Later this summary provided the basis of Roosevelt's radio speech on the Sunday night following: *

As submitted to Pres. [Ballantine]

The purpose of this program is to give to the country as promptly as possible adequate banking facilities and an adequate and sound currency and to restore confidence.

It is, therefore, proposed:

(1) That under the Presidential Decrees of March 6th wholly solvent banks of the country shall be opened for business Friday morning. There are many banks, members of the Federal Reserve System, well distributed throughout the country, that the Secretary of the Treasury would be able to pass immediately as sound banks. These banks could be authorized to open for business on Friday morning.

(2) Other banks not members of the Federal Reserve System and other members of the System not specifically named in paragraph (1) could, no doubt, promptly satisfy the Secretary of the Treasury on further investigation that they are solvent banks. Such banks could thereupon be permitted to open for business.

Banks [Roosevelt] as fast as humanly possible [Roosevelt] Can't cover every soluble [Roosevelt]

(3) Steps should be taken at once to reorganize all banks not now wholly solvent so that they might open at the earliest possible date as new banks of unquestioned solvency. In order to expedite this program of reorganization it might be practicable to consider dealing first with these institutions in cities of populations of 100,000 and over (of which there are 93), leaving institutions outside of these cities to run along such local plans as have been devised and under the protection that is afforded by the general emergency control.

(4) To supplement this plan and to insure an adequate supply of currency, the Federal Reserve banks should be authorized to make loans direct to corporations, firms, or individuals on their notes secured by Government securities and to issue Federal Reserve bank notes secured by such Government securities, or by notes collateraled by such securities. This will enable any holder of Government securities to procure Federal Reserve bank note currency direct from Federal Reserve banks. There are approximately eleven billions

* A copy of this document, carefully identified and with a few marginal notes by Roosevelt, I secured from Ballantine's papers. This handwritten note by Ballantine was attached: "You can use statement that N.Y. Clearing House Banks—have excess cash—will give currency for needs—no hard and fast rule."

of dollars of such securities outstanding in the hands of the public other than banking institutions.

(5) In order to enable any solvent bank to open for business under this program to procure currency sufficient to liquidate all of its deposits, if demanded, Federal Reserve banks should be authorized to lend to any bank regardless of its size on its sound assets. As any bank authorized to open is to be sound this would permit all loans in amounts sufficient to pay off all of the deposits of such a bank, if demanded.

(6) In order to provide adequate Federal Reserve bank currency to satisfy the possible demands of this program Federal Reserve banks should be authorized to issue Federal Reserve bank notes, not only against Government securities, or notes secured by such securities, but also against any member bank note secured by sound assets.

(7) During the early stages of this program and until further notice, the embargo on gold payments, except under license, should be continued and appropriate steps should be taken to penalize the continued hoarding of gold or currency. The continuing to hold gold or currency in excess quantities should be considered hoarding.

As we have seen, Walter Wyatt had been active at the Federal Reserve Board during the planning in February and early March. He was a most competent draftsman. On Sunday, at the suggestion of Ballantine, he had been called to the White House to help in preparing the President's proclamation closing the banks. He remained there working until midnight Sunday night. On Monday and Tuesday he was occupied with drafting the many telegraphic regulations made necessary by the proclamation. Because of his high competence and his familiarity with the plans, he was called to the Treasury by Ballantine at 11:00 P.M. Tuesday to begin work on the Emergency Banking Act, which was to be submitted to Congress on Thursday. He was informed about the items that had been approved by the President.

Wyatt tells the following dramatic story of the drafting of the bill: *

I did not obtain the [Federal Reserve] Board's approval or even attempt to do so; and I don't know to this day whether they ever approved it. I was working for you, Mr. Woodin and the President; and the Board had been functioning so slowly, unconstructively and critically that I felt that the job could not be completed in time if we had to clear it with the Board. You undertook to care for that end of the job and I sent them copies of each draft as they came off the typewriter; but I stuck to the

* Letter to Ballantine from Wyatt, August 1, 1944.

drafting job and had no contact with the Board except as follows: Eugene Meyer came in once and asked me not to take advantage of the emergency to try to get the unified banking system which he had advocated for ten years and which the Board had unanimously told Congress a year before was "essential to fundamental banking reforms"; Goldenweiser came in about the Federal Reserve bank note provision; George Harrison came in about something—I believe the provision about the recapture of gold—and one or two others about matters of detail. We completed a draft some time Wednesday morning and you took it to the White House while I flopped on a couch for an hour or two rest. You came back with a request for a lot of changes (which I thought came from the White House but some of which might have come from the Board) and we got out another draft in time for a conference with Congressional leaders that afternoon or evening. Further changes were suggested and another draft was completed . . . and sent to the printer about 3 o'clock Thursday morning. If the Board gave any clearance or suggested any substantial changes during that time, I did not know about it; but I had a vague impression that you were having a struggle with them. Goldenweiser says the bill never was cleared with the Board, but that Meyer and some of the members of the Board's staff reviewed a draft and suggested a few changes. My notes contain this passage: "After spending 12 hours trying to pick the bill to pieces, Morrill, Harrison [i.e., Floyd Harrison], Goldenweiser and Smead made only one important suggestion and their total suggestions amounted to less than ½ page." I don't remember that; but it was typical of the way the Board's staff functioned at that time and that was why I felt it would be hopeless to try to clear the bill with them.

Wyatt adds his observation that

the relations between Mr. Meyer and the Treasury people were so strained that they were hardly on speaking terms. Jesse Jones was so hostile to the idea of purchasing preferred stock in banks that it took Eugene Black and White House pressure several months to get him going on the program for which he now takes so much credit. Likewise the President was so strongly opposed to the guaranty of bank deposits that he came near vetoing the Banking Act of June 16, 1933; but it is now pointed to as one of the great accomplishments of the Administration.

As Wyatt notes, several people were in and out of the drafting process, although Wyatt carried the main responsibility.

The story in the development of the bill is taken up from here by Ballantine himself:

"As I sat with Walter Wyatt during the night before Congress was to come in, it seemed a good deal to hope that we had in the amendments to the banking act all that would be requisite for the plan. We took the draft up to Senator Glass . . . at 9 o'clock in the morning [of the 9th]. After some discussion the act received his sanction and later that of Chairman Steagall [of the Banking and Currency Committee] . . ."

Walter Wyatt recalls that he did not go with Ballantine. Instead, Ballantine insisted that he go home and "get some sleep." Ballantine promised to explain the bill to Glass and do whatever else was necessary. Wyatt had just fallen asleep when the phone rang. It was Senator Glass, who demanded that Wyatt come to his office immediately and explain "this dad bummed bill." Wyatt dressed and hurried to the Senator's office. Glass had a Confidential Committee Print of the bill and was going over it with Ballantine, Eugene Meyer, George L. Harrison and a few others. With several copies of the committee print, Wyatt was asked to draft some amendments in an adjoining room. There he found Chester Morrill, secretary of the Federal Reserve Board, an experienced legislative draftsman and a favorite of Eugene Meyer's. From time to time, various people drifted into the room to tell Wyatt and Morrill about amendments that Senator Glass wanted. Some were "quite substantial." Wyatt and Morrill carefully wrote them in longhand on several copies of the bill.*

* Wyatt in his March 16, 1966, letter explains:

"Sec. 3 of the bill as agreed upon at the White House and taken to Senator Glass, added Sec. 11(n) to the Federal Reserve Act in a form which would have enabled the Federal Reserve Board to require all member banks to deliver to the Federal Reserve Banks all gold coin, gold bullion and gold certificates and to accept in payment therefor any other form of lawful money. This was almost completely rewritten so as to vest the power in the Secretary of the Treasury, instead of the Board, and to require payment to the Treasurer of the United States, instead of the Federal Reserve Banks. It was also broadened to apply to all individuals, partnerships and corporations, instead of only to member banks. I was told that this had been suggested to Senator Glass by George L. Harrison. It was later used by Morgenthau to try to make the Federal Reserve Banks and Federal Reserve Agents pay the gold in their possession into the Treasury before Roosevelt devalued the dollar; but Eugene Black persuaded the President to get legislation specifically authorizing the Federal Reserve Banks to deliver to the Treasury the gold, gold certificates and gold bullion, including that held by the Federal Reserve Agents as collateral for Federal Reserve notes.

"On the insistence of Senator Glass, Sections 4 and Title II, the Bank Conservation Act, were amended so as not to apply to nonmember state banks, thus making it impossible to retain any control over them after termination of the bank holiday. In fact, Senator Glass insisted that, instead of being licensed by the Secretary of the Treasury, they be turned back to the state authorities, and this was done with many unfortunate consequences! I believe that New Jersey reopened all nonmember state banks, regardless of their insolvency, and I know that many insolvent state banks were opened by state authorities all over the country, and they had to be restored to solvency before they could be insured by the F.D.I.C.

"Sec. 304 was amended so as to authorize the R.F.C. to buy or lend against preferred stock issued by state banks, as well as national banks. As originally drafted, this section had made it mandatory for the R.F.C. to buy preferred stock in national banks when requested to do so by the Secretary of the Treasury with the approval of the President; but this was amended so as to be permissive, instead of mandatory. Because of Jesse Jones' hostility to the preferred stock idea, this

After all changes had been laboriously recorded on the several copies and checked, one of the Confidential Committee Prints was dispatched to the Government Printing Office to be used for the bill which bore Senate designation S.1. Another went to Chairman Steagall of the House Banking and Currency Committee.

Waving the copy over his head, Chairman Steagall added to Congress' most exciting moments by striding down the aisle of the House chamber, shouting, "Here's the bill. Let's pass it." It is said that Steagall had the only copy when the House passed the bill.

The Senate proceedings were more sedate and orderly. Senator Duncan U. Fletcher of Florida, chairman of the Banking and Currency Committee, called his committee members together. Senator Glass explained the measure to the assembled committee. As he spoke, Walter Wyatt prepared remarks which Glass had asked for and delivered them to the Senator as the discussion was under way. Wyatt also explained various phases of the bill at Glass's request.

Some time during the night of March 7, Awalt told the twelve regional chief national bank examiners to telegraph to him a list of the national banks, divided into groups. These came in on Wednesday, March 8. Then, to show the geographical location of the various banks according to their status of solvency, these banks were indicated by varicolored pins on a map of the United States. After this map was completed, Awalt sent it to Roosevelt, who was delighted with it.

While the more solvent banks showed a fair geographical distribution, it was obvious that the country would be paralyzed if more were not opened. The proposed legislation would accomplish that. When the Senate Banking and Currency Committee was considering the bill on the afternoon of March 9, Awalt was the only witness. Glass explained the bill. Awalt was asked how many national banks could be opened. He answered that, without the legislation, only 2,600; but with the enactment of the bill, 5,000.

I have stressed from time to time that the measures taken to meet the banking emergency were all essentially within the limits of orthodox capitalism. Over the nation people, despite their present discomforts,

made it very difficult to carry out the program of strengthening the capital structure of banks which were reopened with impaired capital, and the President finally had to practically take the matter out of the hands of Jesse Jones by appointing a committee himself to act for the R.F.C. in the matter. This committee or 'division,' which was announced by the President on October 23, 1933, included Jesse Jones as an ex officio member; but it was headed by Harvey Couch and included Eugene Black, Governor of the F. R. Board; Dean Acheson, Under Secretary of the Treasury; Lewis Douglas, Director of the Budget; J. F. T. O'Connor, Comptroller of the Currency; Walter J. Cummings, Chairman of the Board of the F.D.I.C.; Henry Bruere and Frank Walker. The President designated Governor Black to head a subcommittee on cooperation with member banks. 19 F.R. Bull. 672–673."

had little thought but that "happy days" would come again. But there was latent danger, which we were too busy to contemplate, that socialists or those who believed in planning might put over some sort of substitute for a free economy. Broadus Mitchell, whose associations and writings place his philosophical position as essentially socialistic, says:

> Some felt at the time, and have continued to believe since, that this was a moment when the country, and Congress, would have followed the President in making the banks national property. If that had been done, the other chief sectors of the economy could have been subsequently socialized. Such an action would have meant that the New Deal, instead of reforming glaring defects in order to preserve the capitalist system, would have set about superseding it.

But Mitchell as a conscientious observer of the realities, adds this:

> The President scouted the idea. Wise decision or not, this was probably the inevitable one. Under emergency conditions the interests and training of all the responsible participants dictated that course. It would have required men long schooled in collectivist advocacy to put the country on a different tack.*

Mere advocacy of collectivism does not train individuals to operate an economic system. Even Lenin admitted this in 1920 when he said, in a letter which is quoted by Sidney Webb: "I do not know of any socialist who had dealt with these problems. What must be done after a socialist take-over is a subject upon which socialist writers have been mostly silent."

When one inspects the actors on the scene at this time, especially Roosevelt himself, it becomes clear that there was little danger that the hopes of socialists might be realized. The Roosevelt I knew then was as interested as was Woodin in maintaining the private character of the banks. And the expert people upon whom we were compelled to depend were certainly of the firm belief that capitalism would work again if certain defects were removed.

There is a note of regret in Arthur Schlesinger, Jr.'s brief and cursory account of the banking emergency. He seems to deplore that passing of the golden moment when the banks could have been nationalized. He says, "Indeed, as Tugwell later acknowledged, Wall Street and the orthodox economists had a monopoly of *expertise* in this area. America had no one outside the charmed circle, like John Maynard Keynes in Britain, who might have conceived a genuine reform." †

As I reflect upon those days, I am thankful to Providence that Keynes

* Broadus Mitchell, *Depression Decade* (*The Economic History of the United States,* Vol. IX) (New York: Rinehart, 1947), pp. 132–33.

† Arthur M. Schlesinger, Jr., *The Coming of the New Deal* (Boston: Houghton Mifflin, 1959), p. 5.

had not yet reached Roosevelt's ear. But even if he had, he would have met strong resistance.

Schlesinger also says:

> The decision to save the system rather than to change it had come about almost by inadvertence. The first problem, as the President saw it, was to banish fear. If he was to restore confidence in the system, he had to offer policies which bankers themselves would support. And he had no real alternative to the restoration of the existing structure. It is true that Rexford G. Tugwell, another member of the campaign brain trust, now Assistant Secretary of Agriculture, had a scheme by which the postal savings system would take over the deposit and checking transactions of banks, while separate corporations would assume the job of commercial credit; but Tugwell's advice was not sought in the banking crisis. . . .
>
> There was restiveness in Congress about the President's approach. "I think back to the events of March 4, 1933," Senator Bronson Cutting of New Mexico later wrote, "with a sick heart. For then . . . the nationalization of banks by President Roosevelt could have been accomplished without a word of protest. It was President Roosevelt's great mistake." On the night before Congress convened, Senators Robert M. La Follette, Jr., of Wisconsin, and Edward P. Costigan of Colorado, two leading progressives, called at the White House to urge Roosevelt to establish a truly national banking system. But they found Roosevelt's mind made up. "That isn't necessary at all," La Follette later recalled Roosevelt saying. "I've just had every assurance of cooperation from the bankers." The very moneychangers, whose flight from their high seats in the temple the President had so grandiloquently proclaimed in his inaugural address, were now swarming through the corridors of the Treasury.*

This is a remarkably naïve account of a major event in the early New Deal if we realize that this historian's entire account of the early Roosevelt era is a highly prejudiced plea for national economic planning. To say that it was "by inadvertence" that the decision was made to save the system is a glaring misstatement. No one who had any part in the emergency in Washington had any other idea in mind from the beginning. There was no time to speculate upon the alternative between restoration and the chaos of revolution. I knew of no such plan of Tugwell's that Schlesinger describes and which he says was submitted to Roosevelt. Roosevelt certainly never mentioned it. For to turn the banking system over to the postal savings system would be as absurd as to turn the railroads over to the postmasters. For the railroads were in trouble, too. The historian is in further error when he says that the emergency plan originated with the bankers. The bankers had no plan at all.

Also, the statement that there was restiveness in Congress is one of

* *Ibid.*

those fractional truths that are no truths at all. Perhaps Cutting, Costigan, and La Follette toyed with the idea of nationalizing the banks, but in La Follette's speech when the emergency legislation was before Congress he made no such proposal, though he was severely critical of the banking system and the bankers. And if Cutting had any such idea, he was silent when the bill was under consideration in the Senate.

Chapter Twelve

Congress Adopts the Emergency Plan

WHEN the Seventy-third Congress met in extraordinary session at noon on Thursday, the ninth, it was the center of attention of an anxious and unhappy nation. Little was known of the plans that had been developed, and what was known was not understood. Bankers over the whole country, except a few in the metropolitan centers, hardly knew whether they were in business or not. Newspaper accounts were mostly speculative. And members of Congress themselves, with a handful of exceptions, knew that they were going to pass something the nature of which had not been disclosed.

Those people in Washington who had time to attend the sessions (and there were many of them), and those who could gain access to Congressional galleries (and those spaces were limited), crowded into their places. Sensing potential disorder, the new Vice-President, John N. Garner, sternly admonished the spectators that while the Senate was happy to welcome them as guests, they must, under the rules of the Senate, indulge in no disorder "verbal or otherwise." This warning had to be repeated many times in the hours that followed.

The House was called to order by the clerk, South Trimble, and it was announced that the credentials of members were noted as having been filed. Henry T. Rainey of Illinois, the choice of the Democratic caucus, was elected Speaker. This roll call indicated a majority of 302 and a minority of 110.

After some preliminaries, the President's message calling for emergency banking legislation was read, and Joseph W. Byrns of Tennessee, the majority leader, announced that there would be forty minutes of debate on the measure—twenty minutes allotted to Henry B. Steagall, chairman of the Committee on Banking and Currency, who was in charge of the bill, and an equal time to the ranking Republican on the committee, Louis T. McFadden.

Since the House had not adopted rules for the new session, the Speaker announced that the rules of the preceding Congress would be used in considering the bill. Byrns then announced that the bill, which had not been read at the moment and which was not even in the hands of members, would not be subject to amendment.

Before the bill was read, Bertrand H. Snell, the Republican leader, noted that it was "entirely out of the ordinary to pass legislation in this House that, as far as I know, is not even in print at the time it is offered . . . there is only one answer to this question, and that is to give the President what he demands and says is necessary to meet the situation."

After the bill was read, Steagall spoke in general support of the bill in terms that were inspirational rather than explanatory. For the opposition, Robert Luce of Massachusetts and McFadden briefly indicated that, while they regretted some features in the bill and the lack of time for amendments, they would support it. There were a few further questions, and the bill was passed without a roll call.

This bill, designated H.R. 1491, then went to the Senate. The identical Senate bill, designated Senate 1, was laid aside. The bill passed by the Senate and signed by the President was the House bill.

The new Senate had already met on March 4 in special session, according to custom and a proclamation by President Hoover. On that day the oath was administered to the new Vice-President and the newly elected or appointed members were sworn. After the Presidential inaugural ceremonies, a number of routine matters were disposed of. The nominations of the new Cabinet members were confirmed after a brief discussion about whether Woodin, the prospective Secretary of the Treasury, had disposed of stock holdings in line with the law on that subject. A memorial service was held for Senator Thomas J. Walsh, who had died on March 2.

The Senate met again on Monday, very briefly, to confirm the nominations of six designees to lesser positions. These included my own nomination as assistant secretary of state.

The Senate on Thursday, the ninth, first elected its officers, Joseph T. Robinson as majority leader, and Charles L. McNary as minority leader; both men were held over from the previous Congress. Because of the appointment of Claude Swanson to the Cabinet, Senator Key Pittman of Nevada was elected President Pro Tempore along with other Senate officers. Then the standing committees for the new Congress were approved. The President's message on emergency banking legislation was read, and since the bill was not yet in print for the members, a short recess was taken. After that, Senator Fletcher, chairman of the Banking and Currency Committee, introduced the President's bill, and it was referred to his committee for consideration until four o'clock.*

When the bill was introduced there were only a few printed copies for the Fletcher committee. Printed copies for other members were not ready until the committee reported.

To expedite action, Robinson announced that bills, resolutions, or joint resolutions not related to the "present emergency" should be deferred. For some reason, however, Robinson permitted Senator George W. Norris to introduce a joint resolution that Norris contended had a great deal to do with the "present depression." It was his legislation to create the Tennessee Valley Authority, which he had vainly promoted for some years. It was received and referred to the Committee on Agriculture and Forestry. That was the origin of the parliamentary career of the TVA.†

At four-thirty that afternoon the Senate resumed regular business, and Fletcher presented the banking bill. There were no committee amendments. The identical House bill as passed was already before the Senate, and this became the subject of consideration.‡

At the outset of the debate, Senator Arthur H. Vandenberg expressed interest in provisions in the bill to permit the comptroller of the currency to open such banks as were in his judgment solvent. Vandenberg's concern was not with the authority of the comptroller, which had always prevailed, but whether the comptroller's determination of solvency would rest upon values as of that particular day. Fletcher replied that he did not think so. Also, he assured Vandenberg that while provisions in the bill would benefit state banks, they would remain subject to state authority if they were not members of the Federal Reserve System.

This launched a considerable interruption by Senator Huey Long. He presented an amendment that would permit the President to "declare" any state bank to be a member of the Federal Reserve System. Despite assurances from many Senators that any state bank that chose to join the Federal Reserve System might do so if it assumed the conditions and responsibilities of such membership, Long launched into an attack upon the big banks, which, he said, had loaded the small state banks with paper that proved to be worthless. "The condition of our state banks," he said, "is due to the impositions of the big banks." He was, he said,

* Of all the members of the Senate present that day, only two remain as this is written in 1966: Richard B. Russell of Georgia, and Carl Hayden of Arizona.

† It is an almost forgotten fact that the members of the Senate sat briefly that day as a court of impeachment. Federal Judge Harold Louderback of the northern district of California was the subject of this proceeding.

‡ The text of the bill as passed by both houses and signed by the President, as well as the various proclamations, official statements, regulations permitting limited banking transactions, etc., are in the *Federal Reserve Bulletin* for March 1933 (Volume 19), beginning at page 113.

not pleading for the "little bank of Pelahatchee or the big bank in New York City; I am talking about the men and women, the bootblacks, the farmers, and widows who have money in these little State banks, just the same as other depositors . . . in the big banks. You are proposing to take every dime they have away from them, and when Friday morning comes it will be a hanging day for that kind of people." He apparently liked the expression "hanging day," for he adverted to it from time to time as other Senators tried to reply. "Now, Friday is our usual hanging day in our state," he said.

During the entire debate on the bill, the chair was occupied by the President Pro Tem. Senator Pittman, after Long's argument had continued for a considerable time, cut him off by saying that the question was on the adoption of the Long amendment. This enabled him to give the floor to the venerable Senator Glass, who said:

"Mr. President, Congress is dealing in an unprecedented way with an extraordinary and desperate situation in the country.

"Under the proclamation of the President and of the governors of many of the States, all the banks in the country are now closed. The proclamation of the President automatically expires at midnight tonight; and, unless some remedial legislation is enacted before that hour, we will have an indescribable condition of distress in the United States tomorrow.

"This bill undertakes to apply, in the emergency, remedial powers vested in the President of the United States, the Secretary of the Treasury, and the Comptroller of the Currency. It broadens—in a degree that is almost shocking to me—the currency and credit facilities of the Federal Reserve Banking System, and largely extends these facilities to State banks which are not members of the Federal Reserve Banking System, that have never endured one penny of the expense of the establishment of the system or of its maintenance, and do not do so today.

"This talk about closing all the State banks is based upon a total misunderstanding of the provisions of the bill. We do not close, by act or by implication, a single, solitary State bank in the United States—not one. These banks are within the jurisdiction and under the authority of the respective States, and every one of them may be opened at daybreak tomorrow morning by authority of the respective States."

From there on, Glass dominated the debate. His distinction as the best-informed, most experienced member of the Senate on fiscal affairs was generally acknowledged. As a member of the House he had managed the Federal Reserve legislation in 1913. He had served as Secretary of the Treasury from December 1918 to February 1920. And as every member knew, Glass had been Roosevelt's first choice for that position until he finally declined less than three weeks before. He was also familiar with the bill pending that day because he had been consulted by the people who were working on it in the Treasury.

Long's contention that state banks were not sufficiently protected in the emergency legislation was, despite its exaggeration, the expression of a concern which several Senators voiced that afternoon. Step by step, Glass described the measures that had been taken in the bill to care for state banks. With no inconsiderable impatience, he denied Long's contention that there was a conspiracy of big banks to close the "little fellows."

MR. LONG: How many banks are there in the United States?

MR. GLASS: When I had the last report there were about 19,000.

MR. LONG: And you are going to open 5,000 and close 14,000.

MR. GLASS: We are not going to close one, and the Senator does not know what he is talking about when he says "close 14,000." There is not a line or a sentence in the bill which authorizes the closing of any bank. They are all closed now, are they not?

MR. LONG: . . . Were you not told that this would mean that 5,000 national banks could open, that if this subscription of preferred stock were allowed they could open 5,000, and without it they will open 2,400, but even with it all 900 national banks would not open and 14,000 State banks would stay closed?

MR. GLASS: No; I was not told anything of the kind, and if anybody who would tell me that there is a word or sentence in the bill that closes a State bank, I would tell him that he did not know what he was talking about.

MR. LONG: I ask the Senator if he has not understood that under this bill, or was it not told to the Senator and did he not understand that under this bill, of the 19,000 banks in America, 5,900 of which are national banks, 900 national banks would not open and 14,000 State banks would not open?

MR. GLASS: The Senator from Louisiana has such ignorance of the whole problem and such a lack of appreciation of things that he wants the President of the United States to cover 14,000 State banks into the Federal Reserve System without knowing a thing in the world about them.

Glass was more patient with some of the other Senators who were concerned about state banks. He said:

"There is not a desirable State bank in the United States which is not authorized to make application and gain membership in the Federal Reserve Banking System before noon tomorrow—not one. But it is idle to talk about the President issuing an edict declaring State banks to be members of the Federal Reserve System—State banks which have persistently for eighteen years remained outside of the fold and protection of the Federal Reserve Banking System; State banks over which the Federal Government has not even the power of examination or espionage of any description; State banks which may do a variety of banking business not tolerated in the Federal Reserve Banking System. Yet it is proposed that the President of the United States, destitute, necessarily, of any knowledge of the condition of these banks, with no possible opportunity in weeks and weeks to ascertain their condition, shall cover them in arbitrarily by a blanket order and have them become members of the Federal Reserve Banking System, enjoying all the privileges of the System.

"I said a while ago that there are provisions of this bill so broad and so liberal that no friend of the Federal Reserve Banking System, in ordinary times, would tolerate them for a moment. Under the provisions of the bill, when member banks shall have exhausted their eligible paper they may then bring their 'cats and dogs,' if you please, to the Federal Reserve bank, and with the assent of the Federal Reserve Board have them discounted under this bill, the whole thing submitted to the judgment of the Federal Reserve Board and banks."

Glass also made it clear that state banks could borrow from banks that were members of the Federal Reserve System and that the bill allowed "the Reconstruction Finance Corporation, upon the initiative of the Secretary of the Treasury, and with the approval of the President, to subscribe to the preferred stocks of the state banks."

In the course of the debate Glass put his finger on the basic situation, which had had so much to do with the creation of the crisis. This "was the multiplicity of state banks and the lack of proper supervision of them by state authority.

"So largely with currency. Every banker ought to know the business of the patrons of his bank. They do in Great Britain. They do in Canada. In Canada at the beginning of the fiscal year every patron of a bank, every business man, has to file with the bank his budget for the year and his probable requirements in credit and currency. If during the year he undertakes to exceed his requirements, as filed, he has to give the banker a reason for it.

" 'Little banks'? Little corner grocerymen who run banks, who get together $10,000 or $15,000, as it may be, and then invite the deposits of their community, and at the very first gust of disaster topple over and ruin their depositors! What we need in this country are real banks and real bankers. If a struggling young man wants to get a place here in Washington as a stenographer or typist, he has to have a civil-service examination; and yet we have people all over the country from one end to the other calling themselves 'bankers,' and all they know is how to shave notes at an excessive rate of interest. They are not bankers."

Glass's discussion of the power granted in the bill to the Federal Reserve to issue Federal Reserve bank notes was occasioned by a question from Senator David A. Reed of Pennsylvania:

MR. REED: Lest the impression get out that this is a novelty in the field of finance, I want to ask the Senator if it [is] not true that they were issued during the World War, to some extent secured entirely by Panama Canal bonds, and if it is not true that in English finance such notes have been repeatedly issued by the Bank of England, so that there is nothing novel about them?

MR. GLASS: The history of the case is just this, in a word. For fifty years the whole banking community and business public denounced our bond-secured currency, and effort after effort was made to rid us of it, so that when the Federal Reserve law was enacted we provided that the Federal Reserve banks might purchase from the member banks their United States 2s which carried the circulation privilege, in an amount not exceeding $25,000,000 per annum, in order that we might literally and eventually abolish the bond-secured currency, and substitute for it the Federal Reserve currency, issued upon commercial, industrial, and agricultural transactions, which would be emitted upon those transactions, and automatically retired at the maturity of the transactions. Before the Federal Reserve banks could make large purchases of these bonds the World War came on and interrupted the whole proceedings. So that the Federal Reserve banks now have a very limited amount of these bonds upon which they are authorized by law to issue Federal Reserve bank notes. In the pending bill we very tremendously enlarge the authority of Federal Reserve banks to issue Federal Reserve bank notes on United States bonds, whether they carry the circulation privilege or not.

MR. REED: What I am driving at, Mr. President, is that bond-secured currency is not a new thing in the world.

MR. GLASS: Not by any means.

MR. REED: Although we would all like to see it done away with.

MR. GLASS: We would like to see it done away with, but it will be a long time now before it will be done away with.

Senator Robert M. La Follette, Jr., who had succeeded to his father's seat in the Senate in 1925, made a somewhat lengthy speech in opposition to the bill. This young man, whose views met with limited acceptance by most of his colleagues but who was widely respected and personally liked, did not elicit an answer from the bill's sponsors. Perhaps that was because, as the text of his remarks shows, he failed to reveal what alternative he had to offer. His general contentions were that the banking distress was indistinguishable from the general problems of the depression; that what was needed was to put more purchasing power in the hands of the people; that the New York banks that were members of the Federal Reserve System were much more solvent than even the Federal Reserve members elsewhere in the country and, of course, than the state banks everywhere; that there was grave danger that their strength, plus the government aid they would receive under the terms of the bill, would give them power to dominate a reorganization of the entire banking structure; that such a reorganization would consist of the big banks acquiring control of all banks and a consolidation in a few "group-banking units"; and that the preferred-stock provision of the bill would invite "widespread speculation, manipulation and abuse by insiders."

The alternative that he must have had in mind was only hinted at in two or three expressions. He said that, since there was such a disparity in strength between what he called "the sheep and the goats," the resources and liabilities of all banks "should be merged respectively." He said further that "if I could have my way, I would insure control by the President during the emergency." There was also a curious reference to permitting the creation of new purchasing power by state action. Whether, as has been said by some historians, this meant that La Follette favored using the distress in the banking system as the occasion for a complete and permanent government banking system is not clear. But the overwhelming sentiment of the Senate and, I believe, of the House that day was to follow orthodox methods of re-establishing the system that had hitherto prevailed.

When La Follette finished his speech, the President Pro Tem put before the Senate an amendment which had been offered by the blind Senator from Oklahoma, Thomas P. Gore, as a substitute for the Long amendment. It was rejected.

Then Long demanded a yea-and-nay vote on his amendment. The President Pro Tem ruled that this demand was not sufficiently seconded. Long asked that there be a standing vote, which the President Pro Tem ordered. He ruled that there was insufficient support for a yea-and-nay vote. The question was put, and the chair ruled that the amendment was rejected.

There were some additional comments, and then Robinson asked for the yeas-and-nays on the passage of the bill. It was so ordered, and the vote was 73 yeas and 7 nays. Among the absentees there were announced two more who would have voted nay.

Those who voted against the bill on the roll call were Borah, Carey, Costigan, Dale, La Follette, Nye, Shipstead.

And, as the *Record* has it, "So the bill was passed."

The time of adjournment: 7:52 P.M.

Chapter Thirteen

Unfreezing the Banks

THE tasks imposed upon the Administration and the Federal Reserve System by the Emergency Banking Act were either explicit or implicit in its four titles:

Title I "approved and confirmed" the authority exercised by Roosevelt under the 1917 legislation and also permitted him to exercise like authority in any national emergency. It recognized that certain activities must be carried on in banks that were otherwise closed. Those powers might be exercised by the Secretary of the Treasury, subject to the approval of the President.

Title II provided for the reopening of certain national banks with impaired assets under "conservators" appointed by the comptroller of the currency. These conservators were to release such amounts of deposits as the comptroller deemed safe. They were also to receive deposits, which would be segregated from the other liabilities of those banks and which were to be subject to withdrawal. The conservators could, with the approval of the comptroller, plan and put reorganization into effect with the consent of 75 per cent of depositors or two-thirds of the stockholders.

Title III provided for the issuance of preferred stock by national banks, which might be bought by the RFC or by the public. The RFC was also authorized to take such stock from state banks.

Title IV provided for the issuance of Federal Reserve bank notes (already described). It was provided, however, that after the emergency these notes would be issued to banks only on the securities of the United States, not, as in the emergency, also upon 90 per cent of other "sound" assets.

The President, after signing the act, issued a proclamation continuing the holiday indefinitely.

The next day, March 10, Roosevelt issued an executive order authorizing the Secretary of the Treasury to provide regulations for certain limited banking transactions by member banks of the Federal Reserve System. He also extended this power to the banking authorities of the states. These transactions were to apply to certain extraordinary emergency situations. The President's order also empowered the Secretary of the Treasury to issue licenses for reopening banks. This actual authority would be exercised by the various Federal Reserve banks serving as agents for the Secretary of the Treasury. His order also prohibited the export or removal of gold from the United States and denied withdrawal of gold from any bank. These gold regulations were subject to interpretation by the Secretary.

Following this, a steady stream of regulations, interpretations, and special permissions poured out of the Treasury, all bearing the name of the Secretary.

On Saturday, the eleventh, the President issued a statement assuring the country that "technical difficulties which operated to delay the opening of the banks . . . have finally substantially been overcome by tireless work on the part of the officials of the Treasury and the Federal Reserve System" and that it would be possible to reopen the banks on Monday, Tuesday, and Wednesday. On Monday, he said, the banks in the Federal Reserve cities that were members of the Federal Reserve System would be opened under licenses. He added that state authorities might, if they deemed it wise, open banks which were not members of the system, under licenses in those Federal Reserve cities. Further, he said that on Tuesday banks in the 250 cities having clearinghouse associations would be licensed to open. And banks elsewhere would be opened on Wednesday. He added in his statement that he would speak over the radio on Sunday night at 10:00 P.M. about what had been done about the banks and what remained to be done.

All this was easier said than done. For each provision in the new act that was directed at reopening imposed a tremendous burden on the individual who was responsible for a specific operation.

It should be noted that all state banks not members of the Federal Reserve System would be opened at the discretion of the state banking authorities of the various states. Many of the people in Washington, including Awalt, felt that this was a mistake but they realized that with the limitations on their knowledge of the condition of those banks, they could not assume that discretionary authority.

The task of sifting out the sound banks that were within the jurisdiction of the Federal government was difficult enough for them to handle in the limited time available. A great part of the decision-making fell upon Awalt. He and his staff had at hand material data on these banks, but it had to be supplemented by information gathered by telegraph and telephone.

There was little time for deliberation. The office of the comptroller had to sort out and classify the banks under its jurisdiction as the sound, the unsound, and the doubtful. Considering the miscellaneous mass of information about what were called assets, this involved quick value judgments, almost in the nature of speculation. For none could be sure until later how high the tide of confidence would rise at the time of reopening.

Everyone was aware that in the rush serious mistakes might be made —some banks would be reopened that should have remained closed, and others would be closed that might have weathered the storm if reopened. The benefit of the doubt, considering the confidence of everyone in the anticipated effect of the President's appeal on Sunday night, would be on the side of reopening. But the burden of responsibility would have to rest upon the Secretary, the undersecretary, and the acting comptroller of the currency.

A matter of procedure immediately arose. This involved a dispute between the Treasury and the Federal Reserve Board.

Under the law, Woodin would have to issue licenses for reopened banks belonging to the Federal Reserve System, both national and state. The governor of the Federal Reserve Board, Eugene Meyer, objected to the demand of the Treasury that each of the Federal Reserve banks in each district should approve of the reopening of the banks in their respective districts. The Federal Reserve Board did not want these banks to assume such responsibility. It held that the Treasury alone should shoulder this burden. The argument over this was fairly warm.

The Treasury was finally successful in this dispute. The district Federal Reserve bank would approve, the chief national bank examiner would recommend, and the comptroller's office would on that guidance recommend that the Secretary of the Treasury issue the license.

I was present when perhaps the most important and dramatic decision about reopening was made. It well illustrated the necessity of harmony between the Treasury and the Federal Reserve banks. It concerned the reopening of the great Bank of America. This bank, controlled by the Transamerica Corporation, had been built up by A. P. Giannini. There were deposit liabilities of $600,000,000. It had at that time 410 branches over the state of California and immense holdings beyond the state.

In his rise, Giannini had made plenty of enemies and had engendered much jealousy in the higher banking circles of the state and elsewhere. But he held a large proportion of the remaining savings of the people of the state in his institution. I was familiar with the paramount importance of the Bank of America in the economic life of California, for my family was living there at the time and I had spent considerable time there in the preceding two years. I had stressed the importance of this bank in the discussions with Woodin. A failure to reopen would shake the state to its foundations. But the bank was undoubtedly on the critical list and the Federal Reserve Bank in San Francisco was none too friendly to its reopening.

The regional examiner had reported an examination completed in July 1932 and said:

"A continuation of existent economic conditions and the present management will place this bank in jeopardy, nor may relief be expected from any of its affiliate corporations, all of which have troubles of their own." *

But a report of a later examination was made to Awalt which convinced him that the bank should be allowed to reopen. Nevertheless, it was clear that, considering the immense amount of deposits which might be withdrawn, and considering the nature of the bank's assets, the Federal Reserve Bank in San Francisco would have to provide sufficient funds to make it possible to reopen and stay open. It was Awalt's opinion that if the Bank of America failed to reopen, such banks as the Continental National Bank of Chicago would be affected and the entire situation in the West would be shaken.

Awalt decided, since the new examiner's report did not show the bank to be insolvent, that it should be reopened. He recommended this to Woodin.

Woodin and Awalt then talked with Roosevelt, but the President said it was a matter for their decision. Since they felt as they did, he said they should call the governor of the Federal Reserve Bank at San Francisco, John U. Calkins, and persuade him to agree to the reopening.

When Woodin called Calkins, only he and Awalt and I were present. Calkins was at first adamant that the bank should remain closed. Woodin insisted that the comptroller's office had information that the bank was solvent. Finally Woodin put the case bluntly, "Are you willing to take the responsibility for keeping this bank closed?" Calkins was shaken by this and also by the figures Awalt had supplied, which Woodin recited. Calkins refused to take the responsibility and Woodin ended the matter by saying, "Well, then, the bank will open."

There have been various versions of this story, one of which erroneously asserts that the reopening was achieved by the Hearst interests. A better account is by Thomas M. Storke, a Santa Barbara newspaper publisher who was in an anteroom of the Secretary's office with Senators Johnson and McAdoo awaiting the verdict. Storke says:

The chief of the Federal Reserve in San Francisco, John U. Calkins, had recommended that the Bank of America remain closed on Monday

* Awalt, unpublished manuscript.

morning. He presented a set of figures which seemed to prove that A. P. Giannini's financial colossus was on the brink of insolvency. Giannini, however, claimed that Calkins had personal reasons for wanting to tear down the Bank of America and had supplied Secretary Woodin with figures which were a year out of date. He said that the Bank of America had made a healthy recovery during that previous year.*

Storke adds that after the reopening the Bank of America paid its first dividend in two years.

After Woodin had made the decision I stepped out of the Secretary's office and found Senators Johnson and McAdoo anxiously waiting. Storke was with them. I told them the good news.

The RFC advanced $30,000,000 on the preferred stock of the bank. Within four months the bank and Transamerica paid off the last of that loan.

There were other moments of tension in those days, and there were some mistakes. But the record stands as a tribute to the judgment of tired men, including—at the very center of things—Awalt, whose office staff had to be enlarged to twice its former size.

The few mistakes made in reopening were buried under a mountain of wise decisions. One of the problems was solved by the creation of a new bank in Detroit and the paying out of frozen deposits through this bank buttressed by a large loan from the RFC.

The operation directed by Jones at the RFC was less critical than that which went on at the Treasury. But it continued long after the days of reopening. For the advances on the banks' preferred stock or debentures required careful examination of the condition of each bank that required help.

There was also feverish activity at the Federal Reserve Board and the twelve Federal Reserve banks.

But it was on an assured note that Roosevelt announced on Saturday that "the technical difficulties" had been surmounted.

When the dawn on Sunday, March 12, came, the die had been cast but the immense task of reopening the banks remained. This had to be orderly, but to make it so involved a mass of detail. The exceptions specified by Woodin's statement had to be implemented. This required the preparation of innumerable directives. Gloyd Awalt and his subordinates were still wading through bank figures to separate the sound from the unsound and to calculate the exact degree of solvency essential to a resumption of business in the week ahead. Jones and his RFC were busy with the process of accepting the preferred stock or debentures of banks and providing loans on this security. The three days' steps of reopening had already been fixed, but the banks had to be notified.

* *California Editor* (Los Angeles: Westernlore Press, 1958), pp. 344–45.

In the White House the critical hour was approaching when Roosevelt would muster all his capacity to induce badly confused and frightened depositors to return to the reopened banks the currency and gold they had withdrawn in the panic that had passed.

I had little part in the preparation of this memorable radio address, the first of what came to be called "fireside chats." It had been announced on Saturday that it would be given over the radio at 10:00 P.M. Sunday night. I spent several hours on that Sunday at the Treasury and the White House, but there were so many other subjects demanding my attention that the serious job of helping with the Sunday night speech was left to others. On Friday I had had to work with Lewis Douglas on the economy message, and after that it was necessary to keep in touch with the people "on the Hill" who were engaged in the difficult job of pushing this bitter act of renunciation through Congress.

Charles Michelson, who during the Hoover years had been employed on the staff of the Democratic National Committee and was retained by Farley, was available. His professional capacity as what he called the "ghost" suggested the idea to someone, perhaps Stephen Early, that he prepare a draft for the Roosevelt speech.

During the campaign and later Roosevelt had never been happy with Michelson's compositions. The fruitful "ghost" was too slap-dash in his writings, and in this instance Michelson knew very little about the plans that had been made in the week after the inauguration. In his book, *The Ghost Talks*, Michelson confesses that "technically these matters of deep finance were, of course, clear over my head." He prepared a draft of a speech, however, and brought it to the White House and handed it to Ballantine, who was a frequent consultant to the President during those days.

After a cursory reading of Michelson's draft, Ballantine and I realized that it lacked precision and substance. I therefore turned it over to Ballantine for a complete rewriting job. This was most essential, for whatever Roosevelt was to say to the country must be factually in conformity with the procedures that were under way and were planned for the week ahead. Ballantine did more than an editing job. He substantially composed a new draft. Ballantine delivered this to Roosevelt. His recollection later was that he did not submit the Michelson alternative to the President.

Roosevelt, falling back upon his simple, homelike style which he had so often used before, then dictated a draft, with Ballantine's version before him. But in doing so, he was careful to follow the procedural details in the Ballantine draft. I may or may not have gone over the final draft. I cannot rely upon my memory on that point, and have no written notes on the subject.

I offer this detailed explanation because in 1944, after the appearance of Michelson's book, there was an exchange in the press between Ballantine and Michelson.

Michelson states:

> In a footnote in his volume published some time later Professor Moley said the speech was entirely rewritten by Arthur Ballantine, which was my first information that that gentleman had ever seen the draft. It must have been handed him by Moley. The actual preparation of the speech followed the procedure which I have described in regard to other speeches. I went over to the White House with my draft (I never saw or heard of any other), and the President lay on a couch and dictated his own speech.*

Ballantine replied to this in an article in the New York *Herald Tribune:*

> My recollection is very clear that what actually happened was exactly what is stated by Ray Moley, whom in many connections Mr. Michelson praises so highly.
>
> I have a very distinct recollection of Mr. Michelson handing me his draft on Saturday morning. He thought I should look the draft over for the Secretary. On taking a rather quick look at it I felt that there were a number of things in it which needed rather extensive change. Mr. Michelson seemed to be pretty tired from his hard work, and I suggested that he take some rest and that I would do some work on the draft. He welcomed the suggestions. I then prepared a draft with needed changes, and took this to the White House. I do not recall distinctly whether or not I also took Mr. Michelson's draft, but I would not say that I did. I do not know how the President prepared the final draft, as I was not present, but it was clear to me that the draft which I had revised was before him and was extensively used in giving form to his telling presentation.

In the final composition of the speech that Sunday afternoon I do not know whether, as Michelson said, Roosevelt reposed on a couch. But I can testify that, homey though it may sound, it was not his customary way of dictating statements or speeches.

Nor am I able to pick from the phrases of the speech as delivered what Ballantine contributed and what Roosevelt wrote on his own. There is the unmistakable phraseology of Roosevelt in the text.

Its tone suggests the way a kindly and worldly-wise high-school principal would tell a freshman class the rules of the school and the way they should behave in joining their classes. It was simple and colloquial, and also explicit in describing what had been done to make the banks safe, what former depositors should do when their banks reopened, what order would be followed in the reopening of various institutions, and, above all, that it would be better to return the money to the banks than to keep it. "I can assure you that it is safer to keep your money in a reopened bank than under the mattress."

* Charles Michelson, *The Ghost Talks* (New York: G. P. Putnam's, 1944), pp. 56–7.

The exact steps that had been taken by the Administration and Congress were outlined, which indicated how fully Roosevelt had been briefed by Ballantine and Woodin. He explained why a holiday had been necessary, to provide for the banks the necessary currency to meet all demands. And, because it was clear that some banks would not reopen during the first week or until later, he offered reassurance to the less fortunate depositors of those banks. He said, "One more point before I close. There will be, of course, some banks unable to be reopened without being reorganized. The new law allows the government to assist in making these reorganizations quickly and effectively and even allows the government to subscribe to at least a part of new capital which may be required."

He explained how completely orthodox the entire plan had been. "There is nothing complex, or radical, in the process."

Finally, he returned to the theme of his inaugural. "Confidence and courage are the essentials of success in carrying out our plan. You people must have faith; you must not be stampeded by rumors or guesses. Let us unite in banishing fear. We have provided the machinery to restore our financial system; it is up to you to support and make it work. It is your problem no less than it is mine. Together we cannot fail."

There were, it was estimated, 20 million radios turned on that night, and an estimated 60 million were listening.

The response to this appeal has been common knowledge in the generation since. It is true that large sums were withdrawn to meet necessitous situations. But the return flow of currency was far greater than the withdrawals. The New York Federal Reserve Bank alone reported an excess return of $10 million in currency. All over the nation people were redepositing the money they had taken out in the panic.

Abroad, signs of confidence in the dollar appeared. At the resumption of official foreign exchange on Monday, only a few hours after Roosevelt's speech, the dollar advanced sharply from the level of March 3, at which time it had been very profitable to withdraw gold from the United States. The pound sterling dropped 6½ cents to $3.39½ and the franc dropped 4⅛ points to 3.92⅜ cents.

The New York Stock Exchange reopened on Wednesday, and prices rose steadily, with transactions exceeding three million shares. This was the largest volume since September, when prices were in a spectacular decline.

The increase in stock prices over March 3 was more than 15 per cent, the largest single day's rise in the memory of the exchange.

One of the most distressing subjects that had occupied the bankers' meetings in the week before had been the necessity looming ahead for a Treasury refinancing program involving $800,000,000 in new certificates of indebtedness. It was on this point that Traylor had reproved me when I suggested that Roosevelt could assure that the subscription would be taken by the public.

On Saturday, relying on the prospect of the drastic cut in government spending, the Treasury announced that bids would be received on the following Wednesday. When the new issue was put on the market it was oversubscribed by more than 100 per cent. To sweeten the issue, the interest rates were set at 4 and 4½ per cent, the highest since World War I. But the gratifying element in this response was that without recourse to an offering directly to the public, the normal procedure of accepting bids from the banks was followed. Also, the new certificates promised redemption at maturity in gold coin at the current standard of value.

The reaction of depositors to the President's appeal and the reopening of the banks exceeded our most optimistic expectations. The great majority of the depositors were assured by the reopening and the means taken to keep the banks open.

But a sizable number of the depositors were still left anxious and unhappy. For all the banks did not reopen after the holiday; some remained closed for a time, and a few were closed permanently.

Here the statistics must be stated with many qualifications.

Arthur Ballantine, writing fifteen years after the holiday, says that by the end of March there had been returned to banks over $1.2 billion in currency, half of which was in gold coin, bullion, or certificates. By April 12, when the original licensing had been completed, 12,817 of the 17,796 banks that had been open and operating two months before the holiday were fully open again with deposits of $31 billion. By the end of the year, there were 14,440 commercial banks in operation with $33 billion in deposits.

Ballantine also points out that very few banks were reopened with conservators. Some of these, however, were banks of considerable size. Many others were opened because they took advantage of the help of the RFC.

The return of gold in various forms was so great during and after the holiday that the President did not issue his drastic executive order "Forbidding the Hoarding of Gold and Gold Certificates" until April 5.*

On the day after the President's executive order, Woodin elaborated and explained its meaning. His statement permitted gold for use in industry or art to be held until May 1. An exception was made to permit "any one person" an amount not exceeding $100 and also the retention of gold coins of recognized value to collectors of rare or unusual coins.

An accounting of the aftermath of the holiday by Friedman and Schwartz amplifies Ballantine's figures concerning the banks that re-

* Ballantine, "When All the Banks Closed," *Harvard Business Review,* March 1948.

mained closed and those that were opened.* They say that after the 12,000 banks were reopened under license, approximately 5,000 were left "in a state of limbo." Of these, 300 were opened later, and 2,000 were either consolidated with other banks or permanently closed. Others were reorganized under new names.

This is a relatively modest figure, considering the great multitude of banks of various kinds spread over the nation, some with extremely rickety foundations. Glass had pointed out in his comments during the debate on the Emergency Banking Act that banking practice was so loose and banking regulation so incompetent in many states that a large number of so-called banks were running and receiving deposits with little capital and no real banking talent to manage them. Some were, to use Glass's term, "rotten."

Measured by these conditions and also by Glass's estimate of the number of banks that should remain closed, the number of banks which resumed business and paid off their depositors in whole or in part was most remarkable. Friedman and Schwartz say that "by the end of June over 2,300 of the banks holding nearly half of the *restricted* deposits were licensed to open, 388 closed." It is true that those closed banks held a very large amount of deposits.

It was this "mopping-up" operation that Jesse Jones faced at mid-year.

While some banks availed themselves of the opportunity to borrow working capital on the security of their preferred stock or debentures, Jesse Jones was far from satisfied with the bankers' reaction. He was firmly convinced that the banking community had invited trouble traditionally by working with inadequate capital. And he continued his campaign to break down their reluctance to borrow from the RFC for a long time after the period of the emergency.

After the Glass-Steagall Act had been passed with provision for the guarantee of deposits by the Federal Deposit Insurance Corporation, Jones set to work with deadly seriousness to induce banks to shore up their capital with RFC loans.

On August 1 he made a radio address urging cooperation. But when this produced only scant response, he asked permission to speak before the American Bankers' Association at its convention in Chicago on September 5. He faced a not-too-friendly audience. He was heard in silence. But at an evening meeting later, he decided to answer the criticisms of his earlier pronouncements with brutal realism. He said:

"I made one speech today and you did not like it. Now, I suppose, I ought to say something to redeem myself in your eyes. What I say here is being said at a private dinner, and is entirely off the record; and if there are any newspapermen here, they will so treat it. . . . Half

* Friedman and Schwartz, *A Monetary History of the United States.*

the banks represented in this room are insolvent; and those of you representing these banks know it better than anyone else."

His fierce conviction had its effect. There was considerable support for him among bankers. But a serious task still confronted him because the banks, in order to qualify for Federal deposit insurance, had to satisfy the government before January 1 as to their soundness.

Jones encountered opposition in the Administration at this point, and in October he was summoned by Roosevelt to discuss differences with Eugene Black, Lewis Douglas, and Henry Bruere of the Bowery Savings Bank in New York. They were critical of the way Jones was meeting the banking situation and apparently wanted to set up a new agency.

Jones replied that they grossly underestimated the need of the banks for new capital. "They tell you that it will take $600,000,000 dollars to make the questionable banks qualify for deposit insurance. They know less about it than I had given them credit for. I tell you it will take one billion two hundred million dollars to do the job, double the amount they think. The RFC can and will do the job, in the required time. Furthermore, these men all put together could never do it." Roosevelt said:

"Boys, I am going to back Jess. He has never failed me yet. Henry, you and Lew and Jess get together and work out a plan."

Jones's plan was already in operation, but he agreed to meet Bruere and Douglas at breakfast the following morning.

After Douglas and Bruere had left, Jones went back into Roosevelt's office.

"I would like for you to make me a promise," Jones said to Roosevelt.

"What is it?" the President inquired.

"Promise me that you will forget that there is a bank in the United States; and I promise you there will be no more bank trouble."

While it was necessary to extend the time for some 2,000 banks to qualify for deposit insurance, the necessary loans were made during 1934.

Years later, the reckoning showed that the RFC invested $1,171,411,000.56 in the capital structure of 6,105 banks. This was very close to the estimate Jones had made in October 1933.

In 1956, twenty-four years after the first loan had been made, the books of the RFC showed that all but two banks originally helped had redeemed their securities. The total loss at that time was only about $5,000,000.*

* This account of the aftermath of the bank crisis is based upon Jones's *Fifty Billion Dollars,* and *Jesse H. Jones* by Bascom Timmons.

Chapter Fourteen

Economy, a Key to Confidence

IF we were to lay side by side the expressions of Roosevelt about government spending and those of the more recent Presidents Kennedy and Johnson, we could scarcely believe the three authors were not only American Presidents but members of the same political party. Deficits were then matters of concern, even alarm. Now they are regarded as evidence of growth and enlightened public policy. The public—or a considerable part of it—has first abhorred, then tolerated, and finally embraced the concept of unbalanced budgets.

It was not until Roosevelt was well into his second term that he found economic rationalizations for spending large sums of government money. As late as 1936 he submitted what he called a "conservative" executive budget to Congress. In 1933 he subscribed to views as frostily thrifty as those of his predecessor Calvin Coolidge.

In the campaign of 1932 Roosevelt and his advisers were deeply committed to economical government. Among the memoranda submitted to Roosevelt by members of his Brains Trust, there was a memorandum by Adolf Berle in which he not only pointed out the growing Hoover deficits, but suggested methods of eliminating them. Beginning in 1920 there had been eleven years with sizable surpluses, and the indebtedness of the government had been reduced from its wartime high in 1919, \$25.4 billion, to \$16.2 billion in 1930. At the time of the inauguration in 1933 it had run to \$22.5 billion. This, according to Berle, represented a serious and rising burden on the credit of the United States. A manufacturers' sales tax was suggested as a means of fiscal relief.

Hugh Johnson wrote a blistering speech assailing the profligacy of the Hoover Administration, which Roosevelt delivered with singular emphasis at Pittsburgh on October 19, 1932.

Earlier, as well as in that speech, he declared his determination, if elected, to redeem the Democratic platform's promise to cut expenditures by 25 per cent and to balance the budget.

I had no doubt then and have none now that Roosevelt was perfectly sincere in this dedication to government economy. He had been a measurably economical governor of New York. In his personal life he always indicated a streak of Dutch thrift, no doubt inherited from ancestors who had been shrewd and canny businessmen.

More than a month before the inauguration, I had discussed his budgetary plans with him. We both agreed that with vast unemployment and lagging business, reductions in spending would be hard to get through Congress. And we realized that to accomplish real economies, the effort had to be made at the very beginning of the "honeymoon" after the inauguration. Also, that to by-pass the special interests of members, economical legislation must provide for wide delegation on spending to the President.

In making this decision, there was a factor other than saving money and thus relieving the pressure on the government's credit. For Roosevelt had promises of economy in his campaign record and there was also the need to inspire the people of the country to invest and provide opportunities for re-employment. Thus a determined expression of frugality in government spending would be essential to the generation of public confidence.

As noted earlier, Swagar Sherley had been Glass's choice for Secretary of the Treasury. He had very orthodox views on finance, and Roosevelt had offered him the directorship of the Budget Bureau. He declined, but was very helpful in preparing the plans for economy.

Roosevelt in late February called Lewis W. Douglas and offered him the appointment as director of the budget. Douglas hesitated, since he had served as Congressman-at-Large for Arizona since 1923 and had attained a good degree of seniority in the House. But after a few days he accepted, with certain conditions:

> I finally acquiesced and suggested certain conditions under which I would accept the position. One of them was that the campaign pledge to reduce expenditures ought to be honored, especially since, in my view, there would be a banking crisis and the credit of the United States would be, at least, temporarily impaired or, if not impaired, it would be under some temporary shadow. Under these circumstances, certain reductions in authorization for expenditures could be approved by the Congress. In any event, if the banking collapse, which I anticipated, were to come about, it was vitally important to revive the confidence which would, by the collapse of the credit institutions, have been impaired.
>
> To all these things and others FDR gave his unqualified consent. I recollect saying to him . . . that by accepting the position of Director of the

Budget, I was bringing my own political career to an end, because I had no illusions about the effect it would have upon my future in political life.*

Douglas was well prepared for the labors involved in preparing the necessary legislation and in carrying out its strictures in the Budget Bureau. A year earlier, as a member of the House, he had introduced a resolution providing for the appointment of an Economy Committee. The resolution directed the committee to make recommendations to the House and, especially, to examine, in the interest of economy, the haphazard provisions for compensation to veterans of World War I. Many, it was claimed, were receiving benefits for disabilities that were not at all connected with their war service.

The resolution passed the House. John McDuffie of Alabama was appointed chairman, and Douglas was a member. Douglas recalls that Byrnes was active in the Senate, but nothing was done there on the subject. The McDuffie committee's recommendations were debated in May 1932, but with a general election ahead and powerful veterans' organizations opposing changes, not much was accomplished that year.

Even before Douglas' appointment as budget director had been announced, he had been working on plans to reduce expenditures. He enlisted the help of General Frank T. Hines, head of the Veterans Bureau, and the unofficial help of Sherley and Dean Acheson. A comprehensive bill was prepared before the inauguration, and Douglas gave it the attractive title "A Bill to Maintain the Credit of the United States Government."

In the preparation for and final drafting of the bill, Douglas had the help not only of Hines, Sherley, and Acheson but of Congressmen McDuffie and Cliff Woodrum of Virginia.

During the banking holiday, on March 8, the bill was taken to Roosevelt and explained. He agreed to have it submitted with a strong message on Friday, the tenth, the day after the banking legislation was submitted.

On Thursday, while Congress was at work on the banking legislation, Douglas and I spent the entire afternoon at the White House. Roosevelt had assigned the writing of the message to us.

Roosevelt had elected to remain in the Oval Room in the White House to await action in Congress on the banking bill. To keep close to him, Douglas and I worked on the message in the Lincoln Room which, prior to the building of the office annex, had been the official office of Presidents.

I redrafted the text Douglas had prepared and sought to embody in the message not only the provisions in the Douglas bill but strong collateral language stressing the urgency, which Roosevelt believed required

* Letter to the author from Douglas under date of May 4, 1964. Most of the facts which follow are taken from that letter.

prompt action by Congress. For this was not only a message directed at Congress, but a reminder to the public of the concern of Roosevelt for sound fiscal administration. Certain key words were these: "Upon the unimpaired credit of the United States Government rest the safety of deposits, the security of insurance policies, the value of our agricultural products, and the availability of employment. The credit of the United States Government definitely affects these fundamental human values. It, therefore, becomes our first concern to make secure the foundation. National recovery depends upon it."

Then this warning was added to those who had been calling so insistently for "pump-priming" government spending:

"Too often in recent history liberal governments have been wrecked on rocks of loose fiscal policy."

That section was often used in later years by the critics of Roosevelt's subsequent spending policies.

Every argument for prompt action was used, particularly the need to meet the big refunding operation which the Treasury was to face the next day.

Also, to avoid amendments that might emasculate the plan, Roosevelt reminded Congress that "The details of expenditure, particularly in view of the great present emergency, can be more wisely and equitably administered through the Executive."

The major features in the bill were the title giving the President discretion to reduce veterans' benefits and cut "across the board" the salaries of all officers and employees of the Federal government.

The Budget Bureau estimated at the time the bill was written that payments to veterans would be reduced by $470 million and salary-cutting would amount to something like $150 million. In the aggregate, this meant a prospective cut of nearly 13 per cent in the contemplated expenditures in the next fiscal year.

The bill and message went to Congress on the next day, March 10.

Altogether, the bill, with the message, was a considerable shock to members. In the past the veterans had generally been given whatever they had the capacity to generate support for in Congress. There had been continuous revisions upward since the war, and the aggregate system of benefits was planless and formless. Not the least of the painful provisions in the bill was the stricture regarding government salaries. This was, so far as I have been able to determine, the first time in history when members of Congress voted to reduce their own salaries.

When the bill was presented in the House, a most unusual parliamentary situation prevailed. No committees had been appointed. The new speaker, Henry T. Rainey of Illinois, was in the chair. After the message was read, Joseph W. Byrns of Tennessee, the majority leader, presented a resolution giving power to the Speaker to appoint a select

Economy Committee of five members "for the purpose of considering and reporting. . . . upon the subject matter contained in the message of the President. . . ." The bill reported by that committee should have a privileged status. After a brief exchange the resolution was agreed to. The speaker appointed to the Economy Committee McDuffie as chairman; Milligan and Woodman, Democrats; Taber and McGugin, Republicans.*

Since the Senate was already completely organized, the bill was referred to the Committee on Finance, the chairman of which was Pat Harrison of Mississippi. It was considered there over the weekend and reported with minor amendments on Monday, the thirteenth.

The McDuffie committee reported the bill to the House on Saturday, the eleventh, and under the terms of a resolution by Byrns all points of order were waived and debate was limited to two hours—one hour to be controlled by McDuffie, the other by John Taber as ranking Republican. In response to a question, the Speaker ruled that there would be no privilege of amendment.

John E. Rankin of Mississippi, who had long been a tireless supporter of veterans' legislation, provided most of the opposition. He bitterly complained about the limited time for debate and later spoke in opposition. But under the strict rulings of the Speaker, the debate was concluded as ordered; a motion to recommit the bill was offered but in a division it was rejected; and the bill on a yea-and-nay vote was passed, 226 to 139.

Subsequently, there was plenty of oratory and protest, but the bill with the extraordinary power vested in the President remained.

It is true that since the power given to the President under the bill would not become effective until July 1, there was time later for deliberation and new legislation. But this was not the issue in those March days. The country had been treated to an example of swift and drastic action. And the passage of the bill in one day gave the nation a greatly needed injection of confidence which, along with the restoration of banking operations, marked the end of the long economic decline and the beginning of the recovery that followed.

In the Senate, action was less summary. Motions to recommit were rejected by a heavy vote. A few amendments, added to those recommended by the Harrison committee, were adopted, but most efforts to amend were rejected. Opponents and critics of the bill had their day under Senate rules.

Henry Fountain Ashurst of Arizona, perhaps the most fluent and

* McDuffie was not only popular and respected in the House, but was well known and helpful to those of us who were close to Roosevelt. He was a source of great strength in the session which followed. In 1935 Roosevelt appointed him to a Federal judgeship.

charming man in the Senate, had been under heavy fire from many of his constituents, some of whom had gone to his state because of tuberculosis. The question whether this disease was or was not connected with their military service had never been and perhaps could not have been accurately determined. Their suffering and their demands for benefits, however, were a vital political matter. Ashurst said:

"I have received, as doubtless many Senators have, a large number of telegraphic dispatches respecting this bill. One of the dispatches ends as follows: 'I feel it my duty to advise you that your future service is in grave danger if you uphold granting Presidential power.'

"Another reads: 'Your attitude very unsatisfactory. You are taking $6,300,000 from Arizona, and are politically dead unless you change your attitude.'

"Mr. President, some time ago I made the astonishing and for a while, to myself, distressing discovery that the perpetuity of the American Government did not absolutely depend upon the re-election of one Henry Fountain Ashurst to the Senate of the United States.

"When a Senator makes such a discovery, the fact seems incredible. It seems as if the stars above his head had faded and the earth had slipped beneath his feet. But as time rolls on, such a discovery proves to be a real antidote to megalomania; and the further flight of time brings to the discoverer a serenity and a humility to be envied by the world's greatest philosophers.

"It may be, Mr. President, that the perpetuity of the American Republic does not depend upon my re-election to the Senate; but the perpetuity of the Republic may indeed depend upon granting to the President the authority for economies called for in his message to Congress."

The bill with amendments was passed in the Senate on March 15 by a recorded vote of 62 to 13, with 19 not voting.

On March 16, McDuffie announced in the House that the Senate bill had been received, that most of the amendments added in the Senate were not vital to the bill, and that his Economy Committee had agreed to accept them. He then offered the Senate amendments en bloc, saying that they only reduced the economies in the original bill by $25 million. There was some more discussion, and plaintive speeches by Rankin and Wright Patman of Texas. The vote on the amendments accepted by the Economy Committee was 373 to 19, with 37 abstentions.

The President signed his approval of the bill on March 20.

It was inevitable that such a measure, enacted under such emergency pressure and involving such a multitude of individual human situations, would cause hardship. This came not from the specific provisions of the bill but from its administration, with the wide discretion it gave to the President. Douglas himself recognized this before many months passed.

His present judgment is this:

I do not recall that there was any legislation during the Hundred Days which amended the bill and which affected to any degree the original plan. I did find to my amazement, however, that in the administration of the legislation, some veterans, whose disability was directly connected with their war service, were sustaining substantial reductions in their compensation. I, forthwith, wrote and told F.D.R. about it and suggested that we set up throughout the country reviewing boards, to ensure that compensation to directly connected disabled veterans was not reduced. This process of review extended over a period of several months and had the effect of restoring to the directly connected disabled the reductions they otherwise would have continued to experience. If my recollection is correct, in 1934, the period of presumption regarding service connected disability was modified and some of the savings in veterans' compensation were accordingly eliminated. . . . I have written this to exonerate the President from any attempt to injure those whose disabilities were directly connected with their war service and, more especially, those who received wounds on the battle fields.*

James F. Byrnes, who more than any other Senator was responsible for the passage of the Economy Act then, said this in his memoirs, published in 1958:

Unfortunately, in exercising the discretion granted to fix the amount of compensation for various disabilities, the Veterans Administration cut some benefits too deeply and made the whole proposal very unpopular.

Later in the same session of Congress, when the appropriations bill for the independent government agencies and offices was introduced, providing funds at the reduced rate authorized by the Economy Act, the controversy over the cuts flared up again. The veterans' organizations had mobilized to reverse the defeat in the Economy Act. In a statement President Roosevelt said he thought the service-connected cuts were deeper than intended and promised to review those cases, and he suspended the plan to close some regional offices of the Veterans Administration until that situation was reviewed. The President agreed to limit pension cuts to war-disabled veterans to 25 per cent and to leave on the rolls 150,000 veterans whose disabilities were presumed to have originated in the war. The House stood by his compromise. In the Senate an amendment repealing more of the cuts was adopted. The House rejected the Senate's amendment. Shortly after midnight the Senate agreed with the House version, nine Democrats who had previously voted against our cuts changing to support the President. The Bill was adopted 45 to 36.

In March, 1934, economies in the independent offices bill again aroused a controversy. An amendment was added not only restoring increased allowances for veterans, but authorizing the restoration of the pay cuts for federal employees, including salaries of members of Congress, which had been reduced in 1933. Lew Douglas, Cliff Woodrum and I recommended that the

* Letter from Douglas to author, May 4, 1964.

President veto the bill. After much deliberation he exercised his veto. We did all we could to sustain that veto, but failed.

It was a resounding defeat for Mr. Roosevelt and for us. In my opinion it entirely changed the President's attitude toward economy measures. He evidently concluded that whatever may have been the wish of the Congress in 1933, it was no longer willing to support him in his efforts to economize. Then, too, new advisers to the President had come on the scene, most of whom believed in a liberal spending policy. The action of the Congress convinced the President, who was no follower. He immediately became the leader of those who were advocating liberal spending.*

* Byrnes, *All in One Lifetime* (New York: Harper, 1958), pp. 75–76.

Chapter Fifteen

Reflections on the Great Banking Crisis

MEANWHILE, with a great majority of the banks open and back in business and the Glass bill for permanent reform moving in Congress, the new Administration had bought the time and the public confidence for broad economic recovery. Those of us who had passed through those anxious and laborious days were encouraged to believe that with the spectacular expression of confidence that followed Roosevelt's appeal on the Sunday night before the reopening, and the repairs to a capitalist society that had been made and were planned for the immediate future, the great depression was at least at the beginning of its end.

The claim that had been made irresponsibly after the election, that the root of the trouble had been fear of Roosevelt and his advisers, seemed then to have been dissipated, although it has echoed through the years since, notably in Hoover's memoirs and in partisan books and articles. But Roosevelt, with the tools in his hands that had been available to Hoover but were unused, had set to work with unparalleled vigor just as he had promised in his inaugural address.

There was much to be done in the months ahead in shoring up a still impaired economy. And there were times when it seemed that new troubles were threatening in certain sectors of the economy. But the storm had spent itself. I still feel as I did in 1939, when I wrote that "capitalism had been saved in eight days." Now, in reviewing the years of the great depression, I feel that the decisive event that turned the tide was the brilliantly successful rescue of the banks. Surely nothing so gripped the imagination of the American people and gave them assurance that their nation was sound at heart and capable of providing them once more the means of a good life.

It would certainly have been better, twenty years later when he wrote his memoirs, if Herbert Hoover had not claimed, first, that there was a crisis and that Roosevelt had caused it, and then that there was no crisis severe enough to justify the closing of the banks. It would have been more illuminating and more favorable to Hoover's public record if he had said that there was a crisis but that the tools used by Roosevelt in meeting it had been shaped by his own Administration.

My personal participation in banking affairs was peripheral after the reopening of the banks on that happy Monday in the second week in March. My relations with Woodin continued officially because of my responsibilities for the European debt negotiations and the subsequent demands of Europe for monetary stabilization. Unofficially there had been forged in those weeks a lasting personal friendship which ended only with Woodin's death.

The lengthy details I have given to the story of the banking crisis and its end reveal that many individuals contributed materially to the rescue operation. To display any spirit of partisanship in any citations, what this one or that one did, would violate the very spirit that moved them and sully the story of what happened. Some contributed more than others, but they all gave their skills and devotion to a common cause—the welfare and solvency of the American nation.

Two purposes are foremost in what follows. One is to explain why cooperation between Hoover and Roosevelt failed, and the other is to single out for special tribute those who did the most in saving the banking system.

Why Hoover-Roosevelt Cooperation Failed

In the foregoing accounts of the Hoover-Roosevelt exchanges—first in grappling with the foreign debts and other international economic affairs and subsequently in the bank crisis—the *how* of the failure of cooperation is made clear. There remains to be added this witness's estimate of *why* it failed.

In the arguments over fixing the responsibility for the failure of cooperation between the outgoing and incoming Presidents, partisans of both men, who have had little direct knowledge of what happened, have (if they were Hoover partisans) said that not only the international impasse that ended in the London Conference, but the bank crisis could have been averted if Roosevelt had responded to Hoover's pleas. Others (if they were Roosevelt partisans) have been free to absolve Roosevelt of any responsibility and also to claim that Roosevelt alone was responsible for the outcome of the banking operation.

It may be that my own realistic and intimately based evaluation may please neither side. But I am not concerned here with the judgments of partisans. I am concerned mostly with informing a new generation about certain major events in the history of their country and also with refreshing the memories of those who grew to maturity at that time but who were too far away to know all that happened. Certainly it would be absurd to attempt to squeeze political advantage from a series of events so far distant in time and concerning individuals most of whom are no longer living.

Beyond their policy differences, Hoover and Roosevelt entertained feelings of personal distrust and antipathy. Perhaps these might be traced back to their relations in the Wilson Administration. Or they could have originated in the 1920's. Roosevelt was a Democratic candidate for Vice-President in 1920. Hoover was already an active Republican then and made two speeches in that campaign. In spite of his illness, Roosevelt was fairly active in the 1920's, especially in 1928 when he ran for governor of New York while Hoover was a candidate for President. Fairly harsh things were spoken about the party in power, and Hoover was personally sensitive about such attacks.

Quite naturally, Roosevelt's speeches in the 1928 campaign were, in part at least, directed at Hoover. And in the years of Roosevelt's governorship there were several policy clashes with the Washington Administration. Moreover, from the time of his re-election in 1930 Roosevelt was regarded as a strong contender for the Democratic nomination. In the campaign of 1932, in criticism of Hoover's handling of the depression there was, at least by implication, the charge that Hoover was indifferent to the human suffering involved. While Hoover was always very sensitive to all political criticism, this must have hurt him more than anything else. For he was a great humanitarian. And now, viewed in retrospect, such a charge even by implication was unfair. It was not because of Hoover's indifference that he failed. It was the ineptitude of so many of his efforts to stem the decline.

It is undoubtedly true that Hoover shared the slighting evaluation of Roosevelt's capacity that was so widespread in the East. He regarded the man who opposed him in 1932 as possessed of little intellectual capacity, as a man of consuming ambition and excessive political opportunism. Hoover also firmly believed, especially toward the end of the campaign, that Roosevelt had surrounded himself with radical and dangerous theorists.

On the other side, there is little doubt that Roosevelt possessed a deep personal antipathy toward Hoover.

Despite the clear need for some contacts between the two men in the period after the election, it would have been difficult to achieve much in view of these personal considerations.

Another factor which marred the possibility of full cooperation was the determination of Hoover to seek vindication, politically or otherwise.

That is made clear in Stimson's comments in his diary. Perhaps this determination took the form of a desire for a return match in 1936. Roosevelt himself believed firmly that Hoover would be the Republican nominee in that year.*

The final proof of the bitterness of Roosevelt toward the man he defeated in 1932 is that he never up to his death asked for any help from Hoover. That act of generosity was left to his successor, who enlisted Hoover's capacities on more than one occasion.

It is unfortunate that these mutual suspicions and animosities should have prevailed in a great national emergency. But they remain as lasting proof of one reason why there was no cooperation.

But there were other, more rational reasons for Roosevelt's reluctance to cooperate. In the negotiations described in Part I of this book, I still believe that Roosevelt could not in conscience have acceded to Hoover's requests for cooperation in dealing with the international debts and other related matters. At the center of Hoover's suggestions was the creation of another commission. The creation of commissions when hard decisions were to be made had been overworked. A new commission to handle the debts and other subjects could not have won the confidence and support either of Congress or of the public.

That is how the idea of cooperation stood when Hoover wrote his letter about the banks on February 18. As I look back at that time, I feel that Roosevelt, without abandoning principle, could have made a reply that would have brushed aside the impossible conditions imposed by Hoover but would have shown a comprehension of the serious nature of the situation and have endorsed action by Hoover on specific steps. But as I have indicated, Roosevelt failed to reply, and when he did reply his excuse for delay was palpably flimsy.

The conditions for alleviating the panic imposed by Hoover as outlined in his own letter and to Roosevelt and his letters to Senators Reed and Fess could not be accepted by Roosevelt. Also, there was a fundamental difference in the views held by Roosevelt and Hoover concerning the reason for the depositor panic. Roosevelt believed that people were fearful for the solvency of the banks. Hoover believed that people were in panic because of their fear of Roosevelt's monetary views. The deepen-

* I have some very material proof of this. After the election in 1936 I received a note from Marguerite LeHand, written from the White House, which said: "Dear Ray: In the President's 'future folder' he found a memorandum dated June 3, 1935, saying: 'How many dollars will you give me against one dollar that Hoover will not be the Republican nominee in 1936? I will give you twelve to one on all the money you can get.'

"He had an idea that he made this bet with you. Do you recall it? At any rate, he says he owes somebody a dollar and he wants to pay it."

A dollar was enclosed, which I framed and have kept along with Missy's letter. I did recall the bet.

ing crisis that faced the country on March 2, when Roosevelt arrived in Washington, suggested a quite different course of action. As I have indicated, March 2 was Thursday, March 3 was Friday, and March 4 was Saturday. Numerous governors had closed the banks in their states. The strain on the remaining states was growing rapidly. Currency and gold were running out of the banks and out of the country in alarming proportions. Hoover's advisers in the Treasury and at the Federal Reserve Board were urging upon him the use of the Trading with the Enemy Act to stop the flow of currency and gold by closing the banks, especially when the Detroit situation worsened. Finally there were only hours before a weekend would intervene. But Hoover was master of the ship. He did not believe that the banks needed to be closed, but sought some action short of that extremity. And in all these suggestions, he wanted Roosevelt to provide an endorsement.

But up to the time when Roosevelt entered the White House, he was not informed about the elaborate plans which, as we have seen, were already prepared in the Hoover Administration. It was hardly fair to expect him to give an endorsement in a matter in which he was ill informed.

Hoover should have acted on his own responsibility and have placed upon Congress the responsibility to validate his action. If, as Hoover said repeatedly, he was afraid that Congress would not support his action, I cannot see any grounds for such a fear.

Congress was in session. In a matter of this sort the strong men were Garner as Speaker of the House, and Robinson and Glass in the Senate. I cannot believe that these men would have invited a catastrophe by refusing to approve the proclamation of a holiday already established by Presidential action. Nor could Roosevelt have dared to rescind the order after he took office without also inviting chaos. For, as we have seen, he believed the Trading with the Enemy Act was valid and usable. Therefore, I believe that Roosevelt's refusal to cooperate up to the time he took office was justified. His answer to Hoover was not that he believed that action either to close the banks or to take the intermediate step of restricting withdrawals was wrong. He merely said that Hoover should proceed on his own initiative.

Let us consider what Hoover actually accomplished by refusing to act unless Roosevelt approved. If he had followed the advice of Mills, Ballantine, and others and acted himself, he would have been able later to claim at least a part of the credit that went to Roosevelt. What he did by his indecision was to set the stage for a great triumph by the man he so cordially disliked and to provide the party he opposed with material for political triumphs for years to come.

For if Hoover had decided to act as advised by his own close associates, all the methods later used were available to him in his own Administration. The proclamation and also the necessary emergency legislation could have been prepared by Mills, Ballantine, Awalt, and Walter Wyatt just as easily on March 2 or earlier as it was after Roosevelt was inaugurated and had given the go-ahead signal.

But Hoover was in the grasp of a fatal indecision. And Roosevelt reaped the acclaim of a nation for bold, calculated, and imaginative action in the crisis. No doubt, he provided the boldness, but the calculation and imagination came from within the Hoover Administration and from Woodin and Jones.

To sum up my judgment on the nagging issue of non-cooperation:

So far as the period from the Hoover-Roosevelt meeting in November at the White House up to the February bank troubles was concerned, Roosevelt acted correctly in refusing to entangle himself with international matters that were entirely within the province of the President. His neglect to reply promptly to Hoover's appeal of February 18 was inexcusable and makes him vulnerable to the charge in the years since that he was playing for personal and political advantage in a grave national disaster.

In the period immediately before the inauguration, however, the responsibility was Hoover's and Roosevelt was justified in declining to share that responsibility, since he was not fully informed and could not unofficially direct emergency measures himself.

When Herbert Hoover was writing his memoirs, he asked me verbally and later in a letter why Roosevelt refused to cooperate with him. In my reply I indicated that I could not speak specifically of Roosevelt's motives, because if his motive had been to let the crisis mount until his accession to the Presidency, he would not have admitted it. But I said this, which Hoover quotes in his memoirs:

> I feel when you asked him on February 18th to cooperate in the banking situation that he either did not realize how serious the situation was or that he preferred to have conditions deteriorate and gain for himself the entire credit for the rescue operation. In any event, his actions during the period from February 18th to March 3rd would conform to any such motive on his part.

It should be noted that I excluded from this comment any judgment on cooperation on March 3 and before February 18. For the responsibility on March 3 and the days before was Hoover's alone.

In the light of the foregoing account, it is not helpful for those who have commented upon the relations between the two men in the interim between the election and the inauguration to make a general charge of non-cooperation against Roosevelt. For there were many sorts of cooperation suggested in many forms, and each must be judged upon its merits and in the context of the time.

Credit Where Credit Is Due

In the public mind, at the time and in the accounts since, Roosevelt was the major figure in weathering the banking storm. He was the President, and he validated the major decisions. But he had an extraordinarily able crew, without whose skills and preparatory plans he could not have succeeded. This, however, does not take from him the credit for the vigor, energy, and contagious optimism that were such decisive factors in recovery.

Even before the departure of Hoover after the inaugural ceremony, when Woodin and I brought Roosevelt the information that we had learned at the Treasury on March 3 and early on March 4, Roosevelt without reservations welcomed the help and direction of what might be called the team of holdovers from the Hoover Administration. Since they had been restrained—even frustrated—by Hoover's indecision so long, Roosevelt's support gave them new energy and determination. They felt that through Roosevelt they had not only the Congress but the country behind them. And Roosevelt's inaugural address and his remarkable appeal the night before the reopening of the banks produced a climate of public confidence that made the going infinitely easier. To Roosevelt's eternal credit, he substantially took over Hoover's team and surmounted the crisis.

The major figure in the direction of affairs during the crisis was Arthur Ballantine. Fifteen years later he wrote his conclusions:

> The disastrous development of the last days generally would not have occurred, I think, had it been politically possible to accomplish in January or February what was done in March after the new Administration came into power. The banks closed on March 6 and could not have been successfully reopened in the week of March 13 if they had really been but "the ruin and debris of a once-powerful banking empire."
>
> The difficulty was that President Hoover, with no power in Congress, wanted to do or join in doing everything to avoid a general banking debacle, while President-elect Roosevelt was against assuming affirmative responsibility until he came into office. Here was a most unfortunate impasse.
>
> To Mr. Roosevelt it might have seemed best for the effectiveness of new measures, and not merely politically best, to take action only after the banks were mired in a crisis, in spite of all the tragedies that the miring was sure to bring about. Of course Mr. Roosevelt could not have given the critical assurance, so much sought by President Hoover, that the dollar would not be devalued, for devaluation was clearly in contemplation in the incoming President's mind, either as a definite plan or as a strong possibility.
>
> It must be remembered, too, that the provisions of the Emergency Banking Act furnishing the additional machinery for banking recovery were worked out by the old Administration in cooperation with established agen-

cies, not by the new Administration, and theoretically the act might just as well have been passed by the expiring Congress as by the new Congress in special session. True, actual closing of the banks gave a dramatic setting for the passage of the measure. But it is hard to believe that the joint or parallel backing of such a measure by the President and the President-elect would not have carried it through before the banks closed.

Actually there was nothing in the Emergency Banking Act, or in the new President's speech, that committed the new Administration on the ultimate treatment of gold and the dollar. The President's speech was indeed firm support for the success of the new banking measure, but again it is hard to see that such a speech could not have been made with equal effect before the closing of the banks or that final remedial steps could not have been taken in time for avoidance of that calamity.*

With all this I am in substantial agreement. I have already given my conclusions concerning the failure of earlier cooperation at the White House level, a failure that perilously threatened any ultimate stability. It is clear that except for the expertness, the information, and the plans at the lower levels of the Hoover Administration, the crisis could never have been surmounted. The new Administration and the Congress that sustained it were in their novitiate. Without direction from those who had been in office, unspeakable chaos might have followed the collapse of banking.

The massive operation that terminated in March was dependent upon the firm directing hands of a very few individuals. Ballantine was the strongest—the indispensable—link between the outgoing and incoming Administrations in those days and in the three months following. He and Roosevelt had been members of the same Harvard College class of 1904, although until the banking crisis there were not, apparently, any close contacts between the two. Politically, they responded to different loyalties.

After his graduation from the Harvard Law School, Ballantine practised law for a time in Boston and then moved to New York as a member of Elihu Root's law firm. He served in minor capacities in the Treasury for short periods after 1917. When Ogden Mills became Secretary of the Treasury after the retirement of Andrew Mellon in 1930, Ballantine first became assistant secretary and then undersecretary of the Treasury. Mills had great prestige because of his years of service in the House of Representatives and as undersecretary and also because of his marked personal capacity, which was recognized even by members of the opposition in the Senate. But Ballantine had his full confidence and carried a heavy burden of the administration in the Treasury.

This made Ballantine especially valuable to Woodin, and a warm affection grew up between the two men. Despite Ballantine's desire to return to his private practice, Woodin and Roosevelt persuaded him to

* "When All the Banks Closed," *Harvard Business Review,* March 1948.

remain as undersecretary until May 15, when Dean Acheson was chosen to succeed him. It should be noted that many of Ballantine's Republican friends criticized him for lingering on. But he felt moved by the necessity of getting Woodin well established in his difficult position.

After Ballantine left the Treasury, Woodin wrote a letter to him on June 14 which went far beyond the formal amenities:

> I have been trying to write you a letter ever since you left here. I think I have written at least sixteen but tore them up and consigned them to the wastepaper basket, because all dictionaries in the English language that I possess do not some way or other seem to have the proper words to express my thoughts. I have even gone so far as to wander into other linguistic lands, Latinesque, if you please, but my dear boy I just cannot find them. All I can say is that the greatest rainbow of the whole affair here since March 4th was my learning to know, admire and develop great affection for Arthur Ballantine. You were certainly a patriot if there ever was one, and I shall never forget how nobly you stood by the ship and very often prevented me from making some of those high dives to which I am afraid I am somewhat prone, which might have ended in broken bones. . . . I certainly miss your dry humor, and lots of other things about you, which, as I said before I cannot find expression for. I trust that sometime in the future our paths will be thrown together again, as there is no one in the world I would love to work with rather than you.*

Roosevelt, as well as Woodin, was appreciative of Ballantine's service and asked him repeatedly to stay on. When Acheson had been chosen, he wrote this note to Ballantine:

> It is a real pleasure to express my great appreciation of the high character of your service to the Government and the country and I send you my best wishes for your future welfare and happiness.

Ogden Livingston Mills was the grandson of Darius Ogden Mills, a famous nineteenth-century businessman and philanthropist who made his fortune after migrating to California during the gold rush in 1849. He spent the later part of his life in New York City.

The grandson graduated from Harvard College along with Roosevelt and Ballantine in the class of 1904. Like Roosevelt, too, he became a

* From my own secondary position as Woodin's *de facto* assistant in those days, I felt the same respect and affection for Ballantine. On one occasion in April when Woodin and I were discussing official business, Roosevelt asked Woodin when he was going to select a new undersecretary. Woodin turned to me and said to Roosevelt that he would like to have me as undersecretary when Ballantine left. It was a flattering suggestion, both undeserved and unexpected. It would have been tempting, for I realized quite well that because of Hull's attitude I was a misfit in the State Department. But I realized by that time how much technical equipment was required in the Treasury, and that I possessed no such knowledge. But Roosevelt closed the issue by saying that he wanted me to continue to assist him in the White House.

lawyer, but preferred politics as a career. Also like Roosevelt, he served in the New York State Senate. He was elected from the Seventeenth District in New York City to the House of Representatives in 1921 and served until he ran unsuccessfully in 1926 for governor against Alfred E. Smith. President Coolidge then appointed him undersecretary of the Treasury, where he promptly assumed most of the burdens of the aging Andrew Mellon. Upon Mellon's resignation, Hoover appointed Mills Secretary.

In the 1932 campaign, he had been a rugged campaigner. Roosevelt respected his capacity so much that he deliberately deferred his attack on the Hoover Administration's fiscal policies until very near the end of the campaign, after Mills had completed his transcontinental speaking tour in October.

It became apparent in these days of the banking crisis that Mills believed all the time that Hoover should have acted on his own responsibility earlier, with or without Roosevelt's cooperation. He was, as we have seen, responsible for many of the vital steps which were adopted in the plans.

He showed the greatest friendliness for Woodin and me in those days, and we both came to respect his judgment and value his advice. His letter to Woodin written on the morning of March 4 is a précis of the steps to be taken in preparing the emergency legislation and in reopening the banks.

Mills was no reactionary, nor was he subservient to the New York bankers. As early as September 1932, he contemplated most of the steps that were later taken by Roosevelt, including the abandonment of gold.

In my judgment, he deserves to rank with the foremost Treasury Secretaries over all the years since Hamilton and Gallatin.

I had conceived a great respect and no little affection for this brusque and masterful individual. This feeling went back to the days in December and January when we had contacts at Hoover-Roosevelt meetings.

Mills passed with high marks the most rigid test of a Treasury Secretary's capacity, which was to win the extraordinary respect of the officials who worked under him.

In the most distinguished sense of the term, Francis Gloyd Awalt was a professional career man. He was a native of Maryland. He practiced law briefly in Baltimore and entered the service of government in the final year of the Wilson Administration. He served as special assistant to the Secretary of the Treasury until 1927 and then had several positions in the office of the comptroller of the currency. He was deputy comptroller when his chief, J. W. Pole, resigned in September 1932. Rather than serve as comptroller, an office that has generally been regarded as a political plum, at the advent of a new Administration, he preferred the title of acting comptroller, which he held during the banking crisis.

The office of comptroller of the currency is the major factor in the Treasury's supervision and control of the banking system. Necessarily the comptroller (or acting comptroller) is subordinate to the Secretary and undersecretary of the Treasury. But the comptroller has wide discretion, and in important instances is subject only to the directives of the President. Because of the great powers of the office, the comptroller is subject to heavy pressure by bankers and members of Congress.

Later when Roosevelt appointed J. F. T. O'Conner comptroller, Awalt continued as first deputy and substantially managed the office until his resignation in 1936.

At that time Roosevelt accepted Awalt's resignation with this unusual tribute:

> I learn with real regret that you are about to leave the Government service after so many able and devoted years in responsible positions in the Treasury Department.
>
> Naturally, I am best acquainted with the remarkably wise and competent manner in which you carried on the duties of Acting Comptroller in the heart of the banking crisis in the early days of my Administration and with the fine assistance you have given to Secretaries Woodin and Morgenthau and to Comptroller O'Conner since then. For this great service you deserve and you have my most sincere gratitude and you deserve also the gratitude of the Nation.
>
> It has been encouraging to me to rely on your continued loyal support and you have my good wishes as you leave the public service with a clear record of work well done.

Awalt left the government after having served under five Presidents and four Treasury Secretaries.

As a rule, historians neglect such individuals, despite their vital part in great events, and write about those whose names are already known to the public. I have searched vainly in no less than six histories of this period for a mention of Awalt. But he was a major hero in the most remarkable episode of that time.

These unnamed people are the architects of the deeds that make the named figures famous. They serve solidly without note or credit. Theirs is "not to be ministered unto but to minister."

These men, their names noted only on the glass in their office doors or in official directories, laboring only on what are called the details of government, subordinate to mediocrities who are the currency of political spoils, when an emergency comes are ready with the means of salvation and are the real governors of the nation. They keep the mechanism strong, regardless of political turmoil and provide the order and continuity under which free men live their lives.

Gloyd Awalt was not a mere repository of figures and information, although the banks of the nation were in reality his next-door neighbors. I was constantly aware in those exciting days that when he presented his facts to Woodin, Mills, and Ballantine he enriched them with a wise judgment of their impact and meaning. In determining a bank's soundness, something more was needed than mere balance sheets. There needed to be a consideration of unwritten factors and a projection of probabilities to come. In the classification of banks that were in his jurisdiction, it fell upon Awalt to determine—mostly with finality—which were solvent, which were insolvent, and which reflected doubt. These basic decisions were, by law and practice, his to make, subject only to reversal by the Secretary or the courts.

Walter Wyatt, a native of Georgia, the major author of the Emergency Banking Act, had served the Federal Reserve Board for sixteen years and came up through the ranks to become general counsel in 1922. In 1946 he became reporter of decisions for the Supreme Court and served until his retirement in 1962. In the relative limits of his professional associations he received many distinctions. He, too, has been missed by the historians of the period, although when the decisions were made to act in the crisis, he had already formulated most of the essential legal papers and had foreseen most of the issues that had to be faced.

I shall consider later the immense administrative capacity of Jesse Jones, who carried on the task of forcing the banks to strengthen themselves long after the crisis. He was the one individual who, despite Roosevelt's objections, was most responsible for the adoption by Congress of Federal deposit insurance. This has since proved itself as the most important factor in banking stability.

In part because of my own associations with Will Woodin and the scant notice of his great contribution by those who have since written of the period, I am constrained to linger on what he meant to the country in the short period during which he served. As I have noted earlier, personal tragedy for Glass had been avoided when he finally rejected Roosevelt's offer of the Treasury position. We had no hint that the selection of Woodin would end in a personal catastrophe. In those days from March to June, I lived near him in the Carlton Hotel and was with him for a time nearly every day. I noted with increasing concern that the strain on him was taking a heavy toll. He complained at times of a sore throat and frequently went to New York to consult his physician. In late June, while I was in London at the Economic Conference, I was distressed to learn that he was at home and was desperately ill. He recovered sufficiently to resume his duties in Washington, but in November his throat trouble had developed further, and he left office, never to return. It was a malignancy, and he died in May 1934.

This deadly attack no doubt would have come had he never assumed office at the Treasury. But it may be assumed that the energies he spent during those critical days might, if conserved, have lengthened his life.

In my book *27 Masters of Politics,* written sixteen years later, I offered this personal estimate of Woodin:

> He was, among all the men I have known, the most kindly, sincere, and unselfish. . . . Achievement in public office can be of two sorts. The first is rounded achievement—the details completed, the shadows retouched, the story told in persuasive and friendly prose. The friends of Will Woodin would covet for him that kind of public service.
>
> But they must content themselves with the memory of another sort of public career—short, broken, the details incomplete—a fragment of artistry left by the maker. . . . In October, against Woodin's advice, Roosevelt adopted Professor Warren's fantastic and, as it proved, ineffective gold buying scheme. Shortly after Woodin retired on leave, Dean Acheson resigned [as Under Secretary] and Henry Morgenthau was appointed Under and Acting Secretary.
>
> Some time after that, I visited Woodin at his home in New York. He was in his library surrounded by his magnificent collection of Cruikshank drawings. With a most unusual touch of bitter sadness, he recalled his final departure from Washington.
>
> "Roosevelt couldn't have been more sweet in what he said about me. But he never asked me to stay." And then he paused a long time, "or to come back."
>
> Roosevelt, however, could not sincerely have expected Woodin either to be able to stay or ever to return. Nor with a clear conscience could he have been the cause of such a sacrifice. It was kindness that left unuttered the words that Woodin had wanted to hear. For Woodin was mortally ill. . . .
>
> Woodin's career, although its impression on history may be dim, may resist the passing of time better than the finished product [of others]. The restless erosion of facts may work havoc with the best planned memorial. The fragment is a fragment. It may pass into history with more assurance of permanence.

Part Four

The Hundred Days

Chapter Sixteen

The Themes, the Plans, and the Improvisations

SATURDAY, March 18, is fixed firmly in my mind because it marked the beginning of the second phase of the Hundred Days period. Roosevelt summoned me for a long private talk about plans. The First New Deal was, in Churchill's phrase, at the end of the beginning. The bank crisis had been surmounted successfully, and the early passage of the Economy Act was assured. But the emergency banking bill and the Douglas economy plans had been thrust upon the Congress by the nature of the emergency. There were left before Roosevelt and the Congress other problems of recovery. Roosevelt had promised "action on many fronts." What were those fronts, and what forms of action should have priority?

Congress had been in almost continuous session since early December. The majority of those who had been returned as members of the new Seventy-third Congress had been wearied during the lame-duck session by long and fruitless wrangling. Many would have loved to have a vacation.

But the leadership had no alternative but to continue. There were promises to keep and there were already on the calendar such measures as the Glass-Steagall bill for permanent banking reform and the farm bill, which had been introduced on March 16.

The day before Roosevelt talked with me, he had conferred with the leaders and they had agreed to keep the Congress in session, presumably for the duration of the spring months.

While there were plenty of campaign promises to keep, there was lack of specifics. There was no over-all plan. There were only pieces of a program and ideas that still lacked formulation. Even the farm bill, on which many people had labored since the New Year, was still a rather rough draft.

Public anticipation ran high, and the inspiration of the banking solution excited a vast expectancy. But if the country could have known how unclear we were, the tide of confidence would have frozen in its course.

It was perfectly plain that relief and recovery were to have priority and that the international complications that had absorbed so much of our time from November to February could wait a while. As I considered the domestic issues we were facing, I bitterly regretted the time we had lost, which could have been used profitably to consider a domestic legislative program.

On March 18 we were at a much greater disadvantage than we had been when facing the bank crisis. For then we had blueprints from Ballantine and other Hoover holdovers, which had been labored over for many anxious months. Now, so far as a legislative program went, we had only a few prefabricated specifics—only general areas to consider and broad objectives to guide us.

It must be confessed, too, that Roosevelt and I were equipped only with the valor of economic amateurs. Neither of us was well versed in economic theory; nor were we trained by much contact with the realities of economic life. Perhaps this was fortunate for the country, because we were not burdened with or committed to long-held economic dogmas. We were wide open to the influx of ideas—new ones and old. Anything seemed acceptable that appealed to our common sense and was worthy of a trial.

Some writers have attempted to define the economic philosophy of Franklin D. Roosevelt. They have had hard going, and when proof failed they have dipped deeply into inference and imagination.

I doubt that either Roosevelt or I could have passed an examination such as is required of college students in elementary economics. As I noted earlier, Roosevelt's knowledge was, like Sam Weller's acquaintance with London, extensive but peculiar. Both of us were bored and confused by long, learned memoranda with which so many people had inundated us over the year since the campaign started in 1932. Most of these were analyses of some isolated economic problem, with proposals for solving it. Only a few, which I shall presently describe, saw the national economy as a whole and saw what was politically possible and usable by Congress and what would stir up a minimum of controversy.

Perhaps the limitation of our economic expertise was an advantage. But whatever its advantage, it was very real. We were rank amateurs in the very domain of knowledge that was of paramount importance. For the depression was an economic disease, and in its treatment it had gotten worse, despite, or perhaps because of, an over-supply of doctors. The advice sought by Stimson and Mills came mostly from the New

York banking community and, as we have seen, these gentlemen not only were grossly ignorant of causes and effect in agriculture and industry, but in the crisis they could not supply a remedy for their own derelictions. Hoover saw things from a wider perspective, but he was hampered by various deficiencies—some personal to him, and some because of his stubborn belief that things would automatically right themselves in the fairly short run.

An informative description of Roosevelt's economic philosophy is Daniel R. Fusfeld's book, *The Economic Thought of Franklin D. Roosevelt and the Origins of the New Deal.* The author has carefully checked Roosevelt's formal education in economics at Groton, Harvard, and the Columbia Law School: "F. D. R. learned little at Harvard or Columbia that might fit him to meet the problems of the great depression of the '30's, in particular, or the problem of economic instability in general." * Not only were the courses for which he had taken the general examinations small, specialized corners of economic life, but they had been taken three decades before, when he was certainly not a studious young man. Moreover, in those thirty years the American economy had passed through revolutionary changes.

What Roosevelt knew in 1933 came from two sources: his political career, in which bits and pieces of economic affairs were the subject of executive action and legislation; and the "seminars" before the nomination in 1932, when I had taken various economists to spend evenings with him in Albany. Those discussions were mainly concerned, however, with issues suitable for use in the campaign. That sort of "education" sporadically went on during the confusion of the campaign.

I had been a college and university teacher for eleven years before joining the campaign, but my subject had been what is generally known as political science. Its center of interest was only collaterally related to economics. As I have noted earlier the greatest influence I had felt was a book, very popular during the Progressive era, which I had read while a graduate student (and re-read later), Charles Van Hise's *Concentration and Control.* This book, by a famous president of the University of Wisconsin, presented the case for the irresistible growth of large corporations. He saw the necessity that they should not be broken up. Instead, he pointed out that they should be controlled at the national level of government.

But if Franklin Roosevelt and I on that March day in 1933 were deficient in economic knowledge, we projected into our calculations a very broad view of the national scene and, I still believe, a large measure of common sense.

Although most of the speeches in the 1932 campaign dealt with specifics—agricultural relief, the protection of workers, help for the

* New York: Columbia University Press, 1965, Chapter 2.

railroads, electric power, and fiscal management—most had conformed to a central theme. Hugh Johnson, a productive source of speech ideas during the campaign and later a notable figure in the Administration, stated this theme in a book that appeared in 1935:

> There is something about this depression that doesn't speak well for what we call our common sense. We have suffered for five years. And for what? The fields are just as green and fruitful, the skies are just as blue as they were in the 1929 boom, when everybody was going to get rich and poverty was to be no more in the land. The birds and the beasts seem to be faring about as well as ever—except those in care of men—and, so far as one can see just riding through, there is nothing much the matter with the country—until we get to the Lords of Creation—the vaunted human race. . . .
>
> We have mechanized our industries and specialized our people. Families are no longer self-contained, economic units that can be put on wheels and trundled into a new environment to start things over again. Our nineteeth century safety valve of cheap or free new lands and a constantly expanding country has ceased to exist. The old order of our frontier days is gone forever and by no man's designing. All this has brought benefits, but it has also brought great griefs. The roaring, clacking engine of our industry and commerce has become a vast and highly active machine of which no individual is more than an integrated part. Each performs a specialized function. In most cases living income comes as a matter of determination by a power with whom there is no bargaining in any true sense. The individual worker accepts the wage scales decreed by employers and is thankful, and his separation from the particular ratchet in which he revolves may be a real tragedy. At his doorway there is no longer an open road to high adventure in a new and brighter country, and even if there were such a road, his specialization has unfitted him to take it.
>
> In March, 1933, we had almost achieved economic collapse. Of the credit and product and hoarded reserve of domestic industry and labor and agriculture (indeed of all our people) *too much had been concentrated on production—too little on distribution and consumption.* The people's financial resources were thus squandered, either through their own unwise investment or the equal madness of their bankers. The results were a grotesque speculative structure of values; an elephantine production and service plant; a creeping paralysis of consumption and employment which began as far back as 1926; a decay of agriculture which began even further back in 1921; and an interior cavity in domestic absorptive and resisting power which started coincident with this diversion and impairment of the proper income of all people, but which was concealed until 1929 by an expansion of all kinds of credit—an expansion like a bubble—the skin of which became so tenuous and thin in 1929 that no power on earth could have saved it.
>
> If you want to know where the consuming power of America went, you need only look around you and see it congealed in icebergs of unnecessary building and un-needed plants—and in the dead leaves of the worthless securities which financed them, and our fatuous foreign loans. Suppose that,

instead of so freezing such vast sums a prudent part of them had been distributed in wages and dividends or conserved in cushions of credit invested in more stable securities—does anybody doubt that we would never have suffered this Gethsemane? . . .

We did not concede that we must try to balance production and consumption and that the best way to increase both is to *push them up together.* The way to do that is to try to balance and correlate the income of great groups. We must not let too much of profit and the people's credit and savings run into unwise speculative obligations of debt for the purpose of increasing production. We should try to direct more of it toward the uses of distribution and consumption, so that farmers and workers and *all* producers can constantly consume more and more in order that there may be more employment, more business, more profit, and that the people of this bountiful country can enjoy to the full the fruit of their own labor and the resources which are now locked away from them. We did not act on the principle that *it is the distressed and backward economic areas which topple the structure of prosperity, make depressions, and that the exploitation of any class is a downward drag on the progress of the whole people!*

If we could have perfect balance among all producing segments—agriculture, capital, industry, workers in industry, the services, and the segment engaged in transportation and distribution, there would be almost no limit to our consuming capacity. Of course, that is Utopia and can never be attained. My only point is that all law, all administration, and all popular effort should be directed toward that goal instead of away from that goal. I think that the *essence of the New Deal is to point toward that balance.* I think that the *essence of what preceded the New Deal was to point away from that balance.**

The clear implication of this concept of balance was interdependence —that in a civilization that is tied together by modern conditions each part is dependent upon all others. If agriculture suffers, the market for industry is constricted. If crushing debt pervades great areas of national life—debts incurred when the security behind them was vastly overappreciated—the capacity to pay either interest or principal is either paralyzed or people will have to forgo spending for other necessities. This cuts the volume of consumption so that producers will suffer, too. If in a flush period like 1923–1929 people—little people—bought securities that proved worthless, they would be thrust out of the consumers' market, and more goods would pile up unsold. And if the mechanism of money control, a sole responsibility of the Federal government, were unbalanced by unsound policies, prices and profits would shrink everywhere, and millions of jobs would vanish.

All this was so simple for people to understand and so true that it was stressed in the campaign. Roosevelt's speeches were full of this

* Hugh Johnson, *The Blue Eagle from Egg to Earth* (Garden City: Doubleday, Doran, 1935), pp. 158–62.

idea. We couldn't recover, in Adolf Berle's phrase, "half boom and half bust." Our economy, Roosevelt said, was "a seamless web."

It was therefore apparent, as Roosevelt and I considered the future in March, that there must be action on many fronts at the same time. That was a major necessity.

The fundamentals were easy to grasp. But in the formulation of a program we were faced by great differences among those who had offered advice and participated in the campaign. The New Deal, in fact, became a composite of the remedies proposed by five distinct groups:

1. There were those who favored traditional remedies for an economic setback—solutions such as government economy, use of the credit of the United States to relieve certain debt situations, the restoration of the private banking system. The exponents of these traditional remedies were such men as Lewis Douglas, Jesse Jones, Will Woodin, Ralph Robey, Swagar Sherley, and Bernard Baruch. "Business will just have to go through the wringer," Baruch jokingly commented to me, greatly to the consternation of Tugwell and Berle, who were present at the time. Robey, Sherley, and Baruch did not hold official positions in the government, but in those early days they were all welcome in the counsels of the President. Of those who held office, Jones had the greatest lasting influence.

2. Then there were the money managers, who would control prices and economic tides by altering money values. Cheaper dollars by altering gold content and the remonetization of silver were the depression cures offered by Pittman, Wheeler, and other Western Senators; by Professor James Harvey Rogers of Yale, and Cornell's currency magician, George F. Warren.

3. There were the "regulators" and trust-busters, still thinking in terms of the Progressive era, like Louis D. Brandeis, Felix Frankfurter, and many of the young Frankfurter protégés.

4. There were those who favored a measurable degree of economic planning by the government. Berle and Tugwell were in this group; Hugh Johnson and Henry A. Wallace were, in a somewhat different manner, also sympathetic with planning.

5. Finally, we had the government ownership and "government in business" people such as Harold Ickes and Senator George Norris of Nebraska.

The New Deal as it emerged had a little of all these philosophies in it. Roosevelt's lack of firm convictions proved to be a means of holding together this widely assorted group of advisers. He was willing to try them all, and he used many methods at the same time.

An examination of the many measures passed in the Hundred Days Congress illustrates this many-sided approach.

On the farm front some step, it seemed, should be taken to reduce price-depressing surpluses. It was believed that the determination of prices should be geared to the domestic market and not be fixed in the international market.

In monetary affairs, deflation must be checked and a measure of inflation established. This was called "reflation" at the time. For the value of a dollar had risen sharply from 1930 to 1933. Roosevelt roughly calculated that 1926 prices should be re-established.

It also seemed essential that the sale of securities must be regulated at the Federal level, with strict requirements for full disclosure imposed upon the seller. The old dictum "Let the buyer beware" would not work in a modern capitalist economy, for the buyer could not know enough to "beware."

Finally, cutthroat competition must be checked by some means of self-government in industry.

So far as the relief of individual hardship was concerned, this was regarded as a temporary necessity. The Federal credit, which was still unimpaired, should be used for Federal help. But in the light of the larger objectives we had, individual relief was regarded as incidental.

There was nothing revolutionary in such a program. The maintenance of the capitalist system, with individual enterprise as its base, we took for granted. Hoover's dire warnings during the campaign about shattering the timbers of the Constitution were uncalled for. They were part of the desperate appeal of a candidate who realized that defeat was facing him. Roosevelt wanted nothing but the restoration of the balance in our economy, after which, presumably, old and traditional freedoms would be restored.

But to accomplish these ends, a measurable intervention of Federal authority was essential, and we felt that this could be a wise risk. For the chaos that might result from inaction might bring really revolutionary measures profoundly affecting the future of the nation.

As we contemplated the legislative measures that would be necessary to these ends, we found that we already had a number of attractive proposals.

When Roosevelt talked with me on March 18 about a legislative program, I had sorted out, from the innumerable plans and ideas with which we had been inundated and which had been routed to me by Roosevelt and Howe, a few that seemed most useful.

What was needed was a program sufficiently comprehensive to reach all the major sectors of the economy; practical enough to commend itself to the Congressional leaders; and, above all, sufficiently simple and attractive to excite public interest and confidence.

Since Tugwell, Johnson, Berle, and I had enjoyed more direct and continuous contact with Roosevelt in the campaign, I considered for a moment bringing these people together for a session with Roosevelt.

But I dismissed the idea because there were sufficient differences among them to cause delay and confusion. Johnson, especially, had always been difficult to manage in a group. I fared better by probing his brain in individual contacts. Tugwell had already talked with Roosevelt several times and was at that time fully occupied with the farm bill.

And so I selected what seemed to be the best of all the general plans, a memorandum which Berle had submitted to me on November 10.

Two or three years earlier, when I had attended faculty meetings of the Columbia Law School, I had been impressed by Berle's keen and comprehensive understanding of economic affairs. This was why I invited him to join our group in the spring of 1932. He agreed and gave much of his time to the preparation of speech material.*

As a member of our group, Berle was exceedingly useful in the campaign. He was quick to catch the essence of what Roosevelt needed and was remarkably articulate in what he said and wrote. He supplied texts, figures, and phraseology for several speeches and was substantially the author of the speech delivered by Roosevelt at the Commonwealth Club in San Francisco.

As is often the case with a strong individualist with a scintillating intelligence, he was not always popular with those who worked with him. I learned in 1933 that he had not been a favorite with Professor Felix Frankfurter, who demanded something akin to discipleship from his best and favored students. The two differed strongly in many matters of public policy. Berle did not seek office in the Administration beyond part-time work on railroad matters with the RFC.

During the final month of the campaign I saw him frequently, but since he was not needed for the speeches during that period, he devoted himself to the writing of a plan for Congressional action after the inauguration. This was embodied in the memorandum he submitted to me in November. He arranged his proposals in two categories, one "fundamental" and the other "curative."

Under the first, he listed a farm-relief act and industrial stabilization. He defined farm relief as the domestic allotment plan or some other measure designed to increase the purchasing power of the farmer.

Berle added that so far as industrial stabilization was concerned there should be "limited protection to industries to get together under suitable

* Many of those who knew Berle at that time spoke of him as "an infant prodigy." His academic record amply justified this characterization. He was only nineteen when he graduated from Harvard College. A year later he had his M.A., and in 1921 he graduated from the Harvard Law School. He saw service in the World War and was attached to the American staff at the peace negotiations in 1919. He practiced law in New York and was appointed to the Columbia Law faculty in 1927. In 1932 he published a book with Gardiner Means which attracted wide favorable attention. It was *The Modern Corporation and Private Property* (New York: Macmillan, 1932).

supervision or stabilization plans, provided they afford reasonable probability of greater employment, protection of the consumer and are kept under control."

This subject of industrial stabilization had only been hinted at during the campaign. But Berle's suggestion bears a remarkable likeness to the National Industrial Recovery Act.

Berle's specifics for "curative" legislation included: "(1) Federal regulation of security issues and publicity of account, covering public utility holding companies, etc.; but to be considered also with reference to companies of large size and national scope bidding in the capital market. . . . (2) A federal incorporation act, which is tied up with the foregoing. . . . (3) Possibly, a branch banking act. This is Carter Glass's proposal. . . . (4) A thoroughgoing coordination of the various credit emitting agencies such as The Home Loan banks, The Federal Farm Loan banks, The Federal Joint Stock Land banks, (possibly) the Reconstruction Finance Corporation. . . . (5) The revision of the federal receivership laws. (This is largely to provide for the probable railway reorganizations which will have to take place. . . .) . . . (6) Some revision of the Interstate Commerce Act providing for regulation of motor trucks and additional unification of railway facilities to eliminate unnecessary competition. . . ."

Berle concluded, "On my own responsibility I have been collecting material in those fields in which I happen to have special facilities, notably: (A) Industrial stabilization plans; (B) Federal regulation of security issues, publicity of account, etc.; (C) Federal incorporation . . . ; (D) Revision of the federal receivership acts; (E) Revision of the Interstate Commerce Law. . . . I have also been collecting some material on branch banking; and some material on the currency matter; though this is by way of supplementing the collections which must be in existence elsewhere." *

After this chapter was written, I submitted it to Berle for checking and suggestions. In a letter to me under date of February 3, 1966, he made this addition to the foregoing list of subjects:

> You do not mention—and perhaps should—the feeling of most of us, myself especially, that a larger share of the national income ought to be steered toward the lower income levels including farmers. This we did, consciously, through lowering interest rates, credit arrangements and so forth. This was not socialist: it was common sense. They needed the money; business needed the customers; everybody needed employment. We thought private organization would do it, but were prepared to do this through public sectors expenditures if need be—the result, in any event, would be mixed.

* A. A. Berle, Jr., "Memorandum to R. M.," November 10, 1932; in R. M. Files.

I agree that this was in our minds in that early planning phase and it was achieved, as Berle says, in the course of the legislative and administrative arrangements that were a part of the Hundred Days operations.

Berle adds this in his letter:

> I was half-way between a philosophy of "getting the old boat going again," on the one hand, and the socialist and near-socialist conceptions proposed by some of our friends. Essentially the Frankfurter group proposed to depend on ultra free markets and return to a small-scale production. Like you, I thought Van Hise's *Concentration and Control* was more logical.
>
> I think you should mention one other fact. At that time academic economists did not soil their hands with practical questions. Application of their science is almost entirely a post–New Deal phenomenon.

I thoroughly agree with these comments by Berle.

In our March 18 conference Roosevelt dictated to me a list of the major legislative measures that seemed to him to deserve priority. These were temporary relief for the jobless and the needy, agricultural adjustment, farm- and home-debt refunding, banking reform, a Muscle Shoals setup of some kind, simplified bankruptcy procedures, and regulation of corporations. The last-named at that time was an utterly vague concept. Above all, Roosevelt stressed the raising of prices and provision for reemployment.*

* R. M. Notebook, March 18, 1933.

Chapter Seventeen

Congress and the President

IT is recorded in the memoirs of the Earl of Kilmuir (David Maxwell Fyfe) that after the devastating defeat of the Conservative Party in 1945 a strange lot of Labour members appeared in the House of Commons. One of the surviving Conservative members said, "Why, they are just like a lot of damned constituents."

There were "wooly-headed" theorists with nothing to offer but the doctrinaire socialism they had picked up in the universities and their reform clubs, impecunious and rabidly radical journalists, social-settlement workers, trade-union leaders with no experience in statecraft, old rabble-rousers from the industrial Midlands, Scotland, and Wales, and a few of high birth who broke ancestral ties and sought the distinction in Labour that was denied by their peers among the Conservatives.

In trying to manage this motley crew, Clement Attlee had more headaches than had Churchill, who once more felt the freedom of opposition. The Cabinet that Attlee managed to contrive was strong in agitation but dreadfully weak in administrative talent. The overwhelming popular vote that had brought this aggregation to office was not a mandate for socialism. It was inspired only by the desire to express resentment against anyone who might have contributed to the strains and suffering of a long war.

In drawing a sharp contrast between this Labour majority in Britain and the Seventy-third Congress, which served with Roosevelt in 1933, I would not deny that the United States had its own share of reformers, agitators, and crackpots. A few of the new members who were elected with Roosevelt were of that element, but they were kept under control by the rules, traditions, and habits of the two houses of Congress and by the powerful influence of old experienced members.

Roosevelt's sweeping victory over Hoover in 1932 brought into Congress a large Democratic majority. In the Seventy-second Congress, after the election of 1930, there were in the House 220 Democrats and 214 Republicans. Republicans kept control of the Senate by one vote. But in the new Seventy-third Congress the party ratio in the House was 310–117 and in the Senate 60–35. Despite this big change in the party balance, which meant that many new and inexperienced members came to Washington, several circumstances prevented things from getting out of hand:

1. There was the seniority system, which in the 1960's has been derided and opposed. This system placed experienced and generally sound men as chairmen of vital committees.

In the Senate there were Ellison D. Smith of South Carolina, Agriculture; Carter Glass of Virginia, Appropriations; Duncan U. Fletcher of Florida, Banking and Currency; Hubert D. Stephens of Mississippi, Commerce; Pat Harrison of Mississippi, Finance; Key Pittman of Nevada, Foreign Relations; Clarence C. Dill of Washington, Interstate Commerce; Henry F. Ashurst of Arizona, Judiciary.

In the House there were Marvin Jones of Texas, Agriculture; James P. Buchanan of Texas, Appropriations; Henry B. Steagall of Alabama, Banking and Currency; Sam Rayburn of Texas, Interstate and Foreign Commerce; Hatton W. Sumners of Texas, Judiciary; Robert L. Doughton of North Carolina, Ways and Means; Edward W. Pou of North Carolina, Rules.

2. As the foregoing list indicates, nearly all the chairmen were from the South and were of a generally conservative temper. More often than not, they were backed in a showdown by ranking Republicans on their committees. These, too, were veterans.

3. The Democratic control of the House for two years, with Garner as Speaker, had provided experience in methods of operation that was valuable in the special session. It is true that the House majority had been a fairly irresponsible body during the years 1931 and 1932. It played politics with the prospect of a Presidential election ahead, and despite my admiration for Garner, I realized that he had encouraged the habit among the majority to play politics with the nation's ills. But now, with a Democratic President and with Garner gone, the House showed its capability of real statesmanship.

4. This was no Congress to be stampeded or cajoled. Roosevelt well knew it. Congressional veterans regarded Roosevelt as a wonderful man, but they realized that he had been absent from Washington during the twelve long years when they labored with problems and policies at the national level with Republican Presidents.

I was almost always present when Roosevelt conferred with Congressional leaders. Since my experience had been in academic life, I conceived a parallel in which a young and untried college president must deal with grizzled and time-tested professors. Roosevelt was aware of a decided attitude of considered reserve among the Congressional leaders, and he proceeded with the greatest of caution in dealing with them. At first, Roosevelt's restraint when he met with Congressional leaders approached awkwardness. He followed the political custom of calling them familiarly by their first names, but it took a year or more to develop a real camaraderie.

But in those early days, they knew so much about the government over which he presided, and for many months he knew so little about it, that he was at pains to exercise great care in what he said. Moreover, his innate tact was without fault.

I came to realize then, and the impression has grown since as I have watched Congresses come and go, that in general the leaders of the Seventy-third Congress were extraordinarily capable and intelligent individuals. There were probably as many first-rate men in that Congress as there had been at any time in history since the golden years of the Virginia Dynasty.

5. Roosevelt's deferential attitude toward Congress does not mean, however, that he did not exercise the subtlest sort of influence over its leaders. This was created by the very special mood of the President during that period. He was exhilarated by the success of the attack on the banking crisis and conveyed his buoyancy to everyone with whom he came in contact. His carefree, confident spirit was contagious, and Congressional leaders were quick to get the infection.

6. Moreover, those of us who came to Washington with Roosevelt soon conceived a deep respect for the place of Congress in the Federal establishment. Some of the professors who had made light of Congress in their classes came to realize that this coordinate body was a solid and formidable factor in our government. We became aware, moreover, of the traditional jealousy that prevailed between the two houses and also the easily aroused resentment in both houses at the suggestion of Executive encroachment. Since Roosevelt exercised great care in those early years in dealing with Congress, there was no trouble. But when, after his smashing victory in 1936, he proposed the reorganization of the Supreme Court, and later, in 1938, when he attempted to purge Democratic Senators, he was faced by the reality of the system of checks and balances. The two houses might have their mutual differences, but when they were faced with a powerful Executive they drew together and strongly resisted him.

7. In the Hundred Days period, when my relations with members of Congress were manifold, I was profoundly thankful that in the 1932 campaign I had enlisted Senators Byrnes, Pittman, and Walsh to work with me. I had learned a lot from them.

8. The friendly and cooperative relationship between Roosevelt and

Congress in those days is the more remarkable when it is remembered that Roosevelt had been elected over Hoover with a majority of more than 7,000,000. Considering the dire distress of the country at that time, the popularity of Roosevelt after his inaugural speech and the saving of the banks, his own innate instincts to experiment, and the access to him of radicals of all sorts who came unofficially to Washington, the wonder is that reform did not get out of hand. In large part, the country was saved from chaos by the conservatism of Congress and the restraint of the President. Those of us who labored to maintain a liaison between the President and Congress were for the most part extraordinarily thankful for the intelligence and common sense of the members of Congress with whom we had to deal. I once answered a critic who complained that we did too much and too soon, "If you only knew how many absurd ideas we killed, you would praise us for moderation."

9. In Roosevelt's conferences with leaders and with chairmen of committees, he often brought in members of the Administration or others who were concerned with the problem that was the subject of discussion. In these conferences he skillfully committed himself to the role of moderator, listening attentively to the suggestions that were offered and carefully refraining from injecting his own views until the conference had been concluded. Sam Rayburn, chairman of the vital Interstate and Foreign Commerce Committee, told me more than once of his impression when several people were arguing something among themselves in the presence of Roosevelt. Rayburn said that while Roosevelt did not act as the active proponent of a point of view, he was "the best jury to listen and decide that I ever saw."

10. It has been accepted as a fact, largely because Farley has repeated it so often, that Roosevelt deliberately withheld appointments in the executive departments during this period in order to hold members of Congress in line for favorable votes on his legislative proposals. This was not nearly so important a factor as Farley has claimed. It was not necessary to twist the arms of legislators in those days by the promise or expectation of favors to come. Roosevelt did not need to do this to get favorable votes for his program. There simply wasn't time to consider in detail such matters of patronage, and members of Congress well realized that since they were there to achieve recovery of the economy, their continuance in office would be assured by what they themselves accomplished in their legislative tasks. If the country recovered, there was no need for them to worry about re-election. In any event, matters of patronage have been vastly overestimated as a means of winning Congressional votes. I cite Sam Rayburn's judgment. He told me on more than one occasion that when he secured an appointment for some friend or constituent, the result was generally the creation of "nine enemies and one ingrate."

Chapter Eighteen

The President's Assistant

EIGHTY or ninety years before the Hundred Days, John Bright said that the Chancellor of the Duchy of Lancaster was the "maid-of-all-work" in the British Cabinet. The bearer of this title in bygone years had exercised authority as the custodian of the Crown's property in that area and had oversight of its courts for the Crown. But in the course of time these functions passed to others, and he had nothing left but the possession of the Lancastrian title. He has since been a minister without stated responsibilities. He is attached to the Government, to do whatever is assigned to him by the Prime Minister.

For the short period of the Hundred Days I had that sort of status in the Roosevelt regime. My official title, assistant secretary of state, had little relevance to what I did.

I operated with a great deal of freedom. The President's orders and suggestions were my first consideration, but often I assumed the initiative without consulting him, as I did when the National Industrial Recovery Act was in its earliest stages.

The source of my influence was in my recognized long relationship with Roosevelt, in my personal and friendly contacts with certain members of Congress and with Farley in the National Committee, and my close friendship with Secretary Woodin. Within rather narrow limits and largely because of my relationship with Roosevelt, I had some influence in the State Department.

I was indifferent to any change in my official status because I felt that, considering my past relations with Roosevelt, I could be more useful and more independent of intra-departmental conflicts and because I intended to remain in the government only until my classes at Columbia resumed in September.

Rex Tugwell has since defined my status before the inauguration:

> Our experience during the fall and winter—Ray Moley's and mine—would never be repeated. Beginning shortly after the election and continuing until the spring, Ray was, for all practical purposes, a Cabinet in one person; and I was his second. There was no real third.

Tugwell makes the interesting point that "this was the last of the long intervals between election and the inauguration. The old stretch of four months, devised for a country without rapid transportation, was a dangerous hiatus in the circumstances of 1932–1933." *

The more important Cabinet appointments were not made until late in February.

Thus, there was an unbroken continuity in my relations with Roosevelt into the period of the Hundred Days. Tugwell was deeply involved in his new job as assistant secretary of agriculture and the legislative problems involved in the farm bill. The new Cabinet members were engaged in learning "the ropes" in their departments. I had only casual contacts with them. I survived, not necessarily as the fittest, but by virtue of my earlier relations with Roosevelt.

The daily routine was a conference with Roosevelt after he finished his breakfast in bed about 8:30 to 9:00 A.M. There the legislative situation was reviewed, information was exchanged about miscellaneous subjects, and messages were planned. When a message or speech was to be written, we talked it over and I retired to the Cabinet room to draft it. When Roosevelt reached his office at ten-thirty or so, there was then a short period with him to read over my draft and amend it. A message generally went to Congress when it assembled at noon.

Roosevelt, after the breakfast dishes were taken out, usually spent about an hour in bed, and that hour was the period when I had my conference with him. It was necessary for Lewis Douglas to discuss budget matters with him at that same time. Since Douglas was concerned with many matters of policy that went beyond the duties of his office, he had a chance to discuss these with Roosevelt. Douglas and I agreed roughly to divide this hour between us, and we both stayed throughout the hour before Roosevelt dressed and went to his office. During that hour, McIntyre came in with his list of appointments for approval, and Steve Early discussed matters that related to the President. Mrs. Roosevelt also came in, with lists of the people who had been invited to dinner.

My status was well understood by McIntyre, Early, and Missy Le-

* Rexford G. Tugwell, unpublished manuscript entitled "Transition." The "lame-duck" amendment (Article XX) was ratified in October 1933.

Hand of the White House staff, and my relations with them were exceedingly pleasant. Except for an occasional argument, there was a complete understanding with Howe so far as my comings and goings were concerned.

I had been able to work on a satisfactory basis with Howe throughout the previous year and now, since the issues that were coming before Congress were not even remotely understood by Howe, he had little to do with the legislative program.

If I were to bring the function that I performed somewhere within the reaches of exact definition, it was to establish a series of lines of communication:

1. I maintained constant contact with Congress, especially with the members I knew well. In the Administrations of Truman, Eisenhower, Kennedy, and Johnson a definite member of the White House staff was assigned to Congressional relations, in a sense as a lobbyist for the Executive. There was no such definition of responsibility in those days, but as a matter of practice I had that function, especially with the members of Congress who were most valuable to Roosevelt in his legislative program. My acquaintance with members of Congress was somewhat specialized, but it was most intimate with Senators Byrnes, Glass, and Robinson and with Sam Rayburn in the House and two or three others, including the astute chairman of the Judiciary Committee, Hatton Sumners.

2. Through Will Woodin, I maintained a close contact with the Treasury and measurably maintained a line of contact between that department and Roosevelt.

3. There were many people completely outside the government who were important to the legislative program. Among these were men like Bernard Baruch, whose advice and assistance were always important. I also had the assignment of maintaining contacts with certain elements in the press, notably with the Hearst people and with Roy Howard of the Scripps-Howard papers.

4. Early in the Administration, Frances Perkins invited me to lunch, and her explanation of what I might do stands out sharply in my memory. She said that after her experience with Roosevelt in Albany, where she was commissioner of labor, she realized that it was necessary that someone be a means of communication that could not be maintained by casual appointments with Roosevelt. She said that people could talk to me at length and count on me to convey the essence of what they had in mind to Roosevelt at a propitious time, when I was able to get his full attention. Perhaps this was deeply embedded in her mind because Roosevelt in his personal contacts with Mrs. Perkins was fairly abrupt and not always attentive to her somewhat lengthy discourses on social philosophy. She felt this isolation and was anxious to develop a

means of communication that would serve her purposes better. Such contact with other Cabinet officers, however, did not prevail, although my relations with them were friendly. For all of them sought, quite properly, their own means of communicating with the President.

During the remaining weeks of the Hundred Days Congress, my pace required a physical durability that even now is a mystery to me. I watched over the formulation of many plans for legislation (except, notably, the agricultural bill, the TVA, the farm- and home-loan bills) and the plans for their administration; tried to unravel the snarls and quiet the clashes of opinion that cropped up among the many architects of legislation; listened to and tried to understand the many suggestions that were routed through me to Roosevelt by many people in government and in private life; kept a hand in the conferences in the State Department that related to the coming Economic Conference at London; maintained in the State Department a firm control over the debts of the various European countries, although these were technically Treasury matters. It was impossible to plan ahead, for some new problem would emerge almost hourly, and some new task would be assigned by Roosevelt at our routine meetings.

My office in the old State, War, and Navy Building, across the street from the White House, was generally only a place to get and answer mail and to make appointments for visitors.

During the months from February to July I lived at the Carlton Hotel, a short walk from my office in the State Department and the White House. In New York my apartment near Columbia University was still available when I needed it.

My family, consisting of Eva Dall Moley and twin sons, Malcolm and Raymond, Jr., born in 1924, remained in Santa Barbara, California, in those years. It was important, it seemed to me, to keep the children clear of the schoolboy political arguments so common in those hectic years 1932 and 1933.

My office staff consisted of six people. Shortly after the inauguration I acquired from Marvin McIntyre a young man who had been his assistant during the 1932 campaign and who served for a while in the White House. He was Januarius A. Mullen, the son of the Democratic national committeeman from Nebraska. Mullen, among his other qualifications, was a lawyer and I secured for him status as assistant legal adviser in the State Department. He also had credentials as a member of the State Department intelligence group. Mullen knew almost everyone of importance in the new Administration and served well as a contact. Through McIntyre he continued to have the run of the White House. He and I engaged an apartment in the Carlton Hotel where he was constantly with me to assist in many political and personal matters. Later, he accompanied me on my trip to London during the summer.

He was my greatest source of information about what was going on outside my daily routine, and he had excellent relations with the working press.

I brought with me to Washington two young women who had been my assistants in New York since 1931. One was Celeste Jedel, who earlier had been an honor student of mine at Barnard College and who graduated in 1931. She had an extraordinarily brilliant mind and could help with the multitude of tasks that fell upon me in the 1932 campaign and thereafter. Officially, she was made an assistant legal adviser in the State Department but was assigned to my office. She was then only twenty-two years of age.

Another young woman, Annette Pomeranz, also came with me from New York. She served as a personal secretary and was officially on the State Department payroll.

I inherited from my predecessor in the State Department a fine career woman, Mrs. Helen Cook, who was exceedingly helpful in maintaining relations within the department. There was also Katherine C. Blackburn, who served during the campaign as "librarian" for the Democratic National Committee. I employed her in my office in Washington at Howe's request. Her duty was to care for the innumerable plans, memoranda, and papers. Under the pressure of those days we cut the red tape surrounding an appointment such as this one by having it listed on the rolls of Jesse Jones's RFC, since that agency was not restricted by civil service.

I spent Thursdays in New York until the end of the term at Columbia, because I had never dropped my courses at Barnard College. I was able, with the beginning of the new term in February, to have my courses scheduled for one day, one at 9:00 A.M. and another at 1:00 P.M. I entered my courses in the Columbia catalogue for the academic year 1933–1934 because at that time I had every intention of returning to academic life.

My relations with the press were mixed. There were six or eight reporters who were my most frequent visitors, and, while I was not a source of sensational news, they felt I was helpful to them in providing background and understanding of what was going on. I was always completely candid with them, trusting to their friendly discretion in what they wrote for publication. The most important and interesting of these was Ernest K. Lindley, a staff man for the New York *Herald Tribune*. Generally I saw these reporters in the late afternoon.

I set aside a few hours on Friday afternoons to go over the week and talk about further plans with Willard Kiplinger, who had established his newsletter ten years earlier. I liked Kiplinger, trusted him, and withheld practically nothing in informing him. In later years he told me that some of my reflections and disclosures about what was going on had frightened him. This was because he had grave misgivings about such freedom in talking with any journalist. But I knew he was capable of guarding such confidences and would protect me in what he published. Our talks, however, were two-way affairs. He had spent many years in Washington, first as a financial writer and later as editor of his newsletter. His advice about Washington ways and the information he offered about what people were saying about Roosevelt and the new Administration and about me were invaluable. I was, after all, quite unfamiliar with official life, and in the position I occupied I was isolated from the casual gossip that flowed so abundantly in the capital. Kiplinger saved me from many a slip.

There was one problem I tried my best to avoid—patronage. In late December I expressed my position about appointments to Farley in a letter:

> I am going to take this occasion to put into words the policy I am following very strictly in all my dealings. It is simply that in all matters of appointments I am absolutely and entirely maintaining a hands-off attitude. . . . I do not consider that my function involves any question of appointments whatsoever.

I did not then and never have taken the position that appointment as a reward for political service is bad or that a career man is per se preferable to an amateur. I certainly did not believe that civil service had forever abolished politics in government or that it was an unmixed blessing. The criterion is qualification for the office, tempered by preference for those who have served the party.

I added this in my letter to Farley:

> If and when you want any advice from me on these appointments, I should certainly not follow the policy of advising the retention of existing officials except when they are of the most indispensable kind. . . . It is perfectly possible to find men, in a country as large as our own, who supported the Governor loyally and who are at the same time capable in a high degree of doing this work.*

In those early months I was asked by Farley to alter this policy so far as certain diplomatic appointments were concerned. Farley, who knew that Hull had decided not to concern himself with diplomatic appointments, had found hard going with Undersecretary William Phillips, who was a career man himself. And so Farley turned over to me a file on Democratic prospects, designating in each case what they had contributed in effort and money to the 1932 campaign. He asked me to use my influence with Phillips and Roosevelt in providing suitable appointments for these people.

* Raymond Moley to James A. Farley, December 22, 1932. R. M. Files.

Several interesting and occasionally outlandish cases were involved.

High on the list for a diplomatic post was Claude Bowers, a political columnist for the Hearst newspapers and a favorite orator at Democratic conventions and other meetings of the faithful. Bowers had written popular political histories and wanted an embassy where there would be leisure to write. Belgium was his preference. But when I spoke to Roosevelt about this, he said, "Claude is a funny-looking fellow. The Belgian Court is very fastidious. So let's send him to Spain, where there won't be much to do." When the Spanish Civil War broke out, the Ambassador and his entourage were moved out of the country temporarily. Bowers' literary plans were badly shattered. Later they were resumed in Chile.

Mayor James Curley of Boston had his heart set on being Ambassador to Italy. He had earned priority because in the pre-convention campaign he had supported Roosevelt instead of Smith, who was highly popular in Massachusetts. Certainly, here was an obligation which could not be lightly held. Phillips, a Bostonian of distinguished antecedents, was horrified by the idea of Curley as Ambassador in Rome. He begged me, with quite uncharacteristic passion, to block this appointment. Roosevelt compromised by offering to appoint Curley to Poland. Curley rejected this and announced that he would run for governor of Massachusetts. He did so and won.

Chapter Nineteen

Curbing Agricultural Anarchy—the AAA

REVIEWED now over the long perspective of years since 1933, the efforts of government to grapple with and contain the product of America's fertile soil have been a cycle of futility. Roosevelt himself must have had some intimations of the strength of the giant force with which he was contending when he presented his farm program to Congress on March 16. For he said in his message that he was proposing an experimental plan; if it failed to work, he would be the first to admit it. Later, he did not admit it. But he tried something else after the Supreme Court had invalidated the Agricultural Adjustment Administration in 1936. Presidents, Congresses, farm organizations, and economists have been struggling with the problem ever since.

For government by its intervention in this area of our economy has faced a titanic natural force, which, by the application of newly discovered scientific methods, has become all the more formidable. Surpluses have mounted with every new plan to curb them, and only the seemingly inexhaustible credit of the United States has been able to prevent catastrophe.

I am reminded of *The Pit*, a moving novel written by Frank Norris many years before the New Deal. A Chicago businessman was afflicted with a raging obsession. He wanted to corner the market in wheat. He crushed other speculators who opposed him. He trusted to his daring and his wealth. Finally he realized that he was contending with something more than the "shouting and excited men in the Board of Trade":

> It was the harvest, it was the Wheat—the very earth itself . . . those scattered farmers, who because he had put the price so high, had planted as

never before . . . the Wheat had grown itself; demand and supply, these were the two great laws the Wheat obeyed. Almost blasphemous in his effrontery, he had tampered with these laws and had aroused a Titan. He had laid his puny hand upon Creation and the very earth itself, the great mother, feeling the touch of the cobweb the human insect had spun, had stirred at last in her sleep and had sent her omnipotence through the grooves of the world, to find and crush the disturber of her appointed courses. . . . The new harvest was coming in.

The harvest sickled down Curtis Jadwin and those around him. Like Milton's Lucifer, he had dared to defy the omnipotent.

Roosevelt in the early spring of 1932, with a daring that almost paralleled that of the fictional Curtis Jadwin, promised the nation's farmers to raise the relative value of their income. The political premise of his campaign for the nomination was that his delegate strength must be found in agricultural states. For the industrial and financial East had other candidates and regarded Roosevelt with misgivings. Somehow, he realized, there must be found a program that not only would be effective in winning farm votes but could provide for agriculture a balance in what had become, since World War I, a badly disjointed national economy. The Armistice had marked the beginning of hard years for most farmers.

For reasons that need not be explored here, the farmers in the years before 1914 had enjoyed a fair competence. In fact, when the Department of Agriculture created what was known as the "parity index," it considered the five years ending in 1914 as normal. "Parity" was the expression of the relationship between an index of the prices the farmer received for his product and an index of industrial prices—that is, the prices he paid for what he bought.

The war from 1914 to 1918 had created a vast market abroad for the American farmer, and he was exhorted by his government to plant more and more. Acreage expanded and production increased prodigiously. When peace and the resumption of planting in Europe followed, exports were sharply reduced. American agriculture suffered from an abundance of its own creation. All through the 1920's, with rising prosperity on the industrial front, the farmers were to a greater and greater degree afflicted with stagnant or falling prices for their crops. As Hugh Johnson put it, "the red flags of distress" were flying in the farm states long before the crash in 1929 initiated a great industrial contraction.

Throughout the twelve years of Republican Administrations there can be little doubt that Herbert Hoover as Secretary of Commerce and President had largely dominated the government's policies toward agriculture. He stubbornly maintained that agriculture could prosper only as the rest of the economy prospered. Farm leaders, farmers' organizations, members of Congress, and economists sought continuously for a solution of the agricultural imbalance, but the executive department only measurably acceded to proposed plans. The McNary-Haugen plan to promote exports was vetoed twice, and its supporters looked to something else as a means of relief.

Politically, therefore, Hoover had created the best of all issues for a Democratic opponent in 1932. And Roosevelt was determined to make use of that opportunity.

But what plan or plans should be presented in the campaign for the nomination and later in the election campaign? It was clear that Roosevelt must in a Democratic convention have the support of the farm states, since his strength in the industrial Northeast was spotty. The first consideration that faced the group that I was gathering to help provide Roosevelt with issues and answers was an attractive agricultural program. In our collaboration we addressed ourselves to this with a confidence that could only be attributed to our inexperience. Al Smith had presented the McNary-Haugen plan in 1928. While his defeat cannot be attributed to that, the response to his rather labored discourses on agriculture was not notable.

We were quite aware of the plight of agriculture but we were not entrusted with the power of government. We were concerned primarily with getting the nomination and, after that had succeeded, with winning an election against a Republican President who had altogether lost the confidence of the traditionally Republican farm states.

Thus we were concerned with politics as well as with economic education. Roosevelt told us more than once that unless we won the nomination and the election nothing we wanted could be done. There was also the necessity to educate a good part of the country, which had no direct knowledge of the plight of Midwestern and Southern farmers, as well as to put before the farmers themselves something that might arouse their hopes for relief. But we were foresighted enough to realize that our plan must be reasonably practical and workable after the election had been won. And we were infected with the boundless confidence of Roosevelt, who believed that, once he was elected, all sorts of means for relief would be found.

On one aspect of farm relief we were all in accord. We rejected out of hand the populistic concept that farm relief could be achieved by tinkering with the currency, either by greenbackism or "free" silver. A large sector of Congress was still wedded to the notion that if more money were created, the farmers' prices would rise and their tribulations would cease. But we realized the economic fact that merely increasing the volume of money would not only provide farmers with higher prices, but would also force them to pay higher prices for what they bought. Something must be proposed that would limit production to domestic needs and at the same time free the farmer from prices determined in the international market. This, we learned, would involve a vast pattern of planning.

Planning was a concept that had won a great deal of popularity in academic circles—in part because of the Soviet experiment, which was still looked upon with a considerable amount of sympathy, and in part because of the lessons that Americans as well as others had learned from Germany's mobilization in the war. The perversion of the Russian revolution by an iron and cruel dictatorship had not become apparent at that time except to a few more perceptive observers. In Britain, planning was already supplanting socialism as the theme of the Labour Party.

Something specific had to be proposed, for Roosevelt had cast the die in these words in his "Forgotten Man" speech in April 1932:

> Approximately one-half of our whole population, fifty or sixty million people, earn their living by farming or in small towns whose existence immediately depends upon farms. They have today lost their purchasing power. Why? They are receiving for farm products less than the cost to them of raising these farm products. The result of this loss of purchasing power is that many other millions of people engaged in industry in the cities cannot sell industrial products to the farming half of the Nation. This brings home to every city worker that his own employment is directly tied up with the farmer's dollar. No Nation can long endure half bankrupt. Main Street, Broadway, the mills, the mines will close if half the buyers are broke.
>
> I cannot escape the conclusion that one of the essential parts of a national program of restoration must be to restore purchasing power to the farming half of the country.

This was the key to Roosevelt's forthcoming campaign. At least by implication, it was a promise to come up with something that could solve what was known as the great farm problem. To me, it was something more than a problem. It was a mystery. I knew little more about it than what I had read in the newspapers.

I sought the advice of my colleague at Columbia, Rex Tugwell. He was familiar with the efforts for farm relief that had been made in the 1920's and had been used in a peripheral way in the Smith campaign in 1928. He explained in simple economic terms the nature of the problems related to farming—first to me; then to Sam Rosenman, Roosevelt's counsel; to Basil O'Connor, Roosevelt's law partner; and finally to Roosevelt in Albany.

It appeared that during the 1920's a plan that went under the name of its Congressional sponsors, Senator McNary and Congressman Haugen, had dominated the efforts of reformers. Five versions of this plan had been introduced in Congress—in 1924, 1925, 1926, 1927, and 1928. It had passed both houses twice, in 1927 and 1928, but had been vetoed both times by President Coolidge. The stinging phraseology of these veto messages was widely attributed to Herbert Hoover, who stood out in the Coolidge Cabinet as an agricultural expert because of his work on the production and supply of food in the Wilson days.

While the various versions of the McNary-Haugen plan differed in specifics, the essential purpose was to create a two-price system for the staple crops with a resulting parity with other products that entered the marketplace. A government agency would determine domestic requirements, and the balance would then be sold on the world market, presumably at a loss. The assumption was made that a better balance between supply and demand on the domestic market would so enhance farm prices that losses abroad could be made up by the levying of an "equalization fee." The cost of dumping abroad, to be assumed by the farmer, it was argued, would be much less than the higher income from domestic sales that would accrue to the agricultural producer. The plan also included a firm reliance on tariffs to keep foreign production out of our market.

The rallying cry in this plan was what was called "tariff equality." This meant to the farmer that he would be protected in much the same manner that the manufacturer had been in times past. As it was, he had been compelled to sell at a price determined abroad, while he bought what he needed in a market protected by tariff.*

The major figure in the campaign to promote the McNary-Haugen plan since 1920 had been George Peek, an Illinois farm-implement manufacturer. In the early Harding days he had strong support from Henry Wallace, Sr., Secretary of Agriculture. Some of those associated with Peek were Bernard Baruch; Hugh Johnson, who himself was engaged in manufacturing farm implements for a time; Chester Davis; and Frank Lowden, former governor of Illinois. Considerable sums were contributed to support an educational campaign among farmers and to lobby for the plan in Congress. Most of the leaders of farm organizations supported the plan.

When Hoover became President he proposed and secured the creation of a Federal Farm Board as a substitute for the McNary-Haugen plan. Among the purposes of this Farm Board was the promotion of co-ops and stabilization corporations. But because of the deepening depression and the mounting distress of the farm population, the Farm Board by 1932 was unpopular in the farm states. When the Farm Board, for instance, finally gave in and bought wheat and cotton, it could not dispose of it.

After the failure of the McNary-Haugen plan because of the Presidential vetoes, various people had been thinking about and working on an

* The complicated details of these McNary-Haugen bills are not relevant to this account.

alternative plan. In a book on the farm problem by Professor J. D. Black of Harvard, which was published in the 1920's, there is a chapter on an early version of the domestic allotment plan.

The individual who deserves major credit for the development and acceptance of the domestic allotment plan in the New Deal was M. L. Wilson, a professor at the Montana State College at Bozeman. In the winter of 1931–1932 Wilson presented the plan to Hoover's Federal Farm Board. At that time Henry I. Harriman, president of the Chamber of Commerce of the United States, became interested. Early in 1932 an informal committee was formed to work on the plan, consisting of Wilson, Harriman, Henry A. Wallace, and Beardsley Ruml of New York. It was from this group that Tugwell first developed an interest in the plan. The House Committee on Agriculture appointed a subcommittee to consider it, and, as a result, a bill was introduced on June 4, 1932. A month later, no doubt stimulated by what Roosevelt said in his acceptance speech, another bill was introduced, on July 7, by Congressman Clifford Hope.

Since Tugwell felt that this plan would be a valid basis for a campaign issue, I asked him to find someone who would supplement our efforts by getting it in shape for a basic speech. He attended a meeting of farm leaders in Chicago in June and when he returned to New York he told me that the man we needed was Wilson.

Tugwell had thoroughly briefed Roosevelt on the plan, and Roosevelt agreed to discuss it in his acceptance speech, which I had under preparation with the assistance of Tugwell, Berle, and others. The language in that speech, largely supplied by Tugwell, was:

> . . . The practical way to help the farmer is by an arrangement that will, in addition to lightening some of the impoverishing burdens from his back, do something toward the reduction of surpluses of staple commodities that hang on the market. It should be our aim to add to the world prices of staple products the amount of a reasonable tariff protection, to give agriculture the same protection that industry has today.
>
> And in exchange for this immediately increased return I am sure that the farmers of this Nation would agree ultimately to such planning of their production as would reduce the surpluses and make it unnecessary in later years to depend on dumping those surpluses abroad in order to support domestic prices. . . .
>
> Farm leaders and farm economists, generally, agree that a plan based on that principle is a desirable first step in the reconstruction of agriculture. It does not in itself furnish a complete program, but it will serve in great measure in the long run to remove the pall of a surplus without the continued perpetual threat of world dumping. Final voluntary reduction of surplus is a part of our objective, but the long continuance and the present

burden of existing surpluses make it necessary to repair great damage of the present by immediate emergency measures.

In July, after the nomination, Tugwell, Henry Morgenthau, Jr., and I persuaded Roosevelt to invite Henry A. Wallace, son of the former Secretary of Agriculture, and Wilson to Hyde Park for further consultation, and I went to work on the farm speech, which was tentatively scheduled for Topeka in September, during Roosevelt's Western trip. Although I put the pieces together in an omnibus speech, I had the collaboration of many people. I estimated later that at least twenty-five people either submitted memoranda or read over the speech and made changes or corrections. But the very heart of the speech was contributed by Wilson. This section follows:

It will be my purpose, my friends, to compose the conflicting elements of these various plans, to gather the benefit of the long study and consideration of them, to coordinate efforts to the end that agreement may be reached upon the details of a distinct policy, aimed at producing the result to which all these efforts and plans are directed—the restoration of agriculture to economic equality with other industries within the United States. I seek to give to that portion of the crop consumed in the United States a benefit equivalent to a tariff sufficient to give you farmers an adequate price.

I want now to state what seem to me the specifications upon which most of the reasonable leaders of agriculture have agreed, and to express here and now my whole-hearted accord with these specifications.

First: The plan must provide for the producer of staple surplus commodities, such as wheat, cotton, corn in the form of hogs, and tobacco, a tariff benefit over world prices which is equivalent to the benefit given by the tariff to industrial products. This differential benefit must be so applied that the increase in farm income, purchasing and debt-paying power will not stimulate further production.

Second: The plan must finance itself. Agriculture has at no time sought and does not now seek any such access to the public treasury as was provided by the futile and costly attempts at price stabilization by the Federal Farm Board. It seeks only equality of opportunity with tariff-protected industry.

Third: It must not make use of any mechanism which would cause our European customers to retaliate on the ground of dumping. It must be based upon making the tariff effective and direct in its operation.

Fourth: It must make use of existing agencies and so far as possible be decentralized in its Administration so that the chief responsibility for its operation will rest with the locality rather than with newly created bureaucratic machinery in Washington.

Fifth: It must operate as nearly as possible on a cooperative basis and its effect must be to enhance and strengthen the cooperative movement. It should, moreover, be constituted so that it can be withdrawn whenever the emergency has passed and normal foreign markets have been re-established.

Sixth: The plan must be, in so far as possible, voluntary. I like the idea that the plan should not be put into operation unless it has the support of a reasonable majority of the producers of the exportable commodity to which it is to apply. It must be so organized that the benefits will go to the man who participates.

If the farmer chose to raise more than his allotment, he could sell that part of his crop in the world markets for what he could get. But since this internationally fixed price was generally lower than the cost of production, he would have a strong incentive to use the extra land for other purposes, such as the raising of "legumes," or permit it to lie fallow.

By the time Roosevelt had delivered his Topeka speech, he was quite familiar with the plan and would refer to it in his extemporary back-platform speeches. He had a habit of explaining the relative fall of farm prices by saying that the farmer now had to carry two wagon-loads of his produce to town to buy the same shoes, machinery, and other manufactured goods that one wagon-load would have bought in the period before the World War.

To avoid any suggestion of government coercion, the plan was essentially voluntary. The farmer might or might not sign up for the subsidy as compensation for restriction of production.*

After the election, Tugwell, along with Wallace and Wilson, and responsible members of Congress worked out a bill embodying the plan. I had little to do with this phase except that in early January Tugwell told me of the frictions that developed because of Henry Morgenthau, Jr.'s projection of himself into the negotiations with Congressional leaders. I called Morgenthau and told him that Roosevelt wanted this matter to be handled by Tugwell. He was very disagreeable. He said he would not recognize Tugwell's authority to act for the incoming Administration unless Roosevelt personally ordered him to.

Tugwell and I were convinced that Morgenthau had anticipated, with some confidence of success, that he would be appointed Secretary of Agriculture. This ambition of his had become evident throughout the preceding year. Certainly he believed that in these preliminary conferences with the House committee he was acting as Roosevelt's representative. He asserts this in his diary.†

Morgenthau and Roosevelt, neighbors in Dutchess County, had been

* In the famous decision of the Supreme Court in 1936 invalidating the AAA, Justice Roberts, speaking for the Court's majority, said that the processing tax and the spending of it for subsidies imposed contractual obligations and therefore involved coercion. It would, he said, force farmers to regulate production, and this was an unconstitutional invasion of the powers reserved to the states. It was, as one commentator has put the Court's opinion since, "an unconstitutional means to an unconstitutional end."

† *From the Diaries of Henry Morgenthau, Jr.,* by John Morton Blum (Boston: Houghton Mifflin, 1959), pp. 38–42.

on rather intimate terms for some years, and during Roosevelt's governorship Morgenthau had been conservation commissioner. During the campaign Morgenthau told me, modestly, I believed then, that he realized that his capacities permitted him to perform only two functions. One was to supervise the arrangements for the candidate's transportation; the other was to confer with farm leaders over the country and to enlist their support for Roosevelt. But Roosevelt, so far as agricultural policies were concerned, looked to Tugwell and to Wallace and Wilson. There was no doubt in my mind that Morgenthau's father, who was constantly popping in and out of the Roosevelt circle of acquaintances and had in the past been an effective money-raiser for the Democratic Party, seriously coveted the secretaryship of agriculture for his son. I was also convinced that Roosevelt, while maintaining cordial relations with the Morgenthaus, never seriously considered this appointment. In fact, on the day before my unpleasant contact with Morgenthau, Roosevelt had given me his choices for Cabinet offices and had Wallace scheduled for Agriculture.

But the ambiguity of Roosevelt's instructions led to an airing of differences between the Wallace-Tugwell views and those of Morgenthau before the House committee. Morgenthau was accompanied to the meetings by Professor William I. Myers of Cornell.

The Myers-Morgenthau ideas for farm relief were for the most part derived from the curious monetary policies of Professor George Warren, also of Cornell. Myers had no confidence at all in a plan to restrict agricultural production. While Morgenthau believed in such a plan for an emergency, he opposed it as a permanent measure. He favored what he called a multiple approach—provisions to eliminate speculation in commodity futures, aid to cooperatives, reforestation, refinancing of farm mortgages, and Warren's idea of manipulating prices by revisions in the price of gold.

Thus Tugwell, Wallace, and Wilson were confronted by opposition from two sides. There was George Peek, who had been a sponsor of the McNary-Haugen plan and favored marketing agreements to dispose of surpluses abroad on the one hand, and Morgenthau, with his miscellaneous ideas, on the other.

Wilson, however, had paved the way for the domestic allotment plan when he explained it to the Hoover Federal Farm Board in December. The board later—and somewhat reluctantly, because of Hoover's views—commented on it rather favorably.

After there had been several meetings with Marvin Jones, chairman of the House Committee on Agriculture, and after long arguments with Morgenthau and Myers, F. P. Lee, a legislative draftsman, was given the job of drafting a bill. It included some of Morgenthau, some of Peek, and, also, as its central provision, the domestic allotment plan.

Its title was the Agricultural Adjustment Act. This bill passed the House on January 12, 1933. But after some debate in the Senate, it was laid aside pending the coming of the new Administration.*

After Wallace and Tugwell moved into the Department of Agriculture, they directed various individuals and bureaus there to prepare the complicated administrative arrangements which would be essential to the operation of the AAA.

With some modifications of the Jones bill, which had passed the House in January, a new bill was prepared in March, and Wallace called a meeting in Washington to provide briefing for farm leaders.

Because of the short time before the oncoming planting season and the variety of ideas to be reconciled, Wallace would have preferred a shorter measure covering only the domestic allotment plan. But opposition and misunderstanding still prevailed, and so the omnibus bill was decided upon. Tugwell believed that "in the more calculating and less heated atmosphere of the Department of Agriculture a selection could be made of any or all devices."

While Hugh Johnson and George Peek were far from convinced that the domestic allotment plan would work, they were less vocal in opposition than was Morgenthau. They largely voiced their objections in the bosom of the New Deal family. On March 9, on a train from New York to Washington, Johnson delivered an impassioned tirade to me against the domestic allotment plan on the ground that it would subsidize nonproduction. He favored the McNary-Haugen plan with a high tariff on agricultural imports. The receipts from the tariff would be distributed to the farmer in proportion to his output. There should also be, he said, government supervised "dumping" abroad and marketing agreements to control the flow of produce into the nation's markets. But he was completely against curtailing output.†

But Johnson and Peek lost out to Wallace, Wilson, and Tugwell in March. Johnson wrote to me on March 30:

> Of course, you know that we did not draw that farm bill and have not been able to influence it. We have done everything we could to help Wallace to get a better bill but only by talking to him. We have refused to dis-

* After Roosevelt assumed office he healed Morgenthau's shattered ambition to become Secretary of Agriculture by entrusting him with preparations for centralizing all farm-credit operations in what became the Farm Credit Administration. Here Morgenthau gathered several of his advisers, Myers, Herman Oliphant, formerly a professor in the Columbia Law School, and others. At that time, he consulted with me about the title he himself should have in this agency. He believed that the title "governor" sounded better and provided more prestige than the title "administrator," which was given to other heads of agencies. And so it was that the Farm Credit Administration became the only agency except the Federal Reserve System to have a "governor."

† R. M. Diary, March 9, 1933.

cuss it even with members of Congress or anybody else because while we believe we have the right to fight in the bosom of the family for what we think is right and is right and sound, we do not think we have the right to snipe or sabotage to anybody outside.

Johnson added:

The farm bill breaks my heart. I began this farm fight twelve years ago and I think I know as much about it as anybody in the country. The bill was drawn without any consultation with either B. M. [Baruch] or myself and when we were called in, it had gotten so far that we could not do anything to make it practicable.

However, Johnson concluded on the note that even the domestic allotment plan could be made to work "if it is skillfully administered."

When I thanked Johnson for his letter, on April 1, I said, "I am suggesting to Henry Wallace that he get in touch with you if and when the bill is passed, and get your advice about setting up the administrative machinery. I am passing word on to the President, too, about your letter and the fine spirit you and B. M. have manifested in connection with this legislation." *

The President's message on the farm relief bill was one of the shortest of the session. There was little time to describe the various sections embodied in it. My records fail to show a draft prepared either by Tugwell, Wallace, or me. I was present, however, when it was written, mostly in dictation by Roosevelt himself. It merely pointed to the necessity for action by Congress "to increase the purchasing power of our farmers and the consumption of articles manufactured in our industrial communities, and at the same time to relieve the pressure of farm mortgages and to increase the asset value of farm loans made by our banking institutions."

He then mentioned the "deep study and joint counsel of many points of view" in preparing the bill. This apparently reminded him of the opposition to the domestic allotment plan by Morgenthau and by Peek and Baruch. And so he added the famous expression that indicated his desire not only to make everybody happy but to give himself an escape if the plan failed to work:

I tell you frankly [this was a typically Rooseveltian expression, just as was the word "definitely" when he was being most indefinite], that it is a new and untrod path, but I tell you with equal frankness [again a Roosevelt cliché] that an unprecedented condition calls for the trial of new means to rescue agriculture. If a fair administrative trial of it is made and it does not produce the hoped for results, I shall be the first to acknowledge it and advise you.

* R. M. Files.

He then called attention to the necessity for quick action because "the spring crops will soon be planted and if we wait for another month or six weeks the effect on the prices of this year's crops will be wholly lost."

But fifty-seven days elapsed before the act was ready for his signature. Because of this delay Wallace was compelled to resort to extraordinary methods to get rid of some production.

Chapter Twenty

Curbing Agricultural Anarchy—1933 to 1936

THE farm bill was finally passed on May 12, 1933. It had something for everybody, including the old sponsors of the McNary-Haugen plan. Title I of the act set up the domestic allotment plan, providing benefit payments from the processing tax for farmers who curtailed voluntarily their production of seven basic crops: wheat, cotton, corn, hogs, rice, tobacco, and milk. At the same time, the Secretary of Agriculture was authorized to enter into marketing agreements with processors covering all farm products. These agreements were to be exempt from the provisions of the anti-trust laws. This latter provision came close to the ideas of Peek and Johnson.

Title II was the revised version of the famous Thomas amendment, which is considered later.

Roosevelt had also proposed, on April 3, a bill offering mortgage relief. The Emergency Farm Mortgage Act of 1933 saw light of day as Title II of the legislation and provided for the issuance of bonds by the Federal land banks and the purchase and refinancing of farm mortgages.*

Meanwhile, the principle of mortgage relief was extended to include the urban, middle-income homeowner when Congress, on Roosevelt's

* *The Congressional Digest,* November 1933, p. 266; Roosevelt, *Public Papers,* II, pp. 102, 180, 182. Another agricultural reform was put into effect by an executive order of the President (March 27, 1933) which consolidated the existing farm credit agencies into the Farm Credit Administration; on May 27, Henry Morgenthau, Jr., was appointed Farm Credit governor. In June, Roosevelt's action was confirmed by the Congress in the Farm Credit Act, which further expanded the new agency's powers.

recommendation, created the Home Owners Loan Corporation (HOLC). This agency was provided with a $200 million Treasury subscription and was authorized to raise $2 billion more through the issuance of 4 per cent bonds. Its function was to check the mounting rate of foreclosures by taking mortgages off the hands of individuals and institutions that could no longer grant extensions to borrowers. Loans taken over by the HOLC were rewritten at a 5 per cent rate, and fifteen years were allowed for repayment. Appraisal fees, delinquent taxes, and the like were consolidated with the principal.

The Farm Act was so comprehensive that it gave Roosevelt a large area for political and personal maneuverability. Both Morgenthau and Peek were mollified by appointments in which they could operate largely independently of Wallace and Tugwell.

Morgenthau, as I have indicated, fell heir to the job of managing the farm credit operations. Peek, at the suggestion of Baruch, was made administrator of the AAA.

Wallace and Tugwell, before and after the bill was finally approved, had their hands full with the administration of the immense Department of Agriculture. And although the AAA was nominally a part of the department, Peek had measurable independence in his emphasis on the various provisions of the bill.

Because of the influence of Baruch and Peek (despite Johnson's claim that they were not consulted), the act was loaded with authorizations for marketing agreements and export subsidies. Peek was thus able to experiment with these.

One of the first problems faced by Tugwell after he took office in the Department of Agriculture was to find a satisfactory solicitor of the department. Here we encounter, once more, the indefatigable activities of Felix Frankfurter. The available evidence shows that Frankfurter's influence prevailed in the selection of dozens of lawyers in several of the departments. On his recommendation Nathan Margold was appointed solicitor of the Interior Department, Charles Wyzansky solicitor in the Labor Department, and, in May, Dean Acheson was made undersecretary of the Treasury. As soon as these and other key people were installed, the beneficiaries of Frankfurter's influence turned to Cambridge to recruit people for lesser posts. Thus, a very considerable number of Frankfurter protégés were scattered throughout the Administration. And these people in turn looked to Frankfurter for advice and counsel. Moreover, there prevailed for some years among these protégés a sort of fellowship. One of them referred to the aggregation of Harvard lawyers as Frankfurter's "well-integrated group." Once when Roosevelt showed signs of turning to other advisers, the same protégé suggested that they might resign in a body as a protest. Needless to say, this threat was never carried out. Some found access to the White House and became very influential in later years.

Tugwell sought the advice of Frankfurter in looking for a solicitor for his department. Max Lowenthal was first considered, but was unavailable.

When the attempt to get Lowenthal failed the choice turned to Jerome Frank, who had graduated from the University of Chicago Law School. When Wallace presented Frank's name as solicitor of the department, Farley objected, largely because of mistaken identity. But since the AAA needed a general counsel, Frank was given that job and there he, with plenty of advice from Frankfurter, recruited a large staff. The position of solicitor of the Agriculture Department was filled by an Iowa lawyer who was not a Frankfurter protégé.

Schlesinger says in his *The Coming of the New Deal* that Frank, in recruiting the legal staff, regarded knowledge of farming as "the least of requirements; he had a lawyer's confidence that men trained in the law could master anything." Tugwell says that Frankfurter recommended most of the curiously assorted talent. There was little screening to eliminate people with Communist affiliations or sympathies. Among those supplied were Lee Pressman, Alger Hiss, Nathan Witt, and John Abt.*

When Chester Davis succeeded Peek in late 1933, Wallace agreed with him that most of this strange crew, including Frank, should be fired. This was accomplished forthwith.†

There were several others, who were certainly not subject to any ideological suspicion. Abe Fortas and Thurman Arnold came from Yale. Adlai Stevenson was brought in, according to his own testimony to me in writing, by George Peek because of their acquaintance in Illinois.

My own contacts in those days never included any of the Frank group. But in the years that followed I knew a number of others who would be classified now as ultra-liberal and anti-free-enterprise. My reaction was not that the infusion of these people was a factor that threatened Communist control or even measurable influence. The important point, it seemed to me, was that a government, especially those agencies of the government that are concerned with the regulation of

* For an account of the activities of this radical group see Schlesinger, pp. 52–53. This account also mentions Harold Ware, who was not an employee of the government at that time. He was the son of the veteran agitator Ella Reeve Bloor.

† In later years when it was publicly known that some had Communist affiliations, Wallace and Tugwell were criticized for carelessness. That charge is not valid, for Wallace had provided the authority to get rid of them when he knew the facts. The AAA was independently administered, and Tugwell knew little of their activities. Tugwell said this to me in a letter under date of April 15, 1965:

"As to Frank's coming I enclose several communications from Felix Frankfurter. This is how he [Frank] came in. As for the Commies, . . . Wallace and I could not have known they were there, or even seen them, except casually."

business, is badly served by people who have no faith in the survival of individual enterprise. I made this clear in correspondence I had a few years later with Jerome Frank. For as Clement Attlee once said, "A socialist party cannot hope to make a success of administering a capitalist system, because it does not believe in it."

The position in which Peek found himself became more and more intolerable as the hot summer of 1933 moved into September. He was not in sympathy with what was essentially the heart of the act. He was suspicious of the man who had been appointed over his protests as general counsel. He certainly distrusted Frank's staff. And his tariff ideas were sharply opposed by Secretaries Wallace and Hull. And so he resigned. But Roosevelt, who was anxious to retain him in the government, made him president of the Export-Import Bank, another preposterous miscalculation.

For in his new job Peek was brought squarely into conflict with Cordell Hull. Peek believed not only in tariff protection but in bilateral trade agreements, or "swapping." These views were anathema to Hull, who adhered to conventional "most favored nation" methods of international trade. And when anyone disagreed on these matters, Hull believed him to be not only mistaken but dishonest and unpatriotic. And so, after a few months of conflict with Hull, Peek retired to private life.

Anyone who attempts to evaluate the results, economically, of the experiment with the domestic allotment plan faces serious complications. The orderly reduction of production could not be effective in 1933 because the act was passed too late in the planting season to have any effect upon that year's crop. Then there was the appointment of Peek, who subordinated the domestic allotment provisions of the act to his favorite methods of marketing agreements and other devices. Results in 1934 were complicated because nature capriciously selected that year to impose upon the farm states the most severe drought in seventy-five years. The effect of this scarcity substantially helped the system of voluntary crop limitation. A not-too-sympathetic economist, Broadus Mitchell, offers this evaluation:

The droughts of 1934 and 1936, the former being the more severe, were the worst in seventy-five years. Much of the area between the Appalachians and the Rockies was struck, cutting crops in 1934 by a third and in 1936 by a fifth. This result in general fell in with the crop restriction policies of the Department of Agriculture, and the second drought reduced yields the year after the control features of the AAA had been invalidated by the Supreme Court. The droughts increased prices of farm products, farm incomes and the purchasing power of these incomes. The effects of the droughts on agricultural prices continued beyond the immediate reduction of products, for carry-overs were diminished. As a consequence, in 1937, with bumper crops, and despite the drop in prices of farm products toward the end of the year, farm income had a buying power equal to that of the predepression period of 1924–1929. Farm prices themselves were above prewar level but nonfarm prices had risen still higher.*

Tugwell's opinion after three decades is that the Conservation Act was a much better plan than the one it replaced in 1936. However, he feels that the people who administered the AAA during its short life did "as good a job as was possible, considering the past years of controversy, the heated situation in the farm states, the egos of the farm leaders, the determination of the farmers to get paid for all they wanted to raise regardless of the market. It did quiet the troubles, make the farmers prosperous again more rapidly than was done for labor, and on the whole saved a practically revolutionary situation." †

In 1964 I solicited the retrospective views of Henry A. Wallace on the achievements of the AAA program and other subjects commented upon in this chapter. His reply, in part, follows:

> As you know, the original AAA tried to pay its way with the processing tax. My doctrine had been that Federal power should not be used beyond the point where the amount paid by the consumer (including the processing tax as a part of the consumer's cost) was beyond that during the period 1910–1914.

That was the period upon which the "parity ratio" was calculated.

> In other words the consumer should not pay a higher percentage of his dollar for farm products because of Federal legislation. I tried to spell this out to Jerome Frank but he misunderstood and therefore wrote legislation which set up a consumers' division which under Fred Howe (a very fine person) was composed largely of city people who did not understand farmers. Jerome Frank also appointed largely city people who did not understand farmers. People like Lee Pressman and Alger Hiss.
>
> My association had been with the Farm Bureau people, to a lesser extent with the Farmers' Union and above all with Chester Davis and George Peek. When the show-down came, Rex was out of town . . . I listened to both sides but in the final show-down went with Chester Davis largely on the advice of M. L. Wilson and John D. Black of Harvard. I had great respect for their wisdom. The so-called liberals shrieked to high heaven when I discharged at Davis' insistence Jerome Frank and Fred Howe and Lee Pressman (Hiss left a short time after). . . . So we have a situation where my name has always been mud with the Jerome Frank type of liberal. . . .
>
> I agree completely with you and Rex and everybody that the Soil Conservation plan was a great improvement over the original AAA. In fact in 1920 and 1921 I had centered on this approach in editorials entitled, "Less Corn, More Clover, More Money." I had battled for this approach at the January, 1922 Presidential Agricultural Conference held in Washington,

* Mitchell, *Depression Decade,* p. 202.

† R. G. Tugwell to Raymond Moley, April 15, 1965.

when my father was Secretary of Agriculture. I first met George Peek and Hugh Johnson in May, 1933.

It was probably impossible at the depth of the depression to ask half a billion dollars to finance a farm program. So we all did the best we could in May 1933 and God was good to us and the farmer and the country when the Supreme Court destroyed the processing tax. After January 1936 when the processing tax was destroyed I was amazed at how ready President Roosevelt and even Secretary Henry Morgenthau were to go along with straight appropriations from the Federal Treasury to finance benefit payments for soil conservation and crop control purposes. This approach did get corn off the hillsides and saved hundreds of millions of tons of soil from being washed off the land to silt up the rivers.*

Wallace adds this to his comment:

For certain periods of time I feel that Rex served as Roosevelt's conscience. Rex was responsible for the Rural Resettlement Administration and for that finest part of it known as the Supervised Loan, a technique which will prove of inestimable value in the undeveloped areas of the world for the next 50 years. Rex also had vision in pushing for the acquirement of an enlarged area of land for the Beltsville Experiment Station. . . . Rex was as far ahead of me in sensing certain things as I later turned out to be ahead of the American people.

After the Supreme Court declared the NIRA to be unconstitutional in 1935, serious doubts were raised about the AAA. And so a group of millers challenged the legislation by refusing to pay processing taxes. The case was decided on January 6, 1936.†

Justice Owen Roberts delivered the majority opinion, declaring the processing tax unconstitutional. Agreeing with him were Chief Justice Hughes and four other members of the Court. Justices Stone, Cardozo, and Brandeis dissented. The dissenting opinion was rendered by Stone.

The Court through Roberts took the position that the matter at issue was a state concern and was beyond the powers of Congress, and that the use of the processing tax to induce a limitation of farm products was in fact coercion. Thus, the Court's opinion was that the end as well as the means was unconstitutional:

The power of taxation, which is expressly granted, may, of course, be adopted as a means to carry into operation another power also expressly granted. But resort to the taxing power to effectuate an end which is not legitimate, [which is] not within the scope of the Constitution, is obviously inadmissible. . . .

If the taxing power may not be used as the instrument to enforce a regulation of matters of state concern with respect to which the Congress has no authority to interfere, may it, as in the present case, be employed to raise

* Henry A. Wallace to Raymond Moley, May 27, 1965.

† United States v. Butler, 297 U.S. 1.

> the money necessary to purchase a compliance which the Congress is powerless to command? . . . The regulation is not in fact voluntary. The farmer, of course, may refuse to comply, but the price of such refusal is loss of benefits. The amount offered is intended to be sufficient to exert pressure on him to agree to the proposed regulation. The power to confer or withhold unlimited benefits is the power to coerce or destroy. . . .
>
> Since, as we have pointed out, there was no power in the Congress to impose the contested exaction, it could not lawfully ratify or affirm what an executive officer had done in that regard.

Even in the context of those days when Roosevelt had so severely and, I believe, unnecessarily criticized the Court for its decision in the previous year striking down the NRA, there was no need for the violence that marked other parts of the Roberts opinion. For he went on to draw a grim picture of the possible extension of this power to the destruction of all local self-government in the states. This sort of language merely added to the flames of controversy.

The opinion of Stone seems to me to present a more reasonable view of the case. In response to the contention over the end in view, which was the curtailment of production by voluntary means, Stone said that in "the present distressed state of agriculture, . . . nation-wide in its extent and effects, there is no basis for saying that the expenditure of public money in aid of farmers is not within the specifically granted power of Congress to levy taxes 'to provide for the . . . general welfare.' " Stone went on to say that the imposition of the tax was not in the opinion of the dissenting justices a means of regulation, but, rather, that the way the proceeds of the tax were used was in effect coercive regulation of the farmers. But, Stone added, "The suggestion of coercion finds no support in the record or in any data showing the actual operation of the act. Threat of loss, not hope of gain, is the essence of economic coercion. . . . But there is nothing to indicate that those who accepted benefits were impelled by fear of lower prices if they did not accept, or that at any stage in the operation of the plan a farmer could say whether, apart from the certainty of cash payments at specified times, the advantage would lie with curtailment of production plus compensation, rather than with the same or increased acreage plus the expected rise of prices which actually occurred. . . . It is a contradiction in terms to say that there is power to spend for the national welfare, while rejecting any power to impose conditions reasonably adapted to the attainment of the end which alone would justify the expenditure."

At one point in the Stone opinion there is a hint of the issue that was later to burst into a political conflict between the President and Congress. For he said, "the suggestion that it [the power of the purse] must now be curtailed by judicial fiat because it may be abused by unwise use hardly rises to the dignity of argument. So may judicial power be abused."

It is not because of the Court's rather narrow construction of Federal power or the labored interpretation of coercion, which were rejected by the Court in the years that followed, that I believe that the Stone dissent was sound. For it is my opinion that the Court, in later years and with new members, stretched not only the general welfare clause but the interstate commerce provisions in the Constitution to an altogether dangerous degree. It is because in the context of the time, and in the situation which Congress sought to remedy, the wholly voluntary use of the processing tax was valid. Its use was to reward farmers who were willing to cooperate in achieving a national purpose.

It should be noted that the decision of the majority did not destroy other provisions of the AAA—only the processing tax and its use.

Chapter Twenty-one

The Federal Almoner

IT was a long, long trail from the Roosevelt who entered office in 1933 to grapple with the great depression and its human consequences to the Lyndon B. Johnson who in 1964 initiated the war on poverty. Some writers claim that the origins of the present dominant concern of the Federal establishment with welfare are in the First New Deal. That is debatable. Perhaps, however, there is some justification for saying that the reforms in Federal relief, employment provisions, and social security in 1935 might be recorded as the origin of the present welfare state. But even these reforms only slightly suggested what ultimately emerged.

The history of the rise and flowering of Federal welfare lies beyond the purview of this story, for the evolution of the various improvisations in relief and work relief lie beyond 1933. But to understand what happened in 1933 to ease the hardships inflicted by the economic collapse, we must leave the world in which we now live and plunge into another and almost forgotten era when the traditions and constitutional limits of Federal responsibility for welfare were narrowly drawn. In those years, the public as well as its representatives assumed that when personal distress came the individual must look to his own personal resources first, then to philanthropic and religious agencies, and, as a last resort, to the crude and parsimonious provisions of the community or county.

But since the immense impact of the depression was without precedent, both Roosevelt and Hoover before him were compelled to improvise. They faced a situation for which theories and constitutional precedent offered very little guidance. Both Presidents were at first most reluctant to plunge the Federal government into the task of relief. Both were quite aware of the perils that might attend direct help for individuals. It should be added that Roosevelt rather than Hoover was forced not only to create some means of relief but to fend off those who would use the emergency to institute visionary and impractical schemes. For Roosevelt was regarded as a reformer, and reformers of all kinds rallied to his cause with their nostrums.

Roosevelt faced the essential need that temporary relief was to be only a prelude to recovery. Structural reform had a later priority.

The first priority had been the restoration to people's minds of confidence that a return to normal conditions was possible. I have already shown that this was achieved not only by the inspiring words of Roosevelt but by the material results of the bank rescue operation. Next, it was necessary to provide relief for the institutions at lower levels upon which countless individuals depended. At the same time the still unimpaired Federal credit needed to be used to finance programs for employment through Federally supported public works.

The concept of Federal responsibility that Roosevelt had in those early months and for a year or two later differed little from that of his predecessor. There were a few innovations in 1933. All were consistent with Roosevelt's pledge in his 1932 speech of acceptance and his inaugural address. Every effort was made by Roosevelt to avoid direct relief to individuals except through provision for work. And as things developed in the years 1933, 1934, and 1935, there was more and more insistence upon constructive and useful projects rather than mere made-work.

It seems tragic that in the half century after 1914, during which Herbert Hoover dedicated himself to public service, fate and political chance should have made him President of the United States in the four years from 1929 to 1933. He was caught in the center of a catastrophe, the causes and imminence of which he had persistently pointed out from his position as Secretary of Commerce. In an Administration of which he had been a vital member, he had the misfortune to see his forebodings ignored. Others had sown the wind. He was fated to reap the hurricane.

He reached the Presidency and left this mortal life the most experienced, the most successful, and the most renowned administrator of relief that the modern world has seen. But he was denied re-election by an electorate that charged him with cold indifference to personal distress, which grew with intensity as the economic system faltered to the verge of collapse.

In 1914 Hoover was in England when the world felt the impact of war. He abandoned his professional career and dedicated himself to the service of the unfortunate in many nations. He never accepted for himself the payments due him in the many offices he held. His labors in

Europe during and after that war eased the sufferings and saved the lives of millions caught in the wake of hostilities. And his moral and religious commitment to help the needy earned him the tribute of many nations when his life ended in 1964.

Politics can be a cruel business. As the time approached when Hoover sought re-election, opponents sought advantage by charging not only that he had been incompetent in ministering to the distressed but that he had been without feeling and concern. The character of the man himself is the answer to the second of these charges. Facts now apparent dispose of the first. For while struggling to stabilize and energize the economic system, in which lay the permanent cure for unemployment and distress, he worked tirelessly to devise means for temporary relief, first through private efforts and then through Federal authority.

After the stock market crash had shaken the vital producing elements of the economy, Hoover ordered a census of the employed and the unemployed. The Department of Commerce reported in April 1930 that there were 45 million gainfully employed, 2,429,000 looking for work and 755,000 temporarily laid off. Thus, the unemployed totaled 3,184,000. Perhaps one or two million families suffering some distress were provided measurable relief through local efforts, public and philanthropic.

But when the number of unemployed increased in October of that year and local relief began to feel the strain, Hoover created the President's Emergency Relief Organization, with Colonel Arthur Woods as administrator. In August 1931 Woods was succeeded by Walter Gifford, who served through 1932. This organization created three thousand state and local committees and charged them with mobilizing voluntary relief over the nation.

In February 1931 Hoover rejected a strong sentiment in Congress for Federal appropriations for relief purposes. He believed that because of the difficulties in administration and the danger of political influence, Federal relief should be used only as a last resort.

In appraising this hesitation we must not depend upon the knowledge of hindsight. At the time responsible people knew from experience how recovery might come, as it had come before, after a year or two of recession. They had every expectation that economic revival might be, as Hoover himself said, just "around the corner." For this and his optimistic utterances in his campaigning in 1928 he was castigated.

In 1928 he had envisioned an ever-growing economy which could provide a hitherto unknown standard of living for all Americans. That vision was a possibility in our economy. It has been proved since. But his words were hurled contemptuously at him when conditions grew worse. Now, in the 1960's, two cars in the garage is a commonplace and two chickens are in many a pot.

Hoover was an early exponent of enterprise within the constitutional province of the Federal government, and in the late fall of 1931 he urged the Federal departments to provide 750,000 jobs on Federal public works during the winter ahead. Early in 1932 Hoover secured an authorization from Congress for large purchases of surplus farm products held by the Federal Farm Board for relief of the hungry. Finally, in February 1932, with unemployment at 10 million, Hoover, still rejecting the idea of direct Federal relief, secured the approval of Congress for loans of $300 million from the new Reconstruction Finance Corporation to the states for temporary relief.

Meanwhile, in New York Governor Roosevelt recommended and the legislature created a Temporary Emergency Relief Administration. In making this proposal, he said that "the distribution of relief of the poor is essentially a local function." His TERA was merely to supplement local efforts. In February, Roosevelt sent a telegram to Senator Robert Wagner supporting emergency Federal relief, but warned that "it should not be regarded as a permanent government policy."

Thus, there was at the outset of the campaign of 1932 little difference between Roosevelt's and Hoover's policies on relief. In fact, Roosevelt in his 1932 campaign was most cautious in attacking Hoover on the subject of relief. In a book published in 1937, *The Hoover Policies* by Ray Lyman Wilbur and Arthur M. Hyde, both former members of Hoover's Cabinet, the authors say, "No such charge [of inadequacy in Hoover's interest in relief] was made during the campaign of 1932."

When in March Roosevelt called for a relief program, his specifics, except for the Civilian Conservation Corps, differed in no essential respect from Hoover's policies of the year before.

The Democratic platform in 1932 went only so far as to say that the Federal credit should be extended to a state only when "the diminishing resources . . . make it impossible . . . to provide for the needy."

When Roosevelt signed the Unemployment Relief Act on May 12, 1933, he said, "The first obligation is on the locality; if it is absolutely clear that the locality has done its utmost but that more should be done, then the State must do its utmost. Only then can the Federal government add its contribution to those of the locality and the State." It should be noted that this meant grants to state and local governments, not direct relief from the Federal government to the individual.

Early in March, Frances Perkins had outlined to me a plan for grants-in-aid to the states for direct work relief. She said that La Follette, Costigan, and Wagner agreed with this approach. Since she had also talked with labor leaders, "she was very much upset by F. D. R.'s idea of hiring, etc., men working on public works and paying them at the rate of $1 a day. This was well and good, she said, 'so far as reforestation is concerned but when it is applied to public works it tends to bring down the price of free labor.' " *

Later that day I told Roosevelt about my conversation with Mrs. Perkins, but instead of replying directly, he outlined his plan for what he then called a Civilian Reclamation Corps. This was a unique feature in Roosevelt's plans for unemployment relief.† It was directed toward providing employment for a considerable number of young men between the ages of eighteen and twenty-five, in a disciplined organization, to do useful tasks in the out-of-doors. This would not only provide the means of doing many small services to the cause of conservation, but would at the same time take out of the cities and off the streets young men who would be the last to get employment under normal conditions.

I incorporated this idea in a message draft that Roosevelt sent for criticism and comment to the Secretaries of War, Labor, Agriculture, and Interior:

> I propose to the Congress the creation of a Civilian Reclamation Corps, to be recruited from the ranks of the unemployed, ratable to the proportion of unemployment existing in the several states.
>
> The actual work to be undertaken covers a wide field, many of the projects being already a component part of our national policy. All of them call for a high proportion of manual labor. They would cover roughly the fields of reforestation on national and state lands, prevention of soil erosion, flood control, power development, inland waterways, and inter-coastal communications.

The draft suggested that the work relief be planned by established agencies of the Agriculture, Interior, and War departments, while recruitment would be the responsibility of the Labor Department. Housing, clothing, food, and medical care would be provided for in camps administered by the War Department. Though there would be no military training, a short-term technical enlistment, terminated if employment was secured, and simple order (Roosevelt struck out the word "discipline") would be necessary. Roosevelt was convinced that his Civilian Reclamation Corps would "give useful work to five hundred thousand men between now and next summer" and estimated the cost at $500 million for a year.‡

* R. M. Diary, March 14, 1933.

† It has come to my attention that an account by Governor Phillip La Follette indicates that work camps had been established in Wisconsin some time earlier and that Senator Robert La Follette, Jr., had discussed them with Roosevelt.

‡ R. M. Files. As will be noted, the word "reclamation" was changed by the Cabinet committee to "conservation."

A memorandum dated March 15 and signed by George Dern, Harold Ickes, Henry Wallace, and Frances Perkins promised the public-works advocates their ardently sought opportunity.

In response to your memorandum of March 14, 1933, the undersigned have considered not only the draft of the bill with regard to the Civilian Conservation Corps, but also the whole program of relief for industrial unemployment. We are of the opinion that there are three items to be considered in this program:

1. Federal appropriations for grants in aid to the various states for direct relief work. (The details of such a Bill are now practically agreed upon between Senators Wagner, Costigan, La Follette and Secretary Perkins.)

2. A measure for a large practical, labor producing program of public works under the control of a Board which can allocate them in such a manner as to drain the largest pools of unemployment in the country, and also arrange to taper off the public works, when, and if, industrial employment picks up.

3. A measure providing authority for the President to recruit a Civilian Conservation Corps for forestry work under the direction of the Army, Labor Department and Forestry Service.

The four Cabinet members urged that the work of the CCC be confined to forestry and soil-erosion projects lest the Conservation Corps produce a depressing effect on the wage levels of free labor. They also suggested that the three measures be introduced at the same time, but presented as three separate bills.*

On March 15 the President had instructed me to have Senators La Follette, Costigan, and Wagner, Secretary Perkins, and Harry Hopkins in his office the next day for a discussion of relief.†

In speaking of grants to the states for relief work, the President said that "the balance appropriated to the RFC is sufficient to carry on with until May." However, he did request that a Federal relief administrator be appointed to coordinate relief work.

Finally, in this original version of his message, Roosevelt could see no obstacles to the immediate employment of individuals in forestry, soil erosion, and similar work "which does not interfere with normal employment. . . . I estimate that 250,000 men can be given temporary employment by early summer if we can start the machinery within the next two weeks. By the use of unobligated funds now appropriated for public works, no additional burden on the Treasury will be imposed at this time." ‡

* R. M. Files.

† R. M. Notebook, March 15, 1933.

‡ Work Bill, in R. M. Files, 50–55. The final draft of this message on relief and public works is to be found in Roosevelt, *Public Papers,* II, 80–81.

Roosevelt's final draft of the relief message submitted on March 21, which differed in some respects from the draft I had prepared earlier, follows:

To the Congress:

It is essential to our recovery program that measures immediately be enacted aimed at unemployment relief. A direct attack on this problem suggests three types of legislation.

The first is the enrollment of workers now by the Federal Government for such public employment as can be quickly started and will not interfere with the demand for or the proper standards of normal employment.

The second is grants to States for relief work.

The third extends to a broad public works labor-creating program.

With reference to the latter I am now studying the many projects suggested and the financial questions involved. I shall make recommendations to the Congress presently.

In regard to grants to States for relief work, I advise you that the remainder of the appropriation of last year will last until May. Therefore, and because a continuance of Federal aid is still a definite necessity for many States, a further appropriation must be made before the end of this special session.

I find a clear need for some simple Federal machinery to coordinate and check these grants of aid. I am, therefore, asking that you establish the office of Federal Relief Administrator, whose duty it will be to scan requests for grants and to check the efficiency and wisdom of their use.

The first of these measures which I have enumerated, however, can and should be immediately enacted. I propose to create a civilian conservation corps to be used in simple work, not interfering with normal employment, and confining itself to forestry, the prevention of soil erosion, flood control and similar projects. I call your attention to the fact that this type of work is of definite practical value, not only through the prevention of great present financial loss, but also as a means of creating future national wealth. This is brought home by the news we are receiving today of vast damage caused by floods on the Ohio and other rivers.

Control and direction of such work can be carried on by existing machinery of the departments of Labor, Agriculture, War and Interior.

I estimate that 250,000 can be given temporary employment by early summer if you give me authority to proceed within the next two weeks.

I ask no new funds at this time. The use of unobligated funds, now appropriated for public works, will be sufficient for several months.

This enterprise is an established part of our national policy. It will conserve our precious natural resources. It will pay dividends to the present and future generations. It will make improvements in national and state domains which have been largely forgotten in the past few years of industrial development.

More important, however, than the material gains will be the moral and spiritual value of such work. The overwhelming majority of unemployed

Americans, who are now walking the streets and receiving private or public relief, would infinitely prefer to work. We can take a vast army of these unemployed out into healthful surroundings. We can eliminate to some extent at least the threat that enforced idleness brings to spiritual and moral stability. It is not a panacea for all the unemployment but it is an essential step in this emergency. I ask its adoption.

CCC came into being eight days later, and the Emergency Relief Bill, appropriating $500 million for distribution through the states and setting up a Federal Relief Administration, passed Congress and was signed by the President on May 12, 1933.

The disposition of these two features of Roosevelt's relief program left as a subject for many discussions and much argument the question of a large appropriation for a public-works program, to be discussed in the next chapter.

On May 22, Harry Hopkins arrived in Washington and assumed the direction of the Federal Emergency Relief Administration. From the moment of his arrival he was to be the major figure in Federal relief and in efforts to develop Federal projects that might supplant relief with employment.

The first time I heard of Hopkins was at a family luncheon at the governor's mansion in Albany in 1932. Roosevelt commented that Jesse Isador Straus, who had acted as chairman of the New York Temporary Emergency Relief Administration, had resigned and had suggested as his successor Harry Hopkins, who had been his deputy. No one at the table seemed to know much about Hopkins. Roosevelt and Mrs. Roosevelt knew him only by name. He had been a professional social worker in and around New York since his graduation from Grinnell College in Iowa. For a time he had been director of the New York Tuberculosis and Health Association, but when Straus offered him a position in the TERA he quickly accepted, and at once demonstrated his capacity for quick and, it should be added, expensive activity. During his final months as governor, Roosevelt appreciated these traits, and when the FERA was created decided to call Hopkins to Washington.

Hopkins combined vigorous dispatch in distributing the funds entrusted to him with unorthodox, not to say radical, political and social ideas, most of which were derived from the emotional impact he had experienced in dealing with the poor and unfortunate in his social work. There was never any evidence that he had studied these questions in any depth.*

By autumn of 1933 it was evident that the need for relief was greater than had been anticipated. Roosevelt came to the conclusion at about

* For a sympathetic but colorful appraisal, see Schlesinger, *The Coming of the New Deal*, pp. 263–69. Also, the wholly laudatory profile in Robert Sherwood's *Roosevelt and Hopkins* (New York: Harper, 1948).

that time that direct relief in the form of doles could never be adequate as a solution and that some provision for work was demanded to sustain and improve the morale of the employable unemployed. Everyone in the Roosevelt Administration looked with fearful misgiving toward the advent of another winter. Competent observers of trends actually expected the late fall to usher in an economic relapse after the high hopes of the spring and summer. For the early recovery had been largely psychological, aided considerably by the President's re-employment agreement under the NRA. Sustained confidence would have to have something more tangible than cheerful assurances from the White House.

Since, as we shall see in the next chapter, little could be expected immediately from the Public Works Administration, which had been created under the National Industrial Recovery Act, a Civil Works Administration was created on November 8 by an executive order.

Roosevelt transferred $400 million to the new agency from PWA and what was left of FERA funds, and appointed Hopkins administrator. With a minimum of bureaucratic red tape, Hopkins, an expeditious spender, authorized a wide range of projects that could be started immediately. Almost anything involving employment was undertaken. By January, Hopkins had more than four million on the payroll.

Thus, action prevented conditions from worsening during the winter months, and in the spring CWA was liquidated.

Chapter Twenty-two

Work Projects Supplant Relief

ROOSEVELT consistently kept faith throughout his first two terms with a principle he had capsuled in his inaugural address: "Our greatest primary task is to put people to work." To this he later added security, thus fulfilling a pledge in his 1932 acceptance speech to provide two values of basic importance to individual life, "work and security."

As these promises evolved into national policy, many experimental methods were tried. As we have seen, the Civil Works Administration, operated by Hopkins, supplemented relief to tide over the hard winter of 1933–1934. Later that operation was discontinued; a clear policy was announced that was to supplant relief entirely.

In the Hundred Days there was created not only the FERA but a large and more costly public-works program with Interior Secretary Ickes as its administrator. This more ambitious program, which carried with it an appropriation of $3,300,000,000, was incorporated in the National Industrial Recovery Act as Title II. It was a compromise with the people who had for more than a year been advocating a $5,000,000,000 public-works program as a means of providing employment.

Roosevelt's reasons for rejection of the larger expenditure were that $5,000,000,000 represented only a rough and uninformed guess of what would be needed to provide jobs; that it would plunge the Federal government into very large deficits; that the Hoover Administration had plans for worth-while projects involving less than $1,000,000,000; that public works of the type suggested would involve long delay before many jobs would be created; and, a most serious objection, that the advocates of such spending had quite different ideas among themselves about what was to be achieved by such a program. These objections proved valid after $3,300,000,000 was appropriated in 1933.

Among the advocates of public works three points of view emerged:

1. There were those who believed that large expenditures on permanent public improvements, involving as they did large demands for materials, would help to activate such heavy industries as steel and machinery. Under this concept the number of jobs actually created on the project itself would be relatively small as compared with those created in the industries that furnished the materials. In the idiom of 1933, this was called "pump-priming."

2. Another school believed that government spending supplied through deficits would increase the money supply. This would be inflationary (in the 1933 idiom, "reflationary") and would lift wages, prices, and profits. One zealot said to me at the time that the $3,300,000,000 would be better used if it were scattered by aircraft over the country in one-dollar bills. I suggested that two-dollar bills would be more appropriate because in the resulting inflation a dollar would mean so little.

3. It is not clear whether Ickes was interested in either of the foregoing theories. He wanted to use the money to build large and useful public improvements—highways, buildings, airports, and, above all, immense dams that would not only control water flow but generate electricity in wholesale lots. He was most concerned in public ownership of public power generation and distribution in competition with "evil" private utility companies. Since he had control of the money, his concept prevailed. Ickes was less interested in quick recovery than in pursuing his theories of public ownership.

In 1932 the most prominent advocates of the $5,000,000,000 public-works idea had been former Governor Alfred E. Smith and the Hearst press. Among the Brains Trust veterans, Tugwell was wedded to it. In 1933 there was strong support for a big public-works project (La Follette, Wagner, Costigan in the Senate and Frances Perkins in the Cabinet). But Roosevelt still harbored his doubts and agreed to the $3,300,000,000 appropriation in order to get the rest of his NIRA adopted.

Strong pressure for a broad program came from another source, which sought Roosevelt's agreement through me. Frankfurter told me in February that I must see Justice Brandeis. In a memorandum under date of February 9 he sketched out the Brandeis views:

> Real improvement can come only with his [Roosevelt's] declaring at the opening of the Extra Session a comprehensive program. It must be of such magnitude that it will . . . effect the needed change. The change will come if he will go in for (1) the whole reforestation plan (2) control of waters plan (to be paid for at first by loans, then by high estate and income

taxes . . .). That plan if broadly and quickly entered upon could put two million men to work, directly by the U.S. and the States, within six months; and another million or two indirectly.

Brandeis, according to this Frankfurter memorandum, regarded the Tennessee Valley project as "fine in quality but deficient in quantity." In other words, he would have pulled out all the stops to meet the emergency. Whether the Tennessee Valley project was self-liquidating was not the prime criterion to be considered, for "this is a permanent investment, which, if the policy is right for America, will be productive." Moreover, "we should treat the early public works expenditures . . . as advances in anticipation of large tax returns which will come in when our super-rich die."

Frankfurter wrote to me again on February 26 regarding the Brandeis views:

> It is most important that the very concrete, carefully thought out and strongly felt views of Brandeis reach F.D.R's mind, and I think by direct communication. You ought to see Brandeis because he wants to see you. But you should arrange, without fail, to have Brandeis put his views on the public works program, and the modes of financing it before R. at the earliest moment.

I have no record of my discussion with Brandeis except for the notation in my appointment-memorandum that "On March 8—Felix will be at the Brandeis home and I will pick him up at 9:30." I do recall clearly the discussion I had with the old Justice, and some painful recollection of the very hard chair on which I squirmed while Brandeis presented his views. As is indicated in the Frankfurter memorandum and letter, he urged the broad public-works program. It was to be financed by closing the loopholes in the Federal tax laws. The result, he promised, would be the addition of some $2,000,000,000 a year to the Federal Treasury. I assume (I do not specifically remember) that Brandeis had his opportunity to present these views to Roosevelt directly.

If carefully examined with a practical view in mind of the problems involved, it will be clear how vague and impractical the ideas of even these two men were. This was especially true in what they said about the usefulness of public works in meeting a grave emergency. If the views of such men of eminence were so devoid of practical sense, one can imagine what lesser advocates were dreaming about at that time. For anyone, perhaps with the exception of people who had spent their lives reading and writing legal abstractions, could see that public works of such magnitude could not possibly be useful in meeting an emergency. Their views of financing such works by plugging loopholes in the tax law and by waiting for the super-rich to die, despite the distinction of their source, were frivolous to the point of absurdity.

All these ideas had been presented more than a year before, and after careful consideration had been rejected.

Roosevelt's decision to divorce the administration of the public-works program from the rest of the National Industrial Recovery Act was based not only on his practical assessment of the difficulty of getting anything like an expeditious relief of unemployment, but on his appraisal of the mentality of Harold Ickes, the man he selected to administer the program. Under any administrator, the projects would be slow in development. Under Ickes it would take a year or more even to start them. Thus Roosevelt frustrated the proponents of public works despite his gesture of consenting to the $3,300,000,000 appropriation.

Very few of those who had advocated public works as a cure for unemployment were influenced by the writings of John Maynard Keynes. Most argued only from their common sense plus plenty of imaginative assumptions. Keynes later argued with elaborate formulas that one job created on the public project would generate many jobs in the private sector where the materials were created. This was his so-called "multiplier theory," which might be described as the concept of ripples of employment running away in all directions from the splash of the public expenditure.

But those who argued from their own calculations or even from Keynes's theories overlooked many practical considerations. In the first place, the Federal project must be instituted where there is already a considerable pool of unemployment. In those days before public housing or urban improvements were thought of, most people were still supported by the land. The direction of "ripples" of re-employment coming from projects to the private sector were unpredictable. They might and might not affect the industries most in need of revival. Moreover, any large public project is slow in getting under way. There must be a careful appraisal of many alternative projects by some authority. There must be elaborate engineering studies. Contracts must be let, and many applicants must be examined for their capacity to deliver.

Finally, the amount expended upon government public works and enterprises, except in time of war when waste is the rule rather than the exception, is only a part of the stream of an immense economy such as ours. A few billions in public expenditures, especially in those days, could not be compared with the tens of billions produced in a revived private economy. The gap in employment was too wide for any such government method, and that gap was widening in 1933. Moreover, as Lewis Douglas repeatedly pointed out, the fiscal impact of big Federal spending could not be neglected. Deficits had supplanted the surpluses in the Harding, Coolidge, and the first Hoover years. And deficits, which would be sure to mount under Roosevelt, would alarm investors and deflate the confidence that had set in after the rescue of the banks.

Roosevelt's appraisal of Ickes was abundantly validated as the PWA slowly prepared to get under way in 1933. The operation proceeded at a snail's pace. Ickes' manner of speech was reckless and almost as incandescent as Hugh Johnson's. But as an administrator he was slow and cautious. He had spent his life fighting politicians and political methods in Chicago. Hence he rebuffed Farley and others who suggested projects that might be politically expedient. And because members of Congress were regarded as products of the political system, he distrusted all their suggestions. The members reciprocated his rebuffs with strong but helpless profanity. He even moved the quiet Rayburn to strong language when he stalled a long time about building a dam on the Red River, which bounded Rayburn's district on the north. Businessmen—especially contractors—were written in the Ickes book as profit-mongers and rascals.

It has been said in extenuation that Ickes' physical ailments made him crusty and sharp in his dealings with those who sought his co-operation. But I prefer to believe that even without his pains and insomnia he would still have earned the characterization, which he loved, of "curmudgeon." He was deeply suspicious of almost everybody. As time went on he conceived his office to be a shining and clean island in a sea of evil. Schlesinger admits, despite his ardent belief in public works as a cure-all:

> Honesty was for him [Ickes] a rare and fleeting commodity, of which he had the good fortune to command an American monopoly. His egotism was so massive that he remained perfectly unconscious of its existence . . . he could not but conclude that anything which extended his power served the republic.*

With the exception of a few reporters who paid off his confidences with lush praise, Ickes seemed to hate all newspapermen and publishers. Later he wrote a book in which he violently attacked the press. And it is no credit to him that the few reporters with whom he had close relations were among the least worthy representatives of their profession. Presumably the expression "Honest Harold" originated with these sycophants. His suspicions were so magnified that he established a staff of investigators numbering at times in the hundreds. These people were supposed to pry into the affairs of everyone who had relations with the public-works program but their surveillance extended to the whole Interior Department as well. These sleuths not only pried into the lives of contractors and others who had business with the Ickes domain, but extended their concern to fellow employees in the government service. They even spied on each other. A year or so later, one of the half-dozen top officials in the Interior Department came to me in New York and

* Schlesinger, *The Coming of the New Deal,* p. 283.

told me that his desk had been opened and searched nightly by the Ickes spies. I knew this man to be of unimpeachable integrity and realized that this sort of treatment so distracted him as to make his services practically useless. He wanted me to report this to Roosevelt. I cannot remember whether I did so, but if I had, it would have only intensified Ickes' zeal in the witch hunt.

Perhaps Ickes' most serious disqualification was that in those early months of crisis he really had little interest in economic recovery. It was like appointing a general to command the front line who was not interested in winning the war. Foremost among the Ickes ambitions was the building of massive physical monuments to honor his administration. This would take time but he hoped to live to see them completed. He was like an Egyptian pharaoh whose greatest contribution to his country was the building of his tomb.

But with plenty of prodding from Roosevelt, a great many important projects were completed with public-works money. There were highways and bridges, post offices and courthouses, tunnels and docks. Roosevelt saw to it that several warships were built with public-works funds. Ickes' distrust of business was overcome when funds were supplied to complete the electrification of the Pennsylvania Railroad from New York to Washington and to build the Thirtieth Street Station in Philadelphia. It may be, however, that this was done to improve access and egress to and from Washington for traveling bureaucrats.

Friction between Ickes and Hopkins was an early development. For Roosevelt liked the speed with which Hopkins dispersed money for the needy and his ingenuity in providing made-work. Hence from time to time Roosevelt by executive order took considerable sums from the PWA to help Hopkins in his efforts. This became a constant source of complaint which is all now duly recorded in Ickes' incredible *Secret Diary*.

After Morgenthau became Secretary of the Treasury, there was more friction over spending programs. Morgenthau vainly sought to bring the budget into something like controllable balance. And there was friction between the Secretary of the Treasury and Hopkins for the same reason.

After the liquidation of the Civil Works Administration in 1934, smaller works projects were carried on through Hopkins' FERA. But during 1934, when there was a measurable improvement in the economy, Roosevelt, Hopkins, and Perkins gave a great deal of thought to the future of relief and job-producing public works. The success of the CWA had provided many useful lessons. Something more substantial was needed for the future.

Therefore, a new plan would be unfolded in the President's annual message in January 1935. Following a custom established in 1933, I was called to Washington for a few days in December to help in its preparation. Roosevelt had outlined to me the plan for converting relief into work projects.*

Stephen Early had called for memoranda from various departments, notably from State and Agriculture, which embodied suggestions of what the respective Secretaries wanted the President to mention. But the main feature of the message was to be the new program of work-relief. Hopkins and Perkins came in and talked to me about the plans as I was working in the Cabinet room preparing the draft, which was to summarize the evolution of relief and work-relief and to present the outlines of the new policy.

In the preceding June I had written the President's preliminary message to Congress outlining the plans for social security and unemployment "insurance." I had served rather inactively during the months that followed on the President's advisory committee, which was charged with drawing up suggestions to guide the committee in drafting a social security bill. This, as well as the immediate plans for supplanting relief with work projects, was to be included in the message.

In this message, which I had a major part in drafting, the President disposed of further responsibility for relief in these words:

> More than two billions of dollars have also been expended in direct relief to the destitute. Local agencies of necessity determined the recipients of this form of relief. With inevitable exceptions the funds were spent by them with reasonable efficiency and as a result actual want of food and clothing in the great majority of cases has been overcome.
>
> But the stark fact before us is that great numbers still remain unemployed.
>
> A large proportion of these unemployed and their dependents have been forced on the relief rolls. The burden on the Federal Government has grown with great rapidity. We have here a human as well as an economic problem. When humane considerations are concerned, Americans give them precedence. The lessons of history, confirmed by the evidence immediately before me, show conclusively that continued dependence upon relief induces

* The fact that Roosevelt was aware that politics was already thriving in relief administration and that he wanted to get the Federal government out of relief altogether is shown by a letter which he wrote to Colonel House under date of November 27, 1934:

"I suppose there will be a general attack on relief fund expenditures. As a matter of fact, politics crept in to some extent. . . .

"What I am seeking is the abolition of relief altogether. I cannot say so out loud yet but I hope to be able to substitute work for relief. . . .

"There will, of course, be a certain number of relief cases where work will not furnish the answer but it is my thought that in these cases all of the relief expenditures should once more be borne by the States and localities as they used to be."

a spiritual and moral disintegration fundamentally destructive to the national fibre. To dole out relief in this way is to administer a narcotic, a subtle destroyer of the human spirit. It is inimical to the dictates of sound policy. It is in violation of the traditions of America. Work must be found for able-bodied but destitute workers.

The Federal Government must and shall quit this business of relief.

I am not willing that the vitality of our people be further sapped by the giving of cash, of market baskets, of a few hours of weekly work cutting grass, raking leaves or picking up papers in public parks. We must preserve not only the bodies of the unemployed from destitution but also their self-respect, their self-reliance and courage and determination. This decision brings me to the problem of what the Government should do with approximately five million unemployed now on the relief rolls.

About one million and a half of these belong to the group which in the past was dependent upon local welfare efforts. Most of them are unable for one reason or another to maintain themselves independently—for the most part, through no fault of their own. Such people, in the days before the great depression, were cared for by local efforts—by States, by counties, by towns, by cities, by churches and by private welfare agencies. It is my thought that in the future they must be cared for as they were before. I stand ready through my own personal efforts, and through the public influence of the office that I hold, to help these local agencies to get the means necessary to assume this burden.

In phrasing this passage, I drew certain conclusions from my own experience several years before in Cleveland. I served on a committee of the Associated Charities, and the highly respected head of that organization said more than once in advising us, "Remember, charity is a narcotic. Your major concern is to re-establish a home with a breadwinner who has a job. Relief is only for an emergency to be kept as short as is humanly possible."

Roosevelt's message outlined the new policy:

There are . . . an additional three and one half million employable people who are on relief. With them the problem is different and the responsibility is different. This group was the victim of a nation-wide depression caused by conditions which were not local but national. The Federal Government is the only governmental agency with sufficient power and credit to meet this situation. We have assumed this task and we shall not shrink from it in the future. It is a duty dictated by every intelligent consideration of national policy to ask you to make it possible for the United States to give employment to all of these three and one half million employable people now on relief, pending their absorption in a rising tide of private employment.

It is my thought that with the exception of certain of the normal public building operations of the Government, all emergency public works shall be united in a single new and greatly enlarged plan.

With the establishment of this new system we can supersede the Federal Emergency Relief Administration with a coordinated authority which will be charged with the orderly liquidation of our present relief activities and the substitution of a national chart for the giving of work.

This new program of emergency public employment should be governed by a number of practical principles.

(1) All work undertaken should be useful—not just for a day, or a year, but useful in the sense that it affords permanent improvement in living conditions or that it creates future new wealth for the Nation.

(2) Compensation on emergency public projects should be in the form of security payments which should be larger than the amount now received as a relief dole, but at the same time not so large as to encourage the rejection of opportunities for private employment or the leaving of private employment to engage in Government work.

(3) Projects should be undertaken on which a large percentage of direct labor can be used.

(4) Preference should be given to those projects which will be self-liquidating in the sense that there is a reasonable expectation that the Government will get its money back at some future time.

(5) The projects undertaken should be selected and planned so as to compete as little as possible with private enterprises. This suggests that if it were not for the necessity of giving useful work to the unemployed now on relief, these projects in most instances would not now be undertaken.

(6) The planning of projects would seek to assure work during the coming fiscal year to the individuals now on relief, or until such time as private employment is available. In order to make adjustment to increasing private employment, work should be planned with a view to tapering it off in proportion to the speed with which the emergency workers are offered positions with private employers.

(7) Effort should be made to locate projects where they will serve the greatest unemployment needs as shown by present relief rolls, and the broad program of the National Resources Board should be freely used for guidance in selection. Our ultimate objective being the enrichment of human lives, the Government has the primary duty to use its emergency expenditures as much as possible to serve those who cannot secure the advantages of private capital. . . .

The work itself will cover a wide field including clearance of slums, which for adequate reasons cannot be undertaken by private capital; in rural housing of several kinds, where, again, private capital is unable to function; in rural electrification; in the reforestation of the great watersheds of the Nation; in an intensified program to prevent soil erosion and to reclaim blighted areas; in improving existing road systems and in constructing national highways designed to handle modern traffic; in the elimination of grade crossings; in the extension and enlargement of the successful work of the Civilian Conservation Corps; in non-Federal works, mostly self-liquidating and highly useful to local divisions of Government; and on many other projects which the Nation needs and cannot afford to neglect.

The budget message described the methods by which Roosevelt intended to implement this program. It meant a deficit for the fiscal year ending on June 30, 1936, of $4,424,549,000, the largest before the war expenditures in 1941. And a considerable proportion of these extra expenditures was made through the Works Progress Administration.

If our present immense and varied welfare programs had their origins in the 1930's, the date must be 1935 rather than 1933.

Chapter Twenty-three

Toward Industrial Self-Government

AT noon on April 25 I returned from the Capitol to the Carlton Hotel for lunch. In the lobby I met Hugh Johnson, who had just returned from South Carolina with B. M. Baruch. I was delighted to see him, for I had a number of problems on my mind on which I needed his stimulation and guidance. The wide range of his interests and his powerful and creative mind had always seemed to cast new light on our concerns.

I was glad to see him, too, for personal reasons. When I had last seen him, in March, he had expressed grave misgivings about the agricultural bill, already the law of the American farmland. This added frustration to the hurt he felt because no place had been offered him in the Administration after nearly two months. Despite his rough exterior, Johnson had the sensitiveness of a child, and he had reason to feel that he deserved something better than neglect from an Administration which had come to power in part because of his valiant services in the campaign. Not only did I want to see this service officially recognized, but I felt that we sorely needed him in the Administration.

During lunch, however, he first turned the conversation to something which he said had deeply offended Baruch. It seemed that a gossip had told Baruch that I had made a slighting and wholly unjust remark about his services in the Wilson Administration. There was no truth in the story, and I suggested that we get this detail straightened out with Baruch, who was in his apartment in the hotel. We went up to see him, and my explanation restored Baruch's good humor and our friendship remained unimpaired.

But during the hour I conceived of a task for which I believed Johnson of all people was best suited. And so I outlined to Johnson and Baruch the perplexing problem of devising some plan for industrial recovery. Both had been associated with Wilson's War Industries Board, Baruch as chairman and Johnson as his trusted lieutenant.

I told them of the many plans for industrial recovery that had been submitted to Roosevelt, which had been turned over to me to analyze, sort out, and bring together in a single plan. Even then, several people in the Administration were working on the subject. There was John Dickinson, assistant secretary of commerce, an old friend whom I had recommended to Roper, and Frances Perkins, who was conferring with labor leaders and a few industrialists.

A month earlier I had turned over a number of the plans to James Warburg, and he had submitted a program on April 4. This I believed to be inadequate, and nothing had happened since, except the work of Dickinson and Perkins.

But at the moment Roosevelt was facing an emergent situation. Hugo Black had introduced a thirty-hour-week bill in the Senate, which with the strong support of labor leaders was making some progress. Roosevelt believed that such a scheme—merely to spread out the available work—would fail to reach the heart of the problem. What was needed was not to thin out the jobs then available, but a measure to create new employment and to stimulate industrial confidence.

I suggested that Johnson take all these plans, including Warburg's summation, and with Baruch's advice and by cooperation with everyone concerned prepare legislation that Roosevelt could submit to Congress. Johnson enjoyed the prospect and Baruch warmly approved. Since it was of vital importance to offer a substitute for the Black bill as soon as possible, I suggested that Johnson return with me to my office in the State Department, where I would turn over all the plans to him and provide space to work. Two years later, Johnson recalled this incident in his book:

> . . . one day when B. M. Baruch and I were returning from a hunting trip in South Carolina we met Ray Moley in the Carlton Hotel, Washington. He said that the draft of an Industrial Act was an immediate necessity and, recalling our many studies of the subject, our frequent talks with him, and B. M.'s experience in the mobilization of Industry, asked if I could not be loaned to him to draw up such a bill. . . . Mr. Baruch readily assented, and I went over to Ray's office that afternoon. Indeed I never went back to New York from that day to the end of my service except to get my clothes and rarely even so much as saw my own family.*

There was an unused office in the old State, War, and Navy Building next to mine. I dumped all the plans and correspondence on the desk

* *The Blue Eagle from Egg to Earth,* p. 193.

and told Johnson that this ended my responsibility for industrial-recovery planning unless he wanted to consult me or to iron out differences with Dickinson and Perkins. It was a hot day. Johnson took off his coat and tie and plunged into a job that was to make him, next to Roosevelt, the most talked-about member of the Administration during the year ahead. For that office was the birthplace of the National Industrial Recovery Act. Later, when the bill had been written and was enacted by Congress, and when Johnson was designated as administrator of the NRA, the operation soon proliferated in the Commerce Building.

In 1930 and 1931 the huge American industrial economy had slowed to a mere crawl. Millions of workers were displaced; thousands of companies closed their doors. In this vast complex the most difficult of all industries to reactivate were the "heavy" ones—industries that produce for other industries.

It had been all well and good to say, as Roosevelt had repeatedly asserted, that with agriculture relieved of some of its debt, low prices, and great surpluses, the farmers would provide a market for industrial products. But as we saw it, agriculture would require a year to provide the stimulus for such a revival. Something was needed sooner that would bear directly upon the industrial establishment. Roosevelt had relayed to me innumerable recipes for industrial revival. Over the greater part of a year, I had talked with many people who had ideas. In March and April the accumulation of plans in my files was a haunting reminder of a responsibility that lay ahead. Outstanding among them were those of Gerard Swope, John R. Oishei, M. C. Rorty, Senator La Follette, Fred I. Kent, H. S. Rivitz, Henry S. Dennison, and Henry I. Harriman. Harriman in particular, at that time president of the United States Chamber of Commerce, had given the subject much thought over a long period of time. He had talked at length with Roosevelt regarding his plans on many occasions during 1932, and on February 10, 1933, sent me a document entitled "An Economic Program" in which he elaborated his ideas.

To stimulate employment and recovery Harriman advocated the legalization of a practice that had become common in the 1920's—the use of trade associations to eliminate destructive competition and to encourage national economic planning. Harriman suggested that "the Clayton Act, under which the Federal Trade Commission is organized, be amended to provide that trade practice conferences may abolish any unfair operating condition in the trade." The labeling of a practice as unfair would require approval by better than a simple majority of such a conference—say 60 or 70 per cent—as well as by the proper government agency. These conferences would also regulate "such matters as maximum hours of labor and minimum rate of pay."

Harriman further suggested that corporations be permitted to take joint action in the direction of balancing production to demand, with the proviso that agreements limiting and allocating production be filed with some designated government agency. If the Federal agency showed no objection within sixty days, the agreement would become operative; but the agency retained the continuous right to review such agreements with an eye to the public interest.*

Whereas Harriman's proposals were geared to relaxation of the anti-trust laws by FTC approval of trade associations' agreements, other plans would attain recovery by stimulating production and consumption through a great public drive. Some advocated large expenditures for public works and the subsidization of plant improvement and enlargement. Others proposed government loans to industry to tide it over the gap between increased costs of employment and the pickup of purchasing power that would ultimately come about. And there was every possible combination of these ideas.

When in March I placed the problem and the materials I had gathered in the hands of Warburg, who was working with me on the preparations for the Economic Conference, I asked him to consult such men as Professor Moulton of the Brookings Institution, Fred I. Kent, and Adolph C. Miller of the Federal Reserve Board. In the memorandum Warburg gave me on April 4, entitled "Industrial Rehabilitation by Reemployment," he described a two-fold cleavage. One group, he reported, believed that manufacturing could be revived through government loans to selected industries. On the other hand, Kent and Warburg (and "partially converted" Oishei and Edgar Kaufman) favored a government guarantee to industry against losses for a stipulated period in return for an agreement that it share in any profits of industry. Warburg also, claiming the support of Kent, Walter Stewart, Lew Douglas, and Adolph Miller, suggested the stimulation of the movement of producers' goods as opposed to concentration on consumers' goods.

Warburg appended to his report a draft of a proposed Presidential message to Congress that argued for the rehabilitation of industry through government aid and "regimentation." In the proposed message the President would state: "I shall submit to the Congress a bill for the regimentation of industry and ask of Congress its immediate passage." †

I was not satisfied by this conscientious memorandum and laid it aside with the belief that thinking on the subject in business and government

* Henry I. Harriman, "An Economic Program," February 10, 1933, R. M. Files. While trade associations had existed in the 1920's to minimize destructive competition, maintain prices, and divide markets, they faced two problems: uncertainty as to their legality under the Sherman and Clayton Acts and, following from the first, inability to enforce decisions in view of their doubtful legality.

† R. M. Files.

circles had not crystallized sufficiently to justify further moves at the time. This conclusion, and the reasons therefor, I described to Roosevelt the same day I received the Warburg document. We agreed that nothing should be done as yet regarding national economic planning for industry.

Only two days later this decision was rejected when the Senate passed the Black thirty-hour-week bill on April 6. This was an impractical attempt at work-spreading by legislating a thirty-hour week for persons engaged in the production of goods that entered into interstate commerce. Roosevelt was quick to realize that, should it pass through the House, it could only paralyze industry, not revive it, and immediately appointed a Cabinet committee under Secretary Perkins to work out a substitute. My notebook contains Roosevelt's reaction to the Black bill under the category of "Threats." *

But the Perkins substitute in the form of amendments to the Black bill produced an even greater sensation than the Black bill. The New York *Times* described her as "astonished" and "amused" by the claim that her proposals "had been heralded as a demand for a broad and sweeping control of industry, with the Secretary of Labor in the role of dictator." Mrs. Perkins had in mind the retention of the thirty-hour principle for most industries and permission for certain industries or sections to work forty hours in case of emergency. In addition, borrowing from the terms of the New York State minimum wage legislation, she proposed the creation of minimum wage boards where it appeared to the Secretary of Labor that wages in an industry or plant were below the fair value of service rendered or below a fair living standard. After her receipt of a report from such a board, the Secretary could put its recommendations into effect through a "directory order." The Secretary of Labor was also to be given the power to relax anti-trust laws and authorize the making of trade agreements of various types.†

The Perkins substitute was a great shock to employers. Henry I. Harriman registered his opposition to regulation by government boards and suggested instead agreements entered into voluntarily by the majority of a particular industry. The basic issue at stake was industrial self-regulation versus government imposition of standards of conduct. Matthew Woll of the American Federation of Labor opposed the Perkins minimum wage proposal lest minimum wages become maximum wages.‡

Opposition to the Perkins proposals came from other quarters. John

* R. M. Notebook, April 10, 1933; April 13, 1933.

† New York *Times,* April 20, 1933 and April 26, 1933.

‡ *Ibid.,* April 28, 1933.

Dickinson, assistant secretary in the Department of Commerce, wrote to me on April 28, 1933, as follows:

I saw in this morning's paper that Miss Perkins yesterday put herself on record more emphatically than before in favor of the so-called Black 30-Hour Bill in its present form. I am attaching a set of three memoranda which I presented to Miss Perkins. . . .

I am bringing the matter to your attention because I cannot help feeling that it would be, both from an economic and political standpoint, very unfortunate and, *I believe, politically disastrous for the Administration if it were to be put in the position of making the Black Bill as it now stands with Miss Perkins' amendments an Administration measure, and if the bill were to pass.* [Dickinson's italics.] *

Dickinson presented a host of economic arguments against the Black-Perkins measure, which he scored as "economically unfortunate for the country." He saw the thirty-hour rule for all industries as too rigid, and in cases of extraordinary need the exception limited to forty hours for ten weeks as too narrow. Further, the Perkins scheme for determining hours and wages would permit a separate case to be made for each plant, which could only produce a "monster bureaucracy" in the Labor Department. He pointed out that "a general reduction in the number of working hours per man, not accompanied by an upward movement in wages, would not increase buying power, but is almost certain to make conditions worse. The reason for this is that the earnings of wage earners employed in 1932 were already so low that no general benefit could be derived from reducing them further by spreading the wages among a larger number."

Dickinson proposed a measure along a line different from that of the Black bill and closer to the forthcoming NIRA scheme:

1. Prohibit from interstate commerce the products of night work by women or children or of sweated labor, defining sweated labor in some detail as, for example, labor employed more than 54 hours a week. . . .

2. Permit the members of an industry after conferences to agree upon and propose a code of labor standards covering maximum hours . . . and other labor standards, including machinery for the determination of minimum wages for the industry, said code to be binding when approved by the Secretary of Labor. The Secretary's approval shall be conditioned upon the code in his opinion providing for proper protection to labor. . . . Provide that violation of the code shall constitute unfair practice.

3. Empower the Secretary of Labor to call for a conference of his own motion.

4. Provide that during the existence of the emergency if after such a conference has been called by the Secretary the members of the industry are unable to agree on a code of labor standards, the Secretary may promulgate

* John Dickinson to Raymond Moley. R. M. Files.

such a code for that particular industry, effective for the period of the emergency.

I quote Dickinson's views at length, since he very shortly was to participate in the drafting of the National Industrial Recovery Act. Dickinson's letter, moreover, reflects the fact that I, too, had entered into the picture—on Tuesday, April 11, when Roosevelt directed me to contact the various groups in Washington that we knew were pondering the question of business-government cooperation. Specifically, he mentioned the Brookings Institution and the Chamber of Commerce.

News of my assignment leaked out on April 14 in an Arthur Krock story published in the New York *Times*:

> A plan to mobilize private industry under the government for expansion in the production of articles and materials in normal demand, this expansion to be coeval with the administration's public works activities, is being developed by the President's closest advisers, and they hope to persuade him to attempt it.
>
> Certain types of industry, under the plan, would be assembled and regulated by a government agency reminiscent of the War Industries Board. Competition would be regulated; hours of work and minimum rates of pay would be fixed. . . .
>
> The thought behind the plan is that a public works program standing by itself, even if five billions is expended upon it, will not sufficiently reduce unemployment or make use of the new purchasing power. . . .
>
> Among the important administration advisers who are giving thought to the plan is Assistant Secretary of State Raymond Moley, who is represented as being "sold" on the general idea. If this is true, then its adoption is but one step away, since there is no adviser in whom the President reposes more confidence. With others in the administration who have been trying to evolve a coordinated program, Mr. Moley has not been content with what is known here as "holding the line." . . . The real objective of the administration is to restore the normal business conditions, with people at work and domestic and foreign trade fluid once again.

Although Krock's account overstated my role in the plan to achieve industrial resuscitation, it was nevertheless well informed regarding the current of our thinking. During the two weeks following Roosevelt's delegation of authority to me, I devoted as much time as I could to schemes for government-business cooperation. But the Thomas amendment, the arrival of Prime Minister MacDonald, and other pressing matters kept me from getting on top of the job. At least I knew I could not move swiftly enough to stave off the menace of the Black bill (with Perkins' amendments) and the equal menace of a rapid inflationary rise unaccompanied by any sound attempt to raise purchasing power in wages and salaries.

After Johnson had been working a day or two, he discovered that

Roosevelt had casually invited several people to work on plans for industrial recovery. In addition to Dickinson and Secretary Perkins, Senator Robert F. Wagner and a few of his colleagues were considering plans for a big public-works program. Dickinson was interested chiefly in a plan that would relax the anti-trust laws sufficiently to permit cooperation within industries. Tugwell, despite his labors in agriculture, was casually interested, and so was Donald Richberg.

Richberg was a Chicago lawyer whom I had known in 1932 and who had worked with me on Roosevelt's Salt Lake City speech on the railroads. I entertained a very high opinion of his competence as a lawyer and his clear and concise habit of thought. For the most part his clients had been railway labor organizations, and for these reasons I suggested to Johnson that he use Richberg in working out the provisions in the bill that concerned labor.*

When Johnson told me about the confusion he encountered because of so many other plans in preparation, I suggested to Roosevelt that he bring all the architects to his office—Johnson, Dickinson, Perkins, Richberg, Wagner, and Lewis Douglas—and secure some sort of agreement. I attended the meeting but remained silent while they argued. Roosevelt ended by telling them to shut themselves in a room, iron out the differences, and bring him a bill on which they could agree.

The result was two drafts, one by Johnson and the other by Dickinson. Richberg assisted in the Johnson draft. One evening the group called me in to mediate, but I refrained from any interference, largely because I did not consider myself competent to do so. Finally, however, a compromise measure emerged which Roosevelt accepted and sent to Congress with a message.

At that time, which was early May, I had before me the drafting of a speech to the country called the "Second Fireside Speech," to be delivered on May 7, and the NIRA message to accompany the completed bill, which was to go to Congress on May 17.

Since the theme of the bill was cooperation within industries without undue restraint by the anti-trust laws, it seemed to Roosevelt that the word "partnership" in describing the relationship between private industry and government would be appropriate. This was the phraseology used in the Fireside Speech: "It is wholly wrong to call the measures

* Roosevelt admired Richberg and was determined to have him in the Administration. Various jobs were suggested, including comptroller of the currency, counsel for the Bureau of Internal Revenue, and solicitor general. He would probably have accepted the latter office, but Felix Frankfurter advised against it. Richberg worked with Johnson on the NIRA bill and after Johnson's selection as administrator was named chief counsel of the NRA. He remained there until 1935. During a large part of the time in which he served with Johnson, there were sharp differences which are described from his point of view in his book, *My Hero* (New York: Putnam's, 1954). These differences are also described in Johnson, *op. cit.*

we have taken government control of farming, industry, and transportation. It is rather a partnership . . . not partnership in profits, for the profits still go to the citizens, but rather a partnership in planning, and a partnership to see that the plans are carried out."

The key words here are "partnership" and "planning." They meant partnership in planning by government in collaboration with private interests. This was, it seemed to me, a very important matter of policy.

In discussing the message with Roosevelt, I recalled that the word "partnership" had been sharply debated by Theodore Roosevelt and Wilson in the campaign in 1912. T. R. favored the idea of government partnership and intervention in business. Wilson specifically denounced the concept of partnership. He said that if there were any partnership, the dominating force would be big business as the stronger partner. He held that the role of government should be restraint of unfair business practices. When the problem of enforcing the anti-trust laws arose, the "Donnybrook" system should be followed—"Hit the heads you see." That was the essence of Wilson's New Freedom.

Roosevelt promptly replied that, despite his admiration for Wilson, his preference was for the T. R. policy. He did not believe in reform through "trust-busting." In terms of ideology, Franklin Roosevelt, so far as the relationship between business and government was concerned in 1933, was essentially the heir to the policies of T. R.*

Congress debated the NIRA bill at length. The measure passed the House without difficulty, but there was heavy opposition in the Senate. The conference report was passed in the Senate on June 13 by a vote of 46 to 39, and Roosevelt approved the measure on the last day of the session, June 16.

The National Industrial Recovery Act combined two of the most favored approaches to recovery:

Title I declared a national emergency, which justified a partial suspension of the anti-trust laws. It provided that the various members of an industry could, with the collaboration of the government, draw up codes that when approved by the President would have the force of law throughout the entire industry and be enforceable by the courts. A code would specify certain provisions for the protection of labor and other

* Planning was a controversial concept within the early New Deal. Tugwell and Johnson were planners. But the immediate inspiration in each case was different. Some, including Tugwell, had been impressed by their observation of the early Soviet plans. Johnson was thinking about industrial mobilization in World War I through the War Industries Board. The source of both, it can clearly be shown, was Germany's total mobilization in 1914, so clearly described in Walter Rathenau's vastly influential book in that year, *Germany's Raw Materials Management*. After the Supreme Court had decreed the fate of the AAA and the NRA, Roosevelt turned away from planning until the advent of World War II. This change bitterly disappointed Tugwell and many other New Dealers.

provisions covering fair competition. Because of the requirement of Presidential approval, Roosevelt might amend or amplify the code. In certain instances in which no agreement could be secured among the members of an industry, the President could impose a code. This I believed at the time was flagrantly unconstitutional. It was a weakness that I feel certain played a large part in the subsequent decision of the Supreme Court to scrap the whole apparatus.

Title II authorized the President to create an emergency Public Works Administration. To this was attached authorization for the expenditure of $3.3 billion. The administrator could spend money for a wide variety of public works which, as the act was later administered, included highways, dams, Federal buildings, and even naval construction.

Perhaps because of the doubt in Roosevelt's mind about "pump-priming" and also because he had certain reservations about the capacity of Hugh Johnson as an administrator, he decided to divorce the administration of the two operations provided in the act. In a Cabinet discussion it was suggested that the Secretary of the Interior should become public-works administrator and Hugh Johnson the administrator of the codes.

Roosevelt believed that because of Ickes' innate caution and suspicion and also because of his inimical attitude toward political favoritism, the money would be spent slowly and grudgingly. He believed that Johnson, driving and impulsive, would spend the money with great expedition.

When the decision to divide the responsibility for administering the act was announced to Johnson at a Cabinet meeting, his protests were furiously vocal. But after a great deal of coaxing by Secretary Perkins, Johnson agreed to serve, and the show was on the road.

Johnson moved at a furious pace. Three weeks after the approval of the act, a textile code was adopted and approved. A great rush of people representing many industries came to Washington. Johnson's administrative staff mounted with bewildering speed. The great spaces in the Commerce Building were soon filled with people hurriedly recruited and only casually briefed. Reformers seeking employment found a niche somehow in the operation, some of them wholly unsuited for any sort of administrative work. The concept of recovery as distinguished from reform was forgotten, and the codes, hurriedly drawn, embodied restrictions upon and concessions by industries that had been the subject of debate for many years.

By the simple means of getting together the representatives of an industry to write a code, who perforce were whipped on by the patriotic need for a great national effort, fundamental changes in the relationship between labor and management and an industry and its customers were made overnight.

A month after the act became law, Johnson decided that, even with the speed at which code-making was proceeding, there was need for something of a more general nature. And so he created and the President approved a blanket code called the President's Re-employment Agreement (PRA). This was at the moment the most effective of all the formal steps toward recovery. For the terms of this agreement were subscribed to by 2,333,000 employers with 16,000,000 employees. Those who subscribed to this agreement pledged themselves to employ no one under sixteen years of age, to pay a fixed minimum wage, to avoid unnecessary price increases, and to provide a 35-hour week for factory workers and 40 hours for others. The impact was almost immediate. Between June and October, 2,462,000 were re-employed. This achievement, widely advertised by Johnson and Roosevelt, provided a surge of confidence and an economic stimulant that carried into the next year.

Johnson was most dubious about the enforcement provisions of the act. He was also anxious to lose no time in litigation, which in every instance would carry with it the dreaded review of the act by the Supreme Court. Therefore, he sought by a tremendous publicity campaign to secure voluntary compliance.

The rush to Washington of businessmen and lawyers was so great that by August 546 codes had been submitted, and before the end of the year 1,000.

In his great drive Johnson created the famous Blue Eagle, to be shown in thousands of windows, over the doors of countless factories, and imprinted upon the goods of code members. He employed all sorts of performers to help carry the message to the country—public relations people, employers, labor leaders, actors, artists, and others. He himself was the stellar attraction. He took the stump and traveled widely over the nation when he was not laboring in his office. The administrative machinery spread not only through the Commerce Building. Branch offices popped up in every important city. Nothing like this, short of war, had been seen in any nation since Peter the Hermit and others incited the Crusades. It submerged all the other activities of the New Deal. Indeed, it almost became synonymous with the New Deal. And Johnson for a time eclipsed the President in the headlines.

The history of the NRA after 1933 is beyond the scope of this account. The frustrations of Johnson, his mistakes, the violations of codes as prosperity slowly returned to industry, the innumerable reorganizations and Roosevelt-sponsored investigations assured the decline and fall of NRA even before the Supreme Court invalidated it in May 1935.*

* For two accounts of the later history, see Broadus Mitchell, *Depression Decade,* Chapter VII; and Arthur Schlesinger, Jr., *The Coming of the New Deal,* pp. 87–176. Also Hugh Johnson's account in his *The Blue Eagle from Egg to Earth,* and Donald Richberg's *My Hero.*

Schlesinger, whose commitment to national economic planning runs through all his writings on the New Deal, seems to have remained firmly committed to this idea, even though the Supreme Court had spoken and the NRA had reached the end of its usefulness:

> The more enduring achievements of NRA lay not in the economic but in the social field. Here NRA accomplished a fantastic series of reforms, any one of which would have staggered the nation a few years earlier. It established the principle of maximum hours and minimum wages on a national basis. It abolished child labor. It dealt a fatal blow to sweatshops. It made collective bargaining a national policy and thereby transformed the position of organized labor. It gave new status to the consumer. It stamped out a noxious collection of unfair trade practices. . . .
>
> More than this, NRA helped break the chains of economic fatalism which had so long bound the nation. The Blue Eagle campaign changed the popular mood from despair to affirmation and activity. The psychological stimulus gave people new confidence in their capacity to work out their economic salvation. . . . It accustomed the country to the feasibility of government regulation and taught people to think in terms of national policy for business and for labor.*

Schlesinger adds that "it trained personnel for the responsibilities of government service in a time of crisis." This, he suggests, is why so many individuals who in one way or another had participated in NRA activities were able and willing to serve in the great industrial mobilization when preparations for war began in 1940.

With much of this appraisal I heartily agree. For by subsequent legislation and by custom and the actions of individual companies, a great deal of the idealistic reform so forcibly taught by the NRA has come to be accepted practice.

There can be no doubt about the lifting of the morale of the public and of the business community. Under the incredible stimulus of Hugh Johnson, new hope and new confidence grew in every sector of American life.

But, like the medieval preachers of the Crusades, Johnson fell a victim of his own optimism. The codes under which industries could find the way to recovery and internal peace should have been created after more deliberation and study. It would have been wiser to have limited code-making during the first year to a few of the large, key industries. However, stimulated by his early successes, Johnson attempted too much too soon. As gradual recovery took hold, the old forces of competition took over. These forces, however they may be deplored by the orthodox planner and despite their often ugly mien, are the lifeblood of progress. As I witnessed events after I left Washington in the fall of 1933, it seemed to me that Roosevelt might best have terminated NRA and sub-

* Schlesinger, *op. cit.*, pp. 174–75.

stituted a broad program of industrial legislation. But he believed that a permanent institution capable of long-term reform had been created.

As Roosevelt and Johnson penetrated more deeply into industrial life, they met more and more frustrations. The innumerable factors involved in industrial life, the conditioning factors that bear upon industry, the human elements that are always present, the incapacity of any government bureaucracy to understand the infinitely complex conditions in a competitive society, and, finally and not the least important, the selfishness of many industrial leaders who after the panic of a crisis subsides return to their old ways—all these should be a lesson to those who believe in over-all national economic planning.

When the emotional impulses that gripped some businessmen as well as labor leaders and carried them to such heights of idealism in 1933 had subsided, the old habits returned. After the hurts of the depression, they were willing to agree to anything. But when they returned to the routine of the life they had left temporarily, the old habits came back: "The burned fool's bandaged finger went wabbling back to the fire."

Some of the dedicated advocates of economic planning who had greeted the NRA and the AAA as the dawn of a new civilization were convinced that Roosevelt had betrayed them when he failed to re-create a modified NRA after the Court action in 1935. They should have realized, as Roosevelt seemed to sense, that planning of an economy in normal times is possible only through the discipline of a police state. They cannot have the cake of free enterprise and also eat it away by government directives. Government is a suitable instrument for negative action. It can be effective when it tells industry what it may not do. But it cannot summon the talent to create positive means for operating a free economy. The planning concept can provide a few guidelines but not many. Economic planning on a national scale in a politically free society involves contradictions that cannot be resolved in practice. The bones of the Blue Eagle should be a grim reminder of this reality.

There is a certain meanness in retrospection. But as we look back, we see that it would have been wise if Roosevelt and Congress had anticipated the collapse of NRA in the middle of 1934. Legislation could have been written to use the broadened interpretation of the commerce clause to put into effect many of the reforms of the NRA that were achieved temporarily by the codes. Even the Supreme Court of that time might have approved most such measures—the abolition of child labor, the guarantee of collective bargaining, the protection (not the promotion) of unions, even maximum hours and minimum wages. Instead, after the decision of the Supreme Court, the Wagner Act was thrust into industrial life, a measure that heavily weighted the scales against the employer. Thirteen years were required before correction could be made by the enactment of the Taft-Hartley Act.

In early 1935 Roosevelt had convinced himself that there were no limits to the power of the President and Congress in an emergency. And so, despite the fact that NRA was a palpable failure, he asked Congress in February to extend its life for two more years. He said, "the fundamental purpose and principle of the Act are sound. To abandon them is unthinkable. It would spell the return of industrial and labor chaos." *

I am sure that Hugh Johnson, as early as 1933, doubted the constitutionality of the provisions of the act that permitted the President to revise codes and thus give them the force of law. That is why he desperately sought to induce compliance by persuasion and also to avoid so far as he was able, any judicial test of the act. When after 1933 the power to *impose a code by the President* was used in cases in which the members of an industry could not agree, there were few with any sense who believed that the current Court or any court would approve of such delegated legislative power.

On May 29 the blow fell. The Supreme Court by unanimous decision in the famous Schechter case (295 U.S. 495) threw out the act as unconstitutional.

The decision of the Court was written by the Chief Justice, Charles Evans Hughes. In his opinion Hughes stated: "Extraordinary conditions do not create or enlarge constitutional power." He said that the power conferred by Congress upon the President to impose or even approve codes was an unconstitutional delegation of power. "Such a delegation of legislative power is unknown to our law and utterly inconsistent with the constitutional prerogatives and duties of Congress." Under this ruling it would even be doubtful if Congress itself possessed the power to enact such codes directly.

In a singularly eloquent concurring opinion (in which Justice Stone joined), Justice Cardozo said that the authority exercised by the President under the act was ". . . delegation running riot. No such plenitude of power is susceptible of transfer."

Roosevelt, in a press conference that was elaborately staged, struck back at the Court a few days later. The outstanding aspect of his long argument was that he believed that the question of delegation might have been cured in a new act, but that the interpretation of the Court of the interstate powers of Congress turned back the Constitution to the "horse and buggy" days. This phrase he specifically permitted reporters to quote directly.

There was great activity in and around the White House after this. Everyone, it seemed, had an alternative plan. I was summoned, among others. I suggested that it still seemed possible for the government to

* I had no part in writing this message. Its language suggests that Richberg had a hand in it.

encourage the creation of purely voluntary codes to be enforced by contract and for Congress to pass legislation empowering the President to reconcile the provisions of the codes with the anti-trust laws through consent decrees. I believed that it would be possible to construct a constitutional amendment to permit such voluntary action.

Roosevelt, beyond giving his support to the Wagner bill then before Congress, did nothing. But at that time, and especially in the next year when the AAA was struck down, he developed an animus toward the Court, which was to come to a crisis in early 1937 with his proposal to enlarge and reorganize the Court. No doubt, like James I in his long struggle with Lord Coke, Roosevelt believed that under the cover of legalism the Court was attacking him personally. His confidence in his ability to secure the passage of that revolutionary plan was created by the immense majority his party had received in 1934 and his own triumphant re-election in 1936. In the defeat of his Court reorganization he discovered to his intense distress and indignation that he no longer had public opinion behind him on all things.

Chapter Twenty-four

Off the Gold Standard

ONE morning in April, Will Woodin entered the bedroom where Roosevelt lingered after his coffee. The President greeted his Secretary of the Treasury by saying that he had taken the country off the gold standard. A smile came to the pixy-like face of Woodin and he replied, "What? Again?"

This fairly well expresses the difficulty of fixing with exactness the date when the United States abandoned the gold standard. The restrictions upon the withdrawal of gold coin, bullion, and certificates in the proclamation of March 6 under the 1917 act were a clear indication of what was to come later. Another relevant date was April 5, when Roosevelt's executive order prohibited under penalty the hoarding of gold. Or the abandonment might have been in several executive orders which followed in April.

Meanwhile, an old, nagging problem faced the President. In the 1932 campaign Roosevelt had been under heavy pressure by leaders in the Western copper- and silver-producing states to remonetize silver. There was also considerable agitation in the East, in part by individuals close to the Democratic Party who were speculating in the white metal. Roosevelt sought to appease the silver proponents by inserting in a speech or two the expression that he would, if elected, "do something for silver."

Once his Administration got under way after the bank crisis, Senators from silver-producing states demanded that this promise be redeemed. Most of them favored the adoption of the old Bryan formula, "the free coinage of silver at a ratio of 16 to 1." With them joined members of the farm bloc who saw the remonetization of silver as a means of raising farm prices through inflation. Roosevelt, while he intended to raise prices through monetary means, remained opposed to the silver formula.

In late February one of the foremost silver advocates, Senator Burton K. Wheeler of Montana, invited Woodin and me to have dinner at the home of Jonathan Bourne, Jr., who had represented Oregon in the Senate and was one of the oldest and most ardent "progressives." We were subjected that evening to three hours of argument for silver. We had little to say ourselves, for my experience in those years made it perfectly clear that it is useless to oppose verbally the ardent expositions of those who believed that silver was as important an issue as it had been in 1896.*

After leaving Bourne and Wheeler that night, Woodin and I discussed the somewhat boring adventure on the way back to our hotel. Woodin's objection was that if silver were remonetized and coined freely as legal tender, there would be a general reopening of old and abandoned mines and the market would be flooded. I shared Woodin's apartment on that visit to Washington, and after I went to my room and partially prepared for bed, I heard Woodin tinkling away at the piano. I asked him what he was doing. He said that he was composing a lullaby. I suggested that he give his composition the title "Lullaby to Silver." He accepted the idea, and when the composition was published later that name appeared in print.

But in April our jest was brought down to the hard and practical business of counting noses in the Senate. For Wheeler was in deadly earnest. In January he had proposed a bill providing for the remonetization of silver. It had been defeated by a large majority, but that was in the lame-duck Congress. Now we were dealing with a Congress infused with the spirit of bold innovation. And so when the agricultural measure came to the Senate floor, Wheeler offered his 16-to-1 proposal as an amendment. It seemed sure of at least a dozen votes from silver-producing states. But there was also great support from the Midwestern farm states and measurably from the South, which supported free coinage because it was believed to be inflationary. It was true that monetary affairs were quite different from what they were in the Bryan years. But it was believed by advocates of the amendment that silver remonetization would help. There were strong indications in April that, despite the objections of Roosevelt, the Wheeler amendment would win in the Sen-

* The silver advocates had pat answers for every objection. In discussing the subject with Senator Key Pittman, I once suggested that when the United States raised the price of silver the Chinese might flood the market with silver obtained by melting down vast quantities of silver ornaments, tableware, and other forms in which the stuff had been used for centuries. Pittman replied, "You don't understand Chinese psychology. When they have anything and its market value rises, their desire to keep it becomes intense. That silver in China will never be a problem."

ate if put to a vote. This would have been Roosevelt's first serious defeat, and he was determined to seek inflation in his own way and in his own time.

Roosevelt let it be known that if the Wheeler amendment were adopted, he would veto the farm bill in its entirety. In the debate on the Wheeler proposal, Senator William E. Borah asked Majority Leader Joseph T. Robinson whether this alleged threat was true. Robinson replied that it was. Borah then declared that, while he was sympathetic to the Wheeler proposal, he would be compelled to vote against it.* No doubt, this gesture of Borah turned the tide, and the amendment was defeated 43 to 33.

On the morning of the day the vote was cast, Senator Carl Hayden of Arizona came to my office. He said that while he represented a state with large interests in silver (mostly as a by-product of copper) and while he personally favored the Wheeler amendment, he was reluctant to vote against Roosevelt's wishes. I suggested that he absent himself from the floor but keep account of the roll call. If the vote appeared to be very close, he might vote "Nay." But if defeat seemed certain, he could appear and vote "Yea." On April 18, the day after the vote, Hayden wrote to me saying, "I waited until the tally showed over 30 votes for 16 to 1, and then voted 'Nay.' " †

But the defeat of Wheeler's proposal did not end the threat, for at least ten Senators had voted against their convictions that Congress should take affirmative inflationary action. It was clear that either Roosevelt himself must take command of monetary expansion or Congress would impose it.

Senator Elmer Thomas of Oklahoma, almost immediately after the Wheeler vote, offered an amendment to the farm bill that would authorize the President to do any or all of the following: (1) to issue greenbacks in meeting all forms of current or maturing Federal obligations and in buying up United States bonds; (2) to fix the ratio of the value of silver to gold and to provide for free coinage of silver by proclamation; and (3) to fix the weight of the gold dollar by proclamation.

Here were all the dreaded proposals for inflation bound up in a way to elicit all of the support in Congress for inflationary measures.

Early in the morning on April 18, the day after the vote on the Wheeler amendment and the introduction of the Thomas amendment, I had a telephone call from Senator Robert J. Bulkley of Ohio. He said that unless the President acted promptly, the Thomas amendment would be adopted, and he urged me to inform Roosevelt of the serious nature of the situation. Almost immediately I received the same news from

* Burton K. Wheeler, *Yankee from the West* (New York: Doubleday, 1962).
† R. M. Files.

Senator Byrnes. I asked Byrnes to join me at the White House and talk with Roosevelt during his breakfast hour.

Byrnes, with his uncanny capacity to judge senatorial opinion, told Roosevelt that the Thomas amendment was certain to have a majority and that the best that could be done was to persuade Thomas to accept a revised and not so mandatory a version. Roosevelt agreed to this, and on a printed copy of the Thomas proposal he wrote in longhand these words: "Ray Moley—Byrnes, Thomas, Treasury." This, he explained, meant that I should take charge of the amendment and, working with Byrnes, persuade Thomas to accept a revision. The purpose was to give the President discretionary authority among a selection of methods to promote a rise in prices, especially farm prices. Thus, instead of compelling the President to follow a course determined by Congress, it would permit him to use his own judgment about timing and method.

Byrnes in his memoirs describes what followed that morning meeting:

> Together we thoroughly canvassed every possibility and at length Mr. Roosevelt drew up a memorandum which he asked us to draft in the form of an amendment. That evening, with Senator Key Pittman of Nevada, we prepared a rough draft which that night Moley took to the President for any changes he might suggest. Meanwhile, since the Thomas amendment was due for consideration at twelve the next day, I was given the task of approaching its author and seeing that he kept an open mind. I asked him to go with me to see the President, who did an excellent sales job—in fact, so good that Thomas said he would be glad to substitute most of our draft for his own. Moley, Pittman and I then began the job of final drafting. When Thomas finally offered the amendment to the agricultural bill, there was strong opposition, but the Senate approved the amendment and the bill by a good majority. Later it passed the House by an overwhelming vote.*

The provisions of the amendment as revised and passed gave the President six methods of increasing the currency. These are outlined by Broadus Mitchell:

> The inflationary options were as follows: (1) to persuade the Federal Reserve banks to buy government obligations in the open market to the extent of $3 billion, without tax on reserve deficiency, in order to put more lending power in the hands of the banks. If the reserve banks refused, the Treasury might (2) issue $3 billion in United States notes (fiat "greenbacks") in exchange for government bonds, 4 per cent of these notes to be retired annually. These notes and all other coin and currency were to be full legal tender. Or (3) the President might adopt bimetallism, fixing the relative weight of gold and silver. Or (4) he could reduce the weight of the standard gold dollar (which was in fact not procurable) by not more than 50 per cent. These last three devices were to be used only in case the reserve

* James F. Byrnes: *All in One Lifetime,* p. 77.

banks refused to make the open-market purchases. Besides, the President might (5), for six months, accept silver at not more than 50 cents an ounce—then 10 per cent above the market price—in payment of debts due the United States from foreign governments, to a maximum value of $200 million silver certificates to be issued against most of this bullion. Lastly, (6) in wording which bowed to restraint where all the rest of the measure embraced expansion, the Federal Reserve Board might increase or decrease reserve requirements.*

That evening of the eighteenth when I delivered the revision to Roosevelt, there was a dramatic scene at the White House. A meeting was scheduled for that evening after dinner to discuss the coming meetings with Prime Minister MacDonald and other British representatives who were at that time crossing the Atlantic on their way to Washington.†

Assembled in the Oval Room with Roosevelt were Secretaries Woodin and Hull, Senator Pittman, Lewis Douglas, Herbert Feis, who was economic adviser in the State Department and under Roosevelt's February directive my subordinate; James Warburg, who had been advising on foreign fiscal matters unofficially; William Bullitt, who had been appointed an assistant to the Secretary of State, and I. The purpose for which the meeting was called was forgotten when Roosevelt told us that he had decided to accept the Thomas amendment with the revisions agreed upon earlier that day. All the people present were stunned except Pittman, Woodin and I, who had known of the decision earlier that day. Hull was characteristically silent. Bullitt said little. But Douglas, Warburg, and Feis were vociferous in opposition. The argument went on for two hours. Roosevelt calmly stood his ground.

After the others had left, Byrnes (who had arrived after the others), Pittman, and I worked on a draft, with refinements earlier suggested by Roosevelt. I accompanied Pittman to his home to talk over procedure for the next day and returned to my hotel after midnight. There I found in my room Douglas and Warburg, still discussing what they passionately regarded as a calamity. One of them said as he left the room, "This is the end of Western civilization." This has been attributed to Douglas and also Warburg. I am not sure, although it sounds like one of the cosmic conclusions of Douglas. Warburg himself, in his book *The Long Road Home*, attributes the expression to Douglas.

At any rate, I learned later that Douglas and Warburg walked the streets discussing the subject far into the morning.

There was more work on the draft amendment by Byrnes, Pittman, and others in the office of the Foreign Relations Committee. On the

* Mitchell, *Depression Decade,* pp. 137–38.

† See Chapter 32 for the reasons for and history of these conferences in Washington.

twentieth Douglas accepted the inevitable with certain reservations. These he urged upon the President, and two were accepted, which appear in the first two provisions of the revised Thomas amendment. They stipulate that in certain contingencies the President should direct the Secretary of the Treasury to negotiate with the Federal Reserve banks to conduct open-market operations in the obligations of the Federal government to an amount not to exceed $3 billion, the object being to put more lending power into the banks. If, however, the Federal Reserve Board and banks refused to do this, the President had other alternatives. One of these would be to issue $3 billion in greenbacks under an act of February 25, 1862, for the purpose of retiring outstanding Federal obligations. Such notes, once issued, "should be legal tender for all debts public or private." They were to be retired, however, at the rate of 4 per cent annually.

But as indicated above, the President had an abundant collection of powers to promote inflation. Finally, the Federal Reserve Act was amended to permit the Federal Reserve Board to increase or decrease, "at its discretion, the reserve balances required to be maintained against either demand or time deposits." *

The new version of the Thomas amendment was adopted by the Senate on April 28 by a vote of 64 to 21, and the House passed it on May 3 by a vote of 307 to 86. Meanwhile, with Roosevelt's executive orders in April prohibiting the export of gold, the United States was definitely off the gold standard. On June 5 the President signed a joint resolution of Congress that abrogated the gold clause in public and private contracts. This was the logical conclusion of the many earlier executive and legislative actions.†

The permission granted to fix the value of gold in terms of dollars was not used until later when the price was fixed at $35 an ounce, which was less than the statute permitted. The provision, largely the invention of Pittman, by which the President was permitted to accept silver to the amount of $200 million at a price of 50 cents an ounce was not extensively used, although the last installment from Britain, which I negotiated, accepted silver in an amount of $7 million in value as a token payment of $10 million in June. The greenback permission was never used.

* Byrnes, *op. cit.*, pp. 77–78.

† In 1935 the Supreme Court sustained these various actions in full. It held that the gold clauses in private contracts were invalid because they were in violation of the constitutional power of Congress to fix the value of its money. So far as the abrogation of the gold clause in its own securities was concerned, the government had exceeded its powers, but plaintiffs could claim no recourse because they had not shown loss. The minority of the Court spoke of its "abhorrence" at the "repudiation and spoliation of citizens by their sovereign." With this minority opinion many responsible people agreed, notably Carter Glass.

A great deal has been written and said about Roosevelt's belief at that time in the idea of Professor George F. Warren of Cornell, that prices could be regulated from time to time by changes in the value of gold. I heard nothing from Roosevelt about the Warren theory in those days in the spring, but later, in August, he began to toy with the idea of using it to raise prices, which had lagged in midsummer after the early rise. By October he fully embraced it, but after a few months' trial it proved ineffectual and was abandoned.

I still believe, as I did when the Thomas amendment was revised and accepted and also in 1939 when I wrote my account in *After Seven Years*, that Roosevelt's course in accepting the abandonment of gold was the inevitable consequence of all that had happened before. The pressure of inflationary sentiment was the major reason for Roosevelt's decisions regarding money matters in April. Rationalization, the business of making a virtue of necessity, came after the decisions were made. It is true that these rationalizations were to become the intellectual channels through which an absurd monetary policy was adopted in October, when, in the vernacular, Roosevelt decided to give the Warren theory "a whirl." The absurdity of this action was made greater, and Roosevelt gravely marred his image as a responsible statesman, by the early-morning bedside guesses with Morgenthau about what the price of gold was to be "that day."

It is true that Roosevelt had a comforting way of rationalizing, then and later, his more serious blunders, just as he tried ineffectively later to excuse his blasting of the London Conference in July. But his critics even to our own day are also misusing reason when they blame the decisions in early 1933 as the root cause of the disastrous fiscal policies that still afflict us.

Those critics fail to grasp the meaning of the climate in which we were working in those spring days in 1933. There was a preponderant sentiment in Congress for almost any sort of device to raise prices and to correct the devastating deflation, which had gone on since the dawn of 1930. Washington had as its guests in those early weeks of the Administration almost every survivor of those radical movements of the past, including Populists and Greenbackers. Even such a powerful influence as Arthur Brisbane, who wrote daily in scores of newspapers, was calling for fiat money. The fact that Wheeler's proposal to resurrect the panaceas of Bryanism came so close to adoption must prove the reality of Congressional sentiment favoring anything that looked like inflation. I am willing to accept—I was then—Carter Glass's characterization of Thomas, Wheeler, and others as "wild men." But they were men with whom we had to deal. And they were tremendously influential in a bewildered and harassed Congress. I felt that Roosevelt's incredible skill in dealing with personalities and situations could frustrate these extremists better than could any economic fundamentalist. And he succeeded beyond the expectations of almost everyone around him.

It is ironic that since 1933 the real menace to fiscal soundness has been the very thing that Roosevelt so seriously sought to grapple with in his economy bill. Deficit financing has proved to be the peril that we have faced for the past quarter of a century. Budget deficits have become common practice. And in the Administration of President Kennedy deficits were accepted not as a burden to be endured, but a blessing to be cherished. The trouble began four years after 1933, when Roosevelt's appetite for reform outran his capacity for assimilation, and the progressive reforms that we designed in the early New Deal gave way to a belief in spending. This at first made Roosevelt its captive and then found in him its eager proponent.

Chapter Twenty-five

Toward a Responsible Securities Market

THE Securities Act, which was signed by the President on May 27, 1933, differed in three important respects from the farm legislation and the National Industrial Recovery Act:

1. As it was written in 1933, it was regarded as a reform designed to be a permanent means for Federal policing of the issuance and sale of securities. It had its constitutional basis in the interstate commerce clause. Its impact on the economy was negative and it retarded recovery.

2. It was conceived and drafted by individuals who subscribed to a public philosophy entirely different from that held by the planners who were so prominent in the farm and industrial legislation. There was a deep split in the early New Deal between the so-called Brandeis school —consisting of Frankfurter, Samuel Untermyer, James M. Landis, and Benjamin V. Cohen—and believers in national economic planning like Hugh Johnson, Tugwell, and Wallace. Roosevelt, who held no firm convictions on either side, believed that in the interest of experimentation both should have a hand in what was going on.

3. While the AAA and NRA successfully promoted recovery, at least in the first year, the Securities Act proved to be a grave mistake. The drastic nature of its terms so constricted the business of selling securities that it had only a negative effect upon recovery. Perhaps this freezing of the securities market would have been inevitable. For an impoverished public had little to invest. In any event, recovery in the securities market had to wait until a much more workable measure was drafted and enacted, the Securities Exchange Act.

Some accounts assume that the Securities Act was passed as the result of the public indignation generated by the sensational investigation of banking and investment practices by Senator Duncan Fletcher's Senate Banking and Currency Committee with Ferdinand Pecora as its counsel. It is true that this investigation revealed some of the practices that the securities legislation was designed to prevent. However, it more directly emphasized the necessity for the reforms enacted in the Glass-Steagall Act, which was signed on June 16.

But Roosevelt nearly a year earlier had made securities selling an issue in the campaign. He called for reforms in a radio address at Albany on July 30, 1932, and at Columbus on August 30. In the Columbus speech he said, largely following the provisions in the Democratic platform:

> Government cannot prevent some individuals from making errors of judgment. But Government can prevent to a very great degree the fooling of sensible people through misstatements and through the withholding of information on the part of private organizations, great and small, which seek to sell investments to the people of the Nation.
>
> First—Toward that end and to inspire truth telling, I propose that every effort be made to prevent the issue of manufactured and unnecessary securities of all kinds which are brought out merely for the purpose of enriching those who handle their sale to the public; and I further propose that with respect to legitimate securities the sellers shall tell the uses to which the money is to be put. This truth telling requires that definite and accurate statements be made to the buyers in respect to the bonuses and commissions the sellers are to receive; and, furthermore, true information as to the investment of principal, as to the true earnings, true liabilities and true assets of the corporation itself.
>
> Second—We are well aware of the difficulty and often the impossibility under which State Governments have labored in the regulation of holding companies that sell securities in interstate commerce. It is logical, it is necessary and it is right that Federal power be applied to such regulation.
>
> Third—For the very simple reason that the many exchanges in the business of buying and selling securities and commodities can by the practical expedient of moving elsewhere avoid regulation by any given State, I propose the use of Federal authority in the regulation of these exchanges.
>
> Fourth—The events of the past three years prove that the supervision of national banks for the protection of the public has been ineffective. I propose vastly more rigid supervision.
>
> Fifth—We have witnessed not only the unrestrained use of bank deposits in speculation to the detriment of local credit, but we are also aware that this speculation was encouraged by the Government itself. I propose that such speculation be discouraged and prevented.
>
> Sixth—Investment banking is a legitimate business. Commercial banking is another wholly separate and distinct business. Their consolidation and mingling are contrary to public policy. I propose their separation.
>
> Seventh—Prior to the panic of 1929 the funds of the Federal Reserve System were used practically without check for many speculative enterprises.

I propose the restriction of Federal Reserve Banks in accordance with the original plans and earlier practices of the Federal Reserve System under Woodrow Wilson.

Finally, my friends, I propose two new policies for which legislation is not required. They are policies of fair and open dealing on the part of the officials of the American Government with the American investing public.

This remembered pledge came long before the Fletcher-Pecora investigation. And the President's efforts to have a securities act drafted began in March, while the more sensational revelations of the Fletcher committee came in April and May. Some discussion of methods had preceded the inauguration. The amputation of the investment affiliates from the banks was already written in the Glass bill in the Seventy-second Congress.

Samuel Untermyer of New York, whose fabulous career at the bar made him famous for sixty years, had studied the practices involved in the issuance and sale of securities for a long time. In 1912 he had served as counsel for an investigation by the House Committee on Banking and Currency. This was renowned as the Pujo investigation of the "money trust." It had considerably shaken up the financial world. Untermyer's skill as a lawyer, his reform preachments, his colorful personality, and his capacity to draw the attention of the press and the public made him one of the talked-about figures of his time. He was also one of the most controversial individuals who ever lived.

A year and a half before Roosevelt's election I had first encountered Untermyer. Judge Samuel Seabury, after a sensational investigation of the New York City magistrates' courts, had been commissioned by Governor Roosevelt to investigate the New York County district attorney's office. The district attorney at that time was an elderly ex-judge, Thomas T. Crain. Seabury employed me to present a statistical analysis of the official record of the district attorney's office under Crain. I served in this investigation as Seabury's principal witness.

Untermyer was Crain's attorney, and after I had presented the case for Crain's removal he subjected me to two days of intensive cross-examination. Although in the end Seabury failed to recommend the removal of Crain, I believed, and a large part of the press agreed, that I had proved my case. But Untermyer had been a formidable opponent. Seabury let Crain off with a severe criticism, and he was not renominated by the Democratic organization.

From that point, incidentally, the career of Thomas E. Dewey began; first, as a special representative of the governor and, later, as district attorney.

My passage at arms with Untermyer had considerable attention in the press and established what I believed to be a mutual respect, which developed into a sort of friendship. Therefore, after Roosevelt had recommended remedial securities legislation, I had many letters from and conferences with Untermyer on that subject.

I greatly welcomed his help because I realized that Untermyer, beyond dispute, had more knowledge and more constructive ideas about reform than anyone else.

On December 7, 1932, Untermyer pointed out in a letter that he had been "trying for over twenty years to bring about Federal regulation of the Stock Exchange." He said that such legislation had been one of the fourteen recommendations of the Pujo committee. Twelve of these had been enacted into law, but efforts to regulate the New York Stock Exchange had failed.

On December 21 I asked Untermyer to communicate further with me on the subject. (He had already sent me the Pujo report.) I said in my letter: "I spoke to the Governor last week about the necessity for some planning with regard to the enactment into law of his campaign pledges regarding the regulation of the Stock Exchange and securities issues, and we agreed it would be most wise to ask you to give some thought to the subject and while on your vacation . . . to communicate your suggestions to me."

Then, because of the pressure of other work and a short illness, I put Untermyer in touch with Adolf Berle and Charles Taussig. The latter had been of some help in the campaign and was associated in business with Berle.

For a while things went smoothly enough as Untermyer got down to work. In early January he wrote telling me that in December he had turned down an offer from Senator Norbeck to act as counsel for the Senate Committee on Banking and Currency in the lame-duck Congress in an investigation that had been the subject of a Congressional resolution. Untermyer said he was unhappy about "the circumstances surrounding the organization of the Committee" and doubted that its personnel were "such as would furnish the proper scope and authority for a thorough investigation as the basis for constructive remedial legislation."

I suspected, however, that Untermyer's reluctance to participate in the projected Senate investigation was based less on these objections than his desire to assume a stellar role in formulating a new securities and exchange bill for Roosevelt.

On March 4 Senator Fletcher assumed the chairmanship of the Banking and Currency Committee and thereafter conducted the investigation, with Ferdinand Pecora as counsel.

However, in mid-January Taussig had written a letter to Untermyer saying that "it would be desirable to continue the investigation after March 4th under the aegis of the new administration, and I think it would be fine if you act as counsel for the committee."

Taussig had no authority for making such a suggestion. He was serving as my representative and I was serving Roosevelt, and neither Roosevelt nor I had any thought of suggesting to a Congressional committee that they employ any specific individual as counsel. But Taussig's letter led Untermyer to believe that we were behind the suggestion, for on March 5 he wrote to me that "as soon as the Committee is re-constituted, if it desires to have me go forward with an investigation in the first instance in support of the proposed legislation, I shall be prepared to do so."

In my reply I gave no encouragement to Untermyer's ambition to serve as counsel for the Fletcher committee, but to avoid any further indiscretions on Taussig's part I suggested that Untermyer henceforth direct his correspondence to me alone. While I believed that, even then and despite Roosevelt's popularity, there would be opposition in the Senate committee to any interference from the White House in its choice of counsel, I realized that Untermyer would have been preferable to the man ultimately selected. For Ferdinand Pecora's experience had been that of an assistant district attorney in a generally incompetent office. This I knew because of my own investigation of that office two years before, when I was working for Seabury.

Untermyer shared my doubts about Pecora. In a telegram to Taussig on March 1 he said that the mere exposure of Wall Street's sins would produce sensational headlines but would serve no useful purpose in laying the basis of constructive reform. He added that "Pecora unfortunately understands absolutely nothing about intricate exchange machinery and could not lay foundation."

Taussig, who sent me a copy of Untermyer's telegram, noted that according to Senator Costigan the committee "will engage Untermyer if requested to by F. D. R." But F. D. R. had no such idea in mind.

The first specific step toward securities and exchange legislation had been a draft bill sent to me by Untermyer on January 18, 1933. This bill would have placed the regulatory machinery in the Post Office Department, an obvious attempt to guarantee the measure's constitutionality. I had told Untermyer—and Roosevelt agreed—that it would be unwise to burden what was essentially a service organization with such a complex system of regulation. The idea of thrusting an immense regulatory machine into the midst of the Post Office Department violated my sense of administrative efficiency and legal responsibility. Untermyer, however, did not agree.

After talking with Roosevelt, I concluded that Untermyer could be of valuable assistance in the drafting of a bill, and with Roosevelt's express consent I conducted the correspondence with Untermyer through February and early March.

In mid-March, however, I suddenly discovered that the President had asked Attorney General Cummings and Secretary Roper to prepare securities legislation. They had brought in Huston Thompson of the Federal Trade Commission, and Thompson had already prepared a bill.

I am sure that Roosevelt brought in Cummings, Roper, and Thompson not to cause embarrassment but, rather, through sheer forgetfulness. It was not unusual for the President to ask several people to perform the same task, only to find himself confronted with a multiplicity of proposals. It was equally typical of Roosevelt to resolve such a situation by bringing everyone together "around the conference table," where he could soothe injured feelings and compromise all differences.

The Thompson bill provided, quite sensibly, that the regulatory machinery be placed under the Federal Trade Commission, but otherwise it was seriously deficient. For it dealt with securities marketing only, whereas Untermyer's bill embraced also the regulation of stock and commodity exchanges. The Thompson bill, moreover, was deficient in legal draftsmanship and displayed a lack of knowledge of finance. Nevertheless, I arranged for a meeting of the principal parties with Roosevelt on Sunday, March 26.

That peace conference was a frost. Untermyer was openly contemptuous of the Thompson bill, and Thompson kept shooting at the weakness of the Untermyer suggestion that regulation be placed in the Post Office Department. Untermyer's views were incorporated in a letter to Attorney General Cummings, which excoriated the Thompson bill as "mischievous besides being quite unnecessary." Untermyer, however, cooled off sufficiently to include in his measure some of the provisions from the Cummings-Roper-Thompson bill.

Apparently, Roosevelt's thought was to permit Thompson to draft a securities measure and let Untermyer proceed with another bill regulating the stock and commodity exchanges. He decided that there would be time for both, or that if Untermyer could not deliver his bill in the time remaining in the session, it could go over to the next year. It proved to be unfortunate that he let the whole subject go over for a year. For the division between the two subjects was impractical and there was not sufficient time to create legislation that involved such highly technical and detailed questions of administration.

However, Roosevelt, abundantly equipped with optimism, blithely submitted a message to Congress, which I composed with some misgivings, calling for "Federal supervision of traffic in investment securities in interstate commerce."

A few days later, the Thompson bill was introduced in both houses of Congress. Members assumed that this was the legislation Roosevelt had in mind.

Immediately there arose a storm of protest from lawyers and bankers. I received such protests in letters, telegrams, and personal calls. I recognized the justification of these complaints, for Thompson had produced a hopeless and unintelligible confection. But I could do nothing but refer the complaints to the respective chairmen of the two committees on interstate commerce, Senator Dill and Congressman Rayburn.

Rayburn said that he and his committee had examined the Thompson bill and did not like it. He asked me to get someone else to draft a new bill. I decided to call upon Frankfurter.

In response to my call he asked me to send him a copy of the Thompson bill and added that "three of us will arrive at the Carlton Friday morning. Please reserve room for us."

The three consisted of Frankfurter, James M. Landis, a junior member of the Harvard Law School faculty, and Benjamin V. Cohen. Cohen, Frankfurter said, had had experience in the drafting of state laws.

It was my first meeting with Landis and Cohen, who were destined to remain in Washington for many years and gain celebrity. On that morning I noted only that they were very serious young men, impressed with the assignment that so unexpectedly had come to them. This was my first impression. But after they had been working with Rayburn's committee and staff—especially with Middleton Beaman and on the periphery Thomas G. Corcoran, who was already serving, despite his job with the RFC, as a Frankfurter general-utility man in Washington—I had further impressions. They entertained a deep suspicion of bankers, of Wall Street lawyers, and of corporation lawyers in general. Rayburn gave them wide latitude in the drafting, and the bill that finally emerged was their own product.

On the day of their arrival, after Cohen and Landis left for Rayburn's office, I had a talk with Frankfurter. I told him of the various objections to the Thompson bill by the lawyers and bankers from New York, some of whom he knew. Frankfurter, despite his suspicions about the self-interest of the big New York law firms, agreed that the bill about to be drafted for Rayburn's committee should enjoy the benefit of consultation with people who were experienced in the securities business. One banker, W. Averell Harriman, I knew quite well and I brought him and Frankfurter together. Both seemed to agree that the British Companies Act, which was at that time nearly a century old, might well be the model. Harriman then proposed two of his lawyer friends as consultants with Landis and Cohen. These were Arthur H. Dean and Alexander I. Henderson.

With the assurance from Frankfurter that Henderson and Dean would be acceptable as consultants to Landis and Cohen, I had reason to believe that a fair and workable bill would be prepared. I had neither the knowledge of the technical subject nor the inclination to intrude on the actual composition of the bill, but I was concerned to see that the lawyers actually would work together. And Rayburn and his committee were favorable to cooperation with practical people in or close to the securities market.

Rayburn insisted that Henderson and Dean be consulted, and Landis and Cohen agreed with them to eliminate some but not all of the provisions in their draft to which the New York lawyers objected.*

There was little agreement between the Frankfurter protégés and the New York lawyers, and at one point Frankfurter telephoned to say that even Landis and Cohen were getting on each other's nerves. But a bill was whipped out and, without hearings, Rayburn secured the affirmative vote of his committee. Its passage in the House was easily accomplished, since Rayburn had endorsed it and members were unacquainted with the subject matter. All they knew was that it was a measure to provide Federal supervision of securities marketing under the Federal Trade Commission.

The parliamentary situation was seriously complicated because the Thompson bill was making progress in the Senate. I received two frantic telegrams from Frankfurter on April 27 and 28 characterizing the Thompson bill as "innocuous and unconstitutional" and urging: "It is really vital to avoid progress on the Thompson bill until the House gets and passes its bill. Am aware of the exigencies that press upon the President's time but urge strongly his intervention to prevent jam and jeopardy of his securities regulation proposal."

Whatever the merits of the arguments of the people from New York who objected to the House bill, it was apparent that some means must be found to sidetrack the Thompson bill. I immediately talked with Majority Leader Robinson and Jim Byrnes. On April 29 Robinson wrote to Frankfurter: "In re your telegram to Mr. Moley criticizing the Securities Bill as reported by the Senate Committee on Banking and Currency. . . . In all probability we will not proceed to legislate on the subject until the House has acted. This I understand is in conformity with your suggestion."

With a remarkable exercise of parliamentary skill, Robinson and Byrnes contrived to have the Thompson bill pass in the Senate, after which it went to conference. Then when the House bill was passed, it was substituted for the Thompson bill in conference and passed by both houses. The President signed the measure on May 27.

* In Schlesinger's *The Coming of the New Deal,* p. 442, it is recorded that John Foster Dulles of the big law firm of Sullivan and Cromwell was selected by some of the New York lawyers to confer with Landis and Cohen. I have no specific recollection of this, but it is possible, for many emissaries from New York came down to consult with Rayburn and his Harvard draftsmen, and Dulles may have been among them. Schlesinger naïvely comments that Dulles was "ill-informed about the problem." This is an amazing statement, for Dulles had spent his life in this field and Landis and Cohen had only theoretical equipment.

Frankfurter sent me a congratulatory telegram: "Your constant help was indispensable in obtaining sound securities bill." I appreciated the compliment. But I had grave doubts about how the bill would work.

Despite my sympathy for Roosevelt's effort to redeem his campaign promise to reform the marketing of securities, certain serious and realistic considerations presented themselves. Certainly the government possessed the power and the duty to protect the investor. But the process of selling was in the hands of the people who were subjected to regulation. These people believed the law to be unfair and unworkable. They also believed that the people who had drafted it and who had cavalierly rejected their well-meant advice were ill-informed about the realities of the market.

Here a fundamental appeared that is relevant to any legislative act. The bill lacked the consent of the governed. I once defined this term as it applies to all legislation:

> What, then, is consent? Is it mere resignation to the inevitable? . . . Is it agreement secured under duress? . . . In the long history of the common law, which is still in large measure the application of common sense and fruits of experience to human situations, these questions are answered in the negative. . . . Consent is real when those involved freely, knowingly, willingly, and with a part in creating the situation enter into the benefits and responsibilities of the situation. Consent is not present when a decision is made in the face of a virile and sizable opposition.*

It was clear that this bill lacked such consent. It had been hurried through with inadequate debate. There had been no hearings and, since it was adopted in conference, the Senate had little opportunity to consider the House bill. There had been deep distrust between the lawyers from Harvard and the lawyers in New York. I had been impressed by the arguments of individuals from New York in whom I had genuine confidence. They were not arguing against a bill. They realized that such Federal regulation was necessary and inevitable, but they objected to certain features in the bill which they felt were too drastic and, under conditions that existed in the market, unworkable.†

I was also convinced that this permanent reform had been an inappropriate one to push during a short session in which recovery should have enjoyed first priority.

Finally, I was uneasy because of Untermyer's contention that there should also have been provisions for regulating the stock exchanges. For this measure dealt only with the issuances of new securities and left

* Moley, *How to Keep Our Liberty* (New York: Alfred A. Knopf, 1952), p. 8.

† Two of the people in whom I had the most confidence were Robert A. Lovett of Brown Brothers, Harriman & Co. (who served later with distinction as the second Secretary of Defense in the Truman years) and William C. Breed, counsel for the Investment Bankers Association.

unregulated the market in which the vast bulk of securities already issued were bought and sold. This doubt soon was strengthened. By late May a dangerous speculative spree started in the exchanges, which ended with a sharp decline in mid-July.

There had been time to wait, for people simply did not have much money to invest.

But with the new law on the books, the Federal Trade Commission was measurably reorganized. Landis, Robert E. Healy, and George G. Mathews were appointed, presumably to dominate the enforcement of securities selling.

The outcome was exactly what the bankers and lawyers from New York had predicted. The market for new securities was virtually frozen during the year that followed. Bankers and lawyers were unwilling to advise investors to risk entanglement with a law that might be enforced with Draconic severity. For the new members of the FTC were regarded not only as amateurs but also as men possessed of irrational prejudice.

Undiscriminating people described the securities bill as the "Truth-in-Securities Act." And it was claimed that the failure of new securities issues was a "strike" by the people in Wall Street.

But as the year passed, even Roosevelt realized that the act in its existing form was unworkable and that a new bill with machinery to regulate the stock exchanges must have priority in the 1934 session of Congress. Rayburn, too, was convinced that something must be done to loosen up the constrictions of the original legislation and that its administration should be divorced from the Federal Trade Commission and vested in a new commission.

Chapter Twenty-six

Permanent Banking Reform

ON June 16, when Roosevelt signed the Glass-Steagall Act for permanent banking reform, he commented that "this bill has had more lives than a cat." It was the product of three years of prodigious labor by Carter Glass. He had fought off frustrations on every side. The farm bloc Senators sought advantages for the little banks and inflationary money policies in terms that suggested the Populist tirades of the late years of the nineteenth century. The big bankers, who resisted change, had seemingly been oblivious to the shady practices in their midst until Senator Fletcher's investigation revealed them to the public. Hoover as President agreed with Glass's ideas up to a point, but disagreed sufficiently to delay action. Roosevelt until his inauguration had been only casually interested in banking problems, and after the bank crisis had subsided he was too busy to take much interest in what Glass was doing in the Senate. Moreover, he realized that if he interfered he might find himself in an argument with the venerable Virginian.

In 1931, after nearly a year's effort, Glass formulated a series of reforms which included most of the features of the bill which finally was passed two years later.* In 1932 Glass made some progress but the Senate leadership, anticipating the impending political campaign, removed the Glass bill from the calendar. Then the campaign and the recess of Congress brought about another delay. The lame-duck session saw the bill reinstated on the Senate calendar, but amendments so crippled the measure that when the Senate voted for it in January it was clearly an unsatisfactory measure, and debate was resumed immediately.

* Smith and Beasley, *Carter Glass,* pp. 304–305.

During most of February, Senators Huey Long and Elmer Thomas staged a filibuster that almost drove Glass to desperation. And then for three weeks emergency banking legislation and the Thomas amendment fully occupied the attention of Glass and other supporters of the bill.

Meanwhile, the Fletcher hearings unearthed so many irresponsible, even scandalous, practices that by June Glass found his efforts supported by an aroused public opinion. And so his bill was finally passed by both houses during the final days of the Hundred Days Congress.

The Glass-Steagall Act of 1933 can hardly be classed as a New Deal measure. Roosevelt was sympathetic, but had no active part in pressing for its passage. Most of the people who were close to the White House in April and May were so busy with their own legislative programs that Glass was left to his own devices.

This narrative, for that reason, is not concerned with the legislative history or details of the bill, except for the final inclusion of the provision for a Federal guarantee of bank deposits, which was widely discussed during the crisis but was opposed by Roosevelt.

The major features of the bill as finally passed were these:

1. The Federal Reserve Board was given wide authority to prevent speculation in securities, real estate, and commodities. But this was supplemented by the Administration's Securities Act, an integral part of the Roosevelt program, which had been passed in late May.

2. Payment of interest on demand deposits by member banks was prohibited, thereby eliminating a dangerous form of competition for deposits.

3. Beginning on January 1, 1934, no officer or director of a member bank could serve as an officer, partner, or director of a security-selling firm or a private bank, and by June 1934 no member bank was allowed more than twenty-five directors.

4. Mutual savings and Morris Plan banks were made eligible for membership in the Federal Reserve System.

5. National banks were put on a parity with state banks in branch banking operations.

6. It was provided that within a year member banks were required to divorce their security affiliates and private banks were required to stop selling securities. If they chose to keep their deposit business, they must submit to periodic examinations.

This divorcement of commercial banking from securities selling was a long-overdue reform. It was shown in the Fletcher hearings that securities selling had been the root of many of the discreditable practices which had shaken public confidence in banks generally. This reform—the divorcement of commercial banks from their securities affiliates—had been a part of the 1932 Democratic platform. It had also been a major purpose of Glass from the beginning.

Finally, and most important of all in its contribution to bank stability, was the addition to the Glass bill of an amendment providing for the Federal guarantee of bank deposits. This had been considered during the bankers' meetings during the holiday, and Jesse Jones had strongly favored it. But Roosevelt was opposed to it, and there was insufficient time to incorporate it in the emergency banking legislation.

Jones had been an early advocate of this reform and had supported it from the moment he had joined the RFC in early 1932. When Glass reported his bill in January 1932, Jones discussed the subject with John N. Garner, then Speaker of the House. Garner was most sympathetic and said that both Glass and Hoover had ignored this most important element in creating depositors' confidence. Garner talked with Henry B. Steagall, chairman of the House Banking and Currency Committee. Later, in April, Steagall told Garner of the political popularity that such a measure would enjoy, saying, "This fellow Hoover is going to wake up someday and come in here with a message recommending the guarantee of bank deposits; and, as sure as he does, he'll be reelected." *

Garner agreed, and Steagall cleared a bill with his committee and secured its passage by the House on May 25, 1932. But in the rush to adjourn before the party conventions, both the Glass bill and Steagall's were passed over.

After the election and when the bank crisis grew more ominous, Garner and Senate Majority Leader Robinson conferred with Hoover and Mills. Instead of a deposit guarantee, the Glass bill had a provision at that time for a lending corporation to speed up payments to depositors in closed banks. They all agreed at that time that in the emergency the Glass bill should be passed without delay. And when Garner and Robinson later met with Roosevelt there seemed to be no objection by the President-elect.

Later, Roosevelt told Garner that he had decided not to agree. Garner then told Hoover of his regret that he could not carry out the agreement.

In February, Hoover had written to the Federal Reserve Board, asking its opinion about "some form of Federal guarantee of bank deposits." The board replied that it "is not at this time prepared to recommend any form of Federal guarantee of bank deposits." †

In Bascom N. Timmons' authorized biography, written during Jesse Jones's lifetime and with complete access to the Jones papers, there is this account:

> On March 3 Franklin D. Roosevelt arrived in Washington for his inauguration, when the bank crisis was at its height. Speaker Garner, who was to become Vice-President the next day, accompanied by Senator Augustine

* Bascom N. Timmons, *Jesse H. Jones,* p. 177.

† Hoover, *Memoirs,* Vol. III, pp. 211–12.

Lonergan, of Connecticut, called on the President-elect at the Mayflower to make another appeal. Garner held hope that, if Roosevelt would not agree to the broad-scoped Glass Bill, he might at least agree to deposit guarantee.

"We passed the Steagall Deposit-Insurance Law in the House nine or ten months ago," Garner said to Roosevelt, "and it is still in the Senate Committee. Hoover is now for some sort of guarantee. If you will support it, we can get together on a bill and have it the law of the land when you take office."

Again Roosevelt refused his consent. "It won't work, Jack," he said. "The weak banks will pull down the strong."

Garner replied, "They are about all down now anyway, the weak and the strong. You will have to come to a deposit guarantee eventually, Cap'n." *

There the subject stood until immediately after the holiday, when Jones, who was indefatigable in his determination to see this reform enacted, found unexpected support from a stalwart and respected Republican Senator, Arthur H. Vandenberg. The Michigan Senator gave Jones a copy of his deposit guarantee plan. Jones said, "Give us some legislation like that, and the people will put their money in the banks instead of stuffing it in their socks. A man ought to be able to insure his bank deposits against loss, just as he can insure his home against fire loss. In time, accounts should be insured up to 10,000 dollars. But start with 2500 dollars immediately. That will care for most depositors." †

Jones told Vice-President Garner of the Vandenberg conversation but thought no more of it for some time.

On May 19, 1933, the Senate, with its heavy calendar of emergency legislation, was sitting as a court of impeachment in the trial of Harold Louderback, a district judge.

Vice-President John Nance Garner, who was presiding over the court, left his chair on the dais and walked down to the seat of Senator Vandenberg on the Republican side. The Vandenberg amendment would accomplish about what Garner had expected to accomplish in the Steagall bill which he pushed through the House in 1932.

"Arthur," Garner inquired, "how fast can you get on your feet?"

"As quick as any man in the Senate, I think," Vandenberg replied.

"You'll have to do a damn sight better than that," said Garner. "You have to be *faster* than anyone. Where's that deposit-insurance amendment of yours?"

"It's never been out of my pocket," said Vandenberg.

"Well, I am going to suspend this court in a few minutes and go into session of the Senate, and recognize Carter Glass to bring up some more banking legislation. I want you to get on your feet and get your amendment out of your pocket, and I think we will get it in the bill," Garner said.

* Timmons, *op. cit.,* p. 184.

† *Ibid.,* p. 193.

Vandenberg said he would be alert.

"All right," continued Garner. "I am going to look for you. My best eye is the one I use on the Republican side of the chamber; and besides, with fifty-nine Democrats and thirty-seven Republicans, there is less congestion on your side, and you are big enough for me to see."

In a few minutes the court suspended and the Senate began considering the Glass-Steagall Banking Bill. Garner again went to Vandenberg's seat.

"I was just talking to Carter Glass," the Vice-President said. "Next to me, he is the most cantankerous man in the world; but he is in good humor now, and I don't think he will fight your amendment too hard."

With Garner sitting in the seat next to him, Vandenberg offered his amendment to insure immediately bank deposits up to 2500 dollars. It was overwhelmingly adopted.

When the bill reached conference between Senate and House, President Roosevelt sent a note to the conference asking that they reject the Vandenberg amendment in toto. The conference refused the demand of the President.

The new banking law creating the Federal Deposit Insurance Corporation was signed by President Roosevelt on June 16, despite his objection to the Vandenberg amendment.*

In all the years after, Jones regarded this as a profoundly important banking reform. Ironically, Roosevelt, despite his last-ditch opposition, in later years claimed credit for the legislation.

In their *Monetary History of the United States, 1867–1960,* Milton Friedman and Anna J. Schwartz say that "Federal insurance of bank deposits was the most important structural change to result from the 1933 panic, and, indeed in our view, the structural change most conducive to monetary stability since state bank notes were taxed out of existence immediately after the Civil War." †

In an article on the deposit guarantee legislation of 1933, Carter H. Golembe quite correctly points out that this reform "was the only important piece of legislation during the New Deal's famous 'one hundred days' which was neither requested nor supported by the new Administration. Deposit insurance was purely a creature of Congress. For almost fifty years members had been attempting to secure legislation to this end, without success; while in individual states the record of experimentation with bank-obligation insurance systems dated back more than a century." ‡

It was the indifferent success or failure of the early efforts of states to provide deposit insurance to which Roosevelt, Glass, and others pointed in opposing the idea in early 1933.

* *Ibid.*, pp. 194–95.

† Friedman and Schwartz, *op. cit.*, p. 434.

‡ *Political Science Quarterly,* June 1960, pp. 181–82.

The Vandenberg amendment, which was incorporated in the Glass bill, provided for a temporary system of deposit insurance preceding the adoption on July 1, 1934, of a permanent system. This temporary period was extended to July 1, 1935, by legislation adopted in 1934. Finally, the system in approximately its present form was incorporated in the Banking Act of 1935.

The Vandenberg amendment merely superimposed a new agency, the Federal Deposit Insurance Corporation. All banks that were members of the Federal Reserve System were required to have their deposits insured by the FDIC; but non-member banks might be admitted by the corporation. This authority contributed greatly to the persuasive capacity of Jones to have banks enlarge their capital by RFC loans in late 1933 and early 1934. At first, insurance was limited to a maximum of $2,500. Beginning on July 1, 1934, the maximum was raised to $5,000, and in 1950 to $10,000, which has been in effect since.

Since 1950, the FDIC has had the right to make examinations of banks at its own discretion. Thus, at least in principle, member banks are subject to examination by three agencies: the Federal Reserve System; the comptroller of the currency if they are national banks, or their state banking authorities if they are state banks; and the FDIC. Non-member banks are subject to examination by two agencies: state banking authorities and the FDIC.

Federal deposit insurance has certainly contributed measurably to a sensational decline in bank failures and in losses by depositors. According to the calculations by Friedman and Schwartz, the number of suspensions per year from 1921 to 1933 inclusive ranged from 366 to the panic year 1933 when 4,000 suspended. The losses by depositors in those years ranged from $38,000,000 to $540,000,000. From 1934 to 1960, the number of bank suspensions was at no time higher than 82 (in 1937), and down to only two in 1960, while losses by depositors declined in the same proportion. In those 27 years there were seven during which no losses at all were borne by depositors. And the loss to depositors per $100 of deposits was negligible.

These statistics are the coldly drawn proof of Jones's remarkable sense of public psychology. He realized that panic comes when those whose small deposits represent the difference between security and need are the victims of fear. Thus, he believed that if small depositors could be assured, the dreadful impact of last-minute panic could be prevented.

Large depositors generally have means that are not measurably left in the care of the banks. The failure of a bank is less likely to spell their ruin. Such large depositors also have means of anticipating the approach of danger. They have expert advice, or they provide their own counsel. Big depositors can be talked to and reasoned with. But the "little fellows" are the ones who comprehend danger too late. And they are more susceptible to rumor which

> Doth double, like a voice and an echo,
> The numbers of the fear'd.

Therefore, the concept of insuring at a small maximum of deposits, such as $2,500 or $5,000 or $10,000, eliminates the peril of a panic from small depositors. And with this assurance, hundreds of banks that have crashed might have been saved.

I might add that the peril that haunts stock, or real estate, or commodity markets lies too often in the small owners or investors.

Chapter Twenty-seven

The Tennessee Valley Authority

THE Tennessee Valley Authority had little to do with the surge of economic recovery that began with the successful conclusion of the bank crisis. It was not proposed as experimental or temporary, as were most of the other measures passed in the Hundred Days, for it was an institution built for all time. Its benefits, the realization of which took a year or longer, affected only a relatively small proportion of the people of the nation. It was a new Federal agency that took over activities and interests that up to that time were within the province of various departments in Washington. The act was only incidentally a relief measure, and it could not provide more than a sprinkling of jobs in the critical year 1933.

But the spectacular originality of the plan more surely cemented the liberal elements in the country than anything else that Roosevelt proposed.* And because it excited the interest of those who believed in the "progressive" ideal of more Federal intervention in business and local government, it became a cherished monument to Roosevelt's statesmanship and his fame as a reformer.

Nevertheless, it was an oddity thrust among many other more immediately relevant measures which came to be known as the First New Deal.

Muscle Shoals had always been a section of the meandering Tennessee River that had been a barrier to river navigation. Because of the rapid movement of the water at that point, it provided a favorable

* The word "liberal" in its present meaning was then only beginning to supplant the old word "progressive."

spot for the construction of a dam or dams for navigation, flood control, and the generation of electric power.

Nitrates are useful not only for fertilizer but for the manufacture of explosives, and their production needs a large amount of electric power. Since explosives were in demand during the First World War, the Federal government decided to build a power-generating dam and a nitrate plant at Muscle Shoals. The war ended before these installations could be in operation, and they stood relatively unused in the years that followed. (The dam was named after President Wilson.)

In 1921 Senator George Norris began what was to be a long struggle in Congress to bring the projects to completion and to operate them directly by the Federal government. Norris was a dedicated exponent of government power production and distribution. In Nebraska he had been effective in having the state take over the major power company, and by the time he began the Muscle Shoals fight the entire state he represented was served by government-owned power.

There is ample evidence that until 1933 Norris was interested only in the power aspects of the project. He included navigation and flood control in his various bills to bring the project within the constitutional powers of the Federal government. Here, however, was a contradiction of purposes that has always attended Federal dam-building. For the way to prevent floods is to build dams that in normal times must be relatively empty. But for power production to attain maximum efficiency, the dam must be high and the reservoir above it must be full at all times. When there are floods, a dam with a full reservoir is incapable of capturing the flow. But a low dam with plenty of emergency reservoir space is incapable of producing much power.

Navigation through high dams must be accommodated by locks and by special channels. Moreover, in the Northwest, where fisheries constitute a major industry, ladders must be built to permit the passage of fish up and down the river.

The difference between power and flood-control purposes was well illustrated when the state of Ohio built extensive facilities for flood control after the disastrous Dayton flood in 1913. The dams built on the river carried plaques saying: "The dams of the Miami Conservancy District are for flood prevention purposes. Their use for power development or for storage would be a menace to the cities below." It is important to note that the engineer in charge of building these facilities was Dr. Arthur E. Morgan, later to become chairman of the TVA.

If both power and flood control are desired, there can be developed what are called multiple-purpose dams. In these instances, one dam is in reality built upon another dam. The high power dam is built first, with its full reservoir. Then a series of sluices is constructed, and the dam is built higher. When gates are installed to control these sluices, the human element enters and disaster ensues if the gates are not opened quickly enough. Multiple-purpose dams such as are now operating in the Tennessee Valley require reservoirs to store the water. These inundate the best sort of farm land. This sort of construction is very expensive.

In the early 1920's Henry Ford expressed a desire to lease the Muscle Shoals project. But Congress rejected his offer and resumed construction of the Wilson Dam and the nitrate plant. The hydro power component was completed in 1925. Thereupon the Alabama Power Company and a large chemical company sought to relieve the Federal government of what seemed an unproductive investment.

Senator Norris, however, opposed any plan for private operation and between 1921 and 1933 introduced nine bills providing for Federal ownership and operation. Six of these failed. One was vetoed by President Coolidge and another by President Hoover. The last of these bills was introduced when Congress met on March 9 to act upon the banking legislation.

From the time of the Reclamation Act of 1902, which had the strong support of President Theodore Roosevelt, the Federal government had been interested in river development. These early operations were for purposes of navigation and flood control. Irrigation was another function of these operations. All this was clearly within the constitutional province of the Federal government. But until the 1920's the power generated at these projects was small and incidental. However, it was provided by Congress that such power as was developed could be sold and the proceeds of the sale were to be put into the reclamation fund. In this legislation it was provided that in the sale of this power preference was to be given to "municipal purposes." Endless controversy developed as to what this expression meant. Was it merely intended to mean that cities and the people were to get the benefit of buying this power, or did it mean that it must be sold to municipally owned and operated agencies? In short, was it a declared policy of promoting public power activities by this preferred sale to smaller public power agencies? Ultimately, by Executive action and further legislation, it was decreed that in the sale of Federally generated power, preference should be given to public rather than private agencies. In practice it has meant that when a private company is dependent upon a contract with the Federal government for some of its power, it is compelled to yield if and when a public power agency demands it.

It is interesting that Herbert Hoover himself, as Secretary of Commerce, should have initiated the movement for comprehensive Federal planning of great river basins. This momentous suggestion was made in a speech in Seattle in 1926. Later, he initiated the building of the great dam and power installation in Black Canyon, which now bears his name. Secretary Ickes, possibly with the knowledge of Roosevelt, spitefully decided that this dam should not be called by the name of the former President, although Secretary Wilbur had so christened it. Ickes decided that it should be called Boulder Dam instead. Since Ickes and Roosevelt were in office when the dam was completed and dedicated in September 1935, they were the speakers on that occasion. A great deal of criticism had descended upon Ickes two years earlier when it was known that he intended to remove the name of Hoover, but in his speech at the dedication he carried out what he recorded in his diary in this way: "One thing I did in my speech was to try to nail down for good and all the name Boulder Dam." * His efforts were without permanent avail, for in 1947, when Republicans were in control of Congress, the name Hoover was restored by Congressional action.

The Hoover project, however, was carefully guarded by provisions for its operation. It should remain in Federal ownership and be administered by the Bureau of Reclamation. But under carefully drawn contracts before construction was started, the power generated was sold to the Los Angeles Department of Light and Power and the Southern California Edison Company. Under this arrangement, the original cost is being liquidated by the proceeds from the sales. These customers come to the "bus bar" of the dam for the power and thus eliminate the cost to the government of its own transmission lines.

Roosevelt, in his speech on power development in Portland in September 1932, used a text that I had prepared in collaboration with Senators Key Pittman and Thomas J. Walsh. He pledged his support to the Federal construction of four great dams—at Boulder Canyon (already in construction), Bonneville on the Columbia near Portland, Muscle Shoals in the Southeast, and St. Lawrence in the Northeast.

These were, he said, to be "national yardsticks" to facilitate the regulation of rates by government agencies. As I understood this term and as the Senators who collaborated with me in preparing the speech understood it, this meant that with the government operating such pilot operations it would be possible to learn more about costs than through the books of private companies. The expression which he also used in the speech was "the birch rod behind the door." This meant that if private companies failed to serve the public properly, the Federal government could enforce better service by threatening to serve it directly. But he made it clear that he had no intention to thrust the Federal government into competition with private enterprise:

> I state to you categorically that as a broad general rule the development of utilities should remain, with certain exceptions, a function for private initiative and private capital. . . . State owned or Federal owned power sites

* *The Secret Diary of Harold L. Ickes,* Vol. I (New York: Simon and Schuster, 1953), p. 445.

can and should and must be properly developed by Government itself. That has been my policy in the State of New York for four years. When so developed by Government, private capital should, I believe, be given the first opportunity to transmit and distribute the power on the basis of the best service and the lowest rates to give a reasonable profit only. The right of the Federal Government and State Governments to go further and to transmit and distribute whenever reasonable and good service is refused by private capital gives to Government—in other words, the people—that very same essential "birch rod" in the cupboard.

This speech and the policy enunciated were very well received by the very private companies that Senator Norris had been denouncing for years. It seemed to those of us at the time who were working on the speech—and, I believed, to Roosevelt himself—to be a gesture of cooperation and friendship. That is how the Roosevelt policy in the controversial field of electric power stood at the end of the campaign and, I assume, in the months of November and December.

But while the Portland speech served to prevent the eruption of a hot controversy that would involve many highly technical matters in the campaign, there were two factors that were certain to revive the subject after the election. One was that Norris was unhappy about Roosevelt's endorsement of the "birch rod" idea. He loyally supported Roosevelt in the campaign but still held firmly to his belief that the development of the Muscle Shoals project should include the construction by the Federal government of transmission lines to market the power directly to customers.

Another factor was Roosevelt's deep distrust of the private power companies. I had received a strong hint of this earlier in 1932 when Samuel I. Rosenman resigned as the governor's counsel to become a State Supreme Court judge by appointment of the governor. I suggested Robert H. Jackson (later Attorney General and U.S. Supreme Court Justice) as a replacement for Rosenman. Roosevelt rejected the suggestion because he said that Jackson was a public utility lawyer. I knew Jackson well because he and I had been members of the Commission on the Administration of Justice in New York, which was created in 1931. After Roosevelt's refusal to accept him as governor's counsel I asked Jackson what his relations with public utilities had been. He said the only utility he had represented had been the independent telephone system in Jamestown, where he lived.

I am not sure that between the election and the inauguration Roosevelt had conferred with Norris, but I learned later that he had talked at some length with Dr. Arthur E. Morgan. Morgan's ideas of what should be done in the Tennessee Valley extended not only to the Federal development of the power facilities of the Wilson Dam and the nitrate plant there, but to a vast Federal enterprise to improve the economic and social resources of the valley. Thus the plan as it developed in Roosevelt's mind was more of a creation of Morgan than of Norris, whose major concern was public power.

Roosevelt had not discussed this larger plan with me and I learned of it only in the newspapers when he presented it in preliminary rough form to reporters on the twenty-second of January, when he visited Muscle Shoals. Norris accompanied him, but was quite surprised when he heard of Roosevelt's expanded version of a project on which he had labored for many years. He was, however, tearfully overjoyed by this authentic support of his cause. On that day in January, Roosevelt told the reporters that he wanted to put Muscle Shoals "to work" and hinted broadly of some great government enterprise fitting together "industry, agriculture, forestry, and flood control."

On February 3 Roosevelt at Warm Springs elaborated his ideas about the Tennessee Valley proposal. He told reporters that he wanted "the widest experiment ever undertaken by a government." It would include reforestation, flood control, power development, restoration of land, elimination of sub-marginal land, implementation of navigation, and the attraction of industry by the inducement of cheap power. He even plunged into estimates of the amount of "horsepower" that would be available.

This out-Norrised Norris, for the Senator had not been interested in any phase of the development except power. On the other hand, Roosevelt had been talking with Senators and Congressmen in the region who were not much interested in power but wanted Federal help for the land through the production of nitrates. Senator Hugo Black had said, "I care nothing for the power, it is infinitesimal in importance." Thus, Roosevelt when confronted with several objectives, embraced all of them.

I had little to do with the TVA proposal. When I read the account of Roosevelt's Warm Springs press conference in the newspapers, I was so busy with many other assignments that I had little time to analyze the implications of what he said. I believed erroneously for a time that he merely had outlined this plan to supply cheering headlines at a moment when other news was scarce and the public was deeply disturbed by the mounting bank crisis.

But when I had my conference with Roosevelt on March 18, I learned that he was very serious about the plan and was determined to give it a prominent place among the proposals he intended to present to Congress. My first reaction to the idea was that since it involved a long-term project, it might well wait over until the next year. However, I made no comment on the plan at the time, and I do not remember, nor have I any record to show, that I had any part in preparing his message on the subject. A little later I suggested to him that, while the reactivation of the power facilities of the Wilson Dam was in line with the proposals of his Portland speech, it would be best to follow the course Congress had adopted at the time the Hoover Dam was built and sell the power at the "bus bar" under contract to public and private distributors. Roosevelt curtly answered that I should talk with George Norris. "It's his baby." I realized that this would be a waste of time.

I was not aware then that during the controversy in the 1920's over the disposition of Muscle Shoals, the United States Army Corps of Engineers had been directed to study the subject. In March 1930 the chief of the corps had sent a report to the House of Representatives, saying that if Congress decided that flood control was desirable in the Tennessee Valley, low single-purpose dams would be more effective and more economical than high multiple-purpose dams, for high dams would flood some 600,000 acres of good farm and timber land. The corps recommended that if power dams were constructed under licenses from the Federal Power Commission, the Federal government should assume only the cost of locks and minor work necessary for navigation. But when reform is under way, expert advice is ignored. And Congress passed the Norris bill.

On April 10 Roosevelt sent his message to Congress proposing the creation of a Tennessee Valley Authority. The word "authority" was borrowed from New York State, where it was used to designate certain institutions created by two states, New York and New Jersey, to operate tunnels and bridges connecting them. The text of the message put into general terms the glowing concepts Roosevelt had described in the earlier press conference:

> The continued idleness of a great national investment in the Tennessee Valley leads me to ask the Congress for legislation necessary to enlist this project in the service of the people.
>
> It is clear that the Muscle Shoals development is but a small part of the potential public usefulness of the entire Tennessee River. Such use, if envisioned in its entirety, transcends mere power development; it enters the wide field of flood control, soil erosion, afforestation, elimination from agricultural use of marginal lands, and distribution and diversification of industry. In short this power development of war days leads logically to national planning for a complete river watershed involving many States and the future lives and welfare of millions. It touches and gives life to all forms of human concern.
>
> I therefore suggest to the Congress legislation to create a Tennessee Valley Authority, a corporation clothed with the power of Government but possessed of the flexibility of a private enterprise. It should be charged with the broadest duty of planning for the proper use, conservation and development of the natural resources of the Tennessee River drainage basin and its adjoining territory for the general social and economic welfare of the Nation. . . . Its duty should be the rehabilitation of the Muscle Shoals development and the coordination of it with the wider plan . . . If we are

successful here we can march on, step by step, in a like development of other great natural territorial units within our borders.

Roosevelt's familiarity with power problems had largely been limited to his experience as governor of New York. In that state there had been a controversy for several years during the governorship of Alfred E. Smith. This centered largely in the relations of the state with the major company that was exploiting the power generated at Niagara Falls. There were economic factors at stake, but the subject was mainly political. For it was claimed by Democrats that the power interests, mainly in the northwestern part of the state, were very influential in Republican affairs. But there was little in this localized situation that might provide guidance in such an immense area as the Tennessee Valley. In carrying on Smith's controversy with the private power interests, Roosevelt had brought in as advisers a good many public-ownership zealots who had been prominent in their movement elsewhere.

On the day after Roosevelt's message went to Congress, two bills were introduced in the House. John E. Rankin introduced the Norris bill as a House measure and John J. McSwain of South Carolina, chairman of the Military Affairs Committee, introduced a quite different bill.

On the next day Ellison "Cotton Ed" Smith, chairman of the Senate Committee on Agriculture, without holding hearings reported the Norris bill and it was placed on the calendar for action.

Lister Hill, a member of the McSwain committee, introduced a bill that stressed the nitrate aspects of the project. This bill, which had the support of a majority of the House committee, stressed the development of nitrates to assist the farmers of the valley. It was believed by these members that power was secondary to the manufacture of nitrates. In any event, it was believed that the moderate amount of power developed at the dam as then envisioned would mostly be used in manufacturing nitrates. In this the Congressmen, according to Judson King, a close friend and adviser of Norris's, were reflecting the wishes of a great majority of the people in the Tennessee Valley. They wanted help in making their land more productive. The distribution of electric power seemed secondary.

Thus there was a division in Congress on the relative importance of the various elements involved in the plans. Some wanted only nitrate production; some wanted power development to be sold to the private companies at the "bus bar." Others wanted to create a vast power development with Federal lines supplying customers directly.

The private companies, who had been quieted by Roosevelt's mild Portland speech, were now aroused and representing them there appeared before the House committee Wendell L. Willkie, who had been made president of the Commonwealth and Southern Corporation in

January. Commonwealth and Southern was a holding company which controlled the six great operating companies in the Tennessee Valley region. Willkie, who represented himself as a Democrat, hailed the idea of Roosevelt for the development of the region with enthusiasm. But he pointed out that this development could be made without the government's building of transmission lines. He said that such lines would duplicate the present facilities of the private companies and in such a competition with the great resources of the government the investments of these companies, amounting to $400 million, would be destroyed. He even cited Governor Roosevelt's favorable attitude toward selling Federally generated power to the companies at the "bus bar."

When nearly a month later the various bills went to conference, the differences were resolved and the main body of the Norris bill emerged and was signed by the President.

On the main points of dissension—the concentration on nitrate production and the building of transmission lines—the bill passed the questions on to the members of the newly created authority. The board was authorized to recondition the nitrate plant and to sell the product to any extent that it desired. The board was likewise authorized to build transmission lines or to sell the power at the "bus bar" at its discretion.

The bill provided for three directors to manage the corporation.

In making the appointments, Roosevelt followed his habit of seeking to reconcile the irreconcilable. His tremendous urge to achieve many objectives in one operation had blinded him to the many problems that lay before the administrators of the act. There were many points of view among the people with whom Roosevelt had discussed the subject. There was in this proposal the difficulty of digesting these diverse plans because of the pressure of so many other problems in those days. It was to be assumed that the generation of power at the Wilson Dam would be a simple task. But how should this power be distributed to its beneficiaries?

The imaginative concept expressed in the message included the improvement of living standards for the people in the valley. This was an ambiguous objective, for those people needed many things enjoyed by their fellow citizens in the cities. Most of them were genuinely poor people eking out a living on the land. The nitrate plant at Muscle Shoals could provide a limited amount of fertilizer, but that would only be a small help and production was very costly. No means had yet been devised to retire sub-marginal land. This might involve legal and constitutional problems of a serious nature.

The Wilson Dam and others to be built would flood a great deal of the most productive land of the valley. The farmers there would have to be induced to pack up and move to less productive lands in the hills.

Neglected also was the fact that the new corporative government unit would take over many of the activities in the region that were already being operated through the big departments in Washington. Soil conservation, reforestation, research, and other aids for farmers were within the province of the respective departments, and some division of responsibility must be arranged.

Finally, government power operations would inevitably compete with and seriously affect the private companies. And the situation here was quite unlike that which had faced Roosevelt as governor of New York.

All these perplexities must be dumped upon the board, which Roosevelt must choose. And in his choice of the members he immediately found that, while he conceived of a nice allocation of their functions, the differences of opinion within the triumvirate were destined to shake the TVA for years to come.

Because Roosevelt had so many objectives in mind in projecting the TVA, he decided that he needed as its first directors three individuals of widely diverse talents and capabilities. For chairman he selected Arthur E. Morgan, with whom he had discussed his ideas on several occasions. Morgan was an engineer who at that time was president of Antioch College, a small institution that had been founded as an experimental enterprise in education by Horace Mann in 1852. As an engineer, Morgan had directed the construction works in the valley of the Miami River for the state of Ohio after the disastrous Dayton flood in 1913. But Morgan was more—or less—than an engineer. He was possessed of vast dreams for the economic and social regeneration of mankind through the mediating influence of government. He saw in the Tennessee Valley an area in which he might carry out some of the dreams he had nurtured for years. His concept of reform, however, involved peaceful and cooperative action. He was wholly sympathetic, so far as the private power companies were concerned. They would be partners in the enterprise, not competitors or enemies. "I am not going to fight the power companies," he said.

The next appointment was David E. Lilienthal, who at the time was chairman of the Wisconsin Public Service Commission. Lilienthal was a graduate of the Harvard Law School, where he had, along with so many other young students, been a friend and protégé of Felix Frankfurter. Since he had been appointed in Wisconsin by the La Follettes, there is no doubt that Senator Robert La Follette was most influential in pressing his selection upon Roosevelt. But there is also no doubt that Frankfurter had a decisive hand in commending Lilienthal to Roosevelt. Ideologically, he belonged to the Brandeis-Frankfurter school, which held to the view that while private enterprise should be retained in any reform, all public utilities should be subjected to drastic regulation. To the members of that school, these public utilities—the railroads, the power companies, and all others that possessed measurable monopoly —should be viewed with deep suspicion.

Like others in the Brandeis-Frankfurter school, Lilienthal had little faith in planning. He regarded Morgan's ideas of regeneration as pure moonshine. Morgan, however, seemed unaware of this and he added his influence to that of others in recommending Lilienthal.

The third member of the triumvirate was H. A. Morgan, president of the University of Tennessee and a dedicated student of agricultural problems.

Almost immediately after the appointment of these directors, friction developed. A common suspicion of Arthur Morgan's concepts of uplift brought Lilienthal and H. A. Morgan into an alliance against the chairman. To resolve this, the directors as early as August 1933 decided to allocate the administrative responsibilities among themselves. Arthur Morgan was to direct and supervise the big construction project. Lilienthal was to look after legal problems, rate-making, and relations with the private utilities. H. A. Morgan was to concern himself with the problems of agriculture in the valley, including the production and selling of nitrates.

While this administrative method of assigning functions to a directorate was common in New York, it is not consistent with orthodox governmental practice. For a board is supposed to make policy and vest the implementation of the policy in an over-all administrator. But since the board differed so widely about the purposes of the new institution, the three major functions were thus allocated. And out of this rather clumsy allocation of responsibilities came a feud that continued for some years. With plenty of Federal money to be spent, the Wilson Dam and the nitrate plant were completed and put into operation, and other dams and installations were pushed ahead.

The discord was not to remain quiet. For Lilienthal's journals reveal that he talked about the difficulties with many people.*

The feud rumbled in the press and supplied plenty of gossip in Washington. In 1936 Lilienthal's term expired, and despite the objections of Arthur Morgan and bitter opposition in Congress, Roosevelt reappointed him. This marked the twilight of Arthur Morgan's influence. Planning, after the death of the NRA and AAA, fell from favor, and in 1938 Roosevelt demanded and secured the resignation of Arthur Morgan. After that, for practical purposes Lilienthal ran the show.†

* *The Journals of David E. Lilienthal,* Vol. One, *The TVA Years* (New York: Harper & Row, 1964).

† The development of the operations of the TVA beyond 1933, the intra-board struggle between Arthur Morgan on the one hand and Lilienthal and H. A. Morgan

The popularity of the TVA, despite the controversy among the original directors and the opposition of the private power companies, encouraged Roosevelt in 1937 to propose in a message to Congress the creation of such authorities for the various watershed regions in the nation. Nothing came of this grand design at that time, but in 1944 the President recommended a Missouri Valley Authority which failed of enactment in its original form but influenced the extension of wide Federal authority in that region. In 1949 a Columbia Valley Administration was proposed and that failed of enactment.

The Federal government since then has contented itself with setting up various public power administrations that in one way or another direct the marketing of power produced by Federal dams and facilities.

And so the Tennessee Valley Authority stands unique as a vast experiment in paternalism. The strong opposition of state and local interests has prevented the idea of the national expansion envisioned by Roosevelt before World War II.

on the other, and the long legal contests in the courts extending into the middle 1930's lie beyond the scope of this book. A vast literature, much of it influenced by the prejudice of its authors, has accumulated.

Chapter Twenty-eight

The Hundred Days in Retrospect

THE fame of the Hundred Days Congress lingers on after the passing of more than three decades. The legislative record it set, the impression it created on the public, its impact upon the economy of the nation, and the incredible speed with which important legislation was planned, considered, proposed, and enacted had no parallel in the earlier history of the republic. Nor has there been any parallel since, except under the exigencies of the war that began eight years later. I make very limited claims to the gift of prophecy but I venture to suggest that only in some equally great economic emergency will anything like the events of those spring days from March 9 to June 16 be repeated.*

The unique character of the Hundred Days was due to the conjunction of several most unusual contemporary circumstances:

There was a nation emerging from a long period of distress and disillusionment. There had been an election that gave the winning party an indeterminate but sweeping mandate for change. A new President had

* As this is written, comparisons have been made between Roosevelt's Hundred Days and the great mass of legislation passed in the 1965 Congress under the Presidential leadership of President Lyndon B. Johnson. No doubt, the amount of legislation passed in that more recent session was more voluminous. But much of it had been inherited from the Kennedy years and it was more specifically directed to the field of welfare. Its enactment occupied the larger part of a year. It is possible, however, to trace much of this more recent legislation to the beginnings in the Roosevelt years, especially to the social security, welfare, and work-relief measures that were enacted in the 1930's. The origin of the expression the Hundred Days was in the designation given to the short restoration of Napoleon after his return from Elba and before the Battle of Waterloo. I do not know who first applied this characterization to the short special session of the Seventy-third Congress.

been inaugurated whose personality inspired glowing optimism in Congress and the nation. And this President was blissfully free from dogmatic preconceptions.

There was also a Congress whose leadership included an extraordinary degree of competence and experience. Most of its leaders had been schooled as members of the minority for twelve years. They were worldly-wise and thoroughly familiar with what had happened in those years, although they had lacked responsibility beyond the fact that the House had been Democratic since 1931.

There was also a great intellectual ferment in the land among those possessed of the capacity and knowledge necessary for reflections upon the unhappy course of the depression.

In 1932 and 1933 the overshadowing problem was recognized as economic. And reformers, businessmen, and professors had formulated innumerable plans for recovery and reform. This tide of remedies flowed into Washington after the inauguration. Remedies either beat out their lives in competition with other remedies or found the opportunity to fertilize some corner of the new dispensation. As Emerson said of the American Transcendentalists, "What a fertility of projects for the salvation of the world!"

In addition to the old reformers there was a heavy influx of young lawyers and some economists, mostly from Harvard and other universities, and a considerable number recruited by the infatigable master of placement, Felix Frankfurter. Many of these had been unusually capable in their academic careers. They were liberally sprinkled among the departments where Cabinet members were in need of personnel. A certain dedication to reform characterized the thinking of these people. For Frankfurter was always likely to attribute brilliance to students who shared his ideological sympathies. Their self-confidence was boundless. But they were quite unacquainted with the art of administration and unfamiliar with the practical workings of the economic system.*

As we have seen, there were solid men about, upon whom fell much of the labor of planning and administration. There were holdovers from the Hoover Administration like Jesse Jones and Arthur Ballantine; also reliable party men who had enjoyed experience in the Wilson Adminis-

* A habit developed among newspapermen to describe these newcomers as members of the Brains Trust. But this was a gross exaggeration, for the Brains Trust had been dissolved by me after the election and never again met in a group. Indeed, it got so that everyone who had a college degree and carried a briefcase was perforce regarded in the press not only as an "intellectual" but as a "brains-truster." Many proved to be useful but many were nuisances. But since law offices as well as business had been prostrated in the depression, the government offered almost the only opportunity for employment and also the stimulation of working in an exciting place.

tration, a few businessmen, level-headed professors, and others. There were the capable men in Congress who were close at all times to our operations.

As we approached the time, after the banking crisis had subsided, to propose and secure the enactment of a legislative program, there was the assurance of public confidence, which was recovering from the long agony of the depression and the most recent moneyless nightmare of the bank holiday. In March the public seemed to shake off its doubts and was hospitable to anything new which the President and Congress had to offer. People believed that things were being done for them or would be done for them. It was not important that they should know exactly what these remedies were to be. It was enough to know that something was happening that had not happened before.

Mythology is an infection that afflicts all written history. It finds lodgment in contemporary press reports or in gossip and, like a malignancy, grows as the years pass. It confronts any serious historian and imposes upon him prodigious labor in sifting fact from fiction.

The written accounts of the period we are considering here are no exception to this rule. An enormous literature on the New Deal has accumulated consisting of books, articles, memoirs, and the deposits of "oral history." There are reliable accounts of specific phases of that many-sided scene, and one or two serious and reliable histories. But there are other accounts whose reliability is marred by lack of access to sources, by reliance on hasty interpretations that appeared in the contemporary press, on stories passed on by word of mouth, or on utter fabrications.

Political motives have had their corrosive effect. Democratic orators and writers persisted for some years in the habit of "running against Hoover." On the other hand, the roots of all our present problems and discontents have been attributed to the actions of Roosevelt and Congress. Some histories from academic sources have been embellished by interpretations that are projected by the ideological predilections of their authors.

Some of the most persistent sources of misunderstanding have been memoirs left by contemporaries. Many of these have been carelessly written from memory by their authors. And, as is quite understandable, such contemporaries have in many instances grossly exaggerated the importance of what they did or what someone whom they disliked did or did not do.

The elimination of mythology is especially important since those who write the textbooks will carry this story to succeeding generations.*

* In offering this retrospect on the Hundred Days, I cannot claim complete comprehension of all that happened. But I have at least the benefit of personal participation in the events of that period at the very center of activity. I have also an excellent

In this account, it becomes essential at the outset to revise all and eliminate some of the widely accepted generalizations about the Hundred Days. They concern what plans were made before Congress met on March 9, how such plans originated, who helped to formulate them, whether they were mutually consistent one with the other, and what happened after they were submitted to Congress.*

Several points need to be made plain at the outset:

1. Despite Roosevelt's frequent claim that "we planned it that way," there was no predetermined, over-all plan. There were some plans and memoranda, based upon the issues raised in the campaign. And in general something like the details in these suggestions were adopted. But since it was a sort of rescue operation, improvisations were the rule.

2. Most of the measures passed in the Hundred Days did not originate in the White House. While the messages and some of the bills were transmitted by Roosevelt, the actual parentage of the measures and plans was widely scattered throughout the Administration, the Congress, and in unofficial quarters. There was a great deal of collaboration and there were many compromises. The relative influence of the many people who participated in shaping legislation cannot be estimated. And in the legislative mill, many amendments were added.

3. The Seventy-third Congress was no "rubber stamp." Its leadership was rich in talent and experience. The concept of an assembly line from the White House to Congress cannot be sustained by the facts.

4. Collectively, the measures passed by the Seventy-third Congress and the many Executive orders of Roosevelt did not constitute a "revolution." There were a number of innovations. But the body of the enactments was built upon and conditioned by traditional institutions and practices. Those who were responsible for the direction of policy regarded a capitalist economy and free political institutions as fundamental.

What some writers about this period fail to realize, and what some zealots who were on the periphery of our activity at the time failed to comprehend, is that we were not creating the institutional structure of a new nation. We were dealing with the temporary ailments of a highly industrialized modern civilization in which trial and error, experimentation and individual enterprise had shaped its national traditions, methods, and economic philosophy. There were a few who believed that capitalism was in a process of dissolution. But they had little influence on

memory, which is sharpened by the notations, records, correspondence, and diary in my papers. I am, moreover, deeply impressed by my responsibility to the cause of historical accuracy.

* I am not burdening this text with an account of the debates in Congress on the measures described. These are available in the *Congressional Record* of the Seventy-third Congress.

what happened. While some of those pessimists, even Communists, found lodgment in office, their contribution was negligible.

5. A large majority of the measures passed were regarded as experimental or were specifically designated as temporary. This Roosevelt himself made clear when he sent the farm bill to Congress. The haste that characterized the writing and the Presidential endorsement of that bill was made necessary because spring planting was already under way.

6. Some of the measures passed, notably the revised Thomas amendment to the farm bill and the National Industrial Recovery bill, were literally forced upon Roosevelt because of the threat of much more radical proposals, which were already milling about in Congress and which, unless some substitute was devised, might have been passed.

7. Most of the measures adopted were, in the year or two that followed, drastically revised. Two were declared invalid by the Supreme Court. Those measures, the NRA and the AAA, were originally passed amid grave doubts of constitutionality in Congress and in the Administration. They were passed because it was believed that they would have an impact that would create recovery before the Court could get around to their consideration.

8. The early New Deal was far from homogeneous. The various acts passed represented a number of divergent points of view. Roosevelt and the Congressional leaders were practical men. Often when confronted with alternatives they accepted both or all. It was thought best to adopt them and eliminate one or another after a trial.

9. Some of the measures passed were designed for recovery. Others aimed at relief. Only one or two, such as the TVA, were professed reforms. But the distinction among these three "r's" was hard to draw. Underneath all was a determination to achieve a psychological effect upon the country by the appearance of "action on many fronts." Roosevelt believed that the very quantity of the legislation passed would inspire wonder and confidence. Nearly everyone who participated and knew what was happening realized that these measures *per se* could not promote economic recovery. They would, however, create a climate in which natural forces would assert themselves. A passive Administration could never have succeeded. It was believed quite generally and widely enunciated on the stump in the campaign in 1932 that the Hoover Administration had failed because it was too timid in applying remedies. The American people wanted their government to do something, anything, so long as it acted with assurance and vigor. The American people needed inspiration far more than they needed direction. Few could understand what Congress was doing. But their sources of news told them that a lot of things were being done that had not been done before. That, we believed, sufficed. Roosevelt's attitude was that if many reme-

dies were tried, some might work and the rest could be scrapped. If the patient could be kept happy, Mother Nature would come to the rescue.

The foregoing considerations suffice as a corrective to the mythology that has been so prominent in the years since. They are essential to an understanding of the significance of the Hundred Days. The results were in no small degree due to the spirit manifested by Roosevelt himself. He admitted that he was moving along an "untrod path." And the credit that has been accorded him for imparting his optimism to a receptive country is richly deserved.

There can be no question about Roosevelt's faith, like that of Theodore Roosevelt, in a very considerable degree of Federal intervention in business and agriculture. There were reassuring gestures about state and local responsibility, but the reality was Federal intervention, subsidies, grants-in-aid, and bureaucratic direction.

The new President plunged with gusto and confidence into what his cousin Theodore had called the "twilight zone" between the national government and the states.

It seemed to me at the time that this thrust of Federal intervention was necessary and inevitable. The states, and especially the cities, were in dire fiscal straits. The catastrophic drop in values and business stagnation had eaten into their sources of revenue. Many cities were bankrupt. The Federal credit was still sound—largely, it should be noted, because of the fiscal prudence of the Harding and Coolidge Administrations, which had greatly reduced the national debt. In fairness, it must be admitted that Roosevelt's Administration lived for some time off the fat of its predecessors.

While I could reconcile myself to this massive expansion of the Federal establishment, my conservative instincts developed by my earlier study and teaching of constitutional institutions led me to hope that the balance might be restored after the emergency. But as time has passed, the trend has continued. Political expediency, the unlimited sources of revenue provided by the Federal income tax and deficit financing, the greater integration of the nation because of new means of communication and transportation, the dedication of many leaders of opinion to the concept of a centralized authority and "strong" Presidents, the chronic fiscal distress of the cities—all these have hastened the trend.

But not the least of the forces that have so altered the Federal-state balance was Roosevelt's appetite for authority, which was so manifest in later years. The centralization compelled by the war and the rise of Federal welfarism have since profoundly altered the institutional structure of the republic.

In those days in 1933 there were many circumstances, aside from Roosevelt's reach for power, that altered the character of the Presidency as an institution. There was the emergency, which ignited many schemes for change that, if adopted, would have been disastrous. These perils were met by Roosevelt, as in the case of the Thomas amendment, by inducing the progenitors of such schemes to agree to give the President discretionary authority. He argued in such instances that he wanted "room to turn around." Thus there passed to the Presidency vast authority that had never been exercised in peacetime. And Congress, wearied by long months of debate, was willing to throw many major problems into the lap of the President and hasten an early adjournment.

The ultimate effect of such delegation seemed at the time to be an academic question, which we had little time to ponder. History, we realized, would have its inevitable way with us. But if we achieved recovery, our risks would be charitably weighed in the balance.

The one factor I failed to anticipate was the effect of this vast delegation of power upon the man who exercised it. But even if I had anticipated a transformation in the Roosevelt character, there was nothing I could have done about it.

As I look back at those days in Washington from mid-March to June, my mind is arrested by their contrast with those of exactly a year before. In my first task in writing a pre-nomination speech for Roosevelt, I had used the expression "the forgotten man." It seemed to be suited to the mood of a country that had suffered through more than two years of despair, frustration, and privation. People were sorry for their families, their neighbors, their country, and themselves. They grew to believe that their government indeed had forgotten them.

The expression was the title of an essay by William Graham Sumner written in the 1880's. I was quite aware when I used it that Sumner's "forgotten man" was not of the same breed as the people who were in need of encouragement in 1932 and 1933. Sumner's forgotten man was self-reliant, self-sufficient. He never felt sorry for himself.

It was unfair to fix the blame for forgetfulness on Herbert Hoover, who had aged with the burdens of his office, but unhappy people are neither considerate nor tender when they are dealing with a public servant. In those spring days in 1933 after the bank crisis, however, the public mood had undergone a profound change. A vitalizing optimism pervaded the country. And upon this tide were launched the measures of the Hundred Days.

As I look back over the years of my life I realize that this period—from the night of March 3, when Woodin and I went over to the Treasury to work with Mills, Ballantine, *et al.*, to the sixteenth of June, when Congress adjourned—was not only the most exciting but intellectually the most rewarding of my life. My relations with Roosevelt, which were strained during the conflict with Stimson and Davis, were restored to the close comradeship that had prevailed throughout 1932. Moreover, I formed friendships with members of Congress that lasted long after my departure from the Administration. I absorbed a grasp of practical statecraft, which has been invaluable in later years when my profession as a political commentator has called for an understanding of what goes on in government. The burdens were very heavy, painful decisions had to be made, and I had to ignore the inevitable infighting and jealousies within the Administration and also the sharp thrusts of the press. So far as publicity was concerned, I had to take the bitter with the sweet with equanimity.

Sometime in May my intimate friend Willard Kiplinger told me that a good many articles were being prepared for national magazines and newspapers that, while mostly flattering, would thrust me into a sea of publicity, which might not only irritate my relations with colleagues in the Administration but excite the concern of Roosevelt himself. This projection into national prominence would be a mixed blessing at the best. But in the position I occupied there was little I could do about it. My rule forever after was to accept criticism by this formula: Your friends won't believe it, your enemies will believe anything that is adverse to you. But if you don't answer, 99 per cent of the public will forget it.

I emerged from that brief experience a wiser individual and a more competent witness of the meaning of public affairs.

Part Five

Contemporaries

Chapter Twenty-nine

In the Administration

IT would have been far more agreeable and less arduous to the writer, and perhaps more interesting to most readers, to have limited this story to sketches of the personalities of those who people the pages of this book. For the epigram attributed to Carlyle, Emerson, and several others that there is no history, only biography, has an element of truth. The New Deal was to a degree made by people, living alongside one another, working together, disputing, and agreeing. Some struggled for recognition, others quietly did their bit to create the many-sided, many-colored, heterogeneous product called the New Deal.

But personalities, however positive, fade into a complex of events, of many forces, human and natural, all with a common enemy: that thing called the depression, which was born of so many circumstances that its origins were not then clearly defined and have never been adequately identified. Explanations vary according to the predilections of the authors.

To have limited this book to the personalities of those who participated in the rescue would have torn the fabric of the story. Such an account would have seemed like a picture of many people all working on crossword puzzles or problems in books of arithmetic. Even the story I have told is limited to what was seen and heard by one of the participants.

There were scores, perhaps hundreds, whom I saw and at least temporarily knew in varying degrees of intimacy. A few I knew well and with them forged ties of friendship and common ideals that remained for years after. Most vanished from my concern after my period of service ended.

In the position I occupied, so near the focal point of decision, it was difficult to form lasting ties with anyone. For since my responsibilities moved so rapidly from one subject to another, my contacts were mostly temporary and the interests shared were few. This induced at least one memoirist, James P. Warburg, to charge me with what is commonly called fickleness. I became close and confidential for a time, he has written, and then withdrew to other individuals and other interests. I regret that I invited this impression. But it was the penalty I paid for the role I assumed.

In my detachment from the political scene, which became final in 1936, there were many regrets abount sundered relationships. But there was a solid compensation. For this detachment told me who were real friends and who had cultivated me for expediency's sake. I learned the difference between the profession and the reality of friendship. It was quite an experience to witness this sorting out.

Since I was so near the center of the new Administration during the months after the inauguration and since the climate of Washington at that time was so pregnant with the spirit of reform, I saw as strange an influx of visitors as has been witnessed since the days of Jackson. But in Jackson's time the people who came were mostly backwoodsmen and office-seekers or specimens from the political ghettos in the cities who were mobilized by Van Buren. These people contented themselves with knocking about the physical fixtures, especially the White House furniture. The 1933 newcomers were a different sort. They came with innumerable schemes to rearrange the institutions of the republic. Some were livid ghosts of old and forgotten reform movements of the past. There were Greenbackers, Populists, silverites, taxation cranks, socialists, and even a sprinkling of Communists. These people greeted what they conceived to be a new dawn. They came

Singing songs of expectation
Marching to the Promised Land.

Government in operation has few niches for people of such strange antecedents and limp qualifications. Minor jobs were found for some in the new agencies. But since so many wanted a revolution shaped to their own specifications, there was not enough revolution to go around. Most of them drifted back into the fading twilight from which they came.

Henry Mencken, from his literary throne in nearby Baltimore, saw all this gathering of the discontented, and it provided him material for some of the best of his sardonic observations:

> At every time of stress and storm in history one notes the appearance of wizards with sure cures for all the sorrows of humanity. They flourished, you may be certain, in Sumer and Akkad, in the Egypt of all the long dynasties, and in the lands of the Hittites and Scythians. They swarmed in Greece,

and in Rome some of them actually became Emperors. For always the great majority of human beings sweat and fume under the social system prevailing in the world they live in—always they are convinced that they are carrying an undue share of its burdens, and getting too little of its milk and honey. And always it is easy to convince them that by some facile device, invented by its vendor and offered freely out of the bigness of his heart, all these injustices may be forced to cease and desist, and a Golden Age brought in that will give every man whatever he wants, and charge him nothing for it. . . . Let them trust the wizards manning the spoons, and they will presently enter upon fields of asphodel, where every yen that is native to the human breast will be realized automatically, and all the immemorial pains of doing-without will be no more, and what goes up need never come down again, and two and two will make five, five and a half, six, ten, a hundred, a million. . . . Even the dumbest yokel does not succumb to even the most eloquent hawker of snake-oil on days when his liver and lights are ideally quiescent. It takes a flicker of pain along the midriff to bring him up to the booth, and something more than a flicker to make him buy. In the present case there are qualms and tremors all over the communal carcass, for the whole world was lately mauled by a long, wasteful, and fruitless war, and the end of that war saw many millions of people reduced to poverty, terror, and despair. . . . The resemblance of all such arcana to the theological revelation must be plain to every connoisseur of buncombe. There is something transcendental about their very absurdity, and their agents quickly take on a truly sacerdotal cockiness. They always deny the fact heatedly, and the communist apostles, in particular, are sensitive about it, but, as I shall show presently, its truth is always evident.*

Truly there are so many, especially among the better-educated classes, who should know buncombe when they see it, but who are so intrigued by the wiles of politicians and rabble-rousers that they, too, are carried along by the belief that things are so bad that something must be done, and therefore that anything that is done with sufficiently dramatic effects will be better than nothing. And there is some validity for Mencken's observations when we consider that masters of money and men high in government had been blind to the lessons of the debacle that followed the Florida land boom, and believed in their hearts and their purses that stocks and other securities could never come down. Perhaps it was the follies of the great boom that induced so many missionaries of a new order to leave home and swarm into Washington in those days.

But the cranks were not all in Washington. Many of them were abroad in the great farm belt in the Middle West and in California, lashing sober tillers of the soil with their messages of indignation and winning supporters for their nostrums by the thousands. There were also plenty of radicals mouthing Marxian dialect in the cities. Workers without work were their willing victims.

* The New Deal Mentality," in *The American Mercury* (May 1936).

The subjects of the sketches that follow include none of those cranks. I have arbitrarily chosen a few of the people whom I knew best and with whom I worked. All had important influence in their own right. And collectively they show the infinite variety of the people who were present in and around the First New Deal.

I have already characterized several very important figures who participated in the rescue of the banks. Also I have commented upon the members of the Cabinet in earlier chapters, and outstanding figures at the London Conference are considered later. Other notable individuals in Congress, such as Senators Joseph T. Robinson, Norris, and Vandenberg, I have omitted because my contacts with them were slight and casual. Finally, I omit some figures well known to history, such as Harry Hopkins, whose ascendency came in the years after I left the government.

In the Official Family

The White House Staff

Louis McHenry Howe, who for the final three years of his life had the title secretary to the President, had earned his grim eminence by long years of dedicated service to Roosevelt.*

Howe was a jealous guardian of Roosevelt's interests but he never forgot his own. Hoover had employed three secretaries with equal status, and that is what Stephen Early and Marvin McIntyre expected. But when they received their commissions they were amazed to find that Howe had induced Roosevelt to designate them as "assistant secretaries." Howe also sought to locate Marguerite LeHand, long Roosevelt's personal secretary in Albany, in the White House residence rather than in the office annex. But she frustrated Howe's plans by taking possession of a small office next to the President's. These tricks of Howe's to establish his primacy did not provide affectionate relations with these nominal subordinates. But Howe's concern was that no one should come between him and the President. In some instances, such as his relations with Samuel I. Rosenman, there had developed strong mutual dislike.

* *Roosevelt and Howe* by Alfred B. Rollins, Jr. (New York: Knopf, 1962) is not only a scrupulously objective portrait of Howe but in its vivid style is one of the outstanding biographies of our time. The author concludes that "Time and History would deal harshly with Howe. He had none of the sense of order and importance that would inspire him to make a record for posterity. . . . Louis had left one monument that could never be erased. No one would ever write about the twentieth century without mentioning Franklin Delano Roosevelt. No one would ever be able to write about Roosevelt without mentioning Louis McHenry Howe."

I feel certain that it was due to Howe's maneuvering that I was not established in a position Hoover had recognized by the title administrative assistant to the President. I am sure also of Howe's expectation that placing me in the State Department would arouse the bitter jealousy of Hull.

I had known Howe at least five years before the campaign of 1932, and realizing his possessive interest in Roosevelt, I kept as much of his good will as he ever vouchsafed to anyone by constantly consulting him and in other ways using as much tact as I could command. During his last long illness, when he was confined to the Naval Hospital, I visited him whenever I was in Washington and invariably showed him drafts of speeches and messages I had prepared for Roosevelt. In a burst of confidence on one of those occasions he said, "Keep close watch. Franklin is very impulsive."

Actually, Howe was not influential in determining issues and decisions either in the 1932 campaign or in the Hundred Days. He was most interested in political strategy and in appointments. Slowly in the year after the inauguration his influence with Roosevelt as well as his health declined. Finally he was moved to the Naval Hospital and he was limited in the use of the telephone. This was done not only to save the President's time but to prevent Howe from calling members of the Cabinet and Congress with orders which he made clear came directly from the President.

Many people commented after Howe's death that Howe had been a "moderating" influence on Roosevelt. I never believed that. Fortunately both never had the same "brain storm" at the same time.

There were times when Howe's influence on Roosevelt was very dangerous. This was shown when by casual reading of the newspapers he convinced Roosevelt in February 1933 that the bank crisis was not serious. Also when, as a fellow passenger on the *Indianapolis*, he encouraged Roosevelt to destroy the London Conference. In that instance he drew his information from the stock market quotations.

Marvin McIntyre, although he, too, was plagued by a frail body, managed the most difficult tasks of appointments secretary with good judgment and efficiency. Stephen Early was not only an individual of superlatively gracious manners but of inflexible honesty with the press. He was the most competent and most respected Presidential press secretary of modern times. His task was not easy, because of Roosevelt's indirectness and occasional deceitfulness and his outbursts against the newspaper publishers and some reporters. Early, more often than not, was the staunch defender of newsmen in the face of Roosevelt's determination to denounce them.

Few ever realized how important it was to the national interest to have Missy LeHand constantly at the elbow of the President. She had every virtue and every talent needed by the super-confidential secretary of a man in high office. I can well remember that when I had sought unsuccessfully to get Roosevelt to omit some unnecessary dig in a speech, I would ask her to come to my aid. She would listen to the passage and then say, "Mr. President, that really doesn't sound like you." This appeal was invariably successful.

After the breaking of my relations with Roosevelt in 1936, I was more than happy that my friendly relations with Early and Missy remained as they had always been.

The mortality of the people around Roosevelt was very heavy. Gus Gennerich and Howe died in the first term. Missy and McIntyre in the second.

Jesse Holman Jones

In the literature of the Roosevelt years there has been a singular neglect of the major role played by Jesse H. Jones, who dominated the immense lending and purchasing operations of the Reconstruction Finance Corporation. And when among the various histories Jones is mentioned at all, these historians have openly revealed their ideological bias by slighting characterizations of the man.

But without Jones's management of that agency I doubt whether recovery would have been possible. Certainly without the RFC the banks could not have attained stability. And in many other operations the RFC played a meaningful part. One of the members of Jones's legal staff told me that the functions of most of the alphabetical agencies created in 1933 might with slight amendments to the law have been taken over by the RFC.

From the moment when Jones took over the chairmanship of the RFC in March 1933, he revealed himself as a masterful administrator in an Administration that was sorely lacking in executive talent. It is my considered opinion that Jones was not only the most competent administrator in the Roosevelt era but probably the most successful civil administrator in the nation's history.*

In early 1932, the support of Speaker Garner and of Joseph T. Robinson, Senate Democratic leader, was necessary to the enactment into law

* In 1955, at the suggestion of the author, I edited Bascom N. Timmons' comprehensive biography of Jones. In the course of that task I examined the available documents, especially those dealing with Jones's twelve years in Washington. The Timmons book is *Jesse H. Jones, the Man and the Statesman.* It is on the basis of that examination that I have ventured the opinion expressed above. There is also Jones's own book, *Fifty Billion Dollars,* written with the collaboration of Edward Angly. This is a personal and documented story of the RFC before and during World War II. In Hoover's *Memoirs,* Vol. III, there is an account of the creation of the RFC and the appointment of Jones as a member of its board.

of Hoover's proposal to create the RFC. Hoover agreed that he would permit Garner and Robinson to name two members as the price of their support. Garner selected Jones, and Robinson, Harvey C. Couch.

Jones himself had already urged his Democratic friends in Congress to support Hoover's proposal. There had been two successive chairmen but when Roosevelt was inaugurated this office was vacant. During the first days of the new Administration Jones asked me no less than three times to remind Roosevelt to fill that vacancy. When, on the third occasion, we went to Roosevelt, Jones said that with the heavy burden of the banking rescue coming up there should be a chairman. Roosevelt said, "I thought that you were the chairman." The appointment was made forthwith.

There is no exaggeration in the claim made by Jones that in the twelve years of his chairmanship the RFC handled no less than $50 billion. And it is a well-deserved tribute to Jones's administrative skill, honesty, and common sense that in that vast operation there was no serious scandal and no important waste.

Jones operated wholly within the rules and traditions of an orthodox business. Except in the unusual cases, loans were not to be made without a fair prospect of repayment. Risks had to be taken, but they were shrewdly calculated. Political pressures had to be met, but Jones was sufficiently canny and politically sophisticated to understand and to frustrate such efforts. In the midst of the rapid changes that characterized those early months, powerful members of Congress who themselves were unacquainted with much of the unorthodox goings-on in the Administration placed immense confidence in Jones as a stabilizing element in the government. Indeed, such was the confidence that Congress bestowed upon Jones that in 1941, when he was appointed Secretary of Commerce, Congress at the insistence of the appointee placed the RFC in the Commerce Department. In 1945, when Roosevelt ruthlessly compelled Jones to step aside to make room for Henry Wallace in the Commerce post, Congress withdrew the lending agencies from that department.

The management of a large bureaucracy and the businesses with which it had relations presented no problems to Jones, for he had been a manager of business since the age of fourteen. He was not a banker, but in the early years of the depression he had been able to guide the policies of Houston bankers with amazing skill. His many earlier enterprises had given him an understanding of businesses from farming to international exchange. He also had a genius for selecting excellent subordinates and for delegating to them a liberal amount of discretion. In an oil country he never dabbled in the oil business, except on one occasion when he traded in oil leases. In his later years he was essentially a builder, and many of the great buildings that now mark the

Houston skyline were built by Jones and then leased or sold to large corporations. His building operations in those years extended to other cities, even as far away as New York.

While Jones was strictly orthodox in the business principles he maintained in the RFC, he was quite unorthodox in his methods. When it seemed necessary, he took chances that to those around him seemed dangerous. But his judgment rarely failed him.

One of the marvels of the time was how he got on with Roosevelt, whose business experience was most limited and who was one of the most capricious and disorderly administrators who ever occupied the Presidency. Roosevelt, a creature of what he himself called "brain storms," often asked Jones to do something that the RFC chairman knew to be unwise. One of these occasions was Roosevelt's suggestion that the RFC buy the Empire State Building in New York to house Federal agencies. On this occasion, as on others, Jones listened, withheld argument, but contrived inconspicuous but valid reasons for inaction. Roosevelt apparently never before had to cope with such strategy. And, as Jones well realized, Roosevelt would forget his directive under the pressure of other concerns. Roosevelt scrupulously avoided any clash with Jones, because he well knew that the RFC was regarded in Congress as the most popular and trusted of all government agencies.

Jones had to contend with two other problems. One was the banking community, which had learned little from the depression and which for some time held tenaciously to practices hallowed only by their traditional observance. And he had at all times to contend with the visionary radicals in the Administration. As we have seen earlier in this story he won over the bankers with plain talk and vigorous action. The radicals he ignored until during the war he won a battle with Henry Wallace.

The capricious and cruel act of Roosevelt in 1945, when he asked for Jones's resignation as Secretary of Commerce to make room for Wallace, can be explained only by the failing health and erratic mentality of a dying President.

Lewis W. Douglas

The only time I ever heard Roosevelt mention the name of a possible successor was in the early months of 1933. Lewis Douglas and I had been conferring with the President at his bedside that morning and after Douglas left I expressed my admiration for the manner in which Douglas was operating the Budget Bureau. Roosevelt replied that "in twelve years he would be an excellent candidate for President." Thus Roosevelt revealed not only the feeling he had for economy in government but his early determination to seek a third term.

Douglas was a member of a family with very large property interests in Arizona. He had already served two terms in the House of Representatives from his state and had been elected to a third term when Roosevelt prevailed upon him to become director of the budget. Douglas was a Democrat of the old school and was as rigorously dedicated to orthodox fiscal policies as was Grover Cleveland.

Douglas saw in the office to which Roosevelt appointed him the opportunity to return it to the power and prestige it had had under the first budget director, Charles G. Dawes, in the early 1920's. At that time President Harding—and this is one decision for which that unfortunate President deserves much credit—placed the budget director on a parity with the members of his Cabinet and permitted Dawes to wield the knife without stint upon the estimates of the departments.

Because of his close relationship with the President in those early months, Douglas exercised powerful influence in making policy. Douglas' outstanding contribution was his authorship of the Economy Act.

The fraying of the Douglas relationship with Roosevelt began as soon as the President began flirting with radical fiscal policies. This began with his acceptance of the powers under the Thomas amendment and continued until he decided to try the Warren plan in October.

Douglas not only argued valiantly every morning with the President but put his objections in the form of memoranda which he left with Roosevelt. This sort of thing always infuriated Roosevelt. He kept no diary or memoranda himself and was suspicious of anyone else who did so. He commented to me on one occasion that "Lew seems to be trying to establish a record."

It is possible that Roosevelt's adoption of the Warren plan led to the final break. Douglas resigned in early 1934 and continued his opposition to the Roosevelt policies in private life.

A reconciliation of sorts was achieved when Roosevelt took the side of the Allies in the late 1930's.

Finally when Acheson, who had also made his peace with Roosevelt after 1940, became Secretary of State in Truman's Administration, he obtained the appointment of Douglas as Ambassador to the Court of St. James's.

Hugh S. Johnson

Of all the people who surrounded Roosevelt in 1933 I find it most difficult to write without emotion about Hugh Johnson. After his death, I wrote this:

> For to recall the days of my association with him, the causes in which we were joined, the disappointments we shared, the manner of the man and the atmosphere in which he moved through the last great ten years of his life is to feel again his vitality, his cosmic pretensions, his torrential

emotion and his armored divisions of words. It means, too, a return of the feeling that came with his death—bitter regret that he burned his precious vitality so recklessly, that he could not have seen the frustration at the end of the war he opposed so earnestly, that he could not counsel us on the problems of its tragic aftermath.*

With all the externals of the tough realist, a ruthless engine of discipline and command, and a volcano of invective when roused, he was beneath it all an individual of tender and copious emotion, a sentimentalist and a dreamer of fine-spun fancies.

Johnson graduated from West Point in 1903. Douglas MacArthur was a classmate. He showed great promise in the Army, but his restless mind turned to law for a time. When the United States entered the war in 1917, Johnson returned to the Army and there he helped plan and administer the selective service system. This earned him promotion to the rank of brigadier general. Later he served with Baruch in the War Industries Board, where no doubt he conceived the idea which he later embodied in the National Industrial Recovery Act.

I first met Johnson on the day following Roosevelt's nomination in Chicago. He was then serving as economic adviser to Baruch, who offered Johnson's services to the candidate. He was then attached to my group of policy advisers. I welcomed this addition because Johnson's conservative views, I believed, would be a healthy corrective for some of the more radical plans and ideas of the academicians. In the preparation of campaign speeches Johnson was of immeasurable help. He not only had an encyclopedic knowledge of economics and business but had the robust and colorful style so essential in a campaign that was destined to be limited to dry economic issues.

Johnson was not a team worker. He would vanish for several days and then appear with a full-blown draft of a speech. Then when I edited his material to bring it into the mainstream of the campaign strategy and also to temper some of his incandescent language, he would scream with agony.

He had some of the universality of knowledge that was the mark of the scholars and preachers of the Middle Ages. He was at home in public finance, business, law, agriculture, industrial production, military affairs, literature, and American folklore. I am always hesitant to use the word "genius," but Johnson's capacity to absorb, retain, and articulate knowledge calls for no other characterization. At one time he had written some children's stories.

When the NRA got under way, the whole nation was treated to the delights we had enjoyed in the campaign. For the first half year Johnson staged a show the like of which Americans had never before seen. He

* *27 Masters of Politics,* p. 165.

exhorted, scolded, and inspired. He denounced businessmen who faltered in their cooperation. He quarreled with his subordinates. But the rise in employment in 1933 justified his labors.

For a year and a half Roosevelt regarded Johnson's efforts as exactly what was necessary to dramatize the New Deal. But, as we have seen, the NRA bogged down, in part because Johnson tried to do too much too soon.

The wearied warrior resigned and began writing a column for the Scripps-Howard newspapers. There he exercised his independence to oppose most of Roosevelt's policies. When the drift toward war began, he became vigorously anti-interventionist. He called this phase of Roosevelt's Administration the "Third New Deal." Johnson died in 1943.

Johnson's volatile temperament drove him when faced with frustration to overindulgence in alcohol. After a few days of this he would find recovery at an inn overlooking the Hudson River and West Point. There he would gaze at the ivied halls and playing fields of his beloved alma mater. He would recall with profit the lesson of integrity and self-discipline that he learned so many years before. On several occasions I saw him when he had returned after this soul-searching, and there was always something of spiritual majesty after winning this battle with himself.

After his resignation from the government, which ended his immense efforts to teach industry self-control and self-discipline, I quoted for him Carlyle's benediction over the career of Robert Burns:

> Granted, the ship comes into harbor with shrouds and tackle damaged; the pilot is blameworthy; he has not been all-wise and all powerful; but to know how blameworthy, tell us first whether his voyage has been around the earth, or only to Ramsgate and the Isle of Dogs.

With misty eyes Johnson responded, "You can say that again—and again."

Johnson carried a soft heart in that hard shell.

Rexford G. Tugwell

On almost every minor issue confronted by the early New Deal, Hugh Johnson and Rex Tugwell were in sharp conflict. But on the two principles that distinguished the Roosevelt Administration in its first year they were in firm agreement. Both believed in putting domestic recovery first and both favored a measurable degree of planning at the Federal level. My convictions mostly were Johnson's but I sought to maintain a neutral position when the members of our group were in conflict.

Tugwell was a colleague of mine at Columbia, but since we were in different faculties and departments I knew of him only by hearsay before

1932. Before I asked him to meet and discuss policies with Roosevelt he was deeply depressed about the state of the nation. He firmly believed that the business community was incapable of recovery except through massive intervention by the Federal government. He had visited Russia in the late 1920's and was deeply interested in the Soviet government's use of economic planning. But, like many others who saw the Soviet experiment, Tugwell was repelled by its ruthless denial of personal liberty. He always believed that personal and political liberty could be reconciled with national economic planning.

In 1933 Tugwell's major interest was in agriculture but, as his book published in that year, *The Industrial Discipline*, shows, his interests extended into industrial life. He also believed with me that our road to recovery lay in protecting our economy from international entanglements until we had gotten our domestic house in order. He accepted the status quo in tariff protection, not on the ground that such protection would help business but because he believed it helped to isolate the United States and thus provide room for a planned and orderly economy. Tugwell's economic thinking closely resembled that of the British socialists who as time went on submerged their socialism under the guise of national planning.

Tugwell was the first of the professors whom I escorted to Albany to spend an evening with Roosevelt. The reaction of the two men to each other was immediately favorable. Roosevelt loved the stimulation of unorthodox ideas, although his considered decisions as governor were, with the exception of those concerning public electric power, quite orthodox. While Roosevelt rejected many of Tugwell's ideas, the professor's range of interest provided for him a sort of intellectual cocktail.

Tugwell's reaction to Roosevelt from that first meeting in Albany was the beginning of an admiration that almost approached a romantic dedication. This is abundantly shown in his book *The Democratic Roosevelt*. In writing of that first meeting Tugwell says, "I was taken out of myself. . . . That my inquiring has gone on since that spring day in 1932 is my credential for writing this book. It will be understood, since I have said this, that meeting him was somewhat like coming in contact with destiny itself. It was a tremendous, unnerving experience, only to be realized and assimilated over a long time."

My mind was more worldly. I realized when I saw this conversion that with this devotion I had found a man who would be an invaluable factor in the structure I was trying to create to help Roosevelt win the nomination and the election.

In those preliminary days up to the time of the Chicago convention, it was Tugwell who converted Roosevelt to a major, if not the major, issue in winning both the nomination and the election. As I have said in an earlier chapter, it was Tugwell who explained the domestic allotment plan to Roosevelt and then, at my instance, brought to our group M. L. Wilson, who had been a main exponent of the new plan for agriculture. When, after his acceptance of Tugwell's argument, Roosevelt was reminded by Henry Morgenthau, Jr., that he had written an article earlier that year in support of the McNary-Haugen plan, the governor replied, "Well, that was last February."

It was Tugwell who brought Henry Wallace to Hyde Park to see Roosevelt after the nomination and persuaded Roosevelt to appoint the Iowa editor Secretary of Agriculture, despite the vigorous efforts of Morgenthau, supplemented by his father, to get that office for himself. Wallace, after his selection in 1933 had been announced, persuaded Tugwell to join him as assistant secretary and later promoted him to the newly created office of undersecretary.

While the adoption by Roosevelt of the domestic allotment plan was a major contribution to the 1932 campaign, Tugwell was helpful in many other ways in the two months that followed the nomination. In August Tugwell, who was annually afflicted by hay fever—a most unfortunate weakness in a farm expert—was compelled to find a more friendly climate. When he returned in early October, he said that he was unhappy over what he called Roosevelt's compromises in his speeches and statements. As I understood him, he had hoped that the planning concept, which was applied to the agricultural sector, might have been advocated for other elements in the economy. Years later he still felt the hurt of our expediency. He said in a letter to me in 1965, "Roosevelt did tell us that nothing we wanted could be had unless the election could be won. I think that we felt that he did compromise too much. And the Pittsburgh speech [which was a strong orthodox statement of fiscal policy] was a disaster from the long-run point of view. We didn't like the Brandeis reform in the Columbus speech. It seemed that it had nothing to do with recovery."

I respected these sentiments of Tugwell's, but I agreed with Roosevelt that in a campaign for the Presidency there must be something for everybody. And since Hoover and the opposition orators were already harping about the dangerous views of Roosevelt, we believed that with the election practically won, ideology must yield to political necessity.

As time went on, Tugwell's perfectly sincere but maladroit expression of his views brought upon his sensitive head bitter criticism in the press and in Congress. The early experiments which emanated from his office in the Department of Agriculture provided plenty of fuel for attack. Direct criticism of Roosevelt was softened by the vast popularity he enjoyed in his first term. But a great deal of harsh comment was directed at the "men around the President." Tugwell, despite his mild manner and most friendly disposition, became a national symbol of radicalism. Old poems and other writings of his were unearthed and given prominence in the press.

Tugwell stoically met these attacks without in any way yielding his convictions. There was a close affinity between Tugwell and Wallace. Wallace was much more visionary and radical than Tugwell and less intellectually equipped to grapple with the opposition. But Tugwell was regarded as the more dangerous of the two. Wallace was also less equipped to meet the heavy administrative burden of running immense departments, and much of the labor fell to his subordinate. People close to Wallace called him a "mystic," and plenty of evidence accumulated to justify that characterization.

James A. Farley, always the pragmatist politician, brought to Roosevelt in 1936 the complaint that Tugwell was a dangerous political liability. There was also opposition to Tugwell by the internationalists, including Hull and several members of Congress who were committed to tariff reduction as an economic cure-all. Finally Roosevelt, with Wallace's consent, yielded and Tugwell left the Administration in 1937.

He was in business for a while and then became chairman of the New York City Planning Commission under Mayor La Guardia. In 1941 Roosevelt appointed him governor of Puerto Rico. His sympathy for the inhabitants of what he called that "stricken land" and his pleasant relations with the island's political leaders made his stay as governor a relatively happy interlude in his life. Later he returned to university service and writing.

It is not without significance that so many historians of the Roosevelt years, especially those with a liberal bent, have given so much attention to Tugwell. For he was the most dedicated and articulate spokesman for the planning phase of the First New Deal. Thus he had influence upon this decisive period in our history. He was not able to see many of his ideas adopted as national policy, but his dissents from orthodox thinking substantially enlarged the range of American thought.

I am appalled to speculate upon what might have happened if more of Tugwell's ideas had been adopted. But that is because my concept of national progress differs from his. But even in the limited area of our agreement my own philosophy has been enriched by my association with him.

In the course of years many of one's friends are estranged or drop away because of ideological or political differences. Others are dropped because they have no sincerity in what they support or are seeking undeserved advantage. But I have always maintained my respect for this man Tugwell, who might have attained much more of what the world calls distinction. And I have been happy to be reminded by my all too infrequent contact with this old friend that he entertains a warm affection for me although he has always wished that I might have found more agreements with his views.

James A. Farley

Of all those who worked with Roosevelt in the First New Deal, the image of Jim Farley has remained most clearly etched in the public mind. This is in large part due to the love and admiration of his innumerable friends, his exemplary business and personal life, his many public appearances, and his pains in maintaining friendly relations with the press. He is honored by Republicans because of his break with Roosevelt, by Democrats because of his unshaken loyalty to the party, and by others because he is known as a politician who is honest, decent, and personable.

Indeed, as time has passed, his fame has become so great that many regard him as the man who discovered Roosevelt, won him the nomination and, because of his political talents, assured his "boss" unprecedented political success. With this legend we need not argue, although there were many others, including Roosevelt himself, who contributed to that success story.

Edward J. Flynn was from the beginning of Roosevelt's candidacy Roosevelt's major strategist and political mentor. It was Flynn who selected Farley to travel over the country and win delegates who favored Roosevelt's nomination. Farley, a master salesman, carried out this assignment so well that from the beginning of the active pre-convention campaign there was never any doubt about Roosevelt's lead in delegate strength.

But it was Flynn who remained at home close to Roosevelt and designed the strategy that proved so effective when the going was rough. There was also the dedicated Howe. Thus Farley was never the sole manager of Roosevelt's fortunes. He was the natural choice for national chairman because he knew more people of importance in the party, was better liked by politicians of all sorts and conditions, and was superb in compromising differences and in preventing intra-party strife. But Roosevelt's political management was a three-man affair until Howe's death, and after that the essential power slowly passed to Flynn.

Farley was a splendid team worker. Throughout the campaign political and policy decisions were kept strictly apart. Farley seldom if ever made any suggestions to me or to Roosevelt about matters of policy or the content of his public commitments. And I scrupulously kept hands off political management. This distinction carried over into the activities of the new Administration. Only when Farley asked did I do anything about appointments after the inauguration, and that was confined to a few diplomatic posts that were given to large contributors to the 1932 campaign.

As Postmaster General, Farley ran a good and efficient store. Only when Roosevelt impulsively canceled the mail contracts with the airlines and the mails were for a time carried by Army flyers was there serious trouble, and Farley blamed the resulting tragedy upon the Secretary of War.

No doubt the first four years of Roosevelt's Administration were the happiest of Jim Farley's life. The great victory in 1936 was the crowning event in his long political career. The victory was accompanied by Farley's prediction that Landon would carry only two states, Maine and Vermont. This established the reputation of Farley not only as a manager without a peer but as an incomparable prophet.

The first month of the second term revealed a serious rift among the Democrats in Congress over the "Court packing" proposal. In this fight Farley was loyal to the President and sought without success to win support for the measure in Congress. But I doubt whether his heart was engaged in these efforts.

From there on the Farley-Roosevelt relationship began to fray. The reasons for this, as Farley was to tell in his book *Jim Farley's Story* in 1948, were not only political but personal.

It might have been wise if Farley had omitted the personal factors in the estrangement from his writing. He keenly felt a hurt because Roosevelt during their relationship had confined their contacts to the office and their discussion strictly to political affairs. No doubt this feeling was deepened because Roosevelt and Flynn enjoyed more or less continuous contacts of a social nature. In Farley's earlier book *Behind the Ballots,* he says that Roosevelt didn't have a snobbish hair in his head. But in 1948 there is a broad suggestion that quite the opposite was true. I am inclined to agree with Farley's 1938 estimate, because I never discovered snobbishness to be one of Roosevelt's traits. In fact, he permitted himself to be insufferably bored with some of the people whom Mrs. Roosevelt brought in for luncheon or dinner. And in the relationships with Flynn and Farley, no doubt Roosevelt enjoyed the broad interests of Flynn more than the rather specialized concerns of Farley.

This personal factor, however, would probably never have been mentioned by Farley unless there had been serious political differences developing after 1937.

Roosevelt in 1938, angered by the opposition in his party to the Court bill and also by outspoken criticisms by some of the Senators, decided that he would seek to prevent the re-election of a number of these opponents. Farley was deeply disturbed about this, because it was not only a serious threat to party unity but because he believed it to be a futile gesture. He spoke of his dissent not only to Roosevelt but quite freely among his friends. Farley's practical judgment proved to be right, for Roosevelt lost his fight to prevent the renomination of the Senators he opposed. He also failed to secure the renomination of McAdoo, whom he supported. It was a bitter blow to Roosevelt's popularity, which might well have defeated him in 1940 except for the coming of the war in Europe.

At this time Farley, encouraged by his friends and by his enjoyment of great popularity, entertained an ambition to seek higher office. He sought repeatedly with little success to elicit from Roosevelt his plans about running for a third term. Farley wanted the Presidential or the Vice-Presidential nomination in 1940. But if Roosevelt ran, Farley was barred by the Constitution, which specifies that the electors of a state cannot vote for both a President and a Vice-President from their own state. Therefore he urged upon Roosevelt the desirability of conforming to tradition and retiring. In that case, Farley argued, Cordell Hull would be a fine candidate. This would have opened the way for Farley as Vice-Presidential candidate. In rejecting the idea of Hull as a candidate Roosevelt merely said: "Did you ever see Hull's desk?"

Roosevelt suggested that, since Herbert Lehman was reluctant to run again for governor of New York, Farley should consider that alternative. Roosevelt's argument for this was sound. He told Farley that the road to the Presidency was through winning an elective office of some consequence. And the New York governorship had served admirably in the past in helping to get a Presidential nomination.

Farley's rejection of this suggestion was probably the major political mistake of his life. For with Roosevelt's support he could have won the governorship and in 1942 would probably have been re-elected. Beyond that almost anything might have happened.

But Farley was unable to get Roosevelt to say that he intended to run for a third term. From that time on, a scattering of delegates pledged themselves to Farley as a Presidential candidate. There was considerable disaffection among the delegates about the renomination of Roosevelt, but finally the word came from the White House that Roosevelt was to be named and Harry Hopkins was sent to Chicago to make the nomination certain. Farley believed that he had the pledges of from 120 to 150 delegates. This included, he thought, the entire Massachusetts group. But as the pressure from the White House was applied and party leaders tried to avoid a contest, the Farley support crumbled.

Farley tells that someone among the Roosevelt supporters telephoned to Ambassador Kennedy in London asking that he instruct his son, Joseph, Jr., a Massachusetts delegate, to switch to Roosevelt. The elder Kennedy rejected the suggestion and young Joe voted for Farley.

Garner also had not discouraged support for himself.

Altogether it was a sullen and confused convention. The aged Carter Glass was there and made a speech placing the name of Farley before the delegates.

But when the roll was called Farley had 72½ votes, Garner 61, Senator Tydings of Maryland 9½. Roosevelt had the rest.

Farley then moved to make the nomination unanimous and it was done. Under great White House pressure, Henry Wallace was nominated for Vice-President.

Later, Roosevelt begged Farley to continue as national chairman. Farley refused, and Flynn was named to succeed him.

Farley went through the amenities and gave Roosevelt his endorsement. He did so in 1944 with words that conveyed no enthusiasm.

But Farley's devotion to the Democratic Party remained—after his religion—the passion of his life. And ever since Roosevelt's death, Farley, with little discrimination, has conspicuously supported every Democrat who has aspired to high public office. This unfailing dedication to the party label has measurably impaired the reputation as a prophet he earned in 1936. For some of his predictions have since been almost absurdly incorrect.

There is a certain lack of consistency in this dedication to the nominal Democratic Party. For the Democratic Party of which Alfred E. Smith was leader back in the 1920's and in which Farley rose to fame bears little resemblance to the party that Roosevelt so fundamentally re-created. On many occasions when I have met Farley in later years his friendly greeting has been, "Ray, when are you coming back to the Democratic Party?" My answer has been, "What party? The party in which you and I grew up is dead as the Whigs and the Know-Nothings."

There is a certain irony in the Farley image of a man who did so much for Roosevelt and who was ungratefully injured. On balance the Farley-Roosevelt rift cannot be charged against Roosevelt.

But many other persons, such as Smith, who left the Democratic Party and Roosevelt on the high level of principle have been denounced as ingrates and turncoats. Between the motivations of Farley in leaving Roosevelt and those of Alfred E. Smith and others there can hardly be a comparison.

Chapter Thirty

In Congress

John Nance Garner

One of the more classical miscalculations in American political history was the belief in the East among bankers and businessmen in 1932 that while Roosevelt could be trusted to understand their point of view because of his aristocratic background, Garner, his running-mate, was a dangerous radical. Conservatives prayed that Roosevelt might live.

Slowly these people came to realize that whatever stability the careening ship of state might attain would be due not to the captain but the first mate.

The earlier opinion may have been due to what the press told about the rugged manner, the salty speech, and the unconventional life that Garner lived. Indeed he was portrayed as a sort of "character," a glorified clown, who spent his time inventing wisecracks or selecting the funny hats he preferred to wear. Perhaps this image of the man from Texas came into being because newspapermen in Washington lost the capacity to take a man as he seems to be. They have seen so many phonies come and go and are so afraid of falling victim to pretense that they conclude that nothing is what it seems to be.

Against the background in which he lived, Garner was unusual. His mode of life contrasted sharply with the show that goes on in the national capital simply because he intended to live his life as he wanted to live it, and the least of his wants was public attention. He refused to go out to dinners because he wanted to go to bed early and get up early. He smoked cigars of his liking and played a bit of poker. When late afternoon came, friends in Congress gathered in his office "to strike a blow for liberty," as he called it, which translated meant bringing out a bottle or two, exchanging the latest gossip, and sometimes talking about matters of high policy. At home in Uvalde he went hunting because he liked to hunt and to live out of doors. He wore Amon Carter's gift hats because that sort of headgear is worn in Texas and because they didn't cost him anything.

In 1933 he had seniority over everyone else connected with the Roosevelt regime, for he had served fifteen terms in the House when he was elected Vice-President. He had seen six Presidents come and go and, by my calculation at the time, when he retired he had known no less than three thousand members of Congress. The district from which he came in 1903 was as large as Pennsylvania and its border on the southwest followed five hundred miles of the Rio Grande.

Sharpened by those many years in Congress, Garner had an amazing mastery of fiscal policy. His capacity, as a member of the Ways and Means Committee, to outwit Treasury experts' estimates was legendary. With little research assistance and aided only by a pencil, paper, and a keen sense of values, he offered an annoying opposition during the many years of Republican control.

His mind was like a field sparingly planted. He never tried to raise too much per acre. What grew there needed the air and sunlight to fill out and nourish itself. His mental life was no aggregate of half-suffocated plants, and there were very few weeds. The principles that guided his votes and his sparing vocal support were few. But they were of the sort which have stood the test of centuries.

The President he loved and respected most was Woodrow Wilson. From that great constitutionalist he learned more than any books could supply. He told me once of his relations with Wilson. While Claude Kitchin, as majority leader of the House, outranked Garner, Wilson had conceived a strong aversion to the man from North Carolina because he had voted against the declaration of war. Garner's relations with the President ripened into a friendship that provided long private conversations at the White House on legislation, politics, and life in general.

In the Hundred Days, Garner accepted without much debate the measures favored by the President, and his shrewd appraisals and wise advice to the members of both houses who frequented his office materially contributed to the support Roosevelt enjoyed in Congress. But in the Cabinet meetings and in private talks with the President he freely spoke his mind. It was, as I have already shown, due to the sagacity of Garner as presiding officer in the Senate that the guarantee of bank deposits was attached to the Glass bill, despite the doubts of the author of that bill and the President's firm opposition.

In the years after 1933, the true character of Garner's constitutional and political convictions came to be well known. These cheered and reassured conservatives and infuriated the radicals. Slowly, as the toxic effect of the overwhelming victory in 1936 possessed Roosevelt, the contacts between the two men sharpened into disagreement. As Garner described it to his friends, the two major differences were spending and concessions to labor unions. Here there would be no reconciliation.

Meanwhile the popularity of Garner grew. He was the man in Washington whom visitors wanted to see. Newspapers gave him ample space. Businessmen liked him because he offered a possible alternative to Roosevelt. Party men loved him because of his regularity. Congressmen and Senators respected him and sought his advice. The traditional impotence of the Vice-Presidency no longer applied to him.

He was firmly committed to the two-term limitation, but by 1939 he shrewdly concluded that Roosevelt wanted a third term. He decided not only that he would not accept renomination for the Vice-Presidency but also that he should do what he could to frustrate Roosevelt's ambition to shatter the two-term tradition. And so he announced in late 1939 that he would accept the Presidential nomination if the offer came to him. He had no organization and no hope of stopping Roosevelt, but he wanted to offer a tangible protest against a third term.

What happened was that in an angry and confused convention Roosevelt was nominated because he said in effect that, while he was reluctant to run, the international situation compelled continuity. Also, by the use of Presidential pressure, Roosevelt secured the Vice-Presidential nomination for the thoroughly unpopular (with the party) Henry Wallace.

Garner returned to Washington in January to preside over the Senate for the last time and to accept the tributes accorded him on his retirement. When asked what he intended to do he replied, "I am going home to live to be ninety-three years old." As this is written he is in his ninety-sixth year. He never revisited Washington.

James F. Byrnes

In recent years, in complicated and overcrowded Washington a major White House functionary is charged with Congressional relations. Skilled in the arts of persuasion and officially known as the President's man, he manages the Chief Executive's legislative measures in Congress, consolidates the committed, persuades the uncommitted, and when necessary overrides a member's convictions by promises of patronage.

In the less complicated era of the Hundred Days that responsibility was largely vested in James F. Byrnes, the junior Senator from South Carolina. Byrnes had little committee seniority, for he was then serving in only his third year in the Senate. But he had other advantages which made him, next to Garner and Majority Leader Robinson, the most influential member of Congress. He knew everyone there because he had served in the House from 1911 to 1925, and in 1930 had defeated the racist and demagogic Cole Blease in a hard fight in the Senatorial primary. He was not only Roosevelt's favorite Senator but was very popular among his colleagues. The venerable Carter Glass was official chairman of the Appropriations Committee, but because of his labors with the banking bill and his age, he bestowed upon Byrnes most of his authority for managing that powerful group.

Byrnes's close association with Roosevelt began shortly after the Chicago convention in 1932, when he called upon the nominee at Hyde Park. I was present when they were discussing campaign plans. I was deeply impressed by Byrnes's fine intelligence, his sharp mentality, his extraordinary knowledge of the issues that had come before Congress since he entered the Senate. And so, since the policy group I had assembled at that time was heavily loaded with academic men, I asked Roosevelt to add Byrnes to my Brains Trust. This was easily arranged, since Byrnes was not a candidate for re-election that year. Later I secured the help of Senator Key Pittman, and the two Senators were my constant companions throughout the campaign. They were used only sparingly in preparing speeches, but their sage advice and wide acquaintance with party personalities saved us many mistakes. The essential conservatism of the two also helped to dissipate the dangerous idea that Roosevelt had surrounded himself with wooly-minded theorists.

From that association with Byrnes there grew a personal friendship between us which has lasted through the many years since. Few men in American history have had so diversified a career in public office as Byrnes—distinction in the House and Senate for twenty-four years, membership in the Supreme Court, the direction of the most important civilian war agency from 1942 to 1945, and Secretary of State after Roosevelt's death. These official responsibilities came not through the usual political processes or because Byrnes was a sycophant before the throne. They came in large part while Roosevelt was living because the President respected his judgment even when he disagreed, and because Byrnes had the love and respect of his party in the Senate. He missed the Vice-Presidency in 1944 and, as fate decreed, the Presidency in 1945 through as wry a process of wire-pulling—and of rug-pulling—as we have had in our political annals.

Byrnes had loyally left the Supreme Court to serve as a sort of economic minister in the war, and, since Roosevelt had decided to drop Henry Wallace as a running-mate that year, Byrnes had every reason to believe that he was Roosevelt's choice for the vacancy. Byrnes had conferred with Roosevelt about his ambition for the nomination for Vice-President and was assured that the President would welcome him as a running-mate. Byrnes therefore went to the convention in Chicago to consummate what he thought was an agreement. When he arrived there it seemed that the party leaders were already receptive to his nomination.

But at this point the powerful hand of Edward J. Flynn moved into the situation. Flynn's account of his argument against Byrnes is this:

> In a subsequent meeting with the President I told him of my conclusion that Wallace would be a serious handicap to him on the ticket. The problem then was to find a man who would hurt him the least. A review was made of the other candidates. Byrnes, who was the strongest candidate, wouldn't do because he had been raised a Catholic and had left the Church when he married, and the Catholics wouldn't stand for that; organized labor, too, would not be for him; and, since he came from South Carolina, the question of the Negro vote would be raised. For these reasons he would, as I said, hurt the President." *

Thus it seemed at that time that while being a Catholic was a fatal bar to a place on the national ticket it was even worse to have been a Catholic and to have left the Church. This would array against such a candidate anti-Catholics on one side and Catholics on the other. But Flynn was calculating only upon the effect of such a nomination on the vote in New York. It seems that Roosevelt was not convinced, because he told Flynn to talk with National Chairman Robert E. Hannegan and other leaders about it. It is clear from all of the accounts of two principals—and I have had the story from both Flynn and Byrnes—that Roosevelt because of failing health and energy was less than positive about whom he wanted at that time. However, it was believed by the leaders in Chicago that Roosevelt preferred Byrnes, for they said as much to Byrnes when he arrived at the convention city. Finally, after a violent argument with the President, Flynn convinced him that Truman rather than Byrnes should be chosen. For, as Flynn said to me later, he believed that no one could help a ticket with Roosevelt at its head and that Truman, because he was less known, would "do him the least harm." It is out of such cynical considerations that nominations are sometimes made and the republic is governed.

After his retirement as Secretary of State, Byrnes returned to South Carolina and in 1950 was elected governor. His major contribution during those four years of office was a vast program for rebuilding Negro schools. These stand as a final monument to one of the South's most distinguished and most honored elder statesmen. It is worthy of note that because of these new schools and the generally moderate attitude of Byrnes and his successors toward the race question there has been less trouble and racial unrest in South Carolina than in some other Southern states.

* Flynn, *You're the Boss,* p. 180.

In recent years Byrnes, like so many whose roots were in the pre-Roosevelt Democratic Party, has cut the ties with the present leadership. He supported Eisenhower twice, also Nixon and Goldwater. In this protest he has called himself not a Republican but an "independent" Democrat.

Key Pittman

Most of those who have written accounts of the period under consideration in this book have not been kind—not even fair—to Senator Key Pittman of Nevada. The major indictments have been three, and these seem to have convinced commentators that in the history of the New Deal he was a negative influence. He has been condemned because of his preoccupation with the interests of silver in our economy and in our currency. He is charged with excessive zeal in getting patronage for his state. And his convivial habits have been censured, even ridiculed. Since among all of those who have written of this period I am the only one who had a close and intimate relationship with the Senator, I am concerned here not only with a recital of that association but in correcting some of the tales that have interested younger historians.

The first two of these charges can easily be disposed of. When Pittman first entered politics in Nevada the state was new—almost primitive. There were no traditions of long tenure such as had made things so easy for Borah in Idaho or Hiram Johnson in California. In every one of Pittman's six battles for his seat, the fighting was tough and the electorate judged candidates by what they had done for the state. And since nearly 90 per cent of the state was Federal property, this meant Federal patronage and help for its major economic support, the mining interests, especially the interests of silver.

This concern for local interests has never been absent from the political life of any state. Massachusetts today compels its Senators to fight lustily for the retention of obsolete shipyards and its dying textile interests. Oklahoma dearly covets the Federal improvement of the Arkansas River, and Texas of the Trinity. A state's representatives in Congress are judged by these efforts in behalf of local interests. This is one of the prices we pay for representative government.

But Pittman's concerns were not limited at all by these local necessities. It was the wide knowledge of national issues generally and the experience he had enjoyed in studying and debating these affairs that attracted my attention when I first met him and caused me to ask Roosevelt to add him along with Byrnes to my policy group. I was desperately seeking to round out my group to include the practical political experience and knowledge of those who had intimate contact with what had been going on in the Congress during the twelve years of Republican rule. Pittman fitted these requirements admirably. For Pittman had not only been a very active Senator during that period but earlier had been a stalwart supporter of President Wilson's domestic and foreign policies. In Wilson's efforts to bring the United States into the League of Nations, Pittman had been one of those Democrats on the Foreign Relations Committee who begged the President to agree to reservations—Pittman called them "understandings"—less rigid than those proposed by the Lodge group but sufficient to win ratification in a divided and distracted Senate. At that time Wilson called Pittman to the White House and asked his opinion. When Pittman gave his opinion Wilson ended the interview. Our foreign policy, indeed the course of our history, might have been quite different if the stubborn President had accepted the judgment of those loyal Democratic Senators.

In the campaign Pittman was of inestimable service to Roosevelt's cause. For the candidate trusted Pittman and knew of his loyal support when he was seeking the nomination. In many a decision when I needed help, Pittman with the utmost frankness offered wise advice to Roosevelt, even when it meant opposing an earlier conclusion. On two touchy subjects, public power and the tariff, Pittman not only advised but collaborated in preparing the speeches delivered by Roosevelt in Portland, Sioux City, and Baltimore.

Pittman was useful in that campaign for the Presidency in many other ways. He was very popular with political figures over the nation who from time to time visited the campaign train, and he served well in interpreting the candidate to these people, who were so important in their states and communities. He quieted many doubts and soothed many hard feelings. His popularity in the Senate was later shown when, after the new Congress assembled, he was named President Pro Tem of the Senate.

In the West the most troublesome question before Roosevelt was what he should say in those states whose depressed economy had been so dependent upon the price of silver. Neither Roosevelt nor Pittman believed it wise to go all the way to Bryan's formula for remonetization at the ratio of 16 to 1. But something had to be said, and the formula successfully used was Pittman's suggestion that the new Administration would "do something for silver."

After this campaign experience a firm friendship and mutual trust developed between Pittman and the new President. When the Thomas amendment was proposed and there was a great danger that its passage in its original form would seriously impair our plans for recovery, it was Pittman who contrived, along with Douglas and Byrnes, a modification that placed discretionary power with the President. And it was Pittman who "sold" the revised amendment to Thomas. No one but a known friend of silver could have accomplished that.

Since so much sniggering has marred the pages of supposedly responsible history-writing about Pittman's indulgence in alcohol, this subject needs to be faced squarely. To begin with, most of the stories that have been inserted in historical accounts are to my personal knowledge gross exaggerations or untruths. As anyone knows, the atmosphere of politics is always heavily laden with the fumes of alcohol. It is a life in which most participants live under constant strain. There are few who on this score can afford to cast the first stone. Political life lacks the measured routine of a more sheltered career. The strains of campaigning under almost inhuman conditions, the rigors imposed in legislative debates, the perils that threaten any holder of a public office from those who seek to replace him are heavy loads to bear.

In Pittman's case we have a brilliant mind coupled with a highly sensitive nervous system. Over the years alcoholic indulgence on a moderate scale ended in a case of genuine alcoholism. This, as any one familiar with this curse of modern living knows, is as authentic a disease as is paralysis or catalepsy. To make light of it or to view it with moral censure is as cruel an anachronism as paying admission to view the inhabitants of a Bedlam. I simply offer my own testimony on the Pittman case, based upon almost daily contact for thirteen months from July 1932 to September 1933 and casual contacts until his death.

Only twice in that period did Pittman's affliction overwhelm him. Once it was at the very end of the long campaign in late October. It was then brought on by a long frustrating meeting of the members of the Brains Trust in the Roosevelt Hotel in New York. Pittman argued heatedly with some of the more radical members of our group, who wanted Roosevelt, on the very eve of victory, to abandon the cautious course that had signalized his final weeks. In this Pittman was not only right but his caution was shared by Roosevelt himself. But the strain was too much and a week of excess followed in the privacy of his hotel suite. Byrnes and I, who were with him, made sure that this should be a strictly private matter. The other occasion was at the London Conference, where again he was frustrated, this time by the general demoralization of the American delegation. If half of the stories about that affair had been true, Pittman, despite his privileged position, would have been committed to protective custody. But I can vouch for the fact that when this spell had passed he made as much sense as any other American present and also that the silver proposal that he sponsored was the only tangible American achievement in the conference.

The early (and more readable and authentic) chapters of Fred L. Israel's biography, *Nevada's Key Pittman*, tell a saga of self-help and absorbing adventure. Pittman was born in Mississippi. His parents died before he was twelve. The care of Key and his three brothers passed to relatives. Various snatches of education were picked up by a genuinely talented boy, and after a few years of drifting he read law in Seattle and was admitted to the bar at the age of twenty. It was a time of deep depression and his legal work afforded only the bare necessities of life. Then in 1897, when the gold rush to Alaska began, he cast his lot with that adventure. Somehow he survived and prospered in the Far North. After three years, another gold rush opened in Nevada and he went there. He was so competent in mining law and there was so much litigation in those days of the gold rush that he became a notable figure in the new state. After one unsuccessful try he was elected to the United States Senate in 1912. This was the only elective office he held thereafter. He died only a few days after winning re-election in 1940.

Hiram Johnson

The significance of Hiram Johnson in the early New Deal is not because he contributed in any important respect to the decisions made then or to the measures enacted. It is, rather, that he stood as a reminder of the faith and philosophy of an earlier generation of reform to which was attached the name Progressivism. There was much in the early stages of the Roosevelt era that, as I have shown, derived from the two decades before when the President and many of those around him first concerned themselves with political affairs. But as the First New Deal ended and new influences and new personalities emerged, Progressivism faded and Hiram Johnson withdrew first into independence and finally into opposition. Then after 1938, when Roosevelt moved ever more dangerously toward the orbit of the gathering storm in Europe, Johnson once more displayed the energy and fire which had characterized his opposition to Wilson's League of Nations. He finished his career, as it began, an unreconstructed liberal in the domestic field and irreconcilable to foreign entanglements.

The career, activities, and ideology of Senator Hiram Johnson more clearly represent the extent to which early Progressivism extended into and came to be differentiated from New Dealism than those of any other individual. An authentic biography of Johnson is missing from the vast political literature of the period between 1910 and 1940. It needs to be written if we are to understand how Progressivism, a product of the best intentions and of an authentic need, shaped the thinking of a whole generation. Also, how some of its reforms misfired or were perverted into mischievous distortions of our political life. And how a man like Johnson found the atmosphere so distasteful that in 1940 he rejected Roosevelt and returned to his early Republican allegiance.

Johnson was no thundering exponent of constitutionalism like Borah. He began essentially as a reformer, a virile enemy of the unholy alliance between certain monopolistic business interests and politics. Nothing could have been more appropriate than his nomination as Vice-President on the ticket headed by Theodore Roosevelt. In the Senate later, he was a complete individualist. He opposed Wilson's peace plans not because he was a complete isolationist, as so many writers have claimed, but because he distrusted the intentions of our former allies in Europe and the Eastern interests in the United States who sought closer relations with them. So far as the Pacific and Far East were concerned, he fully recognized our immense stakes there and was willing to defend them. As a Republican he opposed the policies of the Republican regimes from 1921 to 1933 and in 1932 supported Roosevelt against Hoover. His relations with Roosevelt were excellent until his basic respect for the unwritten Constitution was affronted by Roosevelt's effort in 1937 to reorganize the Supreme Court. His early determination to check business-in-politics could not carry him so far as to support certain socialistic tendencies in the Roosevelt Administration, chiefly exemplified by the policies of Harold Ickes.

As an individual Johnson was deeply emotional—a warm and affectionate friend, but a bitter critic toward his enemies.

One of the most unfortunate outcomes of the efforts he and other Progressives made to limit the power of political parties by such reforms as the initiative and referendum and non-partisanship was to impair almost fatally the responsibility of party government. California still suffers from the perversion of Johnson's reforms. But his hold on the imagination and affections of his state and many other Western states continued to the end. He hardly needed to campaign at all for his successive elections to the Senate. He died in 1942.

Huey P. Long

Largely because of the mutual distrust, not to say antipathy, that prevailed between Roosevelt and Senator Huey Long, I was delegated by the President in 1933 to maintain a contact with the Louisiana dictator.

His influence was not only supreme in Louisiana but extended into all the neighboring states. A point was reached at the summit of Long's power at which he could by his influence assure the election of his friends in both Arkansas and Mississippi. And in the Senate, while the veteran members disliked Long, there was a healthy respect for his ruthlessness in debate.

I spent many hours talking with Huey Long in the three years before his death. When we talked about politics, public policies, and life generally, he cast off the manner of a demagogue as an actor wipes off greasepaint. There could be no question about his extraordinary mental—or, if you will, intellectual—capacity. I have never known a mind that moved with more clarity, decisiveness, and force. He was no backwoods buffoon, although when the occasion seemed to offer profit by such a role he could outrant a Heflin or a Bilbo. But the state of Louisiana reveals ample evidence of his immense contributions to the happiness and welfare of its people. As his power in that state grew to be secure and absolute, the virus of success took hold. There can be no doubt of his purposes: first, the complete consolidation of his power in Louisiana; second, his use of his forum in the Senate to grasp national attention; and, finally, to direct a campaign of national "education" through the states toward a Presidential nomination for himself at some future time, perhaps in 1940.

I am unable to estimate the potential of Long's strength as he looked toward a third-party nomination in 1936. But I am certain that Roosevelt and James A. Farley entertained a healthy belief that in a close election he might throw the election to a Republican. Polls taken by Farley's National Committee gave Long 10 per cent of the preferences. This threat definitely influenced Roosevelt's policies in 1935. For after the NRA had been declared unconstitutional, Roosevelt pressed upon Congress a drastic, half-baked "share-the-wealth" tax scheme. Perhaps one of the reasons for Roosevelt's change in direction was this threat, which reached its summit just before Long went to his gaudy grave on the capitol grounds at Baton Rouge.

Many times in the course of our friendly talks I implored Huey to rise above demogoguery and use his great capacities to act like a statesman. I told him what everyone came to know after his death: that although his objectives might be sincerely held, his accomplices were unworthy of him. He always protested that he made or sought no personal gain. But there was tragedy in his deliberate squandering of his talents for tawdry ends. He misused his fine mind, battered it, as a child might treat a toy the value and purpose of which he could not understand. He used his skills for the enrichment of his shoddy friends and for petty revenge upon his enemies. He used his mind to destroy the very foundations upon which his real reforms in Louisiana could permanently rest. He destroyed many things with his mind. And among them was himself.*

Sam Rayburn

As the seemingly interminable reign of Sam Rayburn over the House of Representatives moved on through the 1950's and into the 1960's, and his name became legendary and honors were bestowed upon him by Congress and his party, I often asked myself what I could have missed when I knew him so well in the 1930's. What made for such greatness?

* Some of the text of this appraisal of Huey Long I have taken from my book *27 Masters in Politics.*

In 1949, after he had been Speaker for nine years, I wrote this in a sketch about him: "Sam Rayburn, like Garner, hasn't swelled with his official rise. He has seen enough of greatness and the great through his keen reflective eyes to know the transitory nature of high place."

Now I doubt the validity of that appraisal. For with security in his status in the House and with his party so firmly in power he willingly permitted, even sought, more and more power in his hands than any Speaker since Joseph G. Cannon sixty years ago. Rayburn won his eminence by impressing his colleagues with his simplicity, his humility, his salty common sense, and his toleration of differences. But with power once attained and long held, he imposed an iron discipline on his parliamentary party. He made successive changes in the House rules and in the Rules Committee that substantially restored to the Speaker the powers that the Democratic Party, with the help of rebellious Republicans, had torn from Cannon in 1910. And curiously, despite his own love of power, he permitted the independence of the House to be compromised by his obedience to a new Democratic President.

Finally he conceived and directed the planning of one of the most monstrous and ugly edifices in Washington, the Rayburn office building.

One morning when I was having breakfast with Rayburn in his simple bachelor's apartment in the Anchorage, I asked him what advice he gave to young members. He said that he told them, "The way to get along is to go along." Perhaps that explains his own rise to power.

This advice drawn from Sam Rayburn's book of life meant fidelity to the party majority and obedience to the Executive—when the President was a Democrat. Those who choose to live by this rule enjoy many advantages. In a legislative body they can skip all the hard labor of reading bills and listening to the arguments for and against them. Their conscience is never torn by doubts, because they never use it. No loneliness needs to be endured, because such people will always have plenty of company. It seemed to me fitting that I titled my article about Rayburn in 1949, "He'll Never Walk Alone." This, I have reason to believe, terminated a friendship that had endured since 1933. Rayburn had lived by the dictates of regularity and hated to be reminded of it.

Rayburn never pondered the profoundly important constitutional or policy questions involved in the measures that came before the House. Because of his position first as majority leader and later as Speaker, he found it unnecessary to enter into debates. His speeches from the floor were short, few, and far between.

What he said on one of those occasions suffices to explain a lot about Rayburn. It was shortly before the Taft-Hartley Act came to a vote. He said that very few of the members had taken the time to read the bill. "I do not know all that is in this bill. Few do or can. But from what I know of it, I know that what you are doing here is not fair. The bill is not fair. I'm not going to vote for it."

He did not add that the real reason he was going to vote against it was to try to save his friend Harry Truman the embarrassment of a veto.

Even Rayburn's protégé in the House, Lyndon B. Johnson, voted for the bill and later voted to sustain it against a veto.

It did not seem to disturb Rayburn's placid and steady course to monumental esteem that the rules he followed were a peril to the status of the House in our system of government. Something of the fine tradition of the House as an independent body died during the long years when Rayburn was Speaker. That was his contribution to posterity—along with the Rayburn office building.

Chapter Thirty-one

Unofficial Advisers

In any Administration, but especially in as informal a one as Roosevelt's, the role of unofficial adviser and friend is as important as that of anyone in office. These people play a large part in shaping the President's decisions and in directing policy not because any law says so but because the President likes them, respects them, and seeks them out. He can count upon their lack of interest in personal gain or preference. Such individuals shun public office for a variety of reasons. Their private responsibilities bar the way to a full-time job in government. They may dislike the publicity and the onerous routine imposed by office. They are available when needed. They can advise without accepting public responsibility. Their status with the President is not bound by the shackles of priority or protocol. They can come and go as they wish or as the President wishes. They are intimate friends of the President and he can unburden himself of what is on his mind without any fear of gossip or tale-bearing. They can even escape the surveillance of the press.

Edward J. Flynn

A strong argument can be made for the proposition that if there had been no Edward J. Flynn, Roosevelt could not have reached the Presidency. But in the annals of his time Flynn will probably be written off simply as the boss of the Bronx. The anonymity of Flynn in the years before and after the election of 1932 was a calculated choice made by Flynn himself. Farley and others took the bows. Flynn, so far as he could, kept in the background. But in every critical moment when great decisions were made he could be found at Roosevelt's side.

Perhaps the lesson he learned, that the influence of a major political strategist should be felt but not seen, came from the man to whom he owed his beginning in politics, Charles Francis Murphy, the mighty leader of Tammany Hall for twenty-two decisive years. I ended a sketch of Murphy's life which I contributed to the *Dictionary of American Biography* with the words, "his life was a masterpiece of reticence." The same might be said of Flynn. Only in the final years of his life did Flynn break through the self-imposed bounds of reticence. He told me that he would like to give some lectures on politics and write a book of reminiscences. I had a large class in politics at Columbia and Flynn appeared for three or four lectures. The calm bearing of the man, the depth of his understanding of political life, and the sophisticated manner in which he told his story delighted and informed the students. Shortly after that I persuaded him to dictate the text that appeared as his book, *You're the Boss.*

When Farley withdrew in 1940, Roosevelt persuaded Flynn to serve as chairman of the Democratic National Committee during that year's political campaign. In 1945 Roosevelt took Flynn with him to Yalta. I have already described how Flynn, singlehanded, persuaded Roosevelt in 1944 to drop Wallace from the ticket, to reject the strong claims of Byrnes to the Vice-Presidential nomination and to accept Harry Truman instead. When the Democratic Convention came very close to denying Truman the nomination, it was Flynn in the background who convinced the President that, while to nominate Truman was a risk, the nomination of Wallace would invite disaster.

Flynn's definitive part in promoting Roosevelt for the Presidency began when he assumed a major part in Roosevelt's campaign for governor in 1928. On the night of the election it was apparent that Smith would lose New York State by a considerable majority and that Roosevelt's election as governor was very doubtful. Flynn dispatched trusted agents to a number of upstate centers to make sure that the vote count would be accurate. No doubt Roosevelt's slim majority of 25,000 was due to that action of Flynn's. After Roosevelt's installation as governor he appointed Flynn to the sinecure office of secretary of state. The duties of that office were purely perfunctory. Flynn's real job was to serve as Roosevelt's closest political adviser and mentor. It was Flynn who selected Farley to canvass the country for delegates and it was Flynn at the center of things who directed operations at the Chicago convention which nominated the New York governor. During the campaign that followed it was Farley who held the office of chairman and dealt directly with the leaders. But it was Flynn who remained closest to the candidate.

In 1902 there was a contest for the leadership of the borough of the Bronx. Murphy selected Flynn to break the impasse, and for years thereafter Flynn was the undisputed master of that immense urban complex of races, nationalities, and other minorities. According to the accepted pattern of American politics, any such city area with a tightly organized machine and a supreme leader at its head would be badly or indifferently governed. For the machine's vote in the Bronx was always in the neighborhood of 80 per cent. But despite recurring scandals in the other boroughs of the city the Bronx enjoyed clean and efficient government.

The reason for this lay in the character, astuteness, and methods of Flynn. He held that a stupid or corrupt official was a fatal handicap to continued party success. The people gave him their votes. He gave them good government.

But in administering the affairs of the Bronx, Flynn violated all the common rules of political leadership. He was no mixer. Few citizens of the Bronx ever saw him. His circle of friends was small. And only his district leaders had access to him. To those leaders, whom he selected with great care, he delegated all the ordinary amenities of political association. In his book he described the life he lived in almost regal isolation:

> I intended to keep my personal life entirely separate from my political life. As a result, while I have enjoyed a personal friendship with each of the members of the Executive Committee over a long period of years, it has never been an extremely intimate association. I have not visited the homes of any of these men and women, nor have they been inside mine. I meet them only when occasion requires. Personal relationships . . . are apt to cause jealousy and dissatisfaction.*

To dispose of political business Flynn maintained an office at the County Building (near the Yankee Stadium), where he met his leaders at stated hours or by appointment.

Flynn was a graduate of Fordham University. He subsequently studied law and formed a partnership with a boyhood friend, Monroe Goldwater. The firm's office was in Manhattan, and Goldwater, a very able lawyer, directed the large practice, which ranged over all aspects of civil law. It was not a mere political law office.

Since Flynn managed his borough largely through his district leaders and Goldwater looked after the law practice, Flynn enjoyed plenty of leisure. This he spent in wide and sophisticated reading. Occasionally in the Roosevelt years he would, with a trusted lieutenant, take long automobile tours through the country to learn political trends and opinions at first hand.

Flynn was far ahead of most political leaders in detecting the liberal trend among American voters. It was on the basis of this ap-

* *You're the Boss,* p. 61.

praisal that he advised Roosevelt in 1935 to alter the philosophy and direction of Democratic policies. He described to me at the time this shift of emphasis in the Roosevelt policies from the agricultural areas to the cities. He said:

"There are two or three million more dedicated Republicans in the United States than there are Democrats. The population, however, is drifting into the urban areas. The election of 1932 was not normal. To remain in power we must attract some millions, perhaps seven million, who are hostile or indifferent to both parties. They believe the Republican Party to be controlled by big business and the Democratic Party by the conservative South. These millions are mostly in the cities. They include racial and religious minorities and labor people. We must attract them by radical programs of social and economic reform."

Flynn was thus responsible along with Roosevelt for a profound change in the Democratic Party and in national policies, a change the results which we are continuing to witness today. I personally regretted this change, but Flynn was a realist and his strategy, whatever one may think of its consequences, meant a new life for the Democratic Party.

Joseph Patrick Kennedy

During the past ten years the American people have witnessed the rise to power and place of three young men named Kennedy by the calculated use of burning ambition, intelligence, wealth, work, and a certain amount of personal charm. But if we isolate from these virtues the element of personal force and determination, these sons are but pale progeny of their father. For in their character there was, especially in John F., an inheritance from a softer, sweeter mother. There was also the softening factor of inherited wealth. The father made what he had by his own efforts and shrewdness. And the influence of those more sophisticated factors that come with a wider range of interests and a somewhat different education have tempered the original pattern of the Kennedy inheritance. The high offices attained by the sons are but blossoms on the paternal tree.

My own impressions go back to my relationship with Joe Kennedy, which began on a June day at the governor's mansion in Albany shortly before the Democratic Convention assembled in Chicago. I was there because it was necessary to make some final revisions in the speech of acceptance. Roosevelt introduced me to his visitor, a ruddy-faced, vigorous, and highly colorful talker. I arrived just as Kennedy was leaving and I well remember that when he paused at the door he turned to Roosevelt and said, "I will keep my contact with W. R. [Hearst] on a day-and-night basis."

A week later, after the nomination, I met Kennedy again. He was at breakfast in his apartment at the Ambassador with his friend Herbert Bayard Swope. Because Louis Howe had jealously rejected the speech of acceptance that I had drafted, which Roosevelt and Sam Rosenman had edited in Albany, and had written one of his own composition overnight, I was anxious to gather as much help as I could to win support for the earlier draft. I read the text and Kennedy's first comment was highly favorable. It was, he said, "bullish."

Subsequently Roosevelt invited Kennedy to accompany us on the long campaign trip to the West Coast and back, and there in the friendly intimacy of the campaign train the man from Boston became one of the inner circle. I permitted him to read the speeches before their delivery and welcomed his shrewd suggestions. His political inheritance from his father and his understanding of very practical economic affairs were valuable. Kennedy was accompanied by a friend and employee and man of all tasks, Eddie Moore, formerly secretary to Kennedy's father-in-law, Mayor John F. Fitzgerald. Moore was a lovable individual who soon became a favorite of the Roosevelt staff and the newspapermen. His infinite capacity to make friends made up for much of Kennedy's shortcomings in that respect. Kennedy loved Eddie Moore and in recognition bestowed his name upon his fourth son, Edward Moore Kennedy, now United States Senator from Massachusetts.

Except for what Kennedy told me from time to time, I knew little of the political obligation that the Roosevelt pre-convention organization owed to Kennedy. According to Richard J. Whalen's account, Kennedy had given the Flynn-Farley organization $25,000 and lent the Democratic Party another $50,000. In addition he raised $100,000 from his friends, mostly from Wall Street.*

I cannot vouch for these amounts. Kennedy himself told me that the amount advanced either as a gift or loan in the pre-convention months was $20,000. But the devious ways in which contributions were routed in those days makes exact amounts hard to arrive at. At any rate, Kennedy had given or loaned a hard-pressed Roosevelt cause a lot of money and in a depression year when money was very essential to an organization.

Whalen suggests that Kennedy's interest in the Roosevelt cause involved a cold, calculating streak of opportunism. It was evident to Kennedy, who in the course of amassing a fortune (which even then was probably about $10 million) had learned as much about financial affairs as anyone in Wall Street, that there was plenty of stupidity, mischief, and downright rascality in financial circles, and also that

* These figures are from Whalen's excellent and objective book, *The Founding Father* (New York: New American Library, 1964).

revelations already made, with more to come, would generate a wide demand for reform. He realized that such a demand would be an overpowering political force, and that it was therefore good politics to be on the side of the angels. I am inclined to conclude that Kennedy's contempt for the stupidity and reaction of those financial interests was the major source of his indignation.

At any rate Kennedy ranged himself ostentatiously on the side of Roosevelt and, after the crusade had been concluded with a triumph at the polls, he quite realistically, and I believe properly, thought that he would be rewarded with a high place in the new Administration.

But there was something I did not know at the time but which Whalen tells about in his book. It seems that early in the pre-convention months Kennedy had been introduced to Louis Howe in the little master's disorderly nest on Madison Avenue. At that meeting Howe knew that Kennedy had been a successful Wall Street operator, and he had made up his mind that neither the Kennedy name nor his money was wanted. When Howe decided to be discourteous, he operated with the virtuosity of a master. From that moment the mutual feelings between Howe and Kennedy developed into a venomous hatred.

It must have been due to this antagonism of Howe's, supported as Howe was by Mrs. Roosevelt, who regarded him as her political mentor and inspiration, that after the election there was little except mere formal communication from Roosevelt to Kennedy. Kennedy's concern about this neglect turned very soon to deep indignation. It increased as the Cabinet posts were filled and other plums were distributed. After accompanying Roosevelt to Jacksonville in February, I spent two or three days at Kennedy's home in Palm Beach. There I heard plenty of Kennedy's excoriation of Roosevelt, of his criticisms of the President-elect, who, according to Kennedy, had no program—and what ideas he had were unworthy of note. There must have been hundreds of dollars in telephone calls to provide an exchange of abuse of Roosevelt between Kennedy and W. R. Hearst. The latter by this time was wondering why he had ever supported Roosevelt in the final hours before the nomination.

There was little I could do in 1933 either to pacify Kennedy or to move Roosevelt to offer some substantial recognition of his obligation. But while I never developed a real affection for Kennedy, I sympathized with his disappointment. Our friendship reached a point when during the Hundred Days Kennedy invited me for lunch in New York. I remember the place well—it was at Robert's on West Fifty-fifth Street. After a few preliminaries, Kennedy came down to the business he had in mind. He said that my status in Washington required a certain standard of living that my limited private means could not sustain. Therefore, how would it be if he solicited some of his friends to contribute to a fund to provide me with the means to live as I should? I was sure then, as I am now, that there was nothing in this to suggest a bribe. I was already willing to do what I could to get him recognition but had failed. I expressed my appreciation for his concern, which I regarded as a simple act of friendship. But I added that I expected to stay in Washington only a few months and then return to Columbia. I was already receiving a salary from the government at the rate of $6,800 a year, and since I still maintained my classes at Columbia, I had that salary too. I had no elaborate tastes, and if I had I was too busy to enjoy such diversions. But I added that if I ever needed a loan I would certainly come to him.

He then said that there was no moral stigma in such a supplement to the income of a person in public office. "John W. Davis had such a fund when he was Ambassador to England." I said that such a matter was for anyone to decide for himself but that I was not in need of any help. This refusal in no way impaired our relationship and the matter was not mentioned again, although I saw Kennedy often in the years that followed.

I wish I could say that I was astute enough to realize that if I finally succeeded in getting Kennedy into the Administration the revelation of such a fund, either as a loan or a gift, would raise some nasty observations in the press harmful to Kennedy and to me. I declined simply because I preferred to live as I had been living and to maintain a freedom from financial obligations. In politics the rule I lived by was a matter of proportion. One does not get sticky about small gifts and entertainment. It would be an affront to my own position and influence if such gifts as a bottle of liquor or a Sulka tie or a cask of needle beer (all of which I accepted at times) could be regarded as a bribe. Also it would be a reflection upon the donor to believe that my influence could be purchased at such a meager price.

One must keep his sense of values in such things. During the period before the inauguration I received a letter from a man whose name meant a great deal in the Democratic Party. He said that he was serving as guardian for some children and it would help him mightily in investing their trust funds if I would inform him about Roosevelt's plans concerning the gold standard. I didn't flap my wings and ignite my halo. I simply answered that I didn't know. This happened to be the truth. But if I had known, the answer would have been the same and I would have begged forgiveness for my lie. Men in politics and elsewhere live by their own codes and I never felt the urge to assume a protectorate over the morals of the people I knew. Friends are too valuable in non-material ways to abandon them merely because one disagrees with their standard of morality.

When, as I have already described, the opportunity came in June

1934 to win the recognition that finally came to Kennedy, I was able to override both the prejudice of Howe and the reluctance of Roosevelt. And Kennedy splendidly justified my judgment in his first Federal office, chairman of the Securities and Exchange Commission.*

Felix Frankfurter †

In the early years of World War II, Richard Gardiner Casey, Australian Minister to Washington, resigned to accept an office in the British Cabinet under Churchill. This shift of allegiance from one sovereign state to another was an uncommon matter, even in the British Commonwealth. Casey's superior, the Prime Minister of Australia, thought so too and vigorously protested. Casey said in his reply that in making his decision he had been advised by Felix Frankfurter and Harry Hopkins.

This amazing participation of a Justice of the Supreme Court in job placement in a foreign nation hardly created a ripple of news here. For over the years Frankfurter had come to be known as America's most eminent provider of jobs for people and people for jobs.

This activity went on under at least six Presidents, Republican and Democratic. Possibly, since Frankfurter was a protégé of President Taft's Secretary of War, Henry L. Stimson, he might have been active even then. As for Presidents Eisenhower and Kennedy and their relations with Frankfurter, I have no direct knowledge.

I am only incidentally concerned here with Frankfurter the jurist, the law teacher and philosopher. But in the years before his investiture with the robes of a Justice, despite the protection of academic life and his acute passion for anonymity, I knew enough to rate Frankfurter as a politician of superior, highly original talents.

Frankfurter was small, slight, sharp, talkative, and prodigiously energetic. John Garner once told me that Frankfurter reminded him of James Gibbons, America's first cardinal. And this made me ponder what Frankfurter might have achieved if invested with the red hat and placed in Renaissance Italy, when politics and religion were meshed in close alliance.

Frankfurter was born in Austria and knew no English until he was twelve years old. His record was outstanding at the City College in New York and the Harvard Law School. His habitat was almost entirely limited to Cambridge, New York, and Washington. In 1920 I brought him to Cleveland to participate in a survey of criminal justice over which I had direction, and it became quite clear to me that he

* My account of how that appointment came about is in substantial agreement with that of Baruch and Whalen.

† In this sketch I have used without quotation some of the text of a profile of Frankfurter in my book *27 Masters of Politics.*

regarded the Middle West as alien territory. He infuriated me when he calmly told me that his primary task there was to educate my board of directors.

After he graduated from the Harvard Law School, he had the remarkably good fortune to be employed by Henry L. Stimson, who was then United States attorney in New York City. This, his first important contact with a man who was destined to go far and wide in public life, was of immense influence in his life. He followed Stimson into the War Department when Taft appointed Stimson Secretary of War in 1910. Later he was fortunate in knowing Louis Brandeis, who was able to secure for him a place in the Harvard Law School faculty.

In those early days of progressivism and in that litigious atmosphere, Frankfurter attained the pattern of his public philosophy. Problems of economic life were matters to be settled in a law office or in court or around a labor bargaining table. His mind was legal and controversial, never broadly constructive. The government was the protagonist. Its agents were its lawyers and commissioners. The villains were the corporation lawyers. In the background were owners and managers whom Frankfurter never knew at first hand and whose practical problems he never tried to understand.

It was this blindness that caused his influence to be thrown behind the writing of the Securities Act in 1933 without giving a fair hearing to the practical people who had to operate in the market and sell securities. That is why the original legislation so dismally failed and why something else had to be provided in 1934.

Despite his immense intellectual curiosity, his numerous contacts in academic and professional life and in government, and his copious reading, Frankfurter's economic ideas remained in this no-man's-land between the realities of industry and the practical problems of governing a nation. He knew practically none of the industrial leaders of his time, the men who had forged the immense might that won two wars. The only two important businessmen whom he was constantly quoting were oddities and non-conformists, Lincoln Filene of Boston and Samuel Zemurray of the United Fruit Company.

There was good fortune in Frankfurter's relations with Stimson. That planetary figure—austere, sophisticated, ambitious, and wily—was an avenue of influence for nearly forty years. Frankfurter, who would certainly have been devoid of influence in Hoover's Administration, found the way clear through Stimson to place his protégés in the State Department and even to provide Hoover's Wickersham commission on prohibition with a director and several of its working staff members. It is quite probable that this was repaid through the use of Frankfurter's influence with Roosevelt that led to Stimson's return to the Cabinet in 1940, despite his earlier denunciation of New Deal policies. I also venture to suggest that Frankfurter can be charged with contriving the lamentable appointment of John Winant as Ambassador to Britain during the war.

Frankfurter's circle of friends was not so wide but it was very select. And within it there was no little mutual admiration that found its way into print. An example of such encomia is Archibald MacLeish's introduction to a collection of Frankfurter's writings published when he ascended the bench.

But Frankfurter's relations with Justices Holmes and Brandeis must stand as the most important of Frankfurter's exercises in friendship. A man on the Supreme Court, especially an elderly man, has some need for articulation, promotion, and interpretation other than the limited means imposed by his office. Frankfurter became a sort of missionary. It was routine for Frankfurter to supply these Justices with assistants from the Harvard graduates whom Frankfurter deemed worthy of such a post-graduate training. They were not only bright young men but their brightness was of the sort that Frankfurter could recognize. Fred Rodell of the Yale Law School, in an article on Frankfurter, says this of Frankfurter's relations with his students:

> The dull and mediocre students, the slow-witted, got short shrift. Moving too fast or too subtly for them, he left them behind—and as a result they had no more use for him than did he for them. . . . But the bright boys, the end men of his minstrel shows, revered him.

But this falls short of an interpretation of Frankfurter's estimates of students. As I have indicated earlier, Adolf Berle was one of those students and he was very bright indeed. But he disagreed, and that was regarded as a disqualification.

Frankfurter by a count that may or may not have been complete placed nineteen clerks in Holmes's office and twenty-one were selected for Brandeis. Other Justices were supplied in a few instances.

After Roosevelt's Cabinet was appointed, Frankfurter placed his men in two of the departments as solicitors. Dean Acheson was appointed undersecretary of the Treasury and Jerome Frank and several protégés were appointed to the legal staff of the AAA.

Frankfurter's activities in job placement extended into the major law schools. And in two other instances he contrived the appointment of a publisher and of an editor in large city newspapers. In the latter instance, another journalist of great talent deserved and was being considered for the appointment. Frankfurter was opposed to him. He secured letters and telegrams of protest from several of his friends on the bench or from eminent lawyers to block the man he opposed and to secure the appointment of an old friend.

In placing these protégés in important places of influence, Frankfurter seemed to have little motive except to place his selections where he could use them in furthering the policies he favored or opposing measures of which he disapproved. There was also the quite generous desire to help young men along in their careers.

But in matters in which he was interested he was vigorous in his effort to project his ideas into legislation or in administrative policies. During the period when I was close to Roosevelt there accumulated what is now a fat dossier of letters, telegrams, and memoranda, the content of which he asked me to transmit to Roosevelt or to someone else in the Administration or Congress. In the days when Harold Laski was prominent in the British Labour Party, that abundant fountain of radical ideas routed his communications through Frankfurter and me for Roosevelt's consideration. I have a batch of these, too, in my files. But when I submitted them to Roosevelt I added my own comments and the President, at least in those years, was little interested in transplanting British socialism.

When I discontinued my contacts with Roosevelt in 1936, I could provide no further means for the transmission of Frankfurter's suggestions. And Frankfurter was one of the considerable number of old friends who terminated their relations with me at that time.

In 1934 and 1935 Roosevelt told me that as vacancies appeared he intended to appoint Frankfurter, Joseph T. Robinson, and Hiram Johnson to the Supreme Court. The latter two were dropped from consideration later, but Frankfurter remained on the priority list. Frankfurter knew this, and he remembered that when Justice Holmes displeased Theodore Roosevelt because of his position in the Northern Securities case the relations between the President and the Justice cooled. The Roosevelts, when they selected a Supreme Court Justice, expected not merely faithful interpretation of the law but ideological conformity with the ideas of the President who appointed them.

With this history in mind, Frankfurter kept silent when Roosevelt proposed to reorganize the Supreme Court in 1937. In my last long conversation with Frankfurter, after I had appeared in opposition to the proposal before the Senate Judiciary Committee, I told the prospective appointee that I understood his silence despite his earlier writings against the enlargement of the Court. He offered no denial but after that I had no more letters or telegrams. And when I wrote congratulating him on his appointment there was no reply.

As a Justice, especially after the death of Roosevelt, Frankfurter became a vigorous proponent of conservative views. Perhaps he had been conservative all the time, despite his long association with radicals. Perhaps he believed that the liberalism of those earlier years had been perverted in later years. Perhaps as he grew older he entertained new respect for constitutional limitations. I was never close enough in those years to know much about his private motives.

Bernard M. Baruch

Although the name Baruch appears frequently in this story, it is not easy to specify what he contributed to the First New Deal. There were major and easily identified contributions by others who have been the subjects of these sketches. Roosevelt won the nation's confidence and ignited the people's hopes. Hugh Johnson supplied the color and drama that so vitally contributed to re-employment. Frankfurter found men for jobs. Tugwell gave Roosevelt his major issue, the farm plan. Jesse Jones's canny judgment in the RFC gave the means of survival to many facets of the economy and also brought to the bankers a sense of their responsibility. Byrnes used his parliamentary skill to facilitate the adoption of Roosevelt's program. Farley kept the politicians satisfied with patronage. And later Flynn devised the strategy that ended the First New Deal and reshaped the Democratic Party.

But Baruch's hovering presence in those early days led to nothing very specific.

He had contributed Hugh Johnson to the cause and he gave generously to the needs of the party. And his close ties with members of Congress helped maintain peace with the Executive.

Indeed, when Baruch's life ended in his ninety-fifth year the obituaries were largely limited to characterizing him as "adviser to Presidents" and to listing his many philanthropic benefactions. Even in his memoirs, *The Public Years*, it is clear that his advice to the Presidents who succeeded Woodrow Wilson was more often neglected than adopted.

Perhaps that was because his great caution and his desire not to offend clothed his advice in such general terms that it was impossible to fit it into the practical decisions of responsible statesmen. In his memoirs he gives most of a chapter to extolling Eisenhower. But when the nominations were made he says that both Stevenson and Eisenhower sought his views. "I told them both that in my opinion the control of inflation, the strengthening of our defenses, and the securing of peace were the major goals." These generalities were hardly useful in a long Presidential campaign. They were like telling a schoolboy that he must study hard and listen to the teacher if he wants to learn.

Sometimes his efforts to protect himself were absurd. As I shall show later, I sought his advice, during my mission to London, about the compromise declaration which I asked Roosevelt to approve. Baruch stoutly supported the plan. But after Roosevelt rejected it, he wrote to Roosevelt warmly commending him for his courage.

After Roosevelt's nomination in 1932 I escorted some of my policy group to Baruch's office. I hoped that he might have some useful suggestions for the campaign. He shocked my professorial friends by saying, "Business must go through the wringer and start over again." One of those present exclaimed that such a course would produce "riots in the streets." Baruch replied, "There is always tear gas to care for that." This I am sure was merely a way of playing with his young guests.

For this harsh judgment was not Baruch's considered opinion. As the campaign went on, he heartily agreed with the policies announced by Roosevelt, especially the farm program. For Baruch had given a great deal of attention and material support to remedies for the plight of agriculture. In the 1920's he and George Peek and Hugh Johnson labored indefatigably to have Congress adopt the McNary-Haugen plan and twice succeeded in getting Congress to adopt it, only to meet vetoes.

Baruch's financial help created close ties with Farley and Howe. Whenever cash was needed, someone went to Baruch and he always responded. On the night of election when the victory was being celebrated, he whispered to me, "I gave two hundred thousand dollars."

Baruch had established a towering reputation during the First World War. Wilson accepted him as a warm friend and named him as head of the War Industries Board. This agency did a great deal to mobilize American industry. He was prominent in the proceedings at Versailles. As Wilson's other friends gradually dropped or were dropped, Baruch remained close. And during the eighteen months when the President was incapacitated, Baruch and Mrs. Wilson and Dr. Cary Grayson were the people through whom there was a very limited access to the invalid.

The greatest hurt Baruch ever suffered was when, during the Nye committee's investigation in the 1930's of war profiteering, there were irresponsible charges in Congress and elsewhere that he had profited from his relations with the Administration during the war. That I have always been convinced was wholly false. Such a charge lacerated Baruch's feelings for two reasons. First because he was passionately dedicated to American interests. Although he lived in a financial community in which many were so dedicated to international affairs that they often overlooked American interests in striving to accommodate other nations, Baruch stood apart from that influence. And another reason why Baruch resented such a charge was his sporting instinct. To profit from "inside" information to him would be like shooting birds in a cage or catching fish in a barrel. He made what he had—and he never had a great fortune—by matching wits and judgment with professionals in the marketplace.

He once told me that he was a speculator only in the philosophical sense of the word, never as the term was used in the financial community.

He bought and he sold with amazing foresight from the beginning of his career. As the great boom of the 1920's came ever closer to disaster Baruch clearly perceived the weakness in the economy, especially the folly in our government policies. He safely withdrew from the market months before the crash.

After Wilson left the White House, Baruch's contacts with Republican Presidents were few and casual. He knew Harding and had several interesting visits with Coolidge and Hoover. But during that period, when the Democratic Party was very weak in Congress, Baruch established strong and mutually useful ties with members high in the opposition. These relations with several Senators were accompanied by modest contributions when they were running for re-election. This, when the Democrats assumed power in both houses in 1933, meant that Baruch's influence was a fact with which Roosevelt had to deal. And he proved to be very helpful in maintaining good relations on "the Hill" for the Administration.

In the pre-convention battle for the nomination in 1932 he was, as he admits in his memoirs, "no Roosevelt enthusiast." I am convinced, although he never admitted it, that he cautiously encouraged the movement to stop Roosevelt. In my book *After Seven Years* I said that he was "among the Smith supporters." After this was published he called me to say that it was not true—he was for Governor Ritchie of Maryland. But when he published his memoirs his recollection seemed to have failed, for there he stated that he was not a Ritchie supporter.

The penalty Baruch paid was imposed by Roosevelt after his inauguration. For at least six weeks the President did not call upon Baruch for any advice about the critical problems which he was facing. This, I am convinced, deeply disappointed Baruch, although after Hugh Johnson had been enlisted to prepare the plans for the National Industrial Recovery legislation, Baruch's contacts were more frequent. But if, as is quite doubtful, Baruch expected to assume the position of influence that he had during the Wilson years, it was never accorded him.

The reticence of Roosevelt in his contacts with Baruch was puzzling to many of the friends of both men. For Baruch's wisdom might have been extremely useful to an occasionally befuddled President. As I look back at the incidents that marked this semi-detachment, several compelling reasons come to mind. In the first place, Baruch had been one of the towering figures in the Wilson Administration, and those people—among whom were most of the Cabinet officers—had had grave doubts about the stability and capacity of the young assistant secretary of the Navy. Roosevelt also distrusted anyone who had been prominent in Wall Street. He feared that the public would misinterpret any seeming dependence on Baruch's advice. Moreover, Roosevelt's attitude toward Baruch was like his earlier rejection of Alfred E. Smith's advice after he was elected governor. Above all, Roosevelt was determined to be a statesman in his own right without let or hindrance from his elders. It is also true that Baruch deeply distrusted many of Roosevelt's more radical friends, subordinates, and advisers. For Baruch, while he favored the new agricultural and industrial legislation, was basically a very conservative person who always regarded government in business and inflation as twin threats to the economy. He certainly doubted the competence of most of the Roosevelt Cabinet—notably, later on, Henry Morgenthau, Jr., Secretary of the Treasury.

Baruch's immense caution was not mere dissimulation but a manifestation of his habit of carefully examining the ground before taking the first step. Woodrow Wilson once compared Baruch with an elephant that, coming to a bridge, tries the strength of the structure with one foot and then the other and then finally decides to let some other elephant cross the bridge first.

Baruch had none of the reticence in speech that might become a man of such caution. For he talked volubly. And much of what he said the listener could let pass without note. But interspersed in the flow of words there were real nuggets of pure wisdom.

He always was passionately loyal to his friends. My relations with him were not altered when my contacts with Roosevelt ceased, even though Baruch came much closer to Roosevelt during the war years. No one will ever know how many he helped in the innumerable ways that were possible to a man of such means and influence.

Part Six

International Frustrations

Chapter Thirty-two

Great Expectations

I have not checked the history books to learn what Henry VIII and Francis I accomplished at the Field of the Cloth of Gold. But everyone knows it was a great show. While the pageantry of that earlier event was absent when Roosevelt played host to Prime Minister MacDonald and ex-Premier of France Eduard Herriot and a flock of lesser dignitaries in Washington in April and May 1933, the bounding expressions of good will were exhilarating to all who were present or who read about it in their newspapers. The various embassies did their utmost with dinners and cocktail parties, and since these extraterritorial oases were most popular with the press and the bureaucrats in those Prohibition days, international good feelings reached dizzying heights. I well remember the obese Herriot standing in the greeting line at the French Embassy extending the right hand to the guests while his left hand reached for a succession of chocolate dainties.

The lurking peril that underlay these external manifestations of agreement was that Roosevelt by inviting all these missions from foreign lands was creating the impression that he was the major proponent of the forthcoming Economic Conference. That is why his subsequent action that brought the conference to its untimely end was such a shock abroad.

As we have seen, there had been a rather vague commitment by Roosevelt to these preliminary conferences during the weeks before his inauguration. The outcome of the pleas of France and Britain for debt negotiations had been an agreement, in which Stimson participated, that after Roosevelt assumed office there should be discussions in Washington to consider both the debts and the subjects that would come up during the projected Economic Conference. And at that time I insisted and Roosevelt agreed that the debts were to be kept apart from the other matters in the conference agenda and that that distinction should be made clear by having separate British and French negotiators. This distinction was not strictly observed, for after the foreigners arrived everyone seemed to be concerning himself with all sides of the questions at issue between the United States and the European countries. For it had been firmly resolved in both London and Paris that the debts should be mixed with the subjects for which the conference was to be convened.

Roosevelt, who wanted agreeable souls to come from Britain and France, had communicated his preference for MacDonald and Herriot through diplomatic channels. It took quite a bit of doing to get the Tory leaders in the British Cabinet to permit MacDonald to represent the Crown at these preliminaries. They no doubt felt what the Vicar of Wakefield might have if his son had asked once more to go to the fair. But when MacDonald appeared he was flanked by two guardians—Sir Frederick Leith-Ross, the economic adviser to the British government, and Sir Robert Vansittart, the immensely competent permanent under-secretary of state for foreign affairs—along with a goodly supply of experts. The French government must have had the same feeling about sending Herriot, for he was flanked by Charles Rist, the respected economic adviser to the French government, and three other hardheaded bureaucrats. Italy sent its Finance Minister, Guido Jung and a staff; the Third Reich, the indestructible Hjalmar Schacht. Invitations had been sent to eighty other governments, most of which were represented at the discussions by their permanent diplomatic missions in Washington. But from Canada came Richard Bennett, the Conservative Prime Minister, and the Irish Free State sent a member of De Valera's cabinet, Joseph Connolly, with whom I was to develop a lasting friendship.

Representing the United States in the many conferences of experts were James P. Warburg, William C. Bullitt, and Herbert Feis.

The long series of contacts with the Hoover Administration had given me a fairly good comprehension of the debt issue. With the directive of Congress to guide me, and with Roosevelt's determination that the debts were not to be an issue in the Economic Conference, I felt reasonably sure of myself in this area of discussion. But I had recognized the need for more people who could be depended upon to deal with the many other subjects that would be under consideration in the preliminaries to the conference.

Herbert Feis was at hand in the State Department, where he held the title of economic adviser. He had been especially recommended to me by Frankfurter, upon whose recommendation Stimson had employed him. And in the assignment of my duties that Roosevelt had given me in February, I was to supervise the Feis office. He was able and trustworthy.

Some time before February, I cannot recall when, I had met James Warburg at his office at the Bank of Manhattan in New York, where he held the title of vice-chairman. He was the son of the distinguished banker Paul M. Warburg and had had an excellent training in banking at home and abroad. He had been sympathetic with Roosevelt's cause in the 1932 campaign and later. He not only had the technical background essential in the matters we would face in preparing for the conference, but he had a quick and inventive mind and a fine command of language. In his memoirs he said that when he met Roosevelt at the Sixty-fifth Street house in February, the President-elect expressed warm admiration for his father and recalled that financier's timely warnings of economic trouble in March 1929:

> "Ray Moley tells me," he said, "that you are one of the white sheep of Wall Street." I replied that this flattering distinction more appropriately belonged to my father and that so far as I knew, a white sheep does not necessarily beget white lambs. At this F. D. R. chuckled and said: "I didn't know you were a farmer like me. Anyway, I want you to work with Ray Moley on the banking and currency situations." *

From then on until the end of the Economic Conference, Warburg was constantly in Washington and London. His services were outstanding.

Another who was of great value was William C. Bullitt. As a very young man he had been an attaché to the American Commission to Negotiate Peace in 1918 and 1919. Wilson during that period had sent him to Russia but later ignored his report that the Bolsheviks were likely to hold power for a long time. Frustrated by this and by criticism from Lloyd George, Bullitt told his story to the Senate Foreign Relations Committee. For this disclosure he was consigned to the diplomatic doghouse and spent the years that followed in private life.

I made his acquaintance late in 1932. I arranged to have him talk with Roosevelt in New York after the election. He had been in Europe in 1932 and had many contacts there, especially with Ramsay MacDonald.

I decided to work for his reinstatement in the State Department and despite the heated opposition of William Phillips secured his appointment as assistant to the Secretary of State. After his services in Washington and London, Roosevelt appointed him our first Ambassador to the Soviet Union.

The talks among the experts started, even before the various missions arrived, with meetings at the State Department with Ambassador Sir

* James Warburg, *The Long Road Home* (Garden City: Doubleday, 1964), p. 107.

Ronald Lindsay and T. K. Bewley, who had been sent over from London as counselor to the embassy. Hull attended these, and when it was possible to get away from the legislative program I attended.

Later when the missions arrived these talks were enlarged. The discussions ranged over several subjects, including the tariff, monetary affairs including a consideration of some sort of restoration of silver in the systems of the major countries, and occasionally the debts. Since the participants in these talks were bound by the policies of their respective countries, very little of a concrete nature emerged.*

While it was well understood by everyone on the American side that we would not permit the debts to be a subject for action at the conference, the British and French and to a degree the Italian representatives very definitely had in mind getting some sort of concessions in Washington. But while MacDonald and Herriot were still at sea, the news went out that the United States had definitely and finally left the gold standard. This, along with the vast powers delegated to the President by the Thomas amendment, shifted the immediate concern of MacDonald, Herriot, and Jung and all of the experts who accompanied them to monetary stabilization. This expectation ran squarely into the determination of Roosevelt to raise domestic prices by some sort of monetary policy the exact nature of which was not yet clear in his mind. And while he spoke freely of his desire to do something about stabilization and indeed made certain private commitments, which were not to be known generally until long after, our differences from our European friends became clear even while our guests were in Washington.

MacDonald feared that the abandonment of gold by the United States might set off a monetary race that would have disastrous effects upon Britain's export trade and bring a halt to the rise in employment in the United Kingdom. Herriot and his colleagues feared that this action by the United States, together with monetary manipulation in Washington, would force France off the gold standard.

To ease the anticipated shock, Warburg devised a plan that might be called a modified gold standard. This was presented to the foreign representatives when they arrived in Washington. At the outset it received a very interested and friendly reception by the foreign experts. This plan in brief provided:

> 1. Monetary policy should embrace every possible effort to bring about a rise in the world price level. For this purpose the central banks of all countries should consult with each other and pursue vigorously a policy of cheap and plentiful credit.

* There is a fairly extensive account of these discussions in my *After Seven Years* and in Warburg's memoirs, *The Long Road Home*. I am not cumbering this present narrative with the details of these, since subsequent events made them irrelevant.

2. So far as possible there should be a removal of exchange restrictions.

3. There should be re-established an international monetary standard as a necessary step to world recovery. The Warburg document said that "gold seems to form the medium most likely to be acceptable as the international measure of exchange values. This, of course, does not necessarily involve the re-establishment of the old exchange parities." The gold reserve ratios should be lowered. In earlier versions of this plan it was said that 25 per cent in gold and given percentages in gold or silver should be the standard.

4. Special consideration should be given to silver "as a corollary to a general rise in the price of commodities." The countries with large stocks of silver should limit sales on the world market and central banks should be encouraged to consider holding an increased proportion of silver in their reserves. Moreover, there should be international agreement to replace paper notes by silver coins. This emphasis on silver was not only to make the plan palatable to the considerable number of American Senators receptive to the idea and also to restore confidence in the Far East by dignifying silver by means of including it to some extent in the gold family.*

This proposal implied that its specifications could not be attained for some time. Therefore some intermediate arrangement should be agreed upon to stabilize the currency relations to prevent currency warfare. Perhaps it was believed there might be a short-term stabilization agreement with a fixed ratio between the pound, the dollar, and the franc, each country contributing money to a joint fund for such stabilization.

I am not sure, considering what happened later, that Roosevelt read—or, if he did, was interested in—this proposal, which by implication at least suggested that the United States would welcome stabilization in some form. Or perhaps he was willing to use the plan as a basis of talk, with the ultimate decision to be made by him alone.

Bullitt claims that Roosevelt proposed a stabilization agreement to Herriot when he was in Washington. But, according to an article by Jeannette P. Nichols, Bullitt said of this that "when the relieved Premier Edouard Herriot and Professor Charles Rist cabled the offer, Finance Minister Bonnet in Paris yielded to fears that such an agreement would strike their electorate as a currency innovation of an inflationary character. . . . So Bonnet cabled Herriot and Rist that France was strong

* R. M. Files.

enough to proceed independently of the United States; he flatly refused Roosevelt's offer of stabilization."

Bullitt says further that when Bonnet refused the offer the second time, the French asked Roosevelt to keep that offer open. The President refused.*

I knew of no such offer by Roosevelt to the French but I have no reason to doubt Bullitt's statement.

Even before these conferences were held, we were well aware that a revised gold standard was not an end in itself, nor was monetary stabilization, temporary or permanent. I made this note on April 30: "While generally desirable" our major aims could only "be achieved by [the] rest of [the] program." Meaning our domestic program for recovery.

Moreover, we were quite aware of the efforts of the British to depreciate sterling. Thus, Adolf Berle sent a telegram to me on April 26 saying that the British Treasury was buying gold bullion. "Purchases apparently made from stabilization fund amounting to increase in gold values four shillings per week with corresponding depreciation of sterling. Would tentatively indicate Treasury was immediately artificially depreciating sterling." †

It is noted in my diary for May 6, 1933, "Our monetary proposals have had a not unfavorable reception with the delegations to date." But such optimism had to be qualified by British, French, and American reservations on almost every topic under consideration, including money. When late in May the dollar fell on the world's exchanges, marking the beginning of a brief and delusory speculative spree, Roosevelt shifted course. He was no longer interested in stabilization.

This was a turn in Roosevelt's thinking that shook Warburg. And it should have dampened the enthusiasm of Hull. But apparently it did not. As the end of May approached, Hull was still dreaming of cooperative international action toward the reduction of tariff barriers.

The atmosphere in Washington in those days in late April and early May was charged with a dangerous euphoria. The saving of the banks, the rapid formulation of the measures for Congress and the speed with which they were passed, the rising confidence in the country, the upspring of the economic indicators, and the delights felt by Roosevelt himself with the powers and perquisites of the Presidency created a climate of such optimism that it seemed to many people in Washington that nothing in the way of international complications was impossible of solution by mid-year. The very character of the visitors MacDonald and Herriot made them easy victims of this contagion. Both

* Jeannette P. Nichols, "Roosevelt's Monetary Diplomacy in 1933," *American Historical Review,* LVI (January 1951), pp. 301–302.

† R. M. Files.

were given to large propositions and we-must-work-shoulder-to-shoulder-to-save-the-world talk. The excitement of meeting with Roosevelt, who was a new star rising over a troubled world, possessed both of them and to a degree everyone around them, excepting the case-hardened experts. In their talks with Roosevelt and others whom they met, all sorts of things were discussed other than the knotty economic affairs that the conference would be required to face. Despite the ominous differences that so concerned some of us who had been laboring unsuccessfully to get agreement among ourselves, to say nothing of the recalcitrance of the foreign experts, the sweep of optimism went on. With monetary stabilization and tariffs foremost, it seemed to them that the conference toward which so many of us had been looking with such misgivings would provide quick answers. And above all, Hull seemed, despite his discomfort about my participation in what he regarded as his exclusive province, to be very happy.

Occasionally MacDonald, doubtless reminded of the realities by cables from home, had his doubts. After an evening devoted to talk about a reduction of tariffs or at least a respite from tariff increases during the period of the conference, he remained overnight at the White House. I was on my way to my morning conference with Roosevelt the next morning when I met him pacing the floor in the large hallway on the second floor. It seemed he had not only tariffs but breakfast on his mind. He halted me to say: "See here! I'm not so sure about this tariff truce now. In bringing it about, you people are like a man who, having finished his breakfast, says to his friend who is coming from his room, 'Let's have a truce on breakfasts.' " I inferred that some of his advisers had been talking to him either after the meeting the night before or early that day. Or perhaps in the night he began to wonder whether he had made any dangerous commitments while under the beguiling influence of Roosevelt.

However, after having talked about tariffs and stabilization, and because of the pleasant mood which prevailed at all the meetings, the three principals, Roosevelt, MacDonald, and Herriot, came to the serious question of the time when the conference should meet. Everyone was so friendly, so cooperative, and so hopeful! Why put off the great meeting of the nations that might produce the solution of the world's ills?

It was with grave misgivings that I learned that Roosevelt had agreed that the conference should open on June 12. It seemed almost incredible that this was the same Roosevelt who in December had enjoined Edmund Day to seek at the Preparatory Commission to put off the meeting of the conference until it became clear over here that our domestic program was well under way. And at that moment in April not more than half of Roosevelt's legislative program had been adopted by Congress.

And so it was agreed to meet in June. It seemed that Roosevelt calculated that it could not meet earlier than June 12 because Congress would be in session until about that date. And MacDonald pointed out that if the date were set in July there would be insufficient time before British statesmen and other big shots went north for grouse shooting. And so with Congress on the one hand and the grouse on the other, only a month was available to rescue the world from its economic malaise.

Cheerful joint statements poured out of the White House after the various meetings, statements that reported progress but, as we shall see, deeply committed Roosevelt later to a monetary course that he was to repudiate when our representatives reached London.*

When the day for MacDonald's departure arrived, Roosevelt presented him at a crowded press conference in his White House office. MacDonald, trained in the House of Commons—that great school of extemporary speech—was at his magnificent best. The import of what he said was that he had enjoyed a wonderful visit and was leaving "as free" as he came. This was no doubt accurate, for nothing had been decided except the date of the conference.

Herriot, who left three days later, was equally polite and vague. He had talked with Woodin as well as Roosevelt, and since he and the Treasury Secretary were both music lovers he left with him an inscribed copy of his book on Beethoven. He said, "A week ago we might very well have wondered whether the World Economic Conference could meet at all, and in the event of its meeting, at what date it would meet. Now we know for certain that it will begin its work on the twelfth of June. . . . On certain points we have already brought our views much nearer to each other; an excellent way of proceeding, which President Roosevelt has rightly advocated, while he launched new motions concerning the world disarmament and security." This in a somewhat awkward translation reflected the giddy climate of the moment. But while Herriot was speaking, Hitler was beginning to study the war maps.

Of all the statesmen who were afflicted with the euphoria of those spring months it seemed certain even then that the Secretary of State was most blind to the realities. Years later in his memoirs he was to say this, "For a time before I left for London, it looked as if no serious obstacles would arise to my putting into effect the ideas I had entertained for nearly thirty years on the necessity for lowering tariffs and other trade barriers. At the State Department we began to draft a bill for submission to Congress authorizing the Executive to negotiate reciprocal

* These joint statements, to which I shall refer later, are printed in *Foreign Relations of the United States, 1933,* I, pp. 492–93 and 499–501.

trade agreements based on the unconditional most-favored-nation principle." In the understatement of the decade, he observed that "some signs of approaching trouble" for his tariff ideas now had appeared in the form of the NRA and AAA with "their own remedies for recovery." He realized that these measures along with the abandonment of gold and Roosevelt's determination to raise prices would be troublesome, but he took comfort because Roosevelt on April 3 "in a message to Congress on farm-mortgage refinancing, said he would ask for authority to initiate 'practical reciprocal tariff agreements . . . to break through tariff barriers' . . ." Hull could see no contradiction here nor could he understand the caprice that led Roosevelt to make that suggestion when he had no intention to open up the Pandora's box of tariffs in the special session.*

But Hull had been specifically warned from a not unsympathetic source. For Feis had written to him on March 23 when he submitted a draft of a reciprocal tariff bill, which had been written in the State Department:

> May I take the occasion to venture the judgment that I do not think it would be advisable for the President to introduce this bill immediately. It is one that would stir the whole of Congress and cause a current of confusion. Since the fate of much other legislation is undetermined, I believe it unwise to hazard the whole relationship between the President and Congress on this bill. My judgment in this connection is strengthened by the fact that under existing world conditions I would not expect serious immediate results in the application of this policy. For one thing, monetary conditions remain highly unsettled. I do not consider that it is certain that the present value of the dollar of the United States would be retained. Furthermore, we may have to face the question of competition from countries whose currency is depreciated.

Feis further suggested to Hull that informal negotiations take place with the British, Canadians, and one or two Latin-American countries to see if any possibility of reciprocal tariff reductions existed; then "we could put through a bill of this type." On March 24 Feis sent me a copy of the above memorandum and repeated his conviction that a reciprocal tariff bill would arouse "a great amount of questioning and debate," in both the country at large and the Congress. At best it should not be introduced until late in the current special session.†

When some polite consideration of tariffs was given in some of the discussions with minor officials from France and Britain, Hull seemingly had forgotten the Feis warning and entertained hopes not only that Roosevelt would present the reciprocal bill to Congress but that at the

* Hull, *Memoirs,* I, pp. 248–49.
† R. M. Files.

coming conference he might get either a tariff truce or a general agreement to lower rates by perhaps 10 per cent. Warburg proposed a tariff truce for the duration of the conference to the British representatives and the idea was tentatively accepted, although, as I have indicated, MacDonald had doubts about it after a night's sleep. When he wrote to Roosevelt under date of May 8, MacDonald elaborated on these doubts. He said that, while he favored the idea, Britain's European competitors had been hard at work "setting up new barriers to damage our trade . . . I told you of the unfortunate effect on our minds of the behavior of some European governments when we ourselves tried to get a tariff truce at Geneva a few years ago, and nothing could persuade me to go through the same experiences." Newspapers and the House of Commons, MacDonald continued, saw the new truce proposal as "a sacrifice of our interests alone of all our competitors." He concluded that the English people wanted "a standard of protection as low as our own." I am not sure that Roosevelt did not show this letter to Hull, but if he did it should have dampened the ardor of the Secretary before he announced his objectives when he sailed for Europe.*

When the organizing group for the coming conference met in May to consider final arrangements, Norman Davis, as eager as Hull to project tariff affairs into the agenda, secured a proposal for a tariff truce. Hull regarded this as a "splendid job." †

But as Ernest Lindley, an extraordinarily well-informed newspaperman, wrote later, the exceptions and interpretations made by the eight participants in this agreement were "numerous and vitiating. The British, who had just cornered Argentina's exchange in a discriminatory trade agreement, coolly went ahead with the formation of their protected trade system." Shortly after, when Roosevelt was confronted with the real meaning of the proposed truce, he hesitated a day or two in applying a cotton-processing tax because it meant a compensating rise in the tariff on cotton products. Then he decided and gave the word to go ahead with the tariff increase.‡

In negotiating with the British we were confronting a relatively small country that by the sophistication of its trading methods had spread its power over the whole world. The advantage of the United States in this instance was almost solely due to its economic might, certainly not to the talent it had developed to represent the government in trade affairs. Our trump cards were the debts and the freedom of action permitted by the terms of the Thomas amendment. We had already made it clear that Congress had spoken the final word about compromising the debts.

* R. M. Files.

† Hull, *Memoirs,* I, p. 602. This so-called agreement is in *Foreign Relations, 1933,* I, p. 587ff.

‡ Lindley, *The Roosevelt Revolution,* p. 186.

The reluctance of Roosevelt about stabilization was wholly in the interest of our own recovery.

The joint statements issued when the visiting statesmen departed did commit the United States to include stabilization in the concerns before the conference. And there was sufficient ambiguity to permit multilateral interpretations of what was meant. Moreover, I was quite aware from my long and close experience with Roosevelt that when an agreement became uncomfortable he was adept at contriving an escape, and when that failed he would simply repudiate it. This is virtually proved in a letter that he wrote to MacDonald after the dissolution of the conference.

But there was ample room to change his mind in the actual wording of some of the joint statements. In the one he issued with MacDonald the escape words were "ultimate reestablishment of equilibrium in the international exchanges," also "when circumstances permit," and also the qualification that such a standard should operate "without depressing prices."

As to what he said when he talked privately with these statesmen, I cannot be sure, but nods of the head or such replies as "fine," conveyed quite different impressions to strangers than they did to his intimates. Those around him were not deceived by such assurances.

Despite these warnings and reservations the general atmosphere created by Roosevelt's active participation in the talks and his great talents in acting as a host had created the impression that a great deal should be expected from the coming conference. Lindley made the shrewd observation later that "in the eyes of the public at home and abroad [he had become] the chief sponsor of the World Economic Conference and the international approach to recovery." *

Meanwhile, Hull apparently missed the implications of Roosevelt's reservations and warnings and seemed unable to grasp the hard fact that Roosevelt had little or no belief that much could be accomplished in tariff reform or immediate monetary stabilization at the coming conference.

I was perhaps in a better position to see the conflict between international agreements in this field and our domestic program. By mid-May I was convinced that the time for sobering, even painful, reconsideration had arrived. I feared, if the conference opened with high and illusory hopes and then grim realities rose like a cloud over the proceedings, that the attendant shock would seriously affect our own recovery, which had been so notable since the inauguration, the solution of the bank troubles, and the early enactment of the domestic program. Such an international disaster might well erase much of the gain we had already made at home.

* *Ibid.*, p. 182.

Since much historical comment has been concerned with what I did at that moment, and since Hull in his memoirs lays so much blame at my door for my outspokenness, it is necessary to get these events into the perspective of the time.

I had been directed by Roosevelt in February to manage with his knowledge and approval the preliminaries to the conference and to conduct the debt negotiations subject to Roosevelt's approval. This was with full knowledge of Secretary Woodin, whose department had most of the responsibility for both debts and monetary affairs.

In making my decision to drop a bit of cooling water on the heated anticipation of what the conference could accomplish, I was faced by a number of options.

My status as a nominal subordinate to Hull would be untenable even if I remained silent. Moreover, as I shall explain later, I was already committed to edit a new magazine. I also had made an earlier decision to return to my job at Columbia in the fall of that year. My courses were listed in the catalogue.

To resign at that time, however, would have been unthinkable. This would not only stir up a good deal of gossip hurtful to the Administration but would also leave undone a number of tasks that lay immediately ahead—the debt negotiations prior to the pay date of June 15, the remaining work on the Congressional program, and the final arrangements for the conference. As for transferring me to the White House as an assistant, there was Louis Howe barring the way.

Another option, which unfortunately did not occur to me at the time, would be a transfer to the Treasury as an assistant to the Secretary. Such a transfer could be made by Roosevelt by a stroke of the pen. For an "assistant to" did not—then, at least—require Senate confirmation, which an "assistant secretary" did. This could easily be explained to the press, and Woodin would have welcomed the change.

But there is no need now to ponder over what might have been.

The immediate question at that moment in May was whether I should try to clear the atmosphere by saying publicly what could be accomplished in London and what could not.

I was not alone with these doubts, for a good many people in the Administration and in Congress had told me that they shared my views. But they were not in a position where they could say so. I was free to speak because I was leaving in any event.

I had agreed a week or two before to write a weekly article for the newspapers, which would be distributed by the McNaught Syndicate. This was with the approval of the President. And the first piece was advertised to appear early in June. It had to be filed on May 18. I decided to use the Economic Conference as a subject and say what it could and could not be expected to accomplish. I wrote this and submitted it to Roosevelt for approval on May 18. He read it in my presence and not only approved it but to my astonishment said, "As a matter of fact, this would be a grand speech for Cordell to make at the opening of the conference." I submitted it for publication.

At about that time I received an invitation from the Columbia Broadcasting network to give a talk about the coming Economic Conference. This speech was substantially the same as the article that Roosevelt had approved.*

In the radio address I cautioned that, considering the "icy atmosphere of economic fear" that prevailed throughout the world, not too much could be expected at London. "The delegates may, as individuals, join in a common spirit of give and take, but their conclusions will always be modified by what their parliamentary bodies will be willing to approve." While the article and the speech were in meaning identical, this passage in the article Roosevelt had approved is no doubt what Hull resented most:

The problems most difficult of solution will be related to trade, the barriers against trade and the readjustment of these barriers. Tariffs and other restrictive devices are deeply rooted in the policies of the various countries and are closely integrated parts of their economic life. All of the nations, including our own, have been moving toward self-support for a long time. Industrial and agricultural life has developed in that direction with remarkable rapidity of late. Manufacturing has grown in even such remotely industrial countries as China and India. American capital and industry, by the establishment of factories abroad, have themselves gone far toward the acceleration of this tendency. The inexorable laws of cheaper production and reduced costs of transportation help. Thus a combination of forces is arrayed against extensive attacks upon trade barriers. Moderate results must be anticipated. The groundwork can be laid for many bilateral agreements and a more enlightened point of view. But we shall not have a vast new commerce on the seven seas, even after a successful Economic Conference.

I was merely echoing what Roosevelt had said in the campaign in 1932 when I wrote this:

Too many people are likely to think that because the depression is world-wide its causes rest solely on international conditions or that the solution for this world-wide depression is solely through international remedies. This erroneous impression is based upon the notion that we suffer in one country only because other countries are depressed. The fact is that a good many of the economic ills of each country are domestic. . . . They are predominantly internal, not external. Much of the remedy, then, must be what the nations do within themselves.

* The texts of the speech and the article are printed as appendices in my book *After Seven Years.*

In the article I stressed further the benefits that could come from such a meeting of representatives from many nations:

In the face of this realization, however, it is well to remember that the meeting at London is to be not only an international conference but a conference of nations. That suggests a great value to be captured which had almost entirely been overlooked by commentators on the subject. Enlightened leaders of many nations come and live together for many weeks. These men are likely to be those who have had much to do with domestic policy as well. They find that a large part of recovery has to do with the domestic policy of each individual country. They compare notes, match experience and gather for the sake of their own country's policy, the best of a varied assortment of the experiences of other countries. . . . We can learn from practical methods abroad. We do not need their political theories, but we do need their technical advice. Much can be gained for us and for all other nations by such an exchange of ideas at London this summer.

If we can picture the Conference in advance, not as a scene for the performance of miracles, not as a glorified market place, but a means for the development of a common understanding of universal difficulties and for the final solution of many, although not all of international problems of exchange and trade, we should look forward to it with genuine and justified optimism.

In the years since I have learned that the redoubtable Philip Snowden in Britain was saying almost the same thing.

This expression of mine still seems to me the most realistic appraisal of the prospects of the conference that appeared at that time. There is nothing in my short official life for which I have fewer regrets. It not only served as an antidote for the prevailing over-optimism, which the Eastern internationalist press reflected, but in the light of what happened it was a prophecy come true.

I had to face certain various reactions. The New York *Times* and the Baltimore *Sun* heartily disagreed. Walter Lippmann said in a letter to me that he had read my speech "with the greatest of interest, and found to my own great comfort that I had been thinking along almost parallel lines. . . . I feel sure that you are on the right track." *

When I met Hull in the lobby of the Carlton Hotel two days later I told him that I regretted that the newspaper comment on my speech mentioned a "clash" between us. He expressed no concern at all at that time about my article or my speech. But there is no doubt that he was mortally offended.

In his memoirs he says that my speech was "broadcast repeatedly through Europe, thereby impairing the standing of the American delegation, especially myself. In the circumstances Moley deserved a severe

* R. M. Files.

call-down from the President, but unfortunately Mr. Roosevelt sometimes gave his intimates undue liberties over his other friends." *

It is doubtful whether under the circumstances any sort of delegation, however able, could have accomplished much at London. But the members were selected by Roosevelt with little regard for their special qualifications in any negotiations of a serious nature. Hull says in his memoirs that he was not consulted by the President, and that may have been so. Roosevelt did discuss the personnel with me on April 18, but except for two who were chosen shortly before their departure for Europe his mind was already made up. The selection of Hull as chairman seemed to be assumed, although the major subjects for consideration at London were more properly within the domain of the Secretary of the Treasury. But Woodin was deeply immersed in the banking system and in monetary affairs at home. He was also, even then, in failing health. So after recognizing that the Secretary of State should be chairman, it seemed to Roosevelt that the chairmen of the two committees in Congress that dealt with foreign relations should be included. These were Senator Key Pittman and Congressman Samuel D. McReynolds of Tennessee. In order to represent the "progressive" group in the Senate he first offered, through me, the assignment to Hiram Johnson. But Johnson declined because, as he told me, he wanted no part in negotiating with the European countries that had been so remiss in paying their honest debts. La Follette and McNary were considered. I am not sure that Roosevelt asked either of them. Finally, two days before the delegation sailed, he persuaded Senator James Couzens of Michigan to go. Couzens was nominally a Republican, but he generally voted with the Democratic majority in the Senate and was regarded as "progressive" in his views. Roosevelt probably regarded Couzens' protectionist and soft-money views as a suitable means of restraining Hull's ideas on the tariff. For what seemed to be purely sentimental reasons Roosevelt chose James M. Cox, who as Presidential candidate in 1920 had been his running-mate. Cox was orthodox in his views on money, a low-tariff advocate, and, judged by his speeches when he was a candidate in 1920, he was a strong exponent of Wilson's internationalist policies and the League of Nations. On his way overseas and in London he came to be considerably influenced by Warburg.

Ralph W. Morrison was the last member to be selected. I had not heard of him before, and so far as I know Roosevelt had enjoyed only a hand-shaking contact with him. But James A. Farley, prompted by Vice-President Garner, urged his name, no doubt because he had

* Hull, *Memoirs,* I, p. 249. It is notable that Hull wrote this nine years after I had written in my *After Seven Years* that Roosevelt had approved this expression of my views about the prospects of the conference.

been a considerable contributor to the campaign in 1932 and because Garner knew him in Texas. He was a man of considerable wealth. An immense ranch in Garner's district and a beautiful hotel in San Antonio were among his possessions. He also had large interests in Mexico, largely utility property. There was nothing at that time to indicate Morrison's ideas about the issues to come before the conference.

Recognizing the lack of capacity of these selections, I noted in my list when I talked with Roosevelt the name of Owen D. Young. This, written in ink, was crossed out in pencil, apparently by Roosevelt.

Hull later claimed with some justification that, since he had not selected the delegates, he could exercise no discipline over them in London. Like Wilson in 1918, Roosevelt had created a very weak group to meet the sharp representatives of other, older, and more experienced foreign representatives.*

Roosevelt left the selection of the experts largely to me. I listed Warburg as financial adviser, Bullitt as executive officer, and Feis as general director of the experts because of his proved ability and his status in the State Department. For chief of press relations Charles Michelson, who had been employed by the National Committee since 1928, was chosen. Early suggested Elliott Thurston, financial writer on the Washington *Post*, and he was taken as assistant press officer. This was an excellent choice, for he knew as much about the economic issues as any of the experts and delegates. Subsequently he held for many years a responsible position with the Federal Reserve Bank.

I showed the list of experts to Hull for his approval. He made no suggestions except that there be added two names, one of which was crossed off by Roosevelt later.

Roosevelt and Woodin designated Professor Oliver M. W. Sprague of Harvard to represent the Treasury in financial and monetary matters. Sprague was a capable and well-recognized expert and had served earlier as an American adviser to the Bank of England. To represent the Federal Reserve, George L. Harrison, president of the New York Federal Reserve Bank, was chosen. Sprague and Harrison were close to the delegation but were not responsible to it.

When I reviewed the list of delegates and experts with Roosevelt, he casually asked me why my name was not included as a delegate. I said that I would prefer to remain in Washington but that in accordance

* When Henry L. Stimson visited MacDonald on July 15, 1933, he noted in his diary something of MacDonald's opinion of the American delegates. It was a most uncomplimentary evaluation, which stressed their inexperience, their general lack of understanding of the issues, and their unrestrained leakage to the press. For these reasons MacDonald said that the British and their representatives could not talk freely with them.

with our plans I would be willing to go over later as his emissary for a short while.*

When the delegation met at the White House for a final briefing, Roosevelt read a set of instructions, copies of which were dispatched to each member personally. These had been prepared by Warburg and Feis. Apparently Feis wrote the first one, which dealt with tariffs, and the rest were by Warburg.†

The instructions given the delegation embodied six resolutions that the President believed should be adopted by the conference.

The first resolution called for the establishment of a tariff truce for the duration of the conference. The second resolution asked for the establishment of general principles of coordinated monetary and fiscal policy to be followed by various nations in cooperation with each other for the purpose of stimulating economic activity and improving prices. More specifically, governments and central banks should make credit readily available to private enterprise; there should be a synchronized program of governmental expenditures to stimulate employment, industry, and commerce. The third resolution was aimed at the removal of exchange restrictions. The fourth related to the "laying of the groundwork for an adequate and enduring international monetary standard." The American delegates were instructed to attain monetary stabilization "as quickly as practicable"; to secure agreement on a new modified gold standard, one with lower legal minimum reserve; to seek an agreement that would prevent further debasement of subsidiary coinages; and to pave the way for central bank agreement that "80 per cent of their metal cover shall be in gold and 20 per cent shall be optionally in gold or in silver." The fifth resolution was designed to "lay the foundations for a gradual reduction and removal of artificial barriers to trade" such as tariffs, quotas and embargoes.

In the aggregate these resolutions were largely identical with what Warburg and Feis had proposed to the foreign missions when they visited Washington earlier. They had not been discussed carefully with the delegates and I doubt that Roosevelt regarded them as very important. But he saved the delegates from the embarrassment of going to London empty-handed.

Baruch and I attended this casual briefing session. We left the White House with a deep sense of foreboding. It was perfectly clear to us that there was lack of understanding as well as difference of opinion among

* Warburg, Bullitt, and Feis were disturbed by my preference to decline membership in the delegation, but I assured them that I could be more useful in Washington and would join them later in London.

† The texts of these are printed in *Foreign Relations, 1933,* I, pp. 622–27. The more vital part of the fourth resolution I quote on pages 480–81.

the delegates concerning these instructions. All efforts to bring that session down to specifics had ended in foggy generalities. But the die had been cast and there was nothing left for us but to hope for the best. The main part of the group was to sail the next day.

Hull alone was shining with hope. As he boarded the old S.S. *Roosevelt* on May 31, he told reporters that there was, given world conditions, "The strongest reason for an agreement among the countries to lower trade barriers and stabilize the currency exchange, with a corresponding restoration of international finance and trade. . . . There should be an agreement as to the fundamentals of the situation in a few weeks that should equally apply to currency stabilization as well as to trade barriers." *

I was at the dock to say good-bye to the group. As the tugs pushed the ship into midstream and it throbbed with the thrust of its own power, there seemed to be something symbolic in the scene. The old ship with its cargo of official Americans was facing into the fogs and winds of the Atlantic. Those hopeful argonauts would, I believed, be facing fogs and winds of another sort when they reached their destination.

I left the dock and returned to Washington. For there was unfinished business there.

* New York *Herald Tribune,* June 1, 1933.

Chapter Thirty-three

The Debts Stalemate

IT will be recalled that in the contentions in which Tugwell and I were engaged with Stimson in January we insisted that the projected exploratory talks preceding the London Conference should be sharply separated from debt negotiations. In the end Roosevelt, after what Stimson called "wobbling," agreed with us. In his communications with the British and French, Stimson reluctantly made this clear. However, we were to learn when the new Administration took office that the British and French had no intention to recognize this distinction.

My reason for insisting on this distinction was that the debts had been bilateral transactions. They were not subjects for international action. By the Dawes and Young plans, moreover, the amount of the obligations had been whittled down to normally bearable semi-annual payments on account. Hoover's *quid pro quo* idea, that we should trade debt concessions for some vague trade advantage, we rejected because, as I mentioned before, we had the quid while nobody seemed to be clear about what the quo might be. And as for mixing up the debts with the preparations for the international Economic Conference, I had even stronger objections. I was determined that in this instance the United States should not buy its way into an international conference.

Thus it was understood that while we were willing to talk about debts and also to talk about the coming conference, the foreign nations involved should send separate negotiators. By this means the debts could be entirely eliminated from the program for the conference.

The British, however, were determined to mix the debts with other matters of mutual concern. And they made this clear in a long memorandum, which Stimson received just before the inauguration. This was a routine matter placed before Hull when he took office.

It stated at the outset that "the depression cannot be effectively remedied by isolated action" and that solutions must be sought through "international action on a very broad front." It regarded the report and agenda of the Preparatory Commission of Experts as a useful basis of discussion. It also regarded Anglo-American cooperation as essential. It then indicated the subjects to be considered in such a cooperative effort:

1. A rise in the general level of world prices, especially those of farm commodities.

2. Monetary action in Britain and the United States "to ensure the provision of cheap and abundant short-term money" as well as coordinated action between the central banks.

3. Stabilization of currencies. Diminution of trade had made a "currency" breakdown inevitable, with few countries able to remain on gold. "A large number have remained nominally attached to gold, but only by imposing restrictions which are destructive of trade and financial intercourse between nations." The British indicated that they wanted a general return to an international monetary standard.

4. Abolition of exchange controls—a serious threat to international trade.

5. Relaxation of trade barriers in the form of prohibitions and quotas as well as general agreement to reduce tariffs. Here the British hedged because of (a) their existing treaty obligations; (b) a "comparatively low measure of protection" afforded their own tariff system; and (c) "an enormous excess of United States exports to this country over British exports to the United States." They could not, they claimed, absorb larger quantities of American goods. They were willing to discuss a reciprocal tariff agreement, the freezing of tariffs for the duration of the conference, and an arrangement for gradual reduction of high protective tariffs to a more moderate level.

6. Bimetallism they characterized as "impossible of adoption," thus agreeing with the conclusions of the Preparatory Commission. The silver problem would be solved "not by a rise in the price of silver as such" but through "a rise in the general level of commodity prices, which would bring up the value of silver at the same time."

7. Finally, and to the British most important, they wanted satisfactory settlement of the debts question, or at least an assurance that this would be agreed to. They asserted that "the existence of these debts constitutes, as the Preparatory Commission have said, an insuperable barrier to economic and financial reconstruction, and there is no pros-

pect of the World Economic Conference making progress if this barrier cannot be removed." *

And so apparently the debts were the price we were supposed to pay. But the other propositions were either to catch the eye of Hull, who wanted tariff barriers removed, or the silver bloc, which wanted special treatment for silver if not a return to bimetallism.

While these subjects, so far as the debts and preparations for the conference were concerned, came clearly within the responsibilities Roosevelt had assigned to me on February 3, Hull had turned to Norman Davis to draft a reply.†

Quite accidentally I came upon Davis on March 6. He was working on a reply to the British note in an office in the State Department. Despite our previous differences, he was cordial enough and was quite willing to show me the preliminary draft he had prepared. At first glance his reply seemed to have observed the dicta that Roosevelt and I had formulated on the debt question. The British, he had written, had given debts a "peculiar primacy" over the other matters noted in their memorandum, and to this thesis "The Government of the United States is unable to agree." Further, "It is the judgment of this government that the importance of these debts as a cause of the depression or as a major element in its continuance has been overestimated and overemphasized." So far so good, I thought. But on the next page the Davis draft acknowledged "that the debt question cannot be satisfactorily or successfully dealt with as an isolated element in the world situation of today; it must be brought within the scope of a broad program of international effort looking toward economic rehabilitation, an increase in trade, and a decrease in unemployment, by removing or reducing the many artificial obstacles to normal trade between nations which now prevail." ‡

Beneath the diplomatic jargon to which Davis was so addicted, this was an expression of economic cause and effect that Roosevelt had already rejected. He did not believe that the maintenance of the debts, whether the installments were paid or not paid, would in any way hinder recovery here or abroad. The course of events proved Roosevelt to be right. For while the debtors for the most part failed to pay, the obligations were kept inviolate to the present day. And we and Europe had recovery.

I succeeded, at least for the moment, in eliminating Davis from the

* The British memorandum, entitled "British Policy on Economic Problems," is in *Foreign Relations, 1933,* I, pp. 465–71. Also in typewritten copy in R. M. Files, dated February 1933.

† Davis had returned to Washington for the inauguration.

‡ R. M. Files.

drafting of a formal reply. I had in mind a draft that would satisfy Hull and Feis—a reply that would preserve the principle that the debts should be kept separate from the preparations for the conference and also eliminate the debts from consideration at the conference itself. I said in my draft reply to the British that "nothing is to be gained by partial solutions," and if paragraph 15 of the British memorandum considers that a new settlement of the intergovernmental debts be a precedent "to a solution of the questions outlined in the tentative draft agenda prepared for the Economic and Monetary Conference, this Government must express entire disagreement." In this connection, it is perhaps well to note that the last sentence of the British memorandum misinterprets the conclusion of the Preparatory Commission on this point. "The Government of the United States is prepared to discuss these debts with the British Government at the same time as—but separate from—the questions on the tentative draft agenda." *

When Hull, Feis, and I finally came up with a reply to the British on March 22, it substantially followed the same language as my draft. It called any attempt to establish an order of priority in the settlement of the various problems "undesirable" and insisted that any discussion of the debts be held separately from the rest of the questions on the tentative draft agenda.†

Ever since Warburg had joined our group, he had been concerned with devising two formulas. One was a revised gold standard, which has already been described. The other he called the "Bunny." This proposed the cancellation of all interest payments and a substantial reduction of the principal in the light of the depressed conditions that had arisen since the last agreements had been made in the 1920's. The debtors would reaffirm their obligations by depositing a note for the new amounts with the Bank for International Settlements. These notes were to be secured by a deposit of 25 per cent of the principal amount in gold bullion plus another 5 per cent in gold or silver. The remainder of the debts would be dealt with by a sinking-fund agreement under which each debtor would make certain annual payments to the BIS. The BIS, as trustee of the fund, would apply all payments received from the debtors toward the purchase in the open market of United States obligations. These securities and the 30 per cent in bullion would be delivered to the United States at the terminal date of the plan. Meanwhile, the BIS would issue its gold certificates to us for notes lodged with it, against which we, in turn, would issue Treasury certificates that could be used by us for the rehabilitation of industry, public works, and the like, or to retire our existing public debt. This ingenious plan attracted many of the foreign experts, but as things developed it came to nothing.

* R. M. Files.

† *Foreign Relations, 1933,* I, pp. 472–73.

Despite our plan to keep the debts separate from the other questions, the many meetings between the statesmen and experts hopelessly intermingled the two issues.

The attitude of Congress concerning the debts had always been a firm determination to keep them inviolate even if unpaid. And the gathering of foreign representatives in Washington, especially when such figures as MacDonald and Herriot were there, was bound to raise questions in Congress. For that reason Roosevelt was exceedingly careful to turn the subject whenever the debts were mentioned.

While MacDonald was in Washington, he and Roosevelt repaired for the greater part of a day for a private talk. In preparation for this, I drew up at the request of Roosevelt a one-page memorandum containing the essential facts about the debt of Great Britain—amounts, payments, etc. Then, to sharpen the subject still more, I had the page retyped with the more essential facts in red. Whether this was used I never knew. No doubt there was much conversation about many interesting subjects—war reminiscences, MacDonald's appraisals of his colleagues in the national government at home, the delights of Washington in the spring, and possibly the joyous walks in the Scottish countryside about which the Prime Minister had written so entertainingly eight years before.*

Presumably whenever the debt question came up Roosevelt diverted the talk with some more interesting anecdote. At any rate, on the day following this excursion Roosevelt told me that MacDonald knew practically nothing about the debts. He said that the Prime Minister confused the amounts due between pounds and dollars and millions and billions.

So far as Warburg's "Bunny" was concerned, I doubt whether either MacDonald or Herriot had any knowledge of it while they were in the United States.

However, with an eye to allaying any suspicion in Congress, a joint Roosevelt-MacDonald statement was given out which said:

"During the day the Prime Minister and the President have discussed the problems of the debt of the British Government to the United States Government. Both have faced the realities and the obligations and both believe that as a result there is laid the basis of a clearer understanding of the situation affecting the two nations. It would be wholly misleading to intimate that any plan or any settlement is under way. It is the simple truth that thus far only preliminary explorations of many different routes have been commenced. The point to be emphasized is that with the most friendly spirit progress is being made. After the

* *Wanderings and Excursions* by J. Ramsay MacDonald (London and New York: Jonathan Cape and Harrison Smith, The Travellers Library; first published in England in 1925 and reprinted in New York in 1929).

Prime Minister's departure these conversations can well continue in London and Washington."

A similar statement described the "results" of Roosevelt's debt meeting with Herriot on April 28.

The next day Roosevelt, apparently more sanguine about Britain's meeting her June payment, directed Lewis Douglas and me "to talk with the British on debts." Also he made it clear that no one else, including Hull, was to know of these discussions. Leith-Ross had been persuaded to remain after the departure of MacDonald.*

Douglas and I were glad to have this opportunity to discuss the debts in private with Leith-Ross and to get his reactions to Warburg's "Bunny" plan. To enlarge the group would lead not only to confusion but to the peril of a leak, which might stir up things in Congress and over the country. At the moment we saw nothing amiss in carrying on such discussions without telling Hull, for the debts were not in any event a State Department responsibility and both of us were close enough to Woodin to know that he would not mind. Little did we realize, however, that a wry embarrassment would come of it later.

Douglas and I spent most of May 1 and 2 at the British Embassy talking with Leith-Ross and Bewley, the embassy counselor. They were interested in the idea of the "Bunny" and had various suggestions to make for amending it. One was that the payment to the Bank for International Settlements need not be in bullion but in the form of a note only.† Presumably Leith-Ross, who immediately left for England, would take this proposal to the Cabinet and send a reply.

At this point, the problem that confronted us was not a wholesale debt settlement but a way of determining how the June 15 payment could be made. Leith-Ross told us in our talk on May 1 that if the British government had to make the payment it would. But it would be a terrific hardship.

However, a week later the question took another form. In a personal and unofficial message MacDonald dispatched to Roosevelt on May 8, MacDonald sought a way out short of payment of the June installment. He intimated what I had not known before, that Roosevelt had encouraged the Prime Minister to believe that the President could suspend the June payment. This MacDonald urged him to do on the ground that, while it would be impossible to manage an over-all debt settlement in the time remaining, the solution of the June embarrassment would permit the conference to get off on a friendly note. However, I had already told Leith-Ross that Roosevelt could not suspend payment without the consent of Congress, and that in view of the legislative situation he did not want to ask.

* R. M. Diary, April 29, 1933; *Foreign Relations, 1933,* I, p. 837.

† R. M. Diary, May 1 and May 2, 1933.

On Thursday, May 18, by a regrettable mischance I was absent from my office and in New York. (Each Thursday I had reserved for meeting my two classes at Columbia.) It happened to be the day on which the cable promised by Leith-Ross came from the British government. Ambassador Lindsay called my office saying he had a cable from his government and also a personal letter from MacDonald to Roosevelt. He was told that I was in New York. He hesitated to call me there and so he carried the cable and letter to Hull.

When he told Hull the substance of the cable, it became clear to Hull that Douglas and I had carried on conversations with Leith-Ross without his knowledge. He coldly told Lindsay that he had better take the documents to the President.

Lindsay, who had not known that we had carried on these discussions without the knowledge of Hull, was shocked. He called my office and left this note:

"I asked the Secretary of State a certain question. He referred me to the President. What shall I do next?" *

I certainly could sympathize with Sir Ronald's amazement. For he was a career officer of the old school of proprieties and protocol. The informality that Roosevelt practiced with his subordinates was something he had never encountered before. But he was certainly without blame for what he did.

Whatever the suffering Lindsay might have endured could not undo the damage that had been wrought in my relations with Hull. When I returned to the State Department, Hull was even more silent and formal than ever. And since explanations would only serve to notify him that Roosevelt himself had ordered these meetings, I made no attempt to explain. If by this time he still failed to understand that I was serving Roosevelt directly and that the debts were not his responsibility but the Treasury's, further explanations would serve no purpose at all.

Although the circumstances were regrettable, it was only proper that Hull should make some reply to the British note. He took the position that something agreeable to the British should be worked out so that the conference might not be threatened by the debt controversy, and so he drafted a note to the Ambassador saying that it should be understood that the President's hands were tied by action of Congress and the British might make some proposal which could be submitted to Congress.†

Since Roosevelt had no intention to submit any proposal concerning the debts to Congress, this note was not sent. Roosevelt held that the debts must be kept out of the conference. But whether he would submit

* R. M. Diary, May 18, 1933.
† R. M. Files.

any proposal to Congress was a question that at the moment he was not prepared to answer.

Hull, who wanted Roosevelt to save the conference by some debt gesture to the British, noted with deep concern a reply that Roosevelt made to MacDonald indicating in a most friendly way that the principles hitherto established concerning the debts would be firmly maintained and that the conference could succeed without any consideration of the debts at all. These debts, he added (following the formula adopted in the November conference with Hoover), could be discussed with British representatives in Washington.*

At that moment it seemed to me that there was something far more important than pacifying Hull. It was to find a way to save the British from two unthinkable alternatives. One was a default and the other was a demand for the full June payment, which would impose a painful strain on their resources.

It was quite clear that Sir Ronald was undergoing painful apprehensions about that June payment. To default on an obligation openly and clearly assumed was a deviation in principle which the British must avoid. The British pound for generations had the respect of the world. "Sterling" meant exactly what its more common use proclaimed.

I felt that some means must be devised to reach an honorable and fair adjustment of that June payment. I talked with Roosevelt about it and he suggested that the American custom should prevail under which an individual's credit is maintained if when a debt is due he does his best to pay what he can, however small, on account. After I talked with Lindsay, the British government suggested a "token" payment of five million dollars. This we considered too small, and we countered with the suggestion of ten million. Then, after consulting Pittman, we took advantage of an amendment sponsored by him that permitted payment in silver. We arbitrarily fixed a price in silver below the world market, which enabled the British to pay in silver that cost them seven million in American dollars. And so the June 15 payment was successfully met at that figure. That was the last dollar, however, that was ever paid. It was also the last payment made by any debtor except Finland. These debts stand on the Treasury's books today.

This proposal to the British for the settlement of the June payment was not only conveyed by me to Lindsay but was embodied in a confidential letter from Roosevelt to MacDonald. It could be amply justified to the public. For the British at that time had paid $1,447,270,000 on account, the French only $200,000,000. And the interest rate paid by the British had been much more than that charged to the other debtors.

* R. M. Files; Roosevelt to MacDonald, May 22, 1933.

Since December the French had been harping on a formula of their own making that suited their reluctance to pay anything. They wanted us to find "some new fact." Warburg and Bullitt had shown the "Bunny" to the French representatives in confidence and, as was usual in the practices of the French government, the suggested compromise immediately appeared in the French press. This was exceedingly annoying to us, because such a publication might stir up public comment in the United States and trouble in Congress. Warburg and Bullitt were then told to inform the new French Ambassador, André de Laboulaye, that this violation of a confidence made further discussions impossible. Also that we would await further proposals from the French government.

Laboulaye came to my office and after hearing the formula "pay or plead inability to pay" replied that his government would accept neither of these alternatives. I ventured to reply that out in Ohio where I came from this sort of debtor was called a "dead beat." He thanked me and left.

Other debtors went through the routine of pleading "inability to pay." But the Finnish Minister said that his government intended to pay the installments in full and on time. This gave Roosevelt the idea that a beginning of a general revision might be to start with Finland. The honesty of the Finns would be recognized and a revision favorable to them would excite little opposition in the United States. But the Minister came back and said that his government wanted no revision. It would pay. By this Finland won a dividend of good will in the United States that has probably amply compensated for all that it paid on the debt. The Finns and their products won a warm place in the hearts of all Americans.

And so, as far as my participation was concerned, that is the end of the story of the debts.

Chapter Thirty-four

Confused and Demoralized Negotiators

THE misfortunes of the ill-starred American delegation began on the high seas. Some sense of this is conveyed by what Hull wrote in his memoirs fifteen years later:

> As I sailed aboard the steamship *President Roosevelt* from New York on May 31, I had in my pocket a copy of the Reciprocal Trade Agreements Bill which was now on the President's desk. I expected to be able to show this to the other delegations at London and to use it to prove to them we were sincere in our efforts to reduce tariffs and also had the power to do so. . . .
>
> Thereupon I began receiving aboard the steamer wireless messages from Washington concerning new legislation to raise—not lower—tariffs and impose import quotas. . . .

This was but the beginning of Hull's unhappiness. He says further that on June 7, while still at sea, he dispatched this message to Roosevelt:

> I earnestly trust reports are unfounded that Congress will not be asked for executive authority to negotiate reciprocal commercial treaties. . . . My deliberate judgment is that, in addition to most seriously handicapping the mission of our delegation . . . it would be a major error to defer until 1934 any authority thus to negotiate this type of commercial treaty.*

Roosevelt's reply was, in the idiom, a "kick and a lick." He informed Hull that he considered the introduction of any tariff legislation by him to be not only "inadvisable" but "impossible of achievement." But to

* Hull, *Memoirs,* I, pp. 250–51.

soften the impact upon Hull, he added that Hull would enjoy full authority to negotiate reciprocal treaties, and to arrange for further negotiations in Washington. The results of these, Roosevelt said, could be submitted when Congress reassembled. This meant 1934.

Hull wrote in his memoirs that this message was "a terrific blow. It swept from under me one of the prime reasons for going to London." "It was a dismal and hopeless prospect." ". . . there was no hope here for me." *

This state of affairs was communicated by Hull to other members of the delegation, and dissent arose. For some of the members, notably Pittman and Couzens, were not at all sympathetic with Hull's tariff views and understood Roosevelt's appraisal of the Congressional situation.

Later, after this initial shock had been only measurably absorbed and the delegation was in London on the eve of the opening of the conference, the question arose as to the authority of the delegation at the conference to make any move toward general agreement on trade barriers. Cox and Bullitt cabled Roosevelt:

"Hull deeply distressed by reports from America that you and administration are no longer supporting his desire and that of delegation to reduce tariffs and remove obstacles to international trade. Advise urgently that you should send him as soon as possible personal cable telling him that you are behind him and that you should issue a liberal early statement that administration policy in regard to removal of barriers to international trade has not been altered. We hope that you will be able to take this action today. . . . Regards. Cox, Bullitt."

The generality and awkwardness of this message was no doubt due to the emotional state that prevailed in and around the delegation, which was especially marked in the deep dejection of Hull himself.

Roosevelt again applied the stick followed by the balm. In a message that, to say the least, was prompted by affection rather than reason:

"Please do not worry about situation here in regard to tariff reductions and removal of trade obstacles. The eleventh hour rows in Congress over domestic problems made general tariff debate dangerous to our whole program. I am squarely behind you and nothing said or done here will hamper your efforts. There is no alteration of your policy or mine. Remember, too, that if we can get treaties signed we can call special session of Senate along in the autumn, to consider ratification." †

This unwillingness to hurt and the habit of speaking in soothing generalities was characteristic of Roosevelt. It was also a manifestation of his unwillingness to face the facts and of his disingenuous habits when it seemed essential to escape the consequences of a hard decision.

* *Ibid.*, pp. 251–53.

† These messages are in *Foreign Relations, 1933,* I, pp. 633–34.

The fact was that at that very moment a drastic revision of Hull's optimistic speech prepared for the opening of the conference was already on the way from Washington. It was absurd to claim, as Roosevelt did, that it would be practical in the autumn to call the Senate to consider treaties negotiated in London or Washington.

It is no doubt probable that Roosevelt calculated that, with the existing attitude of European powers toward tariff or trade concessions, Hull would meet nothing but frustration, and therefore there would be nothing to present to a recalled Senate. But it was clear even then that by autumn the domestic program would be meeting its most severe test and that to call the Senate would provoke a sweeping debate on all sorts of subjects, including the National Industrial Recovery Act, which was at that moment being subjected in Congress to severe opposition. It did not pass until the last day of the special session.

It was this confusion of pretenses and policies between Roosevelt and Hull and most of the delegation that was to characterize the course of events until the conference expired in July.

The depressed mood of Hull communicated itself to the whole party on the S.S. *Roosevelt* and, as was inevitable, communicated itself to the newspaper correspondents who were on board. Already there were differences arising between the low-tariff people and such arch exponents of protection and easy money policies as Pittman and Couzens. The information that reached us in Washington confirmed this unfortunate situation. The American delegation, when it arrived at Plymouth, was already disorganized and impotent.

In Washington, Roosevelt was coming to a realization not only that his delegation was incompetent but that he himself had lost interest in the conference. And in his thinking he was drifting farther by the hour from any belief in the capacity of attaining recovery through international action.

The conference itself, which opened on June 12 as planned, was launched on a discordant note. MacDonald in his opening speech, no doubt irritated by the lack of progress at that time in the debt negotiations, violated the understanding that the debts were not to be an issue at the conference. He prodded at this sore spot in relations with the United States.

He said that "behind the subjects I have mentioned is another in the front rank of importance. . . . I refer to the question of war debts which must be dealt with before every obstacle to general recovery has been removed and it must be taken up without delay by the nations concerned." *

This MacDonald statement was a clear breach of faith. Not only had

* R. M. Files.

it been understood since November that the debts and the measures that were to come before the conference were to be dealt with separately, but the American delegates had been instructed before they left that they had no authority to deal with the debts whatsoever.

Hull was not only disquieted by this MacDonald reference to the debts but he was suffering from other troubles. And so he failed to appear the next morning to deliver his opening speech. This was regarded as an expression of displeasure over MacDonald's reference. It was, however, motivated by the fact that his prepared speech had not been revised in line with the instructions that had come from Washington.

Hull had drafted the speech on shipboard. On June 10 he cabled the proposed address to Phillips. The speech, which in essence was a paraphrase of speeches Hull had been making for years in his lifelong crusade against economic nationalism, might well have served even the most severe critic of Roosevelt's domestic policies. It said in part:

> Ignoring all realities nations have strenuously pursued the policy of economic isolation—each futilely and foolishly striving to live a hermit life. However diverse were the contributing causes of the present depression, it is now manifest that this frenzied effort of each nation as nearly as possible to seclude itself in a closed economic compartment, under the delusion that it would thereby be immune from world conditions, has been the largest single cause of the present universal collapse. . . . The cherished idea of the extreme type of isolationist that each nation singly can by boot strap methods lift itself out of the troubles that surround it has . . . proved wholly fruitless. . . .
>
> When every nation is visited by a disastrous panic at the same time, it is for the isolationist a mere coincidence. For him no panic has an international character, cause or cure. He credulously believes that . . . each [nation] by its own local program can at will restore full prosperity.

In this draft Hull went on to denounce "trade barriers," long his favorite topic, and to conclude that "this conference should proclaim that economic nationalism as imposed upon the various nations is a discredited policy." *

Roosevelt, Phillips, and I examined this speech on Sunday, June 11, and again on the next morning. It was clearly the escape of a pent-up torrent of indignation about the policies of Roosevelt in the campaign of 1932, which had kept Hull relatively silent during those months at his home in Tennessee, and also the domestic program so far pursued by Roosevelt and Congress since the inauguration. Perhaps he failed to realize this divergence of policy. Perhaps he intended, when he had an international platform to make his position clear, that he would have his

* R. M. Files.

say regardless of the consequences. And it must be noted that he was still smarting about Roosevelt's refusal to bring his reciprocal trade plan before Congress. At any rate it seemed necessary, to avoid any response from Europe charging that the Roosevelt Administration was among the sinners and isolationists described by Hull, to modify these remarks.

I deliberately refrained from amending the speech myself. For my position had already been made known in May, when Hull bitterly resented my outspoken radio speech. And I well knew that if I participated in any revision, Phillips would eagerly convey the news to Hull.

But Roosevelt used the blue pencil liberally on the draft and instructed Hull as follows:

"We must be very careful about the substance of this paragraph, which you will probably wish to recast. It is at variance with the President's campaign speeches, notably that at Louisville, wherein he differed with President Hoover as to the latter's theories that other nations were responsible for the world depression. The President throughout the campaign maintained the view that the United States was the first offender."

Hull was further instructed to "tone down" certain phrases and sentences in the draft, especially in his philippic against economic nationalism.*

When the final text of the speech Hull delivered came through, there seemed to be little evidence of the corrections and revision made in Washington.†

The "boot strap" references were there as well as the arraignment of economic nationalism and isolationism.

Meanwhile things were going from bad to worse in London. "In London all was confusion. . . . Hull, still dejected over the trade agreements disappointment, could not bring himself to assert authority. Without a firm hand on top, the heterogeneous band felt free to indulge its fancies. The morning meetings turned into aimless, shapeless discussions, filled with gossip, backbiting, stump speeches, and irrelevance. . . . The delegation, in short, displayed neither leadership . . . nor cohesion. The Conference would probably have failed with the best delegation in the world. It could never have succeeded with this one." ‡

* R. M. Files. Also R. M. Diary. For some reason, which is not clear to me, these instructions to Hull are not included in *Foreign Relations, 1933,* I.

† This text is printed in full in *Foreign Relations, 1933,* I, pp. 636–40. See particularly paragraph 7.

‡ Schlesinger, *The Coming of the New Deal,* pp. 210–11. As authority for this appraisal Schlesinger cites "Feis, memorandum of July 17, 1933," in Feis's personal papers; also various page references from Warburg's "Reminiscences" (1952) in the Oral History Research Office, Columbia University. Both Feis and Warburg were firsthand witnesses.

But far more serious, so far as the fate of the conference was concerned, than Hull's tariff griefs and MacDonald's unfortunate reference to the debts was the insistence of the French, strongly supported by the British government and delegates, that some sort of immediate stabilization of the currencies be agreed upon by the United States. This they regarded as a prerequisite to any serious consideration of other issues. But while it was within the stated responsibilities of the American delegation to consider long-term monetary objectives, the position fixed by Roosevelt was that any immediate agreements of stabilization should not encumber the work of the conference. Also the clear fact was that any such immediate agreement was not relevant to the powers of Hull or the delegation. This was a Treasury affair.

This Roosevelt had made clear in a message to London on May 31, sent by Phillips to Ambassador Bingham:

> Advise Foreign Office, for the information of the Government and of the bank officials, that Doctor Oliver M. W. Sprague, representative of the Government of the United States and Mr. George L. Harrison, Governor of the Federal Reserve Bank of New York, will sail on the S.S. Olympic on Friday, June 2nd, to discuss with British and French Government representatives and representatives of their central banks methods to stabilize the monetary stituation.*

One of the most unfortunate circumstances in those early days of the conference was the habit of American delegates individually to talk to the press. To stop this, Bullitt prevailed upon Hull to issue a directive against such interviews. But this could not deter Senator Couzens and Cox. They had so long been free agents in this respect that they were contemptuous of any discipline from the chairman of the delegation.†

Meanwhile, untroubled by the problems of the delegates, Sprague and Harrison proceeded with talks with Montagu Norman of the Bank of England and Clément Moret of the Bank of France.

* *Foreign Relations, 1933,* I, pp. 627–28.

† There were bizarre incidents that attended this failure of discipline, even self-discipline. These were eagerly seized upon by the press and widely disseminated in the comments published in Europe and the United States. Many of these bits of gossip found their way into the history books. Those with an appetite for such material will find considerable to their taste in Schlesinger, *op. cit.,* Chapters 12 and 13; in James P. Warburg's memoirs, *The Long Road Home;* in Feis's *1933: Characters in Crisis;* and also in the incredible mishmash *The Secret Diary of Harold L. Ickes.* All the delegates and many of the other participants are dead. The issues raised then are no longer relevant to our present concerns or to the long trail of history. I shall spare the reader this sort of thing in this story, limiting my account as strictly as possible to the major matters of high policy, which are still relevant in a world in which the international and the intra-national approaches to human affairs are still subjects of debate among sincere and intelligent individuals.

On the same day that Roosevelt had dispatched his message about Sprague and Harrison, he approved a dispatch from Phillips to James P. Warburg authorizing him to act as liaison between the Sprague-Harrison team and the American delegation. On June 8 Hull asked the President, probably at the suggestion of Warburg, that the latter participate fully in the Sprague-Harrison discussions. Roosevelt through Phillips granted this authorization immediately.*

The talks between the British and French banking representatives and Sprague, Harrison, and Warburg brought forth a tentative agreement as early as June 15. The news of this proposed *de facto* agreement leaked out and there was a sharp rise of the dollar in world exchanges and a corresponding decline in American stocks and commodities. This alarmed Roosevelt, Woodin, and me, since this sort of thing ran counter to our own domestic "reflationary" goals.

For public consumption Woodin issued a statement, which I wrote, to the press:

> Various reports from London published today concerning an agreement by American delegates to stabilization in some form have been brought to my attention. Such reports cannot be founded in fact. Any proposal concerning stabilization would have to be submitted to the President and to the Treasury and no suggestion of such a proposal has been received here. The discussions in London in regard to this subject must be exploratory only and any agreement on this subject will be reached in Washington, not elsewhere.†

This denial by Woodin served to rally the stock market.

Privately, Woodin sent a cable to Sprague saying that "we are wholly in the dark regarding the negotiations of the past week leading up to this proposed plan and request that you inform us immediately and fully of its causes and of the points at which it is proposed to stabilize." ‡

Meanwhile at the White House, also on June 15, Roosevelt and I drafted a cable for the President's signature asking for definite information about the rumors:

> For Secretary of State and Cox and Sprague . . . All kinds of wild reports here about stabilization at some fixed rate, some reports saying around 4 dollars and other reports at other rates. I feel sure all these reports are not founded on any fact. Of course any proposal must in any event come here for approval or disapproval by Treasury Department and me. [Roosevelt] §

* *Foreign Relations, 1933,* I, pp. 628–29.
† Roosevelt, *Public Papers,* II, p. 245.
‡ R. M. Files.
§ *Foreign Relations, 1933,* I, p. 641.

In response to Woodin's request a long cable came from Sprague on Friday, June 16.* He said that after continuous negotiations with representatives of the British and French central banks (presumably Norman and Moret), he along with Harrison and Warburg had worked out an agreement for temporary stabilization for the duration of the conference only. It was understood that long-range plans in the monetary field were still to be subject to discussion and negotiation in the conference.

The Sprague cable confirmed our fears that something might be contrived that would play havoc with our plans for domestic recovery. The terms of the agreement were that through cooperation among the banks of issue "the Bank of England and the Federal Reserve Bank of New York shall in effect maintain [exchange] rates within a spread of 3 percent in relation to the gold franc." This agreement would "result in a dollar-sterling middle rate of four dollars per pound." Under these circumstances Britain would give assurance "that they will not use the equalization fund . . . to affect the price of sterling," while the United States would promise not to use the powers under the Thomas amendment during the period of the conference "except in exceptional and unforeseen circumstances."

In order to stabilize at four dollars to the pound, the plan also proposed that the Bank of England and the New York Federal Reserve Bank would each, if necessary, "expend up to 3 million ounces of gold equivalent to 60 million gold dollars." Sprague went on to "presume that the Federal Reserve Bank of New York would be acting at the request of and for the account of our Government." The implication was clear that the U.S. Treasury would make good any gold losses incurred by the New York Federal Reserve Bank.

Later that afternoon Warburg cabled a message directly to the President endorsing the Sprague proposals and saying that it was necessary that some such agreement be accepted to allay fears that the United States would not be unnecessarily violent and willful in its monetary policy. Warburg asked that Roosevelt authorize a statement that the United States and Britain would stabilize on a gold basis as "the ultimate objective of their policy."

After the receipt of these messages, Roosevelt called a meeting at the White House at which Woodin, Dean Acheson (who had been appointed on May 12 undersecretary of the Treasury), and I were present. It was decided there that $4.20 would be more reasonable. We agreed that while a tentative and flexible agreement was desirable to calm the fears of the

* The full text of this and others that were subsequently exchanged in the next few days between London and Washington are printed in *Foreign Relations, 1933,* I, p. 642ff. Copies of most of these are in my files. I have not believed it necessary at this time to quote these at length in this account.

gold-standard countries, we were not going to bow to the extreme demands of the British and French.

The original draft of Roosevelt's reply, which was formally directed to Hull but for the guidance of Cox and the information of Sprague, Harrison, and Warburg, included this passage:

> It is my thought that instead of an agreement based upon mutual action, it might be possible for us to announce unilateral action by the United States by which if the pound goes to $4.25 we will expect to be willing to export gold to an amount of fifty to eighty million dollars to hold the dollar within that limit.*

After this was written, Roosevelt decided to eliminate these softening words—not because they did not represent his position at the moment, but because he did not want to mitigate the brusque tone of the rest of his message. His reply to the cables of Sprague and Warburg, sent on June 17, therefore was somewhat more uncompromising than his actual position at that time. He wanted a more favorable bargaining position.

Thus the President told his negotiators in London that he could not approve a bilateral statement by the United States and Britain to the effect that they would under proper conditions ultimately stabilize their currencies on a gold basis. He made the point emphatically that he wanted a "re-establishment of currencies based on gold or gold and silver by all nations and not by three or four only." †

The terms of the President's reply and rejection of the plan communicated by Sprague and Warburg were so explicit that they deserve in the light of later events to be cited in full:

> As a general principle, I am at present opposed to any agreements aimed at close stabilization of pound and dollar with small leeway either way, especially at present approximate levels.
>
> It is my thought that at this time we should avoid even a tentative commitment in regard to any definite program by this Government to control fluctuations in the dollar.
>
> It seems wiser to content ourselves for the present with an informal statement that if the pound should rise to an excessive point, say $4.25, that we will then consider unilateral action of some kind, the exact nature of which would depend on the circumstances then confronting us.
>
> On the other hand, if exchange goes the other way, resulting in commodity price declines in this country, we must retain full freedom of action under Thomas amendment in order to hold up price level at home.‡

* A copy of this original message is in my files.

† It is well to keep this passage in mind because later, when I transmitted an agreement that would have encompassed both gold and non-gold countries, presumably most of those at the conference, he rejected it. He probably forgot when he rejected that innocuous declaration that he had said this on June 17.

‡ *Foreign Relations, 1933,* I, p. 646.

This statement of Roosevelt's, which was most carefully considered by Woodin, Acheson, and me and most meticulously composed by Roosevelt, was at that moment and later his position.

In Washington the President's message was designed to warn the American negotiators of Roosevelt's intention to keep his hands free for any action he believed would be useful in stimulating the rise in prices which he deemed essential to domestic recovery. He was not at all impressed by the position of the French and British that temporary stabilization was an essential prerequisite for a successful conference. And he was now a little nettled that the American negotiators were out of accord with his domestic objectives. Perhaps he even remembered that on the evening at the White House some weeks earlier, when he announced his intention to accept a modified Thomas amendment, that Warburg and Feis had joined with Lewis Douglas in almost hysterical opposition. And he assumed that Sprague and Harrison, whom he knew only slightly, were hard-money men. Cox he discounted because he believed quite correctly that his former running-mate was so uninformed about international monetary affairs that he had fallen under the influence of Warburg.

The state of mind in London among the negotiators and some of the delegates after receiving this rejection reached the proportions of despair. Their contention, expressed in private, was that Roosevelt had changed his mind after they had sailed. But this contention, which was vigorously proclaimed later, was wrong. They should have known better.

Harrison decided that the end had come to all hopes for temporary stabilization and he packed his bags and sailed for home. Warburg and Sprague, along with Cox, still believed that they could change Roosevelt's mind. On Sunday, the eighteenth, they dispatched a cable to Roosevelt stressing that their stabilization agreement would be "of purely temporary nature designed to facilitate work of conference in laying permanent groundwork." Moreover "if during the conference national emergency should make it necessary we can withdraw." This of course Roosevelt already knew because it was in the agreement itself, which he had already answered. However, they persisted and, apparently chastened, they said they would work for a better bargain in the dollar-sterling rate, widening the spread from $3.80 to $4.20. "Believe any greater spread than this would result in making it too easy for speculators to work against stabilization." Finally they argued that if we refused to cooperate in reducing currency fluctuations it would be claimed "that having sent special representatives to discuss temporary stabilization we [meaning Roosevelt] have now changed our minds. . . ." *

* *Ibid.*, pp. 647–48.

Warburg cabled Roosevelt privately the same evening saying that until our "attitude toward exchange stability during the conference is clear" there would be little likelihood that any other ideas would take root. He asked for endorsement in principle "even if we have not been able to meet your wishes completely on technical details." This was a gross understatement because the technical details were regarded by Roosevelt as the essence of the position he had taken.*

Roosevelt did not reply to this directly, but sent a cable from the destroyer *Ellis* which was taking him to Nantucket, where he was to board the sailing ship *Amberjack* for a vacation. That cable authorized Warburg and Sprague to suggest our willingness to keep the pound from going above $4.25.†

On the twentieth in a cable also sent from the *Ellis*, Roosevelt told Hull, "I think it best in every way for us to stand on the principles and suggestions outlined in my cable of June 17th. You are in position to insist upon consideration of the larger and more permanent program, working towards a means of exchange among all nations. Remember that far too much importance is attached to exchange stability by banker-influenced cabinets. In our case it means only a very small (perhaps 3) per cent of our total trade measured by production." ‡

Meanwhile, the delegation members and staff found some respite from their discomfort and a bit of satisfaction in politicking. The conference was to have two commissions, one dealing with economic affairs and the other monetary affairs. The chairman proposed for the latter was Cox. After much negotiation it was agreed that Cox should be chairman of the Monetary Commission. It proved to be an empty victory, for monetary matters had reached a stalemate.§

Further troubles dogged the hapless delegation. At a meeting of the delegation on Saturday morning, June 17, the proposition was advanced that the United States suggest to the conference a horizontal 10 per cent tariff cut. This was rejected by all of the delegates except Hull and Morrison, but it was agreed that the idea could be discussed by the appropriate committee of the Economic Commission.

That same afternoon it was learned that Hull had signed a list of proposals for consideration by the conference. This was sent to the secretariat and was mimeographed and given to the press. When this was revealed to the members of the delegation, there was a spate of personal comments to the press by members. Pittman explained that the list of topics was not an expression of American policy but subjects to be explored. Morrison told reporters that he was delighted that stabilization had been rejected by Roosevelt. Couzens said to the press that "He in-

* *Ibid.*, pp. 646–47.
† *Ibid.*, p. 649.
‡ *Ibid.*, p. 650.
§ *Ibid.*, p. 641.

tended to voice his opinions on all matters at any time to the press—regardless of whether they agreed with the delegation point of view."

Alarmed by this free talk to the press, Bullitt suggested to Hull that he give instructions to the delegates that they must not make public statements "without his [Hull's] approval." Hull refused to issue such an order, saying that since he had no part in selecting the delegation he could not provide any discipline.

News of these statements of members had reached Washington, and on June 19 Phillips sent the following cable to Hull (curiously enough it is not to be found in *Foreign Relations of the United States, 1933,* I):

> Strictly Confidential for the Secretary from Phillips. I am a good deal worried by the press reports this afternoon emanating from London. . . . It looks to me as if members of the delegation were expressing their individual views too fully with the result that the picture is being represented over here of disagreements among the delegation and a lack of unity of purpose. . . .*

It was this evidence of open disagreement, bickering, and confusion of purpose that led Roosevelt to the conclusion that someone must be sent to help get things straightened out in London. And since it had been agreed earlier that I was to be one of a series of liaison officers or messengers, this meant that this formidable, perhaps insurmountable, task be assigned to me.

* R. M. Files.

Chapter Thirty-five

My Mission to London

THERE was a great fuss in the press about my mission to London in the summer of 1933 and the story, with many fictional additions during and since, reached the proportions of a "whodunit" crawling with spies, hidden and sinister purposes, clashes of personalities, and hurt feelings and reputations.

But there was nothing secret about my mission and its purposes. Under normal conditions it would have been routine. But normal conditions did not prevail.

The American delegation had been hastily thrown together. Its instructions were capable of all sorts of interpretations. The agenda, prepared months before for the conference itself by a group of international experts, was unclear and internally contradictory. Our untrained and unbriefed American delegates were pitted against foreigners who knew what they wanted and who believed they knew how to get it. And, worst of all, the central figure in it all was a President of the United States who had selected a most unfortunate and most inaccessible place to spend a leisurely vacation. It is still the opinion of Mullen, who was my assistant through it all, that Roosevelt deliberately designed his vacation to avoid responsibility for what might happen. As it did happen, however, he emerged as the man who wrecked the whole affair.

The story had humor as well as pathos and tragic overtones. I propose to tell it as simply as possible and without the romantic coloring with which participants at the time and historians since have cluttered it up.

It seems a pity to break away the festoons of fable that have grown about the incident. Such imaginative literature, after all, can break the monotony, which so frequently accompanies the course of public life.

The bare bones must be exposed, however, so that they may dispel the romantic aura that has been accorded this bit of life among civilized nations. History has a plain responsibility to be something more than a compendium of old wives' tales.

When and how and by whom was the plan made for my mission to London? Why was that specific time selected? What was my attitude about going when I grew to realize that the conference would end in failure? How was my last-minute reluctance to go resolved? What did I do and why? What did Roosevelt do and why? What were the reactions to Roosevelt's capricious policies among the sober and more or less wise statesmen who were there representing foreign nations? What did the members of the American delegation and their experts do and how did they behave? And in the perspective of time, does it seem that I was wise in going at all?

Some time in May, perhaps three weeks before the members of the delegation had been selected (except that it was obvious that Hull should go as chairman), Roosevelt told me that, in order to create liaison between the delegation and himself, three emissaries should be sent over in chronological order. The first of these was to be Warren Robbins, protocol officer in the State Department and a cousin of Roosevelt's. The second was not then selected. The third was to be Tugwell and he was to go in mid-July.*

As I have indicated earlier, Roosevelt asked me why I did not want to go as a delegate when I showed him the list of the staff that should attend the delegation. I declined because I had serious doubts about the conference being able to accomplish anything so soon and I didn't want to be embroiled in the difficulties that I anticipated would meet the delegation. Also I was at that time managing the debt negotiations and, since Congress would be in session beyond the time when the delegation would sail, I felt that I could be more useful to Roosevelt in Washington than in London.

And so I suggested that when Robbins had returned and had reported his findings to Roosevelt, and Congress had adjourned, and the debt payment date of June 15 had been passed, that I might go late in June. Roosevelt agreed to this suggestion.

There was no secret about this plan for me to go. Bullitt, Warburg, and Feis were told about it and protested because they wanted me to go with the delegation and with them on May 31.†

On May 9 I wrote a letter to James C. Bonbright, a colleague of mine

* This plan is verified by Tugwell in notes he sent to me in 1965. Mullen suggests that Hull was not informed of this plan. I am sure, however, that he knew. At any rate Robbins must have informed him when he went and returned in June, for Robbins was a close subordinate of Hull's.

† R. M. Diary, May 16, 1935.

at Columbia, saying that I "expected to be in London in a short time." Senator Byrnes knew it, because I have a letter from him recommending a young woman whom he wanted me to take along to do secretarial work. On May 30 I wrote to my friend Joseph Connolly, who was to be the Irish Free State's representative at the conference: "I am not a member of the Delegation but plan to leave for London about the fifteenth of June." Also my diplomatic passport under date of June 12 stated that I was "about to proceed abroad on official business."

Considerably earlier than this, early in May, before Robert Bingham left to take up his duties as Ambassador, he asked me to stay at the embassy when I visited London in June. And the New York *Times* reported on May 27 that I was planning to go.*

The exact time for my departure was fixed by the considerations I had stated to Roosevelt. It also became more imperative that some sort of contact be established when reports of confusion in London came to us in Washington, and when the various messages on stabilization from Sprague, Warburg, and Cox came for the approval which was refused.

The decision for me to go was announced by Roosevelt at a press conference on June 16. He said, according to a memorandum by the State Department's press officer Michael J. McDermott: "Mr. Moley from the very start has been going over just for a week or two, acting more as a messenger than anything else. Warren Robbins is coming back next week to report. There will be somebody else going over and coming back just a couple of weeks later." †

On Saturday afternoon, June 17, Phillips sent this cable to Hull:

> Moley, accompanied by Arthur Mullen, sails on the Manhattan Wednesday June 21 and expects to remain in London for a week or ten days. The object of his trip is to inform the delegation of the situation here during the last three weeks and bring impressions and views that may be useful to the President. He is accepting an invitation from the Ambassador to stay at the embassy. Phillips, Acting Secretary.‡

In planning for the trip I decided to take Mullen, who was my assistant in the State Department, holding not only the title of assistant legal adviser but also of State Department intelligence agent. Mullen had been an assistant to Marvin McIntyre during the 1932 campaign

* All of these items are in my files. Mullen notes that when he heard Bingham extend his invitation to stay at the embassy he protested. But I could see then no reason to refuse since the embassy was government property and my mission was to be official.

† "Memorandum of White House Conference, June 16, 1933." Signed M. J. McDermott. In R. M. Files.

‡ Copy in R. M. Files. This is another omission from *Foreign Relations, 1933*. This omission, which may have been deliberate, may have been made to support the mystery which Hull later claimed about the fact and the purpose of my mission.

and at the White House after the inauguration. He was twenty-eight years old and a college and law-school graduate. I had asked for his transfer to my office. He was exceedingly helpful in the extremely busy days in April and May. He enjoyed complete daily and hourly access to the White House and to Roosevelt himself. In our months together he showed extraordinary shrewdness in helping me deal with the many situations with which I was confronted. He was intensely loyal.

I decided that Mullen should not only go with me but be present at all of my contacts with the press, the American experts, and foreign representatives. This was very important to me on such a delicate mission, since I was to be the President's representative and whatever I said might by inadvertence or design be twisted and distorted.*

When the time for my departure drew close, I talked with Roosevelt and we considered having Herbert Bayard Swope accompany me. He had formerly been executive editor of the New York *World* and had been a distinguished reporter for the *World* in the war and in the peace conference that followed. He knew many people here and abroad. He had been a loyal supporter of Roosevelt in 1932. Louis Howe had some long-standing reason for disliking Swope and objected to sending him with me. Roosevelt overruled Howe and wrote inviting Swope to accompany me:

> Would be delighted if you could accompany Raymond Moley for a short visit in connection with, but not a part of the Economic Conference. I am sending him soon and feel that your presence would be helpful in many ways. . . . You will be absent from this country only about a month.†

Mullen had enjoyed many contacts with official British representatives in Washington. He learned from them in some way that the official determination of the British government was to stabilize the pound at $3.50. This added to my concern about the whole question of stabilization at that time. I therefore went over the ground carefully with Roosevelt, Woodin, Hugh Johnson, and the people at the Department of Agriculture. I was very anxious to determine what the effect of stabilization at that time might have upon the domestic programs for recovery and for raising prices here.

Woodin explained that Roosevelt's hands must be kept clear of any specific agreement even for temporary stabilization. Hugh Johnson said, when I talked with him:

"An agreement to stabilize now along the lines your boy friends in London are suggesting would bust to hell and gone the prices we are

* This association has been rewarding even in writing this account. For Mullen is in 1966 in full vigor at the head of a manufacturing company in Detroit and has verified substantially everything that appears in this chapter.

† R. M. Files.

sweating to raise. Please get me. I am for a return to gold at the earliest possible moment. But that time is not now." I received the same advice from the Department of Agriculture.

Also, at this time the information from Mullen and the attitude of my associates in Washington made me wonder whether I should go at all. I could, it seemed, carry to London only negative news about the position of the American government. This would put me in the position over there as carrier of bad news. It would be exceedingly embarrassing to me. Mullen whose native shrewdness was keener than mine was vociferously against our going.

Since the President was leaving for a cruise on a sailboat and would be relatively inaccessible, and since Woodin's health had deteriorated to the extent that he was compelled to return to New York for treatments, and since Acheson, the undersecretary of the Treasury, was only newly appointed, I concluded that someone must be at hand in Washington who was capable of meeting the continuing problems raised by our monetary negotiators in London. The eminently qualified person for that stand-by job was Baruch. I asked Roosevelt about this and he was delighted with the suggestion. "As a matter of fact," he said, "I not only had Bernie in mind for that job myself, but I have already spoken to him about it. He is willing. So go ahead with it." So I announced the plan to have Baruch sit in my office and keep himself in readiness to advise Acheson and the President about affairs in London. This, in the form of a formal announcement, was unfortunate. For the newspapers blazoned the news that Baruch was to be a temporary "assistant president." This so frightened the cautious Baruch that he beat a hasty retreat to New York. This was only one of the many complications I learned about as soon as I was on shipboard.

My days after Roosevelt departed for his vacation on June 16 and before my sailing on the S.S. *Manhattan* on Wednesday, the twenty-first, were exceedingly crowded. Roosevelt left with me the draft of his statement of policy * to which I have already referred. I took it with me to my office at the State Department, but considering the pressure under which Roosevelt had written it I decided to wait until the next day to send it. No essential time would be lost because the next day was a Saturday. The next afternoon I went over to the White House and with Stephen Early made contact with Roosevelt in Massachusetts. There were a few slight revisions, which Early incorporated in a new draft. Then, since there was eager expectation of news, a number of reporters were waiting at my office for information about what Roosevelt was sending in reply to the stabilization proposal from London. Since it was officially a Treasury matter, I asked Dean Acheson to come and help me

* See *Foreign Relations, 1933,* I, pp. 645–46.

with the reporters. We did what we could, without handing them the note, to explain the Administration's position. After that my secretary took the note to the appropriate office for transmission.

On Sunday, June 18, there were many loose ends to clear up, correspondence, and gathering things together which I would need in London. I called Swope and Baruch and asked them to come down and join me in the office the next day.

On Monday, the nineteenth, they were at my office most of the day. We went over the stabilization question thoroughly. Then Swope with Baruch's help prepared a general statement opposing stabilization at this time. He believed it might be useful to Roosevelt. This I left with Roosevelt when I saw him later on the *Amberjack*. Then I recalled that the "thank you" notes (or the reverse) should be written to the debtor nations for their payments (or non-payments). These were dictated and dispatched. Finally the reporters came in and I explained my plans for departure and made the remark about Baruch's being around to advise that proved to be so embarrassing to Baruch later.

That evening, while I was with Mullen packing at my hotel, I had a telephone call from James Byrnes. He said he was at the Chevy Chase Club with Marvin McIntyre and that they wanted to talk with me. I suggested that they come to the hotel. In his memoirs Byrnes tells of this visit:

> A few days after the Congress adjourned I attended a summer Gridiron party at the Chevy Chase Club. During the evening Marvin McIntyre, one of the President's secretaries, told me that Ray Moley was leaving that night for the World Economic Conference. . . . He was going as a special envoy of the President. I had come to think a lot of Moley and, believing that he was making a mistake, I left the party with McIntyre for Moley's hotel, where I found him packing for the trip. I told him he could serve the President best by remaining at his side to confer with him about instructions to be sent to the delegation that was already representing us at the Conference; that if it should be announced that he was leaving for the Conference as a special envoy of the President, the delegations from other governments would ignore our delegation and its effectiveness would be impaired. He was sufficiently interested to say that the next morning he would fly to see the President, who was in New England at the time.*

Byrnes and McIntyre were very canny individuals. They were, I realized, tried and tested friends. I told them that their doubts might be on different grounds than my own but that I agreed that I should not go to London. I explained, however, that the message that had been sent on Saturday would be a great shock to the delegation and the stabilization negotiators. So far as the delegation was concerned, I didn't

* James F. Byrnes, *All in One Lifetime,* p. 81.

feel that it could properly comprehend how serious Roosevelt was in rejecting even temporary stabilization.

When Byrnes wrote, twenty-five years after the event, he had been Secretary of State himself and had attended a number of international conferences. That is why he stressed the danger of impairing the effectiveness of the delegation in his account of the advice that I should not go. But in my account, written only six years after 1933, I recorded other telling arguments he made that night. He said that I could only injure myself by plunging into the maelstrom in London. The conference would be a fiasco anyhow, and anyone there would emerge with a damaged reputation. He and McIntyre stressed especially that I should remain close to Roosevelt as before and help advise him in directing the affairs in London by remote control. So why get mixed up in it? I had everything to lose and nothing to gain personally by going. Why not persuade Roosevelt to send someone else?

I recalled to them the fact that my mission had already been announced and that Phillips, at Roosevelt's direction, in his cable to Hull on the previous Saturday, had announced my trip, and also that Roosevelt had told the press about it in his press conference before he left on the sixteenth. I was virtually under orders to go, and no one could countermand those orders except the President himself. I also told them that I had grave misgivings that agreed with theirs.

Byrnes and McIntyre then said that I certainly must go at once and talk with Roosevelt, telling him about their arguments that I should stay in Washington.*

It was about eleven o'clock by that time and Roosevelt was on a sailing boat somewhere off the coast of New England. Since McIntyre was the President's appointments secretary, he made an effort to get in contact with Roosevelt. This failed and we all agreed that it would be best to go at once and confer with him on the *Amberjack*. Mullen, who was a very resourceful young man, called Henry Roosevelt, who was assistant secretary of the Navy, and had him arrange transportation to Martha's Vineyard that night. This was approved by McIntyre, and a hydroplane that had been assigned for the use of the Secretary of the Navy was prepared to leave in the early morning hours. The Navy undertook to carry word to Roosevelt about my coming on a matter of vital importance. Although we had not secured authority directly from Roosevelt, he was notified of our coming during the course of our flight. And so, with the blessings of Byrnes and McIntyre and their expressed

* When I checked this incident with Mullen on September 1, 1965, he made the point that Byrnes was very insistent that I should see Roosevelt at once and clear the whole matter with him. Byrnes authorized me to tell Roosevelt of his advice that I stay in the United States.

hope that the President would countermand my orders to go to London, Mullen and I finished our packing, and at 3:00 A.M. took off from the Anacostia air base. I managed a couple of hours' sleep during the flight. We arrived at Martha's Vineyard and were transported by a cutter to the destroyer *Ellis*, which took us to the *Amberjack*. Mullen was with me when I met with Roosevelt at ten o'clock on the stern of the boat and was present during the two hours' discussion which followed.*

To avoid any misinterpretation about what happened on the *Amberjack*, I am following the account that I wrote in my book *After Seven Years*, which appeared six years after the event. I am also using information that I have unearthed since. All of this is verified by Mullen, who was the only other person present.

It was my custom to prepare carefully what I wanted to talk about when I saw Roosevelt. For his habit of altering the import of what had been said to him and what he had responded was well known to all of his intimates. His will was so strong that he quite easily compelled himself to remember or believe that what he wanted to be true was true. I had no opportunity to write an agenda for this conference during the last hour of our delightful early morning flight over the tip of Long Island and the Sound. But I carefully considered what I wanted to learn from him: (1) I wanted to express my reluctance to go to London and to tell him of the advice given me by Byrnes and McIntyre. (2) Since I would be, if I went, running directly into the center of contention in London, stabilization, I wanted to know exactly how far he would go to save or break up the conference. (3) I wanted a written statement of the purpose of my mission that I could use with the press when I arrived in London.

He scoffed at the misgivings of Byrnes and McIntyre and my own. At this point Mullen, in his direct way, said, "Mr. President, I don't want to go to London." Roosevelt replied, "No, I want you to go and help Ray."

When we came to the all-important subject of stabilization, I reminded him that he had not yet answered the final message from

* In Arthur Schlesinger's account of this incident, he says, "There is . . . evidence that Roosevelt was somewhat irritated by Moley's dramatic descent upon the *Amberjack*." He gives no such evidence and his statement is wholly wrong. Roosevelt had been notified and had arranged to have the destroyer pick us up and take us to the schooner. He seemed to enjoy the visit immensely. And so far as drama was concerned he suggested, to place even more emphasis on my departure, that he would have Mullen and me board the destroyer *Bernadou*, which was nearby, and on Wednesday or Thursday intercept the *Manhattan* on the high seas and put us aboard. This I dismissed as a joke. I was having too much publicity already.

Sprague, Warburg, and Cox, which had been received on Sunday. He thereupon picked up a scratch pad and wrote this with a pencil:

For Hull—

After careful reading of the views expressed in your 40 and 41 and after full discussion here I think it best in every way for us to stand on the principles and suggestions outlined in my cable of June 17th. You are in position to insist on consideration of the larger or more permanent program, working towards a means of exchange among all nations. Remember that far too much importance is attached to exchange stability by banker-influenced cabinets. In our case it concerns only about 3 per cent of our total trade as measured by production. Roosevelt.*

In the conversation that followed I asked for instructions as to what he would be willing to do. He said that the way was still open for some sort of agreement to calm the gold-standard countries and "steady" the dollar if that could be contrived without shipping gold and thus checking the magnificent advance of American prices that had followed our departure from gold in April. I suggested that, in part at least, the rise in prices had been speculative and said that I felt some apprehension about the rapidity of the rise. I said I concurred with him that the agreement Sprague, Warburg, and Cox had suggested would cause too drastic a decline. Perhaps we could devise some sort of action that would somewhat slacken the rise without impairing our recovery and would at the same time check speculative excesses. The memory of 1929 was still fresh in my mind. Roosevelt said that he agreed with this, and then added:

"You know, if nothing else can be worked out, I would even consider stabilizing at a middle point of $4.15, with a high and low of $4.25 and $4.05. I'm not crazy about it, but I think I would go that far."

I replied that Sprague and the others might work something out even more satisfactory than that. "They will probably be putting up proposals to you while I am on the way over."

The verification of this suggestion by Roosevelt is in a telegram that had been dispatched the day before from Roosevelt to Phillips from the destroyer *Ellis:*

U.S.S. "Ellis," June 19, 1933—1 P.M.

(Received 2:50 P.M.)

Believe general situation not greatly altered and still my personal thought that a range with upper and lower limits is unnecessary. London and Paris would combine to put dollar at lower end of range. Why not

* *Foreign Relations, 1933,* I, p. 650. Original copy in Roosevelt's handwriting is in my files, for I had it copied for transmission from the destroyer *Ellis.* (The last sentence quoted above is from the original handwritten copy and therefore differs slightly from the transmitted copy.)

probably try suggestion of our willingness during conference to keep pound from going above 4.25. You can make it perfectly clear that the 4 dollar medium point is in my judgment too low especially at this time of year with tendency of trade balance favorable to us during next few months depressing pound still further.

Talk with Baruch and Moley about advisability of suggesting to Cox a final medium point of 4.15 with maximum point of 4.25 and minimum 4.05. I hesitate to go even that far but it is worth considering.

We should also ascertain whether life of conference means August 12 or perhaps December 12. There is a vast difference.

Am in Nantucket tonight.

ROOSEVELT *

At this point I took from my pocket a brief memorandum that Swope along with Baruch had prepared on the preceding day. It was, I explained, background argument on stabilization. He might find it useful in replying to further dispatches from London. It was essentially an argument against rigid and arbitrary stabilization. He took the memorandum and without reading it put it in his pocket.

He then said that the essential thing I should impress upon the delegation and the others was that his primary objective was to raise the world price level, that I should tell them in detail about what the American recovery program was accomplishing in raising prices, relieving debtors and increasing purchasing power. He referred to a column of Walter Lippmann's that said international cooperation was an admirable ideal provided that it be "a cooperation in powerful, concurrent and concerted measures, and not merely a cooperation which produced a negative and impotent stability." †

I reminded him that Lippmann was then in London. Should I get in touch with him and also John Maynard Keynes, who I knew shared Roosevelt's monetary ideas? They would be useful in advising me and also the American negotiators. He liked this idea, and we added the names of Charles Rist, whom he had met in Washington, and Walter Runciman, a member of the British Cabinet who served as the president of the Board of Trade. The Runciman suggestion came from Roosevelt. I jotted down these names on a page from Roosevelt's scratch pad.‡

Finally I asked him to write out something that would not only make my status clear but explain the purpose of my mission. I also said that I wanted permission to give this to the press. He again turned to his scratch pad and wrote the following:

Asst. Secretary Moley is sailing tomorrow for London at the request of the President. He will act in a sense as a messenger or liaison officer on this

* *Foreign Relations, 1933,* I, p. 649.

† New York *Herald Tribune,* June 14, 1933.

‡ R. M. Files.

short trip, giving the American delegates first hand information of the various developments, Congressional etc. in the country since the Delegation left and conveying the President's views of the effect of these developments on the original instructions given the Delegation before they sailed.

Asst. Sec'y Moley will stay in London only about a week and will then return to give the President full information of the Conference up to that time.*

Mullen and I left the *Amberjack* and returned to the *Ellis*, which put us ashore at New Bedford. There we boarded a Coast Guard amphibian plane and returned to New York. I spent the night at the Biltmore and Mullen flew to Washington to get our baggage. He returned to New York on the night train.

As I was preparing for a much needed night's sleep, Joseph P. Kennedy came to my room. He said, in the spirit of a bird of ill omen, that he had come to warn me. He said that he had reason to believe that Roosevelt was growing "jealous" because of the prominence I had "enjoyed" as an adviser and assistant of the President. Also that I had better "watch out for him."

I was not disposed to be disturbed by this admonition for two reasons: I had never believed nor could believe that Roosevelt regarded me as anything but a faithful packhorse in his great affairs. For eighteen months he had entrusted me with confidences and had imposed upon me very serious responsibilities, and I felt that in the present instance I was acting with full assurance of successfully carrying out his wishes. I also made a mental note of the fact that at that time Kennedy grievously resented the fact that Roosevelt had not yet recognized his support and financial outlays in the 1932 campaign by any recognition in the form of an appointment in the new Administration. I was also quite well acquainted with the in-fighting in politics, which so often characterizes itself in driving discordant wedges between allied individuals. My sleep that night and later was not disturbed by that warning, and I cannot accept it today as valid.

The ship was to sail at noon and when I arrived at the dock I found not only Swope and Mullen but several well-wishers. Among the latter was Edward J. Flynn, whom I had long since recognized as Roosevelt's most intimate and wisest political adviser. He greeted me warmly and offered his best wishes. He told me in later years that he was strongly inclined at that moment to take passage on the ship and accompany me to London. I wish now that he had responded to that hunch. For he could have added his great influence to mine in urging Roosevelt to accept the agreement that was later rejected. He could have been of inestimable value in straightening out the differences that prevailed

* R. M. Files. Original in Roosevelt's handwriting.

within the delegation, for everyone intimately related to the Roosevelt Administration regarded him as Roosevelt's alter ego.

After a brief statement to the reporters, we sailed at noon.

The first two days on shipboard were a welcome respite from the turmoil I had been through during the final days on land. In fact, I had scarcely enjoyed a day off since the turn of the year. Swope made many friends on the ship, and so did Mullen. The first day out I sent a message to Hull supplementing personally the explanation of the purposes of my mission that had earlier been sent by Phillips. As I relaxed, I considered what I should do when I arrived in London. I wrote this note to myself: "It's this—hold the Delegation together, stop strife, make Hull feel reassured. He sees it too simply—keep my thinking straight—nothing selfish." And on the flyleaf of a book I was reading I noted this: "How about a tentative agreement with England, France and Italy—bring this up." *

What news we received came from Miss Pomeranz, my secretary in my office in the State Department, and from Baruch to Swope. There also came some messages from Phillips describing some of the newspaper comments. For a time the information we received indicated that the American delegation in London was pulling itself together. But soon this indication of returning harmony was dissipated. We learned that the stabilization negotiators had submitted a new agreement to Roosevelt and that he had rejected it. After that, paralysis seemed to be setting in.

Then I grew very disturbed when a warning came from Baruch that the word was spreading in London that nothing could be done until I arrived with some new information about Roosevelt's views. This suggestion gained ground, I believed, because the reporters had little else to send to their newspapers. This unfortunate enlargement of expectations about me was reflected in the texts of two editorials that came from Washington. The New York *Times* said on the day after we sailed:

> Few are so credulous as to be deceived by the official explanations of Professor Moley's trip to the London Economic Conference. It is gravely said that he is to furnish "reports" to President Roosevelt. As if the cables were not already crowded with such reports. It is added that Mr. Moley is also to be a kind of "liaison" officer at London. He will be one more of the grand coordinators working under the President. Yet everybody who has followed the dispatches knows that Secretary Hull and his fellow-delegates have been thrown into uncertainty and confusion by statements given out at Washington. These have amounted to flat disavowals of what our representatives have said or proposed at the Conference. The result is that they and all the other members of it are now waiting for the appearance of the Professor *ex machina* to decide how much, or how little, is to be done.

* R. M. Files.

This editorial went on to castigate the American delegation for its divided counsels. It was guilty of gross error when it implied that my radio address (broadcast in May) had been made after Hull's speech at the opening of the conference.

Phillips, who was concerned with giving me no comfort, sent me the text of an editorial in the Baltimore *Sun* that said about the same thing. When this sort of thing was appearing in the editorials of supposedly responsible newspapers, we could well imagine what was running in the gossip columns. Clearly the internationalist press in the United States welcomed this opportunity to "have at me" for what they regarded as my isolationist views.

Obviously I was heading into heavy weather. I asked Mullen and Swope to meet me in my room, and we considered carefully our course of action after arrival in London. We agreed that, according to my instructions, oral and written, my mission was designed to achieve these objectives:

1. To make clear to the members of the American delegation and staff that Roosevelt had confidence in the delegation and in the broad planning that might be achieved in the conference.

2. To convey to the delegation the vital need for harmony and discipline. And to do what we could to restore Hull's morale.

3. To make intelligible to the delegation the latest thoughts of Roosevelt so far as we knew them. This meant their bearing upon the domestic program, which was already under way. The NIRA had been passed more than two weeks after the delegation had sailed.

4. Most important of all, I was supposed to convey to Hull and the stabilization negotiators the limits so far as the pound and dollar were concerned that Roosevelt had told us on the *Amberjack* and in his message to Phillips which was to be conveyed to Baruch and me.

5. At the end of our mission, to give Roosevelt a candid report on the proceedings in London and an evaluation of the performance of the delegation.

We also carefully reviewed my status:

1. From the time when Hull was appointed, it was specifically understood that I was, despite my nominal title in the State Department, responsible to the President. Hull and I had both accepted our appointments with this understanding.

2. Throughout the period before and after the inauguration I had been largely concerned with Treasury affairs and in this I had the full confidence of Woodin. Since the stabilization question fell within the Treasury's responsibility I would, in anything I did, be responsible to Woodin and the President, although Hull should be kept informed. Hull understood this and had stated it to the delegation when he said I was

going to work with Sprague and Warburg on the matter of what he called "temporary stabilization." This he admits in his memoirs.

3. As a liaison between the President and the delegation, I had no responsibility to the delegation. To emphasize this detachment, I had somewhat reluctantly decided to stay at the embassy and to keep Swope and Mullen there with me.*

We realized now that every hour of the voyage was bringing us closer to a hell's brew of confusion, mutual distrust, recrimination, and, worst of all, a devastating flood of newspaper publicity. The most important thing, it seemed to us, was that I should make it as clear as possible by what I said and what I did that I had limited responsibility, in order to deflate the fantastic rumors about what was expected of me. With his skill with words, Swope helped me to compose two statements, one to be released at Cobh, the other at my arrival at Plymouth. After consideration these two were combined in one, which I radioed to Phillips to be submitted to Roosevelt for approval. This was on June 25. Roosevelt replied that the statement was "fully lucid." He added that I should give out no more statements because I was "under the Secretary and . . . not a member of the delegation." The same, he added, should apply to Swope. While I needed no such reminder, I realized from his language that he was aware of Hull's worry about the reports that I was to supplant him, and thus he wanted me to make clear my nominal and official relationship to the Secretary. This determined me that the best way to deflate the reports about my authority was to make very clear my subordination to Hull. It would stop the rumors and greatly ease Hull's apprehensions.

Swope, Mullen, and I then considered the advisability of getting to London as expeditiously as possible. Swope suggested that I ask Bingham to send a plane to Cobh to pick us up from the ship. I then sent a message to Bingham asking whether a plane could be sent. I did not ask him to send one. But he took my message to be an order and sent one anyhow. This added to the publicity and suspense in London. For no doubt the bureaucrats in the embassy, taking the State Department line, gave the matter full coverage in the press.

When the plane reached Ireland, it could not land in the Cobh area

* It may have been for that reason that Phillips or someone else in his bureaucracy withheld from my office dispatches from Hull and the delegation after I left for London. This was reported to me by my secretary after I returned. I well realized that Phillips was bitterly resentful of my status in the government. But this denial of information about what was happening in London seemed to be carrying a personal objective too far. For if I were to be effective at all in London, I should have been told what was happening there while I was at sea. My secretary went to Phillips' office and protested, but without success. What information we received came from the newspaper accounts Baruch sent to Swope.

because of fog but found a landing place nearby. And on it was an official from the embassy with a letter to me from Hull.

A number of Irish newspaper reporters boarded the *Manhattan* and staged a sort of an interview with me. I was most reticent in what I said. Some of them were victims of the war and their disabilities coupled with their lack of adequate nourishment gave the group a woeful aspect. They were a friendly lot, however, and I was able to satisfy them with the story of my father's birth in Dublin and my antecedents' migration to the United States. This seemed to provide them with something for their editors—that and a picture of Mullen.

The mishaps seemed to be continuous. I had decided earlier not to use the plane. I sent Mullen ashore to get Bullitt on the telephone and tell him to meet me at Plymouth, but after two hours he still could not make contact with Bullitt. Meanwhile, the *Manhattan* was under way. Mullen entered a small boat and caught up with the liner, which threw a rope ladder over the side. Mullen had a small bag which he had taken to provide for his necessities if he were to be left behind, and with this in hand he essayed the difficult feat of climbing up to the somewhat rolling liner. Somebody on the small boat had a camera and a picture was taken of Mullen and the ladder swaying about twenty feet from the side of the *Manhattan*. This was printed in a London newspaper, further highlighting a sensational incident of my mission.

After things quieted down, I read Hull's letter, which was sealed and marked confidential. It said:

> Thanks for the message to the Delegation announcing your arrival next Wednesday. We are naturally glad to have all cooperation for you to offer, knowing, of course, of your anxiety to be of maximum service. It is due you, the Delegation and the Administration, to know that for several days the hostile and grossly unfair British and French press, aided by numerous American dispatches, have constantly heralded the view that you are coming personally to interfere with and assume more or less of the functions and undertakings of the Delegation, and that, in fact, you are to be virtually in charge of United States interests in London.
>
> The result of these widespread reports read each morning by the Delegates of all nations here, has been to handicap somewhat the Delegation in its earnest efforts to function in fullest measure. As a consequence of this the expectation is rife in the Conference that you are bringing some proposal which will revolutionize the American program as agreed upon in Washington.
>
> In these circumstances, may I suggest the advisability in giving out your first press statement of your indicating rather definitely the extent, if any, to which you personally, under any special authorization from Washington, propose to participate in or supervise the Delegation with respect to the matters aforesaid. I thus, without reference to the information of the Delegation, quote the language of the press for your full information. . . . it is

important that we function here to the fullest extent in support of a sufficiently substantial program as will make it impossible for our critics to charge our administration with any loss of general purpose, much less of good faith, with respect to the World Economic Conference.*

This was a strange and anxious communication. But it was, considering the plight of the delegation, quite reasonable. It sharpened my determination to deflate the rumors as well as myself through my statement on arrival and later through direct contact with the press.

When we arrived at Plymouth, we were greeted by a number of British reporters as well as George Holmes, an old American friend who represented the International News Service. There was also my assistant in Washington, who had been attached to the delegation staff. I had asked her to meet us at Plymouth so that I might learn of what had happened while we were at sea. Following a procedure that had been routine in Washington, she had made a daily account in writing. This was possible for her because she knew and had the full confidence of some members of the delegation as well as of Bullitt, Warburg, and other staff members.

It was late when Mullen, Swope, and I arrived at the embassy, but the next morning I called upon Hull at his quarters at Claridge's. I gave him a full account of my mission and assured him that the idea, stated in his letter, that I might be "supervising" or directing the delegation was an absurd interpretation of my purpose. I told him how deeply I regretted the interpretations the press and other sources had attached to my visit. And I told him that if he would accompany me to a press conference, I would do what I could to dispel the rumors and clarify my mission. Hull seemed to be delighted with this, and the beginning of my public deflation was arranged for at a meeting of the delegation and at a press conference later that morning. A very large representation of the press greeted us in a room at Claridge's.

Hull introduced me cordially and I responded in kind to him. Then I said that the statement I had given out at Plymouth the evening before was all that I intended to make, but that I was willing, with Hull's consent, to answer questions. There was a barrage of questions, most of them friendly enough. And I answered as well as I could, although I declined to respond to any about the debts and stabilization.†

Over-all, I seemed to have succeeded in deflating myself far beyond my anxious expectations, and of conveying my friendly and cooperative attitude toward Hull. I have ever since entertained a very warm feeling toward Frederick T. Birchall, the veteran correspondent of the New York *Times*, for his dispatch describing that press conference. This feel-

* R. M. Files.
† R. M. Diary.

ing is deepened when it is considered that editorially the *Times* remained my bitter critic throughout the period of the conference and at the time of my resignation two months later.

Birchall wrote in his published dispatch, "Of the day's incidents the Conference debut of Professor Moley was the most interesting and provocative of the most comment, all favorable to the newcomer. . . . He expressed willingness to answer questions, but wanted to keep them within the scope of his mission." Birchall noted my emphasis on "the President's high confidence in the United States Delegation to the Conference and in the distinguished citizen who was Secretary of State and its head. For himself he [Moley] was here to render service to the Secretary in any way he could."

Albert L. Warner cabled this to the New York *Herald Tribune:*

> Publicly Mr. Moley bowed to Secretary of State Cordell Hull's leadership hailing him as "my chief." With the attention of London centered upon him in the most unusual publicity accorded any individual at the Conference, the Assistant Secretary made every effort to keep in the background and deferred to Secretary Hull with almost exaggerated insistence. . . . Mr. Moley declared that he would have no new statement to make, since such would naturally come from Secretary Hull. He took pains to impress on every one that President Roosevelt was delighted with Secretary Hull's efforts. At a special press conference at Claridge's Hotel, Mr. Moley . . . stood quietly beside Secretary Hull while the delegation leader told of his confidence in the progress of the Conference and his hopes for the future.

The correspondent for the NEA, Milton Bronner, wrote later that I had deflated myself "completely, willingly, heartily. . . . Professor Moley was innocent of the inflation of his reputation. . . . That same afternoon of his first day in London, he stood by the side of Hull . . . [and] made his act of deflation short and sharp and unmistakable . . . with the sure skill and efficiency of a great surgeon."

Hull apparently caught the sense of approval of the members of the press, for he made no effort to conceal his appreciation. He took me to his apartment and for the first time in our strange association spoke to me confidentially. He said that the delegation had been "disobedient and recalcitrant." I insisted that he had all of the necessary authority to discipline his group. And in answer to the complaint that there was nothing he could do to deal with any matter of importance, I attempted to assure him that for the long pull there was a need to contrive some international means of currency exchange as well as ultimately more freedom of trade. For the moment at least, Hull seemed to be cheered up.

And for the moment I felt the satisfaction of having entered upon my business in London with marked success.

I could not know it at that moment of these laudatory press dispatches, but I could sense from the course of the questioning and the friendly tone of the press conference that I had won a generally favorable appraisal by the American representatives of the press. I had not always enjoyed a good press, except in the 1932 campaign, although a few American reporters were warm and approving friends. But I had learned something from my experience in press relations and during the past few days I had enjoyed the coaching of Swope, a great reporter and editor. From that time on my relations with the press were quite cordial and, with a few exceptions among the French and British, their published comments were helpful. I had effectively dispelled the idea that I had come as a savior, and that meant that my mission was well launched.*

* Mullen, who was closer to the press than I was thereafter, and whose experience throughout the campaign of 1932 and during the period after the inauguration in Washington was considerable, adds this in a letter to me under date of November 1, 1965:

"The London press was filled with comments about you before and when we arrived. After the first day they were very hostile, I thought, and particularly hostile after your meeting with Chamberlain. You will remember that the meeting with Chamberlain was at the Embassy. He was accompanied by his Secretary and you were accompanied by me, and his proposal was that the pound be stabilized at $3.50. You promptly told him that that was impossible. After Chamberlain left, you called Woodin in New York but the connection was so bad that Woodin was unable to understand you, so you put me on the telephone and I was able to communicate to Woodin what had happened and what the offer was. Woodin expressed astonishment and was shocked at the offer."

Chapter Thirty-six

The Short Life and Sudden Death of a Compromise

IN concluding a cable to Roosevelt on June 22, six days before my arrival, the emotional Cox made this plea, "If you love us at all don't give us another week like this one." But so far as I and the others close to the scene were concerned, the week that followed my arrival surpassed anything that had happened before. At a distance of three decades, its recital seems like wry comedy. But to those who were struggling with the realities, it had all of the elements of tragedy. It seemed incredible when it happened. And now, at this distance, it would be unbelievable except for the cold records as well as the impressions written by others who were on the scene.

The hasty rejection of the compromise declaration by Roosevelt becomes even more regrettable when the widely separated locations in which the major actors in the events of the next three days were situated and the faulty means of communication between them are considered.

The Secretary of the Treasury, upon whose judgment Roosevelt should normally have relied, was very ill at his home in New York. He was suffering from the effects of an acute phase of the malignant growth in his throat, which after a three months' remission was to claim his life early in 1934. Keeping store at the Treasury for him was Dean Acheson, who had only been in office six weeks. While Acheson was a highly intelligent and magnificently trained lawyer with a general understanding of monetary affairs, he knew little of Roosevelt's mercurial temperament and capriciously changing ideas. In charge at the State Department was the acting secretary, William Phillips. A career officer for nearly thirty years, Phillips combined in his outlook and mental equipment the prejudices of a Boston Brahmin with the bent of mind imposed upon all members of the foreign-service bureaucracy. He tried to operate at all times "by the book" and except for occasional blunders, one of which will appear presently, he kept himself fairly well out of any controversial position. Fortunately, these two were supplemented by Baruch, the keenest of all the people involved and the most careful in gathering all the available facts before reaching a decision. Close to Acheson was Lewis Douglas, director of the budget, whose monetary views were strictly conservative and who was well informed and highly intelligent. There was also available in New York by this time George L. Harrison, who had returned after Roosevelt's first rejection of the stabilization plan. He adequately represented the Federal Reserve's views.*

In London there was the delegation. Hull was badly confused and according to later accounts had been seriously considering resignation after Roosevelt had rejected his plea for action on the tariff and later the plans for temporary stabilization of currency during the period of the conference. He was utterly at his wit's end in attempting to control the delegates, who had been recklessly talking with the press about their differences. Cox was not only highly emotional but was handicapped by his complete lack of understanding of monetary affairs. Nothing in his past experience in politics and newspaper publishing had prepared him for this situation. Pittman, despite an occasional lapse, understood monetary affairs, but he was preoccupied with the interests of silver. Morrison refrained from any of the discussions except for his support of Hull's views on trade and his leaning toward a soft-

* In the account of what happened in London, I am relying on several sources, some of which are available to any student of the London Conference from the American viewpoint. One is my account in Chapter VII of my book *After Seven Years,* which was written six years after 1933 and was carefully checked in manuscript by Elliott Thurston, who was a press officer with the delegation in London, and Ernest Lindley, the well-informed Washington correspondent of the New York *Herald Tribune.* There is also a day-by-day and almost hour-by-hour account written by me on shipboard during my return voyage. This consists of a pooling of the memories at that time of Swope, Mullen, and myself and also of Celeste Jedel, who was my assistant in Washington and who had accompanied the delegation as a staff member. This account is in my files and had been made available to Frank Freidel of Harvard and Herbert Feis, both of whom are writing about this period. I have also consulted the newspaper accounts of that period, especially the dispatches from London of Frederick T. Birchall to the New York *Times.* Also many notes I made during the period and, of course, the official cables, which are now available in *Foreign Relations, 1933,* I.

In my recital of what happened in London and Washington and at sea with Roosevelt, I am concentrating almost wholly upon the evolution of the compromise declarations on monetary policy. Clarity demands the omission of the many juicy stories and rumors that were published at the time and some of which have crept into the history books. Some of these stories are true. Most are either exaggerations or fabrications. Almost all relate to people long since dead.

money policy. He had secured his appointment through political influence largely because he wanted to impress upon the Mexican government his status with the Roosevelt Administration. He had large investments in Mexico. Couzens, always a difficult individual, jealous of his senatorial prerogatives, had been outspoken in his discontent with everything that was at issue in London. He also was on the point of resigning. Finally McReynolds, whom none of us knew very well, was a complete blank so far as influence in the discussions then under way were concerned.

On the staff side, Bullitt was a capable executive officer. Warburg, Feis, and Sprague were sound economists, but they were frustrated and perplexed by what they quite properly appraised as a great change in Roosevelt's policies since they had left Washington.

Contending with the Americans in London were the representatives of the gold countries, insisting upon some assurance that might provide the means for remaining on gold. They had been selfishly insistent that unless some stabilization of a temporary if not a permanent character were given them, they would pack up and leave the conference. Finally, there was the British government over which MacDonald presided as Prime Minister and in which Neville Chamberlain was Chancellor of the Exchequer. Leith-Ross we all respected and liked. He was a genuine expert in monetary affairs and had been a source of great strength in dealing with the representatives of the gold countries. But there was no doubt about the strong alliance between the British and the gold countries in their insistence upon some sort of concessions by the United States that might prevent a crisis in Europe. MacDonald was impressed by the fact that his tenure as Prime Minister was not likely to survive long after the conference and he was determined to leave with some elements of high achievement behind him. His presidency of the conference placed him in a commanding if somewhat precarious position.

But the major factor in the debacle was Roosevelt, not only because of his capricious way of arriving at decisions but because during three crucial days he was virtually inaccessible. After I had my final talk with him on the *Amberjack*, he continued his leisurely cruise to the north and east. He spent the days from that June 20 to June 30 sailing along the coast, putting in overnight at various points in Massachusetts and Maine. During the final three days of this cruise he was hemmed in by fog from the Bay of Fundy. On the thirtieth he reached his ancestral summer place at Campobello, where he spent two nights. Then he boarded the cruiser *Indianapolis* for the return trip to Washington. Communication was always slow and messages were often garbled. Dispatches to Roosevelt had to be sent in State Department code and after their arrival in Washington were deciphered and translated into the

Navy code. They were then deciphered for Roosevelt's reading. There was no telephone connection at Campobello that we could use to reach him directly.

Moreover, there was no one with Roosevelt at Campobello or on shipboard who understood the issues immediately involved and who could translate his vague monetary theories into terms that would be intelligible to his advisers in Washington, New York, and London. There was also his sometimes lamentable syntax. All these circumstances explain the general impression among knowledgeable people at that time and since that some of his communications made no sense at all.

On his return trip on the *Indianapolis* he had with him Henry Morgenthau, Jr., and Louis Howe. Morgenthau was a dedicated disciple of Professor George Warren of Cornell, who had curious and, as it later proved, fallacious ideas about controlling prices by alterations in the price of gold. Howe relied upon the stock market quotations for his intake on economic affairs, and he noted that stock prices went up when Roosevelt took the hard line with London and down when there was any sign of a compromise. And so he vigorously urged Roosevelt to reject anything that came from London. It was subsequently shown that both of these individuals were desirous of deflating me. It was also revealed later that my old nemesis, Norman Davis, had been with Roosevelt for twenty-four hours on June 30 and July 1. He, too, had a score to settle with me.

These were the deplorable conditions under which we were compelled to work during the days that followed my arrival in London. I could not know of all of them at the time, but the difficulties in communication were quite apparent.*

It will simplify the story of the first appearance of the compromise declaration, its brief life and its death during the three days after my press conference with Hull, to recite the events day by day.

Thursday, June 29, 1933

Bullitt came early for breakfast with me at the embassy. He first said that he had seen Hull the previous evening and the Secretary of State

* It is a fair question whether Roosevelt should have selected that precise time and environment for a leisurely vacation. A failure of communications was not the only factor in the debacle, for even in his office in Washington he was subject to capricious judgments. But there he was always subject to advice. And that might have saved the situation. Surely he needed a vacation. But so did all the rest of those who were involved in this unfortunate affair. But since he had gaily assumed a major role in the conference and since he had plenty of information before he left Washington about the confusion in London, he might have selected a spot more

seemed reassured about my presence in London and pleased with what I had told the press. So it seemed that the first of my objectives had been accomplished with the deflation of the rumors and speculations about what proposals and solutions I was bringing with me.

Bullitt then confirmed most of what I had already heard about the confused events within and without the delegation since its arrival in London. But he then recited a piece of news that presented an entirely new factor in the situation. He said that the representatives of the gold countries had apparently given up their insistence that the United States agree to some form of temporary stabilization as a condition to further participation in the conference. They had correctly interpreted Roosevelt's various refusals to accept the earlier proposals. In short, they had accepted the loss of this claim and were prepared to compromise on a vague multilateral statement of ultimate principle. Bullitt, who for many years had been on friendly terms with MacDonald and had his confidence, said that when the gold representatives had approached MacDonald about a compromise he was "caught off balance and suggested that the United States should also be approached." A meeting was scheduled for that afternoon between Cox, as chairman of the Monetary Commission, Warburg, and the gold representatives, at which MacDonald would also be present.

While Bullitt was talking, I reviewed in my mind the objectives of my mission that Swope, Mullen, and I had formulated on the ship coming over. These imposed upon me the job of conveying to the delegates Roosevelt's ideas concerning the long-range possibilities of the conference along with other conclusions he had reached after the delegation had left Washington. Another was to do what was possible to restore Hull's morale and as tactfully as possible to allay frictions within the delegation. I also had the suggestion imparted to me on the *Amberjack*, and validated the day before in Roosevelt's message to Phillips, that Baruch and I consider a pegging of the dollar between $4.05 and $4.25 to the pound, which Roosevelt said he, too, might consider.*

The possibility of some sort of innocuous, non-binding compromise, which Bullitt's information suggested, intrigued me. For if this could be accepted by Roosevelt, it might cure most of the confusion in which the delegates had been immersed since their arrival. I had thought of this possibility on my voyage from the United States.

But at that moment a number of conditions and reservations occurred to me:

accessible to rest and relax in. The responsibility for the failure in London cannot be charged to the delegation or the advisers in London, New York, and Washington. History has quite properly placed the responsibility for the debacle upon the President of the United States.

* *Foreign Relations, 1933,* I, p. 649.

1. Hull must understand the reason for my interest in such a compromise and inform the delegation that I expected to join Sprague, Warburg, and others in considering it. This Bullitt said he would immediately arrange.

2. I must see the proposal as soon as possible after Hull had made his announcement. I had deep suspicions about the motives of the gold representatives.

3. I must not take over the negotiations for our side. I had no authority to do that. These negotiations had been imposed upon Sprague, representing the Treasury, Harrison of the Federal Reserve, and Warburg. I could merely advise in the light of Roosevelt's most recent thinking as it had been revealed to me.

4. I could accept for transmission. I had no authority or desire to make policy. That was for Roosevelt to determine.

Bullitt then went to Claridge's to suggest to Hull that he make an announcement that I was to participate in the discussions along with Sprague and Warburg. When I arrived at the morning meeting, Hull made such an announcement, saying that negotiations concerning "temporary stabilization" were to be in the hands of Sprague and me, with such others as we chose to call upon.*

I had another reason for assuming this limited responsibility. The nature of the compromise and our reactions to it must be kept confidential within the small group involved. While Hull should be kept informed, it was not wise to risk leakage to the press or by private communications to the United States. The exchanges were already influenced by a speculative frenzy.†

After this meeting with the delegation, I went with Cox and Warburg to join Sprague and saw for the first time the declaration that had been drawn up by the French, Dutch, and Italians. I was amazed when I read it. It was brief, simple, and wholly innocuous. It was largely a paraphrase of one of the instructions written by Warburg and given to the delegation by Roosevelt on the day of its departure from Washington. That resolution had actually been introduced in the conference by Pittman on June 19. None but the most rabid American inflationist could have objected to this. Certainly what Roosevelt had told me and also what he had said in his June 19 message to Phillips was a greater concession than this. For this suggested no rates at all. It spoke only of "ultimate" stabilization. It was in fact an unconditional surrender by the gold countries.

After I had examined the draft, Sprague and Warburg suggested that

* R. M. Diary, June 29, 1933.

† The instability of the market was well shown a day or so later when I went to the Austin Reed store to buy some shirts. The clerk in accepting American dollars was compelled to call the Bank of England before he made the change in sterling.

MacDonald wanted the United States to be present at a meeting of the gold representatives with him later that morning. My instinct directed the cautious reply that I would not attend such a meeting. I felt that as a liaison between the President and the delegation I should not participate in actual negotiations. I added, however, that I would be glad to meet informally and unofficially with Leith-Ross, Rist, and Jung of Italy, whom I had known well when they were in Washington. I could trust their discretion. This would fill me in about the thinking among the foreign countries at the conference. We met with them in Cox's room. I was very cautious in what I said about the declaration, but indicated that certain changes might be made to eliminate any hint of stabilization. I said I could not submit to Roosevelt anything I felt he would reject, but in any event I had no authority to commit Roosevelt to anything. I could merely act as a means of transmission, a conduit. Leith-Ross applied the diplomatic expression "*ad referendum*" to explain my role in the transaction.*

A few days later when Swope and I were talking with Sir Maurice Hankey, we learned that certain distorted reports had been issued to the French press by the government over there. The meticulous secretary of the British Cabinet showed me the notes he had taken earlier, which were his record of whatever he was acquainted with. I casually noted how he did these notes on long narrow paper. That record completely negates a charge made by some of my critics later that my acquiescence in sending the declaration to Roosevelt was vested with some sort of personal authority to approve. The Hankey record, I assume, is in the archives in London.

Before returning to the embassy I visited with Cox and Couzens briefly in their respective rooms. I had known Cox fifteen years earlier, when he was governor of Ohio and I was connected with the Council of Defense in Columbus in 1918. I had never been an admirer of Cox and in 1920, when offered a choice between him and his fellow Ohioan Harding, I refrained from voting. Nor was I impressed by what he told me that particular day. His talk consisted chiefly of warning me that in the privacy of their rooms Mr. and Mrs. Hull were bitterly critical of me. This gossip seemed to be presently irrelevant, and so I went to see Couzens. He said that he had been unhappy ever since arriving in London. He said that there was a fundamental incompatibility between the American position and that of the other nations at the conference. He disagreed with Hull. He said further that a week ago he had told Hull that he felt he could be of no usefulness at the conference and he wanted to quit. He said that Hull replied that he should "wait until Moley comes." He said that he had again approached Hull about resign-

* R. M. Diary, June 29, 1933.

ing that very morning and that Hull had told him again to consult with me. I would not evade this responsibility. I suggested that, rather than resign and cause more commotion in the press, he should take his wife and spend a few days sightseeing on the Continent or in Ireland.

Shortly after lunch that day I had a visit at the embassy from Neville Chamberlain, who was then Chancellor of the Exchequer, and Leith-Ross. They came from the meeting with the gold representatives and brought a revised draft of the declaration. I discussed the draft briefly with them and then said that, since Sprague represented the Treasury, I would ask him to take the responsibility of sending it to Woodin and Baruch for their comment before it was dispatched to Roosevelt. That evening Sprague sent a lengthy cable to Woodin and Baruch giving background on the proposed declaration and at the same time I sent the tentative text to them. I believed it to be important to get their reaction before it went to Roosevelt.*

That afternoon I paid a brief courtesy call on MacDonald at Downing Street. Our conversation was general in nature. I notified Hull of this visit.

In the evening I called Acheson and asked him to meet with Baruch and Harrison at Woodin's home in New York so that Sprague and I could explain the compromise declaration, describe the situation in London, and get their opinion about the document. This meeting would also enable them to get the information essential to their advice to Roosevelt.

Friday, June 30, 1933

Unfortunately, Phillips without my knowledge telegraphed to Roosevelt the earlier text of the declaration, which I had sent for the consideration of Baruch, Acheson, and Harrison. This error of Phillips' may or may not have had any bearing upon Roosevelt's later refusal. But what happened was that Roosevelt based his rejection upon this draft rather than the final one, which I sent later.†

It is also doubtful whether he had received the message from Woodin,

* The texts of these two cables are in *Foreign Relations, 1933,* I, pp. 664–66. Also, a telegram from Phillips to Roosevelt, giving a revision of the earlier draft that I had telephoned to Acheson, is at page 667.

† According to *Foreign Relations, 1933,* I, pp. 669–71, Roosevelt's rejection was sent from the *Indianapolis* on the early morning of July 1 (2:00 A.M.), while the final text from me was received at the State Department on July 1 at 4:10 A.M. It would have probably taken some hours to get it decoded on the *Indianapolis* and to Roosevelt. By that time the damage had been done. He could not have received my supplementary cable in which I told him that the life of the conference depended upon his reply.

Acheson, and Baruch strongly urging him to accept the declaration. I cannot determine this sequence exactly from the record.*

That morning, Friday, I explained to Hull what had been done. He seemed pleased, and suggested that I meet with the delegates immediately and tell them in a general way what was going on (without, however, describing the terms of the declaration). I also stated that, since I had little doubt about Roosevelt's acceptance of the compromise, Hull should be the one to carry the joyful tidings to the foreign representatives. I realized that the situation in London was intense, and that Roosevelt's acceptance of the declaration would mark the end of two weeks of anxiety and inaction. Hull suggested no opposition to this. In making this suggestion I was acting with the utmost precision. For it was not my function to act as a means of communicating such information to the foreign representatives. It was the prerogative of the chief of the delegation and Secretary of State.†

Couzens and Pittman lunched with Swope, Mullen, and me at the embassy that day. During lunch I received a message saying that Leith-Ross, Jung, Georges Bonnet (France's Minister of Finance and the head of the French delegation), and Jean Bizet (adviser to the French Treasury) were coming to see me that afternoon. When they arrived I was shown the French version of the declaration and discovered, with the aid of my assistant, that the French had twisted some phrases to make the text sound like stabilization to French readers. I insisted upon making the proper corrections. The French yielded, but Jung said, "You are breaking my heart." Perhaps the only funny thing I said in London was my reply, "That is because you have a heart of gold."

After they left I showed the declaration to Couzens and Pittman, who had remained in another room. I felt this to be safe since by this time I assumed that the French had already leaked the text to their press. (They had, incidentally, and it appeared on the front page of the New York *Times* the next morning.) Couzens and Pittman enthusiastically approved the declaration.

Shortly after four I called Woodin's home in New York. Baruch, Acheson, and Harrison were there. Thus there were assembled all of the authoritative advisers upon whom Roosevelt might lean in making his decision. These were the Secretary of the Treasury, the undersecretary, and the governor of the New York Federal Reserve Bank; also Baruch, whom the President had designated in more than one of his messages as his adviser.

After a few preliminaries I turned the telephone over to Sprague. He

* *Ibid.*, pp. 667–68.

† R. M. Diary, June 30, 1933. Unfortunately this was twisted by critics later as a suggestion that I was attempting to convert Hull into a "messenger."

spent nearly an hour explaining the declaration, since these men had not yet received the cable from Sprague and me.*

We arranged to call these advisers again later and, we hoped, after they had received the text of the declaration.

After this telephone conversation I called Hull and reported that while the people in New York had not received our cables they seemed to be fully in accord with our views.

That evening at eight we called Woodin's home again. The same people were there and Woodin had recovered from his earlier collapse. The messages from us had been received and there was expressed complete agreement. After a few questions as to our attitude Baruch said that he, Woodin, Acheson, and Harrison had already written for dispatch to the President their recommendation that he accept the declaration.†

I felt some satisfaction in the progress we had made so far. We had the approval of the declaration by every one of the people designated by Roosevelt as his advisers on this subject: Woodin, Acheson, Baruch, and Harrison in the United States, and Warburg and Feis in London; also Cox, Pittman, and Couzens of the delegation and, so far as I knew, Hull. Nevertheless I had an anxious night ahead. For I well knew the capricious President with whom we were dealing.

Saturday, July 1, 1933

Early the following morning I sent the final text of the declaration to Phillips to be transmitted to Roosevelt wherever he was.‡

Later a very disquieting message from Roosevelt came through from Phillips: "The President has sent telephone message to me from Campobello saying that he will send reply to your Nos. 79 and 80 just as soon as possible. Meanwhile he asks that the delegation refrain from any action or comment." §

The two messages to which he referred were the one Sprague had sent to Woodin and Baruch, which Phillips had forwarded to Roosevelt without authorization, and the one numbered 80—the preliminary draft I had sent for the consideration of Woodin and Baruch. This is further evidence that Roosevelt did not have the final draft in hand

* During this conversation there was a break in New York and we waited until we resumed contact. This we learned later was because Woodin had fainted during the conversation. The people with him at the time feared for his life. But he recovered, and the conversation was resumed from another room in his apartment.

† *Foreign Relations, 1933,* I, pp. 667–68.

‡ The text is printed in full on p. 481.

§ *Foreign Relations, 1933,* I, p. 668. Since there was no telephone at Campobello, this meant that someone had taken the message to the mainland to telephone to Phillips.

when he wrote his reply. But since his message indicated that he might reject the compromise, I sent him a final plea for approval at ten o'clock that morning.*

I then went to Claridge's and met Hull on the staircase. We went to his room and I told him that I feared that we were in for another Presidential veto. Greatly disturbed, he gave vent to his inmost feelings. He recited the many humiliations he had suffered, first by Roosevelt's refusal to introduce the tariff bill and also by the recalcitrance of some of the delegates. He also said that "scads" of newspapermen had been telling him that the feeling still existed that I had been sent over to supersede him.

I could only answer as patiently as I could to this highly generalized comment that I had made my position clear to the press on the day after my arrival in London. Without noting my comment, he continued. He said that he had given up a lifetime seat in the Senate to become Secretary of State and, at least by inference, that it was impossible for him to resign now. Since I was more deeply concerned about what might be coming from Roosevelt than Hull's personal troubles, I took my departure, giving him as much reassurance as was possible.

The hours dragged on after that, with Swope, Mullen, and me remaining close to the code room at the hotel.

At three o'clock in the afternoon the first sentences began to emerge, and they confirmed my apprehensions. I left to find Hull and told him as much as I knew. He was leaving his room to attend a party given by Nancy Astor at Cliveden. Most of the other invitees had already left. As we stood on the sidewalk near his waiting automobile, Hull's anger mounted. He bitterly assailed Swope, who, he said, had been talking too much. But I was quite aware that most of the feelings rising from his frustrations were directed at me. He said that when the message came through I should send it to him at the party.†

It seemed to me, after an analysis of Roosevelt's message, that because of the strange assumption—that the declaration called for immediate stabilization—and the fantastic economic reasoning it contained, it would be unwise to make it public.‡ There was also the chance that some inferences in it might lead to a revision and acceptance. For those reasons and to protect Roosevelt himself from widespread criticism,

* See pp. 482–83 for text.

† Later MacDonald told me that James Thomas, Secretary of State for the Dominions and a member of the British delegation, had told him that when the news of the rejection came there was great rejoicing by Americans at Cliveden because I had been humiliated. Little did they realize that the rug had been jerked from beneath their feet, too; that the country they represented had been grievously injured in the eyes of the world, and that the reason for their presence in London would probably vanish, because of the failure of the conference.

‡ The text and an analysis are at pages 481–85.

it was decided that Michelson should not give it to the press but merely issue a statement that Roosevelt had rejected the declaration "in its present form" and that the delegation would have a further statement on Monday.

I decided that we needed some counsel and reflection before we decided upon the next step. And so, at Swope's invitation, Walter Lippmann joined Mullen, Swope, and me at the embassy for dinner. We decided that Roosevelt might be protected from criticism of his faulty economics if we prepared a statement that the delegation might release on Monday morning. During the dinner we talked with Baruch twice. He expressed amazement at Roosevelt's attitude. He said that neither he nor Acheson could understand what the message meant except that it rejected the declaration. He asked whether any other messages had gone to Roosevelt from London to cause him to alter his course. But it was Baruch's opinion that, since Roosevelt had spoken, there was nothing else we could do. Later we talked with Baruch again, to learn if possible the circumstances under which Roosevelt had written his refusal. All he knew was that only Morgenthau and Howe had been with him on the *Indianapolis* when he made his decision. This provided some clue, but it was hardly believable that these individuals, with their scanty knowledge of the situation in London or of the issues involved and, above all, their ignorance of international monetary affairs, could possibly have swayed Roosevelt from the advice of all of his other advisers.

Earlier that evening I sent a message to Roosevelt through Phillips in which I noted that his rejection seemed to be based upon an earlier draft and not the final version I had sent him. But I added that the changes made in the earlier draft would probably not have changed his mind. I added that Hull would make only a statement that the declaration had been rejected in its "present form." And that an explanatory statement would be made Monday. Then, since I felt that I had done what I could and was heartily sick of the whole business, I added that I bowed to his judgment "with no inconsiderable relief." This meant, in a term so often used by Roosevelt, simply "it is your baby now."

But Swope and Mullen insisted that something must be done to convey the President's views more coherently than he had expressed them. And so Swope, Mullen, and Lippmann worked with me to shape a statement that would be in line with Roosevelt's own suggestion in his message that the delegation might use the import of his message as the basis of a statement of American policy.

This we completed by early morning. But because the second "bombshell" arrived on Monday, this statement of ours was never used.*

* Copies of the various drafts of our unused statement are in my files.

Chapter Thirty-seven

Impotence and Dissolution

IT was my ill fortune, during the four and a half remaining days in London, that in addition to my own responsibilities I was fated to spend an excessive amount of time in a fruitless effort to pacify and to buck up two deplorably depressed statesmen. One was the distracted MacDonald, and the other was the angered and hurt Hull.

I saw MacDonald a number of times. His sense of failure was mixed with his resentment at what he regarded as the bad faith of Roosevelt. I tried to explain, keeping well within the limits of loyalty to Roosevelt, what the President had been trying to say to the American delegation, to MacDonald and the conference. The Prime Minister manifested the warmest feelings toward me but he could not forgive Roosevelt for what he considered the abandonment of the assurances he had been given in Washington.

My other personal concern was to respond as well as I could to members of the staff who said I must quiet Hull's resentment toward Roosevelt and also convince him of my own good faith.

My efforts were without avail. For Hull's bitterness toward me apparently grew with the years. His resentment toward Roosevelt he kept pent up until he wrote his memoirs years later.

MacDonald died at sea two years later, a deeply disappointed man. The conference upon which he had built so much of anticipation and hope had failed, and Roosevelt, he believed, was responsible.

Sunday, July 2, 1933

Early that morning MacDonald called me at the embassy before I had dressed. He said, "This is the Prime Minister. I am at Checquers. I am coming in directly to Downing Street. I will send Hankey around to get you."

After breakfast Elliott Thurston called to talk with me. He was a very warm friend and he believed he was performing an office of friendship by telling me that the disappointment caused by the two Roosevelt messages had rekindled Hull's disapproval of me. I should, Thurston said, have a long talk with the Secretary. I explained that I had repeatedly tried to establish a truce for the duration but apparently I had not been successful. But I would try again that afternoon.

Hankey came later that morning and took me in the Prime Minister's car to a rear entrance of one of the houses on Downing Street. MacDonald was very agitated. He wanted to know what was in Roosevelt's mind when he sent the message rejecting the compromise. He said he couldn't understand it. I could only say that Roosevelt didn't want the conference to break up and that Hull would have something to give out Monday morning. This might allay somewhat the fears of the gold countries. I then made it clear that these meetings with him as Prime Minister were not according to protocol and I asked that he make it clear to Hull that they were on the Prime Minister's own initiative. He said he would but that, since he had been unable to get a clear understanding of Roosevelt's views from members of the American delegation, he had waited to supplement what he knew with my more recent talks with the President.

That afternoon, in response to Thurston's suggestion, I met with Hull in Pittman's room. Pittman, who had known Hull for many years, acted as moderator and advocate in my behalf. Pittman's forensic performance was magnificent. If I had been on trial for my life I could not have asked a more brilliant presentation of my case. He expounded upon my posture toward the Secretary, the reasons why Roosevelt had placed me in the Department of State, and the necessity that in this hour of trial we all must stand together. I supplemented this with a repetition of what I had told the press on my arrival. As an American I could hardly have come to a foreign country to undermine another American. Hull seemed assured and from then on there was no more unpleasantness between us.*

* That evening I had dinner at Simpson's, and Morrison dropped by the table where I was sitting. I had a score to settle with him because he had been quoted in the British press as resenting my "tinkering with stabilization." I had disturbing information, too, about certain other Morrison activities, which need not be recited now. I distrusted him profoundly. And I was at that moment less than tender with his feelings. I charged him with deliberate misrepresentation. He answered that he had been misquoted and was sorry that I had taken offense. Years later on a trip to Mexico I discovered that he was up to the same tricks. It was perhaps fortunate that I had this opportunity to discharge some of my pent-up feelings toward a target as deserving to receive the impact as Morrison. (R. M. Diary, July 2, 1933.)

Monday, July 3, 1933

That morning, as I said to myself when it happened, the other shoe fell. The still-famous "bombshell" message dispatched from the *Indianapolis* arrived at the code room at 3:00 A.M. and copies were ready for the delegates and the staff and the rest of us when we met at Claridge's. Stark wonder, not unmixed with horror and consternation, was on every side. The message speaks for itself:

Herewith is a statement which I think you can use Monday morning as a message from me to you. If you think it best not to give it out in London let me know at once and in that event I will release it here as a White House statement.

I would regard it as a catastrophe amounting to a world tragedy if the great Conference of Nations, called to bring about a more real and permanent financial stability and a greater prosperity to the masses of all nations, should, in advance of any serious effort to consider these broader problems, allow itself to be diverted by the proposal of a purely artificial and temporary experiment affecting the monetary exchange of a few nations only. Such action, such diversion, shows a singular lack of proportion and a failure to remember the larger purposes for which the Economic Conference originally was called together.

I do not relish the thought that insistence on such action should be made an excuse for the continuance of the basic economic errors that underlie so much of the present world wide depression.

The world will not long be lulled by the specious fallacy of achieving a temporary and probably an artificial stability in foreign exchange on the part of a few large countries only.

The sound internal economic system of a nation is a greater factor in its well being than the price of its currency in changing terms of the currencies of other nations.

It is for this reason that reduced cost of government, adequate government income, and ability to service government debts are all so important to ultimate stability. So too, old fetishes of so-called international bankers are being replaced by efforts to plan national currencies with the objective of giving to those currencies a continuing purchasing power which does not greatly vary in terms of the commodities and need of modern civilization. Let me be frank in saying that the United States seeks the kind of a dollar which a generation hence will have the same purchasing and debt paying power as the dollar value we hope to attain in the near future. That objective means more to the good of other nations than a fixed ratio for a month or two in terms of the pound or franc.

Our broad purpose is the permanent stabilization of every nation's currency. Gold or gold and silver can well continue to be a metallic reserve behind currencies but this is not the time to dissipate gold reserves. When the world works out concerted policies in the majority of nations to produce balanced budgets and living within their means, then we can properly discuss a better distribution of the world's gold and silver supply to act as a reserve base of national currencies. Restoration of world trade is an important partner, both in the means and in the result. Here also temporary exchange fixing is not the true answer. We must rather mitigate existing embargoes to make easier the exchange of products which one nation has and the other nation has not.

The Conference was called to better and perhaps to cure fundamental economic ills. It must not be diverted from that effort.*

This meant that the statement that Swope, Lippmann, and I had prepared was as dead as last week's newspaper.

Warburg's comment was especially concise and pessimistic. All of his labors before the delegation sailed—in framing a gold compromise, in writing the President's instructions to the delegation, the long days of negotiation in London, and the many cables which he had sent to Washington—had been brushed away by this truculent message and the earlier one rejecting the compromise. He ended his remarks by saying that he simply did not understand what the President was saying in his communications.†

In my book *After Seven Years* I said this in recognition of what Warburg had done:

I have always felt that Warburg merited much more credit for his part in the preliminaries of the London Conference than has ever been given him. He came to Washington at his own expense, served without salary from March to May, and then went to London. There he served in the face of the most discouraging circumstances until all real hope of continuing the Conference was ended. That his views on monetary questions were at variance with the President's in July was the reason for his resignation; but, in fairness to him, it must be said that he made every effort to implement the President's purposes, so far as they were comprehensible to him. I am sure that the ultimate verdict of history will be on his side, although at the time I was much more willing than he to allow that the President's less orthodox views might possibly bear fruit.

After Warburg had concluded, I said that I knew what Roosevelt meant. In this and previous hints in my conversations with him and in earlier messages to London, he was in pursuit of that old phantom, a commodity dollar, which had haunted him for months. But in this instance, instead of suggesting that he intended to seek such a dollar at home through tinkering with the price of gold or some other means, Roosevelt now wanted such a unit of currency to be internationally

* *Foreign Relations, 1933,* I, pp. 673–74.

† Warburg told me that day that there was no alternative for him but to resign. He did in fact resign three days later in a letter to Hull. "We are entering upon waters," he said, "for which I have no charts and in which I therefore feel myself an utterly incompetent pilot."

used. Whether such a plan would be possible in a world of nations each jealously guarding its right to fix the value of its own currency might be doubted. But that was what Roosevelt was proposing, and he was the final court of appeal for us. As to the taunts to the nations about balancing their budgets, I said that he had also suggested this in earlier messages to the delegation.

Later in Hull's room there was further talk. It was suggested that to protect Roosevelt and the delegation this message, like the one two days earlier, should not be given out. But that was impossible in the light of the tone of Roosevelt's directive. It was agreed that it should be made public at eleven o'clock and that meanwhile Hull and Bullitt should take the message to MacDonald.

That afternoon Hull announced his intention to send Roosevelt a message describing the reactions in London to his message and asking for further instructions.

The rest of the day passed in an atmosphere of utter frustration and despair. The British press screamed with indignation. MacDonald, it was reported by Bullitt, was deeply depressed.

Later that evening I tried to get Roosevelt on the telephone, but found that he was still on the *Indianapolis*.*

Tuesday, July 4, 1933

After a great deal of thought during the night, I decided that I should report to Roosevelt on the general situation prevailing in London as a result of his two sharp messages. Since I had been unable to reach him on the telephone on the previous evening, I decided that I would send him an explanatory cable and discuss the points raised therein on the telephone the next day. And so, without consulting Swope or anyone else, I wrote the following message and Mullen took it to the chancery for dispatch:

> From Moley to the President alone and exclusively, with no distribution in the Department. I shall telephone between 9 and 10 this morning your time today, and this cable is to provide guidance in our conversation. We can discuss topics without references to content by number. The topics follow:
>
> Topic 1. I believe best immediate course would be a recess for from 2 to 10 weeks permitting formulation of your ideas into resolutions.
>
> Topic 2. On personal side Pittman is only member of delegation able intellectually and aggressively to present your ideas to Conference.
>
> Topic 3. Expert group needs strengthening on progressive program.
>
> Topic 4. Reconstituted delegation would be helpful in view of developments, hence desirability recess.
>
> Topic 5. MacDonald not favorable recess because political life depends

* R. M. Diary, July 3, 1933.

upon continuation of Conference. Cox emotionally stirred by MacDonald's plight.

Topic 6. If you reply regarding fourth resolution with a new draft radically different from present form Pittman might get general approval from committee and Conference, but it is doubtful.

Topic 7. Saw Keynes day following my arrival explaining situation to him. We can depend upon him for assistance although he is not in favor with Government here.

Topic 8. I consider your message splendid. It was the only way to bring people to their senses, and do not be disturbed by complaints about severity of language. It was true, frank and fair. [Moley] *

In sending this blunt message describing what I concluded and what I believed should be done, I was almost literally obeying the orders given me on the *Amberjack*. For he had said that I should give him on my return "full information of the conference up to that time." My return to Washington, however, could not be for ten days and by that time there might not be a conference. The situation was so critical that the "full information," if it were to be of any use, must reach him at once. The recess I suggested would enable him to specify what he wanted and to strengthen his representation in London by adding new people who were prepared to present his changing ideas before the world.†

It was not a mere coincidence that Walter Lippmann reached almost identical conclusions. For since Swope and I had been talking with him almost daily, our appraisal of what the conditions were and what should be done were for the most part alike. His appraisal appeared in the New York *Herald Tribune* on the same day. He said:

Mr. Roosevelt cannot have understood how completely unequipped are his representatives here to deal with the kind of project he has in mind. For one thing, they do not know what is in his mind. For another, there is not among them a single man who understands monetary questions sufficiently to debate them. For another, they have been so frequently repudiated that they are demoralized. For another, they are divided among themselves. How can a delegation, which lacks authority, which lacks technical competence,

* *Foreign Relations, 1933,* I, p. 680.

† I shall discuss what happened to this message after I left London later. Here, however, I wish to say that, since I had been completely candid to Roosevelt, I must be equally revealing to the reader of this account. I regret only two items in that message. The final paragraph calling his "bombshell" splendid was pure sycophancy. It was not true. But perhaps I believed there was some advantage in keeping his good will for the time being, for he might be influenced even yet to change course. The other regret is that the word "intellectually" applied to Pittman was used instead of "intelligently." Maybe the coding clerks made the mistake. Maybe I did. It is of no moment now. The message itself represented my views then, and there has been nothing in the years since to alter my opinion of what I should have told Roosevelt at that time.

which lacks unity, which lacks contact with the President, hope to undertake the kind of difficult negotiation for far-reaching reforms which the President desires? It cannot be done. Mr. Roosevelt's purposes may be excellent. He has completely failed to organize a diplomatic instrument to express them. If Mr. Roosevelt means what he says, he must send a new delegation to London which knows what he means and has power to act for him.

At eight that morning I received another telephone call from MacDonald, who asked me to come again to Downing Street. He was distraught and discouraged. He said that this message from Roosevelt "doesn't sound like the same man I spent so many hours with in Washington. . . . A man told me this morning that it sounded like Lloyd George." Then he commented bitterly on what the conference meant to him. He had hoped to make it the crowning event of his long career. He angrily added that he had been placed in a dreadfully uncomfortable spot with the gold countries on one side and Roosevelt's recalcitrance on the other. It was, he said, wearing him down. Only a day or so ago he said that King George had said to him, "I will not have these people worrying my Prime Minister this way." I thought later that there was little this George could do about it; with George III in his prime it might have been different.

There was little I could say, certainly nothing in criticism of the President. But I added that it might be possible to reshape Roosevelt's ideas in somewhat softer language and that I would try to work to that end.

That day Hull sent three messages to Roosevelt. One was dispatched at 3:00 P.M., another at 6:00 P.M., and still another at nine that evening. In an earlier telegram, sent the night before at 10:00 P.M., Hull said, "your very able and courageous statement given wide publicity," and went on to describe the bitter reactions of the gold countries and MacDonald. This made the situation "grave." The second stated that Cox and Warburg had agreed upon a summary of the opinions of the gold representatives and MacDonald. Hull quoted this summary. The third said that "The Conference is probably determined to adjourn. . . . Do you wish the delegation to oppose adjournment? Do you or do you not agree that it is in the American interest at this time to agree to a recess of the Conference?" The fourth said that there had been a seeming determination of the gold countries to recess for a period of months and that he and Chamberlain had opposed this and secured agreement to recess until Thursday. He added:

A majority of our friends here now feel that our Government may go out of one flare-up into another if this regular session continues but that this would be avoided by a recess and the appointment of certain committees with MacDonald and the Steering Committee in charge. . . . I have already wired you for your best judgment as to a choice between these two proposals.*

Roosevelt replied to these in two messages, the first of which switched attention to some tariff negotiations; the second was a much elaborated and not very clear discussion of the domestic problems he was facing and what might be done despite the provisions in the NRA and the AAA to work out some trade compromise. In his messages he expressed his "earnest wish" that the conference continue. "But the United States has no other recourse than to pursue its present program until a more general international one shall have been worked out by your conference." The first of these was dispatched from the *Indianapolis* and the second from Washington.†

These dispatches, however, were wasted in the face of the hurricane that was hovering over the conference. Nor were the spirits of the delegates greatly lifted.

That morning at eleven there was a meeting in Hull's room. Hull, Cox, Warburg, Feis, Swope, Michelson, and I were present and Pittman came in later. There was a generally prevailing opinion that nothing much could be done. Swope and I had talked earlier about getting some sort of reasonable and conciliatory statement prepared for Roosevelt to issue, which would not only explain as rationally as possible his strange monetary theories but serve to encourage the conference to continue. There was little enthusiasm about this, but it was agreed that it should be tried.

Accordingly, and without further consultation with the delegation members or the staff, Swope, Mullen, and I arranged to have Keynes and Lippmann come to the embassy and try to frame such a statement to be issued by Roosevelt. Keynes was delayed by a dinner but he arrived at 11:00 P.M. in his dinner regalia, and we started work.‡

Wednesday, July 5, 1933

The writing of the Keynes-Lippmann-Swope-Moley statement was concluded at about 3:00 A.M. Wednesday. Swope, the old reporter, copied it on the typewriter.§

Our task in composing it began with an outline by Keynes, whose views were closer to Roosevelt's than those of the rest of us. He had already written a newspaper article that said Roosevelt was "magnifi-

* The texts of these messages are in *Foreign Relations, 1933,* I, pp. 679, 681, 683, 684, and 685.

† See *ibid.,* pp. 683–84 and 685–87.

‡ R. M. Diary, July 5, 1933.

§ A copy of this is in *Foreign Relations, 1933,* I, pp. 692–94. See Appendix, pp. 557–58.

cently right." He insisted that our statement should include some formula for "sitting" on speculative bulges, and that it was "chimerical" to believe that, without this, violent fluctuations could be avoided. One copy was immediately dispatched to the President and the other I kept to help me when I talked with him on the telephone.

At five that morning I succeeded in reaching Roosevelt on the telephone. There was not the slightest hint in what he said of disapproval of my action in sending the declaration or my cable appraising the delegation. He was breezy, warm, and affectionate. He said he had received my eight-point cable and appreciated it. He asked whether the situation had improved over the previous day. I said that it had, but only slightly. I added that before we got to my eight-point cable I wanted to tell him that Keynes, Lippmann, Swope, and I had worked out a new statement that might clarify his position and help quiet the situation. I asked about a recess of the conference and he said that two months would be too long. He said that when he had received the proposed statement he would call back.*

Apparently after this conversation Roosevelt, also in response to Hull's inquiries, dispatched the following telegram, which reached us on Wednesday morning:

Washington, July 4, 1933—Midnight.

104. For Hull and Delegation (from Roosevelt). Your 99, July 4, 3 P.M. and 101, July 4, 9 P.M., I think our position should be opposed to any recess because Conference has not yet considered the overwhelming majority of the matters on its agenda.

If we are unable to prevent some form of recess our alternative position should be for a recess of 10 days or say till July 17 and it should distinctly be labeled a recess to allow committees to work.

An adjournment of 60 days is in my judgment a defeatist gesture and we should oppose it. We cannot in any way admit or agree that no progress can be made on economic problems until temporary exchange fluctuations are first settled.

The people and press here are united in praise of our stand and regard the French position as wholly selfish and ignoring utterly the big objectives of Conference.

Am back in White House.

ROOSEVELT.†

Swope, Mullen, and I met with the delegation that morning at nine-thirty. Hull called on me to report on the statement I had promised the day before. I said that I was not at liberty to disclose the names of the authors except that Swope and I had participated in its composition. It was, I said, a milder, more coherent statement of the President's views.

* R. M. Diary, July 5, 1933.

† *Foreign Relations, 1933,* I, p. 688.

I read it to the group. The reaction was very favorable. And it was agreed that Hull and I should talk with the President about it. Hull called it the "Moley memorandum." *

At four that afternoon Roosevelt called back. He had received the memorandum and said that some of it had been somewhat garbled. Since I had a copy we proceeded to work on it sentence by sentence with changes inserted that he suggested. He said it should not appear as his statement but that of the delegation. When we had finished with the corrections, Hull, who was on the line with me, said, "How do you feel about this, governor?" Roosevelt answered, "I think it is all right. But I said to Ray that the real reason behind the other statement was this: If we had agreed to approve stabilization through the Central Reserve Bank [he must have meant central banks], the Federal Reserve Bank would have obligated the Treasury to export gold, and we can't do that. As a matter of fact, I got word . . . that there might have been an earmarking of gold in New York to the tune of half a billion dollars." †

Hull, Pittman, and I took the statement over to MacDonald's office at the Kensington Geological Museum, where the conference was meeting. At Hull's request I read the statement as revised by Roosevelt. MacDonald exclaimed when I had finished, "Oh, Moley, tell us why this kind of message couldn't have been sent on Saturday. It would have saved the conference."

After a few minor corrections it was released later that day as a statement of the American delegation.

Hull sent a message to Roosevelt later that evening saying, "Your approved statement which the Delegation has given out tonight made a good impression on the British as it will on all except most of the so-called gold standard countries." ‡

Since I was to sail the next day, I now felt an immense sense of relief that my mission had ended on this note. We had made the best of a bad situation and had made the best possible rationalization of Roosevelt's position. The subsequent story of the conference is a matter of history for others to tell. The conference after various veerings and spasms died within three weeks.

Thursday, July 6, 1933

I had arranged to go to Southampton by automobile to board the *Manhattan*, but before I left I paid a final visit to Hull. I asked him to

* R. M. Diary, July 5, 1933.

† Since this telephone conversation is not printed in *Foreign Relations,* it is reprinted in full in an Appendix to this book.

‡ *Foreign Relations, 1933,* I, p. 694.

give me any messages he might have for the confidential information of Roosevelt.

He made the following points:

1. Ask him not to change his policies again. It had been very embarrassing.

2. It had been especially difficult for him (Hull), after having a statement prepared for a Monday release, to have the President's statement come in on that very morning.

3. He wanted Roosevelt to know how difficult it had been to work with delegates in whose selection he had not participated.

4. Tell him not to get too radical. Do not take up every new idea.

5. Do not give the progressive Republicans too prominent a place. If they must be included scatter them out more. They will not work with anybody.*

After a stop to visit the Salisbury Cathedral, I arrived at the ship. Swope came earlier by train. A group of British newspapermen were there to question me. I had little to say except that I had enjoyed my stay in London during the past nine days. One reporter contradicted me saying it had been eight days. I managed a rather labored answer, "I said nine days because we still keep July Fourth on our calendar."

On the voyage to New York I brought together in my cabin each day the personal group that accompanied me, for the purpose of piecing together a diary of the happenings in London while we were there. These people who thus pooled their memories were Swope, Mullen, Miss Jedel, and I. We sent and received various radiograms while on the ship, seeking information about the reactions in the United States and also the course of the conference after we left. Premier de Valera, no doubt prompted by Connolly, sent a message of good will and congratulations. I wondered what he was congratulating me about.

On shipboard, where there was time for review, reflection, and conversations with Swope, Mullen, and Sprague, I tried to formulate the objectives Roosevelt had in mind when he rejected the compromise declaration. Edmund E. Day, who was also on board, had seen the conference agenda, which he had helped to prepare, become a labor lost. Roosevelt's purposes as we saw them were these:

1. To avoid shipping gold abroad.

2. To avoid a drastic fall in prices in the United States.

3. To compel the conference to achieve a formula whereby nations could maintain a stable internal price level at the same time that they adhered to a new international monetary standard.

4. To be free in behalf of the United States to devise "the kind

* R. M. Diary, July 6, 1933.

of dollar which a generation hence" would have the same purchasing power as the "dollar value" he hoped to achieve "in the near future."

5. To launch a world crusade for balancing national budgets.

At that time it remained to be seen how or whether these objectives could be achieved. But subsequent events tell what happened to these purposes, and I list the aftermath seriatim in the order shown above:

1. On the morning of July 17 the President told me in the presence of Lewis Douglas, "I have been thinking about the fact that the pound went as high as $4.84½ last week. I have just secretly ordered the Federal Reserve to export gold if it goes above $4.86." I could not resist the comment, "Then the only trouble is that I seem to have been two weeks early." On August 29 the President issued an order permitting the shipment of newly mined gold to foreign buyers.

2. On July 19 prices collapsed. For two days thereafter stocks and commodities crashed downward.

3. On July 27 the conference "recessed" after six weeks of accomplishing nothing. It never resumed.

4. On October 22, 1933, the President announced that he was adopting the Warren plan. On January 15, 1934, the President abandoned the Warren operation, which had proved to be an abysmal failure, and requested a stabilization fund of $2 billion. On March 12, 1939, the Federal Reserve Board advised Congress, "Experience has shown . . . that prices cannot be controlled by changes in the amount and cost of money. . . . Cash and prices do not move together."

5. So far as balanced budgets were concerned, the United States proceeded to set a glaring example of unbalanced budgets. Only twice in the thirty-three years since has the Federal budget been balanced, and these budgets came after Roosevelt's death. Finally, in a more recent period, the Kennedy Administration adopted a policy of planned deficits.

Chapter Thirty-eight

Reflections on the Failure of the Conference

THERE was an element of Greek tragedy in the killing of the London Conference, for Roosevelt destroyed something of which he was one of the parents.

On a lower level in the drama was the seemingly fantastic reversal of the positions of Roosevelt and me toward international cooperation. Ever since the November conference at the White House about the debts, I had been portrayed in the Eastern international press as a major isolationist influence on Roosevelt. Stimson, Hull, and many more in the succeeding Administrations believed me to be a benighted nationalist. But when Roosevelt rejected my plea to approve the compromise declaration, I was left high and dry, marooned with the internationalists, and Roosevelt was excoriated as an extreme isolationist.

That Roosevelt believed that I had been "taken in" by the Europeans in London, there can be little doubt. He did not directly tell me this, but Howe's snarling inquiry about what had "happened to me over there" reflected his boss's opinion. Thus it was made to appear that the President's missionary to the heathen had been caught worshiping the golden calf. This was, as Sir William Gilbert might have said, "a pretty how-de-do."

In my examination of the histories of the London Conference written in the years since, I find there is surprising unanimity in the conclusion that the compromise declaration was innocuous and that Roosevelt gave no rational grounds for rejecting it. But there has been a great deal of confusion about the sequence of events.

In narrative form, there has been presented in the preceding chapters what happened day by day and almost hour by hour in London, Washington, and along the foggy Northeastern coastline. But even at the expense of considerable repetition, I feel it necessary to present the record in sequential order with my own comments upon certain questions raised about those events:

1. What did Roosevelt say and do before the delegation sailed that indicated his enthusiastic approval of the conference and assured his delegates, the Treasury and Federal Reserve experts, and the foreign representatives who came to Washington, that he favored some sort of currency stabilization as a basis of long-term international monetary policy?

2. What grounds did I have for believing that in the light of Roosevelt's earlier commitments and his instructions to the delegation and to me, and despite his seeming doubts after June 1, he would still approve of the compromise declaration?

3. Were Roosevelt's messages of July 1 and 3 really responsive to the terms of the compromise declaration?

4. What authorization did I have from Roosevelt and Hull to participate with Sprague in the dispatch of the declaration to Roosevelt and to urge his approval?

5. What were Roosevelt's later reflections on his action in breaking up the conference, as evidenced in a letter written later to MacDonald and in his subsequent monetary policies?

6. Finally, what have been the verdicts of responsible historians on his rejection of the compromise and the impact of his action upon the conference and subsequent developments in Europe?

These questions I shall answer seriatim:

1.

In the long series of exchanges in December and January in which Roosevelt, Hoover, Stimson, Norman Davis, Tugwell, and I participated, it was taken by all hands for granted that the conference projected at Lausanne in mid-1932 would be held and that the new Administration would fully cooperate. Roosevelt fully assented to the return of Edmund E. Day and John H. Williams to Europe to complete the conference agenda.*

Tugwell and I were fearful that the conference would be convened too soon after Roosevelt's inauguration, and it was only by persistent efforts on our part that it was postponed. Roosevelt, without much deliberation, agreed with MacDonald and others to have it meet on June 12. It should have waited until the autumn, after the New Deal measures enacted by Congress had been given a chance to start recovery

* See Chapters 1, 2, and 3.

and suitable revisions of the original conference agenda had been made. That is why I ventured to state publicly in May my caution against great expectations.

Roosevelt assumed leadership in preparing for the conference early in April by inviting discussions in Washington with foreign representatives to shape the issues to be considered by the conference. Invitations to send special missions went to the United Kingdom, France, Germany, Italy, Japan, Argentina, Brazil, Chile, China, Canada, and Mexico. The remaining forty-two participating countries were asked to be represented in such discussions by their permanent diplomatic missions in Washington. This loud, clear call certainly notified the world that the United States was open to do business in international monetary and economic affairs. In a press conference on April 19 Roosevelt expanded on his desire to raise commodity prices and said that he hoped international action might supplement domestic policies.

A reporter asked him, "Is it still the desire of the United States to go back on the international gold standard?"

Roosevelt: "Absolutely; one of the things we hope to do is to get the world as a whole back on some form of gold standard. . . . One of the things they are talking about—the economic end of the conference—is a different gold ratio, a different gold reserve to currency." *

No doubt he was talking about the Warburg plan for a revised gold standard. At the termination of MacDonald's visit on April 26 the President and Prime Minister issued a statement saying in part:

> The ultimate re-establishment of equilibrium in the international exchanges should also be contemplated. We must when circumstances permit re-establish an international monetary standard which will operate successfully. . . . These questions are all inter-related and cannot be settled by any individual country acting by itself. The achievement of sound and lasting world recovery depends on co-ordinating domestic remedies and supplementing them by concurrent and simultaneous action in the international field. . . . It is the hope of both Governments that it may be possible to convene the Conference for June.†

A joint statement on April 28 by the President and M. Herriot of France, said, in part:

> We have noted with deep satisfaction that our two Governments are looking with like purpose at the main problems of the world and the objectives of the World Economic Conference. The Government of the United States and the French Government have been able already to announce their full agreement in regard to the necessity of a prompt meeting of this Conference, the object of which must be to bring about a rapid revival of

* Roosevelt, *Public Papers,* II, p. 140.

† *Foreign Relations, 1933,* I, p. 492.

world activity and the raising of world prices by diminishing all sorts of impediments to international commerce such as tariffs, quotas and exchange restrictions, and by the re-establishment of a normal financial and monetary situation.*

Roosevelt's commitment to stabilization was even more explicit in a joint statement on May 6 by the President and Guido Jung, Italy's Finance Minister:

We are in agreement that a fixed measure of exchange values must be re-established in the world and we believe that this measure must be gold. . . .

It must be attacked as a unit. Along with the measures which must be taken to restore normal conditions in the financial and monetary field, and stability in international exchanges, must go hand in hand measures for removing the obstacles to the flow of international commerce.†

Even Herr Schacht came in for a resounding slap on the back:

. . . we feel that the creation of stable conditions in the monetary field is equally important. Economic and monetary questions are so interdependent that the adjustment of both must necessarily go hand in hand.‡

And so it went in joint statements with representatives of the other countries during the month of May. In substance, all these statements stressed monetary stability.

In Roosevelt's second fireside radio address, on May 7, for which I wrote the draft, he largely devoted himself to the domestic program then before Congress or already adopted. But in terminating his report to the nation he told about the discussions with the Foreign Ministers in Washington, mentioning four great objectives: reduction of armaments, cutting trade barriers, re-establishment of friendly relations, and "the setting up of a stabilization of currencies, in order that trade can make contracts ahead." He spoke of the "helpful" response of the foreign visitors. "The international conference that lies before us must succeed. The future of the world demands it and we have each of us pledged ourselves to the best joint efforts to this end." §

One morning in mid-May Bullitt came to my office with a directive from the President. Apparently Bullitt, who had an expansive imagination in international affairs, had convinced Roosevelt that in order to prod the Disarmament Conference, which was lagging, and to stimulate interest in the forthcoming Economic Conference, he should make a

* *Ibid.*, p. 500.

† Issued by the White House as a press release May 6, 1933. *Foreign Relations, 1933,* I, p. 504.

‡ Issued by the White House as a press release May 12, 1933. *Foreign Relations, 1933,* I, p. 505.

§ Roosevelt, *Public Papers,* II, p. 167.

grand gesture through an appeal to heads of states; that is, at the highest level of statecraft. I was to write this in, as Bullitt put it, "the old organ-roll style." I was already in mortal fear lest anticipation for London would rise too high, but I complied with what was officially known as the appeal of "Roosevelt to various Chiefs of State" on May 16. This went to the chiefs (or kings or shahs or mikados or what not) of fifty-four countries. He said that "the happiness, the prosperity and the very lives of men, women and children who inhabit the whole world are bound up in the decisions which their governments will make in the near future. . . . The World Economic Conference will meet soon and must come to its conclusions quickly. The world can not await deliberations long drawn out. The Conference must establish order in place of the present chaos by a stabilization of currencies, by freeing the flow of world trade, and by international action to raise price levels. It must, in short, supplement individual domestic programs for economic recovery, by wise and considered international action." *

Two days after this, I presented to Roosevelt and secured his enthusiastic approval of my article (which was enlarged into a radio speech) that told Americans not to expect too much from the London Conference!

Since the time was approaching when the delegation to London would sail, Warburg, with my full approval, drew up a series of "instructions" for the American delegates in the form of resolutions to be introduced at the conference. These were read to the delegates by Roosevelt in his office the day before most of the delegates sailed on the S.S. *Roosevelt* on May 31. These were part of an official "memorandum of policy" sent to each delegate over Roosevelt's signature on May 30.†

The fourth resolution is the one that most concerns us here. It is quoted in full later.

Thus in all these official statements Roosevelt, up to the time the delegation sailed, seemed to assume that monetary stabilization would be agreeable to him in some form that might be negotiated by our experts in association with the foreign representatives in London. Hull was shocked when Roosevelt told him that he could not press upon Congress a measure permitting the negotiation of reciprocal trade treaties.

* *Foreign Relations, 1933,* I, pp. 143–44. Addressed to the Chiefs of State of all countries participating in the General Disarmament or International Monetary and Economic Conferences: Albania, Argentina, Austria, Belgium, Bolivia, Brazil, Bulgaria, Chile, China, Colombia, Costa Rica, Cuba, Czechoslovakia, Denmark, Dominican Republic, Ecuador, Egypt, Estonia, Ethiopia, Finland, France, Germany, Great Britain, Greece, Guatemala, Haiti, Honduras, Hungary, Iraq, Italy, Japan, Latvia, Lithuania, Luxembourg, Mexico, Netherlands, Nicaragua, Norway, Panama, Paraguay, Persia, Peru, Poland, Portugal, Rumania, Siam, Soviet Union, Spain, Sweden, Switzerland, Turkey, Uruguay, Venezuela, Yugoslavia.

† See texts in *Foreign Relations, 1933,* I, pp. 622–27.

But when he realized that Hull was so greatly disturbed, he told him that there was nothing to prevent tentative agreements to be confirmed by Congress later. He even went so far in one message to Hull as to suggest that he might call the Senate into session in the autumn to confirm reciprocal treaties. I have already indicated that several exchanges passed between Roosevelt and the delegation in the period before I arrived in London. And while in some of these Roosevelt gave a hint that he was toying with the idea of some new sort of international exchange standard, there was nothing explicit enough to indicate that he had anything clearly in mind other than traditional forms of exchange.*

In one of them he even went so far as to suggest stabilization around $4.25. That is why everyone believed that he would accept the compromise declaration. For if Roosevelt believed that some such figure might be agreeable, he certainly, we believed, would not reject a statement that there would be stabilization at some future time.

2.

What grounds did I have for believing, in the light of Roosevelt's earlier commitments and his instructions to the delegation and to me, and despite his seeming doubts after June 1, that he still would approve of the compromise declaration?

There were not only suggestions he made to me on the *Amberjack* but his message to Phillips sent by way of the U.S.S. *Ellis* on June 19. This prevalidated our conversations. This I have always maintained is the basic document in the case:

> Believe general situation not greatly altered and still my personal thought that a range with upper and lower limits is unnecessary. London and Paris would combine to put dollar at lower end of range. Why not probably try suggestion of our willingness during conference to keep pound from going above 4.25. You can make it perfectly clear that the 4 dollar medium point is in my judgment too low especially at this time of year with tendency of trade balance favorable to us during next few months depressing pound still further.
>
> Talk with Baruch and Moley about advisability of suggesting to Cox a final medium point of 4.15 with maximum point of 4.25 and minimum 4.05. I hesitate to go even that far but it is worth considering.
>
> We should also ascertain whether life of conference means August 12 or perhaps December 12. There is a vast difference.
>
> Am in Nantucket tonight.
>
> ROOSEVELT †

* These several messages between Washington and London are all printed in full in *Foreign Relations, 1933,* I. It is unnecessary to quote them here.

† *Ibid.,* p. 649. This text is quoted in Chapter 35. I repeat it here for emphasis.

This message was dispatched on the day before I conferred with Roosevelt on the *Amberjack* and it follows almost identically what he said to me on that occasion. I was therefore convinced when I arrived in London, and say now, that the compromise declaration was a better bargain than what Roosevelt had himself proposed. Under that agreement the United States would be free to determine its own monetary policy and keep the pound from falling below the four-dollar mark, which Roosevelt was determined to maintain. It also, as I shall note later, linked Baruch with the stabilization situation.

3.

Were Roosevelt's messages of July 1 and 3 really responsive to the terms of the compromise declaration?

Every one of the people in London, New York, and Washington agreed at the time that Roosevelt in his rejection was in effect destroying a "straw man."

This should be evident by an examination of the relevant documents: (1) the fourth instruction given to the delegation before it sailed, and which had been introduced in the conference by Pittman; (2) the declaration itself; (3) Roosevelt's message of July 1; and (4) my message to him on July 1 urging his acceptance.

The fourth instruction given to the delegates:

WHEREAS, confusion now exists in the field of international exchange, and

WHEREAS, it is essential to world recovery that an international monetary standard should be re-established,

NOW THEREFORE, BE IT RESOLVED, that all the nations participating in this Conference agree

(a) That it is in the interests of all concerned that stability in the international monetary field be attained as quickly as practicable;

(b) That gold should be re-established as the international measure of exchange values;

(c) That the use of gold should be confined to its employment as cover for circulation and as a medium of settling international balances of payment. This means that gold, either in coin or bullion, will be withdrawn from circulation; and that contracts, public and private, shall be made payable in the various currencies without reference to gold;

(d) That in order to improve the workings of a future gold standard a uniform legal minimum gold cover for the currencies of the various countries which shall adopt the gold standard shall be established, and that this legal minimum reserve shall be lower than the average of the present reserve requirements;

(e) That the Central Banks of the various nations be requested to meet at once in order to consider the adoption of such a uniform minimum reserve ratio and that a metal cover ratio of 25% be recommended for their consideration. . . .

The final text of the compromise declaration, which was dispatched by me to Roosevelt on July 1:

JOINT DECLARATION BY THE COUNTRIES ON THE GOLD STANDARD AND BY THOSE WHICH ARE NOT ON THE GOLD STANDARD

1. The undersigned governments agree—

(a) that it is in the interests of all concerned that stability in the international monetary field be attained as quickly as practicable;

(b) that gold should be re-established as the international measure of exchange value, it being recognized that the parity and the time at which each of the countries now off gold could undertake to stabilize must be decided by the respective governments concerned.

2. The governments whose currencies are on the gold standard reassert that it is their determination to maintain the free working of that standard at the existing gold parities within the framework of their respective monetary laws. They are convinced of the importance from the point of view of the restoration of world economy and finance of the maintenance by their respective countries of the gold standard on the basis of the present gold parities.

3. The signatory governments whose currencies are not on the gold standard without in any way prejudicing their own future ratios to gold take note of the above declaration and recognize its importance. They reaffirm as indicated in paragraph 1 above that the ultimate objective of their monetary policy is to restore under proper conditions an international monetary standard based on gold.

4. Each of the governments whose currencies are not on the gold standard undertakes to adopt the measures which it may deem most appropriate to limit exchange speculation and each of the other signatory governments undertakes to cooperate to the same end.

5. Each of the undersigned governments agrees to ask its central bank to cooperate with the central banks of the other signatory governments in limiting speculation in the exchanges and when the time comes in re-establishing a general international gold standard.*

Text of Roosevelt's message dispatched by him from the *Indianapolis* at 2:00 A.M. on July 1. It was transmitted to the chairman of the American delegation July 1 at 8:00 A.M.:

Have received Hull's 80, of June 30, and Sprague's 79. In regard to suggested joint declaration I must tell you frankly that I believe the greater part of it relates primarily to functions of private banks and not functions

* As I have indicated, an earlier version was sent to Phillips for the guidance of Woodin, Acheson, Baruch, and Harrison, and this was undoubtedly the text which Roosevelt followed. Since there were very few changes in the final draft, this point is irrelevant.

of governments. Other parts of declaration relating to broad governmental policies go so far as to erect probable barriers against our own economic fiscal development. As to paragraph 1 (a) of suggested joint declaration this language assumes that immediate stabilization in international monetary field will create permanent stability. This I gravely doubt because it would still allow a country to continue unbalanced budgets and other financial operations tending to eventually unsound currencies. France is an example.

As to paragraph 1 (b) we must be free if gold or gold and silver are re-established as international measure of exchange to adopt our own method of stabilizing our own domestic price level in terms of the dollar regardless of foreign exchange rates.

As to paragraph 3 this would be possible only if we are fully free to maintain stable domestic price level as our first consideration. Also it is most advisable to insist on addition of words "gold and silver" to any possible currency reserve.

As to paragraph 4 I do not think this means anything on our part. I know of no appropriate means here to limit exchange speculation by governmental action. I am clear that this is not at the present time at least a government function but is one that could be undertaken only as a private banking function and only if governmental action is not implied or contemplated thereby. In other words, I cannot assent to private action now which might morally obligate our Government now or later to approval of export of gold from the United States.

At this time any fixed formula of stabilization by agreement must necessarily be artificial and speculative. It would be particularly unwise from political and psychological standpoints to permit limitation of our action to be imposed by any other nation than our own. A sufficient interval should be allowed the United States to permit in addition to the plan of economic forces a demonstration of the value of price lifting efforts which we have well in hand. These successful forces will be beneficial to other nations if they join with us toward the same end.

It would be well to reiterate fact that England left gold standard nearly 2 years ago and only now is seeking stabilization. Also that France did not stabilize for 3 years or more. If France seeks to break up Conference just because we decline to accept her dictum we should take the sound position that Economic Conference was initiated and called to discuss and agree on permanent solutions of world economics and not to discuss domestic economic policy of one nation out of the 66 present. When Conference was called its necessity was obvious although problem of stabilization of American dollar was not even in existence.

I have no objection to delegation using the import of this telegram as basis for a statement of American policy.

It may be relevant to add here my message to the President, dispatched on July 1 at 10:00 A.M. and urging his acceptance:

For the President from Moley. By now you have first and final drafts of declaration; also the Woodin-Baruch-Acheson opinion. Sprague and I agree with the general text of the Woodin-Baruch opinion. The situation here requires tonic effect of agreement to this declaration. It in no sense extends beyond our policy already laid down and in fact is a combination of the resolutions in the instructions to delegation and subsequent resolutions of unilateral control. Please note that references to ultimate return to international gold standard permits your suggestion to me to be worked out; also note that references to gold standard are in line with resolutions introduced by delegation and in original instructions to delegation. Also sure reference to central banks are within your statement of June 17th. Important to note that the declaration unites United States and England as distinguished from European gold block.

Really believe success even continuance of the Conference depends upon United States agreement. (Moley.) *

An examination of the foregoing documents reveals the astonishing facts (a) that Roosevelt had not examined the compromise declaration carefully, (b) that he had forgotten his most recent dispatches to London, and (c) that he failed to recall his instructions to me and also his message to Phillips on June 19.

He says that "the greater part" of the declaration "relates primarily to functions of private banks [he probably meant central banks] and not functions of governments." That is not true. For only in paragraph 5 are central banks mentioned, and there it is merely said that the governments "ask" the banks to cooperate. The main body of the declaration specifically relates to the powers vested by the Constitution in Congress "to coin money, regulate the value thereof, and of foreign coin." By legislation the President had received large delegated authority in these premises.

In all his earlier statements, even as late as June 17, he failed to raise this question. He assumed the responsibility of governments to "regulate the value" of their currencies.

His next sentence denies the one that precedes it, where he asserts that "broad governmental policies"—meaning, obviously, monetary policies—could erect barriers, etc. Therefore, that government policies would in essence affect values.

Next, he speaks of "immediate" stabilization. That is not proposed in the declaration. He had rejected this earlier, and the authors of the declaration—who, we should remember, were the gold representatives themselves—had given up any demand for "immediate" stabilization.

But he claims that unbalanced budgets would bar eventual stabilization. As we know, the United States was then and continued to be operating on an unbalanced budget and still was able, in 1934, to join in stabilization agreements.

He says that "as to paragraph 4" he knows of no appropriate means

* *Ibid.*, p. 671.

here to limit exchange speculation by governmental action. It is true that there was no such means in the United States Treasury then. But he knew of the British equalization fund, because on November 22, 1932, at the White House conference, I had questioned Secretary Mills about this British fund, and he had explained it to be a means of checking wide variations in exchange and thus to curb speculation. Later, in 1934, Roosevelt brought about the creation of the $2 billion equalization fund in the United States Treasury, using for this purpose the government's profits from the devaluation of the dollar. He actually had that power at that moment in July but was apparently ignorant of it.*

He then goes on to say that he could not assent "to private action now which might morally obligate our Government now or later to approval of export of gold from the United States." No such "private action" was stipulated in the declaration, only that governments "ask" central banks to cooperate. But, as I have noted earlier, Roosevelt did ship gold two weeks later—too late to save the conference.

He freely used the expression "morally bound," in this statement and for years after, to justify his rejection of the compromise declaration. This is a convenient word—"morally"—to confuse and excuse, just as other noble expressions are the last refuge of some statesmen. But it was a poor time to raise the question of morality when he was refusing to agree to specific commitments that he had made only a few weeks before.

He asked for "a sufficient interval" to permit the United States to raise prices. But the declaration spoke only of ultimates.

Finally, he speaks of England and France as not having sought stabilization for two and three years respectively. But what they were asking in the declaration was not immediate stabilization but the pledge to seek it ultimately at the pleasure of each government concerned.

It is almost incredible that Roosevelt could have inferred that only "one nation out of the sixty-six present" was asking for the declaration. Although he may not have known at the time, before writing that statement he could have found out that the declaration was the joint product of three gold countries—France, Holland, and Italy—and it had the support of Britain and many others. Moreover, the declaration was designed to have the signed agreement of all nations represented at the conference.

While the July 1 message from Roosevelt touched upon the question of unbalanced budgets—meaning specifically France—the full impact of this was not revealed until the July 3 message was made public. But

* The British equalization fund was designed to prevent excessive fluctuations vis à vis the currency. If the pound rose too high, the fund bought francs or dollars or both. If the pound weakened, the fund sold francs or dollars or both.

if he were seeking complete freedom of action for the United States, he was hardly in a position to reproach other countries about unbalanced budgets. He reiterated his claim for U.S. freedom in the very next paragraph.

Finally, he complained in the July 1 message that the conference was called to seek "permanent solutions" for all the sixty-six countries, not "one nation." But the compromise declaration called for agreement by all.

A comparison of the compromise declaration with the "fourth instruction" written by Warburg and officially handed to the delegation shows not only identity of principle but specifically some of the same language.

Thus Roosevelt's rejection of the compromise declaration was such a reversal of his earlier position that our delegates and experts, as well as the representatives of the foreign governments at London, concluded that they were left without any indication of guidelines as to what the conference might do next. This in itself would have ended the conference even if there had not been the supplementary message received on July 3.*

This must have been in Roosevelt's mind also after he dispatched his rejection. For after reflection over a period of perhaps thirty-six hours, he wrote and dispatched his message received July 3.

In that message he repeated the sum of what he had said in the earlier message concerning temporary stabilization and the balancing of budgets, which was, as I have shown, not only not responsive to the compromise declaration but also a vague indication of what he seemed to have in mind.

It said that "such diversion [which was not the point at issue] shows a singular lack of proportion and a failure to remember the larger purposes for which the Economic Conference originally was called together."

But these "larger purposes" were stated in the agenda prepared nearly six months before. He had not challenged these, which included stabilization, during all the spring months. It was therefore Roosevelt, not the members of the conference, who had forgotten.

The real nub of this message was this:

> . . . the United States seeks the kind of a dollar which a generation hence will have the same purchasing and debt paying power as the dollar value we hope to attain in the near future.

Here he was trying to say that he wanted the conference to adopt something in the nature of the "commodity," or "index," or "com-

* See pp. 464–65.

pensated" dollar or some modification of the plan proposed by Professor Warren of Cornell, which had been the subject of many talks he had had earlier with exponents of this idea. It needs a bit of explanation, since in the years since it has been consigned to the limbo of forgotten fallacies.

From time immemorial, concepts of what may be called universality have inspired and tortured the minds of visionary individuals. Innumerable schemes have been projected for a universal language, a single world-wide religion, world law binding on all and respected by all, universal peace, and some sort of world-wide common currency. Time and human nature have had their way with all these strivings for uniformity.

But in international exchange, for certain reasons which I need not elaborate here, gold and silver have become the only measures of exchange that have had acceptance among the nations of the civilized world.

Innumerable efforts have been made to break the "chains of gold" which have dominated currencies. But gold and its companion, silver, have prevailed.

One of these plans, which had considerable attention during the later depression years, was the "commodity" or "compensated" or "index" dollar. Or pound, or franc, or what not.

James Warburg, fresh from the vicissitudes through which he went in 1933, defined this concept in 1934:

> Instead of having a dollar of fixed gold content—which means that a dollar shall be a warehouse receipt for so many grains of gold—it is proposed to have a dollar of varying gold content, but of fixed purchasing power. In other words, people are to be given the assurance that prices of things will not change, in place of the assurance that the price of gold will not change.
>
> If this were feasible, it would undoubtedly make life less complicated. But it is not feasible. To keep the price of gold fixed in terms of money—which is what the gold standard does—is a comparatively simple thing. Gold is a single commodity, a commodity of limited though increasing amount, and it is difficult to obtain.
>
> "Things," on the other hand, include thousands of different kinds of articles, some important, some of no importance. "Things," moreover, include services, such as brain-work and spade-work, the work of a teacher and the labor of a stevedore. "Things" also are subject to sudden unpredictable happenings, such as droughts, storms, and earthquakes—not to mention wars. Under these circumstances it is easy to say that the prices of "things" in terms of money shall be constant, but not so easy to accomplish it.
>
> To meet this difficulty, the advocates of the theory use a price index.

They admit that they cannot stabilize each "thing" in terms of money, but they say: "We can stabilize the composite price of all things."

So they make up their index, which is nothing but a combination of what they consider the important prices, and then propose to keep this index figure constant in terms of money. And it is interesting to note that the way they propose to keep this index constant is by increasing or decreasing the amount of gold in the dollar.*

There are insuperable barriers to such a system either as a means of attaining a common unit of exchange internationally or as a purely domestic system:

1. It would require infinite wisdom to decide what prices should be included in the index, or to weight each price in its order of importance. Wheat is an important article, but bathing suits are less so. How can these infinitely varied articles be properly weighted on an index? We have had enough trouble now in determining a cost-of-living index.

2. How can it be determined when and how the index will be revised? For new articles appear constantly that are widely used.

3. Considered internationally, how can this index be determined? One country will place more value on rice, another on wheat—or bathing suits or woolen underwear.

4. If, after generations, human intelligence is unable to operate the gold standard (as the advocates of a new system claim), how could the intelligence be found to operate this system?

5. This would be subject to infinite exploitation for political purposes. For it would have to be operated by political governments.

6. Imagine the problems involved in foreign trade. How would international balances be settled except by shipping gold here and there?

I was well aware that Roosevelt was toying with this idea long before I left Washington. I knew also that John Maynard Keynes had given it some attention in earlier books and articles. That is why, when Cox summoned me to his room at the Waldorf before he sailed for Europe, I gave him Keynes's 1930 book and suggested that he read the final chapter. Before and after the receipt of Roosevelt's two explosive messages, I had warned the delegates and experts that Roosevelt was considering these novel monetary ideas. But until his messages came, I had not dreamed that he would proclaim them as national policy.†

* James P. Warburg, *The Money Muddle* (New York: Alfred A. Knopf, 1934), pp. 68–69.

† For an examination of this fallacy as well as a critique of the Warren plan, which Roosevelt later adopted unsuccessfully, see *The Monetary Theories of Warren and Pearson* by Walter E. Spahr (New York: Farrar and Rinehart, 1934); *On the Practical Impossibility of a Commodity Dollar* by Benjamin M. Anderson, Jr. (Chase National Bank publication). For an analysis and criticism of the Warren plan and also a discussion of a modified gold standard, see Warburg, *op. cit.*

4.

What authorization did I have from Roosevelt and Hull to participate with Sprague in the dispatch of the compromise declaration and in urging Roosevelt to accept it?

Until as recently as 1964, when I was already engaged in writing this book, I did not believe it to be necessary to respond to this question. It still seems to be obvious that, since I had been sent as a liaison between Roosevelt and the delegation and its staff, and since the chief subject under consideration was the demand for stabilization, this was implied in my mission.

But certain vague passages in Hull's memoirs seem to have raised the question of my authority in the minds of a responsible historian.

Julius W. Pratt, in his biography of Hull, says this:

> In a letter, published in the *New York Times,* February 2, 1948, Moley asserted: "I had authority to negotiate a stabilization agreement and I also had Secretary Woodin's full confidence. I had—and have—documentary proof of this which has never been published." Until such documentary proof is published or made available, we must remain in some doubt as to just what and how much authority the President had conferred on Raymond Moley.*

In earlier passages in his book this doubt does not seem to trouble the author. Moreover it seems to me that before a writer embalms such a statement in a book of reference he should get out of the library and question the individual concerned. I was living and was quite available to such an inquiry at the place where I worked. And I have made it a practice to give time and attention to many other historians of the period. And Pratt seems to have taken pains to talk with many other people mentioned in his book.

Hull in his memoirs does not deny my authority to do what I did. He seems to have been foggy about what I actually did. For he says that "Moley negotiated an agreement to stabilize currencies." Even Pratt admits on this point that Hull "wrote of Moley's mission with obvious exaggeration." He certainly did. For I did not negotiate the agreement. It was not an "agreement to stabilize currencies." Sprague and I merely accepted the agreement for transmission to Roosevelt.

But having made this incorrect statement, Hull goes on to write of the declaration as "Moley's." He says further that when he talked with Roosevelt after his return, the President said that he had no thought of giving Moley any special authority. This is extremely vague. It was

* Julius W. Pratt, *Cordell Hull, 1933–1944* (*The American Secretaries of State and Their Diplomacy,* Vol. XII), p. 51.

not unusual, as has been indicated more than once in the foregoing story, for Roosevelt to exercise wide latitude with the facts to achieve a purpose. And in this case his desire was to smooth the ruffled feathers of a distracted and indignant Secretary of State.

Perhaps Hull had conceived the idea after I left London to shift the responsibility for the failure of the conference from Roosevelt to me. For Stimson visited London at that time and he and Hull, according to Stimson's diary, had a good old gossip feast in which I was the *pièce de résistance*. Stimson was a tireless diarist and this Pepysian statesman duly recorded in his diary a good deal of false gossip about me for generations of historians to see.

However, since this exchange of gossip did not involve the question of my authority, I am not interested in discussing it. But the questions raised by Pratt prompt me to go into a good deal of repetitious and tiring detail as to the purpose of my mission and my authority to do what I did:

1. The purpose of my mission was written by Roosevelt on the *Amberjack* and was made public. It said that I was to serve as a "messenger" or "liaison officer" and to convey to the delegation the President's views of "developments" in the United States as they affected the "original instructions" given to the delegates before they sailed. These views almost entirely related to international monetary affairs. Indeed, there was nothing else under discussion at the time, because some sort of stabilization had been presented to the Americans as a condition for continuing the conference. I could not convey this information unless I were in a position to advise the stabilization negotiators, Warburg and Sprague. I did this in the two days after my arrival, telling them what Roosevelt might or might not accept. I was very careful to operate through Sprague, who represented the Treasury.

Next, Roosevelt's instructions said that I should, upon my return, give him full information about the conference. The fact that this was to be upon my "return" is not relevant under the circumstances that prevailed in London at that time. In the extremely critical situation that prevailed I had to communicate with him immediately. And even then his meanderings on his schooner, sometimes lost in the fog, made cable communication difficult and telephoning impossible. I told him that it was urgent that he accept the compromise declaration if he wanted the conference to continue. When you see a man about to step in front of a moving truck, you don't call the police. You pull him out of danger.

2. I did not project myself into the negotiations out of which came the declaration. That had already been drafted by France, Italy, and Holland. And such changes as were made in it were designed to weaken

the American commitment. These Sprague and I suggested because we knew of Roosevelt's views.

3. As I have indicated earlier, Mullen was with me during my entire conversation on the *Amberjack* and now validates my account, which I submitted to him in October 1965. Roosevelt specifically mentioned the range of pound-dollar stabilization that he believed to be satisfactory —between $4.05 and $4.25. This was confirmed by his message of June 19 to Phillips, in which he stated that I as well as Baruch was to be consulted on this subject. This brought me directly into the stabilization question. Hence, I knew that he had this ratio in mind the last time I saw him. Therefore, I believed that a declaration that involved no immediate decision as to relative currency prices was much less binding than that which he had authorized.

4. In the preceding weeks, I had managed the debt negotiations and had also drafted, for Woodin in Washington, Roosevelt's statements replying to the earlier stabilization proposals. In this I was acting for Woodin just as I had acted during the bank crisis and in the conferences with the foreign delegations when they visited Washington.

5. Because Roosevelt in his message to Phillips said that I was "under Hull" I secured from the Secretary of State a statement to the delegation on June 29 that I was to participate in the stabilization negotiations. When he made this announcement he made it clear that what he called "temporary stabilization" was a Treasury responsibility and not that of the State Department or the delegation. Herbert Feis attended those morning meetings of the delegates and experts and must have heard this statement of Hull's. In his book, *1933: Characters in Crisis*, published in 1966, Feis confirms my statement of what Hull told the delegates.

6. It should be added that in a letter from Frankfurter to Justice Brandeis under date of August 25, 1933 (now in the Brandeis manuscripts at the University of Louisville), the former says:

> Herbert Feis was here (confidentially) straight from Europe. The London Conference on our part was even worse than I had previously known: really a terrible delegation. Hull has sides to him that his face & exterior behavior almost always belie: he is not always candid & he can be aroused to his old hill-billy past. Herbert deeply regrets Moley's withdrawal—says really he was the most potent single factor in bringing to pass . . ." [At this point the handwriting is not legible.]

I am not quite sure what this means, except that when Feis returned from London he had no reservations about what I had attempted to do. He might have had some knowledge of my resignation, which was announced two days after the Frankfurter letter was written.

7. On the *Amberjack*, Roosevelt had agreed that I should get together

in London with Lippmann and Keynes. In my notes written on the boat, I wrote these names and also those of Rist of France and Runciman at Roosevelt's suggestion. This was specifically to discuss the monetary situation and seek their advice. Certainly we were not to discuss disarmament or the Far East.

8. After I had advised Sprague and the foreign representatives, I suggested certain minor changes in the language of the declaration that could, I believed, make it more acceptable to Roosevelt, and I insisted that every one who had in any way been authorized to deal with the monetary question examine a copy and agree to it before it was sent to Roosevelt. This meant Woodin, Acheson, Baruch, and Harrison in New York and Sprague, Warburg, as well as the members of the delegation. It was only after I had solicited and gained their concurrence that Sprague and I sent the declaration to Roosevelt. And I made it clear that I did this, as Maurice Hankey noted at the time, "*ad referendum.*"

9. After the two "bombshell" messages from Roosevelt and after I had secured the statement prepared by Keynes, Lippmann, Swope, and me, and after I had the consent of Roosevelt to send it to him, we had long conversations about it on the telephone, with Hull on the line.* There was nothing, as the record shows, that indicated that Roosevelt considered me to be lacking in authority to continue my participation in the stabilization question. He assumed that I was acting with full authority in this.

10. After my return to the United States and our relationship was resumed for nearly three years, Roosevelt never questioned my authority to do what I did in London, although at the time when I submitted my resignation, and thereafter on two occasions, we discussed the London affair.

11. There is a final consideration. I was no minor bureaucrat. I was a loyal individual with an academic reputation in my own right. Also, I had enjoyed over a period of eighteen months a relationship with Roosevelt that vested me with the management of matters of great importance to him. There had been many times when I had been compelled to act for him without specific written directions. This was implicit in the innumerable responsibilities I carried for him. Also, because he was often less than explicit in his directives and unclear in his thinking, I had often presumed to act and to trust that my action would satisfy him. Every important public statement, speech, and written message he had made in 1932 and beyond the time of his inauguration I had participated in writing. There were some occasions when with little examination or amendment by him he had put these out, without serious

* See Appendix, pp. 559–62.

consequences to him. I am proud to say that in all this I had never committed any serious blunders that might have injured him.

5.

What were Roosevelt's subsequent reflections on his action in breaking up the conference, as stated in his later correspondence with MacDonald and as shown in his subsequent monetary policies?

As is indicated in my telephone conversation with Roosevelt when we discussed the Keynes-Lippmann-Swope-Moley statement, he was already aware that his "bombshell" message had been too harsh. But in a personal letter to MacDonald he expressed regrets that his action should have wrecked the conference. In this candid letter, written in August 1933, Roosevelt acknowledged: (a) that he should have been more forthright in his April talks with MacDonald and others; (b) that he should not have urged the calling of the conference at so early a date; and (c) that the United States had been the "stormy petrel" of the conference. It was, he said, the "march of events" that necessitated a complete change in policy and "I should have told you that monetary stability was out of the question for some months to come."

Once again, as during the interregnum, when compelled to choose between intra-nationalism and internationalism, he had reverted to purely domestic remedies. But this time the price of his indecision and about-face was tragically high. Roosevelt ended this remarkable letter with the promise that "America is not . . . embarking upon economic nationalism and isolation. America will again devote herself to neighborliness when she has put her own house in order." *

6.

Whether the breakup of the London Conference was the tragic overture to the six years of blind nationalism which swept Europe before the war is a subject that will be debated for a long time. I am unwilling to press the question of cause and effect. For there might have been an Armageddon even if there had been no London Conference.

But there have been almost unanimous historical verdicts on these points:

That the compromise declaration itself was innocuous and would not have impaired the efforts of the Roosevelt regime to promote recovery at home;

* I have no way of knowing whether the original copy of this letter was dispatched or, upon reflection, withheld. The carbon copy given to me is in my files.

That his rejection of the declaration, as well as his message of July 3, was unwise, capricious, and, in form and substance, economic nonsense.

In one of the best of the economic histories of the period, *Depression Decade,* Broadus Mitchell says this:

The most serious consequence of the administration's rapidly developing policy of currency management was in the destruction of the World Monetary and Economic Conference which met in London in June and July that summer of 1933. For the President to disappoint assurances of attachment to gold, which he was held to have given to his own country, was one thing; as a domestic matter the ends might justify the means. But the President had committed himself to supporting a last concerted international attempt at exchange and currency stabilization, and the domestic policy which he adopted flew in the face of promises to the rest of the world. In many ways, as has been seen in these pages, Roosevelt carried farther, and made truly effective, means which Hoover had inaugurated or proposed. But his monetary actions, in their international results, reversed his predecessor's efforts, and were intended to do so.

This decision was probably the most momentous one that Franklin Roosevelt made. One may speculate, with cause, whether in defeating the world's resolution to stabilize currencies and thereby promote trade, President Roosevelt did not contribute heavily to the international economic and political deterioration that led to fresh war. Even so, was his decision reasoned, did he seek earnestly to strike a balance between immediate gain and later loss? Or, infatuated with the prospect of rising prices at home, did he hastily condemn others to frustration, discord and the appeal to arms? There was a lighthearted suddenness in his behavior which spoke of ignorance, or certainly of the little knowledge which is a dangerous thing. . . .

This message showed misapprehension of what the declaration proposed, imperfect understanding of monetary principles, and a reversal of his earlier action in encouraging the conference. If announced in that form, it would wreck the conference then and there. The substance of it leaked out, with profoundly disturbing effect. Moley and his friends hastily composed a solicitous explanation of the Roosevelt rejection for official release, but this was not used because that morning, July 3, came a fresh message from the President which amplified the previous one and employed a lecturing tone. The substance of the message was lamented by practically all at the conference, while the manner of it was resented by the Europeans. . . .

If world trade was to be revived, currencies must be stabilized, and quickly. It was worse than idle to talk of postponing this work, for the President's statements portended a rivalry in currency depreciation, and, in throwing the remaining countries off gold, removed indefinitely the reconstruction of the gold standard. Not even time can give a verdict, for international collaboration, then so much desired by all other countries, might not have been effective either. It may be said, however, that the course which the President charted contributed to economic distress in Europe and Asia and thus helped conduct to World War II.*

* Mitchell, *Depression Decade,* pp. 139–40, 143–44, 144–45.

Hull's biographer, Julius W. Pratt, says this:

If it is difficult to explain Roosevelt's rejection of the innocuous declaration on currency policy, it is much more difficult to explain the truculent tone of the "bombshell" manifesto. Himself a recent and still hesitant convert to the Warren theory of price manipulation, why should he have excoriated those who were attempting to accomplish what until a few days before he had publicly proclaimed as a prime American objective? There was an inconsistency here that defied explanation.*

Arthur M. Schlesinger, Jr., says in his evaluation of the conference and Roosevelt's part in it:

Unquestionably Roosevelt's day-to-day management of American policy at the Conference was deplorable. He came to understand only gradually what he wanted himself; and his delegation represented very little beyond their own whimsies and prejudices.†

The declaration I submitted was, according to this historian, "surprisingly innocuous."

Dennis W. Brogan, the foremost contemporary British commentator on the United States and its institutions, presents a similarly grave appraisal of Roosevelt's rejection of the compromise declaration:

The final formula was vague enough. . . . The President's message, when it came . . . rejected even the most limited and apparently innocuous limitation of complete freedom of action in the matter of currency. . . . The conference was dead. The President dismissed the outcry as "petulant" . . . With the collapse of the conference and the obvious failure of the simultaneous Disarmament Conference, the last chance of avoiding by cooperative action a great world crisis, with grave danger of war, was gone. Probably there was little chance anyway; Germany was now in the hands of as resolute and skillful leader as was the United States. But whatever chance had existed was dead.‡

Jeannette P. Nichols, in her article written in 1951, says this:

To one who views the 1933 World Monetary and Economic Conference over the debris of World War II, its principal effect seems to have been to move the nations in a direction contrary to that recommended in the agenda. Instead of easing the adjustment of international diplomacy to the new imperium of internal economic stability, it made reconcilement more difficult. It spurred nationalism in Britain, France, and the United States, with each of them searching out new devices for the waging of economic warfare. For lack of cooperation, they lost precious time and resources, ultimately needed in the confrontation of the Nazis, whose arch manipula-

* Pratt, *Cordell Hull,* pp. 60–61.

† *The Coming of the New Deal,* p. 229.

‡ D. W. Brogan, *The Era of Franklin D. Roosevelt* (*The Chronicles of America,* Vol. 52) (New Haven: Yale University Press, 1950), pp. 60–61.

tor, Hjalmar Schacht, perfected monetary diplomacy as a means to a militaristic state.*

Hull himself says this in his memoirs:

> I believed then, and do still, that the collapse of the London Economic Conference had two tragic results. First, it greatly retarded the logical economic recovery of all nations. Secondly, it played into the hands of such dictator nations as Germany, Japan, and Italy. At that very time this trio was intently watching the course of action of the peace-seeking nations. At London the bitterest recrimination occurred among the United States, Britain, and France. The dictator nations occupied first-row seats at a spectacular battle. From then on they could proceed hopefully: on the military side, to rearm in comparative safety; on the economic side, to build their self-sufficiency walls in preparation for war. The conference was the first, and really the last, opportunity to check these movements toward conflict.†

In a recent history, William E. Leuchtenburg says:

> Yet the failure of the London Economic Conference was deplorable. The United States may have been no more blameworthy than other countries, but, as the most powerful nation in the world, and as the principal creditor, it had a special obligation to lead. The meeting marked the last opportunity of democratic statesmen to work out a co-operative solution to common economic problems, and it ended in total failure. Henceforth, international trade would be directed by national governments as a form of bloodless warfare. In the very year that Hitler assumed power, the collapse of the conference sapped the morale of the democratic opponents of fascism. Roosevelt's policies strengthened those forces in Britain and France which argued the futility of international parleys and celebrated the virtues of economic self-interest. The Nazis hailed the President's message as a "bomb" which ended a futile meeting that was only a "remnant of an antiquated parliamentary order." Roosevelt, declared Hjalmar Schacht, had the same idea as Hitler and Mussolini: "Take your economic fate in your own hands." ‡

NOTE

Robert W. Bingham, the Ambassador to the Court of St. James's, played no significant part in the conference except for one incident in the action described in the preceding chapters, for he was ill in bed at the embassy during my days in London. But he rates a note here because of that incident, which had a minor influence in what happened after my return to the United States.

* "Roosevelt's Monetary Diplomacy in 1933," *American Historical Review,* LVI (January 1951), p. 317.

† Hull, *Memoirs,* Vol. I, pp. 268–69.

‡ William E. Leuchtenberg, *Franklin D. Roosevelt and the New Deal* (New York: Harper & Row, 1963), pp. 202–203.

Bingham was a wealthy owner of a newspaper in Louisville, Kentucky. He was a generous supporter of Roosevelt in the 1932 campaign. Apparently, for some years he had been a warm friend of Colonel Edward M. House. What I never knew until one day in February 1933 was that he had been a House partisan in a bitter feud between House and Baruch during the Versailles Peace Conference.

When his nomination for Ambassador became known, there was potentially violent opposition to confirmation and Bingham, who was in Washington, asked me to help quiet it. I was not willing to see the Administration injured by a row in the Senate, and I succeeded, through Frankfurter, in quieting the opposition. Bingham appeared most grateful for this, and since it had been agreed in May that I was to go to London at some time during the conference, he invited me to stay at the embassy. I said I would, because it seemed that since I was to be an emissary of the President, I should not stay with the delegation at Claridge's.

That is why, since Roosevelt at my request had officially asked Herbert Swope to accompany me, I asked Bingham to include Swope in the invitation to the embassy.

At the time, I was too busy and too stupid to realize that Bingham would regard Swope as "Baruch's man." This may have been one of the reasons why Bingham developed an antipathy toward me. But my relations with Bingham were cordial, and I called on him occasionally in his sickroom to have a chat about what was happening.

The outcome was deplorable, however, because Bingham secured a copy of my highly confidential eight-point cable to Roosevelt and gave it to Hull after I left.* This aroused the indignation not only of Hull but of the other delegates, with the exception of Pittman.

My only reflection on this is that Bingham was less than wise in this disclosure to Hull of my message to Roosevelt. It could not and did not hurt me, because Roosevelt considered my report a routine matter. But it did contribute unnecessarily to the humiliation and discomfort of Hull, whom Bingham was trying to help.

* See pp. 466–67. In showing this message to members of the delegation and others, Hull carefully folded back the words indicating that it was confidential to the President.

Part Seven

Summing Up

Chapter Thirty-nine

The Virtue of Resignation

IN early September 1933, two days after I left Washington free of official status, I was the guest of Vincent Massey in Ontario. I was scheduled to speak at a convocation of the Dominion's Liberal Party, then out of power. Sir Herbert Samuel, the British Liberal leader, had recently resigned from the national government. As he rose to speak, he greeted me as one who had joined with him in the "virtue of resignation."

As I subsequently learned, Sir Herbert was a product of Balliol College, Oxford, where the great Benjamin Jowett had deeply planted the Greek tradition. In the Aristotelian sense of virtue, I felt the meaning of Sir Herbert's expression. For among the many definitions of the word virtue, Aristotle's is most appropriate: "a state of character concerned with choice."

But I had experienced nearly eight strange weeks after I returned from London and before I left my office and my official position at the State Department. It was a period of make-believe. Roosevelt and I agreed that any announcement of my resignation and my new career in journalism should be delayed until the dust had settled on the London episode. For more and more versions of what had happened in London appeared as the delegates and staff returned to the United States, like bits of Napoleon's army returning from Moscow. And these fragments found their way into the press.

I did not mention my plans except in talks with a few friends like Frankfurter, Swope, and Baruch. Roosevelt rebuffed any questions from the press about Hull's or my rumored resignation.

Once during that period when I saw him at Hyde Park, I asked him what I was to say when the newspapermen waylaid me at Poughkeepsie. He said, "Tell them you're not resigning," and I obeyed the order.

While I was still at sea I had received a message from Vincent Astor and Averell Harriman asking for a meeting soon after my arrival in New York. This concerned the plans made in March and April. It had been a well-kept secret. Roosevelt had been told about it by me in April and by Astor in May.

When Warburg returned, he telephoned to me in Cleveland and I met him that day in Washington at the home of Lewis Douglas. There I heard for the first time all about the distribution to the delegates and staff of my eight-point confidential telegram to Roosevelt and of the hullabaloo it had ignited. Since because of its confidential nature and its transmission in code it could not be released to the press, the only news that came of it was that I had been critical of the delegation.

On July 14 I went to Washington and, following my custom of many months, I went to see Roosevelt in his bedroom after breakfast. He was his old cordial, friendly self. I reported casually on London events, and he offered no comment except to say that his message might have shocked the Europeans but that it had enjoyed good press over here. This was hardly true, because Eastern newspapers had taken him severely to task.

Louis Howe joined us and growled to me, "What happened to you over there? Did they take you into camp?"

I didn't bother to make explanations. I had already done that with Roosevelt, and as long as he was satisfied there was no reason to trouble myself about what Howe felt or believed.

There was little that needed doing in Washington during the rest of July and August. I had no stated duties in the State Department. Phillips was minding routine matters there, and Hull returned about the first of August. Roosevelt was very busy with the new agencies created by Congress. He was making no speeches, and his statements were routine.

I spent most of my time in my old office at Barnard College, where it was quiet and cool. And I called my office in Washington only to get reports about what was in the mail.*

Several offers of remunerative jobs came to me in that period. One

* On one occasion when I was in my office in the State Department Huey Long called on me. He said that he was planning a reorganization of the law school at "his" Louisiana State University. He wanted it to rival "his" medical school, which, he said, had won high praise from the Rockefeller Foundation. He needed a dean, and since I was an academic man with, he added, "good sense," he wanted me to find the man. Although I was still a professor at Columbia and was close to the law school, I had been away so long that I was not familiar with the prospects in that field. I had directed the graduate studies of a young man there three years before

was from Will Hays to join his motion-picture organization.* I declined this and all others except the magazine venture, which had been made firm by Astor in late July.

I had a long conversation with Owen D. Young at about that time, and that wise and generous man talked to me like a father. He was unaware of the Astor-Harriman agreement, but he said in substance that I had done an educational job with Roosevelt for eighteen months. "It's like a seminar," he said. "You brought to him the best information available. This job is done. He is on the way, like a great ship which is now in midstream under its own power." No doubt conscious of his own refusal to accept anything but temporary assignments in government, he advised me to stay free of public office.

I also had a number of visits with Frankfurter, one of them in New Hampshire where he was spending the summer. He was most helpful. I had a letter from him in September, after he had left for a year's assignment at Oxford:

> These many months of intimate traffic with you could not have left me with any other conviction than the certain knowledge that your interest in politics is disinterested and that enlightenment and the clarification of understanding about politics are your dominant ambitions. And so I was not at all surprised to find you so wholly without rancor and bitterness; the contrary would have surprised me. And yet I rejoiced to find you so, for you have been tested in your inner security and serenity as few men have been tested in my time. And after all, we are a bundle of feelings and sensibilities, but happily the civilized man is much more besides. To triumph over resentment and wounds may be merely a higher form of pride, but at all events it is a higher form. Nor is anything more poisonous to one's emotional economy than even a sediment of rancor. So may I say again the calm and philosophic perspective in which you view events of the last few months filled me with satisfaction about your own future and enhanced my faith in man's capacity for dignity and disinterestedness. For thereby you will . . .

and considered him suitable for Long's job. His name was Wayne Morse, and he was at that time dean of the law school at the University of Oregon.

"Call him up," said Huey. I did so and turned the telephone over to the Senator. He asked what Morse was getting and immediately offered him something like twice the Oregon salary. That evening I received a telegram from Morse, asking why a Senator should be making such appointments in a university. How about the president and the trustees? I replied that if Long made the offer, the job was his if he wanted it. Morse then consulted his own president at Eugene, who offered a surprising salary increase. And so the future Senator never went to Louisiana. I have often wondered what might have happened if these two firebrands had entertained political ambitions at the same time in the same state.

* I enjoyed Hays's friendship later and at his request wrote a book, published on the occasion of his retirement, describing his services to the motion-picture industry—*The Hays Office* (Indianapolis: Bobbs-Merrill, 1945).

show that little men are little men and men of large measure are men of large measure.*

Meanwhile, Louis Howe was busy seeking a means of avoiding a Hull-Moley clash, which might injure the Administration. Presumably, these efforts were accelerated after Howe had received a confidential letter from Bingham. His first scheme originated in a talk he had with Harold Ickes, whose wide domain included Hawaii. Howe told me that a recent *cause célèbre* in Hawaii had revealed deplorable conditions in law enforcement in the territory and that the administration of justice there was complicated by a mixture of races. How about my going there for three months to study and to report on reforms in the territory's system of law enforcement? Louis added sugar to the suggestion. I was pre-eminent in the field of criminal-law administration. Howe said that Roosevelt approved of the suggestion, but I refused in a conversation with the President. I gave him several reasons: it would involve a postponement of my return to private life; I needed all the time I could spare to plan for the new magazine; it would involve a leave of absence from Columbia.

The next suggestion was more palatable. Roosevelt said that in talking with Attorney General Cummings the question arose as to the need for new Federal legislation regarding kidnapping and racketeering.† Someone with the proper qualifications should explore this subject and make recommendations. Would I accept this assignment?

My understanding of public relations had been sharpened on the grindstone of political and public affairs for years. This proposal offered a remarkable chance to shift the press, so far as I was concerned, from its preoccupation with the London affair, for crime can always take the headlines from diplomatic affairs or intra-Administration frictions. This, I realized, would turn the tide of personal publicity overnight. My competence for this assignment could not be questioned; my reputation in the field of law enforcement was fully recognized. And so, after a talk with Roosevelt and Cummings, I agreed, and the President made the announcement which was reported in the New York *Times:*

> As the opening move in a militant campaign against kidnapping and racketeering, President Roosevelt relieved Raymond F. [*sic*] Moley temporarily of his duties as Assistant Secretary of State today to conduct a special survey of crime-prevention measures for the Department of Justice.
>
> At the same time it was said emphatically in authoritative quarters that the assignment had no political significance and did not mean that Mr. Moley would leave the State Department.

* R. M. Files, Felix Frankfurter to Raymond Moley, September 26, 1933.

† The Lindbergh case had been given great prominence in the newspapers.

There remained only the timing of my resignation and the announcement of the new venture in journalism.*

Finally, Roosevelt and I decided over the telephone on the day for making the announcement of my resignation. It would be on Sunday, August 27, and Roosevelt, with his sense of timing, pointed out that it would get a proper play in the Monday papers. There wasn't much news out of Washington because most members of the Cabinet were scattered on their vacations.

I composed a letter of resignation, which I carried up to Hyde Park that afternoon. Roosevelt was sitting out on the front lawn. He read what I had written and suggested a change.

And so I went to the library and rewrote my letter in longhand, in part on his personal stationery. He was wheeled into his little office and composed his reply.

Raymond Moley's Letter of Resignation as Assistant Secretary of State, and the President's Reply, Both Dated August 27, 1933

DEAR MR. PRESIDENT:

For months I have given long and considered thought to the two happy and pleasant alternatives of either remaining in an official capacity in your administration or of discontinuing my official status to resume my professional interests in writing and teaching. The development of the idea of a national weekly which has now been consummated by Mr. Astor and his associates has provided for me the answer. I have decided that in joining in this new venture I can not only serve you best, but also my own inclinations and interests.

The regret that I should otherwise experience at severing my official tie with your administration is absent on account of the fact that this new work

* I took my time in writing my reports. There were two and they were issued during the year that followed. In preparing for them I consulted the very wise and scholarly Hatton Sumners, chairman of the House Judiciary Committee. One day he was deeply offended by a call from Roosevelt demanding that his committee report out several bills dealing with kidnapping and racketeering that had been prepared in the Department of Justice and dumped on his desk. Sumners said that he had told the President sharply that he, and he alone, would decide which ones were desirable and which were not. He said to me that he and I would sort out these bills and that he would have his committee report out any that we considered desirable, with amendments. The bills from the Department of Justice revealed that they had been prepared in haste. One in particular, on racketeering, would have gone so far as to convict any labor union of criminal conspiracy. Sumners and I made our decisions jointly, and the new legislation was ultimately enacted.

permits me not only to further the ideals common to us both, but to continue to enjoy the friendly association with you that has marked the many months, both before and since your inauguration.

As you well know, my participation in national politics these past two years has arisen from two motives, the one, my friendship for you together with the deep conviction with which I have shared your political views, and the other, my personal dedication as a life work to the writing and teaching of politics and government. This new venture enables me to fulfill both of these purposes in a way that no official or business office would permit.

My service as an official in the Government was professedly temporary. It has continued through the preliminaries of your administration and now reaches a convenient time for its termination. I therefore offer you my resignation as Assistant Secretary of State to take effect, if convenient to you, September 7. As I do so I pledge you my active and continued support of the ideals to which you have given such a hopeful and auspicious realization. I have with many thousands of others found renewed belief in turning the power of government to the alleviation of human burdens and of ordering for the better the economic life of the Nation. We have believed and you have justified us in our belief.

I regard this present opportunity to edit a national weekly as opening the door to a most important means of furthering these ideals.

Friendship for you as a great warrior and chief and a deep sharing of political ideals are precious. These remain and give me encouragement and hope as I undertake this new task.

Faithfully yours,
RAYMOND MOLEY

DEAR RAYMOND:

It is with a sense of deep personal regret that I accept your resignation as Assistant Secretary of State.

I need not tell you that I appreciate and shall always remember your participation during these two years in the development of policies based on our common ideals. You have rendered a very definite service to your country: and your departure from an official position to undertake an editorship will give you opportunity to carry on the task in an equally wide field.

The ending of our official relations will in no way terminate our close personal association. I shall count on seeing you often and in the meantime I send you every good wish and my affectionate regards.

Faithfully yours,
FRANKLIN D. ROOSEVELT

It is notable that Roosevelt went beyond his usual "Dear Bill, etc." formal acceptance of a resignation, which was to become so familiar in years to come. I believe to this day that he meant exactly what he said. The letters were then processed and given to the press for release.

Considering the amazing volume of press coverage of my resignation and the announcement of the new magazine, the verdict seems to have been, on balance, favorable. Those newspapers that opposed the intranationalist trend of Administration policies ranged in their editorial comment from irony to an intense sense of relief at my departure. Supporters of the New Deal were congratulatory and warmly friendly. Nothing could so clearly show the split in opinion between internationalism and American-recovery-first as these comments.

The New York *Times* and New York *Sun*, reflecting as they always did in those days Wall Street's concern with foreign loans and lower tariffs, paid an extraordinary compliment to my influence by saying that a menace to the republic had been eliminated. The *Times* went back to the Hebrew prophets for a quotation:

How art thou fallen from Heaven, O Lucifer, son of the morning! How art thou cut down to the ground, which didst weaken the nations! Art thou also become weak as we? Art thou become like unto us? *

The *Times* and the *Sun* were joined by the Baltimore *Sun*, the Washington *Post*, the Boston *Transcript*, and the old New York *Evening Post* in expressing relief at my departure. The Scripps-Howard newspapers, despite their low-tariff views, said that the Professor was "more erred against than erring." The Hearst papers praised me and castigated Hull. And so did many Midwestern and Southern newspapers. The New York *Herald Tribune* was mildly friendly.

After Roosevelt and I had finished our exchange of letters, I decided it was essential that we have a further understanding. What we said then I quote from my book *After Seven Years:*

"Now, I have resigned. But I am not going to leave Washington voluntarily in this way without defending myself, if that is necessary, with regard to complaints about my conduct that Mr. Hull is rumored to have made to you. We've never discussed the London trip in its details. Not a word of dissatisfaction has come from the Secretary directly to me since his return. But there has been talk of threatened resignations cabled to you and the like. I have a right to ask whether he has made any specific complaint and, if so, to answer it here and now."

Roosevelt answered, "In all honesty, he hasn't. He did hand me an entire report on the Conference which is upstairs and which I haven't read. Suffice it to say that in our conversation he made no complaint except one.

* Swope arranged an invitation for me to join the editorial board of the *Times* at a luncheon. I sharply reminded the group of the disparity in fact between the editorial comment and the dispatches of the London correspondent, Frederick T. Birchall. I also reminded them that in the "Lucifer" editorial they were expressing a low appraisal of their own profession of journalism by likening my "fall" from a minor job in government to journalism to a descent into hellfire.

That was that one day in London you talked to the Prime Minister without asking his permission."

I recited the facts. . . . And then I said, "With reference to the truth of this, I don't ask you to accept my word. But I suppose you will have in mind the fact that, though I've served you in every conceivable kind of confidential capacity, you never had occasion to doubt what I've said. I would just as soon have things out in a three-cornered discussion with the Secretary."

"Of course, that isn't necessary," he said. "So far as I'm concerned the matter is closed." *

Roosevelt then asked me to remain, and he called Hull on the telephone. The Secretary was spending his vacation at Hot Springs, Virginia.

He told Hull I was resigning to edit a new magazine. Then, without warning, he handed the telephone to me over his desk. Hull concealed his intense gratification in a burst of cordiality. He knew this would be a fine career and mentioned how much influence "Marse Henry" Watterson had exercised in the old days in the Louisville *Courier-Journal*. He said he was issuing a personal statement at once. He did:

> Having been on a two weeks' vacation in the mountains of Virginia, I had no information beforehand that Professor Moley contemplated resigning. I may add that I can accurately say in this connection that I have not at any time offered the slightest suggestion to the President or to Mr. Moley relative to any present or future change of the official status of the latter as Assistant Secretary of State. I wish Professor Moley every success in his new field and will at all times gladly co-operate with him in every feasible way both in that field and in all possible joint efforts in support of the President.

On the following day, Astor, Harriman, and I held a press conference at Astor's office and elaborated our plans.

During the days that followed I cleared out my personal papers and belongings from my office in the State Department and arranged for the future employment of my staff. My two personal assistants, who had come to Washington with me, returned to New York to serve with me on the new magazine. Mullen remained for a while in the State Department and then went over to work with George Peek in the Import-Export Bank. Dorothy Crook, a Barnard graduate that spring, and K. C. Blackburn were employed by Louis Howe in a clipping bureau. Mrs. Helen Cook, a career woman, remained in the State Department and was demoted at someone's orders to the stenographers' pool.

I returned to Washington on September 7, the date I had fixed in my letter of resignation. I went to Hull's office and we exchanged cordial

* *After Seven Years,* p. 276.

felicitations. And then I walked down the long hall in the old State, War, and Navy Building, past the intriguing sign over one door, GENERAL OF THE ARMIES, where General Pershing was located, and down the front steps into what seemed a brighter world than I had known for months.

Chapter Forty

"Fresh Woods and Pastures New"

IF it were not that plans made early in the Roosevelt Administration were the major reason for terminating my official status in the government, the account that follows would have little meaning. What I did in the years after that September day when I left Washington is another story.

Those plans were a well-kept secret among those directly concerned—a few close friends and Roosevelt himself. They did not so far as I know ever find their way into the press. That is why in the comments at the time of my resignation, and even in the histories since, my resignation has been attributed to my lack of compatibility with Hull. Even Samuel Eliot Morison in his *Oxford History of the American People* says that Roosevelt had to sacrifice me to appease Hull.

Because of such distortions of the facts, I am constrained to digress long enough to tell how the concept of a new magazine originated, how it was developed, and something of my life as a journalist which has continued until today.

The idea of a new magazine originated in the fertile mind of Mary Harriman Rumsey. She told me about her ideas on a day that I shall remember for two reasons. What she said led to my new and long career in journalism. And while she was telling me about it in her automobile headed for her estate in Virginia, there was a collision, which hurled me through the glass in the limousine. This left a deep scar on my face which is a reminder of that fateful occasion.

Mrs. Rumsey was a dynamic, energetic, and determined woman. She was the daughter of E. H. Harriman, who in the early years of the century changed the railway map of the United States. Of all of the

Harriman children, Mary inherited most of the daring drive of the father. She had been very active in politics with no strong party ties. She had helped in the pre-convention campaign for the nomination in 1932, supporting the candidacy of Alfred E. Smith. In 1932 she actively supported the Republican candidacy of William J. Donovan for the New York governorship. After Roosevelt took office, she worked in Hugh Johnson's National Recovery Administration.

At the time she spoke to me she had decided to get into the newspaper business, and her plan was to bring together several backers and buy the Washington *Post*, which was scheduled to be sold at auction that spring. If this succeeded, would I resign from the government and take over the editorship? I answered that I would.

Far back in 1906, after my graduation from college, I had tried without success to get a newspaper job in Cleveland. After I failed to impress any of the editors, I drifted into teaching. But the lure of journalism had haunted me ever after. As a very young man I had been impressed by a page in the *Saturday Evening Post* written by Samuel Blythe and devoted to political subjects. This came to my mind when Mary Rumsey made her suggestion. For in a daily or a weekly I might enjoy the opportunity to reveal my own ideas for public consumption.

I explained to Mrs. Rumsey that I had decided in February that I would remain in government only during the first and critical months of the Administration and then resume my classes at Columbia. I had no desire to be a nominal subordinate of Hull or in fact to continue in any government job. There is no place in a working administration for an individual who has no real official place in the hierarchy but who exercises influence on policy. The line of command in a government like ours provides for no such indeterminate status. And it should not.

In a letter to Fred Charles, an old Cleveland newspaper friend, I told of this decision of mine to leave after a few months. This letter, which Charles returned to me in September when the commentators were speculating about my resignation, said in part, "I am going to hold the office of Assistant Secretary of State after March 4th for a short time, with the duty of assisting the President on matters of policy, covering the entire range of government." *

After a month during which Mrs. Rumsey and I discussed the idea of purchasing the *Post* with a few potential backers, I was convinced that this was a serious and practical project, and we reached a definite agreement.

I was less interested in editing a newspaper in Washington than in using it as a base for launching a weekly magazine with a national circulation. This idea came to me from what I knew of Horace Greeley's

* R. M. Files.

weekly magazine in pre–Civil War days. It had its base in the New York *Tribune* but it reached all parts of the country and was a very important factor in the political life of the time.

It was decided that Mrs. Rumsey and her brother Averell would contribute $125,000 each and Vincent Astor $250,000 to bid for the *Post*. Mrs. Rumsey brought in V. V. McNitt to represent the backers at the bidding. McNitt was proprietor of the McNaught Newspaper Syndicate, with which I made a contract at about the same time to write a weekly newspaper column. I did this as a hedge in case the other opportunity to enter journalism did not materialize.

Our group failed to get the *Post*. McNitt's bid of half a million dollars was smothered by the bidding of Hearst and Eugene Meyer. Meyer got the newspaper for a reported $750,000.

We then considered purchasing the Boston *Transcript*, which with the decline and demise of the old Boston aristocracy was in financial difficulties. But I had no desire to be an editor in that community. I was a Midwesterner and could not conceive of a magazine based upon a Boston newspaper having a national appeal.

Finally, by June the decision was made to drop the idea of buying a newspaper but instead to establish a new weekly journal of news and opinion. The name *Today* was decided upon after a conference with Arthur Brisbane, whose famous daily newspaper column bore that title. He was agreeable to the appropriation of the name, and in the years that followed was very helpful with advice and encouragement.

After my return from London, my salary was agreed upon during a visit with Astor at Rhinebeck. My personal relations with Astor were closer than with the other backers and he was to provide the major part of the financing and serve as publisher. Subsequently, Astor and Harriman jointly gave me a firm four-year contract, my services to begin on September 7, 1933. When this expired Astor had already acquired complete control of the magazine and I continued as before without a written contract.

In 1957, in order to have the early plans a matter of record, Astor sent me the following letter:

DEAR RAY:

A controversy has existed and seemingly still continues concerning the circumstances which attended your leaving the State Department in 1933 in order to become associated with me and others in a publishing venture. 1933 to 1957 represents a considerable passage of time. Nevertheless I believe my recollections to be substantially accurate concerning the early days of our association.

Sometime in April of 1933 Mary Rumsey, an enthusiastic supporter of President Roosevelt and an equally enthusiastic admirer of you, came to me with the suggestion that she, her brother Averell Harriman, and I acquire a newspaper. After various discussions this was agreed to, provided a suitable publication could be obtained and, furthermore, that your services as editor were to be available, a problem which it was agreed that I would discuss with the President. Upon doing so I found him enthusiastic on the subject of a paper sympathetic to his administration but luke warm when I got around to the matter of his acceptance of your resignation from the State Department. However, he more or less agreed that if and when we finally became organized he would give very serious consideration to releasing you.

At about this time the "Washington Post" was known to be for sale and Mary, Averell and I put in a bid which proved unsuccessful since Eugene Meyer became the purchaser. Sometime thereafter we gave consideration to acquiring the "Boston Transcript" but for various reasons abandoned this plan. In view of the dearth of existing papers that were subject to purchase, we came to a decision to establish a weekly periodical of our own if this were practicable. However, Mrs. Rumsey, Mr. Harriman and I had no intention of entering a field where we were largely inexperienced without the benefit of your services as editor. In consequence I paid a further visit to President Roosevelt in either late June or early July at Hyde Park, told him of our plans and obtained his assurance that he would accept your resignation from his administration. We then went ahead as rapidly as possible with plans which resulted in establishing the weekly magazine "Today."

Twenty-three years have now elapsed and I can assure you that there has never been a time when I have not enjoyed my continuing association with you.

Yours sincerely,
VINCENT

We were all amateurs, even McNitt, whose experience was not in the weekly field, but we hopefully launched the venture in October with our first issue. As I look back at that issue, it was a pretty crude entry into a highly competitive field. Astor appeared on the masthead as publisher, and I was editor. Our format was a rather limp imitation of the *Saturday Evening Post*, with articles and a two-page spread for my editorials.

In the next three years there were many changes and revisions. Our contributors were mostly very notable names, some of them members of the Administration. We were determined, however, and the backers had an abundance of capital. Our policy during the next two and a half years was strongly pro–New Deal. Our basic features as they developed were a Washington letter, written by Ernest Lindley, then correspondent for the New York *Herald Tribune*, my own signed editorial of opinion, and a miscellany originally called "Forecasts and Reviews." The latter has continued to this day in *Newsweek* as "Periscope." My own editorials, which continued in *Newsweek*, originated a feature of signed opinion that is still a unique feature of *Newsweek*.

Three serious deficiencies became more and more apparent by 1937. Our format was not appropriate for competition with the highly successful *Time*. We lacked competent business management. And we all revolted at the idea of a permanently subsidized journal. Also, my earlier connection with Roosevelt and our support of the early New Deal conveyed the impression that we were a house organ for the Administration.

In 1935, when the Administration itself began to change course, it seemed that independence was needed to win public confidence.

A wise and treasured friend, Willard Kiplinger, who was deeply versed in Washington affairs, said to me about that time, "When are you going to be a journalist and stop being a politician?" He pointed out what I was already learning, that whatever I wrote, however sincerely my own, would be publicly regarded as a trial balloon for Roosevelt. A shift, therefore, was in order, because I was already doubting the change in course in the Administration from the 1933 pattern. From then on, independence of party ties and of the Administration characterized our policy.

In 1934 Mary Rumsey met her death through an accident while riding on her estate in Virginia. This presented a very practical problem. The original incorporators had been Astor, Rumsey, Averell Harriman, McNitt, and I. The corporate name was "Today Associates, Inc." McNitt dropped out after the first two months. At first the financial burden was carried 50 per cent by Astor and each of the Harrimans 25 per cent. When Mary Rumsey died, Astor took over her share, which meant his control of the magazine during the years that followed until his death in 1959.

In 1937 we decided upon a complete reorganization. Another weekly, then called *News-Week,* had been started in 1933 with a considerable number of backers. Its publisher was Thomas Martin, a former official in *Time*. The product was a pallid imitation of *Time*. As it lost money, one after another of its supporters dropped away, and by 1937 the properties and liabilities could be had for the asking. We took it over. With a good deal of regret we dropped the name *Today*, because Brisbane had died and we feared that his heirs, who owned the title, would be less generous than he had been.

Then Astor and Harriman succeeded in engaging as president Malcolm Muir, president of the McGraw-Hill publishing enterprise. He brought with him three of his top lieutenants. One of them, Theodore Muller, became publisher of our magazine. My weekly articles of opinion were continued, and another of *Today*'s features became the "Periscope." I continued as editor for six months and then chose instead the title contributing editor.

Since under this arrangement my articles were matters of personal and signed opinion, we conceived the idea, to make our character quite unlike *Time*, of adding a number of other weekly signed contributions. Thus we were able to promote the concept that our news features were measurably limited to objective reporting, but that the articles of signed opinion were the responsibility of the authors. This policy continues today.

Astor probably invested several million dollars before, under our new business management, the magazine showed a profit in 1942, nine years after we started. Ultimately the advances of the backers were all paid back, and in the years since the profits have been consistently rising. The small circulation of those earlier years had risen to more than 2,000,000 in 1966.

Vincent Astor was a Harvard student when his father died in the great *Titanic* tragedy in 1913. This threw upon him the burdens and responsibilities of administering one of America's great fortunes. He was wise and prudent as a man of property, but he never forgot that such economic power had a debt to pay to the society that made such an accumulation possible. His passion for keeping his name out of public notice as to what he did and what he gave permitted those who did not know him well to attach to him the image of just another rich man.

But he maintained a strict detachment and even an articulate resentment for those in his economic status who during the First New Deal were so ready to excoriate Roosevelt's reforms. His friendship with Roosevelt remained. They were old Hudson Valley friends. They shared a love of the sea. He declined office in Roosevelt's first Administration, refusing the offer to appoint him assistant secretary of the Navy, a position which Roosevelt himself had held under Wilson.

In a singular degree Vincent Astor, without ever specifying it or perhaps even realizing it himself, established the editorial and publishing policy that distinguishes *Newsweek* from other publications. He knew how to own a publication without dictating its specific policies. Muir was permitted to experiment and develop the over-all editorial content and business policies under Astor as chairman of the board.

Astor had the instincts of a nineteenth-century liberal. He believed that a commentator will, if left free in the expression of his opinions, maintain a sense of responsibility in himself and for the publication with which he is associated. Thus I was free to choose the subjects about which I wrote, to determine my opinions, and to choose the method of expressing them, even to decide for myself what extra-editorial political activities I might engage in. He never suggested anything that I should write about or criticized what I said. But he maintained his support of Roosevelt, voting for him four times. It might have been that Roosevelt complained to him of some of my criticism, but this never came through to me. When I wrote my controversial book in 1939, Astor read and expressed his admiration for it and suggested the title *After Seven Years.*

After Astor's death, his holdings in the magazine were vested in the Astor Foundation. In 1961 Philip Graham, acting for the Washington *Post*, purchased the controlling Astor stock and later the holdings of other stockholders. Thus by a strong coincidence the original idea of 1933 of associating the *Post* with a weekly national magazine was finally realized. Under the new ownership I continued my articles of opinion under the same conditions that prevailed during Astor's life. That meant complete freedom in the choice of subjects, in the opinions expressed and the form of expression. I am sure that such independence for writers has had few if any parallels in the publishing world. In 1965 I had established what I believe is a unique record of continuity. For by October, thirty-two years after the first issue of *Today*, I had written an article every week without missing, except for four weeks in 1957, when I had Senator Harry F. Byrd as a guest columnist.

Chapter Forty-one

Unofficial Relations

WITHIN the month following my resignation I found my relationship with Roosevelt continuing but with an important difference. I was no longer officially his subordinate. But since the parting had been cordial and since in principle I believed I should support the policies of the Hundred Days, I was willing to help, so far as my new responsibilities permitted, by occasional trips to Washington. There had never been any "boss" or "skipper" business between us, and now there never could be.

He had acknowledged that I had helped him think and to make his thoughts articulate. Moreover, realizing that he could be influenced, I felt that what I could do for him might be good for him, for his cause, and for the country.

In September he asked me to talk with him about what he should say at the American Legion convention, and I responded. Later I was told that Roosevelt was resolved to adopt the Warren gold plan and that he planned to announce it in a fireside chat on October 22. Could I be at the White House that Sunday and help put the speech in shape? Roosevelt knew what I thought about the Warren plan. I was against it. But I responded to the call.

The meeting that day was in a tense setting. In Roosevelt's White House study that morning there sat in a circle George Warren, Henry Morgenthau, Jr., James Harvey Rogers of Yale, Dean Acheson, Henry Wallace, and Henry Bruere, an old friend of the President's and president of the Bowery Savings Bank. Woodin was ill in New York but had expressed himself against the experiment over the telephone. He had said it was illegal, as Roosevelt planned to operate it, and so did Dean

Acheson. Rogers was a strong supporter of silver but doubted the usefulness of the Warren plan. Bruere was there because he had been invited and said very little. But Roosevelt was determined to give the Warren plan a chance. We were there to be told, not asked.

After Roosevelt had expressed his determination to adopt the plan and to announce it that evening, he started in the presence of everyone present to dictate a rough draft of the speech. At one point he hesitated. He had just said that the step he was taking was not a mere offset to a temporary fall in prices but a policy that, by changing the price of gold, would in turn manage prices generally. He then tried to put a hard short sentence at the end of the paragraph. He looked at me and I said, "This is a policy and not an expedient." "That's it," he said, and the sentence went into the speech.

Then, after he had finished a rough draft of what he intended to do, he asked Bruere and me to "put it in shape." We took the transcript into the Cabinet Room and worked it into as cogent a statement as was possible. While we were working, Warren hovered over us, apparently to make sure that there would be no violation of his basic ideas. He was no doubt suspicious of both of us. But we were inexorably correct in portraying the nature and purposes of the experiment. My conscience was clear. I was not there to sabotage the idea. I was inexorably true to the Warren thesis in what we wrote. I didn't believe it would work. But I didn't believe it would do any harm. It was Roosevelt's responsibility. In that instance I was merely a draftsman.

It didn't work. And after a few weeks it was abandoned. It didn't hurt anything except Warren's reputation.

Dean Acheson had valiantly argued against the plan and had presented what should have been decisive legal reasons against the experiment. According to Acheson's own story,* this disagreement was so serious that Roosevelt virtually asked for his resignation, which was forthcoming three weeks later. Woodin's health was failing and he asked for a leave of absence at the same time. Roosevelt then appointed Henry Morgenthau, Jr., undersecretary and acting secretary of the Treasury, and when Woodin resigned, he was elevated to the secretaryship. Thus Morgenthau's long-nourished ambition was fulfilled. He was in the Cabinet after all.

Thereafter, until June 1936, there was scarcely a message or major speech by Roosevelt in the preparation of which I did not participate. I saw Roosevelt almost weekly in Washington—sometimes for part of a day, or sometimes for two or three days at a stretch—occasionally staying at the White House, most often at a hotel.

During the remainder of 1933 and in 1934 and 1935 I spent 132

* Dean Acheson, *Morning and Noon* (Boston: Houghton Mifflin, 1965).

days in Washington assisting Roosevelt. During that period my name never appeared on the White House calendar. I never gave interviews. I came and went by the little back door to the executive offices and to the President's office, a route unwatched by the reporters who spent their time around the White House.

Very few newspapermen knew of these visits. Those few were my warm friends and they respected my anonymity.

It is interesting to me and a source of deep satisfaction that I had a part in the development of two of the most permanent and notable reforms of the early New Deal, which came after my resignation. These were the creation of the Securities and Exchange Commission and of the social security system.

Late in December, when I was called to Washington to help Roosevelt with his annual message, he told me of his decision drastically to revise the Securities Act. He wanted to loosen up its restrictions on the issuance of securities, to create a new commission to administer that phase of the reform, and to regulate the stock exchanges. I reminded him of Untermyer, who in 1933 had favored stock exchange regulation in the 1933 version of the securities legislation, and suggested that he be called in. But Roosevelt said he would have none of Untermyer.

I talked with Rayburn, whose Committee on Interstate Commerce would have charge of the new legislation. He called in as draftsmen James Landis and Benjamin Cohen, who had drafted the 1933 act. Landis had softened his ideas about regulation after his experience on the Federal Trade Commission, which had administered the earlier act. And Rayburn was determined to give the New York lawyers and securities dealers a fair hearing this time, and, so far as he deemed wise, to follow their practical advice.

Roosevelt asked me to keep in touch with the new legislation, and I used as my contact with the drafting Thomas G. Corcoran, a protégé of Frankfurter's. Corcoran had been a favorite student of Frankfurter's at the Harvard Law School, had served with Justice Holmes, and at that time was a member of the legal staff of the RFC.

Cohen was the more competent draftsman and carried most of the work. I kept in touch with Rayburn in the House and with Byrnes in the Senate.

Leading the opposition to the bill was Richard Whitney, then president of the New York Stock Exchange. I published in *Today* an article by Whitney, but in my editorials I strongly supported the measure. It was passed without difficulty and the Securities and Exchange Commission was created with wide powers of supervision over the issuance of securities and the operation of the stock exchanges.

After the bill was passed, Roosevelt suggested that I make up a list of people suitable for appointment to the five-man commission. After considerable consultation with informed people, I submitted this memorandum to Roosevelt in June:

1. [Joseph] Kennedy
The best bet for Chairman because of executive ability, knowledge of habits and customs of business to be regulated and ability to moderate different points of view on Commission.

2. [James] Landis
Better as member than as Chairman because he is essentially a representative of strict control and operates best when defending that position against opposition from contrary view.

3. [George] Mathews
Familiar with operation of blue sky laws and with present Securities Act. He is a Republican from Wisconsin and failure to take him over would antagonize Republican Progressives in Wisconsin.

4. Ben Cohen
He is as able as Landis and more experienced. He has participated to a greater extent than anyone else in the drafting of both Securities and Stock Exchange Acts. His personality would gain friends as people grew to know him. Enormously well thought of by Judge Mack, Frankfurter, etc.

5. Paul Shields
Expresses progressive ideas about regulation by law. Strongly recommended by Averell Harriman. Was associated with Dillon, Reed and probably would be strongly recommended by Clarence Dillon.

6. Gordon Wasson
A resident of New Jersey. Handled foreign securities for Guaranty Company. Has acted as liaison between Wall Street and Landis, Cohen, and Corcoran, because his friendship with them was known downtown. Knows securities business and the act thoroughly, having helped in its drafting. Very well liked by Treasury and Commerce. Would certainly be recommended by the Guaranty and the Stock Exchange and therefore would be acceptable to Wall Street.

7. Frank Shaughnessy
Hiram Johnson would be an excellent judge of him. He is well thought of by Charles B. Henderson of the R.F.C. who knows him.

8. Judge [Robert] Healy
Could be counted upon to be sound and liberal in his interpretation. However, he would be a better member of the Federal Trade Commission.

Party Affiliations:
Democrat—Kennedy, Landis, Cohen, Shaughnessy
Republican—Wasson, Mathews, Healy

Some days after I submitted this list, Ferdinand Pecora, who had been counsel for the Fletcher committee in 1933, told me that he wanted to be chairman of the new commission, and so I added his name verbally to the list.

Landis wanted the chairmanship, too, and I was pressed to support his claim by Corcoran and Cohen. Roosevelt favored my recommendation of Kennedy as chairman.*

For reasons that went back to the pre-convention days in 1932, which Whalen describes in *The Founding Father*, Louis Howe had conceived a violent antipathy toward Kennedy and throughout 1933 he had fought successfully against giving him any place in the Administration. Kennedy was quite aware of this opposition and during the greater part of the year before this present incident cursed Roosevelt in private for his neglect.

I knew Kennedy very well and although I could not admire him as a person and as a business operator, I had several reasons for supporting him for chairman of the new commission. One of these was my admiration for his capacity as an administrator. Another was that he had plenty of money and would not need to use the vital information gained in such a position for further enrichment. Another very important reason was that, according to the ethics of politics, his support of Roosevelt, especially in the critical pursuit of the nomination, should have substantial recognition. These factors I discussed with Roosevelt and he had decided to overrule Howe.

In mid-June when the President agreed that Kennedy should be chairman, rumors spread that he would be Roosevelt's choice. On June 30 I happened to meet Roy Howard of the Scripps-Howard newspapers on a flight to Washington. He told me that it would be very bad to appoint Kennedy. I suggested that he offer his objections to Roosevelt directly, and he did so when he arrived in Washington. He did more. He wrote an editorial opposing the appointment, which appeared in the Washington *News* that afternoon. Later that afternoon, when I saw Roosevelt in his study, he had Howard's editorial on his desk. He squared his body around and said to me, "Send for Kennedy. I'll get Baruch in."

I called Kennedy at his hotel and told him to come over because he was going to get the job. He merely exclaimed, "Nuts!" But he came, and so did Baruch.

Roosevelt pulled out my list of prospective appointees and said,

* Kennedy's various services during the Roosevelt years until his resignation as Ambassador to the Court of St. James's, his subsequent career, and the remarkable ascendancy of his family, have been well covered in recent literature. Richard J. Whalen's biography, *The Founding Father,* is an excellent and unbiased account. See also the profile of Kennedy in my Chapter 31.

"Kennedy is first on this list, and I propose to give him the five-year appointment and the chairmanship."

Kennedy exclaimed, "Mr. President, I don't think you ought to do this." He added that it would subject Roosevelt to severe criticism.

I broke in and said to him—intending to swing him into a vigorous defense of himself—that if there were anything in his business life that might disqualify him for the job, he had better state it then and there.

I had expected the reaction. Through a blue mist of profanity, Kennedy challenged anyone to question his business ethics or his devotion to public service.

Roosevelt then announced his decision for Kennedy and proceeded to name the remaining commissioners.

Since the office of chairman under the law would be filled by a vote of the commissioners themselves, I was told by Roosevelt to notify Landis to nominate and support Kennedy. I then called Landis on the telephone and conveyed Roosevelt's directive. Landis refused to do so, because he had entertained an ambition to have the chairmanship himself. I told him that he would have the order in writing. And so, at my suggestion, Roosevelt wrote a note to the appointees saying that he wanted Kennedy as chairman. I gave the note to James Roosevelt to give to Kennedy for use at the meeting. This was done, and Kennedy was elected. It was an extraordinarily good choice. For Kennedy most competently set up the administrative machinery and when he retired had earned general public commendation.

As it happened, Kennedy and Landis got along well, and when Kennedy resigned Landis was selected to succeed him as chairman.

In June 1934 another major New Deal measure was inaugurated. One morning Roosevelt revealed to Vincent Astor and me his ideas for a system of old-age pensions. He had discussed this with Secretary Perkins, Gerard Swope of General Electric, Owen Young, John J. Raskob, and others. His plan was very general at that time. The money, he said, should be raised by a contributory tax on employees and employers, and the fund should be held and invested by the government. Astor asked him how the fund should be invested, and Roosevelt replied that it should be put into state and municipal bonds. I understood him to mean that payment to beneficiaries beyond their own equity, which they had acquired through paying the tax, should be based upon some sort of means test.

Beyond this, there was need for a long preliminary study. But Roosevelt wanted to present the idea at that time in a message to Congress, and I was assigned the job of writing it.

The message recommended attention to three subjects: one was housing, another was unemployment insurance, and the third was "security against the hazards and vicissitudes of life." It said further that "next winter we may well undertake the great task of furthering the security of the citizen and his family through social insurance." It briefly suggested the idea of a maximum of cooperation between states and the Federal government and said that the funds necessary to provide this insurance should be raised by contribution rather than by an increase in general taxation.

Roosevelt was very anxious in framing this message to stress a conciliatory attitude toward business:

> Ample scope is left for the exercise of private initiative. In fact, in the process of recovery, I am greatly hoping that repeated promises of private investment and private initiative to relieve the Government in the immediate future of much of the burden it has assumed, will be fulfilled. We have not imposed undue restrictions upon business. We have not opposed the incentive of reasonable and legitimate private profit. We have sought rather to enable certain aspects of business to regain the confidence of the public. We have sought to put forward the rule of fair play in finance and industry. . . .
>
> We must dedicate ourselves anew to a recovery of the old and sacred possessive rights for which mankind has constantly struggled—homes, livelihood, and individual security. The road to these values is the way of progress.

I have always been proud of my part in writing that message, for it launched perhaps the most important and permanent reform enacted in Roosevelt's first term.

Roosevelt liked the message, too, and in my presence he told Frances Perkins that I had written "eighty per cent of it."

To prepare a final plan, Roosevelt in June 1934 set up a Cabinet Committee on Economic Security, with Frances Perkins as chairman. The committee provided itself with a staff directed by Edwin E. Witte as executive director. There was also Dr. Arthur Altmeyer, who was an assistant secretary of labor. There was then appointed a technical committee, drawn from various government departments. Later in the year an advisory council of twenty members was appointed, consisting of business and labor leaders, social workers, an educator, and an editor. I was a member of this body, but attended only a few meetings during 1934 and early 1935. Referring to my participation in this group, Mr. Witte says:

> Professor Moley . . . was in closest touch with the committee throughout its entire period of existence. This included complete knowledge of everything that the advisory council was doing. He occupied, however, a very peculiar position, being regarded by both the council and the committee as a personal representative of the President. Consequently, he deemed it

advisable to refrain from active participation in the work of the advisory council.*

The plan, embodied in a bill, was thoroughly debated in the 1935 session of Congress and finally signed by the President on August 14, 1935. There were many amendments added in the course of the debate, which materially changed the plan from that which had been envisaged by Roosevelt and his advisers in 1934.

I have never been happy about the so-called "trust fund," which consisted of the government's I.O.U.'s. But that objection of mine, together with the innumerable extensions of the system since, are beyond the purpose of this story.

* Edwin E. Witte, *The Development of the Social Security Act* (Madison: The University of Wisconsin Press, 1963), p. 54n. This book, published after Witte's death, is the best account of the planning and the legislative history of the 1935 Social Security Act.

Chapter Forty-two

1935—End of the First New Deal

MY friend over the many years since we were first associated with Roosevelt, Rex Tugwell, wrote in 1957 in his book *The Democratic Roosevelt*, "I could not say how many times since 1939 I have been asked, 'What happened to Ray Moley?' I do not yet know how to answer. It is incredible. . . . I can say, of course, that it happened to others—Joseph Kennedy, to William C. Bullitt, to any number of politicians, including Jim Farley, Bronson Cutting, Burt Wheeler. But these defections do not explain Ray Moley's. For Ray, to an extent not matched by any of the others, had sunk himself in the service he assumed."

I should add that many others have asked me the same question, with hardly the same inference suggested by Rex—that there was in my decision in 1936 an element of apostasy.

I can understand the bewilderment of Rex, although if he had read my book carefully in 1939 he might have had the answer to his question. For Rex did not disapprove of Roosevelt's shift in political and ideological strategy, although he was bitterly disappointed because in that shift the concept of national economic planning was abandoned. And while Rex's departure from the Administration was acquiesced in by Roosevelt, and even by Henry Wallace, because he was regarded as a political liability, his belief in the general evolution of the Democratic Party was sufficiently strong to maintain his belief in Roosevelt as a leader and in most of what was adopted in the years after 1935. This overrode any unhappiness of a personal nature. For that I deeply respect him, even though I disagree with his concepts of what was in the national interest.

Rex could not have known of the many efforts I made to dissuade

Roosevelt from his new policies. These had extended over more than a year before 1936. Therefore, Roosevelt himself knew of my views, perhaps better than anyone else. And he should have known that opposition after that was not personal but based upon long-held principle.

And so my answer specifically to the question is in what happened to Roosevelt and the Democratic Party in a period that began some time in 1935 and extended through the election of 1936, and in what happened to Roosevelt's earlier-held ideological principles and political strategy. The account of this change is necessarily intermingled with my own reactions to it. My ultimate decision was to oppose Roosevelt and his new policies. For during this period the First New Deal was abandoned and what might be called a Second New Deal was inaugurated. I shall attempt briefly to describe this change.*

I could not know then, in early 1935, what I was told some years later by Ed Flynn. This was about a decision made by Roosevelt in consultation with Flynn to change his political strategy completely and to impose this change upon the dominant Democratic Party. But there were many indications of the change, which I saw quite plainly and which for a year and a half I opposed as well as I could in many friendly arguments with Roosevelt.

The strategy that directed the campaign for the nomination and election in 1932 had been created by Roosevelt and Louis Howe many years before, when Roosevelt first ran for the New York State Senate in 1910. It might be called essentially agrarian, an appeal to rural elements—farmers and residents of small towns and cities. As Howe and Roosevelt calculated, the large urban vote was by tradition Democratic. It could be counted upon to support any Democratic candidate. But a Democratic candidate who appealed directly, sympathetically, and with understanding could cut into traditional Republican strength, and with that increment added to the rock-bottom and traditional Democratic vote, could win victory in an election.

This was, as Howe described it to me many times, how Roosevelt won election to the state senate and later to the New York governorship in 1928 and 1930. The campaign for the nomination in 1932 was directed by that strategy, and the First New Deal was based upon it.

Moved to the national level, this strategy—especially since the depression had alienated the farm states from the Republicans and since the South could be safely counted as Democratic—was a perfect formula for success.

It was well suited to Roosevelt's early character and philosophy.

A man born and nurtured in the atmosphere suitable to a conservative country gentleman, Roosevelt was by inheritance a Democrat of the old

* A much more detailed account of this transformation is in *After Seven Years,* pp. 299–349.

school of Tilden, Cleveland, and Wilson. He turned by nature to rural scenes. On the sidewalks of rowdy cities he harbored the outdoorsman's discomfort in alien surroundings and unfamiliar crowds. When he entered public life, it was as the choice of a rural county. As a state senator he fought against Tammany and the New York City machine.

Later, as governor, his majority was made secure by Republican votes, for many of New York's upstate Republicans were taken by the man's concern with rural problems and his proven opposition to city machines.

When he was nominated for President, Roosevelt's strength came from agricultural states. Delegations dominated by city bosses bitterly opposed him. And so it followed, in the campaign, that the nagging problem of agriculture came first. The Topeka speech forecast the New Deal farm policy and was instrumental in capturing the Middle Western states. Conservation was included in this category. Tariffs were treated in an oblique manner that satisfied both high- or low-tariff groups. Other lines of experimentation and reform were drawn in other speeches. Finally, Roosevelt pledged thoroughgoing conservatism on fiscal policy, welfare relief from the national government only where states could not carry the burden, Federal provision of "temporary" work (which foreshadowed the WPA and the CCC), cooperation within industry for "regularization and planning" (which foreshadowed the NRA), and provision of "unemployment reserves."

Hence, when he moved into the White House, Roosevelt believed firmly that if agriculture could be made prosperous the industrial areas could revive as a consequence. There were, from the nature of the emergency, measures that had to be taken to save the economy. The banks had to be made secure. For the protection of investors, the issuance and sale of securities had to be regulated at the Federal level. And there had to be priority in relief to people in genuine need.

By the middle of 1934 Howe was slowly sinking into what proved to be his terminal illness. And with his physical decline he lost his influence with the self-assured new President. Howe endured desperate relapses in 1935, and his illness ended fatally in April 1936.

Flynn then emerged as the supreme political strategist. In early 1935 he and Roosevelt had taken stock of their party. Flynn spoke as unchallenged leader of the powerful Democratic machine in the Bronx, and as such he was a great power in the City of New York. In the first eight Roosevelt years, Flynn was the strategist, Farley the technician.

Flynn and Roosevelt noted that, except for cities controlled by Democratic organizations and the traditional Democratic political system of the South, their party was nationally a rather ineffective force. They noted, too, that the Democratic Party had won the Presidency only because the Great Depression had temporarily upset the dominant Republican Party. They recognized that Wilson's two victories in a period of triumphant

Republicanism, extending from 1896 to 1932, had hinged on Republican factionalism. In later years Flynn spoke to me of their decision:

"There are two or three million more dedicated Republicans in the United States than there are Democrats. The population, however, is drifting into the urban areas. The election of 1932 was not normal. To remain in power we must attract some millions, perhaps seven, who are hostile or indifferent to both parties. They believe the Republican Party to be controlled by big business and the Democratic Party by the conservative South. These millions are mostly in the cities. They include racial and religious minorities and labor people. We must attract them by radical programs of social and economic reform."

Hence, the programs most powerfully urged by Roosevelt in the 1935 session of Congress were social security, aimed essentially at urban wage-earners; the Holding Company Act, which undermined the strength of the big power companies; and the Wagner Act, which put government squarely behind the labor movement. Roosevelt's major messages and speeches took on a flavor of strong opposition to business interests. Even Tugwell has said that they were reminiscent of the utterances of William Jennings Bryan.

Welfare measures distributed government aid without much discrimination. The Far West and Northwest were wooed by Roosevelt's public power and reclamation projects. And the South, a prisoner of its one-party system, was taken for granted. However, the South received its share of Roosevelt's attention by liberal policies. Negroes, first in the Northern cities and later in the South itself, were won over, almost to a man, not only by generous welfare measures but by the adoption of gestures against discrimination. The newly created CIO plunged deeply into politics.

Thus, the man who was born to the heritage of a country squire and who had dedicated nearly a quarter of a century to the cause of agriculture became within the space of a few years a leader and idol of the urban masses. A plentiful supply of patronage and Federal grants for housing, relief, and benefits to labor made secure control of great and growing urban centers. Intellectuals were won by Roosevelt's habit of "bold experimentation" and by his conversion to internationalism after 1937. The capacity he showed for adopting the ideas of a new and radical science of economics for the purpose of rationalizing his political policies won him great support in academic circles. And his amazing capacity to dramatize his policies and himself excited a public unable to discriminate among his projects and blinded by the excitement of a masterful show.

The transformation of the Democratic Party was established by the Roosevelt-Flynn strategy.

For a time in the late 1930's Roosevelt toyed with the idea of boldly creating a new party dedicated to his policies. In this he hoped to bring Republicans who were also dedicated to the new Federal centralism into a common fold with liberal Democrats. But this idea was abandoned. The trade name "Democratic" was kept, but the substance of the party's heritage had undergone a metamorphosis. And with the change there came into use the word "liberal" to describe an ideology based upon the enlargement of the power of the Federal government and an abundance of welfare programs.

The bald, practical advantage of the Flynn strategy must have seemed obvious enough to Roosevelt. The drift of population had given the urban centers a substantial majority in many large states. But to adopt such a strategy meant tearing himself loose from many old ideological convictions, from habit and the disruption of many personal associations. I am sure that Roosevelt would not have yielded easily to a strategy based upon an appeal to the city masses. He had by his own admission to me never felt comfortable in urban surroundings. He was at home with farmers, and with upper- and middle-class friends and neighbors. He had not been inimical to businessmen generally, for he had been in business himself and so had his antecedents. He had heartily approved of my draft of his 1935 annual message, which outlined his plans to shift from relief to work projects. And this had a good reception from the business community and the conservative press. In preparing that message, we had a long talk one night about the mistakes of radicalism, how extreme reformist movements in the past had overreached themselves and by attempting too much had ended in failure. He permitted me to conclude that message with an appeal to all interests and classes. "It is not empty optimism that moves me to a strong hope in the coming year. We can if we will make 1935 a genuine period of good feeling."

If that message is laid beside the demagogic message in 1936, we can easily see the vast policy gap he had crossed in the year between.

But in that year several collateral factors served to drive Roosevelt off the course of conciliation and to firm up his decision to adopt the strategy proposed by Flynn:

1. After 1933 there arose highly articulate and mostly intemperate attacks upon Roosevelt, his policies, and the people around him. Some of the critics were Democrats, the very Democratic leaders who had been in control of the national party machinery during and after the Smith campaign in 1928—John J. Raskob, national Democratic chairman from 1928 to 1932, Jouett Shouse, executive of that committee, and John W. Davis and Alfred E. Smith, Presidential candidates in 1924 and 1928. Joining them were a number of nationally prominent business leaders. They formed what was known as the American Liberty League, which issued statements and from time to time held black-tie dinners

with speeches by Smith and others. The Republican Party was altogether too weak after the 1934 election to be a suitable target for Roosevelt and so, no doubt provoked by the increasingly bitter criticism by the league and by some elements in the industrial world and the ultraconservative press, he found first the league and finally business in general a fine target for his ripostes.

2. Roosevelt was subjected to a needling process by some of his intimates who feared that his "era of good feeling" might be a reality. Foremost among these were the sardonic Hopkins, the ever-suspicious Morgenthau, and the "curmudgeon" Ickes. They brought tales to the President—some real but mostly imaginary—of plottings against him that were designed to inflame him against his critics. One story invented by Hopkins, which I heard him tell Roosevelt, was that the Morgan partners held a meeting every morning, then instructed the editorial writers of the *Times* and *Sun* about what they were to write.

3. Two years of labor and strain had so tenderized Roosevelt's normally resistant nervous system that he became exceedingly sensitive to criticism of any sort and from anyone. He was also, because of his political popularity, inclined more and more to believe in the infallibility of his judgments and the omniscience of his knowledge.

4. Moreover, Roosevelt was growing appreciably wearied of the squabbling among the ideologists in his circle of advisers and associates. In an earlier chapter I have enumerated the five major schools of economic redemption. But these had narrowed down in the years since by the demise of the money-managing wizards. The latter had enjoyed their brief moment of ascendancy when Roosevelt adopted the Warren plan, but after that had failed there were few who believed that salvation lay in that direction. It was a bit early then to count orthodox Keynesianism as important except among a few of the economists and some others who, although they were not much versed in economics, believed implicitly and without understanding in deficit spending. And so in 1935 the struggle settled down to the national economic planners and the Brandeisian atomizers—i.e., those who would break up industry into small pieces. The planners were outnumbered and outmaneuvered. After the decline and imminent demise of the NRA, the planners were largely centered in the Department of Agriculture, where Wallace and Tugwell were beleaguered. The energetic Frankfurter had recruited dozens of protégés in many agencies, and they were not only committed with a missionary fervor to their thesis that bigness was a curse (except in government) but highly sophisticated in the arts of palace intrigue. The struggle came to a head after the Supreme Court had destroyed the National Industrial Recovery Act.

There was one art in which Roosevelt was a master in his own right, that of politics. And he realized that a sole reliance on the abstractions of either school would not only confuse the electorate but divide it. His decision was based in part on his common-sense conclusion that a nation could not be governed by any special "ism" unless, like the Soviet Union, it was held together by a totalitarian police authority. Also he was sick and tired of all the nostrums which had so interested him in earlier years. It was possible to unite all schools of radical change by making his cause a crusade with a good wide target to hit at, and that proved to be big business and the rich.

5. To an increasing degree, Roosevelt in the early months of 1935 sensed a threat from Huey Long, who, having made himself the undisputed master of Louisiana, entertained still wider aspirations. The Senator formulated a sort of political formula that would "soak" the rich and attract the poor and discontented. He had a radical farm program, which he described to me in one of our many conversations in his apartment at the Mayflower Hotel. He also had a punitive tax program and plenty of slogans such as "Every man a king"—with himself as the "Kingfish." It was pretty crude stuff, but with unemployment still very large and the farmers unhappy despite a great improvement over 1933, and with a preacher as virile and persuasive as Long, it would win many votes in an electoral showdown with Roosevelt.

Long had a lively dislike for Joseph T. Robinson and Pat Harrison, who were invaluable Roosevelt supporters in the Senate. Long, whose power grew in the neighboring states of Mississippi and Arkansas, planned to slaughter these enemies when they came up for re-election. And beyond the conquest of those neighboring states, Long's ambitions were boundless. As a third-party candidate Long would get, according to Farley's poll-takers, 10 per cent of the vote in a Presidential election. This would be a substantial cut into Roosevelt's strength if the Republicans nominated a good candidate.

There was also discontent with Roosevelt among the "progressive" leaders in the Northwest. The La Follettes were not happy about the pace of Roosevelt's progress, the old silverites were still alive, Borah was growling, and elsewhere strange revivals of Populism were stirring at the grass roots. All this I heard from Floyd Olson, the colorful and powerful governor of Minnesota, when I saw him in Duluth in August 1935. These elements Roosevelt could not quiet by mere persuasion. They demanded something more concrete than words.

6. Roosevelt believed that a "bold" new program would suffice. But the supply of new ideas was running low. Nothing notably important seemed to be on the legislative agenda for 1935 but a social security bill and holding-company legislation, and possibly some sort of new labor measures and a revision of the NIRA. However, social security was still

being considered by the experts. Then, too, the patronage grab-bag was practically empty. Most of the available appointive offices had been filled and the city bosses were crying for more.

7. There was a great deal to do in administrative reform. For new agencies, as well as some old ones, needed reorganization to promote efficiency and economy. But in the lexicon of politics there isn't much "sex appeal" in administrative reform.

8. In 1935, after a bitter struggle between the old craft unions and the advocates of vertical unionism headed by John L. Lewis, the Committee for Industrial Organization was created. One result of this was to plunge the vertical unions directly into partisan politics, a repudiation of the Gompers tradition of impartiality between the parties. The new CIO planned to make a large contribution to Roosevelt's cause in 1936 and to use its machinery actively in the campaign. Roosevelt by skillful negotiation managed to work with both sides in the intra-union war and later through the Wagner Act to throw the influence of the government behind the unionization of certain large industries.

9. A series of decisions by the Supreme Court culminating in the Schechter decision, which destroyed the NIRA, infuriated Roosevelt. He responded with his famous "horse and buggy" press conference. From then on the Supreme Court along with a part of the press and business generally were regarded by Roosevelt as his mortal enemies.

All these factors with several lesser ones combined in 1935 to move Roosevelt toward the Flynn strategy. I was quite aware of what might be the consequences of this change of policies and I realized that the First New Deal was fading into history and the Second New Deal was coming.*

This change meant to me a painful reappraisal of what position I should take as a journalist and as a collaborator in assisting Roosevelt with his speeches and messages. I reached no decisions that year but it was my growing conviction that what was happening would destroy the Democratic Party as I had known it, and that Roosevelt's appeasement of the radicals was bad for the country. But I decided that so long as I had any influence with Roosevelt I would do what I could.

In February, with two friends, Edmund Coblentz and Vincent Astor, I had dinner and an evening with Roosevelt at the White House. In the course of the conversation Roosevelt handed me a brief outline of a tax reform program. He didn't say who had written it, but I suspected then (and this was confirmed later) that the author was Herman Oliphant, whom I had known as a colleague at Columbia and who was at that time chief law officer in Morgenthau's Treasury. He was not a specialist

* I may have been the first commentator to note this distinction between the First New Deal and the Second and to fix the change in 1935. This distinction has since been followed in most histories, notably by Basil Rauch, Tugwell, and Schlesinger.

on taxation, but at Columbia he was well known for his radical and half-baked ideas on social reform. His expressions were regarded by those who knew him as shock treatments for the complacent. The scheme was a "soak the rich" plan. I didn't like it, and Roosevelt at that time seemed only mildly interested in it.

But in June, after the "horse and buggy" press conference, a thoroughly aroused Roosevelt apparently decided that to present the tax scheme to Congress would not only be a means of striking back at his critics but would substantially steal Huey Long's issue. And so one evening Roosevelt read a message embodying the Oliphant scheme to Frankfurter and me and invited our views. Frankfurter, reflecting Brandeis' ideas of paying for public works with heavier inheritance taxes and increased levies on high incomes, was enthusiastic. I argued as well as I could that, since only a few days remained before the end of the fiscal year, Congress could hardly give sufficient attention to any such tax reform. I had definite objections to the undistributed corporate surplus tax, which was part of the reform. It also seemed unfair to the President's loyal supporters in Congress, who had been promised in the January message that there would be no new taxes that year. But Roosevelt was unmoved and said he was going to send the message to Congress the next day. He planned to have Pat Harrison, chairman of the Senate Finance Committee, come to the White House the next morning, and he remarked gaily that Harrison would be so surprised that he would "have kittens on the spot." I was shocked at this reference to a loyal supporter. But when the orders were given, there were no kittens. Rather, Harrison, who certainly did not believe in the plan, loyally lied to the Senate when the message was delivered the next day. Byrnes told me that all of Harrison's friends knew what his feelings were and respected his loyalty and calculated double-talk in explaining a measure he had seen only a few hours before. There was an uproar in both Houses and over the country about the tax plan. For the most part it remained as unfinished business when Congress adjourned. The most serious part of the Oliphant reform was the inclusion of an undistributed corporate surplus tax. This was not new to me, for a lawyer friend of Roosevelt's partner Basil O'Connor had presented it to me and to Roosevelt during the campaign of 1932 and it was rejected as a campaign issue.*

The tax plan and the uproar it created produced the calculated effect. Roosevelt appeared as the scourge of the rich and the big corporations, and the friend of the poor. But the frustration of Huey Long's plan was only a momentary victory. The Louisiana dictator was assassinated in September.

* My objections to this are at pages 310–12 in *After Seven Years.*

It was a torrid summer in Washington. The protégés of Frankfurter took it upon themselves to lobby openly for the holding-company bill with its "death sentence." Senator Hugo Black conducted a tremendous campaign against ship subsidies. And the Wagner bill was supported by Roosevelt as a substitute for the NIRA, which he had decided to abandon. The Wagner Act was weighted on the side of the unions and put the government substantially into the business of helping in the organization of hitherto unorganized workers.

I have already told of Hopkins' decision, which he described to me, to put the vast resources of his work-relief at the disposal of the big-city bosses. That was another step in implementing the new alliance implied in the Flynn strategy.

In July, after viewing the fury and confusion in Washington over the various measures supported by Roosevelt, I wrote a strongly worded editorial in *Today* designed as a protest against the new order of things. It said in part:

> In the heat of conflict, extremists on both sides conceive of the New Deal's activities in patching up our civilization as bitter class warfare. . . . The public is developing a terrific thirst for a long, cool swig of political quiescence. The danger to liberalism at such a moment is that a reactionary party will offer it a long, cool but narcotic swig of "normalcy." The Democrats can, if they will, meet the situation gracefully by the simple process of offering a quiet interlude for adjustment, education and the taking of stock. . . . They [the Democrats] must recognize that every social crusade, from Cromwell to Wilson, has sooner or later come face to face with the stubborn refusal of human nature to rise too high or stay high too long.

Since I called this editorial "On Reading Ecclesiastes," I concluded with this quotation: "To every thing there is a season, and a time to every purpose under the heaven." And as I wrote it, I pondered the Preacher's injunction, "a time to break down, and a time to build up . . . a time to cast away stones, and a time to gather stones together. . . . A time to rend, and a time to sew."

I could not expect that this guarded warning in a magazine of small circulation could affect the tempest of that summer. But I made sure that Roosevelt read it and that he would get the benefit of my advice. For he was entering upon a social conflict rather than a reform movement. But in September, after Congress went home and shortly before Long was assassinated in Baton Rouge, there was unexpected help toward an armistice. And to my amazement, Roosevelt himself seemed to agree with my plea for a period of quiet.

Roy Howard, master of the powerful Scripps-Howard newspaper enterprises, a fairly consistent supporter of Roosevelt and a friend of mine of long standing, must have felt during that summer the same misgivings I had. For on the very day that Congress adjourned he dispatched a letter to Roosevelt asking for what came to be celebrated as the "breathing spell." It read in part:

> . . . any experienced reporter will tell you that throughout the country many businessmen who once gave you sincere support are now not merely hostile, they are frightened. Many of these men, whose patriotism and sense of public service will compare with that of any men in political life, have become convinced and sincerely believe:
>
> That you fathered a tax bill that aims at revenge rather than revenue—revenge on business. . . .
>
> That there can be no real recovery until the fears of business have been allayed through the granting of a breathing spell to industry, and a recess from further experimentation until the country can recover its losses.
>
> I know that you have repeatedly stated your position on sections of the Nation's problems, but as an editor I know also the necessity for repetition and reiteration. There is need to undo the damage that has been done by misinterpreters of the New Deal.

Steve Early discussed this letter with Roosevelt and it was agreed that Howard was to have a conciliatory reply. With Howard's consent I was permitted to revise his letter for publication and to write the President's reply. I was delighted at this opportunity to participate in an exchange that might bring about a restoration of public confidence in Roosevelt's intentions after the heat and confusion of the summer. It proved to be one of those remarkable changes in Roosevelt's mood.

On Sunday, September 1, I drove up to Hyde Park, and there in the quiet of the library I found Roosevelt to be tranquil, indulgent, and quite desirous of meeting Howard's appeal in a spirit of conciliation.

He teased me a bit about my fears about the damage done during the summer. But there was no mistake about agreement that the time had come "to gather stones together." He took my draft of the reply to Howard and added a few gracious phrases of his own:

> I appreciate the tone and purpose of your letter [he wrote], and fairness impels me to note with no little sympathy and understanding the facts which you record. . . . This Administration came into power pledged to a very considerable legislative program. It found the condition of the country such as to require drastic and far-reaching action. Duty and necessity required us to move on a broad front for more than two years. It seemed to the Congress and to me better to achieve these objectives as expeditiously as possible in order that not only business but the public generally might know those modifications in the conditions and the rules of economic enterprise which were involved in our program. This basic program, however, has now reached substantial completion and the "breathing spell" of which you speak is here—very decidedly so.

This exchange of letters was given out a few days later and the effect was remarkable. The public reaction was so favorable that Roosevelt was astonished. Thousands of letters and telegrams came in congratulating the President. Stock issues hit the highest level since September 1931 and the Gallup poll showed later a spectacular rise in Roosevelt's popularity. It had sunk to its lowest level on September 1—50.5 per cent of approval. Roosevelt was delighted and, when I saw him next in mid-September to help draft some speeches for a long trip he was planning, he said with a touch of his old winsome enthusiasm that he wanted to strike a note of peace and unity and harmony again. I gladly responded with drafts full of that spirit. It seemed for the time that we were back in the old days of the spring of 1933.

In the weeks that followed the "breathing spell," there were two subjects to which I gave considerable attention in my editorials in *Today*. One was the implementation of the reciprocal trade authority that had been given to the State Department, which fulfilled the long-cherished dream of Cordell Hull. A trade treaty had been negotiated by the State Department with Canada. The other was embodied in a note by the State Department to the League of Nations expressing sympathy with certain European nations that were on the way to imposing sanctions against Italy because of Mussolini's Ethiopian adventure.

I wrote a series of editorials of protest on these subjects. In discussing the Canadian treaty, I used the word "furtive" because there had been little or no opportunity for hearings on the terms of the treaty by interested parties in the United States. The approval of sanctions seemed to me to be a violation of the spirit and import of a neutrality resolution that Congress had adopted in the previous summer.

I had made no direct criticism of Roosevelt. My comment was directed at the State Department. So far as neutrality was concerned, I had ample authority behind me. For John Bassett Moore, the renowned international lawyer, had prompted my concern in friendly letters. I had been his student at Columbia and our contacts had been resumed when I was in the government.

Roosevelt decided to make an issue of these criticisms of mine and he did something that had scarcely ever taken place in our relations. He wrote a letter defending the Canadian treaty, which in part was directed not at me but at what George Peek had said publicly about the negotiations:

At Warm Springs, Ga.,
November 23, 1935.

DEAR RAY:—

I have not seen the full article but you are wrong about "the furtive character of the negotiations" for reciprocal treaties.

The point which you overlook is this: Full public notice is given long before negotiations are even started. Any person trading with Canada is, or should be, aware that negotiations are on. As a matter of practical fact, many representatives of groups or firms trading with Canada or competing with Canadian products, such as the lumber interests, the cattle interests, the milk interests, etc., actually appear and present their cases thoroughly. In other words, complete knowledge of the facts was obtained and from both sides. There was nothing "secret" about the matter in any shape, manner or form.

The only alternative would be to announce the proposed treaty before initialing, hold public hearings, etc., etc. Suppose there are seven hundred schedules, fifty groups are opposed, six hundred and fifty do not oppose or are favorable. The latter say nothing, get no publicity and leave the entire field of publicity to the fifty opposing groups. Your proposed treaty thereupon fails to an almost certainty.

As to the bilateral treaties, do not get into your head that the most-favored-nation clause eliminates the bilateral feature. A very good example: Under the Canadian Treaty about 20,000 milk cows, i.e., fresh cows, are allowed to come in. That is the maximum quota. That quota would allow every nation in Europe, South America and the Orient to send in cows under the maximum of a total of 20,000 a year. Actually not one cow will come in from the most-favored-nation countries and the only cows to come in under it will be from Canada. So you see how silly George Peek's argument is. In actual practice we are making bilateral treaties insofar as 90% of the articles affected are concerned.

I thought you would like to have this to clear things up.

I will write you in a day or two, or talk to you on the telephone, about the speech. I will get at it today.

As ever yours,
F. D. R.

Professor Raymond Moley,
Hotel St. Regis,
Fifth Avenue & 55th Street,
New York, N.Y.

It should be noted that he did not mention the question of neutrality. However, it seemed to me that the time had come to make my position clear on both points, the procedure in negotiating reciprocal treaties and the unneutral posture of the State Department toward the growing frictions in Europe. And so I wrote a very long letter spelling out my criticisms:

The President November 30, 1935
Warm Springs, Georgia.

DEAR GOVERNOR:

I was delighted to have your frank and earnest note of November 23rd. It gives me the opportunity to speak with equal freedom of matters which I have hesitated to discuss with you and so I shall ask your indulgence for what is going to be, I know, a rather lengthy outpouring. I ask leave to tell you, in this letter, just as I should like to if I were sitting with you, all of the thoughts your note has stirred in my mind.

The issues raised in your letter are of transcendent importance not only to the country and your party but to your own future. I am concerned with these issues on that level, and not on the basis of personal feeling toward members of your State Department. Instead of these differences arising from the events of 1933, it is more truthful to say that those events arose from these differences of opinion which long antedated that time. I found in the State Department under Stimson, even before my official service began there, an atmosphere foreign, it seemed to me, to the vital spirit which characterized the campaign of 1932. That atmosphere has not changed since Stimson's departure. It closed around me and I had not served in office a month before I knew that it would be intolerable. I escaped with my convictions. Those who were in opposition to what it seemed to me were the interests of progressive thought in this country remained.

They remain.

But, as they labor in the shaping of policies that I deeply and earnestly believe to be dangerous, I have left to me the right to criticize, to oppose, and, if possible, to convince you, too, of the existence of the danger.

Now I want to speak to you specifically of the Canadian treaty. I have consistently advocated a general reciprocal agreement with Canada in many private conversations with you and with the Secretary of State before my resignation, in printed articles and in a speech made in Canada after I resigned. I say this to call attention to the record of my belief that we should seek more trade with Canada. Incidentally, I did not, in the editorial about which you wrote to me, discuss the wisdom of a trade agreement with Canada or the specific provisions of the agreements just concluded.

When the existing law on reciprocal trading was before Congress I published a carefully phrased editorial dated March 24, 1934, favoring the bill but indicating my belief that (1) to attempt to carry out the reciprocal-tariff policy while we adhered to the most-favored-nation principle * would lead to serious consequences, and (2) that, in making the treaties, a forum should be provided for discussion "under conditions that conserve the public interest." I have since held firmly to these two beliefs and in the face of that fact I should have been a dishonest journalist had I not spoken my mind once again, even in the face of a popular treaty with Canada.

What troubles me with respect to the present Canadian treaty is the fact that the quotas allowed are "global" and that hence, according to the experts, a certain proportion of the articles admitted will not come from

* Adherence to the most-favored-nation principle binds a nation to grant to a second nation, in certain stipulated matters, the same terms as are then or may be thereafter, granted to any other nations. Some clauses in treaties, embodying this principle, are "reciprocal," requiring that concessions between the signatory states be at all times equal. Others are "imperative" or "unconditional," offering no compensating privileges in return. For years before 1933 our State Department had adhered to the unconditional most-favored-nation principle—even to the point, as Ernest Lindley has remarked, of once asking Brazil to remove the tariff preference which it accorded American automobiles.

Canada at all but from nations from whom we receive absolutely no *quid pro quo* on this deal. To that extent, the treaty is not a trade; it is a gift—at the expense of American producers.

But, as you say, the danger that we will be flooded with imports is avoided by the use of the quota. In other words, economic and political disaster is avoided by the use of the very device which Secretary Hull denounces. If such circuitous calculations must be followed to avoid the effects of adherence to the most-favored-nation principle, why not achieve our ends directly by eliminating the most-favored-nation concessions entirely and by making bi-lateral agreements in which we give and receive definite and specific concessions in trade limited by quotas?

Why bother at all to maintain the fiction of most-favored-nation treatment, if fiction it is, and then attempt (not altogether successfully) to avert the consequences of such action by the quota device?

The answer is that those in whom you have vested the authority to administer the reciprocal-tariff policy want to achieve a general downward revision of tariffs without congressional intervention—an end which will most certainly injure your administration and split your following. And I might add, in this connection, that it is this intent, this fixed purpose to lower tariffs on the part of those entrusted with the administration of the Reciprocal Tariff Act that makes so dangerous the indirect, roundabout method now being followed. If the Act were administered by men of another view, by a Key Pittman, or by a Bob La Follette, one might be less fearful: under the present circumstances, apprehension is understandable.

My education on the tariff question goes back a long time, but the conclusions to which it impelled me really crystallized during your preconvention campaign. You will remember that the reciprocal-treaty idea was set forth by you in your St. Paul speech. The position you took in that speech was not only an astute one, politically, but a sound one, from the point of view of economics.

The tariff plank in the Democratic platform was written subsequently without reference to your expressed views. It was so ambiguous that, despite every effort on my part to comprehend it, it remains to this day wholly meaningless to me. I believe that this was your own reaction to it also and that this was the reason why you quite properly carried into the campaign your own tariff policy.

May I add that it seemed perfectly clear to me at the time that the policy you advocated during the campaign could not be carried out if we adhered to the most-favored-nation principle, and that I took it for granted that we would abandon it.

In this connection, you will remember the communications received from Secretary Hull (then Senator) via Mr. Taussig, during the campaign, and the discussion of his suggestions by you, Senators Pittman and Walsh, and myself. Your Sioux City speech, which rejected the idea of any general tariff reduction, was the result.

When I served in the Department of State, I found opinion there unchanged with respect to general tariff reduction and adherence to the most-favored-nation principle, and, despite earnest consideration on my part, the arguments in support of this position seemed to me to be completely unconvincing. In fact, in May, 1933, I wrote a syndicated article (which you read in advance of publication) expressing my conviction that the London Conference could do little on tariff except to effect an exchange of views.

You will recall the fact, I know, that the general-reduction-by-ten-percent idea was introduced into the Conference and promptly withdrawn. You will recall further the speech of the Secretary of State addressed to the Conference advocating a general lowering of tariff barriers which you and Billy Phillips very considerably amended.

As to the element of secrecy in the consummation of treaties such as the one we have just made with Canada, I must stick to my guns. I made it clear in the editorial to which you refer that I was aware of the "hearings" that are granted, although the Associated Press dispatch which you saw did not.

But, in my opinion, the hearings now granted do not permit sufficiently detailed exploration of the specific points contemplated in reciprocal treaties. To say that if such hearings were granted some of those injured would make outcries so loud as to defeat the treaty is not an adequate answer to the objection that interested parties are not given sufficient chance to present their arguments.

The present method does not ultimately prevent the outcries, in any case. They only come after the event, rather than before, and then they are the more deadly to you politically because those who emit them can howl that they have not only been injured but that they have had no chance to defend themselves—a charge which always gets public sympathy.

I am not convinced, moreover, that a treaty would be defeated if a fair public hearing were given after initialing and before final executive action. At that point there might be introduced into the proceedings the admirable device embodied in Senator Norris' bill vetoed by Hoover and endorsed by you in your Sioux City speech in 1932, thus:

"Another feature of the bill . . . contemplated the appointment of a public counsel, who should be heard on all applications for changes in rates before the commission on the one hand for increases sought by producers, often greedy, or for decreases asked by importers equally often actuated by purely selfish motives, or by others seeking such reductions. I hope some such change may be speedily enacted. It will have my cordial approval."

And now since you have made it possible for me to explain my views on this tariff matter I shall take the opportunity to speak of a much more serious question about which I have even graver apprehensions—neutrality. Here the issue is drawn in much the same pattern—conviction on my part that you hold views with which a vast majority of the country agrees, but with respect to which those through whom you are acting are intent upon making a quite different national policy prevail. I have given a great deal of thought to this of late and, while I have occasionally spoken to you of my uneasiness, I have not outlined the circumstances that cause it.

There are, of course, two extreme views with respect to our foreign policy, the one advocating utter isolation, the other, complete entanglement. If I were to describe your following realistically, I should say that, on the whole, your most loyal followers lean toward the first point of view. The first ballot at the convention in 1932 was a fair indication of the type of men who were supporting you, and the subsequent enlistment into their ranks of the western progressives reinforced this element of your support. Surely such internationalist advocates as the *Baltimore Sun* and the *New York Times* could not be counted as sympathetic supporters. Your domestic policies have accentuated this cleavage—a fact which has warmed my heart and enlisted my enthusiasm.

I realize, however, that you should not take an extreme position and hold dogmatically to it. In this instance, the task is to retain national independence of action but to move so far toward internationalism as is safe and expedient. To do this, however, compels the painstaking pursuit of a hazardous course of action. The success of such an operation required fine instruments and accurate information. Otherwise disaster may result to the nation and to your own loyal following.

Now it required little demonstration to show that the instruments you are using—that is, the men in whom the delicate execution of the job of preserving neutrality is vested—are, almost without exception, of that school of thought that believes that participation in international coercive movements can save us from war. They are of that mistaken group that guided Wilson along the road, first, to war and, beyond that, to bitter disillusion. I say "mistaken" because it was their advice in 1915, 1916, and 1917 which induced us to enter the war "to end war" and to "save democracy" and subsequent events have shown them to be wrong. Apparently they are still firmly in the saddle, some of them in person, some of them through protégés (i.e., as Bingham, of House), others, career men trained under the old dispensation—all of them the intellectual brethren of the naïve Lansing with one foot at Broad and Wall and the other at Geneva. They tell us now, in one form or another, that we can stop wars by engaging in wars to stop wars. These are the men designated to effectuate your decisions and to provide you with the information necessary to guide you on a dark and dangerous road. (And no one knows better than you, I am sure, how settled are the policies of the State Department and how they differ from your own progressive principles.)

This apprehension concerning your international advisers explains why Congress acted as it did last summer when it rejected Section I of the McReynolds Resolution.

The issue was not new to Congress. In March, 1933, John Bassett Moore had written a letter, read in the hearings of the House Committee on Foreign Affairs, exposing the irreconcilability of a discriminatory embargo with law, common sense, or peace. J. B. Moore sent a copy of that letter to me.

Despite this warning and despite an obviously overwhelming opposition in the Congress, the State Department urged upon you the advocacy of a contrary course this August. Those who spoke for the Department failed to point out to you that a discriminatory arms embargo is a denial of neutrality, that to commit an act of war in the name of peace is a clear reversion to the notion of wars to end war. And, while there are those who believe in this principle, I venture to suggest that an overwhelming proportion of the country agrees with Congress that it is a notion which is self-contradictory.

It is true, as the Department argued, that the President may, by maladroitness, involve us in war. But the great power of the President does not in itself justify asking that he be invested with a complete and unreviewable determination as to which of two foreign belligerents is "right" or "wrong." Yet one of the very top layer of your advisers on foreign relations (not the Secretary) said *in writing* that he wanted this power for the President because *in an international crisis Congress might not act and thus sacrifice our vital interests.* This is a strange doctrine indeed!

The Pittman Resolution was passed in spite of these representations and under it you very properly recognized a state of war between Italy and Ethiopia, pronounced the embargo, and uttered the corollary warning. This was excellent.

But following that, a series of pronouncements came from members of the administration which have confused and alarmed me. Perhaps I can best express my feeling by quoting an editorial that I am publishing this week (issue of December 7th):

"Under our form of government, Congress determines what national policies shall be and expresses its decisions in the laws it makes. The members of the executive branch of the government have the duty of enforcing these laws. That is the meaning of their oath of office.

"When a neutrality resolution came up for consideration in Congress last summer, the executive branch of the government asked for discretionary power in imposing discriminatory restrictions and embargoes on American commerce in case of a foreign war. It asked, in effect, to be allowed to choose between nations engaged in foreign war upon the basis of a moral judgment as to the right and wrong of the quarrel. Congress refused this request and announced a policy of strict impartiality in all relations with reference to warring nations.

"That imposed upon the Department of State the obligation of leaning over backward in carrying out a policy which its duty but not its conviction commanded.

"How is the Administration carrying out the neutrality resolution of Congress? Let us look at its record, not legalistically, but realistically.

"In Europe the opinion apparently prevails that economic sanctions on the part of the League designed to coerce Italy will be ineffective unless the United States 'cooperates.' Europe does not care a rap (and let us not forget this for a single moment) what name we choose to call our participation in sanctions or what explanations we make as to the reasons for our policy. The thing that Europe cares about is the *effect* of our decisions.

"The early acts of the government of the United States in carrying out the neutrality resolution of Congress were correct and sound and raised no issues in Europe. But with the growing disposition on the part of our government to restrict the export of oil, scrap iron, copper, cotton, and other articles not included in the statutory embargo on arms, ammunition, and implements of war (and this despite the fact that Senator Pittman,

Chairman of the Senate Committee on Foreign Relations, gave, on the floor of the Senate last August 21st, a definition of the term 'implements of war' which did not include such articles), the tension in Europe has become acute. It has become apparent that the coercing nations of Europe will move against Italy with respect to such items as these only if the United States takes the lead. More ironic still, it is not certain that they will all participate even if the United States does take the lead. This has definitely made us a determinant factor in the general effort to coerce Italy. The members of the League recognize this situation. Italy must certainly recognize our course of action for what it is—the beginning of an almost inevitable logical sequence of acts which, if carried out, would most certainly end in downright hostility to Italy and which would violate the letter and spirit of the neutrality resolution.

"That we have already as a government passed moral judgment on the issue between the sanctionist powers and Italy seems to me to be obvious. The note sent by the Department of State to the League of Nations on October 26th, while it does not name Italy, nevertheless stamps Italy as a wrongdoer, using instead of the term 'League of Nations,' the alter ego of the League Covenant, the Kellogg Pact.

"Anyone who knows the subtleties of diplomatic language knows that when we, as a nation, look with 'sympathetic interest' upon the 'concerted efforts of other nations' to coerce Italy, which we euphemistically call an attempt 'to preserve peace or to localize and shorten the duration of war,' we obviously favor such action. There is no use quibbling about language. The meaning is clear.

"To express 'sympathetic interest' and then to stop with the expression is, of course, one thing, but to give utterance to this expression and then to follow it up with actions that have the effect of implementing 'sympathetic interest' definitely puts us into a position of taking sides in the present European situation. It is a departure from the letter and spirit of neutrality. I cannot say with too much seriousness that taking sides in this fashion will almost automatically make us a party to the wider war that might easily develop out of the present small war."

When in the pursuit of my duty as a journalist I find it necessary to disagree with my friends, it hurts. Nothing so hurts as to disagree with you. All I can do in such an instance is to be terribly sure that I am right and as nearly as possible consistent with myself. On these two subjects of the tariff and neutrality I feel that assurance. I am glad of only one thing, that they constitute a small—however important—minority of the public policies which you profess.

When I must disagree with any of them I share a feeling that the V.P. [Vice President] expressed to me on one occasion last winter. He said, "I love this man in the White House because he is for so many things that I have always hoped for and believed in. And when he does things that I don't believe in, I love him enough to tell him the truth."

Ever with sincere regard and affection,

RAY

There was no direct reply to this letter, but two weeks later the duplicity of European diplomacy left the United States high and dry and alone in its unneutral position. For Britain and France agreed to the annexation of Ethiopia. The long road to Munich began there. And Roosevelt was compelled to withdraw the unneutral demands he had imposed upon American traders.

As the year 1935 drew to a close, it was apparent that the First New Deal was dead in spirit and in fact. The effort to establish self-government in industry had been abandoned after the death of the NIRA. In the Wagner Act the government had allied itself with the unions. The breathing spell was ended. There remained the AAA, which was to die the next year. And under the Ickes administration the PWA was making great efforts to build a public power monopoly. The State Department had reverted to the Stimson policies. And the transformation of the Democratic Party was all but complete with the adoption by Roosevelt of the Flynn strategy.

Chapter Forty-three

1936—The Decisive Year

IN retrospect, it is clear to me that the year 1935 saw the beginning of the end of my relationship with Roosevelt. I hoped, however, that difference of opinion might not terminate a personal friendship that had grown over the years. For I liked the man very much. His infinite charm of manner, his physical courage, his cheerfulness, his patience with many of those misfits in his Administration whom he lacked the stamina to fire, his generosity with me when I made mistakes in carrying out his orders—these qualities made his appeal almost irresistible. Even when with deep misgivings I saw his change of policy, I hoped that I might modify the trend. But it proved to be like two people who after adding up the same column of figures come out with different answers.

He had not answered or mentioned my letter protesting the method of negotiating the Canadian treaty and the unneutral posture toward Italy. But in December he asked me to come to Washington and work with him on the annual message. When I had a preliminary talk with him on December 20, he said that his budget would be regarded as conservative and therefore he needed a "fighting message." The budget was bound to be better than the two previous ones. Since there had been a general economic improvement, the revenues would be larger and, since unemployment was lessening, there would be less need for work-relief.

So far as a "fighting message" was concerned, I had no need to be told who the enemies would be. There were plenty of hobgoblins in his new cosmos. In the absence of actually named villains, there were plenty of sinister but anonymous generalities to be drawn upon. I obediently provided him with those symbolic enemies of the republic and the result was a sort of demagogic masterpiece.

After much whacking of those lurking ghosts, I wrote into the text something that had a two-edged effect. It was the declaration that the New Deal had created "new instrumentalities of public power" that might be used by "the political puppets of an economic autocracy" (meaning Republicans) "to shackle the liberties of the people."

This was pretty corny stuff but it served to remind some commentators that there were powers, created to meet an emergency, that were potentially dangerous. But the faithful followers caught the inference that such powers would be safe if they were continued to be vested in Roosevelt.

When the speech was written I entertained no twitching of conscience, because it was routine political oratory and, since 1936 was an election year, a sophisticated public would take it as normal.

Good beefy rhetoric for headlines! But this rattling of an insubstantial big stick was unimpressive. Progressives in the press and in Congress wanted something more tangible than rhetoric. A typical radical opinion in the *New Republic* was: ". . . in the long run he cannot hope to hold the masses of the people by expressions of sympathy which, no matter how brilliantly or movingly expressed, give hardly an inkling of what, after nearly three years of office, he proposes to do for them."

If he read this and listened to Congressional radicals, he would know that appetites for change, once whetted, grow by what they have already consumed.

The parts of the press that were already critical noted the veiled threat about "new instruments of power." And even as he read the speech to Congress, Republicans guffawed. "It is the first campaign speech," they said.

When I heard the message at home over the radio, my feeling was that of deep regret and self-reproach for the part I had played in mixing this epithetical brew. It was like awakening with a hangover. Time for a decision of my own, I told myself. I had carried the speech-technician business too far. And so far as my own participation was concerned, I would never again help with what I didn't believe. I must prepare for a withdrawal as a speech collaborator. And in my *Today* editorials I must bear on more heavily against the radical trend.

I took steps to ease out of speech collaboration. I had introduced Thomas G. Corcoran to Roosevelt. He was a leader among the Frankfurter protégés, and since Corcoran had a quick mind and a deep sympathy for Roosevelt's new strategy, I suggested that he might help with speeches. Stephen Early had brought in as a sort of literary ghost Stanley High, a former minister and free-lance writer. These I believed could take over with speeches and statements. It would facilitate my withdrawal.

My fear that the campaign against business would go beyond mere words was justified in March, when Roosevelt asked Congress for a tax on corporate surpluses or, as otherwise described, a tax on undistributed profits. After long consultation with Robert Lovett, a partner of the Brown Brothers, Harriman firm, I wrote in the magazine a detailed criticism of the measure. Roosevelt read it and twitted me about it in a friendly telephone chat. In April he asked me to come to Washington and help with a speech he was to make in New York. I responded and left some notes for High and Corcoran to develop.

Later in April, Roosevelt invited me to join him on the Potomac for a weekend over Sunday, May 3. This began as a most pleasant outing, for he and I had wagered something on a horse running in the Kentucky Derby. The horse won, and so on Sunday afternoon I decided to take advantage of Roosevelt's good feeling and have a long talk about his disposition toward business. The talk revolved about my definition of confidence. The discussion went round and round and got nowhere. As I recorded this conversation later, I said, "The conclusion was inescapable . . . that he was a mariner more interested in the voyage than the destination. I, in company with all his associates, was expected to go along for the ride."

I concluded that, while he had no specific program in mind, he was determined in the campaign that year to ask for a vote of confidence—not for something that he proposed to do in the future, but for himself.

On an evening late in May we had another long conversation, this time in his study after dinner in the White House. The discussion started on a sharp note. For he resented an article that had appeared in *Today* that charged him with a vendetta with the press. Its title was "Peeved at the Press" and its co-author was Ernest Lindley, a loyal supporter of Roosevelt who had already written a book praising the New Deal and who had another in preparation. Roosevelt mentioned that he had read newspaper accounts of a speech I had made in New York to a group of businessmen. He said slightingly that it didn't matter what I wrote in the magazine because it was read by few. But when I got into the newspapers!

I replied that when I worked for him my loyalty was altogether given to him. But now I had another loyalty: the people who chose to buy the magazine and read what I wrote. The talk rambled and as we consumed a bottle of Napoleon brandy it became more amicable, and I left at midnight.

In June, as the time for the Democratic Convention at Philadelphia was coming close, Roosevelt telephoned and asked me to come down and "lend a hand" with his acceptance speech. I said I would.

Before leaving for Washington I had a talk with Baruch. He said he had already talked with Roosevelt and had advised that the theme of the acceptance speech should strike a tone of moderation, stressing national unity and public confidence. This seemed to me to be what the occasion demanded. In that moderate tone he could justly point to the record from the day of his inauguration. Recovery had measurably been achieved. There was no need to excite passions. What was needed was to encourage the course of recovery. Roosevelt's re-election was assured. The opposition was weak and scattered.

I talked with Roosevelt about this kind of approach and he seemed to be wholly agreeable. He said that since the speech was to be delivered in the open to a huge crowd it should be short—"about fifteen minutes"—with places well marked by brief, applause-inspiring sentences here and there. And he said that toward the end there should be struck "a very serious note." I prepared the draft according to specifications.

The next day I went over the draft with him and he expressed enthusiasm for it. At least he simulated enthusiasm.

I remained in Washington that night, quite unaware of what was happening at the White House in my absence.

Indeed, I did not know the full story of what had happened that night until Sam Rosenman's book *Working with Roosevelt* came out many years later. Rosenman had been in the White House during those days and was working on a draft of the party platform with Stanley High. Without telling me, Roosevelt had asked them to write an acceptance speech. Their draft, according to Rosenman, was "militant, bare-fisted . . . intended to give battle to the reactionaries in both parties . . . there was very little in it that was conciliatory." After I left, Roosevelt had showed them my draft and asked them to "work it into the draft" which they had prepared. And so they sought to reconcile the irreconcilable "with occasional help from Don Richberg."

There was much more in the finished product that was bare-fisted than conciliatory. It was as if one had taken the portrait of a bishop out of an ecclesiastical frame and had put in its place a likeness of such a hard-riding Populist as Sockless Jerry Simpson.

When I returned to the White House the next morning and saw the product, I was unaware of who had done the mangling, but I realized that all my efforts to stem the radical mood in Roosevelt over the past year had failed. I was neither shocked nor indignant. For I had anticipated the change. I was profoundly relieved. I could now depart in peace.

The new speech was marked by well-worn epithets borrowed from the clichés of battles long ago—"economic royalists," "new dynasties," "concentration of control," "royal service," "privileged princes," "economic dynasties thirsting for power," "new despotism in the robes of legal sanctions," "new mercenaries," etc. It was a clumsy bit of demagoguery. Huey Long would have done it much better.

There were preserved in it some of my expressions, such as a reference to Dante's passage about the warm-hearted and cold-hearted. The slight levity in "Presidents make mistakes" was left. The famous phrase "rendevous with destiny" remained. Roosevelt no doubt left these in the speech to permit his audience to catch its breath.

The revised acceptance speech was far more than a mere rhetorical exercise. It was the expression of calculated policy. Like the earlier, annual message, it sounded the keynote of the campaign that followed. In politics one has to be for somebody and against somebody. Like the medieval English morality plays, there must be devils and heroes. The Flynn statement describes the bedeviled part of the cast. These were the seven million discontented and dissident. These must be mobilized by verbal expressions of sympathy and the promise of programs to benefit them. An unspecified business monster sufficed as the devil. It was relatively easy to stir indignation against business, especially big business. For a long lag of time must pass before the sins of an earlier generation are forgotten. And there was a widespread belief that mismanagement of business had caused the depression. One of Roosevelt's speechwriters in that campaign said most earnestly to me that it was not enough to get business down: "You must turn the knife around in him." A hobgoblin atmosphere prevailed until the last speech of the campaign, when somebody persuaded Roosevelt to say, "I should like to have it said of my first Administration that the forces of selfishness [unspecified, but in the context "organized money"] and of lust for power met their match. I should like to have it said of my second Administration that in it these forces met their master."

It was easy to foresee the course Roosevelt was to take in the campaign that year. And so on that June morning after I read the new draft of the acceptance speech, I took it to the Cabinet Room and with a red pencil corrected some grammatical and stylistic errors. I then laid the draft before Roosevelt and merely told him I was on my way to visit the Philadelphia convention on the way to New York. He beamed and said, "Of course." We exchanged formalities and I left the White House, which I was not to visit again until twenty-five years later when I paid a short visit to John F. Kennedy.

Three days later, Roosevelt called me at my apartment in New York. He was at Hyde Park and in a most friendly manner thanked me for helping him with the speech. Then he generously added that the greatest applause had followed the passages I had contributed. I thanked him for the call.

There, I had every reason to assume, the long story of personal relationship ended.

The speech was public notice that the First New Deal was dead. There was no sharp "break" between us. The ties had deteriorated over so long a span that there was no argument or bitterness or, so far as I knew, diminution of personal warmth. I was glad that it was so.

This conclusion is not what gossips might imagine—or say. Lives are not lived according to the vagaries of gossip-mongers. For men of conviction, lives must be lived by an inward light, however feeble it burns. And I still believe that both Roosevelt and I would have preferred the end to come as it did. We simply came to the crossroads and followed different markers. This meant different routes, different destinations.

The tone and challenge of the acceptance speech confronted me sharply with the necessity for an irrevocable decision. My inclination to terminate my unofficial relations with Roosevelt had been shaping itself for months. But he had made it easy, not to say tolerable, for me to continue. He clearly wanted to continue the relationship which had at that time gone on for four years. He wanted me to "go along." There was the experienced service I could offer, and also, I venture to say, the affection he felt for me. I know that he admired my methods of operation, for he told Vincent Astor about that time that he could work with me "better than anyone else."

I felt the same personal affection for him. There was his infinite buoyance, and his kindness and consideration in our joint efforts.

But there were divergent views now that I could not resolve. And if I had continued, with such differences gnawing in my mind, I could but serve him badly. These differences concerned the impact of a re-oriented party upon the nation. For it was clear enough that the Democratic Party which Roosevelt headed would govern for some years to come and thus in large measure determine the destiny of the nation. The party would be what he chose to make it.

But I wanted my departure to be without rancor or incident. There ran through my mind the "Nunc Dimittis" in the prayer book—"now lettest thou thy servant depart in peace."

I was approaching my fiftieth birthday, and my political convictions had been shaped over a good many years. As a professor and a writer it had been my professional concern to teach and write about politics and government. My convictions were too mature, too deeply interwoven in my habits of thought and action to change now. I was conservative by instinct:

1. There was my conception of the role of party in a free society. In my earlier years as a college teacher I had believed and taught that the two parties should represent sharply different views about the relations between government and the individual and government and individual enterprise. But more observation and reflection had convinced me that in a nation as big as the United States the two national

parties should cut into all classes and interests. In party policies, candidates, and party manifestoes in the past there was measurable blurring of their positions toward the conflicts among interests; there was double-talk and even hypocrisy. But, considering the value which was sought, even double-talk had its usefulness.

2. The concept of a classless society had dominated the spirit of the American nation from its beginning. The ideal was not that one man was as good as another, but that there should be no bar to the man with ambition, capacity, and self-reliance. The stratification of a people in fixed classes or interests had been impossible in a nation ever expanding, ever growing, and in constant flux. No society can stratify in the face of permeable geographical and economic frontiers. This movement of individuals from one economic status to another was, I was convinced, a source of our vast national potential.

3. Despite an earlier concept of the American Constitution, which I had uncritically accepted as a student at Columbia from Charles A. Beard and other professors and which conceived of the making of the Constitution by, for, and of a selfish propertied class, I learned something quite different when I was cheek by jowl with those who directed government in Washington. I rediscovered the Constitution as its makers had designed it.

One must realize when he sees the exercise of naked power by finite men that it must be controlled or balanced by other sources of power. By close observation of the effect of power upon Roosevelt—power that projected its insidious infection more and more deeply with popularity and political success—I came to respect what Madison wrote in *The Federalist*: "Ambition must be made to counteract ambition. . . . It may be a reflection on human nature, that such devices should be necessary to control the abuses of government. But what is government itself but the greatest of all reflections on human nature?"

Tyranny is a sleeping infection in the vast powers imposed upon any President. But when that individual is securely in control of a top-heavy majority, the tyranny inherent in a majority also appears. The aftermath of the election more than showed this peril in the Roosevelt-Flynn strategy.

4. I had also grown aware that our participation in a war that even in 1935 seemed to be brewing in Europe would shake our constitutional fabric at home and imperil the liberties of our people. I was alarmed by Roosevelt's revival of internationalism, which had been dormant in the First New Deal.

5. There was always something lacking in Roosevelt's understanding of modern industry until, at the head of an unprepared nation, he had to call upon it to produce the means of winning the Second World War. His contacts with the leaders of industry before the period we are con-

sidering had been slight. He confused industrial leaders with bankers and "money changers" and traders, although they are a quite different breed. When he wanted to draw an example from the world of manufacturing he used over and over the relatively small DeLaval separator plant in Poughkeepsie to illustrate what he wanted to say. There was the trace of a country squire's or farmer's suspicion of the vast manufacturing industries.

On the other hand, I had known these people fairly well in Cleveland and the Middle West. They were not traders; they were creators of great national wealth. My philosophy conceived the function of government to be limited to making sure that there was fair competition and protection for the consumer. Government should not tell industry what to do. It should limit itself to decreeing what should not be done.

An indiscriminate attack upon business without specifications or name-calling could only hinder the progress of recovery. The free market, if kept free, could right itself. And by 1936 it was recovering. My forebodings were in fact justified in what happened after the demagoguery of the 1936 campaign. For the growth of the national product, which had recovered at the rate of 10 per cent a year, slowed down to less than 3 per cent a year until the war. And unemployment began to rise after 1937. In 1936, the percentage of the unemployed was 16.8. It was 14.3 in 1937. It rose to 19 per cent in 1938, and only fell below the 1937 figure in 1940, when rearmament began.

6. My concept of the American economy centered upon individual enterprise operating in a free market. Government, the servant of the public interest, should keep watch and make sure there is invigorating competition. The operation of such a system rests upon millions of individual parts—those who create enterprises to serve the needs of many; those who contribute labor, which, mingled with natural resources and capital, produces true wealth; those who contribute talent for planning and management; those who consume, whose spending makes profits possible; large businesses dependent upon many small suppliers. Each is essential to the other. This is what I meant when I used the word "interdependence" in Roosevelt's speeches in the campaign of 1932 and thereafter.

The system depends upon billions of individual decisions in the market. There should be freedom in these decisions. Americans vote in the marketplace and reward those who make what they choose to buy. Under broad rules made by the government to enforce fairness and honesty, capital is risked, individuals have the liberty to succeed or fail, and after failure to try again. In this diffusion of decision-making there is national strength. For mistakes here are corrected there. This repudiates either central planning by the government or legal restrictions so tight that enterprise is paralyzed. All this I had learned as I watched the First New Deal's enactments in operation, which succeeded or failed as they departed from those principles.

The Philadelphia acceptance speech had made firm and final my decision to disassociate myself from Roosevelt's new policies, but I faced another problem. What course should I take as an editor and political commentator? While the circulation of our magazine was relatively small, my comments, because of my long association with Roosevelt, would be widely noted by other political commentators. I decided that in that campaign I would observe measurable neutrality between the two candidates. Landon was the unfortunate choice of a Republican Party with a dire poverty of "available" leadership. There were plenty of Republicans who might have made excellent Presidents, but for one reason or another they lacked what is called acceptability. Landon was without political blemish. He had no positive opinions on anything. He had been elected governor of Kansas in two years when the national tide ran the other way. Hearst "discovered" him and promoted his meager virtues. I could summon no enthusiasm for exalting him. And so I limited my editorial comments to observations, except that in mid-October I sharply challenged one of Roosevelt's palpably erroneous claims about fiscal policy. This piece brought me a letter from Walter Lippmann saying it was the best editorial in the campaign.

Since Roosevelt's election was assured from the start, I decided to save my opposition until after he had begun his second term. The opportunity for that was quick in coming, because within two weeks after his second inauguration he proposed his plan for reorganizing the Supreme Court. Then I moved into the debate and because of what I had written on the subject was the first witness in opposition before the Senate Judiciary Committee.

Since I believed in a two-party system and that it is the responsibility of everyone to have a party affiliation, I chose in the years that followed to support editorially Republican candidates and generally Republican policies. I could not remain a Democrat when the nature and objectives of that party had so completely departed from its earlier faith.

It seems strange in a country like ours, in which so many fail to disclose their party affiliation and such a small proportion of the eligibles vote at all, that when a person prominently identified changes his affiliation, there should be so much comment about it. But in Britain, where national parties are so clearly identified and such a large proportion of the eligibles vote in general elections, history is full of statesmen who have crossed the aisle to the opposition. Gladstone began his parliamentary career as a Tory and turned Liberal. Winston Churchill began as a Conservative. He joined the Liberals later and, after twenty years, returned to the Conservatives. Then for several years he became a severe critic of the government. After his summons to the leadership of the war government, he remained as head of the Conservatives until his retirement.

In discussing consistency in politics he wrote this:

"A change of Party is usually considered a much more serious breach of consistency than a change of view. In fact so long as a man works with a Party he will rarely find himself accused of inconsistency, no matter how widely his opinions at one time on any subject can be shown to have altered. Yet Parties are subject to changes and inconsistencies not less glaring than those of individuals. . . . To remain constant when a party changes is to excite invidious challenge. Moreover, a separation from Party affects all manner of personal relations and sunders old comradeships. Still, a sincere conviction, in harmony with the needs of the time and upon a great issue, will be found to override all other factors; and it is right and in the public interest that it should. Politics is a generous profession. The motives and characters of public men, though constantly criticised, are in the end broadly and fairly judged." *

Two comments in that statement of Churchill's apply to what happened with me in 1935 and 1936. Roosevelt substantially reversed the policies of the Democratic Party. The old Democratic affirmation of the constitutional integrity of state and local authority was abandoned. The Federal government intervened, at first slowly but later massively, in areas hitherto reserved to the states and the communities in privately organized welfare and in large parts of economic life.

The strength of the Democratic Party came to be centered in the large urban centers. In every election after 1936 the Democrats lost more counties but gained vast popular majorities from the masses in the cities. Roosevelt created a veritable political revolution. I was frequently asked why I had left the Democratic Party. My answer was that the Democratic Party had left me.

Churchill mentions the sundering of old relationships. But in my case this was incidental. There were innumerable old friends, such as Garner, Glass, Harry Byrd, and James Byrnes, who shared my views but who for reasons peculiar to themselves kept a nominal Democratic affiliation. Even Flynn, the co-architect of the new order, remained my fast friend and a decade later, as I have noted earlier, he asked and received my help in writing his memoirs.

I did not float between the worlds, like Kipling's Tomlinson. I did not believe in non-partisanship. New and important figures rose in the Republican Party and in every Presidential campaign, beginning in 1940 (except in 1956), my help was solicited in their campaigns. I joined in their efforts to turn the tide.

* Winston S. Churchill, "Consistency in Politics," included in *Great Destiny,* edited by F. W. Heath (New York: G. P. Putnam's, 1965).

In 1936 I went to California for the month of August for the first real holiday I had enjoyed in years, far from the preliminaries of the campaign.

When I returned, the ever-conciliatory, lovable Frank Walker came to my apartment. The import of what he said was that Roosevelt and I had been friends too long to part at the beginning of a new campaign. I explained that the disagreement was not personal. It had to do with policy and strategy. To Frank this seemed incredible, even irrelevant. He belonged to the old brigade and so had I.

A day or two later I read in the newspaper that Walker had been at Hyde Park. That evening I had a telegram from Roosevelt inviting me for lunch at Hyde Park on the following Sunday. I went.

It was a pleasant luncheon. Mother Sara presided, and sitting quietly among the guests was General Douglas MacArthur in civilian dress. He had conferred with the President that morning about his new assignment in the Philippines.

After lunch Roosevelt and I went to his little office, where he sat at a desk used by Woodrow Wilson on the ship that had carried him to France after the war. Roosevelt was a proud man, but he brought himself to ask me to accompany him during the campaign and resume my supervision of speech-writing. This, I am sure, was in part due to a superstition that lurks in every political mind. He always wore the same old felt hat in every campaign. I, too, was a symbol of the great victory of 1932.

I made it quietly clear that I wanted to be a journalist this time and write my editorials from my detachment. We briefly discussed Tugwell, and he couldn't avoid saying that Rex had never changed. I knew what this dig meant. But I proffered a bit of advice. I advised him not to rely too heavily on the untried youngsters who were then anticipating a large part in the campaign. I said he ought to have at his right hand a political figure experienced in his own right. I suggested Joseph O'Mahoney, formerly Farley's assistant and then Senator from Wyoming. Roosevelt asked if I would "give O'Mahoney some ideas." I said I would. The occasion for briefing O'Mahoney did not appear. But Roosevelt took him for at least part of the campaign in the West. That was the last time I ever saw Roosevelt or talked with him.

It is best that this long account end on a note of comedy. For in *Working with Roosevelt* Rosenman says that he learned that Roosevelt had, at the instance of Frank Walker, invited me that Sunday to Hyde Park "to discuss the campaign generally and this speech [at the Democratic state convention] in particular." Rosenman and High, with Corcoran, had worked on a draft and had taken it to Hyde Park. There they learned of the plan for my visit:

. . . he [Roosevelt] asked the rest of us to remain out of sight while Moley was in Hyde Park. We did; but Hyde Park is not big and it was not easy to find a hiding place for our group, which included High, Corcoran, Corcoran's secretary (now his wife), Mrs. Rosenman and me.

Mrs. Roosevelt moved us out of the house for a day or two to an apartment over a tearoom about two miles away from the President's residence. The following letter from her is interesting, for it has to do with our involuntary stay at the tearoom:

DEAR SAM

I was humiliated beyond words when I learned from Nellie Johansen that she accepted money for you and Mr. High and Mr. Corcoran for your meals. That place belongs to me and I use it for my guests when the house is full. Nellie simply didn't understand and if I don't tell her each time, she gets confused.

I hope you were comfortable and found everything pleasant. I am enclosing my check for $8.00. Will you please reimburse the other two for their share? . . .

ELEANOR ROOSEVELT

Rosenman continues:

It was not until Moley had left after a day's stay that we were again permitted to come out into daylight.

And so the amenities were observed and, as is always true, good manners proved to be inexpensive. Everyone was happy thereafter, myself included.

Appendix A

Questions Taken by Franklin D. Roosevelt to Conference with President Hoover, November 22, 1932

Can the December 15th payments be discussed separately from the whole question at the present time?

Was there any discussion of failure of Great Britain to include the debt payments of December 15th in its budget estimate?

Can debt matters (in view of the negotiations thus far) be separately discussed with each debtor, or must all debtors be treated alike?

If December 15th payments can be separately discussed, can the problem of transfer be divorced from the question of forgiveness or moratorium?

And can these questions be separately discussed with each country in each case?

What specific results do you consider could be expected to flow from a "period of tranquillity" suggested in the British note?

Would this "tranquillity" be greater if the December 15th payments were not made?

How much is the private debt of foreigners to United States nationals?

How much does that require to be transferred annually in payment?

Specifications:

1. For service charges: interest and sinking fund.
2. How much is in default and is interest being regularly received on the rest?
3. How much is being placed in escrow abroad for the account of American bondholders?

Why, in your judgment, did the debtor nations not avail themselves of the 90-day clause in the debt arrangements?

What are the gold holdings of our chief debtors?

How does this compare with one year ago?

How much gold has each of them withdrawn from the United States which might have been left here to meet December 15th payments?

What change has there been in the debtor countries in the last 18 months?

Is their position with relation to the United States worse than it was 18 months ago?

You have suggested a reconstitution of the debt funding commission.

What is it that you expect this commission will do?

A. Will it re-examine capacity to pay: in relation to (a) the relative situations of U.S. and other countries in 1923–26 and 1932, (b) the relative abilities of various debtors?
B. Will it examine the desirability of readjusting interest rates? If so, on what principle?
C. Will it re-examine the value of the debt? (Our relation to our creditors is the same as their relation to us.)
D. Would the commission be guided by the rate of interest at which conversion can be accomplished in the United States? or in the debtor countries?

Why a debt *commission* at all?

Has any promise been made to European governments that debts will be re-examined because of the conclusion of agreements among European nations to forego reparations payments? (The Lausanne agreement.)

What arrangements were made with Premier Laval?

Does the present move to re-examine the debts represent, in any sense, a fulfillment of informal agreements made with MacDonald and Laval?

What is the position of the Federal Reserve Board in regard to the debt situation?

Has the Federal Reserve Board any understanding with the Administration with regard to a debt policy?

What relation, in the view of the Administration, does the debt question hold to:

A. The objectives of the disarmament conference.
B. The negotiations regarding the Manchurian situation.
C. The coming world economic conference.

Has the Administration:

A. Conveyed any view to the foreign Governments with respect to the foregoing?
B. Given *any instructions* to any of its representatives with regard to the foregoing?
C. Has any member of the disarmament commission asked your views as to the foregoing? And what did you reply?
D. Given any *other* intimation as to the foregoing?
E. Does the Administration have knowledge of any conversations of responsible individuals affecting the situation?

Appendix B

Text of Statement Prepared for President Roosevelt by Herbert Swope, Walter Lippmann, John Maynard Keynes and Raymond Moley, Night of July 4, 1933

In my communication to you of July 2, I endeavored to make clear that I saw no utility at the present time in temporary stabilization between the currencies of countries whose needs and policies are not necessarily the same. Such stabilization would be artificial and unreal and might hamper individual countries in realizing policies essential to their domestic problems. I urged the Conference to move to consideration of its fundamental task of facilitating policies by the different nations directed, not to temporary expedients, but to mitigating and, if possible, remedying the harassing evils of the present economic situation. In the hope that I may be of some help to the Conference, to whose success and friendly cooperation I continue to attach the greatest importance, it may be useful that I should develop this thought somewhat more fully.

In saying that the value of the dollar has not fallen so far as I should like to see it fall, I naturally intended its value in terms of American commodities, which alone matters to us in remedying our maladjustments. The revaluation of the dollar in terms of American commodities is an end from which the Government and the people of the United States cannot be diverted. I wish to make this perfectly clear: we are interested in American commodity prices. What is to be the value of the dollar in terms of foreign currencies is not and cannot be our immediate or our ultimate concern. The exchange value of the dollar will depend upon the success of other nations in raising the prices of their own commodities in terms of their national monies, and cannot be determined in advance of our knowledge of such facts.

I seek no competitive exchange depreciation going beyond actual and anticipated price movements. I have no intention of encouraging American domestic price levels to rise beyond the point required by the American debt structure and American costs. And I have every intention and ample resources to prevent an inordinate and uneconomic rise of prices. There is nothing in my policy inimical to the interests of any other country, but I cannot allow the American government to be embarrassed in the attainment of economic ends absolutely required for the economic health of our country.

If other countries represented at the Conference desire a rise of prices in the same or in a different degree according to the special circumstances of each, I suggest that it is the task of the Conference to consider ways and means of putting into circulation the additional purchasing power by which alone their object can be attained. I see no necessity for uniformity. But no progress can be made until the different needs of the different countries have been elucidated and determined. If there are countries where prices and costs are already in equilibrium, I do not regard it as the task of the Conference, as it certainly is not the purpose of the American government, to persuade or compel them to pursue policies contrary to their own conception of their own interests.

But if it should emerge from the discussion that there is a group of countries whose requirements are broadly the same as those of the United States and if those countries were to make it clear that they were prepared to take appropriate measures for an effective movement in this direction, I should welcome informal arrangements between the Central banks of these countries and the Federal Reserve System of the United States for the avoidance of meaningless and harmful exchange fluctuation which did not correspond to price policies, though such arrangements should be, in my judgment, of a day-to-day character and without embarrassing commitments of either side.

There is also to be considered the policies appropriate to the period after the existent maladjustments in the price structure have been remedied. It is not sufficient to escape from the present evils. It is our duty to consider together how to avoid their recurrence in future. The first task is to restore prices to a level at which industry and above all agriculture can function profitably and efficiently. The second task is to preserve the stability of this adjustment once achieved. The part which gold and silver should play as reserve monies after price adjustment has been secured would seem a further subject suitable for consideration by the Conference. I would link with this the problems of exchanges and of commercial and tariff policies, with a view to the avoidance of unbalanced debtor and creditor positions between nations which have been so fruitful a cause of the present evils. It would be chimerical to hope that much progress can be made in diminishing the excessive hindrances to profitable international exchange during the period before prices have been adjusted, when each country is endeavoring by any means at its disposal to protect what seems a perilous domestic situation. But it is not too soon to consider the general lines of a code which should attain the mutual advantages of legitimate international trading, when the special causes which have led to widespread action of an injudicious and mutually injurious character have passed away.

I conceive, therefore, that the great problems which justified the assembling of the nations are as present today and as deserving of exploration as was the case a few weeks ago; and I find it difficult to conceive that the view which it has been my obvious duty to take on the minor issue of temporary stabilization which was not before the Conference and has not figured on its agenda can in any way diminish the advisability of such discussions.

Appendix C

Memorandum of Conversation via Transatlantic Telephone Between the President, the Secretary of State, and Mr. Moley, Wednesday, July 5, 1933

THE PRESIDENT: I have your despatch No. 203 and it came through rather garbled. I think it is a mistake to make it as a statement from me. I would make it a statement from the delegation and start it this way: "The President has made it clear that the . . ." and then go on with the rest of that sentence. The second sentence is all right. The third sentence, instead of saying I urged the Conference, say "urged the Delegation to seek consideration of its fundamental task" and that is all right for the rest of the sentence. The next sentence, "In the hope that the United States may be of help to the Conference to whose success and friendly cooperation the President continues to attach the greatest importance. It may be useful that we should develop this thought somewhat more fully." The next sentence strike out altogether and I will tell you why. We do not want to say that we are concerned with the value of the dollar. We do not know how far we are going; we are not trying to make it fall in terms of foreign currency. Leave the sentence out, then go on. "The revaluation of the dollar . . ." is all right. "We wish to make this perfectly clear: we are interested in American commodity prices." The next sentence, "What is to be the value of the dollar in terms of foreign currency is not and cannot be our main concern." The next sentence, "The exchange value of the dollar will ultimately depend . . ." and the rest of the sentence is all right. The next paragraph, "Makes no competitive exchange . . ." leave that out altogether, because it is purely a domestic consideration. I would leave out "I have no intention of encouraging American domestic prices." Leave out the last one, "I have every intention . . ." I think that is the thing you can in the Delegation talk about informally rather than in a statement because it is purely an American question. The next sentence, "There is nothing in our policy . . ." and I would add "we are confident that no other country would seek to embarrass us in the attainment of economic ends required for our own economic health." I doubt the wisdom of the next two sentences. Go ahead with the next sentence, "If there are countries where prices and costs are already in equilibrium, we do not regard it to be the task of the Conference . . ." down to the rest of the paragraph. The next paragraph is somewhat garbled and I would leave the whole thing out especially for this reason. There is one thing I want to talk to you about. It came garbled but at the end of the first sentence in that paragraph, "I should welcome informal arrangements between the main countries and Federal Reserve Banks . . ." the difficulty is this; it is the crux of the whole matter. If we approve having our Federal Reserve Banks go into an agreement on exchange with the Bank of France, and the Bank of England—I would make clear if you can do it politely—went off the gold standard and after a year and ten months has not yet said that it was ready to go back in any way. We have only been off for three months and we are not ready to tell how or when we would return. Wait a second. Now, in the paper this morning there is an AP despatch from London that says that the financial secretary of the treasury, speaking for Neville Chamberlain in the House of Commons, said that the Chancellor had expressed the Government's view. Now if ——— made that statement in Parliament yesterday, that is very much our line.

MR. MOLEY: We could say we could subscribe to that.

THE PRESIDENT: Yes, I think we can subscribe to what they want and in the meantime we must retain our absolute freedom to prevent the export of any gold. Now, coming back to the statement, it came through garbled.

MR. MOLEY: Shall I read it back?

THE PRESIDENT: Now I think the sentence beginning "It is not sufficient"—leave that in and the next sentence, "It is our duty to consider together how to avoid their recurrence in the future." The next two sentences are garbled.

MR. MOLEY: Shall I read them?

THE PRESIDENT: Yes.

MR. MOLEY: "The first task is to restore prices to a level at which industry and above all agriculture can operate at a profit and efficiently."

THE PRESIDENT: Leave that in.

MR. MOLEY: "The second task is to preserve the stability of this adjustment once achieved."

THE PRESIDENT: That is right.

MR. MOLEY: "The part which gold and silver will play

THE PRESIDENT: Leave out the word after adjustment. The French hold that gold in the future should serve as a medium for international exchange. We do not go along with that at all.

MR. MOLEY: That is right.

THE PRESIDENT: Gold and silver should not be concerned with international exchange but should be kept by all governments as a permanent collateral behind the whole currencies. I think we ought to make that clear.

MR. MOLEY: Let me read that sentence: "The part which gold and silver should play as reserve monies after price adjustment has been secured . . ."

THE PRESIDENT: Leave out prices.

MR. MOLEY: ". . . would seem a further subject suitable for consideration by the Conference."

THE PRESIDENT: That is right. Then the next sentence is all right, but say "we would link" instead of "I." The whole next paragraph I do not see any need for. It has come through rather garbled. Cut out down to "passed away." The paragraph beginning "It would be unwise to hope"—out with that. The last paragraph is very very garbled. Read it to me.

MR. MOLEY: "I can see therefore that the great problems which justified the assembling of the nations are as present today and as deserving of our exploration as was the case a few weeks ago; and I find it difficult to conceive that the view which it has been my obvious duty . . ."

THE PRESIDENT: Make it "our obvious duty."

MR. MOLEY: ". . . our obvious duty to take on the minor issue of temporary stabilization which was not before the Conference and has not yet figured on its agenda can in any way diminish the advisability of such discussions."

THE PRESIDENT: That is all right. Remember those two points—we cannot agree to anything which would put us in the position of having to export gold and secondly that we would have to add one sentence to the general effect that we have not the slightest objection to the efforts on the part of the central banks of other countries to stabilize their own exchange. That is none of our business.

MR. MOLEY: Now it seems to me the effect of this will be very important. I think we can get England to agree with us on that. Now what would be your desire as to issuing this—after consultation and have them join? You would not join with them. We should not have them join with us in it. It is better to issue it and let them agree to it after issuing it.

THE PRESIDENT: That is all right.

MR. MOLEY: All right, fine.

THE PRESIDENT: You can get me any time you want me from now on. Look, Ray. Make that statement a little more polite. "It is true that the return to the gold standard might be our ultimate objective when proper conditions were assured." We must have complete liberty to choose our own time.

MR. MOLEY: That would put the English in the position of being with us.

THE PRESIDENT: Yes, that is right.

MR. MOLEY: What would you say to the inclusion in this statement of a reference to that, if we can check it properly and see whether that is their view and we subscribe to it.

THE PRESIDENT: Yes, that is right. I would stress the word "might." If you did not use the word "might" don't use it.

MR. MOLEY: I think I will stay here and will not go to Ireland, but will sail from Southampton. That means I sail tomorrow. Here is Cordell.

THE SECRETARY: How do you feel about this, Governor?

THE PRESIDENT: I think it is all right. But I said to Ray that the real reason behind the other statement was this: If we had agreed to approve stabilization through the Central Reserve Bank, the Federal Reserve Bank would have obligated the Treasury to export gold, and we can't do that. As a matter of fact, I got word, and pretty good too, that there might have been an earmarking of gold in New York to the tune of half a billion dollars.

THE SECRETARY: We will go forward here, first, to avoid having this earmarking charge—that we are responsible for any change in the program; and second, to develop as short a recess as we possibly can. I presume it would be better with the Prime Minister agreeing to call it within a week's time which may not be made public.

THE PRESIDENT: Of course if he would agree to call it within a week's time.

THE SECRETARY: I am afraid of its going over sixty days.

THE PRESIDENT: That is the reason why if they made it two weeks we would leave it to his discretion as to whether it would be one week, two weeks or three weeks. You know over there they all go away for August and if the Conference is not called back within two weeks it will have to go over until the middle of September.

THE SECRETARY: Last night they were in such a state of mind that it was almost by accident that we got them to adjourn over—they were bent on the other course. We will do the best we can in the circumstances.

THE PRESIDENT: That is fine, make it as short as you can. You know Bill Woodin is very sick. He has had a very bad throat.

THE SECRETARY: Give him my regards.

Index

(NOTE: *Bibliographical information for works cited in the text is given in full at the first mention of each work. These citations are indexed under the respective titles and authors.*)